Sudden and Gradual

Kuroda Institute
Studies in East Asian Buddhism

Studies in Ch'an and Hua-yen
Robert M. Gimello and Peter N. Gregory

Dōgen Studies
William R. LaFleur

The Northern School and the Formation of Early Ch'an Buddhism
John R. McRae

Traditions of Meditation in Chinese Buddhism
Peter N. Gregory

Studies in East Asian Buddhism 5

Sudden and Gradual

Approaches to Enlightenment in Chinese Thought

Edited by

Peter N. Gregory

University of Hawaii Press · Honolulu

Printed in the United States of America

POD 2025

The Kuroda Institute for the Study of Buddhism and Human Values is a nonprofit, educational corporation, founded in 1976. One of its primary objectives is to promote scholarship on the historical, philosophical, and cultural ramifications of Buddhism. In association with the University of Hawaii Press, the Institute also publishes Classics in East Asian Buddhism, a series devoted to the translation of significant texts in the East Asian Buddhist tradition.

Library of Congress Cataloging-in-Publication Data

Sudden and gradual.

(Studies in East Asian Buddhism ; 5)
Bibliography: p.
Includes index.
1. Englightenment (Buddhism) 2. Buddhism—China.
I. Gregory, Peter N., 1945- II. Series: Studies in East Asian Buddhism ; no. 5)
BQ4398.S93 1987 294.3'442 87-26688
ISBN-10 0-8248-1118-6
ISBN-13 978-0-8248-1118-1

University of Hawaii Press books are printed on acid-free paper and meet the guidelines for permanence and durability of the Council on Library Resources

Contents

Acknowledgments

The conference out of which this volume grew was made possible by a grant from the American Council of Learned Societies, which I hereby acknowledge for its generous support. My particular thanks are due to Robert M. Gimello, who served as co-organizer of the conference and without whom neither the conference nor the volume would have been possible. I would also like to thank Dr. Michael Soulé, director of the Kuroda Institute in 1981; Maezumi Roshi, head of the Zen Center of Los Angeles, which put its facilities at the disposal of the Kuroda Institute for the conference; and the staff of the Zen Center for their unstinting efforts to make the conference a success. My deep appreciation goes to Stuart Kiang, editor at the University of Hawaii Press, for his patience, painstaking care, and moral support. If this volume proves anything at all, it proves that scholars are incorrigible gradualists. Thanks also to Barbara E. Cohen for compiling the index.

Finally, I would like to thank E. J. Brill for permission to include a translation of Paul Demiéville's "Le miroir spirituel," which was reprinted in *Choix d'études bouddhiques* in 1973, and Presses Universitaires de France for permission to include a translation of R. A. Stein's "Illumination subite ou saisie simultanée," which appeared in *Revue de l'histoire des religions* in 1971.

Abbreviations

HTC	*Hsü tsang ching*
IBK	*Indogaku bukkyōgaku kenkyū*
SPPY	Ssu-pu pei-yao
SPTK	Ssu-pu ts'ung-k'an
T	*Taishō shinshū daizōkyō*
ZZ	*Dainippon zokuzōkyō*

Introduction

Peter N. Gregory

The present volume grew out of a conference organized by Robert M. Gimello and myself for the Kuroda Institute for the Study of Buddhism and Human Values. The conference was held in Los Angeles in May 1981 and made possible by funding from the American Council of Learned Societies. As the original title, "The Sudden/Gradual Polarity: A Recurrent Theme in Chinese Thought," was intended to suggest, a central impetus for the conference was the effort to place what had often been seen as a strictly Buddhist problematic within the broader context of Chinese thought and culture.

As expressed in the conference proposal, and later reported in volume 9 of the *Journal of Chinese Philosophy* in 1982, the underlying assumption was that

> while the controversy surrounding the sudden-gradual polarity was not without precedent in other Buddhist traditions, it assumed its greatest significance in the Chinese Buddhist tradition, where its articulation displayed a number of characteristically Chinese features linking it to non-Buddhist modes of thought. The fact that this polarity assumed its particular importance in the Chinese Buddhist tradition suggests that it resonated with, or gave form to, a similar pre-existent polarity within Chinese thought. One of the main objectives of the conference, therefore, was to explore how this polarity formed part of a larger discourse in Chinese intellectual history.
>
> The conference thus sought to take an approach different from those of previous discussions of the significance of the sudden-gradual controversy in Chinese Buddhism. Instead of trying to locate the source of the debate within the Indian Buddhist heritage, the conference attempted to provide a new perspective on the process of Buddhism's accommodation with some of the dominant themes in Chinese intellectual history, as well as Buddhism's effect upon that tradition.[1]

As the volume gradually came together in the years since the conference was held, it has taken a shape in many ways different from the original cast of papers presented in Los Angeles.[2] Some of the conference participants have published their papers elsewhere,[3] some have elected not to rework theirs for publication, and others have written completely different papers for the volume. All of the conference papers that were eventually included in the volume have been extensively revised. The volume has also been enhanced by new papers written especially for it—those by Whalen Lai and Robert E. Buswell, Jr. The translations of the essays by Paul Demiéville and R. A. Stein have been included because of their seminal role in framing western discussions of the issue.

Even though the resulting volume bears a complexion quite different from that of the conference, the working assumption that inspired the conference still operates as an underlying presupposition for the volume and provides an important context in which the various chapters should be understood. Tu Wei-ming's afterword takes up the problem directly, outlining what he refers to as "a peculiarly sinitic mode of approaching the enlightening experience" in a sensitively nuanced reflection on the set of Chinese assumptions underlying the Ch'an notion of enlightenment.

Indeed, the question of the sinitic context informing the Chinese Buddhist understanding of sudden and gradual enlightenment was raised in one of the very first discussions of the issue: Hsieh Ling-yün's *Pien tsung lun* (On Distinguishing the Goal), written in the early decades of the fifth century as a defense of Tao-sheng's theory of sudden enlightenment. Hsieh begins by contrasting Buddhism and Confucianism. He goes on to argue that Tao-sheng's theory combined the best of each tradition, while discarding their particular shortcomings. Tao-sheng thus takes over the Buddhist ability to attain enlightenment while rejecting its gradualism, and adopts the Confucian emphasis on the "single ultimate" *(i-chi)* while laying aside its "almost reaching perfection" *(tai-shu).*[4] Hsieh thus seems to be saying that Tao-sheng's theory represents a uniquely Chinese appropriation of Buddhist enlightenment. Its sudden character derives from the fact that the truth or principle *(li)* to which one is enlightened is the single ultimate. Precisely because it is one and indivisible, it must be apprehended all at once, "suddenly," and can never be disclosed piecemeal. Tao-sheng's subitism thus follows from the nature of the "single ultimate," a notion much closer to Wang Pi's "Neo-Taoist" ontological monism of the one principle *(li)* underlying manifold reality than to Confucian teachings. Tao-sheng's theory of sudden enlightenment *(tun-wu),* which is based on the assumption that enlightenment can only be realized in its entirety, seems to bear out

Stein's contention that the word *tun* has the primary meaning of "all at once."

Tao-sheng's theory met stout resistance on the part of the scholastic establishment, as reflected in Hui-kuan's rebuttal, "On Gradual Enlightenment" *(Chien-wu lun).* Their debate is significant as the first historical instance of the sudden-gradual controversy. Since Tao-sheng's theory of sudden enlightenment, its Neo-Taoist roots, and its gradualist opponents are discussed in detail in the chapter by Whalen Lai, no more need be said about them here. Rather, I would like to take up another aspect of the early debates that reveals an important dimension of the sudden-gradual discourse that is not given its just due in the following pages.

"Sudden" and "gradual" were terms that were not only applied to the nature of enlightenment, but also used to distinguish between the different methods of teaching employed by the Buddha.[5] In this regard Hui-kuan is important not merely as Tao-sheng's gradualist rival but as the figure responsible for devising one of the first systems of doctrinal classification *(p'an-chiao)* in China. According to Chi-tsang,[6] Hui-kuan divided the Buddha's teachings into two major categories: the sudden and the gradual. The sudden teaching *(tun-chiao)* applied exclusively to the *Avataṃsaka,* which fully revealed the truth and was taught only for the most advanced bodhisattvas. All the other teachings of the Buddha were gradual, and Hui-kuan went on to classify them in terms of five periods. Hui-kuan's scheme had great influence on subsequent *p'an-chiao.* Most notably, his classification of the *Avataṃsaka* as the sudden teaching was adopted by T'ien-t'ai Chih-i, as Neal Donner's chapter details, as well as by the early Hua-yen "patriarch" Chih-yen.

In this context, the terms "sudden" and "gradual" were used to resolve a hermeneutical problem particularly vexing for Chinese Buddhists. As the corpus of Buddhist texts translated into Chinese continued to grow, and as Chinese Buddhists gradually became familiar with their contents, they also became aware that the tradition contained a confusing diversity of teachings, some of which even seemed to contradict one another. Since many of these teachings were put forward in the very scriptures themselves, and so constituted the sacred and infallible word of the Buddha, Chinese Buddhists were pressed to devise some means to account for them as a coherent body of doctrine free from self-contradiction. The teaching of expedient means (upāya), taught in the *Lotus* and other Mahāyāna scriptures, offered a convenient way of dealing with this problem, by which the proliferation of teachings could be explained as the result of the different levels of understanding and spiritual readiness of the audiences to which they were addressed. Different teachings were suited to the needs of different beings. The teachings could then be arranged in a hierarchical order, beginning with the most elementary and advancing to the most profound. The progression of the teachings was often pictured as following the course of the Buddha's teaching career, with their order outlining a curriculum of spiritual development.

The *Avatamsaka* posed a unique problem for such a schematic picture of the chronological unfolding of Buddhism. Since it had been acclaimed as one of the most profound teachings of the Buddha ever since its first Chinese translation by Buddhabhadra in 420, it should have rightly been placed at the very end of the progression of teachings as their final culmination. However, since it was also generally accepted as having been the first teaching preached by the Buddha immediately after his enlightenment, it should have rightly been placed at the very beginning. The sudden-gradual polarity solved this taxonomical dilemma by drawing a qualitative distinction between those teachings that resorted to expedients and the one teaching that did not. As the sudden teaching, the *Avataṃsaka* was preached first. It was "sudden" because it directly revealed the content of the Buddha's enlightenment as he experienced it under the bodhi tree; in it the Buddha made no effort to accommodate its message to his audience's limited ability to understand. As a consequence, its meaning was lost on all but the most advanced bodhisattvas. Realizing that beings were as yet unprepared to understand his ultimate message, the Buddha then taught a graduated series of expedient teachings over the course of his teaching career, gradually preparing his followers for his final message, delivered just before he finally passed away. In this context, where the sudden teaching *(tun-chiao)* is contrasted with the expedient teachings, the word *tun* connotes "immediate" in its literal sense of "being without an intermediary."

The doctrine of expedient means thus provided the crux in terms of which the sudden-gradual distinction was made in Chinese *p'an-chiao*. The gradual teachings were gradual precisely because they resorted to expedients as a means to accommodate the Buddha's enlightened insight to the understanding of unenlightened beings. The sudden teaching was sudden by virtue of the fact that it was a direct and unmediated revelation of the truth as the Buddha experienced it. In this way, the two terms could be assimilated with the traditional Buddhist distinction between ultimate and conventional truth: the sudden teaching presented the Buddha's enlightenment from the point of view of ultimate truth whereas the gradual teachings approached the Buddha's enlightenment in terms of conventional truth.

The adoption of the sudden-gradual distinction in Chinese Buddhist classification schemes indicates how it was connected with standard

Buddhist doctrines such as expedient means or the two truths. At the same time, it also reveals how these terms were employed by Chinese Buddhists to resolve the particularly sinitic problem of developing a systematic framework in which the entirety of the Buddha's teachings could be harmoniously integrated. This hermeneutical context also points to the inherent complexity of the polarity. The fact that Hui-kuan found it necessary to introduce the sudden teaching in his classification scheme, and at the same time felt compelled to uphold gradual enlightenment against Tao-sheng's "new theory," indicates that the meaning of the terms "sudden" and "gradual" varied according to context. Before the terms can be understood, one must always ask: sudden or gradual what? As Tsung-mi points out, within Chinese Buddhist discourse the terms are applied both to enlightenment and to the teachings, as well as to practice or cultivation. This is not to deny that there may not be a broad area of overlapping meaning that ties together the usage of these terms in the different contexts in which they occur. It is only to point out that their usage is highly nuanced, and we must be sensitive to how the particular context in which they appear affects their meaning.

While the fluidity of the terms may make it difficult to give the polarity precise definition, it also indicates its richness and suggests the wide range of epistemological, ethical, and ontological issues they encompass. While these issues are all intricately entwined with one another in actual usage, some of the more salient would include:

1. The nature of enlightenment: does it admit of degrees or is it indivisible? Can it be approached through a series of successive approximations or can it only be realized all at once in its entirety?
2. The nature of delusion: is it fundamentally an error in perception or is it woven throughout the whole fabric of the personality? Is enlightenment, therefore, more like opening the eyes or overcoming a bad habit?
3. The nature of ethical and religious practice: is it something that must be consciously and conscientiously cultivated as a necessary precondition for enlightenment, or is it rather the spontaneous and natural outflowing of the very experience of enlightenment itself and hence something to which no special attention need be directed?
4. The nature of religious language: is enlightenment ineffable or can something meaningful in fact be said about it? If ultimate truth is ineffable, can it yet be mediated through language? If language can only function apophatically to say what enlightenment is not, how are students to be instructed on the path?

5. The nature of expediency (upāya): do expedients play a necessary role in the apprehension of ultimate truth or should they be abandoned in favor of a direct intuition of ultimate truth as it is?

One of the particularly significant points implicitly made by the volume as a whole and explicitly developed in the chapter by Luis O. Gómez is that the sudden-gradual polarity is "soft" at its edges. As we have noted, the polarity enfolds a host of complexly interrelated issues. With insight and erudition, Gómez demonstrates that, when the specific historical instances of the sudden-gradual controversy are examined, it is clear that there is no necessary or even predictable way in which the positions taken by the actual participants can be correlated with the complex of issues contained within the sudden-gradual rubric. Hence the subitist on one occasion may well espouse a number of doctrinal positions held by the gradualist on another. Subitists and gradualists, moreover, often appealed to the same doctrine in support of their position. For example, in the most famous instance of the controversy, the exchange of poems that the *Platform Sūtra* alleges were composed by Shen-hsiu and Hui-neng, both parties based their positions on the notion of an intrinsically enlightened Buddha-nature. Furthermore, as John R. McRae observes in his chapter, the terms "sudden teaching," "sudden enlightenment," and "sudden practice" more often carried affective or rhetorical power as slogans rather than demarcating clearly articulated doctrinal positions. In this regard, "sudden" and "gradual" came to function as part of the stock polemical vocabulary used by Chinese Buddhists, in much the same way the more general terms "Mahāyāna" and "Hīnayāna" had been used. The polemical context—in which Ch'an defined itself as a wholly unique "special transmission" over against the more scholastically oriented traditions of Chinese Buddhism, or in which Southern Ch'an asserted its claim to represent the authentic tradition against the claims of Northern Ch'an—again points back to the specific Chinese historical setting in which the sudden-gradual polarity operated.

In his discussion of Shen-hui's emphasis on suddenness as the focus of his critique of Northern Ch'an, McRae concludes that Shen-hui's major contribution to Ch'an lay in his rhetoric. Shen-hui's denunciation of Northern Ch'an meditation teachings as gradualistic entailed a heightened sensitivity to the importance of avoiding dualistic formulations. Shen-hui thus played a key transitional role in the development of the characteristically Ch'an language exemplified in the "encounter dialogue" associated with the Hung-chou lineage and celebrated in the later *kung-an* (J. *kōan*) literature.

With the success of Shen-hui's "campaign" and the eventual emergence of the Hung-chou lineage as the dominant tradition of Chinese Ch'an, the polemical context of the eighth-century debates was superseded by an effort to extend the implications of Ch'an rhetoric to distinctively Ch'an methods of teaching and meditation practice. The chapter by Robert E. Buswell, Jr. skillfully documents this process, showing how the mature *k'an-hua* Ch'an of the Sung can be seen as the culmination of a long process in the internal evolution of Ch'an. *K'an-hua* Ch'an, focusing on the examination of *kung-an,* is both a sudden method of teaching and a sudden form of practice. Buswell sets his argument within the larger context of the sinification of Buddhism, claiming that the process by which the idea of suddenness was extended to Ch'an pedagogy and praxis is coextensive with the process by which Chinese Buddhists continually adapted Buddhism to forms of expression and modes of practice more suited to their own cultural experience. *K'an-hua* Ch'an represents the shedding of the final trappings of Indian Buddhist doctrinal terminology and meditation practices in the creation of what was both a uniquely Ch'an and a uniquely Chinese style of Buddhism.

In the process, the meaning of suddenness was also extended. As a sudden practice, the *kung-an* becomes the means by which sudden enlightenment can be realized. Because the sayings and doings of the masters revealed in the *kung-an* avoid conventional forms of expression, they are able to cut through dualistic understanding and "directly point to the mind of man, enabling him to see his nature and realize Buddhahood" *(chih-chih jen-hsin, chien-hsing ch'eng-fo).* It is the living word of the master, uttered in the intensity of his existential encounter with a disciple, that is able to penetrate to the vital core of religious experience. Suddenness thus comes to mean direct pointing, and the *kung-an* is the paradigmatically sudden method of teaching—a sudden upāya.

The Japanese Rinzai school, which uses kōan as its major form of training, is thus often said to emphasize sudden enlightenment, while the Japanese Sōtō school, which promotes "just sitting" *(shikan taza)* instead, is accordingly said to stress gradual enlightenment. This stereotype fails to take account of the sophisticated Sōtō theology behind its practice of "just sitting"; it also distorts an important dimension of the sudden-gradual polarity as well. The Sōtō theology of "just sitting" contains a psychological critique of kōan practice. If the kōan is seen as a means by which enlightenment is to be realized, then the same kind of criticism that the *Platform Sūtra* had made of Northern Ch'an meditation teaching as dualistic can be applied to the Rinzai advocacy of kōan. To the extent that the student strives for enlightenment, he places enlightenment outside of himself and thereby reifies it. The Sōtō position bases itself on intrinsic enlightenment *(hongaku).* Since our very nature is enlightened to begin with, to seek after enlightenment is only to add to our delusion. The practice of "just sitting," on the other hand, does not posit meditation practice as a means to an end and is therefore nondualistic. Dōgen's emphasis on the oneness of practice and realization echoes the *Platform Sūtra*'s assertion of the inseparability of samādhi and prajñā. *Zazen* itself is the perfect expression of Buddhahood. In this respect, Sōtō theology can mount its own argument that it, indeed, truly represents the sudden teaching, and that its practice of *shikan taza,* which is beyond all means, accordingly is the authentic sudden practice. The modern Rinzai-Sōtō polemic thus reveals that the sudden-gradual problematic is still alive today, as well as furnishing another example of its complexity.

How, then, should we construe the sudden-gradual polarity? In its most general form it can be seen as developing a deeply rooted tension in Chinese culture between effortful cultivation and spontaneous intuition (to adapt Gómez's terms), a tension reflected, in its broadest scope, in the respective stances of Confucianism and Taoism—or between conformity and naturalness, as Richard Mather has characterized it in a perceptive article on the Chinese intellectual world in the third century.[7] Within the Confucian tradition, the polarity could be seen as represented by the different points of emphasis of Hsün-tzu and Mencius, or of the Ch'eng-Chu and Lu-Wang schools of Neo-Confucianism. Even within the latter, it could further be seen as mirrored in the different interpretations of Wang Yang-ming's so-called "four sentence teaching" given by his disciples Ch'ien Te-hung and Wang Chi.

The sudden-gradual polarity not only reflects the uniquely Chinese historical circumstances in which Buddhism, and especially Ch'an, came to define itself in China; it also gave form to a preexistent tension within Chinese thought. Because this tension found its most articulate expression in the Buddhist debates of the eighth century, we are justified in using the Buddhist terms "sudden" and "gradual" to characterize it, without thereby implying that it was a specifically Buddhist paradigm, or that the later extension of these terms to non-Buddhist contexts necessarily reflected a Buddhist influence. In fact, it seems to have been due to their very vagueness and generality that the terms could be adopted by Yen Yü and Tung Ch'i-ch'ang as interpretative categories in their theories of poetry and painting, as Richard Lynn and James Cahill so ably demonstrate in their respective chapters, without thereby imputing any explicitly Buddhist content to them.

Notes

1. P. 471. Without further warning, I have taken the liberty of incorporating portions of my conference report into various parts of this introduction.

2. A summary of the original conference papers appeared in the *Journal of Chinese Philosophy* conference report referred to above. In accordance with ACLS requirements, depository copies of all of the papers were sent to the appropriate East Asian libraries at Columbia University, Harvard University, Princeton University, the University of Hawaii, Yale University, Stanford University, the University of California at Berkeley, the University of Wisconsin at Madison, the University of Michigan at Ann Arbor, and the University of British Columbia, as well as the Tōyō Bunko, Jimbun Kagaku Kenkyūjo, Chinese Academy of Social Sciences, and U.S.S.R. Academy of Sciences.

3. Francis H. Cook's "Enlightenment in Dōgen's Zen" appeared in the *Journal of the International Association of Buddhist Studies* 6, no. 1 (1983): 7–30; and Rodney L. Taylor's "The Sudden/Gradual Paradigm and Neo-Confucian Mind-Cultivation" appeared in *Philosophy East and West* 33, no. 1 (1983): 17–34.

4. See *T* 52.225a–b. A translation of the passage in question is quoted in the chapter by Lai below.

5. See my article "The Place of the Sudden Teaching within the Hua-yen Tradition: An Investigation of the Process of Doctrinal Change," *Journal of the International Association of Buddhist Studies* 6, no. 1 (1983): 31–60.

6. *San-lun hsüan-i,* *T* 45.5b4–14. See also Ōchō Enichi, "The Beginnings of Tenet Classification in China," *The Eastern Buddhist* 4, no. 2 (1981): 91–94 (originally published as "Kyōsō hanjaku no genshi keitei" in idem., *Chūgoku bukkyō no kenkyū,* vol. 2 [Kyoto: Hōzōkan, 1971]).

7. See "The Controversy Over Conformity and Naturalness During the Six Dynasties," *History of Religions* 9, nos. 2-3 (1969–1970): 160–180.

I

The Sudden and Gradual Debates

The Mirror of the Mind

Paul Demiéville

I salute you, child of my soul and of the tide,
Precious treasure of a mirror, sharing the world.
—Paul Valéry, "Narcisse"

The *Platform Sūtra* is supposed to have been preached by Hui-neng (638–713) from the platform of the lecture hall of a Buddhist monastery in Shao-chou, north of Canton, shortly before his death. In its introduction, Hui-neng, the sixth patriarch of the mystical school later known as the Ch'an (dhyāna) school, tells how, at the beginning of his career, when he was an uneducated young novice employed to pound rice in the monastery of the fifth patriarch of the school, he exchanged doctrinal verses with a fellow student named Shen-hsiu (606?–706), against whom the students of Hui-neng would later put forth arguments claiming for their own master the title of sixth patriarch of the school. The verse of Shen-hsiu said:

The body is the tree of the awakening;
The mind is like a clear mirror.
Be unceasingly diligent in wiping and polishing it
So that it will be without dust.

Hui-neng answered with this verse:

Awakening entails no tree at all,
Nor does the clear mirror entail any material frame.[1]
The Buddha-nature is eternally pure;
Where could there be any dust?[2]

These verses, known to all Chinese Buddhists, have given rise to a considerable number of interpretations, the most recent of which is an article by Ch'en Yin-k'o of the Academia Sinica, appearing in the June 1932 issue of the *Tsing-hua Journal* of Peking.[3] Prof. Ch'en, who is one of the foremost contemporary sinologists and the leading Chinese specialist in Buddhist studies, had little difficulty in showing the awkwardness of these verses. He pointed out the more or less folk origin of the *Platform Sūtra,* a work probably composed in the second half of the eighth century for the unlettered classes among whom the teaching of Hui-neng's disciple Shen-hui (684–758) had stirred up a movement of reformist fervor oriented toward quietism[4] and anti-intellectualism.

The Bodhi tree (Skt. *bodhidruma*) under which, according to canonical tradition, Buddhas attain enlightenment *(bodhi),* is a metaphor for the insubstantiality of the body—an unexpected and unorthodox usage, even in this text where numerous terms of classical Buddhism are reinterpreted with new and often startling meanings. The usual metaphor is that of a banana tree, whose stem can be stripped away without disclosing any solid substance. In this connection Prof. Ch'en refers to a saying attributed to T'an-lun, a dhyāna master who died around 627. T'an-lun's approach was thoroughly quietistic: he immersed himself in meditation without ever leaving his cell, cultivating any devotional practices, or studying texts. His master, however, advocated the practice of gradual meditation and, one day, advised him to practice cleansing himself of the passions that obscure the mind by proceeding as one peels an onion:

> Having peeled away one layer after another, what do you find? Purity. [To this T'an-lun replied,] If there were an onion, it would be possible to peel it; but since there is fundamentally no onion whatsoever, what is there to peel?[5]

Prof. Ch'en sees in this exchange, found in a hagiographic collection dating from the end of the seventh century, one of the sources of Hui-neng's verse. The onion would replace the banana tree for geographical reasons. He goes on to say that we can also find the metaphor of the mirror in a text from the beginning of the eighth century, according to which a certain fifth-century patriarch had compared the fundamental purity of the Great Tao, the absolute, to the light of the sun which manifests itself when the clouds that hide it have all disappeared. This patriarch also likened the Great Tao to a bronze mirror, whose natural bright purity is revealed as soon as we wipe away the surface dust.[6]

Doctrinally, the meaning of the verses is clear. Placed like an epigraph at the beginning of the *Platform Sūtra,* which in the complete title of its oldest recension presents itself as an exposition of the "sudden teaching" *(tun-chiao),* these verses oppose this teaching of Hui-neng to the "gradual teaching" *(chien-chiao)* of Shen-hsiu. It is not certain that the doctrinal difference between these two masters was really so pronounced; doubtless this reflects a development in the later tradition. A concern to avoid excessive quietism as well is also apparent in the *Platform Sūtra.* Shen-hui, whom the tradition regards as the main exponent of the subitism attributed to his teacher Hui-neng, says in a manuscript fragment of his *Recorded Sayings* discovered at Tun-huang:

> It is only under the right conditions that one achieves the *seeing* of Buddha-nature in oneself. The effort of digging is necessary in order to obtain underground water; a gem *(maṇi)* is not yet clear without being polished. The *Nirvāṇa Sūtra* says that no beings realize their Buddha-nature in the absence of conditions—that is, Buddhas, bodhisattvas, spiritual guides.[7]

And when someone one day asked him why, if all beings have the Buddha-nature, do some *see* it in themselves and others not, he replied:

> A gem, though it has the nature of clarity, is not yet clear without someone there to polish it. In the same way, beings cannot *see* the Buddha-nature in themselves unless they encounter Buddhas, bodhisattvas, or spiritual guides to arouse in them the thought [of enlightenment].[8]

For the advocates of the "sudden teaching," the seeing *(chien)* of the absolute in ourselves occurs "suddenly," outside all temporal *conditions,* causal or otherwise, without our first having to engage in the practice of *looking (k'an)* at it.[9] "Sudden" *(tun,* Skt. *yugapat* 'all at once', the Platonic *exaiphnes)* has to be understood as the totalistic aspect of salvation, which is related to a unified or synthetic conception of reality, to a philosophy of the immediate, the instantaneous, the nontemporal, which is also the eternal: things are perceived "all at once," intuitively, unconditionally, in a revolutionary manner. "Gradualism" on the other hand is an analytic teaching which claims to lead to the absolute through a gradual progression *(chien,* Skt. *kramavṛttyā,* the Platonic *ephexes)* of practices of various kinds—moral and devotional pursuits, meditative exercises, intellectual studies—all of which constitute an active effort to bring about salvation. It is this active effort that "subitists," in aspiring solely to the passive experience of the absolute, repudiated. The subitists see illumination, salvific knowledge, enlightenment *(bodhi)* in its "fundamental" aspect *(pen-chüeh),* according to which it is necessary for us to remove the veils which obscure the mind so that enlightenment can "begin" *(shih)* to emerge.[10]

Philosophically, both teachings are based on a belief in the intrinsic purity of the mind, which, while pure in its self-nature, is soiled by "adventitious passions." Gradualism insists that effort is necessary to rid it of these foreign impurities, to "wipe and polish the mirror." Subitism considers only its essential purity, to the point of refusing to recognize the existence of any impurity to be removed. For the distinction made between purity and impurity already implies, in effect, a dualism, a relativism antithetical to the nonpredicability of the absolute, which is "empty" of all determination. Buddha-nature *(fo-hsing,* Skt. *buddhatā),* the potentiality to become a Buddha, which is innate in all beings and by which they partake of the nature of Buddhas, itself absolutely pure in essence, is but another name for the absolute. If it is true that it is "eternally pure," this cannot be so in any sense which would have it differ from impurity, from dust—for it is completely identified with the latter.

Such a problem was familiar to classical Buddhism in India, as expressed, for instance, in the following verses attributed to Asaṅga, the great scholar of the fourth century A.D.

> If there were no passions,
> All men would be liberated.
> If there were no purity
> Their effort would be fruitless.
> Emptiness neither has nor lacks the passions;
> It is neither pure nor impure.
> The mind is pure by nature,
> But soiled by adventitious passions.[11]

The work from which these verses of Asaṅga are taken is the *Madhyānta-vibhāga,* "The Discrimination between the Mean and the Extremes." The verses are thus inspired by the desire to steer a middle course *(madhya)* between the extremes *(anta)* of purity and defilement, absolute and relative. These two extremes correspond respectively to the verses by Hui-neng and Shen-hsiu in the *Platform Sūtra.* Hui-neng denies the very existence of both the mirror and the dust which soils it; Shen-hsiu admits their existence insofar as it is necessary to keep them in mind in order to purify the mirror of dust. Their metaphor of dust was further justified by the fact that the standard technical Chinese Buddhist translation of "adventitious passions" *(āgantukakleśa)* was *k'o-ch'en* (guest dust), where "dust" designates the phenomenal world, its contamination and defilement. The Chinese term was borrowed from the vocabulary of early Taoist philosophy.

Śaṅkara, the systematizer of Vedānta, who leaned toward "subitism," asserted that liberation (which according to him consists in identifying oneself with the absolute: *brahman, ātman*) does not admit of any active effort on our part. It is a matter of knowledge, not of works. He held that liberation is inherent in our *ātman.* Yet though it remains hidden from us on account of our ignorance, it would be wrong to think that it could be revealed through purifying the *ātman* by our own effort, *"as the inherent clarity of the mirror can be made visible by wiping it."* In fact the *ātman* can never be the object of any activity, for all activity directed toward an object implies a modification of that object—but the *ātman* is eternally unalterable.[12] These themes in an Indian philosophy that was not Buddhist, but whose thought had been influenced by Buddhism, may serve as commentary to the metaphorical verse in which, around the year 1000, a Ch'an patriarch restated the doctrine of subitism:

> One only streaks the mirror by polishing it;
> Too skillful work ruins the uncut jade.[13]

Such then is the philosophical and religious dilemma posed by the verses in the *Platform Sūtra,* a dilemma which, although not limited to China, was always keenly felt by the Chinese. In the eighth century in particular, all Chinese philosophy centered around the Buddhist controversy over "subitism" and "gradualism"; we can even say that this debate epitomized, though the nomenclature varied, certain themes characteristic of Chinese thought over the centuries. The terms *subitism* and *gradualism,* furthermore, seem worthy to me of being adopted. It is true that they lack elegance and, still worse, only render in an excessively literal manner a complex semantic opposition. "Perfectivism" and "imperfectivism," "totalism" and "evolutionism" would, however, hardly be any better, and I provisionally abide with subitism and gradualism.

But it is not this doctrinal question that I propose to examine here in its breadth. I would like to limit myself to commenting on the metaphor of the mirror as it occurs in the verses of the *Platform Sūtra,* and to exploring its Chinese and Buddhist antecedents, as well as parallels outside Asia. Perhaps this inquiry will raise, by way of response, some doctrinal points worthy of being preserved.

1. Chinese Antecedents

In his article in the *Tsing-hua Journal,* Prof. Ch'en indicates as sources of this metaphor some documents from the Ch'an school which barely predate the *Platform Sūtra.* But these documents are themselves only later reappearances of a current of thought whose deep origins must be sought much earlier, and which appears first in pre-Buddhist Chinese philosophy, in particular that of the Taoist school. Ch'an Buddhism takes inspiration at least as much from Taoism as from the Buddhism of India.

Around 300 B.C., Chuang-tzu resorted frequently to the mirror metaphor in order to illustrate the dispassionateness, passivity, detachment, and disinterestedness of the Taoist sage, who does react to nature, but without ever acting for his own advantage:

> The perfect man *uses his mind like a mirror:* he neither accompanies things nor goes before them;[14] he responds to them without clinging to them. This is what makes him capable of dealing with all things without being tainted by them. . . .[15] The quietude of the sage [his equanimity] is not

quietude in the sense that quietude is said to be something good;[16] it is defined by the fact that nothing [no perceivable or determined being] is capable of agitating his mind. Tranquil water is so clear that it illumines [or *reflects*][17] the very hairs of the beard and eyebrows; its equilibrium is so perfect that it serves the architect as the standard for what is level. If tranquil water is this clear, how much clearer is the soul *(shen)!* The mind *(hsin)* of the sage is quiet, it is the *mirror of heaven and earth,* and reflects the whole multiplicity of things.[18]

In order, therefore, for the mind to be a mirror of the universe, it is essential, according to Chuang-tzu, to calm it, to reduce it to a state of detachment; it then identifies itself with the "virtue of heaven," which is its true nature. Pure and calm, unitary and unchangeable, disinterested and inactive, it is comparable to water.[19] Now water is a mirror, but only if it is calm and undisturbed by anything from the outside. In the same way, the sage must detach himself from everything external:

> To one who is in himself without things staying in him, they show themselves as they are. His movement is [detached] like that of water, *his immobility like that of a mirror,* his response like an echo. . . . He never takes precedence over others, but rather always puts himself behind them.[20]

The whole diverse multiplicity of the perceived world returns for him to oneness; imperturbable in the center of changes, he is touched by neither death nor life, and in Horace's words, "The universe could collapse without involving him." His very calm attracts men:

> It is not in running water that men mirror themselves, but in stilled water; only it, by having stopped, can stop those who stop there [to see themselves in it].[21]

Or again, whoever comes into proximity to a sage has his virtue reflected back, but only on condition that he purify his own mental or spiritual mirror. And here we find the metaphor of the *dust on the mirror:*

> When a mirror is clear, it is because it has not the least amount of dust on it. If there is any dust, the mirror is not clear. Whoever dwells for long near a sage should be devoid of faults.[22]

Most of these themes in Chuang-tzu are taken up, developed, and elaborated in the *Huai-nan-tzu,* a collection of philosophical essays compiled around the middle of the second century B.C. by a group of literati sponsored by one of the princes in the ruling family of the Han dynasty. This work, which is of Taoist inspiration, returns time and again to the metaphor of the mirror. The Great Man, whose detachment extends even to his own thoughts and reflections, is described as doing nothing apart from nature:

> With heaven as a chariot canopy, there is nothing that does not cover him; with earth as the chariot body, there is nothing that does not carry him; with the four seasons as horses, there is nothing which is not at his service. . . . Moreover, he is quick without being agitated, and goes far without fatigue: holding the handle of the essence of the Tao, he abandons himself to wandering in the earthly infinite. Far from intervening actively in the affairs of the world, he pushes them in the direction of their natural movement; far from seeking to fathom the thousand transformations of beings, he strives to return all things to their essential tendencies. *In coming into contact with things, neither a mirror nor water requires thought or intention in order to reflect them,* yet nothing escapes them, not the square or the circle, the curve or the straight line. It is not by chance that the echo responds;[23] the reflection is not always the same.[24]

As with Chuang-tzu, this passivity, which is also sovereignty, has as its precondition a detachment and tranquility of the soul—these being moreover its natural state, for all agitation and passion are fundamentally foreign to it:

> Man is quiet from birth; it is his nature which he has from heaven. Under the influence of things, motion is produced in him; it is there a deterioration of his nature. His soul responds to the things which present themselves to him, and thus his consciousness is roused. This puts him into contact with things, and thus are born within him love and hate, which take on form among things; and his consciousness, attracted to the outside, can no longer return to itself. It is thus that the heavenly order is destroyed in man.[25] Those who are initiated into the Tao do not exchange the heavenly for the human.[26]

The celestial, heaven *(t'ien),* is the original nature of man, which the sage does not allow to be obliterated by human passions. These would cause him to lose the feeling of participation in the totality of nature, in the heavenly order *(t'ien-li).* The word *li* signifies here the whole order of the universe, which embraces and includes all particular entities; it is practically synonymous with the word Tao, the way. It is the absolute, conceived, as always in pre-Buddhist Chinese thought, not as a spiritual and transcendent essence but as a universality in which the diversity of the world is unified, somewhat in the manner of Stoicism.

Passivity, in the *Huai-nan-tzu,* is a passivity with respect to a kind of absolute—for it is surely an absolute, this universality that is set opposite relative entities, and within which they take on order and meaning. And the sage, who never loses his sense of this absolute, this Tao, is compared to *"a perfectly clear mirror in which everything can be clearly seen,"*[27] as also to that other reflective surface, calm water:

> Water is by nature unitary and pure, but mud can make it turbid; similarly human nature is calm and quiet, but desires can agitate it. . . . [All

men] have received from heaven the same senses: ear and eye are sensitive to sounds and sights, the mouth and nose to tastes and to good and bad odors, the skin to hot and cold.

If some people share in the "light of the soul" while others, being spiritually beclouded, "do not shun folly," it is because they differ

in their control of their passions. . . . The soul is the source of the intellect; when this source is pure, the intellect is clear. The intellect is the repository of thought; when the intellect is impartial, then thought is correct. One does not see oneself in the froth of a running current; *one sees oneself in stilled water,* because it is quiet. One does not see one's face in rough iron, but *sees it in the clear mirror,* because it is smooth.[28]

Is this to say that one must imagine first iron, and then the necessity of polishing it? The *Huai-nan-tzu* shows itself here to be resolutely *subitist,* and in the same terms as the verse of Hui-neng:

A clear mirror cannot be soiled by dust; a pure soul cannot be troubled by desire. To wish actively to return the soul from its dispersal among outer things is to neglect the root while seeking [to restore] the branches. To wish to enter into contact with things when there is no correspondence at all between inner and outer, to wish in this way to know by ear or eye the mysterious light [of the soul], is to abandon the light to walk in darkness; it is to lose the spirit of the Tao.[29]

Another chapter of the *Huai-nan-tzu,* while discussing detachment in the practice of government, identifies this "light of the soul" with the completely passive luminosity of the mirror. The latter reflects objects without trying to influence them; in the same way, a good ruler allows himself to be guided by the circumstances which shape his destiny:

Whoever would wish to see himself in the bottom of a well by leaning over the wall around its edge would not be able to see the reflection of the pupil of his eye, no matter how keen his vision: but if he employs the *light of a mirror* to see himself, he can perceive distinctions down to one-tenth of an inch. Thus does an enlightened ruler, without tiring his ears or eyes, and without using up his energy or his soul, let things come to him so as to see his countenance in them, and allows events to occur so as to observe their transformations. . . . He does not resort to random contrivance, but walks in the necessity of the Tao.[30]

The disinterestedness of the sage, which is a consequence of his detachment, makes his judgment so valuable that everyone accepts it:

Even though there are many men of good faith hereabouts, still when possessions have to be managed or wealth distributed, then in order to determine the right portions, one has recourse rather to calculating slips—for in matters of law, one prefers what lacks thought to what is endowed with

> thought. And even though there are many men of integrity hereabouts, still when preserving a precious treasure, one does not neglect to bar the door or verify the seals—for in matters of integrity, one prefers what lacks desire to what is endowed with desire. When a person tells you your faults, you are angry with him; but *when a mirror shows what is ugly, you find this mirror excellent.*[31]

Thus the sage is a man for whom no thought of personal concern—or better, no thought whatever—intervenes between the knowing and the known; his perception is as immediate as the reflection of a mirror. The necessary condition of his moral integrity is an impassivity so perfect that no personal bias is present to distort his judgment as he strives for the wholeness of which the mind is constituted:

> A drum is not destroyed by sound—that is why it reverberates. *A mirror is not destroyed by a reflection—that is why it can reflect.* . . . The sage draws into himself and does not anticipate things. When events occur, he examines them; when things come, he responds to them.[32]

There is another philosopher who uses the mirroring property of water as a metaphor to expound analogous ideas: this is Hsün-tzu (ca. 300–230 B.C.), who is situated chronologically between Chuang-tzu and the *Huai-nan-tzu,* though closer to the former. On the basis of several too hastily interpreted passages and terms, some have made of Hsün-tzu a rationalist. The following quotation shows him as being close to Chuang-tzu. It is taken from one of the principal chapters of the work bearing his name, the chapter entitled "Dispersed Clouds" *(chieh-pi).* This is an exposition of the right procedures for ridding the mind of the "unilateral and partial views" which cloud it over and render it "blind to the great principle" *(ta-li),* to this universality that orders and explains individual beings in their relations with each other. The human mind is here compared to water in a basin: if it is set down properly and not disturbed, the impurities settle into the lower portion of the water while the upper portion becomes so pure, so clear, that

> one can see even the hairs of his beard and eyebrows, and perceive the texture of the skin.

But let a light wind pass over the water, and at once the impurities at the bottom begin to move, and the surface becomes so turbid that one is no longer able to discern in it a good reflection of the whole self:

> Likewise the mind, if it is guided by a sense of the whole *(li)* and nourished by purity, is able to determine the true and the false, to cut off all conjecture and doubt. But if it lets itself be in the least distracted by external things, then its equilibrium becomes jeopardized from the outside, it is internally upset, and becomes unable to distinguish even the grossest detail.[33]

In this text, as in all those from pre-Buddhist times that we have cited here, the point is to purify the mind. This puts the mind into a state of perceiving the external world without confusion, without its losing sight of that aspect of well-ordered totality which was at this time the Chinese conception of the absolute. We meet again in these passages most of the terms in the *Platform Sūtra* metaphor: the mirror, the dust, even the denunciation of the practice of cleaning the mirror. But never is this spoken of as man encountering within himself a purity properly "spiritual," an interior absolute. Such notions were lacking among the Chinese of antiquity. It is rather from India, from Buddhism, that these terms derived the new meaning that they had for the two T'ang dynasty Ch'an masters. We have found in Taoism certain sources for the verses in the *Platform Sūtra;* we must now find others in Buddhism.

2. Indian Antecedents

Indeed, the mirror metaphor is well known in India. It occurs even outside of Buddhism, among the metaphors in the *Upanishads*. Actually, it is not always as mere metaphor that it occurs. In a whole series of *Upanishads,* the *ātman* is identified with one's reflection in a mirror or an eye, with a shadow or an echo.[34] But these texts are clear that a lower concept of the *ātman* is what is meant: it is the "reflected soul," as Senart says.[35] They evidently do not refer to a mediate knowing that is a "reflection" of the absolute, like the speculative knowledge of God that Christianity contrasts with the knowledge of direct acquaintance. This is rather a conception of the soul which is as yet poorly dissociated from that which, among many primitive peoples, inspires them to take the reflection of a man for his true personality, for his "soul."[36] However, one of the *Upanishads* counted as ancient does resort to the metaphor of the dust-covered mirror in a spirit similar to that of the *Platform Sūtra.* This occurs in the context of a passage on yoga, which aims at the realization of the supreme *ātman* in its pure essence:

> Just as a *dust-covered mirror*
> Glitters like fire when it is cleaned,
> So does one who has recognized the *ātman*'s essence
> Attain the goal, deliverance from anxiety.[37]

We move now to Buddhist literature. Here the mirror metaphor is used for a variety of purposes. Most frequently we find the phenomenon of reflection in a mirror used as one illustration—along with hallucinations, dreams, shadows, echoes, the moon in the water, and other effects of this kind—of the illusory character of everything that is not the pure absolute.[38] In Hīnayāna the illusion more particularly refers to sense-objects as material *(rūpa)* or conditioned *(saṃskṛta)* while in the Mahāyāna, notably in the school of emptiness, Śūnyavāda or Mādhyamika, it refers to all "things" *(dharmas)* and entities without exception, since they are "empty" *(śūnya)* of self-nature and are nothing but the product of the play of causes and conditions.[39] The epistemological school (Vijñānavāda or Yogācāra) reserves the comparison with a reflection for a more precisely defined category of phenomena—namely, those objects of consciousness *(vijñāna)* which fall under the rubric of relative or "dependent" *(paratantra)* phenomena—dependent, that is, on conditions outside themselves. In this school the dependent is in fact opposed to both the "imaginary," which is nothing but a product of the mind, and to the "absolute," which is the sole real-in-itself. The reflection is not a real object, but it nonetheless is perceived and it participates in the reality of the object which it reflects to the degree that it is dependent upon that object.[40] "It exists but is not real," says one of the scriptural authorities of this school.[41]

Buddhist exegesis has pushed rather far its analysis of reflections in a mirror, having scrutinized the degree of reality which can be attributed to them, as well as exploring their metaphorical values. Asaṅga, in order to establish the idealist thesis which he has adopted ("all is mind only," "all is consciousness only"), quotes a canonical text that deals with the mental images perceived by the mystic when in a state of meditation—an extreme, but therefore prototypical, case. Are these images, asks Asaṅga, different from, or the same as, the consciousness which perceives them? He argues in accordance with his thesis that they are *not* different, and do not imply the existence of external objects. Thought appears in the double aspect of the seeing and the seen, like a visible object reflecting itself *in the pure circle of a mirror,* where thing and reflection appear to be distinct. In a work where he upholds the existence of the world[42] of sense-objects ("all exists"), Vasubandhu, the brother of Asaṅga, applies himself to demonstrating the inexistence of reflections. He does this in the context of arguing that it is materially impossible for two real things to exist in the same place: only the mirror and the reflected object really exist; the reflection is only an illusory perception.[43]

Another master, one belonging to the school of emptiness, puts to use the resources of the dialectic which is the specialty of this school and states that a reflection is produced neither by the mirror nor by the face, nor again by the person who holds the mirror. Nevertheless it is subject to a conditioned production, for otherwise it would exist eternally, even in the absence of the mirror and the face. In the same way, every knowable thing, every dharma, is produced neither by itself nor by another—yet is on that account no less subject to causes and conditions. In reality, the knowable is "empty" and deceives only non-Buddhists, just as a reflection deceives only fools.[44]

Similarly the *Laṅkāvatāra-sūtra,* one of the principal sources of inspiration for the Ch'an school (which was first called the Laṅkāvatāra school), likens the perceiving consciousness to a mirror reflecting images that it mistakes for real objects.[45] The mind reflects itself in the objects which it has itself created, like images in a mirror:[46]

> Just as an unreal image
> Is reflected in a mirror,
> The one mind, reflected in the mirror of its own perfumings,[47]
> Is seen by the ignorant as a duality.[48]

Thus the major use to which the example of the mirror has been put by Buddhists is as a weapon in this exhaustive analysis of the empirical world, an analysis which is one of the characteristics of their doctrine. But if they undermine the relative, it is only the better to isolate from it the absolute, to release it in its purity, its ineffable independence. We find therefore that "subitist" thinking can derive authority from the Mahāyāna.

There is also no lack of Buddhist texts where the metaphor of the mirror is used in another way, closer to the meaning it had for Taoist philosophers of the Ch'an school. As early as the *Mahāparinirvāṇa-sūtra,* one of the most venerable monuments in the canonical tradition of the Hīnayāna, the realized arhat is defined as the *mirror of the dharma,* that is, of the Buddhist teaching.[49]

Within Mahāyāna, the epistemological school (Yogācāra) posited, as a kind of substrate for the activity of the sensory consciousnesses, a faculty called the appropriating consciousness,[50] whose role is to appropriate sense perceptions so that they may be held in reserve in the nethermost mind. Then, under the influence of certain conditions, new perceptions are able to well forth, fructifying these "germs" in actual acts of objectified consciousness. The Buddhist exegetes will not acknowledge this to be an echo of the *ātman;* but one may wonder, at the risk of committing what would be in their eyes the blackest heresy, whether this "appropriating consciousness" does not represent a kind of carefully camouflaged absolute, reintroduced into Buddhism along with all precautions necessary to preserve the relativist orthodoxy. It is compared to a mirror upon which images are registered *without the mirror itself undergoing any transformation:* as with the *Huai-nan-tzu,* its capacity to reflect images remains intact.[51]

From another point of view, the same school compares the lack of cognitive clarity to a mirror[52] or to agitated water, unable to reflect clearly the face which gazes into it. It is hence necessary for the mind to be *trained* (*bhāvanā-maya* 'made by training') for it to be able to know the absolute.[53] This last thesis is gradualist.

We also find in this school a certain curious doctrine which teaches of the four modes of transcendent consciousness belonging to Buddhas: the first of these is called the *mirror consciousness.*[54] It is a kind of omniscience. The "mirror consciousness" refers to the fact that everything knowable views itself perpetually in the mind of the Buddhas, without limitation in time or space, and without the Buddhas ever being able to forget it—but also without this knowable being present to the Buddhas in acts of perception, nor being in the least affected in its own eternally pure nature. It is in this mirror that all living beings see the objects of their consciousness appear, like reflections, especially objects whose nature is good, salvific.[55] In this sense the Buddhas can qualify as causes of the world, insofar as it is seen by the minds of beings. Yet thereby is this doctrine exposed to the criticism that it posits a creator god, a criticism to which Buddhists have always shown themselves very sensitive.[56] The notion of the "mirror consciousness," which does not seem to occur in India before the fourth century of our era, is reminiscent of certain Western doctrines to which we shall allude below.

3. Western Parallels

The preceding remark will serve as a transition for extending the inquiry to the occidental world, where the metaphor of the spirit-mirror has played a role no less important than its role in China or India. Islamic thought deserves mention here: I limit myself to quoting a few passages from the mystical philosopher Al-Ghazzālī (1059–1111):

> Imagine an oxidized [metal] mirror, with rust covering its surface, its clarity obscured, unable to register our images. Normally a mirror is able to receive images and reflect them just as they are, but whoever wishes to restore this mirror must carry out two tasks. He must first wipe and polish it, so as to remove the rust which does not belong there. Then he has to position the mirror in front of the object which he wants to be reflected. Thus the human soul has the capacity to become a mirror which can at any time be oriented to the true. Just as with the image and the mirror, it receives the imprint of the true when, in a certain sense, it identifies itself with the latter, even though in another sense it remains distinct. . . . Angels do this eternally, just as pure water by nature reflects images in its characteristic manner. But for a human this ability exists only potentially, unmanifested in action. By doing battle against himself, he can attain the status of angels; but if, yielding to his appetites, the human continues to allow rust to accumulate on the mirror of his soul, his potentiality for reflecting the true will be completely eclipsed.[57]

Al-Ghazzālī is a partisan of gradualism:

> When the surface of the mirror is covered with rust, it fails to receive any image—but when it is put opposite the image and the polisher sets about his work, the reflection of the image gradually comes into view. . . . For creatures, spirit comes into being at a certain moment, not before . . . when the spirit is still too little polished to receive the image.[58]

It is clear that such passages already have an occidental coloration. The rust metaphor is Platonic, and can be found among the Fathers of the Greek Church,[59] among whom some also attribute solely to angels the vision of the divine image. Al-Ghazzālī insists on the necessity for the human soul to actively orient itself toward the true, and he speaks elsewhere of the reflection of the *beauty* of God in the mirror of the heart.[60]

We expect to encounter the metaphor or notion of the image in the philosophy of Plato, since for him perceptible reality is nothing but a shadow, an echo, a reflection[61] of ideal models. The metaphor of the mirror figures importantly in a dialogue of debated authenticity, the first *Alcibiades,* which had a great career in Hermetic and Neoplatonic thought, and which, it has been pointed out, contains certain ideas that some other Greek authors attributed to the brahmins of India.[62] In this dialogue, Socrates teaches Alcibiades that the formula of the Delphic oracle, "Know thyself," should be understood in the sense of knowing one's soul. But how to know the soul? In order to see oneself, one requires a mirror, or else what is comparable, the pupil in the eye of someone else. In order to see itself, Socrates continues, the eye has to look at another eye—and to know vision, it must look at the part in that eye where the faculty native to it resides. In the same way, the soul, if it wants to know itself, has to look at another soul, and in that soul, at the "divine" part where wisdom, consciousness, and thought reside. Looking thus at oneself in the divinity of another soul, one discovers God in one's own. To know ourselves is therefore to discover God within us. In the edition of Eusebius,[63] there is inserted here a passage which critics agree constitutes a Neoplatonic interpolation, but which nevertheless recommends itself to our attention. We read there that just as true mirrors are clearer, purer, and more luminous than the mirror of the eye, so too is God purer and more luminous than even the best part of the soul: he is the best mirror of human things, and it is in him that we can see and know ourselves.[64] This develops the meaning of the Platonic text in a transcendentalist direction, which places God outside the human soul and makes of him a mirror presented to man, somewhat like the "mirror consciousness" of Buddhas.

Plotinus (205–270), however, does not seem to have used the metaphor of the mirror to illustrate the relationship between the human soul and God or the absolute, at least not in the sense found in the *Alcibiades*. In the *Enneads,* Plotinus teaches that the lower part of the soul, that which touches and informs matter, is a reflection, as in a mirror, of the ideal or intelligible world.[65] What is at issue here is the unreal aspect of the reflection. Plotinus denies to matter any participation in being, in true reality. Matter is, he says,

> nothing but a phantom in another phantom, exactly as in a mirror, where the object appears elsewhere than it really is. *In appearance, the mirror is full of objects, yet while seeming to have everything, it actually contains nothing.* . . . This reflection leaves matter quite unaffected, like a vision in a dream, like a reflection in water or in a mirror.[66]

Not only does matter not receive real entities, but it also remains unable to appropriate their images. Not only are the images that reflect themselves in it nothing but appearances, but, in contrast to the mirror which is at least a form, it has itself not even a form.[67] Thus in a way similar to the majority of Buddhist authors, Plotinus resorts to the mirror to illustrate the unreality of the perceptible, the material world, a realm absolutely foreign to the spiritual world, which alone possesses being. Elsewhere, however, he does admit a sort of connection between spirit *(nous)* and matter *(hylē),* and follows a myth that also appears in the hermetic philosophy,[68] according to which the soul *(psyche)* is attracted to matter upon seeing there its image *"as in the mirror of Dionysius,"* and leaps from its height down toward this image. But it is only an intermediate part of the soul that is attracted to matter: its higher portion remains on the spiritual plane.[69]

Philo of Alexandria, the Jewish philosopher who lived in the first century A.D., constructed a whole system upon the notion of the image as found in the text of Genesis: "And God said, Let us make man in our image, after our likeness." The metaphor of the mirror recurs constantly in his works.[70] In most cases it is a matter of seeing the suprasensory "as in a mirror," that is to say, in an indirect and mediate way: thus does man's spirit see God in the mirror of things, and thus does the soul contemplate "mysteries" through the mirror of words, and so on.

It is to this current of thought that modern exegesis usually seems to link those Christian apostolic texts that speak of the mirror. As we read in the Epistle of James:

> If someone is a listener to the *logos* and does not put it into practice, it is like a man *who contemplates in a mirror the face of his origin,* and having contemplated, departs and at once forgets what he was.[71]

For "origin" the Greek text has *genesis,* which the Vulgate renders by *nativitas.* We may assume that what is meant is the original face of man, namely, that within him which is the "image" of God and which he rediscovers in the mirror of *logos,* in listening to the Word. But the principal text among these is the one where St. Paul distinguishes between "mirror-like" and "face-to-face" visions:

> Now we see in effect by a mirror, enigmatically; but then, it will be face to face. Now I know partially; but then, I will know as I have been known.[72]

The face-to-face vision of God was reserved for the future life, or at best, for exceptional beings in this life.[73] Normally in this world one has only the "mirror-like" vision of God—reflected, enigmatic, and partial. The Evangelist speaks of the future when he says, "Happy are the pure of heart, for they *will see* God,"[74] and the Epistle of John likewise refers to future time:

> When he appears we will be like him, because we *will see* him as he is. All those who have this hope, founded upon him, *purify themselves* as he himself is pure.[75]

Is not this *purification* that of the dust on the mirror? Elsewhere St. Paul says:

> *Reflecting* entirely on a single unveiled [spiritual] face the light of the Lord, we are transformed into his own image [as it is reflected in us], from light to light, as by the Lord, who is spirit.[76]

Over the centuries a great mass of exegesis developed over the opposition between the two visions of which St. Paul speaks, the "mirror-like" and the "face-to-face": for the whole question of transcendence was at stake. In many of these texts the metaphor of the mirror crops up again. The passage in Genesis about "image" and "likeness" has likewise inspired a wealth of commentary. But I will not attempt to summarize the opinions of the Fathers and Doctors of the Church regarding extremely complex questions which lie beyond my competence—I have already ventured too far into a field foreign to my own studies. Still I shall cite a few examples of this metaphor which I have chanced upon in my reading and which have seemed to me helpful in understanding better its Chinese and Buddhist applications.

Most of the Greek Fathers distinguish between image and likeness, *eikōn* and *homoiousis.* In the second century, Irenaeus defined the *eikōn* as the natural image of God, common to all men, and contrasted it with the *homoiousis,* the divine likeness accorded only to Christians.[77] Clement of Alexandria (d. ca. A.D. 215) interposed the *logos* between God and man: the human spirit is the image of the *logos,* and it is the *logos* which is the image of God.[78] However, unlike St. Paul, Clement does seem to have admitted that in this life a vision of God "face-to-face and *without mirrors*" can be gained,[79] a vision brought about through purification by gnosis, and designated by him as *sudden:*

> When a light is brought suddenly into a banquet room, the guests are surprised and dazzled; but little by little they get used to the light and, exercising their reasoning powers, they are filled with joy.[80]

This vision is also an *eternal* contemplation.[81] Though Clement was of the subitist persuasion,[82] he did not neglect the gradualist point of view. Only those who have purified themselves of their passions can attain to gnosis, the knowledge of God; the spirit must be pure and free of every blemish in order for the image to emerge in it. Faith must not remain "inactive and solitary," but rather requires an active quest.[83]

For Origen, in the third century, the *image* of God is innate to man (in a "sudden" manner) while the *likeness* must be acquired through man's free actions.[84] In the fifth century, Diadochus of Photice postulated between image and likeness a relationship of potentiality and act: the image is the "token" or "pledge" which brings us to aspire to future likeness. Such likeness depends upon a purification that Diadochus identifies with baptism, for it is through baptism that "divine grace fits itself to the features of the divine image."[85] Already in the fourth century, Athanasius insisted on purification, in language redolent with Platonism. In two treatises dating from his youth,[86] he wrote that in order to return to God, man has to remove from his spirit the defilement he has acquired by desiring perceptible things: "Wipe away the spots of sin that dirty the soul," "wash until everything *foreign* to soul is removed." Then having again become one, purified and resplendent, the soul, which is made in the image of God, sees in itself, *as in a mirror,* the *logos,* the image of the Father. We see that the word "foreign" *(to allotrion),* reminiscent of the Sanskrit *āgantuka* and "adventitious dust"[87] of Chinese Buddhism, occurs also in Plotinus.[88]

But it is above all at the hands of Gregory of Nyssa (337–400), who was the greatest representative of the Cappadocian school, and whose role in the formation of Christian thought and mysticism has been clarified by several recent studies,[89] that the metaphor of the mirror undergoes what are for us its most interesting developments. The author of the *Catechetical Discourse* makes no distinction between the divine image and the divine likeness.[90] He proceeds from a kind of "subitism" after the Platonic manner. If man is the image of God, he is so by virtue of his very nature *(kata physin).*[91] He has God within himself, unknown and hidden; conversion is a return to his original state, a restoration:[92]

> The creator who made man in his image deposited into the nature of this model being the seeds of all virtues, so that the good would not have to be

> brought in from outside. . . . And there is no other way to attain what we desire than to give this good to ourselves.[93]

For this it is sufficient to resort to a wholly negative effort, a purging of the passions:

> Freed from the movement of the passions, . . . the soul draws into itself and is able to know itself completely, as it is in its nature; and it contemplates the archetype in its own beauty, *like an image in a mirror.*[94]

The point is therefore to purify the spiritual mirror:

> *The spirit is like a mirror,* receiving a form from the object that appears in it. The nature, which is subordinate to the spirit, cleaves to it, and in turn receives its adornment from this beauty set beside it, *as if it were the mirror to a mirror.* . . . But when matter, which itself has neither form nor constitution, emerges in its deformity, it corrupts the beauty of the nature. Then the ugliness of matter passes via the nature to the spirit itself, with the result that the impression of the divine image is no longer visible there. And the spirit, presenting *like a mirror* only its reverse side to the idea of the all-good, repulses the manifestations of the splendor of the good, and models in itself nothing but the deformity of matter. Thus is evil born.[95]

The metaphor of the mirror occurs here in terms which recall those of the *Platform Sūtra:*

> A piece of iron, when cleaned by a stone of the rust which had shortly before obscured it, reflects in itself the light of the sun and shines back rays. So too the interior man, whom the Lord calls the heart: when he has removed the defiling rust covering over his beauty, he will receive anew the image of the archetype.[96]

For Gregory, as for Platonism, evil is only something added onto our true nature:

> Each person must distinguish himself carefully from what is around him, so that he will not be attached to what is foreign *(to allotrion)* to him. . . . Whoever turns toward that which belongs to human nature, toward the *logos,* will scorn whatever is not *logos.* . . . Man, the image of God, did not originally have as part of his essence the life of the passions. These were added later, and the godlike beauty of the soul, made in the image of the prototype, was obscured by sin, as iron is by rust.[97]

Detachment, the absence of passions, is likened to the *clear mirror* which reflects the divine sun.[98]

Gregory is even less a gradualist than Plotinus. Whereas, according to Plotinus,

> it is a labor *(ergon)* for the soul, burdened by the addition of a foreign element *(to allotrion),* to wash and clean itself in order to be again beautiful and be what it was before.[99]

Gregory in contrast holds that for the soul

> to become that which it was before, the likeness of God, is not our labor *(ergon)*, nor is it in the power of humans to accomplish at all: it is a deed of divine generosity, which has graced our nature, since our creation, with this likeness to it.[100]

Apart from the notions of creator, grace, and likeness, do we not find here taking place between the pagan philosopher and his Christian rebutter the debate of Shen-hsiu and Hui-neng?

Gregory maintained that God cannot be known as an object by ordinary cognition *(gnōsis)*. He can only be known to the extent that he manifests himself to the soul through his grace:

> Blessed are not those who know something of God, but rather those who have him in themselves. . . . According to the words, *the Kingdom of God is within you,* whoever has purified his own heart of all created things sees in his own beauty the image of the divine nature.[101]

Moreover, the property of the mirror is not to be anything in itself but rather to conform to the objects it faces:[102] the Chinese would say it "responds" *(ying)*.

> *Human nature is truly like a mirror: it takes the form of that which its wishes reflect.* When it has turned its back on sin and has been purified by the *logos,* it receives in itself the disk of the sun, and shines with the same light that appears within it.[103]

Christian commentators see this doctrine of passivity as the great innovation of Gregory of Nyssa, in which "under cover of retention of the Platonic terminology, a whole transformation of Platonism" took place.[104] Gregory introduced into Christianity the idea of a transcendent God, distinct from created beings, and also the idea of the grace which he offers us and which we are free to accept or not. We can also see this thinker in another perspective, that of Chinese quietism and "non-doing."

The tendency today is to recognize a strong influence of Gregory of Nyssa in the work of Dionysius the Areopagite, active at the end of the fifth century, who is known to have exerted a profound influence on the whole of Christian mysticism in both its Eastern and Western branches. The metaphor of the mirror occurs with Dionysius under circumstances which recall Gregory of Nyssa.[105] But I will not pursue the metaphor in medieval and modern literature, as most authors merely embroider on themes they have taken from biblical and patristic sources. To be sure, original motifs often come to be mingled with the embroidery, and this is especially the case beginning with the great fourteenth-century revival of mystical philosophy, at bottom Neoplatonic, that within

Christianity announced the dawn of modern times. Ruysbroeck (1293–1381) drew from the doctrine of the divine image and from its elaboration by St. Augustine the very model of a fundamentally trinitarian philosophy, in which the metaphor of the mirror crops up time and again.[106] He sees the creation as a vision that God has:

> Creatures are eternally born, before having been created in time. God saw and contemplated them in himself distinctly, according to the ideas which are in him.[107]

In Ruysbroeck's *Mirror of Eternal Blessedness,* whose title is significant, God's wisdom itself is compared to a mirror, like the "mirror consciousness" of Buddhas:

> The higher parts of our soul are like a *living mirror of God,* where God has imprinted his eternal image and where no other image can appear. . . . Everything that God knows distinctly in the *mirror of his wisdom,* the images, forms, reasons, orderings, all of it is truth and life insofar as this life is himself, for there is in him nothing but his own nature.[108]

To terminate this vagabond inquiry gracefully, after so many quotations which have been more or less distorted in translation, I cannot resist the pleasure of quoting two great French texts from the seventeenth century. The first is by Marie of the Incarnation (1599–1672), an admirable writer who was also an eminent woman of action. As she reported in one of the accounts of her states of prayer,

> there was always present for me the impression of this great abyss of divinity into which I had plunged, and just as vivid an impression of my nothingness and my impurities. *My soul saw itself in this great All as in a very clear mirror,* where I discerned all its defects down to the least atom of imperfection with which it was soiled; and it was this that humbled it, making it hide all the more in its God, to be purified, burned, and consumed by him.[109]

Has the passive humility of the creature before God ever been expressed in simpler and more moving terms?

We come finally to a passage by Fénelon (1651–1715) from his *Explanation of Maxims for Saints on the Interior Life,*[110] a work which was censured for quietism in 1699, two years after its publication:

> Water which has been agitated can neither be clear nor receive the image of nearby objects; but *tranquil water is like the clear glass of a mirror. It receives without alteration all the images of various objects, and keeps none of them.* It is the same for the pure and peaceful soul. God imprints on it his image and that of all the objects he wishes to imprint there. Everything is imprinted, everything erased. This soul has no form of its own, and it equally has every form that grace gives it. . . . Man at this stage can say, "I am com-

> pletely created. Nothing remains of this soul, and everything in it is obliterated as soon as God wishes to create new impressions!"

Would not one think oneself to be reading Chuang-tzu or some quietistic Chinese Buddhist? I would wish us to dream that by investigating distant origins some historic rapprochement would be possible between Fénelon and the Mahāyāna (though what could be said of pre-Buddhist China?)—through the Greek Fathers appealed to by Fénelon for authority, who could in turn have been, like the Neoplatonists to whom they are so close, under the influence of Indian thought (which moreover may itself contain borrowings from Western thought). . . . For my own part, in composing this brief study I have not asked myself any historical questions. If we wish, we may see here a comparative essay, or more simply an essay the point of which is to clarify a Chinese philosophical metaphor by contrasting it with parallels in China and outside China, and particularly with its "reflections" in "mirrors" familiar to us. There are certainly discrepancies among these parallels, for a metaphor, like a rite, can lend itself to extremely diverse uses. To some, reflections in a mirror serve to illustrate the unreality of the phenomenal world. To others, on the contrary, the clear mirror is like the absolute, reflecting back to man his ideal image. Or again, the mirror's property of faithfully reflecting objects without being touched by them is compared to the detachment of the sage, who apprehends reality in an impersonal and immediate manner. These are in short the two aspects of the mirror, the one active, the other passive.[111] For most thinkers, what is significant is the necessity of cleaning the mirror to bring back its clarity, and they liken this cleaning to the purification of the human spirit, which has to purge itself of passions in order to be able to reflect purity. The obscured mirror is then comparable to the impure spirit, which can only know the true in an imperfect and mediate way.

This recapitulation is far from complete. But the resources of the human imagination are after all modest, and among so many disparate documents there are, it seems to me, enough common features for them to be able to illuminate each other on some points.

Translated by Neal Donner

Notes

The translator would like to thank Mme. Elise Olson, whose preliminary translation of this article made his task much easier.

1. The word *t'ai* 'frame, stand' can be used in Chinese to designate mirrors (one does not say "a mirror" but "a frame of mirror," just as one says in French *un pied de salade,* 'a head of lettuce'). This verse can be understood simply in the

sense that the mirror does not exist: "There is not even a frame of the clear mirror!"

2. The text of these verses has come down to us in various versions. The principal variant is in the third line of Hui-neng's verse: all versions that post-date this one (recovered at Tun-huang) have "Fundamentally not a single thing exists" in place of "The Buddha-nature is eternally pure," which is slightly more explicit. See *T* 48.337c–338a, 348b–349a. For other recensions see Matsumoto Bunzaburō in *Zengaku kenkyū* 18 (1932): 54; and in *Bukkyō kenkyū* 2, no. 4 (1938): 46.

Trans: In the second line of Shen-hsiu's verse, Demiéville translates the Chinese *hsin* by *ésprit.* The latter can be retranslated into English as either "mind," which brings us into accord with Yampolsky and other English-speaking Buddhologists, or "spirit," which has a distinctly non-Buddhist flavor. Now even though the point of the paper as a whole is to illustrate the uses which mystics of various times and places have made of the mirror metaphor in their effort to understand the nature of *l'ésprit,* in our translation we have used "mind" in the first (or "oriental") part of the paper (to translate *hsin* from Chinese and *citta* from Sanskrit, as most scholars do today) and "spirit" in the ("occidental") second part. Unfortunately this renders the cultural analogy considerably less striking, but the alternative procedure, to use "spirit" throughout for *ésprit,* yields barbarisms in the Buddhist quotations. Demiéville is able to take full advantage of the fact that *ésprit* covers more semantic territory than "spirit." Besides *ésprit,* he also employs other terms which in other contexts often have distinct meanings, but whose meanings in this paper coalesce: *âme* 'soul', *intelligence* 'intellect', *connaissance* 'consciousness', *coeur* 'heart', and even *ātman*.

3. *Tsing-hua hsüeh-pao* 7, no. 2: 1–4.

4. *Trans:* "Quietism" here means something analogous to the doctrinal posture taken by the seventeenth-century French semi-quietist Fénelon, cited by Demiéville near the end of the paper. This is viewed by the Catholic Church as "a recurrence of the ultrasupernaturalism that has plagued and stimulated the Church from its earliest years. . . . [It reaches] the ultimate moral aberration" (*New Catholic Encyclopedia,* 12:26–27). Spanish quietism in its pure form was condemned (and its principal proponent imprisoned) as heretical by the Holy Office in 1687, only to resurface briefly again with Fénelon in a somewhat amended form. It clearly does not signify merely "a quiet condition or habit, especially of mind" (Webster).

5. *Hsü-kao-seng chüan, T* 50.598a.

6. *Leng-ch'ieh shih-tzu chi,* by Ching-chüeh, *T* 85.1284b. These metaphors are also found in the *Treatise on the Supreme Vehicle,* attributed to Hung-jen, fifth patriarch of Ch'an and the teacher of Hui-neng; but the attribution is in doubt. See *T* 48.377a, 378a.

7. Hu Shih, *Shen-hui ho-shang i chi* (Shanghai Oriental Book Co.: 1930), 108.

8. Ibid., 134.

9. See Plotinus, *Enneads* 1.2.4: "To purify oneself *(to kathairesthai)* is a less perfect virtue than to be purified *(to kekatharthai).*"

10. Taken from the Chinese version of a celebrated philosophical treatise (the

Mahāyāna-śraddhotpāda-śāstra, which is attributed to an Indian author), the terms *pen-chüeh* and *shih-chüeh* have had a grand career in Chinese Buddhism.

Trans: Most scholars now believe this text, *Ta-sheng ch'i-hsing lun,* to be of Chinese authorship. *Pen-chüeh* is of course *hongaku* in Japanese pronunciation, a term whose career in Japanese Buddhism has also been grand.

11. *Madhyānta-vibhāga* 1.21–22, ed. Yamaguchi (Nagoya, 1934), 59–60.

Trans: Demiéville's *ésprit* in the third line of the second verse corresponds to Skt. *citta* (rendered "intellect" by Stcherbatsky). The text goes on, in Stcherbatsky's translation, to say, "[Here] the term 'intellect' is to be taken just in the sense of the Absolute, although the term intellect generally [in other contexts] means the phenomenal Mind."

12. Śankara, Commentary to the *Brahma-sūtras,* tr. Deussen, *The System of the Vedānta* (Chicago, 1912), 403.

13. This verse by Ching-hsüan (943–1027) is cited in an Annamite collection of biographies of Chinese Ch'an patriarchs. This has recently been re-edited at Hanoi by the École Française d'Extrême-Orient.

14. Such a man seeks neither to follow his guests (accompany them as required in Chinese etiquette) nor to walk before them.

15. Literally, without being "wounded" by them. The Taoist sage is invulnerable. In renouncing all activity tied to a particular aim, in identifying himself with the absolute, and in voiding himself of every passion which would impel him to overstep the place assigned to him by heaven (nature), he manages to accomplish his duties and to "mount into the heights" *(sheng)* of things, without participating in them or being in the least tainted by them.

16. He does not pursue it as a virtue knowingly regarded as a good. Quietude is defined apophatically, negatively.

17. I.e., reflects with complete clarity. The concepts "enlighten, reflect, look at, see clearly, understand, know" tend in certain Chinese words *(chao, ming)* to associate and mingle. Shen-hui said, "The clear mirror *illumines (chao),* whether there is an object there for it to reflect or not" (*Shen-hui ho-shang i chi,* 115–116, 212–213). Similarly, the pure mind *illumines* this invisible, this unknowable which is the absolute. In Chinese Buddhism, *chao* technically designates the *gnōsis* function, prajñā. Plotinus likewise speaks of vision as illumination (*Enneads* 1.6.9, 5.3.8, 5.5.8, etc.), and though the semantic link between *speculum* 'mirror' and *speculatio* 'contemplation' (used for the Greek *theōria,* which means a beholding, spectacle, something to be looked at, contemplation) may be historically doubtful, numerous Christian exegetes have made use of it. See for example Thomas Aquinas, *Summa Theologica,* part II, 2.2, question 180 ("Of the contemplative life"), article 3 (where reference is made to St. Augustine); also Suso, tr. Ancelet-Heustache (Paris, 1943), 245; and further the Carthusian monk Guiges du Pont of the thirteenth century, in J. Maréchal, *Psychologie des mystiques,* vol. 2 (Paris, 1937), 279.

18. Leibnitz's monads are essentially "living mirrors" which each reflect the whole universe. The above two passages from *Chuang-tzu* are from chaps. 7 and 13 respectively.

Trans: cf. Burton Watson, *The Complete Works of Chuang Tzu* (New York: Columbia University Press, 1968), 97.

19. *Chuang-tzu,* chap. 15. *Trans:* cf. Watson, 169.

20. Ibid., chap. 33. This doctrine is attributed in the *Chuang-tzu* to Barrier Keeper Yin. The text is further developed in the *Lieh-tzu,* chap. 4. *Trans:* cf. Watson, 372.

21. Ibid., chap. 5. *Trans:* Watson translates, "Only what is still can still the stillness of other things" (p. 69).

22. Ibid., chap. 5.

23. It passively reproduces sounds.

24. It reproduces the diversity of forms. See *Huai-nan-tzu,* chap. 1, SPTK 1.4b–5a; translated by E. Morgan, in *The Great Luminant* (London, 1934), 5–6.

25. He loses the feeling of participation in the ordered totality of the universe.

26. They do not allow their divine nature to be obliterated by human passions. *Huai-nan-tzu,* SPTK 1.5a.

27. Ibid., chap. 2, 2.3b; see Morgan, *The Great Luminant,* 36.

28. Ibid., 2.10a–10b; see Morgan, 49. *Trans:* Note that reference is made to a mirror whose surface is of polished metal—not of glass as would be the case today.

29. Ibid.

30. Ibid., chap. 9, 9.14a.

31. Ibid., chap. 14, 14.5b.

32. Ibid., 8b. I do not take into account the textual emendations proposed by Wang Nien-sun.

33. *Hsün-tzu,* sec. 21, SPTK 15.11a. See Homer Dubs' translation, *The Works of Hsüntze* (London, 1928), 271.

Trans: For a more recent rendering, see Burton Watson's translation, *Hsün Tzu: Basic Writings* (New York: Columbia University Press, 1963), 131–132.

34. *Chāndogya* 8.7.4; *Katha* 6.5; *Kaushītaki* 4.11–13; *Bṛhadāranyaka* 3.9.13–15.

35. *Chāndogya-upanishad,* tr. E. Senart (Paris, 1930), 31.

36. See the comments by A. E. Crawley on the evidence collected in the ethnographic literature, in the *Hastings Encyclopedia of Religion and Ethics,* vol. 3 (Edinburgh, 1915), 696. Adherents to the Freudian conception of the *imago* have called attention to a similar dynamic in children and even animals.

Trans: The *imago* is "the more or less infantile conception of the parent retained in the unconscious" (Webster).

37. *Śvetāśvetara-upanishad* 2.14, tr. Deussen, *Sechzig Upanishads des Veda* (Leipzig, 1905), 296.

38. The art of the illusionist magician is sometimes called in Sanskrit "Indra's net" *(indra-jāla).* Taking inspiration from this term, the Chinese Buddhists imagined a net which is supposed to adorn the palace of the god Indra at the summit of the cosmic mountain Sumeru, a net whose every mesh bears a jewel. All the jewels reflect each other, or more precisely, each of them reflects all the others. This was taken as an illustration of the interpenetration of the one and the many. A further metaphor illustrated the same interpenetration: a person situated between two opposite mirrors in which he is reflected to infinity. See Mochizuki's encyclopedia, *Bukkyō daijiten,* vol. 1 (Tokyo, 1931), 184 and 601. In the course of the *abhiṣeka* (unction) ceremony of the Tantric

school, the new initiate is presented with a mirror in which he is to contemplate his image in order to impress upon himself the illusory character of his personality and of all things. See R. Tajima, *Étude sur le Mahāvairocana-sūtra* (Paris, 1939), 14.

39. See references in Étienne Lamotte, *Le traité de la Grande Vertu de Sagesse,* vol. 1 (Louvain, 1944), 357 n. 1.

40. Asaṅga, *Mahāyāna-saṃgraha* 2.27, tr. Étienne Lamotte, vol. 2 (Louvain, 1938), 123. See also the notes, which bring together numerous references.

41. *Ghanavyūha-sūtra,* quoted in the *Vijñapti-mātratā-siddhi,* tr. La Vallée Poussin (Paris, 1928), 532.

42. *Mahāyāna-saṃgraha* 2.7, tr. Lamotte, 2:94.

43. *Abhidharmakośa* 3.11–12, tr. La Vallée Poussin, vol. 3 (Paris-Louvain, 1926), 34–35.

Trans: Vasubandhu wrote this famous Sarvāstivādin treatise before converting to his brother's brand of Mahāyāna (if indeed there was but one Vasubandhu). It is of course not a Mahāyāna work.

44. *Traité de la grande Vertu de Sagesse,* 1:378ff.

45. Nanjio's edition (Kyoto, 1923), 44.

46. Ibid., 44, 55–56.

47. *Vāsanā* [*Trans:* Demiéville uses *imprégnation* to translate this word], the germs of activity, notably of the imaginative function, with which primal karma has impregnated our mind and which are apt to "fructify" in pseudo-objects, illusory creations of our mind.

48. The duality of subject and object. Nanjio's edition, 186; also cf. 93–94.

49. *Dhammādāsa. Mahāparinibbāna-sutta* 2.8, tr. from the Chinese version by Weller, *Monumenta Serica* 4, no. 1 (Peking, 1939): 61–62.

50. *Ādāna-vijñāna,* often equated with the "nethermost" consciousness *(ālaya-vijñāna).*

Trans: Demiéville and the French translators use *tréfonds* (nethermost, deepest, implying the "sub" of "subconscious") here instead of translating *ālaya* directly as "storehouse" or "repository."

51. *Saṃdhi-nirmocana-sūtra,* tr. É. Lamotte (Louvain-Paris, 1935), 186.

52. *Trans:* to a *dusty* mirror?

53. *Tathatā* is the word here for absolute. *Saṃdhi-nirmocana-sūtra,* tr. E. Lamotte, 224. For the reading *tathatā* I follow Hsüan-tsang's version, *T* 16.701a.

54. *Ādarśa-jñāna.*

55. *Mahāyāna-sūtrālamkāra,* tr. S. Levi (Paris, 1911), 88–89; *Mahāyāna-saṃgraha,* tr. La Vallée Poussin, 681–682.

56. The masters of the Yogācāra school (quoted in the *Vijñapti-mātratā-siddhi,* tr. La Vallée Poussin) strove to refute this criticism.

57. *Mizān al-a'mal,* tr. H. Hachem, *Critère de l'action* (Paris, 1945), 27–28, 21.

58. *Madnun saghīr,* tr. A. J. Wensinck, *La pensée de Ghazzālī* (Paris, 1940), 60.

59. Plotinus, *Enneads* 4.7.10; Gregory of Nyssa, see below.

60. *Ihyā,* tr. Wensinck, *La pensée de Ghazzālī,* 27.

61. These three terms, so familiar in India, are found in the *Republic* in the allegory of the cave and in a passage preceding it, on the divided line (6.510a, 515b).

62. A. J. Festugière, "Grecs et sages orientaux," *Revue de l'histoire des religions,* vol. 130 (1945): 38.

63. Eusebius of Caesarea (260?–340?), theologian and church historian.

64. *Alcibiades* 132d–133c.

65. *Enneads* 6.2.22.

66. *Enneads* 3.6.7. See also E. Bréhier's introduction to the *Enneads* (Paris, 1925), 3.6, p. 91.

67. *Enneads* 3.6.13.

68. *Corpus hermeticum, Hermes Trismegistus* 1.14.

69. *Enneads* 3.9.3; 4.3.12, 17. Elsewhere (1.4.10) Plotinus compares again the polished and immobile mirror to the portion of the soul which reflects intelligence and reason, and which is the condition for sensory consciousness, mental images, and the clear conscience.

70. See Leisegang's index to the Berlin edition, *Philonis Alexandriae opera . . .* (1930), 7.2, p. 447; also H. Willms, *Eikōn, eine begriffsgeschichtliche Untersuchung zum Platonismus,* vol. 1, *Philon von Alexandreia* (Münster, 1935), 37ff. The apocryphal *Wisdom of Solomon,* attributed to an Alexandrian Jew of the first century B.C., calls wisdom "a reflection of the eternal light, an unblemished mirror of God" (7.26).

71. James 1:23–24. *Trans:* The King James version reads (adding verse 22): "(But be ye doers of the word, and not hearers only, deceiving your own selves.) For if any be a hearer of the word, and not a doer, he is like unto a man beholding his natural face in a glass: For he beholdeth himself, and goeth his way, and straightway forgetteth what manner of man he was."

72. I Corinthians 13:12. *Trans:* The King James version does not retain the sense of reflection in a mirror: "For now we see *through* a glass darkly; but then face to face: now I know in part; but then shall I know even as also I am known."

73. There have been endless disputations on the question of whether Moses (Exodus 33:11, 20–23) or again the apostle Paul saw God face-to-face.

74. Matthew 5:8. *Trans:* In the King James version, "Blessed are the pure in heart: for they shall see God."

75. I John 3:2–3; cf. 4:12.

76. II Corinthians 3:18. "Unveiled" corresponds to "without dust." I follow the interpretation of E. B. Allo, *Études bibliques* (Paris, 1937), 95–96. It is also that of Suso, tr. J. Ancelet-Eustache (Paris, 1943), 425. Compare John 1:18, also Clement of Alexandria, Athanasius, etc., as cited below. The word "veil" in the sense of the Buddhist *nivāraṇa* 'covering obscuration, obstacle' is frequent among Christian mystics of all eras.

77. J. Gross, *La divinisation du chrétian d'après les Grecs* (Paris, 1938), 145ff.

78. P. Th. Camelot, *Foi et gnose, introduction à l'étude de la connaissance mystique chez Clement d'Alexandrie* (Paris, 1945), 53 n. 1; 114; 120–121.

79. Father Camelot, ibid., 119–120, first declares that Clement admits this, but later, pp. 130–133, he expresses reservations. The metaphor of the mirror is not frequent with Clement. In the index to his edition, *Clemens Alexandrinus . . . ,* vol. 4 (Leipzig, 1936), 507, O. Stählin indicates only five occurrences. Unfortunately I have not been able to refer to these.

80. *Eglogues prophétiques* 35, quoted in Camelot, 130–131.

81. *Aidios theōria,* ibid., 132, 59–60.

82. Clement of Alexandria is one of the principal authorities referred to by Fénelon (1651–1715) in the dispute on quietism. See P. Dudon, *Le Gnostique de Saint Clément d'Alexandrie, opuscule inédit de Fénelon* (Paris, 1930).

83. Camelot, *Foi et gnose,* 52, 59ff. Cf. also the *Stromates* texts quoted in C. Mondésert, *Clément d'Alexandrie, introduction à l'étude de sa pensée religieuse à partir de l'Ecriture* (Paris, 1944), 106–111. Also quoted by J. Lebreton, in "La théorie de la connaissance religieuse chez Clément d'Alexandrie," *Recherches de science religieuse* 18, nos. 1-2 (1928): 478–481. These texts show to what extent Clement was preoccupied with the problem of "subitism" versus "gradualism," an easily recognizable issue beneath his Hellenic and Christian terminology.

84. Gross, *La divinisation du chrétian,* 174ff.

85. *Diadoque, Cent Chapitres sur la perfection spirituelle,* tr. E. Des Plans (Paris-Lyon, 1943), 33, 137, 153.

86. *Against Heathens* and *Incarnation of the Word,* quoted by Arnou, "Platonisme des Pères," in the *Dictionnaire de Théologie catholique,* vol. 12 (Paris, 1935), col. 2309. Also quoted by Maréchal, *Psychologie des mystiques,* 2:93–95. Cf. Tixeront, *Histoire des dogmes,* vol. 2 (Paris, 1909), 138.

87. *K'o-ch'en* in Chinese, where *k'o* normally means "traveler, stranger, temporary guest."

88. *Enneads* 1.6.5, 5.1.1.

89. (1) G. Horn, "Le 'miroir' et la 'nuée,' deux manières de voir Dieu d'après Saint Grégoire de Nysse," *Revue d'ascétique et de mystique* 29 (1927): 113ff. (2) J. B. Schoemann, "Gregor von Nyssas theologische Anthropologie als Bildtheorie," *Scholastik* 18 (1943): 31ff, 175ff. (3) Hans von Balthasar, *Présence et pensée, essai sur la philosophie religieuse de Grégoire de Nysse* (Paris, 1942). (4) J. Daniélou, *Platonisme et théologie mystique, essai sur la doctrine spirituelle de Saint Grégoire* (Paris, 1944). (5) J. Daniélou, tr., *La vie de Moïse* (Paris, 1942). (6) J. Daniélou and J. Laplace, trs., *La création de l'homme* (Paris, 1943).

90. In his sermon on the Biblical phrase "let us make man in our image, after our likeness" (Genesis 1:26), he does make such a distinction, but the attribution of this sermon to Gregory is in dispute precisely on this account. See Daniélou, *Platonisme et théologie mystique,* 11, 52.

91. Daniélou, ibid., 43, 53.

92. Ibid., 51, 227, 269.

93. Quoted by Balthasar, *Présence et pensée,* 92.

94. Ibid., 91.

95. *La création de l'homme,* tr. Laplace and Daniélou, 131–132.

96. Quoted by Daniélou, *Platonisme et théologie mystique,* 225–226.

97. Ibid., 45. Schoemann supplies other passages in *Gregor von Nyssas,* 177, 182–183, 188.

98. Daniélou, *Platonisme,* 48, 103, 106.

99. *Enneads* 1.6.5.

100. Daniélou, *Platonisme,* 227.

101. Ibid., 221–222. See also Horn, *"Le 'miroir' et la 'nuée,'"* 118–121, and

Schoemann, *Gregor von Nyssas,* 49–50, and esp. 182. For Gregory, the creation of man by God "in his image and likeness" was perfect and instantaneous; but the restoration of the image, disfigured because of the Fall, is a gradual and arduous task devolving upon man, though assisted by divine grace.

102. Daniélou, *Platonisme,* 228.

103. Ibid., 232.

104. Ibid., 229. Cf. the same author's introduction to his translation, *La création de l'homme,* 44–46.

105. *Celestial Hierarchy* 3.2; *Ecclesiastical Hierarchy* 3.1, 10.

106. E.g., *The Spiritual Espousals* 1.10, and *The Book of the Twelve Beguines* 10.

107. *The Spiritual Espousals* 3.5, quoted in A. Wautier d'Aygalliers, *Ruysbroeck l'Admirable* (Paris, 1923), 267.

108. *Mirror of Eternal Blessedness* 8 and 17, quoted in Melline d'Asbeck, *La mystique de Ruysbroeck l'Admirable* (Paris, 1930), 278. According to Nicholas of Cusa (1401–1464), God does not see everything in himself as in a mirror, for in that case his knowledge would be dependent on the world. See his "Treatise on the Vision of God," in M. de Gandillac, tr., *Oeuvre choisies de Nicolas de Cues* (Paris, 1942), 400.

109. A. Jamet, ed., *Le témoignage de Marie de l'Incarnation* (Paris, 1932), 248.

110. *Explication des Maximes des Saints sur la view intérieure,* article 30.

111. See P. Claudel, *L'épée et le miroir* (Paris, 1939), 194.

Glossary

Ch'an 禪
chao 照
chieh-pi 解蔽
chien (gradual) 漸
chien (seeing) 見
chien-chaio 漸教
Chuang-tzu 莊子
fo-hsing 佛性
hsin 心
Hsün-tzu 荀子
Huai-nan-tzu 淮南子
Hui-neng 慧能
k'an 看
k'o-ch'en 客塵
li 理
ming 明
pen-chüeh 本覺
shen 神
Shen-hui 神會
Shen-hsiu 神秀
shih 始
shih-chüeh 始覺
ta-li 大理
t'ai 臺
T'an-lun 曇倫
t'ien 天
t'ien-li 天理
tun 頓
tun-chiao 頓教

Sudden Illumination or Simultaneous Comprehension: Remarks on Chinese and Tibetan Terminology

R. A. Stein

This essay examines the two key words, one Chinese and one Tibetan, that are used to characterize enlightenment in Chinese Ch'an and in Tibetan Buddhism. It subjects to criticism the usual translations of these two terms, translations that emphasize the sudden or instantaneous nature of this mystical experience. While the essay does not deny that this aspect is inherent to the concept in question, it shows that what is really at issue is the simultaneity of two planes that are in opposition yet integral (i.e., the absolute and the phenomenal).

It is well known that the Chinese school of Buddhism called Ch'an (Zen in Japanese) was established at the beginning of the seventh century, and a century later divided into two branches or opposing tendencies. These are generally denoted by the terms "gradualism" (in the north) and "subitism" (in the south).[1] We also know that the same opposition was manifested in Tibet, at the end of the eighth century, in the form of a violent controversy, not between the Chinese proponents of these two tendencies, but between Chinese subitists and their Indian adversaries, who were partisans of gradualism.[2] To this one must add the equally well known fact that the opposition between these tendencies goes back in China to those thinkers of the fourth and fifth centuries who, even though they were Buddhists, were interested in philosophical Taoism, and whose writings were impregnated with a style and sometimes even a vocabulary that stems from that source. Notable among them were Hsieh Ling-yün (385–433), Tao-sheng (ca. 360–434), and Seng-chao (374–414), the author of the *Chao lun*.[3] These thinkers and others of the fifth century already insisted on distinguishing between two or three degrees—high, middling, and low—in the teachings and methods which the Buddha bestowed on people in consideration of their intellectual and moral capacities.[4] They employed in this context the key terms to which our present paper is devoted, *tun-wu* or "sudden enlightenment" as the superior method, and *chien(-wu)* or "gradual enlightenment" as the inferior method, to follow for the moment the translation *(illumination subite, graduelle)*[5] adopted by Paul Demiéville, the scholar best informed on that movement of thought.[6] The same terms were taken up again by Tibetan historians, who speak of *tun-men* or "sudden school" and *chien-men* or "gradual school." Beginning with the Ch'an texts in Tibetan preserved among the manuscripts of Tun-huang (eighth to tenth centuries), the term *tun* is translated by *cig-car* (var. *chig-char*), and the term *chien* by *rim-gyis,* whereas the second element to which those terms apply, the Chinese *wu* (enlightenment, intuitive understanding, direct comprehension, Fr. *saisie directe,* Jap. *satori*), is simply rendered by *'jug-pa* 'entry', because these authors thought first of a door *('jug-pa'i sgo)* through which one enters or a path that one takes.[7]

According to the opinion of the greatest specialists, Ch'an and its antecedents represent a development that was essentially, if not purely, Chinese.[8] The classic genealogy, which has this Ch'an go back to Indian patriarchs, notably to Bodhidharma, was formulated relatively late (in the seventh century), to lend authenticity to the movement. Some authors have, however, pointed out analogies with certain conceptions and practices in Indian Tantrism. Tibetan authors have even identified the views of the Ch'an that was introduced to Tibet with the current of Tantric Indian thought known by the name of Mahāmudrā,[9] but there is a chronological objection to this. The Indian Tantrism to which reference is made is hardly attested to until the seventh or even the eighth century. Should one wish to retain the analogy, it is doubtless preferable to think in terms of parallel development.

The key terms which I shall discuss involve some very subtle philosophical notions whose definitions vary somewhat according to the authors or schools. It is not for me to discuss these ideas, since I am a novice in the field of Buddhism. However, I might be permitted to present some unambiguous observations, of a purely linguistic or philological nature, concerning the semantic field of the term translated by "sudden" (Fr. *subit*) (the second term, "gradual," defines itself simply by reference to the first). I arrived at these observations in the course of my reading when I needed to understand and translate certain phrases. It appeared to me that the use of the same equivalent in every case had sometimes led to inadequate translations. After a small investigation it seemed to me that the semantic field of the original Buddhist term is broader than the French term *subit* 'sudden' indicates. And this purely linguistic finding clarifies, for me at least, an important philosophical notion that seems not to have been sufficiently emphasized before. On this subject I am most grateful for the valuable instruction given to me by the lama who helped me translate an extremely difficult Tibetan text, a man called the incarnate of Dags-po [Dwags-po], Byams-pa rgya-mtsho (hereafter Dags-po Rin-po-che).

Hence the question is to determine whether the Chinese word *tun* and its Tibetan equivalent *cig-char* [*cig-car/chig-char*] really mean "sudden." Certainly, if the great specialists have adopted that translation it is because the texts justify it. But there are nuances. Liebenthal translates *tun-wu* with "instantaneous illumination" where it occurs in Hsieh Ling-yün and Tao-sheng, but he notes in another connection that *tun* corresponds to the Sanskrit *yugapat* or *sakṛt,* meaning not "sudden" but "in one glance," as opposed to *chien* (Skt. *anupūrveṇa* or *kramaśaḥ* 'by degrees').[10] Tucci used "immediate entrance" to translate the Tibetan *cig-car 'jug-pa,* but Wayman in his review shows also the correspondence with Skt. *yugapat*—the elements in question are uncovered all together instead of being arranged successively or being uncovered one after the other[11] (this goes back to the *Laṅkāvatāra-sūtra,* the basic text of early Ch'an).[12]

These definitions are confirmed by the *Mahāvyuttpati* dictionary, but its late Chinese translations (Manchu period) are in a certain disorder. In the edition of Sakaki (who gives late Chinese equivalents), one finds at no. 4516 that *krama-yaugapadya* is translated by Tibetan *rim dang cig-car* 'successively at one stroke' (Fr. *d'un seul coup*) and Chinese *hu tz'u-ti* 'sudden order' and *ch'i yü tz'u-ti* 'simultaneous order'—there was confusion. At no. 6557, *yugapat* is translated by Tibetan *cig-char* 'at one stroke', *lan-cig* 'once only',[13] and *mnyam-pa* 'equal, similar' (compare also *dus mnyam-pa* 'at the same instant, simultaneous'). The following Chinese translations are proposed: *hu-jan* 'all of a sudden, instantaneously', *i-tsun* 'at a single time'(?), *p'ing-teng* 'equal, on the same level', and *i-ch'i* or *i-tsao* 'together, at the same instant'. The edition of Wogihara, ch. 245, no. 155, and ch. 199, no. 111, provides better translations (and permits us to correct the mistakes in Sakaki's edition): *yugapat* is translated by *i-ch'i, i-tsao,* and *p'ing-teng* whereas *krama-yaugapadya* is translated by *ch'i yü tz'u-ti,* that is, "together, completely, simultaneously" and "successively, in order, one after the other." The terms *chien* and *tun* have been added in parentheses. One sees that the meaning "sudden" is absent and that the basic meaning is simultaneity—in time, in space, or on the plane of mental activity. A certain ambiguity is apparently inherent in this concept and in those words that formulate it. This could have had some consequences at the time of these discussions and philosophical controversies. It suffices here to consider various expressions for us to realize the proximity of these notions to each other, their participation in the same semantic field: (1) "at one stroke" (once only), but (2) "all at once" (suddenly), and (3) "outright" (right away).[14] (Note also "immediate," the original meaning of which in both French and English is "being or acting without an *intermediary,*" while the colloquial sense, "all of a sudden, instantaneously," is merely derivative.) It is obvious that if an action is to take place in passing successively from one element to another—a calculation, for example, or a description—it would require time and would take place relatively slowly. If, on the contrary, one could comprehend all of these elements *in one glance,* in an instant, then the action would be quick, instantaneous (but instantaneous does not necessarily imply sudden). The Tibetans have emphasized this aspect very clearly. When Sa-skya Paṇḍita discussed the Indian Mahāmudrā doctrine which the Tibetan Bka'-brgyud-pa and Rdzogs-chen-pa schools received from Nāropa and others, he protested the fact that, according to him, the Mahāmudrā known in his era amounted to more or less the same as the *Chinese* views. He was certainly thinking about the Ch'an of his time, which insisted on the paradoxical, unexpected, sudden character of enlightenment. Here is what he writes:

> In the Mahāmudrā of today and in the Rdzogs-chen of the Chinese fashion, "fall from above" and "climb from below" [on one hand] and "successively" and "simultaneously" [on the other] are only terminological variants. Where meaning is concerned no distinction is made between them.[15]

A fall from above is rapid, while the expression "climb from below" evokes the celebrated parable of the ant who wants to climb a high mountain. In Tibetan, the opposition is linguistically underlined by the consonant alternation *yas/mas* 'from above/from below'. The expression is found again among the Bon-po (whose doctrines are identical to those of the Rdzogs-chen-pa), applied, as is proper, to the opposition between comprehension or "view," which is immediate, and moral practice, which progresses by stages, step by step. One reads, for example, "View falls from above and practice climbs from below, [but] in the end they are reunited in the single drop of absolute truth *(paramārtha).*"[16]

This opposition between rapidity on the one hand and slowness on the other was already explicitly emphasized in the Chinese and Tibetan Tun-huang documents on the Sino-Indian controversy. In one of these (Pelliot 117), the *Sūtra Explaining the Door of Simultaneous Entry [that is the method] of Dhyāna (Ch'an) of the Abbot Mahāyāna,* "simultaneous entry" is designated as a "short or shortened path" (Tib. *nye-lam*, Ch. *chin-tao*), as the "secret door" *(gsang-ba'i sgo)* and as "the door to the path of liberation" *('grol thard-pa'i lam sgo).*[17] Likewise one Bon-po author speaks of the "simultaneous" *(gcig-char)* method of the "rapid path" *(myur-lam).*[18] From there one moves rapidly to the point of exalting the rapid path and depreciating the slow path. As is said in the *Blon-po Bka'-thang* (239a = 21b): "[The *stons-mun,* Ch. *tun-men,* Tib. *cig-car 'jug-pa,* school,] deciding that the absolute truth *(paramārtha)* without duality is one, characterizes the partisans of simultaneity *(cig-car-pa)* as entering the path of the lion, for whom even an abyss or chasm is no obstacle, and characterizes the partisans of gradualism *(rim-gyis-pa)* as entering the path of the fox [fearful and advancing with caution]." Or again (239b = 22a): "The simultaneous knowledge [or comprehension, Fr. *saisie*] which is devoid of discursive thoughts [those that are characterized by their *successive* logical operations] is similar to the lion, king of beasts, who [flaunts] his magnificence."[19] This exalted "royal path" is the "profound path" *(zab-lam)* of Tantrism or Vajrayāna. One also finds it, as everyone knows, in European esotericism.[20] I shall not venture here to enlarge upon the properly philosophical and moral aspect of the distinction in question. But I believe that the violent turn taken by the controversy and the Tibetan king's decision in favor of "Indian" gradualism are explained by the priority given to the practical consequences of the moral conduct that results from following the respective two paths. All the texts in fact associate the direct and rapid path with uselessness (Fr. *inutilité*), hence with the rejection of good works and moral conduct.[21] What permitted this attitude was the making of distinctions both among listeners or faithful followers, who had different degrees of psychological and intellectual aptitudes, and among the different teachings of the Buddha as adapted to these different capacities—an idea that had been widespread since an early date.[22]

These few remarks will suffice, I think, to give an idea of the importance which clothed the ambiguity of the concept we have under consideration, an ambiguity that motivated the adoption of the term "subitism" (Fr. *subitisme*). Is this due to an imprecision of vocabulary? We will see that for the Chinese *tun* this might quite possibly be the case. But not so for the Tibetan expression, which is unambiguous. Since I have no knowledge of Sanskrit, I am in no position to make a similar evaluation of *yugapad*. But Monier-Williams gives in his dictionary for the latter only the meaning "simultaneity" (and derives the word from *yuga* 'yoke', the exact meaning being "to be side by side under the same yoke," referring to a pair of oxen harnessed together under a single yoke, one at each end of the beam). It now remains for us to consider in which sense the concept of simultaneity easily brings with it certain meanings and connotations.

Textual Examples

It is time to consider closely the usage of the terms in question in contexts other than Ch'an, and further in concrete cases if possible. For this we will remain, as far as we can, on the strictly philological or linguistic level. We begin with the Tibetan, which offers no ambiguities.

The expression *cig* (or *chig*) *-car* (or *-char*) consists of two words. The first is a form of the numerical adjective, or the name for the number *gcig* (one). The etymology of the second is less certain. With the initial letter unvoiced, the dictionaries indicate an obsolete word, *car, ca-re, car-re* or *car-mar,* which would mean "always, continually, going on without end," but Chos-grags also gives some examples that imply the idea of "part" or "side": *car brdungs* 'to pound something until flat', *car-la thebs-pa* 'to distribute, align in order by successive parts', and *car-leb* 'flat sides', as when one speaks of hands joined in prayer. On the other hand, with the initial letter aspirated, *char* can be considered the locative case of *chà* 'a part', but Chos-grags indicates at the same time the meaning "pair," and also the meaning "equal to, on the same level." *Char* is indeed the locative case of *cha,* but this interpretation may be excluded, for the phrase *cig-char (char)-du,* with the locative *du,* is often encountered, which would seem to exclude a second locative in *-r.* Some Tibetan speakers occasionally equate *char* with the verb *'char (shar)* 'to appear', but this is more a play of words than anything else.[23] In spite of the apparent impossibility[24] of explaining *char* as locative, the comparison with expressions containing *car* as a component seems to indicate that the meaning "part," implying "distribution by parts," remains underlying. For *cha* exists also as an equivalent to *zung* 'pair, couple' (*cha-gcig* = *zung-gcig* according to Chos-grags).[25] Whatever the case may be, *char* and *car* are employed in general usage with the names of numbers to designate a unitary or a closed group of several elements: for example, *lnga-char* 'all five together', *gnyis-char* 'both together', and so on (Jäschke).[26] Also *gcig-car* (or *-char*) means "at a single occasion" (Fr. *en une seule fois*), and Jäschke indeed translates it with "at the same time, simultaneously" (as opposed to one-after-the-other, successively) in citing the *Dzangs-blun.* It is true that he adds the meaning "at once, of a sudden" (opp. to gradually) in citing Mi-la ras-pa. But the passage that he adduces (the exact source is unfortunately not specified) refers no doubt only to the Mahāmudrā system, of which Mi-la ras-pa was a great exponent. Jäschke could have had a Tibetan informant influenced by the equivalent of "the rapid path," but Chos-grags, an excellent lexicographer, gives *(g)cig-car* exclusively the meaning "together, at the same time" (see note 23 above). He is certainly correct. Neither etymologically nor practically does the expression mean "sudden." All the concrete examples that I have been able to locate confirm the meaning "simultaneous." They are as follows:

(1) The great translator Rva lo-tsa-ba (ca. 1050–1100) "had [then] about 124 disciples. In conferring upon them a consecration *(dbang)* and a teaching, he liberated them *all at the same time (cig-car du)*. . . ."[27]

(2) In a hundred myriad continents, "The twelve acts [of Śākyamuni

Buddha] are displayed *simultaneously (cig-car du)* in a hundred myriad forms."[28]

(3) A saint named Rgyal-sras "appeared simultaneously *(cig-char du)* in three [different] bodies."[29]

(4) Another eminent lama, Nyang Ting-'dzing bzang-po, "saw with his own fleshly eyes the four continents *(dvīpa)* at the same time (simultaneously, *cig-car du*)."[30]

(5) Another miracle of a saint! After his death, "he showed himself again, simultaneously *(gcig-car du)* in the appearance of five illusory bodies" (that is to say, he appeared to the faithful at the same time in different places).[31]

In all the above examples, the translation "sudden" makes no sense. The word can only mean "simultaneous" (Fr. *simultané*). A good confirmation of this is provided by a bilingual text:

(6) There exists a Tibetan translation of the apocryphal Chinese sūtra *Pa-yang shen-chou ching*. Both the original and the translation are found among the Tun-huang manuscripts. One reads, from the Tibetan, "These eight bodhisattvas spoke together (at the same time, *cig-char,* var. *cig-car*) to the Buddha . . . ," and the Chinese translation[32] also has: "spoke all together (*chü*) . . ."[33] We see that, just as in the *Mahāvyuttpati,* the translation does not use the word *tun* to render *cig-car.* The same applies in another bilingual Tun-huang text as given below, a text that recites the transmission of the *Laṅkāvatāra-sūtra,* itself directly relevant to early Ch'an.

(7) Chinese: "Since principle and things are melted together *(chü),* since absolute truth *(paramārtha)* and conventional truth (relative truth, *saṃvṛti*) are seen together (comprehended simultaneously, *ch'i*), and since contamination [of thought] and purity are identical *(i-ju),* Buddha and all living beings are from the beginning equal and coincident *(p'ing-teng i-ch'i).*" The terms employed are the same that the *Mahāvyuttpati* gives as translations for *yugapat.*

The Tibetan translation has combined the first two Chinese phrases into one: "Since principle and things appear simultaneously *(cig-car)* without any duality *(advaya),* and since the defilement and the purity of thought are one, Buddha and living beings, being equal, are of the same essence."[34]

Thus we have returned to philosophy, where the term in question is very frequently used, even in schools other than Ch'an. Here is an example from Mahāmudrā:

(8) "At the end, when he (a saint) is placed in equanimity *(samāhita)* into the state of Mahāmudrā [which is] dazzling light, he treads [crosses] *at a single stroke* (Fr. *d'un seul coup;* simultaneously, *gcig-car, yugapat*) the paths *of all the stages.* By this fact he has realized the state of great

Vajradhara in which are simultaneously present *(yuganaddha),* spontaneously, the four bodies and the five wisdoms."[35]

But it is difficult to imagine a *walk,* which normally implies successive steps, being accomplished all at once in time and space. We will see that one has recourse, therefore, to another metaphor, in which the act of transcendence is spoken of as a *leap.*

(9) The last of our Tibetan examples is the one that seemed to me to justify the present article, because the translation, though done by an excellent specialist, seems inadequate. It concerns "phenomena that are simultaneously reabsorbed in dazzling light." The author of the translation used the term "instantaneously."[36]

As we have seen, the Tibetan term *cig-car* is not ambiguous. There is in it no meaning of "sudden" when it is taken independently of some philosophical notions which themselves imply quickness. This is not the case, however, with the Chinese term *tun,* which is what corresponds to *cig-car* in the Ch'an texts. We can immediately see from the first few concrete examples below that *tun* rather often has the meaning of "sudden," though it may elsewhere mean "simultaneous." (The same ambiguity is present in the Japanese readings: the character is read *ton-to* 'entirely', but also *tomi-ni* and *niwaka ni* 'suddenly, in a hurry, immediately'.) Inasmuch as the meaning "sudden" is neither disputed nor disputable one or two examples will suffice.

(10) "Having grown worried, they inquired and learned that your son had suddenly *(tun,* Fr. *brusquement)* contracted a mild sickness. . . ."[37]

(11) In Taoist circles, a sick person was supposed to recite spells in order to recuperate. "*As soon as* they were pronounced, he was healed of the illness that plagued him."[38] It certainly does seem that we must understand "at one stroke, right away" (Fr. *d'un coup, tout de suite*), but the expression *so-ping* '[everything] from which he suffered, which plagued him', perhaps also implies the idea of complete healing. We see in any case the possibility of passing from one meaning to the other: the patient is healed at the same time as, simultaneously with, the recitation. Let us turn then to some examples where the Chinese word *tun* can only mean "simultaneously," without any suggestion of quickness, instantaneousness, or suddenness.

(12) In the Taoist text just cited, there is a comment on the conditions for the transmission of certain sacred works that are reserved for predestined persons: "It is permitted to transmit [this text, *ching*] to only one person every four thousand years. [But] if there is no desired [predestined] person, it is [also] permitted to transmit it simultaneously *(tun)* to two people every eight thousand years."[39]

(13) The above kind of stipulation was very common in the period

from the fourth to the sixth centuries. Another such book can "be transmitted three times [that is, to three persons] in seven thousand years. [But] if there are [some men] whose names are inscribed in gold and whose family names are inscribed in jade in the registries of the supreme God, it is permitted to proceed with the transmission simultaneously (*tun,* at the same time to three men) in a period of seven hundred years."[40]

(14) In speaking of a drug of immortality, Ko Hung (fourth century) said that a yellow substance can be found in certain stones: "After breaking a stone or rock, one finds in it at least a few tenths of a pint *(ho)* or at most a pint *(sheng).* It is best to swallow [everything] *at once (tun,* Fr. *à la fois),* but even if not much can be obtained, it is all right to swallow it successively. When the amount swallowed reaches three pints, one obtains longevity of a thousand years." We could more rigorously translate "swallow immediately," but I think that *tun* (at once) is in opposition here to "successively."[41]

(15) Concerning Taoist meditation, which consists essentially of visualizing divinities, T'ao Hung-ching (456–536) said at first, concerning the twenty-four divinities of the three-times-eight *ching* (luminosities), "One visualizes the three-times-eight *simultaneously (tun),* at the same time (*i-shih,* a redundancy in the text)." Further on, just after having spoken of the way to visualize the five planets individually, one at a time, he explains what should be done "if one visualizes them simultaneously *(tun).*"[42]

(16) A Taoist rule dating from the seventh century enumerates five kinds of defilement that a Taoist is in danger of contracting (brought about voluntarily, contracted by chance, etc.) and stipulates that one is not allowed to eliminate them simultaneously *(tun).*[43] We will see below that a similar idea is set forth by Tibetan Buddhists.

(17) A Buddhist medical recipe (among the Tun-huang manuscripts) prescribes reducing six ingredients to powder form and mixing them with honey to make a ball. "If one swallows them *together (tun),* he will never be hungry or thirsty again."[44]

(18) A Buddhist work of the Yüan period (thirteenth century) states that "the Buddha appears simultaneously, at the same time *(i-shih tun),* in a hundred myriad illusory bodies in the great chiliocosms."[45]

(19) Another Buddhist text of the seventh century says that "Fa-ch'ang, Hui-ching, Fa-lin, and so forth, some ten persons [monks] simultaneously (all together, *tun*), presented a memorial to the emperor, risking death to ask his authorization."[46]

(20) Passing now to philosophy other than Ch'an, we can cite an example from the Indian Upaniṣadic tradition combatted by Buddhism: "It is not true that all things are caused by God *(Īśvara),* because

all things are produced successively *(kramena).* If the whole world was created by God, then all things would have had to be produced simultaneously (*yugapat,* Ch. *tun*)."[47]

(21) Finally, here is the example that inspired me to write this article, because the translation, though done by one of the best specialists, seems to me inadequate. It is part of the Chinese record on the Ch'an controversy in Tibet. The author presents a slightly corrupted quote from the *Laṅkāvatāra-sūtra:* "Moreover, the dharmakāya is then revealed simultaneously (*tun,* Fr. *simultanément*) with the sambhogakāya and the nirmāṇakāya." The translation of Prof. Demiéville, "reveals immediately and at one stroke *(aussitôt et d'un seul coup),*" seems to me unsatisfactory, the more so because of a note in the text, "in a sudden fashion *(tun, yugapat).*"[48] According to Dags-po Rin-po-che, the simultaneity of the three bodies is characteristic of the Buddha-state. We have seen one example of this concept at example 8, where the fourth body (*sahajakāya,* etc.) is a refinement introduced by Tantrism. The Tantric tradition also speaks of a "secret and precious body" *(rin-po-che gsang-ba'i lus)* in which the three bodies of a Buddha are reunited.[49]

I think these examples suffice to show that the essence of the concept in question is simultaneity. The sudden character of the event is a meaning not present in the Tibetan term (or in Sanskrit). It does, however, appear with the Chinese term. Apart from the meanings of particular terms, the *concept* of simultaneity implies quickness and instantaneousness or immediacy (more than suddenness). In examples 15 and 18, *tun* added to *i-shih* 'at the same time' does perhaps take on the meaning "instantaneous." However, such a sense is usually indicated by particular terms such as Tib. *skad-cig* (= Skt. *ekakṣana* 'in a moment').[50]

The ambiguity is more pronounced in Chinese and could have had consequences on the level of philosophical discussions. Some Chinese historians have thought so. In speaking of the thought of Tao-sheng, his biographer (sixth century) writes, "Now signs serve to [indicate] totally the meaning, but once the meaning has been obtained, the signs are [should be] forgotten. Words serve to explain truth, but once truth is penetrated the words may cease. [However,] since the introduction of sūtras to China, translators have accumulated obstacles, have often adhered too much to the letter, and have rarely seen the perfect sense. . . . We have now established that 'good works are not rewarded' and that Buddhahood is achieved by 'sudden enlightenment' *(tun-wu).*"[51]

As I have said, I will abstain from discussing the subtleties of the different philosophical schools. Interesting examples on the Chinese side can be found in the book of Prof. Liebenthal. I will add only a few words concerning the Tibetan side in order to counter the possible impression that the ambiguity is merely terminological. Such ambiguity is rather implicated in the concept itself. I would also like to suggest that the two tendencies, "subitism" or "simultaneity," and "gradualism" or "successive comprehension" (Fr. *saisie successive*), continue to coexist in Tibet.

According to Dags-po Rin-po-che, the Dge-lugs-pa distinguish two paths for "throwing off the defilements" (which are inherent to discursive thought, *sgrib-pa spong-tshul*)—the "successive" path *(rim-gyis-pa)* and the "simultaneous" path *(cig-car-ba).* In the first, the defilements belonging to each of the three realms (of desire, form, and formlessness: *'dod-kham, gzugs-khams, gzugs-med khams*) are thrown off successively, one after the other. In addition, one distinguishes in each "realm" (Skt. *dhātu*) or domain *(khams)* three degrees of successive throwing-off: greater, middling, and lesser. In the second path one throws off at the same time, simultaneously *(cig-car = lhan-cig),* but not abruptly (Fr. *brusquement*), together and at one time, the three greater degrees; then in the same way the three middling degrees together; then the three lesser degrees together (where "greater" and "lesser" do not refer to the importance of the sins, but to the gross or subtle nature of the contamination). Those able to employ this second method have either wisdom *(shes-rab = prajñā)* or great intellectual power *(blo-stobs chen-po).* But even on this path one cannot eliminate the defilements of all three realms at the same time: thus the Dge-lugs-pa. But the Bka'-brgyud-pa do admit such a possibility, given that the other preceding stages have been achieved in previous lives (via the ordinary path: *lam thun-mong-pa*). The direct path *(thun-mong ma-yin-pa)* of simultaneity *(cig-car-ba)* implies then a direct and rapid road.

We know that Tibetan authors were fond of comparing Bka'-brgyud-pa doctrines to those of Chinese Ch'an. The doctrines of the Rnying-ma-pa school and above all of its branch the Rdzogs-chen-pa could just as well have been made the object of comparison. The latter made use of a different vocabulary (but not entirely new with respect to classical Indian texts) which emphasized the "sudden" break, comparing the critical moment to a leap. They used the two technical terms *thod-rgal* and *khregs-chod.* Since the doctrines and terminology of these schools have as yet hardly been studied, the translations recently attempted by the occasional Tibetanist remain inadequate. Guenther thought at first that two kinds of approach were involved: *khregs-chod* would designate a decision, a momentary act, and *thod-rgal* would mean someone who arrives at a decision *gradually.*[52] Ruegg had recourse to a rather vague translation which remains to be clarified: *shes-rab thod-rgal-pa* 'supreme knowledge'.[53] The definition of Jäschke in his dictionary is definitely erroneous: *thod-rgal che-ba,* "according to context: angry, wrathful," with reference to Mi-la ras-pa (I do not know which context he had in mind).

But an example taken from the *Mgur-'bum* of Mi-la ras-pa has been published: "Everyone is drunk on the beer of *dharmatā* [the 'absolute'], and everyone gives himself up to the game of the state of the leap" (which, as the remainder of the poem indicates, is a state of bliss, of song, of grace, and of happiness).[54] Fortunately the newer Tibetan dictionaries define the term *thod-rgal* well. Chos-grags defines it as *go-rim 'chol-ba'am steng-nas brgal-zin-pa* (to invert or disturb the order of succession, to pass beyond it). The Chinese translators have rendered it "to skip over stages or steps; reserved or disturbed order of succession; to leap or pass beyond."[55] The dictionary of Tshe-tan zhabs-drung[56] quotes a commentary *(rnam-bshad)* on "The Entry to the Leap"(?),[57] which explains that in ancient terminology *thod-rgal* is equivalent to *snrel-zhi* and means "reversed or disturbed sequence."[58] This word *snrel-zhi* is found in the *Mahāvyuttpati,* no. 798, where it is used to translate Skt. *vyatyasta.* Jäschke, p. 320, cites Schmidt: "confusedly, pell-mell," but Chos-grags confirms that *snrel-zhi* = *thod-rgal-ba.* It is immediately clear that the Rdzogs-chen-pa did not invent the term. It signifies a classical notion which has been studied in detail by Prof. Lamotte.[59]

Certainly, a philosophical definition of the concept indicated by the term *thod-rgal* would necessitate deeper study, and this all the more because, where details are concerned, divergences between the schools are possible. Not being qualified for such an undertaking, I limit myself to reporting the information at my disposal. It is Prof. Guenther who knows the issue best. He kindly communicated to me on the subject (letter of 3/24/66) a very interesting extract of a Bka'-brgyud-pa work by Pad-ma Dkar-po (1527–1592). This author affirms that men are divided into three categories in accordance with their intellectual capacities, each being characterized by a particular method of direct comprehension or "enlightenment" *(rtogs-tshul rnam-pa gsum).* These are the "simultaneous" (path) *(cig-car),* the (path of the) "leap" *(thod-brgal),* and the "successive" (gradual) (path) *(rim-skyes-pa).* In another work the same author defines the same categories by the manner in which they "grow" toward the Mahāmudrā *(phyag-rgya chen-po la'ang skye-lugs gsum yod-pas).* The first category, the "simultaneous" path, is illustrated by the siddha Gling-ras-pa (1128–1188): the direct comprehension (enlightenment) of the four yogas arising at the same time *(cig-car-pa ni rnal-'byor bzhi-ka'i rtogs-pa dus-gcig la skyes-pa).* He ignores the subdivisions of the four yogas (four parts each) and reduces them (?) to the single state "without meditation" *(bsgom-med).*

In the second category, the "leap," thanks to the more or less great capacities that were obtained in previous lives, one enters into the first three yogas (excluding the fourth, which is the state "without meditation"), but without being confident of the firmness of the (mystical) experience. Also the yogi *('khrul-zhig)* Nam-mkha'i rnal-'byor explained the expression *thod-brgal* in the following manner: "in uncertain sequence, to pass beyond (in whatever way one can, no matter how) *(go-rims nges-pa med-par gang-thod thod-du brgal-pas thod-brgal zhes bya-ba yin-no).*"

The third and final category, the "successive" or "gradual" path, begins with (the yoga of) the "lesser concentration" *(rtse-gcig chung-ngu)* or with one of the subdivisions of this yoga in order to advance thereafter successively *(rim-pa ji-lta-ba bzhin-du rgyud-la skye-ba).*[60]

It is because of this classification that Prof. Guenther has placed the category *thod-rgal* with the "gradualists" (see note 52). The classification of Pad-ma Dkar-po indicates in fact that this "path" is lower than the path of simultaneity. The Rnying-ma-pa and the Rdzogs-chen-pa seem to give it a more elevated place and practically equate it with simultaneity *(cig-car).* At least so it seemed to me from those textual examples that I was able to collect:

(22) "[A monk] having heard [the doctrine of] the great completion *(rdzogs-pa chen-po)* from the Gu-ru Jo-'bar, there was born in him direct comprehension [enlightenment] (in the manner of) a 'leap' (*thod-rgal du* 'spontaneously, directly, immediately'[?])."[61]

(23) In another case, "The gnosis *(ye-shes, jñāna)* of great bliss *(bde-ba chen-po = mahā-sukha)* frees one from mental defilements *(zag-mad = anāsrava);* it lights him up (burns in him) [in the manner of] a leap *(thod-rgal-du 'bar).*"[62]

(24) "[A monk] was severely afflicted by illness and other disturbances of the senses, but he experienced not the least sensation of pain. Day and night, constantly, there appeared to him visions of a 'leap' *(thod-rgal gyi snang-ba),* visions of the rays of the rainbow, of the drop, of the body, and of the realm [paradise] and nothing else. . . ."[63] *Thod-rgal (-du)* is used with the verbs "to produce" *(skyes)* or "to appear" *('char-ba)* in the identical way that *cig-car(-du)* is used with the same verbs. In both cases the term refers to the supreme experience *(nyams-rtogs* or *-rtogs-pa)* of direct comprehension.[64]

There are two examples below where a second ill-defined term occurs, *khregs-chod* 'firm decision'(?), which does not seem to be opposed to *thod-rgal* but is associated with it.

(25) Someone is practicing *rdzogs-rim* (the "ultimate method" of meditation, *niṣpanna-krama*), which unites body and mind through a psychophysical procedure, and leads the individual to the final state of Buddhahood. A text says of this, "Then he especially relied on the yoga of the spontaneous leap *(lhun-grub thod-rgal gyi rnal-'byor)* and of the firm decision(?), pure from the beginning *(ka-dag khregs-'chod),* [which characterizes] the great completion *(rdzogs-pa chen-po).* Because of this, prin-

ciple itself *(chos-nyid = dharmatā)* became actually present in his mental activity and before all his senses without exception, and he [the monk] was initiated [consecrated, endowed with power] into [the state where] the activities of phenomena [things and thoughts] are the play of the body and of gnosis." In this state, the saint in question becomes the "discoverer" of a "treasury of thought" *(dgongs-ter),* that is to say, of a revealed "text" which he draws from thought itself.[65]

(26) Another saint "had (in meditation) the experience of the 'firm decision'(?) and, having reduced it to its essence, he also experienced the 'leap,' as also the 'oneness and the wind' [the psychophysical experience of oneness in the central artery], and so forth."[66] Here *khregs-chod,* the "firm decision"(?), appears as a preliminary stage to the "leap" which is itself tantamount to the supreme experience of the simultaneous comprehension of the noumenal and the phenomenal. The latter state seems here, in the case of the Rnying-ma-pa, to be identical with the stage of *cig-car,* not inferior to it as in the classification of Pad-ma Dkar-po, the Bka'-brgyud-pa author.

Quite recently, Tucci was able to supply clarifications based on a Tibetan work that was previously unknown.[67] The state of the "leap" *(thod-rgal)* is said there to be superior to that of *khregs-chod.* The former is a view where gnosis *(ye-shes)* and light *('od-gsal)* are based in "space" (*dbyings,* "Existenzialität"). Everything is dissolved into light, even gross particles, and the physical body becomes a rainbow body. In *khregs-chod* the body can be transformed into an atom or a particle of dust, but it does not dissolve into light.

Whatever the case may be, we see that the implied meanings "sudden," "instantaneous," and "paradoxical," which were associated with the term *cig-car* 'simultaneous', have inspired certain schools to search for a term which, by insisting on the leap and the inversion, denotes primarily a break (Fr. *rupture*).[68]

Whether it is sudden (instantaneous) or not, "simultaneous" comprehension designates the supreme experience. It is defined, in opposition to "gradual" or "successive," as the contrary of discursive thought (Tib. *rnam-rtog* or *rtog-pa,* Skt. *vikalpa*), that is to say, as an "enlightenment," an "intuition" in the strict sense of the word, a direct grasp or comprehension *(rtogs-pa = vibodha,* Fr. *une saisie directe).* Mahāmudrā adherents say that those on the "simultaneous path" *(cig-car-ba)* "are able to maintain [a state] without the least discursive thought because from the very beginning they dwell[69] [spontaneously and without intervention, intellect and thought together] in the self-nature of thought." On the other hand, those on the "successive path" *(rim-gyis-pa)* "have to seek the self-nature of thought by meditation [proceeding methodically from one stage to another]."[70] We have seen other examples in which *cig-car* 'simultaneous' characterizes the same direct grasp or comprehension (*nyams-rtogs;* see notes 23 and 64).

To conclude, it seems to me that these concepts and their linguistic expression are all the more interesting to study because they have application to the currently discussed problem of synchronicity and diachronicity. Roger Caillois underlined well the contrast between the "plastic arts" (painting, etc.), which he calls "arts of the instantaneous, where everything is available to be seen at once," and the "discursive arts," such as literature and music, which "necessarily develop over time" or which "imply a succession of events."[71]

But for recitation, too, indeed for every linguistic statement or message, one can speak of "the transformation of sequence into simultaneity."[72] In what we read, the words are composed of successive letters —even in Chinese a character is almost always composed of elements in juxtaposition—and the phrases of successive words. In learning the child must pick them out like beads from a string, but the experienced reader grasps a more or less extended group simultaneously or totally. The same is true of the spoken language. If the Buddhists want to liberate themselves from "discursive thought," it is because the latter proceeds, like "discourse" (whence the French—and English—term), in sequential steps. On the other hand, the supreme meaning appears to them to be connected to simultaneity in space (omnipresence) or in time (synchrony) or in thought (*cognitio intuitiva,* direct and immediate comprehension of unity in multiplicity, of the dharma in the dharmas).

Translated by Neal Donner

Notes

1. See (1) Paul Demiéville, course outlines in the *Annuaire du Collège de France,* vols. 56 (1956), 57 (1957), 58 (1958), 59 (1959), etc; (2) Fung Yu-lan, *A History of Chinese Philosophy,* tr. Derk Bodde, vol. 2 (Princeton: Princeton University Press, 1953), 386ff; (3) Kenneth Ch'en, *Buddhism in China* (Princeton: Princeton University Press, 1964), 350ff. Though many other works could be cited, I confine myself to just a few references here.

2. Paul Demiéville, *Le concile de Lhasa,* vol. 7 of *Bibliothèque de l'Institut des Hautes Études Chinoises* (1952)—this is a basic work of which the second part has yet to be published. See also (1) Giuseppe Tucci, *Minor Buddhist Texts,* vol. 2 (Rome, 1958); (2) the review of the latter work by A. Wayman in *Journal of the American Oriental Society* 78 (1958): 215; (3) Jao Tsung-i, "Shen-hui men-hsia Mo-ho-yen chih ju-tsang," in *Symposium on Chinese Studies,* vol. 1 (University of Hong Kong, 1964), 173-182; (4) Ueyama Daishun, "Donkō to tonkō no bukkyō-gaku," in *Tōhō gakuhō* 35 (1964): 141-217; (5) reviews of Tucci's work by Yamaguchi Zuihō, in *Tōyō gakuhō* 47, no. 4 (1965): 112-122, and in *Shigaku zasshi* 74, no. 5: 261-264. The opposition between the Chinese "subitists" and

"gradualists" could be even more easily transposed into an opposition between Chinese subitists and Indian gradualists, since that sort of ethnic dichotomy had already long before been imagined even in China itself. According to Hsieh Ling-yün (385–433), the Chinese find it easy to "see principle [directly]," but have difficulty "assimilating a teaching," while it is just the opposite for the Indians. The former also dislike "gradual learning" *(lei-hsüeh)* and are open to the "ultimate totality" *(i-chi)*. On the other hand, Indians dislike "immediate comprehension" *(tun-liao)* and are open to "gradual awakening" *(chien-wu)*. See Hsieh's *Pien-tsung lun,* included in the *Kuang-hung-ming-chi, T* 52.224c ff.

Trans: See also the chapter by Whalen Lai in this volume.

3. See (1) Walter Liebenthal, *The Book of Chao* (Peking, 1948), revised ed., *The Treatise of Chao* (Hong Kong: Hong Kong University Press, 1968); (2) the authors cited in note 1 above; (3) T'ang Yung-t'ung, "Notes on the History of Chinese Buddhism," *Yenching Journal of Chinese Studies* 22 (1937): 18, 24; (4) Kimata Tokuo, "A Study on *Pien-tsung lun* of Hsieh Ling-yün," in *Tōhō shūkyō* 30 (1967). During this period the opposition between "sudden" (Fr. *subit*) and "gradual" (Fr. *graduel*) was understood not as an inescapable choice between two irreconcilable doctrinal positions, but as two successive phases in the career of the bodhisattva. The first seven stages of the bodhisattva are characterized by "gradual" progress, but there is a break at the seventh stage, where "sudden enlightenment" *(tun-wu)* is in force. This was the opinion of Chih Tun (314–366); see E. Zürcher, *The Buddhist Conquest of China* (Leiden: E. J. Brill, 1959), 383, n. 157 to chap. 3. See also Paul Demiéville, "La *Yogācārabhūmi* de Saṅgharakṣa," *Bulletin de l'École Française d'Extrême-Orient* 44, no. 3 (1954). In the course of the Sino-Tibetan controversy the Chinese affirmed that "the adept of simultaneous entry is like [the bodhisattva] of the ten stages" (Stein, ed., *Sba-bzhed* [Paris, 1961], 58: *gcig-car 'jug-pa ni sa-bcu-pa dang dra'o*).

4. See Ch'en, *Buddhism in China,* 181, on the teaching of Hui-kuan (d. between 424 and 453) and of Liu Ch'iu (438–495) and, p. 305, on the classification used by the T'ien-t'ai school. For the latter see also Sekiguchi Shindai, *Tendai shikan no kenkyū* (Tokyo: Iwanami shoten, 1969), 72ff.

5. *Trans:* Here and below we occasionally supply Stein's French renditions of terms central to this paper.

6. Similarly in Ch'en and Zürcher.

7. But "to enter" also means "to understand, attain, realize" (*Encyclopedia of Buddhism,* 2:634), though no doubt this connotation remains secondary. It comes from the use of the same verb to translate the Sanskrit term *yuganaddha,* a sort of *coincidentia oppositorum,* or simultaneity of two opposed and complementary aspects (as, for example, the two "arteries," the right and left, are reunited in the central "artery"). The translation of this Sanskrit term, in Chinese *shuang-ju* and in Tibetan *zung-'jug,* literally means "double entrance." The verb "enter" is the same which the Tibetans join to the term "sudden" or more precisely "simultaneous"; now the latter corresponds to *yugapat.*

8. Paul Demiéville, course of 1955–1956, *Annuaire* (1956), 284; Ch'en, *Buddhism in China,* 213; Liebenthal, *Book of Chao,* 177.

9. Tucci, *Minor Buddhist Texts,* has compared the Ch'an positions to those of the siddhas, and Wayman, in his review of Tucci's book, has demonstrated a

strong Mahāsaṃghika influence. Alan Watts, in *The Way of Zen* (New York, 1957), 78–79, has compared Ch'an to the Tantrism of Saraha. Prof. Demiéville, in *Concile,* 41, noted that the Chinese account of the Tibetan debate mentions two "Tibetan" monks who were knowledgeable about Ch'an, one of them being named Pi-mo-lo. This transcription corresponds to Vimala in Sanskrit, and Demiéville thought of Vimalamitra (see his note 3 on p. 41). Now an Indian monk of that name is well known to the Tibetan historians. He lived in the eighth century or near the year 800, and was invited by the king Khri-srong Lde-btsan to Bsam-yas. He probably visited China, spending there a large part of his life, and died there at the sacred mountain Wu-t'ai-shan. For the Tibetans he is the head of the Rdzogs-chen-pa or Rnying-ma-pa school of Snying-thig, a teaching which was transmitted to Klong-chen rab-'byams-pa (1308–1363) and subsequently to 'Jigs-med-gling-pa (1729–1798). Instead of wearing a monastic robe he dressed like a yogi; see (1) *Deb-ther sngon-po,* tr. Roerich, *The Blue Annals,* 1:106–107, 191–192; (2) *Rnying-ma chos-'byung,* 155, 206–208; (3) Tucci, *Minor Buddhist Texts,* 119n. Herbert V. Guenther defines Vimalamitra's philosophy as Yogācāra-mādhyamika-svātantrika and gives further reference in his articles "Indian Buddhist Thought in Tibetan Perspective," in *History of Religion* 3, no. 1 (1963): 85, and "Some Aspects of Tibetan Religious Thought," in *History of Religion* 6, no. 1 (1966): 82. Vimalamitra is the author of the following works: (1) a work on the "simultaneous," *Cig-char 'jug-pa rnam-par mi-rtog-pa'i bsgom-don* (Tanjur, Tōhoku 3910; Cordier, *mdo,* 30.3, p. 316), or in English, *The Meaning of the Meditation of the Simultaneous Entry Without Discursive Thought* (quoted in the *Blue Annals,* 1:192); (2) *The Meaning of the Meditation of Successive Entry* (*rim-gyis 'jug-pa'i sgom-don,* Tōhoku 3938); (3) *Sgyu-'phrul phyag-rgya bsam-gtan* (Cordier, *rgyud,* 75.17). Now Hadano Hakuyu believes that Atīśa (eleventh century) could also have transmitted a teaching of the "sudden enlightenment" type, because of his transmission of *dohā* and his *Dran-pa gcig-pa'i man-ngag* (Tōhoku 3929); see Hadano, "Ei-e no Atīśa shōsei," in *Mikkyō-gaku mikkyō-shi rombunshū* (Commemorative volume on the foundation of Kōyasan) (1965), 421.

10. Liebenthal, *Book of Chao,* 178.

11. Tucci, *Minor Buddhist Texts,* 2:81; Wayman, 215. Cf. Tucci, *Die Religionen Tibets* (Stuttgart, Berlin, Köln, Mainz: W. Kohlhammer GmbH, 1970), 101, 106, "unmittelbare (Enthüllung)," i.e., immediate or direct revelation.

12. See Demiéville, *Concile,* 59 n. 3. The lineage of the Ch'an masters was connected to the transmission of the *Laṅkāvatāra-sūtra*—see Suzuki's translation, *The Laṅkāvatāra-sūtra* (London: Routledge & Kegan Paul, 1932). This lineage was known undoubtedly also at the time of the controversy, for a text referring to it was found among the Tun-huang manuscripts. This text, the *Leng-ch'ieh shih-tzu chi,* is preserved in Chinese (*T* #2307) and in a Tibetan translation (Pelliot 710); see also example no. 7.

Demiéville notes (*Concile,* 18) that in chapter 2 of the *Laṅkāvatāra,* the Chinese *chien* and Tibetan *rim* correspond to Sanskrit *krama* 'gradually', while the Chinese *tun* and Tibetan *gcig-cha* correspond to the Sanskrit *yugapat* 'at one stroke'. See also ibid., 14–15, where he points out the same equivalence. But Suzuki, 49–50, translates "gradual" and "instantaneous."

13. This is perhaps an error for *lhan-cig* 'together'. Note the expression *lhan-cig skyes-pa* (= Skt. *sahaja*), which designates a similar idea, the simultaneous grasp of two or more aspects; see Guenther, *The Life and Teaching of Nāropa* (Oxford: Oxford University Press, 1963), 25 n. 3.

14. *Trans:* Stein offers the French expressions (1) *(tout) d'un coup,* meaning *en une seule fois;* (2) *tout à coup,* meaning *soudainement;* and (3) *sur le coup,* meaning *tout de suite.* All his choices contain the word *coup* 'stroke, blow, knock, hit', which cannot be rendered in each case by the same English word. He wants to convey that "once" and "suddenly" are notions as connected in ordinary French (by the word *coup*) as in Buddhist terminology.

15. *Da-lta'i phyag-rgya chen-po dang*
Rgya-nag lugs-kyi rdzogs-chen la
yas-'bab dang ni mas-'dzegs gnyis
rim-gyis-pa dang cig-car-par
ming-'dogs bsgyur-ba ma-gtogs-pa
don-la khyad-par dbye-ba med

Sa-skya pan-chen (1182–1251), *Sdom-gsum rab-dbye,* fol. 25b, *Sa-skya bka'-'bum* ed. (Tokyo, 1968), 5:309. This quotation was taken up again in a Dge-lugs-pa work on the doctrines of the different Tibetan schools, the *Bya-gton snyan-sgron* by Dpal-mang Dkon-mchog rgyal-mtshan (nineteeneth century), chap. 3, fol. 43a. It must have been very well known, because it was also cited much earlier by 'Brug-pa Kun-legs (around the turn of the fifteenth century) in his autobiography (fol. 69b). We know that Sa-skya Paṇḍita had been in China, and that Ch'an played an important role at the Mongolian Yüan court, alongside Lamaism; see Iwai, *Nichi-shi bukkyō-shi ronkō* (Tokyo, 1957). A description of Ch'an was given to the Tibetan lama Yang Lien-chen-chia, commissioner of Buddhism for the southeast of China, in 1288 (*Fo-tsu li-tai t'ung-tsai, T* 49.720–721). Plates for an important work of the Ch'an vinaya, the *Po-chang ch'ing-kuei* (*T* #2025) were recast by imperial command between 1335 and 1338. This text contains a preface by a Tibetan lama. Later, under the Manchus, we see again an emperor, Yung-cheng (1723–1735), simultaneously patronizing both Ch'an and Lamaism (in the person of his master Lcang-skya qutuqtu), as is shown in his prefaces to his *Yü-hsüan yü-lu* and to the translation of the *Leng-yen ching (Laṅkāvatāra-sūtra),* reproduced at the beginning of *Wei-Tsang t'ung-chih* (Monograph on Tibet); see Ch'en, *Buddhism in China,* 450–451. Returning to the sharp criticism of Sa-skya Paṇḍit, he concludes with a brief history of the Sino-Tibetan controversy. The "bodhisattva" Zhi-ba-'tsho (Śāntarakṣita) supposedly predicted to the king Khri-srong Lde-btsan that after his death a Chinese monk would come to teach the "path of simultaneity" (or suddenness, *cig-char-pa-yi lam*) and would be called "the white one capable of acting alone (once only?)" *(Dkar-po chig-thub).* It was necessary therefore to invite his disciple Kamalaśīla, who was to destroy the Chinese doctrine and preach gradualism instead. But later, when the kings had fallen from power, adherents to this tendency continued to rely on writings on the doctrine by Chinese monks, but concealed this by changing its name to Mahāmudrā. Contemporary Mahāmudrā, he stated, was for the most part the Chinese doctrine *(rgya-nag mkhan-po'i gzhung-lugs kyi / yi-ge tsam-la brten-nas kyang / de-yi-ming-'dogs gsang-nas ni / phyag-rgya chen-*

por ming bsgyur-nas / da-lta'i phyag-rgya chen-po ni / phal-cher rgya-nag chos-lugs yin). I do not understand why Sa-pan attributes the teachings of Dkar-po chig-thub to a Chinese monk. In fact, the name designates one of the Mahāmudrā doctrines attributed to the Indian siddha Maitripa (eleventh century, the teacher of Marpa and Atīśa; see Roerich, *The Blue Annals,* 866, and the *Grub-mtha' shel-gyi melong* 68a). However, in quoting the criticism of Sa-pan, the *Grub-mtha' shel-gyi me-long* says elsewhere (66b) that Sa-pan evokes the *Phyag-chen dkar-po chig-thub* doctrine of Zhang 'Tshal-pa (twelfth century). Sa-pan perhaps wants us to believe that this Mahāmudrā was basically Chinese. Much later again, 'Brugpa Kun-legs (around 1500) speaks of "Mahāmudrā, the view of Chinese monks" (*phyag-rgya ha-shang gi lta-ba, Works,* Kha, 14a). Guenther ("Some Aspects of Tibetan Religious Thought," 71 n. 2) has shown that other authors had varied attitudes towards these "(Chinese) doctrines of Ha-shang."

16. *Gzi-brjid,* Kha, 521 = *lta-ba yas-phub* (error for *phab*), *spyod-pa mas yar 'jeg / mthar ni don-dam thig-le gcig-la bsdu.*

17. Demiéville, *Concile,* 14–15n *(mkhan-po Ma-hā-yan gyi bsam-brtan chag [= chig]-char 'jug-pa'i sgo dang bshad-pa'i mdo).* The Ch'an monk Mahāyaña (Ch. Mo-ho-yen) is mentioned in some Chinese documents, one of which is dated A.D. 730; Jao Tsung-i, "Shen-hui men-hsia Mo-ho-yen," 174. (See note 2 above.) One of his disciples was the Tibetan translator of Chinese texts Rgya Me-mgo (the Chinese head [burnt in] fire; his nickname is explained by the asceticism that characterized early Ch'an: sleeping in the snow, cutting off one's fingers and even the arm); see Yamaguchi Zuihō, in *Tōyō gakuhō* 47, no. 4 (1965): 118–119 (see note 2 above).

18. *Bstan-'byung* 163a ff: *myur-lam gcig-char bkod-don.* The work is a later one (nineteenth century) but summarizes earlier philosophical positions. The same expression *myur-lam* is found among the Dge-lugs-pa (cf. *Mi-dbang rtogs-brjod* 67a–b).

19. See Tucci, *Minor Tibetan Texts,* 2:70, 72, 73.

20. For Dags-po Rin-po-che the "simultaneous" *(cig-car)* comprehension of the Chinese *ha-shang* (the Ch'an monk) consists in being able immediately and directly to contemplate emptiness *(śūnyatā)* or the sixth and last of the *pāramitās,* whereas the "gradualists" *(rim-gyis-pa)* successively contemplate the first five *pāramitās* before being able to grapple with the sixth. The first method is for him "the method of immediate [= right away, without intermediary, *tout de suite*] meditation, the profound way" *(zab-lam lam-sang sgom-tsul),* while the second is called "the broad path" *(rgya-che-ba'i lam).* Elsewhere, for example among the Bka'-brgyud-pa, the two paths are also called "usual, ordinary, common" *(lam thun-mong-pa)* and "extraordinary" *(thun-mong ma-yin-pa),* the latter being a direct and rapid path.

21. We add an example to the indications already given by Demiéville and Tucci. At the time of Bla-chen, the monk who was at the center of the renewal of Buddhism after the fall of the royal dynasty (end of the ninth and beginning of the tenth century) at Dan-tig (in the region of Si-ning), some adherents of "simultaneous entry" *(cig-char 'jug-pa)* denied the utility of virtue and good works (*Amdo chos-'byung* 261b: a work of the nineteenth century but based on ancient chronicles). As a matter of fact, this is the era in which Tibetan histo-

rians note the "barbarian" acts of certain monks (of Tantric inspiration, but the latter connects with Ch'an), who stole and killed, raped women and gave themselves up to debauchery (see R. A. Stein, *La civilisation tibétaine* [Paris: Dunod Editeur, 1962], 49). Tantrism and Ch'an have in common several attitudes which are explained as consequences of the "direct" path: scorn of books and intellectual studies, being active in poesy, dancing and singing, unconventional and paradoxical behavior, attitudes called "crazy"—see Helmut Hoffman, "Die Polaritätslehre des späten Buddhismus," in *Eranos Jahrbuch* 36 (1967): 374–375; and for similar abuses by contemporary American followers of Zen (*satori* through drugs, alcohol, and sexual intercourse) see L. Stryk, "An Exchange on Zen," in *France-Asie* 20, no. 1 (1965): 36–37, 39–40.

22. See note 4 above. In Tibet, too, the Bka'-brgyud-pa assigned the "gradual" or "successive," and the "simultaneous," to two different categories of people with different intellectual ability; see *Grub-mtha' shel-gyi me-long* 69a. Sgam-po-pa (1079–1153) combined Nāropa's teaching of the profound six doctrines with the Bka'-gdams-pa (Atīśa and his disciples) teaching on purification of thought. He gave them to his disciples according to whether the latter were predisposed to the gradual *(rim-gyis)* or immediate *(cig-char)* path.

23. When speaking of Tsā-ri, the holy place of the Rdzogs-chen-pa and the Bka'-brgyud-pa, situated in the extreme southeast of Tibet, people call it "the realm [paradise] where trance [or the mystical experience, direct comprehension] appears in simultaneity" (*nyams-rtogs cig-tu* [= *lhan-cig-tu*] *'char-ba'i zhing;* cf. the *Works* of Pad-ma Dkar-po, na, p. 4, biography of Avadhutipa). The dictionary of Chos-grags explains *gcig-tu* exactly as it does *cig-car,* as "together" *(lhan-du),* "at the same time" *(dus-gcig-tu* or *dus-mnyam-du).* At Tsā-ri (-tra) are located both a mountain and a monastery called Cig-char.

24. I think one could find some examples of double locatives in these texts, especially when the word that ends with the locative in *r* has become more or less independent.

25. Cf. *cig-car 'jug* = *yugapat* and *Zung-'jug* = *yuganaddha.*

26. For an example of *gnyis-char,* see *Amdo chos-'byung,* fol. 274a: someone who, "having asked for religious instruction from lamas and Bon-po teachers, practices *simultaneously both* religions, Tantrism and Bon" *(bla-ma dang bon-po 'ga'-zhig-la chos zhus-pas sngags bon-gyi chos gnyis-char spyod-pa).* See note 31 below.

27. His biography, 124b: *slob-ma lnga-brgya dang nyi-cu-rtsa-bzhi cam byung-ba la dbang gdams-pa gnang-bas thams-cad cig-car grol-te.*

28. F. D. Lessing and A. Wayman, *Mkhas grub rje's Fundamentals of the Buddhist Tantras* (The Hague, 1968), 22–23: "simultaneously demonstrated 100 myriads of times" *(mdzad-pa bcu-gnyis kyi tshul bye-ba phrag-brgya cig-car du ston-no,* repeated twice).

29. *Amdo chos-'byung,* fol. 67a *(sku'i bkod-pa gsum cig-char du bstan)*; cf. example 5.

30. *Rnying-ma chos-'byung,* 207 *(sha'i spyan-gyis gling-bzhi cig-car-du gzigs-pa).*

31. Ibid., 639 *(slar-yang . . . sprul-pa'i sku'i bkod-pa lnga gcig-car du snang-bar mdzad-pas)*; cf. example 3. One can add two similar examples taken from the same work. At p. 506, Nang-ral, in dying, "predicts that he will manifest himself again simultaneously in three incarnations, one of the body, one of the

word, and one of the thought" *(slar sku gsung thugs-kyi sprul-pa gsum gcig-car du byung-bar lung-bstan)*. And at p. 253, someone "appears simultaneously in six bodies" *(sku'i bkod-pa drug gcig-car du ston-pa)* and accomplishes other miracles. These examples seem to prove that terms like *gnyis-car* 'two at once', *lnga-car* 'five at once', etc. (see note 26 above), can be explained as contractions of *gnyis* 'two', *lnga* 'five', etc., and *gcig-car* 'at once, at the same time', as in this case with *gsum gcig-car* or *drug gcig-car*.

32. *T* 85.1424b5: *shih pa p'u-sa, chü pai fo yen*. Ms., 746, 747: *byang-chub sems-dpa 'di-brgyad-kyis cig-char (cig-car) sangs-rgyas la gsol-pa*.

33. *Trans:* Stein contradicts himself here in referring to the Chinese translation. In the previous sentence he stated that it is the Tibetan version which is the translation, the Chinese being by implication the original.

34. *T* 85.1284b8–9: *li shih chü jung, chen su ch'i kuan, jan ching i-ju, fo yü chung-sheng, pen lai p'ing-teng i-chi*. Ms., 710, fol. 20b: *gnyis-su med'pa'i gzhung dang don cig-car byung-ste / yid-la gos-pa* (21a) *dang gtsang gnyis-kyang gcig ste / sangs-rgyas dang sems-can kyang myam snyom ste mdo gcig-go //* For a quick reference on the equality *(p'ing-teng; samatā)* of the Buddha and beings, the coincidence of the absolute and the phenomenal, etc., in the Chinese T'ien-t'ai and Hua-yen schools, see Ch'en, *Buddhism in China,* 307–308, 311–312, 317. Regarding the simultaneous immobilization of body and "spirit" (Fr. *ésprit*), as well as their "equality" *(sama)*, etc., in classical dhyāna, see Demiéville, "La *Yogācārabhūmi* de Saṅgharakṣa," 380 n. 4, and 404, 410–411 (like water and milk mixed together). We find innumerable Chinese and Tibetan examples of this affirmation of simultaneity and unity, and this is the case *in many different schools*. The idea of the deep-seated unity between the Buddha-state (purity) and the state of living beings (impurity) is related to the concept of the tathāgatagarbha; see David Seyfort Ruegg, *La théorie du Tathāgatagarbha et du Gotra* (Paris: École Française d'Extrême-Orient, 1969). This position is exactly that of Tao-sheng in his *Tun-wu ch'eng-fo lun* (Treatise on Realizing the Buddha-state through "Simultaneous Enlightenment").

35. David Snellgrove, *Four Lamas of Dolpo,* vol. 2 (Oxford: Oxford University Press, 1967), 92: *'od-gsal phyag-rgya chen-po'i nyang-la mnyam-par bzhag-pa'i mthar / sa-lam thams-cad gcig-car du bgrod-nas / sku-zhi ye shes lnga'i bdag-nyid zung-'jug rdo-rje-'tshang chen-po'i go-'phang mngon-du mdzad-do*. Correct translation, vol. 1, 178: "He traversed at one go all the stages of the way." On these stages of the bodhisattva, see note 3 above. On the simultaneity of the three or four "bodies" that characterize the Buddha-state, see example 21 below.

36. David Seyfort Ruegg, *The Life of Buston* (Rome, 1966), 103n: *cig-car du snang-ba rnams 'od-gsal du sdud-pa*.

37. *T'ai-p'ing yü-lan,* fasc. 522, quoting a letter from the Three Kingdoms era (fourth century; quoted in turn in Morohashi's dictionary): *nai chih chi chün tun yu wei ping*.

38. *Tao-hsüeh chuan* (fourth–sixth centuries), quoted by Ch'en Kuo-fu, *Tao-tsang yüan liu k'ao,* 2d ed., 2:462): *shang k'ou, so-ping tun yü yeh*.

39. Ibid., 489: *t'ing ssu-ch'ien nien te ch'uan i jen, wu ch'i jen, t'ing pa-ch'ien nien tun ch'uan erh jen*.

40. *T'ai-chen yü-ti ssu-chi ming-k'o ching* (*Tao-tsang* 77, fasc. 2, 6b): *ch'i-ch'ien*

nien san ch'uan, jo yu chin ming yü tzu shu yü ti lu, ch'i-pai nien nei t'ing te tun ch'uan. Similarly at 7a: such a text is "transmitted once in ten thousand kalpas. (But) if there are some true men, it is permitted to transmit it three times in seven hundred years" (*wan chieh i ch'uan, jo yu chen-jen, ch'i-pai nien nei, t'ing te san ch'uan;* the word *tun* is omitted).

41. *Pao-p'u-tzu (nei-p'ien)* 11, p. 46 (*Chou-tzu chi-ch'eng* ed.): *k'o tun fu yeh, sui pu te to, hsiang chi fu chih.*

42. *Chen-kao* (*Hsüeh-ching t'ao-yüan* ed.), fasc. 9, 2a–b: *i shih tun ts'un san pa;* and at 23a, *jo tun ts'un wu hsing.*

43. *Tung-hsüan ling-pao lao-hsüeh k'o-i* (*Tao-tsang* 761, fasc. *shang,* 15a): *yu wu hui, pu k'o tun mien.*

44. *T* 85.1450b20–21: *i shang liu wei, ko wu ho . . . tun t'un fu chih, ling jen chung pu chi k'o.*

45. *Pien-wei lu* (*T* 52.758c26–27): *shih-tsun pai-i hua-shen, ta-ch'ien shih-chieh i shih tun hsien.*

46. *Chi ku-chin fo-tao lun-heng* (*T* 52.383a20–21): *Fa-ch'ang . . . teng shih yü jen, sui tun shang piao.*

47. H. Nakamura, "Upaniṣadic Tradition and the Early School of Vedānta as Noticed in Buddhist Scripture," *Harvard Journal of Asiatic Studies* 18 (1955): 85, quoting the *Mahāvibhāṣaśāstra* (*T* 27.993b17–18 and c4–5) (which is paralleled in the *Tattvasaṁgraha* of Śāntarakṣita, chapter on "Puruṣaparīkṣā"): *chu fa chieh ts'ung tzu-tsai yü lo erh sheng, ku pu tun ch'i,* and *fei i-ch'ieh fa i shih sheng ku, jo wu yin yüan, ying chieh tun ch'i.* Cf. Ganganatha Jha, trans., *The Tattvasaṁgraha of Śāntarakṣita,* vol. 1 (Baroda, 1937), chap. 6: "otherwise all things would come into existence *simultaneously,*" and at p. 95, "yet the producing of things is not simultaneous." Cf. Louis de La Vallée-Poussin, *L'Abhidharmakośa de Vasubandhu, Mélanges chinois et bouddhiques,* no. 16 (1923), 1:311: "If things were produced by a single cause, they would be born all *at the same time,* however everyone knows that they are born successively," etc.

48. *Concile,* 59 nn. 2 and 3: *yu fa-shen chi tun shih pao-shen chi i hua-shen.*

49. Herbert V. Guenther, "Tantra and Revelation," in *History of Religions* 7, no. 4 (1968): 296. Cf. Tucci, *Die Religionen Tibets,* 81, for the three bodies realized together.

50. Cf. Liebenthal, *Book of Chao,* 177.

51. Fung, *History of Chinese Philosophy,* 2:270, quoting *Kao-seng chuan* (*T* 50.366c).

52. "Some Aspects of Tibetan Religious Thought," *History of Religions* 6, no. 1 (1966): 79 n. 26.

53. *Life of Buston,* 76.

54. Helmut Hoffman, *Quellen zur Geschichte der tibetischen Bon Religion* (Wiesbaden, 1950), text p. 394: *chos-nyid chang-gis thams-cad bzi, thod-rgal nyams-kyi rtsed-mo rtse;* the translation, at p. 291, is inadequate. *Nyams* is not simply "thought" as Hoffman has translated, but a state of happiness in which one directly apprehends the "absolute" (cf. the dictionary of Chos-grags: *nyams-khrid, nyams-dga'-ba, nyams-mgur*). The emphasis is on the mystical *experience.*

55. P. 377: *lieh teng, yüeh chi, tz'u hsü ts'o luan, yu shang yüeh kuo.*

56. *Dag-yig thon-mi'i dgongs-rgyan,* Sining ed. (1955), with Chinese.

57. *Thod-rgal ni 'jug-pa'i rnam-bshad las.* I do not know which work is referred to here, but in the *Aṣṭādaśa-sāhasrikā-prajñāpāramitā sūtra* (Ōtani Kanjur, vol. 20, no. 732), chap. 62 is entitled "Thod-rgal du snyoms-par'jug-pa"; in Chinese, "Ch'ao teng chih p'in," or "Entry by a leap."

58. *Thod-rgal zhes-pa ni brda rnying-ba las snrel-zhi zhes-kyang 'byung-bas rim-par 'tshol-ba la zer.*

59. Étienne Lamotte, "Yamaka-vyatyasta-āhara," *Artibus Asiae* 24, nos. 3–4 (1961): 307–310. *Vyatyasta* (= *snrel-zhi* 'inverted', Fr. *placé à l'envers*) is the name of a concentration and also designates a device of literary style (*chiasmus:* reversed words). The author emphasizes the contradictory attitude of the bodhisattva: "to join himself to the world while turning his back on it." This is just what is meant by simultaneity.

60. Pad-ma Dkar-po, *Rnal-'byor bzhi'i nges-pa rab-tu dbye-ba phyag-rgya chen-po'i bshad-pa thams-cad kyi bla-ma,* fol. 2a, and *Phyag-rgya chen-po rnal-'byor bzhi'i bshad-pa nges-don lta-ba'i mig,* fol. 5b.

61. *Rnying-ma chos-'byung,* by Bdud-'joms rin-po-che (written in 1964 but repeating ancient documents), 218: *Rdzogs-pa chen-po thos-pas rtogs-pa thod-rgal du skyes.*

62. Ibid., 520: for *zag-med kyi bde-ba;* cf. Ruegg, *Life of Buston,* 58 n. 2.

63. Ibid., 671: *'du-'khrugs kyi nad-sogs drag zin-pas sdug-bsngal gyi tshor-ba gtan-nas med / nyin-mtshan thams-cad-du thod-rgal gyi snang-ba 'dza'-zer thig-le sku dang zhing-khams kyi snang-ba'ba'-zhig 'tshar-gyin-'dug.*

64. Cf. example 21 above and the case of the saint, who while dancing and singing, "produced [caused to be born in himself] simultaneous and direct comprehension [enlightenment]" (*cig-car-ba'i rtogs-pa skyes,* Chronicle of Dpa'o gcug, ch. na, 18b).

65. *Rnying-ma chos-'byung,* 668: *khyad-par rdzogs-pa chen-po ka-dag khregs-chod dang/lhun-grub thod-rgal gyi rnal-'byor la brten-nas chos-nyid yid-dpyod du ma-lus-par mngon-sum-chad la phebs-te snang-spyod sku dan ye-shes kyi rol-pa la dbang-bsgyur.*

66. Ibid., 594, *rdzogs-pa chen-po khregs-chod kyi nams-bzhes la snyin-por dril-nas* (595) *thod-rgal dang rlung-sbyor sogs-kyang . . . thugs-nyams-su bzhes-pa.*

67. Tucci, *Die Religionen Tibets,* 103, 105.

68. Cf. *tien* 'inverted, upside-down', a term which in Ch'an and in Tibet designates an "inspired" saint, a "madman" of paradoxical conduct. For the Ch'an monk Tao-chi or "Chi, the madman" (1150–1209), see Liu Guan Ying, *Der Heilige als Eulenspiegel* (The saint as fool) (Basel-Stuttgart, 1958), and the review by Paul Demiéville in the *Orientalistische Literaturzeitung,* nos. 1–2 (1961): 92. This monk is also called "the drunk enlightened one" (*tsui p'u-t'i*) and "Great Bliss" (*ta huan-hsi*). While Prof. Demiéville translates the latter name as "the great buffoon," this is nothing more than a paraphrase. As is shown by the Sino-Japanese Tantric deity Huan-hsi t'ien (Jap. Kanki-ten), which is two elephants (Ganeśa), male and female, embracing each other, the word "bliss" alludes to the union of opposites and corresponds to Mahāsukha, the "great happiness" of Tibetan Tantrism (see the example in note 54 above). That the "madman," the inverted one (Fr. *renversé*), is also referred to by Tao-chi as the "Great Bliss" is the more noteworthy because the latter term is used among the Rdzogs-chen-pa and the Bka'-brgyud-pa to characterize the enlightenment

which is "simultaneous" or "leaping" (inverting). This is one of those elements that permit a comparison between Ch'an and the Vajrayāna (see note 9 above).

69. *Trans:* Fr. *sont laissés,* emended from the French text of Stein's article which has *ont laissé.*

70. *Bya-gton snyan-sgron* (see note 15 above), fol. 43a: (a) *dang-po-nyid nas sems-kyi ngo-bo steng-du bzhag-nas cir-yang mi-rtog-par skyong nus-pa;* (b) *sems-ngo btsal-nas sgom-dgos-pa* (see note 20 above).

71. *Cases d'un échiquier* (Paris: Gallimard, 1970), 259.

72. Algirdas Julien Greimas, *Sémantique structurale, recherche de méthode* (Paris: Larousse, 1966), 127. See also Maurice Merleau-Ponty, "De Mauss à Claude Lévi-Strauss," *La Nouvelle Revue Française,* no. 82 (1959), 615–631; Henri Delacroix, *Le langage et la pensée* (Paris, 1924), 39: "Sentence comprehension requires a simultaneous presence from beginning to end, the simultaneity of it all," and at 213, "It is the very essence of discursive thought, as opposed to intuitive thought, that it does not make a connection instantaneously . . . but progresses from one object to another." Finally we find this opposition very much present in Michel Foucault, *Les mots et les choses; une archéologie des sciences humaines* (Paris: Gallimard, 1966), 96–97, where the ideas of Condillac *(Grammaire)* and the latter's contemporaries are presented. For them, language "analyzes a representation in a necessarily sequential order," but "all the elements of a representation are given in an instant," etc.

Glossary

Ch'an 禪
Chao lun 肇論
Chen-kao 眞誥
ch'i 齊
ch'i-ch'ien nien san ch'uan, jo yu chin ming yü tzu shu yü ti lu, ch'i-pai nien nei t'ing te tun ch'uan 七千年三傳, 若有金名玉字書於帝籙, 七百年內聽得頓傳
ch'i yü tz'u-ti 齊與次第
chien 漸
chien-wu 漸悟
chu fa chieh ts'ung tzu-tsai yü lo erh sheng, ku pu tun ch'i 諸法皆從自在欲樂而生, 故不頓起
chü 俱
Fa-ch'ang . . . teng shih yü jen, sui tun shang piao 法常…等十餘人, 隨頓上表
fei i-ch'ieh fa i shih sheng ku, jo wu yin yüan, ying chieh tun ch'i 非一切法一時生故, 若無因緣, 應皆頓起
Hsieh Ling-yün 謝靈運
hu-jan 忽然
hu tz'u-ti 忽次第
i-chi 一極
i-ch'i 一齊
i-ju 一如
i shang liu wei, ko wu ho . . . tun t'un fu chih, ling jen chung pu chi k'o 以上六味, 各五合…頓吞服之, 令人終不飢渴
i-shih 一時
i-shih tun 一時頓
i-shih tun ts'un san pai 一時頓存三百
i-tsao 一遭
i-tsun 一遵
jo tun ts'un wu hsing 若頓存五星

Ko Hung 葛洪
k'o tun fu yeh, sui pu te to, hsiang chi fu chih 可頓服也, 雖不得多, 相繼服之
lei-hsüeh 累學
li shih chü jung, chen su ch'i kuan, jan ching i-ju, fo yü chung-sheng, pen lai p'ing-teng i-chi 理事俱融, 眞俗齊觀, 染淨一如, 佛與衆生, 本來平等一際
lieh teng, yüeh chi, tz'u hsü ts'o luan, yu shang yüeh kuo 躐等, 越級, 次序錯亂, 由上越過
nai chih chi chün tun yu wei ping 乃知即君頓有微病
Pa-yang shen-chou ching 八陽神呪經
Pao-p'u-tzu 抱朴子
Pien-wei lu 辯僞錄
p'ing-teng 平等
p'ing-teng i-chi 平等一際
Seng-chao 僧肇
shang k'ou, so-ping tun yü yeh 上口所病頓愈也
sheng 升
shih pa p'u-sa, chü pai fo yen 是八菩薩, 俱白佛言
shih-tsun pai-i hua-shen, ta-ch'ien shih-chieh i shih tun hsien 世尊百億化身, 大千世界一時頓顯
shuang-ju 雙入
so-ping 所病
T'ai-p'ing yü-lan 太平御覽
T'ao Hung-ching 陶弘景
Tao-sheng 道生
tien 顚
t'ing ssu-ch'ien nien te ch'uan i jen, wu ch'i jen, t'ing pa-ch'ien nien tun ch'uan erh jen 聽四千年得傳一人, 無其人, 聽八千年頓傳二人
tun 頓
tun-liao 頓了
tun-wu 頓悟
wan chieh i ch'uan, jo yu chen-jen, ch'i-pai nien nei, t'ing te san ch'uan 萬刧一傳, 若有眞人, 七百年內, 聽得三傳
wu 悟
yu fa-shen chi tun shih pao-shen chi i hua-shen 又法身即頓示報身及以化身
yu wu hui, pu k'o tun mien 有五穢, 不可頓免
Zen 禪

Purifying Gold: The Metaphor of Effort and Intuition in Buddhist Thought and Practice

LUIS O. GÓMEZ

> . . . *entre tant de documents disparates il y a . . . assez de traits communs pour qu'ils puissent s'éclairer les uns les autres sur quelques points.*[1]

These words from Paul Demiéville's essay on the mirror of the mind epitomize the theme of the pages that I present below.[2] The quotation also expresses the basic assumption of the conference that led to the creation of the papers in this volume. The essays, and their meeting in time and space, presuppose the notion that no matter how disparate the religious, philosophical, and aesthetic ideas may be that we subsume under the terms *sudden* and *gradual,* those ideas share enough of a common ground to make their comparison worthwhile.

In the same paper Demiéville traced across several cultures the image of the mirror as a figure for the human soul or mind. He concluded that the metaphor of the mind as mirror epitomizes theories of "sudden enlightenment."[3] Demiéville's essay suggests that common experiences or views underlie correspondences in poetic imagery, and I use his suggestion as the initial pretext for this paper. Of course, if we consider the ultimate implications of Demiéville's remarks, we are faced with an amount of material that by sheer volume would be unwieldy—to say nothing of the versatility of scholarly expertise that it would require. The present essay will therefore circumscribe its topic by treating briefly, and exclusively, the following questions: (1) What were the main issues *common* to the debates of eighth-century Tibet and China? (2) What can we learn from the questions raised and the solutions proposed during these controversies regarding the nature of the sudden-gradual polarity in this *particular set* of cultural contexts? I also consider (3) the question of common terminology and imagery, since correspondences or lack thereof among abstract conceptions and metaphoric expressions probably tell us much about the nature of so-called parallels in doctrine. And at that point I discuss, albeit cursorily, (4) parallels outside the cultural parameters of eighth-century China and Tibet.[4]

Our point of departure is the hypothesis that there is a complex of doctrines and images, similarity among which points to a discrete religious and intellectual phenomenon that may be adequately described as the sudden-gradual dichotomy or polarity. This general assumption must be followed by a preliminary definition, by intension, of the class of phenomena to be considered. If we accept Demiéville's essay as a guide, the definition can be stated thus: those who assume that the object of religious, aesthetic, or intellectual apprehension is somehow innate in the apprehending subject tend to assume at the same time that the act of apprehension is direct, abrupt, and effortless. The most common metaphor employed by the advocates of this type of position, Demiéville would argue, is the mirror as symbol for the mind: both are *innately* pure, both are able to know (or reflect) clearly, *passively,* and *integrally.* The opposite view would then propose that the object of religious, aesthetic, or intellectual apprehension is not innate, and that the act of apprehension is indirect and gradual, the result of dedicated self-cultivation.

These are, of course, preliminary definitions. I expect to show in the course of this essay that parallels in metaphor and doctrinal formulae can be deceptive, especially if one tries to follow them across cultural boundaries. Even at the outset we can detect serious flaws in the proposed dichotomy—one has only to remember that the mirror metaphor was the common ground for the rival poems of Shen-hsiu and Hui-neng![5] The preliminary definitions will therefore be used only as a working hypothesis, to be examined critically in the pages below, especially in light of the controversies that arose in the Tibeto-Chinese cultural sphere during the eighth and ninth centuries. Since Western scholars have extracted their conceptions of "sudden" and "gradual" from this milieu, it is appropriately the context in which the notion should first be examined.

1. Contexts

This may be the best place to introduce a few cautionary remarks regarding the historical and cultural differences that constrain facile comparisons, since, in the course of developing the argument that follows, greater emphasis will be placed on the comparison of ideas. An obvious point of history is the simple fact that we must count *at least* two separate polemical contexts for the sudden-gradual controversies, and definitely three distinct cultural milieux.[6] The polemical contexts can be defined as two discernible instants in the development of Buddhist thought by constructing the historical fiction of two dates as pivots for the controversies. One context, the purely Chinese, or Ch'an, controversy, we can say centers on Shen-hui's attacks on "Northern" Ch'an, beginning in 732 in Hua-t'ai.[7] The other context, involving Chinese, Indian, and Tibetan Buddhists, centers on a series of polemics commonly known by the misnomer "The Council of Lhasa," and dated by Western scholars as taking place between 792 and 794.[8]

The fact that some of the participants in the latter debate may have been affiliated with the Northern school of Ch'an does not change the tricultural nature of the Tibetan controversies.[9] Even assuming some mechanism for effective and rapid translation into and from the three languages involved, much of the discussion proceeded at cross-purposes, each participant addressing issues relevant only to his own polemic and cultural milieu, yet believing that he was dealing with his opponent's views.[10]

Each of these cultural milieux approached the conflict from a different perspective, derived from its own past. The Chinese concern with sudden and gradual enlightenment was the most intense and long-lasting, simply because the dichotomy was a part of Chinese culture and not an idea introduced with Buddhism. Whenever one speaks of sudden and gradual enlightenment in Chinese Buddhism, one has to keep in mind the broader context of the conflict between cultivation and intuition that separated Confucians and Taoists. Both the intellectual and the social dimensions of this conflict had as great an impact on the development of sudden and gradual distinctions in Buddhism as the issues of doctrine or meditation that were presented as the major points of contention.

On the South Asian side the issues were formulated in other terms and in response to different intellectual and religious contexts. Indian doxography records a Pre-Mahāyāna doctrine according to which a Buddha knows everything in a single thought-instant *(ekakṣaṇa-citta).* This doctrine is associated with certain Mahāsāṅghika schools and it echoes in Mahāyāna texts like the *Avataṃsaka.*[11] It was interpreted by the *Mahāvibhāṣā* technically as referring to the way a Buddha understands the sixteen aspects of the noble truths; but the doctrine may have had a less specific application,[12] possibly arising as a challenge to the spiritual hierarchies created by abhidharmic maps of the path, or as an early theory of omniscience positing a Buddha's instantaneous knowledge of all dharmas.

It is worth remembering that Indian disputes regarding the process and goals of religious practice were not limited to ethical issues (śrāvaka vs. bodhisattva) or problems in the ontology of liberation (tathāgatagarbha vs. śūnyatā). The distinction between the Śrāvakayāna and the Mahāyāna was based upon epistemological and soteriological issues that are not trivial. Apophatic ontologies in India often used a rhetoric that is strikingly similar to some of the expressions used by sudden enlightenment schools in China. In some cases, the *Prajñāpāramitā* literature in particular, a rejection of traditional path theories is derived from an apophatic view of the sacred-profane dialectic. But the scholastic traditions usually did not derive the same implications from a metaphysics of negation or *coincidentia oppositōrum*. As a matter of fact, traditional Indian exegesis of the *Prajñāpāramitā* tended to blunt the radical edge of its negative dialectic when it came to path theory.[13] Thus, although Nāgārjuna's *prasaṅga* may suggest a direct path to enlightenment, his interpreters did not see it that way. What is more, among the Svātantrikas, who qualified his radical apophatism, some assumed positions similar to those of the Chinese proponents of sudden enlightenment (e.g., Bhāvaviveka's analysis of the pāramitās) while others were staunch gradualists (e.g., Kamalaśīla).[14] In the same manner, Indian views on the implications of innate enlightenment do not correspond at all with Chinese views regarding innate Buddhahood—for, in India, innate Buddhahood is often associated with theories of gradual enlightenment.[15] Incidentally, the disjunction between metaphysical and soteriological "suddenness" will not surprise the sinologist, for it is recognized implicitly by Tsung-mi in his "Preface," when he distinguishes direct teaching in doctrine or pedagogy from direct teaching as a method of liberation.[16]

Besides doctrinal parallels, one might consider sociological universals, that is, a pattern in the social implications of the sudden-gradual dichotomy. It can hardly be a coincidence that the defenders of sudden enlightenment in India, China, and Tibet were often associated with movements that were opposed to the religious establishment, especially to the scholastics. In India the proponents of Buddhist doctrines that came closest to what could be called a doctrine of "sudden enlightenment"—the early Prajñāpāramitā and the Tantra—found themselves, at least at the outset, in frank opposition to the scholastic traditions. It seems that in both cases the high tradition made a concerted effort to integrate the radical dialectic and the iconoclasm of these doctrines into accepted systems of path theory.[17]

In Tibet the doctrines of sudden enlightenment were also found in tantric schools that were lumped together or associated with the Bon and their opposition to the establishment (e.g., Rdzogs-chen). Early on these schools became associated with foreign values (Chinese Ch'an) and maverick yogis (Rnying-ma). In China, it was the iconoclasm of Taoism that attracted the sudden enlightenment Buddhists, and the association of the former with shamans and "mad hermits" could not have been lost in the minds of grave Confucian gentlemen.

These considerations, however, do not fall within the purview of the present essay. We will focus, rather, on broad questions of religious ideology, which may be summarized in terms of their Indian roots (though other ideologies and religious styles may be relevant, including Confucian and Taoist concepts as well as the less systematic speculations of the Tantra and the Bon). The fundamental rift as seen in Indian Buddhism can be defined as an ideal polarity between those who understand enlightenment as a leap into a state or realm of experience which is *simple* (integral, whole), *ineffable,* and *innate* (that is, not acquired), and those who see enlightenment as a gradual process of growth in which one can recognize degrees, steps, or parts—a process, that is, which is amenable to description and conceptual understanding, and which requires personal cultivation, growth, and development.[18] Another important distinction is established by noting that in the former view states of bondage and suffering are seen as mere delusion, the result of an error in perception or conception; liberation is therefore similar in nature to opening the eyes. The other side in the dispute considers bondage to be due to attachment and karmic conditioning; liberation is therefore more like changing bad habits than like opening the eyes or curing blindness.

It is possible to explain the difference between these two approaches in terms of the doctrine of the two truths: emphasis on the higher or ultimate truth *(paramārtha)* tends to erase distinctions between the states of bondage and liberation, while emphasis on conventional truth *(saṃvṛti)* brings into relief the gap separating the two conditions. Thus, speaking in broad terms, the philosophical context for the sudden-gradual debate could be reduced to the doctrine of the two truths. Unfortunately, this interpretation is itself gradual enlightenment theory.[19]

Furthermore, the notion of the two truths would have to be expanded to include basic dichotomies that are at the root of Buddhism and that constituted the concrete issue of the debates. These include, apart from the more obvious question of "abruptness" or "speed" (sudden vs. gradual), problems such as (1) the nature of change (with the implicit tension between a kataphatic and an apophatic ontology), (2) the nature of the state of enlightenment (innate or to be attained), (3) the connection between liberation and moral and ritual activity, and, therefore, (4) the primacy of epistemology over ethics (or, rather, cognitive over moral transformation). In the context of these oppositions, one comes to understand that the question of "speed" is only one of several issues debated in the polemics of the eighth century, and perhaps not one of the most important.[20]

2. First Polemic Circle: Shen-hsiu and Shen-hui

The Chinese controversy should be examined first, since it was in the Middle Kingdom that this debate took its classical form. Let us begin by considering issues or polarities implicit in the notion of "speed." To do so we will avail ourselves of a Tun-huang text claiming to contain the teachings of Bodhidharma.

Two passages in the so-called *Recorded Sayings of Bodhidharma (Ta-mo yü-lu)*[21] show distinctly two levels of signification in the concept of "sudden enlightenment." One of these passages begins with a question perhaps foreshadowing Tsung-mi's distinction between the cultivation and the attainment of enlightenment:

> Question: In the cultivation of the way and in its attainment, are there some who delay and some who make haste?
>
> Answer: They are separated by millions of kalpas. Those [for whom] precisely *(chi)* this mind is the way, make haste *(chi).* Those who [first] produce the thought [of enlightenment, and then] proceed to develop their practice, delay [in the way].[22]

This suggests first an obvious distinction of speed, and second a connection between speed of progress in the path and knowledge of the correspondence of delusion and enlightenment. The expression "separated by millions of kalpas" establishes this text as a clear example of the temporal meaning of suddenness. At the same time, "speed" also means directness or immediacy. For persons of "dull faculties . . . do not know . . . that precisely this mind is in itself (or, 'from right now,' *tzu-shih*) unsurpassable enlightenment."[23] Then, more explicitly, the text states: "The mind is the very essence of the way *(tao-t'i);* this is why one can attain the way rapidly."[24]

The specific ontology or psychology assumed (Mādhyamika, or Yogācāra) is not so critical here as the way the philosophical assumption is understood: if illusion and reality, bondage and salvation correspond or meet in the present moment, then enlightenment must be immediate (non-mediate). In this text, therefore, at least two fundamental meanings of "sudden" coalesce: correspondence of relative and absolute, and realization all-at-once. The second of these two aspects also implies (in this particular passage) abruptness or speed.

2.1 Two, Three Poems on the Wall

But these are not necessary implications or correspondences, as can be demonstrated by citing the *locus classicus* traditionally taken to summarize the difference between the Northern and the Southern branches of Ch'an. I use the word "traditionally" advisedly and pregnantly, as the passage in question is clearly biased in favor of the Southern school of Ch'an and should not be taken as an accurate description of the Northern school's position.[25] I refer, of course, to the poem supposedly written by Shen-hsiu on a wall in the south corridor of the fifth patriarch's monastery in Feng-mu shan, and to Hui-neng's reply, which another monk wrote down for him on the same wall.

According to the legend, the fifth patriarch Hung-jen requested from his disciples some proof of realization that he could use as a test in choosing an heir to the "patriarchate."[26] Shen-hsiu, who was head monk and therefore meditation teacher, felt it was incumbent upon him to write a poem proving his understanding.[27] Accordingly, late in the night, when the monastery was asleep, he wrote the following verses on the wall:

> The body is the tree of enlightenment.
> The mind is like a clear mirror.
> One must polish it constantly and earnestly.
> One must not let any dust set on it.[28]

This poem expresses in metaphoric language a conception of the goals and methods of meditation documented in many, if not all, Buddhist schools—meditation as purification of the mind.[29] Hui-neng challenged this ideal in the legend presented in the *Platform,* and Shen-hui attacked it in historical reality. The *Platform Sūtra* attributes the following reply to Hui-neng:

> From the beginning enlightenment has no tree,
> And the bright mirror has no stand.
> Buddha-nature is always pure.
> Where could dust set in?[30]

The Tun-huang and Hsia-hsia versions of the sūtra add a third poem, prefaced by the words "another stanza said." Evidently this is intended as a different version of Hui-neng's reply. This second reply seems to express a different doctrine of enlightenment:

> The mind is the tree of enlightenment.
> The body is a bright mirror.
> The bright mirror is from the beginning pure.
> Where could it be stained by dust?[31]

Nothing in Shen-hsiu's poem suggests that he rejected innate Buddhahood or immediate enlightenment. In fact, his choice of metaphor also points to a belief in the innate purity of the mind. Yet this stanza is usually interpreted in light of the caricature of Northern Ch'an fashioned and promoted by Shen-hui and his school. According to this distortion, the teachings of Northern Ch'an were merely a meditation practice designed for those whose "dull faculties" require a step-by-step approach to enlightenment. As I shall show in the following discussion, nothing could be further from Shen-hsiu's views. Southern "subitism" and Northern "gradualism" overlap and interact more intimately than is suggested by the sudden-gradual distinction.

2.2 Shen-hui and His Contradictions

From the relevant sections in the *Platform Sūtra* one can draw the outlines of what was considered by at least one group to be the characteristic sudden enlightenment theory separating the "Southern" school from the "Northern" gradualists:[32] (a) all-at-once enlightenment, including the notions of speed (Yampolsky, par. 39), suddenness (par. 30), and instantaneity (par. 35) of attainment and the identity or correspondence of delusion and enlightenment, as expressed in such formulas as "from the outset" (*pen* 'originally', 'intrinsically'), "all living beings are enlightened" (par. 17–20, 26, 41, passim), and "enlightenment and delusion are identical" (par. 30, 35, 40). By implication there can be no preparation for this experience, and it is beyond description. Therefore, (b) all discourse about enlightenment is apophatic in nature; that is, one can only speak of it by way of negation: no-thought, no-virtue, and so on (par. 17–18, 34). Only silence seems appropriate; scriptural tradition is irrelevant (par. 28–29, 32). As a further implication, this time for practice, the preceding description of enlightenment entails two additional corollaries: (c) correspondence or identity of meditation *(ting)* and wisdom *(hui)* (par. 13, 15, 31; see also 12, 19), and (d) dynamic detachment or nonpassive renunciation, that is, correspondence of thought and no-thought (par. 14, 17).

All these points are raised in a more polemic mood in the Tun-huang texts believed to contain Shen-hui's words. Although a consideration of all the relevant passages could be of interest, I shall confine myself to only a few sections where the more controversial aspects of the doctrine are expounded. In those sections Shen-hui attempts to draw the line that separates his type of Ch'an from the meditation theory and practice of the Northern school. Moreover, it is in this polemical context that we discover the complexities and inconsistencies of his position. For instance, contrary to what is suggested by Demiéville, innate enlightenment and the concomitant theory of the correspondence of delusion and enlightenment do not lead naturally or necessarily to a doctrine of "sudden" enlightenment.[33] In fact, such metaphysical beliefs raise serious problems for the advocate of sudden enlightenment and put into question much of what is usually accepted as the ideals of Buddhist practice.

Supposedly, the defenders of sudden enlightenment base their doctrines on the famous passage from the *Mahāparinirvāṇa Sūtra* where it is said that all sentient beings possess the nature of a Buddha.[34] This passage is interpreted to mean that enlightenment is innate, or an inherent quality of sentient beings, and therefore directly accessible. No conscious effort or mental cultivation is necessary. In this way a fundamental principle of the doctrine of sudden enlightenment is established: "spiritual cultivation cannot be cultivated."[35]

For Shen-hui suddenness and gradualness do not describe a transition from the realm of delusion to that of enlightenment. At the very least, we must say that for him this polarity is not valid from the perspective of enlightenment. It belongs to the sphere of the relative because all degrees and distinctions are fictions of conventional knowledge. Thus, gradual progress is delusion, and the state of delusion *is* gradualness (the realm of distinctions). Enlightenment, on the other hand, is always instantaneous *(hsü-yü).*[36] An awakening that is not instantaneous would not be whole or complete in itself; it would have parts, and exist only by parts. Such a reality would have to be a phenomenon in the realm of causation.

Accordingly, the arising of the thought of enlightenment (the bodhisattva's mind = *fa p'u-sa hsin*)—in this context a direct manifestation of the absolute *(chih shih chen-ju)*—is similar to cutting through the many strands of a rope with a sword: it occurs with one stroke *(i-chan).* The wisdom of enlightenment cuts through delusions in the same way, all at once *(i-shih).* It is a sudden opening *(huo jan).*[37]

This means that for Shen-hui suddenness is a corollary of the identity of enlightenment and delusion. Thus he affirms: "To know that one's mind is empty and calm from the outset is [what we call] sudden enlightenment." The phrase "one's own mind" does not imply a doctrine of immanence based on solipsistic escapism: for "the mind abides nowhere," and sudden awakening refers to "awakening to the mind while remaining among dharmas."[38]

This is enlightenment as seen from the perspective of the enlightened, but it has implications for the practice that leads to enlightenment. In fact, it tells us something about the nature of knowledge generally—to wit, that one cannot imitate the apprehension of truth, nor can one assay or predict the course of realization, much less bring it about by attempting to reproduce in action its theoretical description. To believe this is possible is to fall into what Shen-hui perceives as the mistake of the "gradualist." Sudden, or direct, enlightenment is only possible through enlightenment itself. Direct, complete awareness is non-mediate awareness.

The doctrine seems simple enough, but it seems to be a critique without a constructive alternative. It entails two major conceptual—and perhaps practical—difficulties: (1) the meaning of delusion, and therefore the need for awakening, is blurred, and (2) it appears to be impossible to say how enlightenment is to be gained, for to say anything already presupposes that enlightenment is not readily accessible or naturally given to all sentient beings.

These issues are taken up in the following passage from Shen-hui's *Yü-lu,* where an unidentified objector challenges Shen-hui with problems that he is at a loss to solve:

Question: If the Buddha-nature and the afflictions *(kleśa, fan-nao)* coexist, why do you claim that the afflictions are not part of the fundamental reality *(pen)*?

Reply: It is like gold and slag, both of which appear together as ore. If one finds a goldsmith who will smelt the ore in his furnace, then gold and slag will be separate. If the gold is smelted a hundred times, it will be a hundred times more pure, but if one tries to smelt again the slag, it will become sand and ashes. . . . All the sūtras and the śāstras of the great vehicle show that the afflictions are only superficial dust *(āgantuka-kleśa)*. Therefore, they cannot be considered part of the fundamental reality. . . .[39]

Here Shen-hui seems to be saying, on the one hand, that enlightenment can be reached only through enlightenment itself. ("We only speak of destroying darkness with light, we do not speak of destroying light with darkness.") On the other hand, he compromises his subitist position, for, in distinguishing afflictions and enlightenment, he has to grant that there must be a process whereby one uproots the afflictions and seeks nirvāṇa.[40]

Accordingly, one should note that the metaphor of purifying gold is used here to depict a process and a duality that would contradict Shen-hui's avowed position. If pushed to its logical conclusion the metaphor reveals an underlying dualistic ontology that seems contrary to Shen-hui's conception of direct or immediate enlightenment.[41] Without question, Shen-hui's innate enlightenment, or fundamental reality, is not one with the sphere of delusion. For him, immediacy does not imply identity, and furthermore, the radical, all-at-once separation required to break loose from delusion does not imply necessarily a once-and-for-all experience of realization (gold can be purified further).

In this passage Shen-hui is seeking a mid-course between, on the one hand, statements from the absolute point of view, such as form the core of the *Platform Sūtra* and are epitomized in Hui-neng's poem, and, on the other hand, statements referring to the methods and realities of practice—which are presumably on the plane of conventional reality. But in setting this middle course Shen-hui contradicts the tone of most of his own writings. Real or imaginary, the objector seems to realize that by distinguishing the fundamental or real from the adventitious or illusory Shen-hui must admit that there is a method and a means of eliminating the veil of unreality. The objector takes issue with this inconsistency:

Question: Why is it then that you say that one enters nirvāṇa without uprooting the afflictions *(fan-nao)*, and that the afflictions originally and in themselves are never uprooted?

Reply: If one were to teach that the afflictions are identical with nirvāṇa, one would not encourage living beings to cultivate the six perfections, uproot all evil, and cultivate all good. If the afflictions were considered part of the fundamental reality, we would not have to discard the fundamental and adopt the accidental.[42]

Shen-hui has seriously undermined his position. For now he seems to be accepting the duality of delusion and enlightenment, and the need for cultivation as well. He proceeds, only to further weaken his avowed "subitism":

> The [*Mahāpari-*]*Nirvāṇa Sūtra* says: "All sentient beings from the outset *(pen-lai)* and of themselves *(pen-tzu)* are in possession of nirvāṇa, of untainted wisdom nature. It is like the nature of wood and the nature of fire, both of which appear together in a pair of firesticks. If one [then] finds an expert fire-lighter who will start a fire with [these] firesticks, wood and fire will be separate." The sūtra says: "One compares afflictions to wood, Buddha-nature to fire." The *Nirvāṇa Sūtra* says: "The afflictions are consumed by the fire of wisdom." The sūtra says: "Wisdom is Buddha-nature." Therefore, if you know that there are such passages in all the sūtras, you should know that the afflictions are not fundamental.[43]

But, one may ask, can there be fire without wood, Buddha without sentient beings?

Shen-hui can only appeal to paradox, but he does so skillfully, by turning the dilemma against his opponents. He argues:

> If you speak of mental cultivation *(yung-hsin)*, does this cultivation involve mental activity *(tso-i)* or not? If it does not, then there would be no difference between us and a common man who is deaf. If they involve mental activity, then they belong to the sphere of the conditioned, and lead to bondage. How are we to attain liberation then?[44]

Shen-hui explains that the only reason one speaks of cultivation or no cultivation is because the opponent has raised the issue. There is no need to contemplate the pure when one realizes the state in which there is no impurity.[45]

This is more than a simple contradiction due to shoddy logic. We cannot overlook the context of Shen-hui's teaching. Not only was it polemical, it was also addressed to his followers, who, presumably, were practicing Buddhists already committed to giving up the "afflictions" in order to seek awakening. Shen-hui must have been aware that statements such as those presented in Hui-neng's stanza represent a point of view that could be meaningful only to a particular audience. The identity of delusion and enlightenment and the rejection of the path and its practice make sense only in the context of a community *already committed* to enlightenment and the path. Shen-hui himself says as much in his "Platform Sermon" or *T'an-yü,* where he declares his teaching to be only for a particular class of pilgrim of the path:

> Good friends, [when I tell you] to discard as useless all you have learned before, those of you who have spent five, ten, or twenty years practicing meditation will be extremely puzzled upon hearing this. When I speak of discarding, I mean discarding deluded thoughts, not the dharma. For all the Buddhas of the ten directions could not discard the true dharma; how could you, my good friends, discard it then? As we are unable to separate ourselves from the space in which we walk, stand, sit, and lie, such is the dharma of unsurpassable bodhi; one cannot discard it. All activities and operations are inseparable from the sphere of the dharma *(dharmadhātu, fa-chieh)*. . . .
>
> Good friends, listen carefully. When I speak of deluded thoughts *(wang-hsin),* what do I mean by this? You have gathered in this room today, yet you crave for wealth, you crave for sensual enjoyment with males and females, you [are] thinking of gardens and houses. This is coarse delusion. You should become free of such thoughts.
>
> But, as regards subtle delusion, you do not know what it is. What is the subtle form of delusion? When you hear someone describe bodhi, you think you must have that bodhi; and when you hear someone describe nirvāṇa, emptiness, purity, and concentrated mind *(ting),* you think you must have that nirvāṇa, that emptiness, that purity, that concentrated mind. These are all delusions. They are the fetters of dharma, false views about dharma. If you make them the objects of your mental cultivation *(yung-hsin),* you will not attain liberation—they are not the mind that is fundamentally and of itself serene and pure.
>
> If you think of abiding in nirvāṇa, this nirvāṇa becomes a fetter; if you think of abiding in purity, this purity becomes a fetter; if you think of abiding in emptiness, this emptiness becomes a fetter; if you think of abiding in concentrated mind, this concentrated mind becomes a fetter.[46]

With these words Shen-hui establishes a clear separation between gross and subtle delusion, or, what amounts to the same, between degrees of delusion. Furthermore, in defining truth and error ("they are not the mind that is fundamentally and of itself serene and pure"), he recognizes a distinction between delusion and enlightenment. In other words, this passage denies two of the presumed characteristics of sudden enlightenment doctrine!

Shen-hui's "gradualist slips" may be interpreted as inconsistencies in his rhetoric, as concessions to persons of limited understanding, or as concessions to his opponents. Or one may prefer to interpret them, with Tsung-mi, as referring to gradual cultivation after sudden enlightenment. If this is the case, we may say, following Shen-hui's use of the metaphor of purifying gold, that slag is eliminated once and for all the first time the gold is smelted. Gold then can be further purified: "if it is smelted a hundred times, it will be a hundred times more pure." But it remains forever gold.[47] The implication is that enlightenment, though complete from the outset, needs cultivation. Like the birth of a child, the attainment of enlightenment is an all-at-once event; but, like bringing up a child, the actualization or development of the enlightened mind requires cultivation.[48]

Shen-hui's apparent inconsistencies reflect a recognition of the logical and practical incompatibility of gradual means and immanent realization. In other words, he cannot avoid the conflict between an obvious necessity for mental cultivation and the need for an accurate description of the resulting experience. A similar concession is implicit in a short passage from the *Platform Sūtra* that has been overlooked or undervalued by Western scholars. The fifth patriarch's reaction to Shen-hsiu's poem is seldom noticed, because it is assumed that in the dialectic of the narrative Hung-jen has to find Shen-hsiu unconditionally mistaken. I do not believe this has to be so; and the passage in question concedes this point. Consider the words pronounced by the fifth patriarch after offering incense before Shen-hsiu's poem: "You should recite this stanza, so that you will see your own nature. If you follow this [type of] practice you will not fail."[49] Yampolsky is inclined to view this as an interpolation, "since later on in the text Hung-jen says that Shen-hsiu's verse does not show true understanding."[50] But "later on" the sūtra only tells us that Hui-neng's stanza was the superior one, not that Shen-hsiu was mistaken. Evidently the text is suggesting that the stanzas express different levels of understanding.[51]

Unfortunately, Shen-hui's doctrine is not clear on the important question of the practice of meditation. On the one hand, with some hesitation and not always unambiguously, he acknowledges the need for "polishing" the mind. On the other hand, he never explains what this "polishing" means. We have no way of knowing whether it refers to some form of meditation practice. Modern scholarship has assumed that he condemned meditation outright: since he advocated direct enlightenment, the argument goes, he could not have accepted the practice of "seated meditation" *(tso-ch'an, zazen).* It seems, however, that we do not need an argument by implication, for a number of passages in the literature *(Platform Sūtra, Vajrasamādhi, Recorded Sayings of Shen-hui)* suggest that some schools of early Ch'an rejected outright the practice of sitting in meditation. One such passage deserves our attention.

> The Master [Shen-hui] asked Dhyāna Master Ch'eng: "What condition of mind *(fa)* should be cultivated in order to see one's own nature *(chien hsing)*?"

Reply: First of all, one should cultivate concentration while sitting *(tso hsiu ting)*. Once concentration is achieved, one should produce insight based on concentration *(yin ting fa hui)*. It is by means of this insight *(chih-hui)* that one is able to see one's own nature.

Question: While cultivating concentration, isn't there necessarily thought-construction *(tso-i)?*

Reply: Yes.

Question: As long as there is thought-construction, even if consciousness is concentrated *(shih ting)*, how can one see [self-nature]?

Reply: As long as one is speaking of this nature, the cultivation of concentration is absolutely necessary. If one did not cultivate concentration, how could one achieve concentration?

Question: When one cultivates concentration, it is from the outset the deluded mind *(wang hsin)* that cultivates it; how could this lead to [true] concentration?

Reply: When one cultivates concentration, there occurs by itself an inner and an outer illumination *(nei wai chao)*, which allows us to see thoroughly and clearly *(chien ching)*. It is with this clarity that one is able to see one's own nature.

Question: [Self-]nature has no inner and no outer. If one speaks of inner and outer illumination, from the outset it is the deluded mind [thinking]. [Under these circumstances,] how could one see one's own nature? The sūtra says: "The [proper] practice *(hsüeh)* of all [forms of] concentration *(samādhi, san-mei)* is movement *(tung)*, not sitting in meditation *(tso ch'an)*." [This means that] the mind follows the flow of all objects *(sui ching-chieh liu)*. How can you call this [sitting] concentration? If you claim that it is true concentration, then Vimalakīrti should not have upbraided Śāriputra for his [practice of] calm sitting *(yen-tso)*.[52]

In this passage Dhyāna Master Ch'eng represents the "gradualist" position of the Northern school. Note, however, that the basic issues are not those we usually associate with "gradualism." Ch'eng's exposition of the basic elements or stages of contemplative practice is in agreement with traditional Indian and T'ien-t'ai definitions: concentration *(śamatha, ting* or *chih)* followed by insight *(vipaśyanā, hui* or *kuan)*. Shen-hui's own approach seems to be one of pure, direct insight. He finds fault in a system that not only separates different aspects of realization, but actually seems to "confuse" some form of conscious observation or conceptual analysis with direct insight.[53] The meditation practice attributed by Shen-hui to his opponents is not direct or immediate in the sense that it makes use of mental effort and construction *(manasikāra, tso-i)* as the means to attain insight.[54] But Shen-hui also criticizes Ch'eng because his method entails a series of dualities (concentration/insight; inner/outer; delusion/enlightenment) that contradict the innate character of enlightenment and obstruct the meditator's realization of the nondual nature of enlightenment.

He also seems to discover some quietistic implications in Master Ch'eng's preference for "sitting in meditation." This second type of objection is expressed in the technical language of Ch'an as follows:

> If someone sits [in meditation] and freezes *(ning)* the mind in order to enter concentration, fixes *(chu)* the mind in order to contemplate purity *(k'an ching)*, arouses *(ch'i)* the mind in order to illuminate externally *(wai chao)*, and restrains *(she)* it in order to experience it internally *(nei cheng)*, this person is hindering enlightenment. As long as one does not respond harmoniously *(hsiang-ying)* to enlightenment, how is one going to be able to attain liberation? Not by continuing to sit in meditation *(tsai tso)*.
>
> If sitting were the correct approach, then Vimalakīrti would not have upbraided Śāriputra when the latter sat in silence in the forest. [At that time] he said: "True silent sitting means not to see *(pu . . . kuan)* one's own mind and body in any of the three realms." Not to see bodily forms *(shen hsiang)* is called correct concentration *(cheng ting)* only when you see no-mind *(chien wu-nien)* at all times. [Then, likewise,] not to see mental signs *(hsin-hsiang)* is called correct wisdom *(cheng hui)*.[55]

Clearly Shen-hui's practice is not sitting nor is it concentration—that is, it is not fixing *(ting)* the mind on an object. It is based on the *Vimalakīrti-nirdeśa*'s description of samādhi as movement.[56] For Shen-hui uses the word "movement" advisedly, in order to define this samādhi as a technique that does not remove or erase the multiplicity of objects from the mind. The term that we have translated here as "movement" is the same word *(tung)* used in other contexts to signify the arising of thoughts in the mind. The point at issue is not so much whether one *sits* in *zazen* or not, but whether thoughts should be allowed to arise in the process of meditation.[57]

This position corresponds to ideas expressed in two passages in the *Platform Sūtra:* the definition of "mental concentration" as the "one-practice samādhi," and Hui-neng's definition of no-thought *(wu-nien)*.[58] The first of these passages uses several terms of the scriptural and the Ch'an traditions in a unique combination:

> The one-practice samādhi *(i-hsing san-mei)* is the constant practice *(hsing)* of single-minded thought *(i-chih hsin)* at all times, whether you are walking, standing, sitting, or lying down. The *Vimalakīrti* says, "Single-minded thought is the place where the way is to be realized *(tao-chang)*, single-minded thought is the pure land."[59]

This apparently innocuous exegesis is in fact a polemic directed against Northern Ch'an views of contemplation, as is revealed by the conclusion to this section of the *Platform Sūtra.* The words, parallel to Shenhui's statements, are attributed to the sixth patriarch:

> Again, there are those who teach you to sit looking into the mind, contemplating purity, without stirring [the mind] or giving rise [to thoughts]. They put all their efforts into this. Deluded persons fail to understand, so they cling [to this method] and fall into error.[60]

Taken together these two passages define the "object" of meditation polemically, as neither a vision of Buddhas and Buddha-fields (against East Mountain doctrine) nor the contemplation of an empty mind (against Northern Ch'an). The oneness of the samādhi is not that of a single technique or a simple object, but that of single-mindedness. According to the Southern school, the sacred character of samādhi is not derived either from a particular sacred object of meditation or from the absence of mental content and activity. The samādhi and its content are defined apophatically, as single-minded detachment from all objects and practices.

The second passage from the *Platform Sūtra* defines the difference between Southern "no-mind" and the quietistic state of immobile contemplation attributed to the Northern school by its rivals:

> Non-abiding is the original nature of man. Thoughts follow each other without abiding; past, present and future thoughts follow one after the other without interruption. . . . As thoughts follow each other there will be no place for the mind to hold on to. If one instant of thought holds on [to something], then successive thoughts will cling. This is called "bondage." If thoughts follow one another without abiding in anything, then one will be free from bonds. Therefore, non-abiding is the foundation [of our practice]. . . .[61]

But what does it mean to say that "the mind does not abide"? This is explained as not clinging to conceptual signs *(hsiang).*

> Freedom from [conceptual] signs means to be free from all conceptual signs on the outside. When you are free from these signs, the substance of your nature is pure. Therefore, no-sign is the substance [of our practice].
>
> To remain stainless in all sense fields *(ching)* is called no-thought. If in [every one of] your own thoughts you remain free from the sense fields, then thoughts will not arise with regard to [any] thing (*fa* = *dharma*).[62]

A few problems arise here, for someone could object that this "separation" from mental conceptions is a passive state. After all, the passage seems to hedge the central issue—is no-mind a mindless state, or a "stopping of the mind"? The definition of "no-thought" that begins the section, however, leaves no doubt as to the intentions of the text:

> [. . .] from ancient times all have established no-thought *(wu-nien)* as the core *(tsung)* [of the teachings], absence of conceptual signs as the substance *(t'i)* of the teachings, and non-abiding as its foundation *(pen)*. Absence of signs is to be free from signs even though you are in the midst of signs. No-thought is not to think even in the midst of thoughts. Non-abiding is the original nature *(pen-hsing)* of man.[63]

In these passages, however, there is nothing to indicate that Shen-hui or Hui-neng excluded sitting in meditation from the practice of Ch'an. The rather facile, but mistaken, conclusion that the Southern school was a revolution so radical that it advised its followers to give up meditation has been repeatedly and justly criticized.[64] The central point of contention was not the question of sitting or not sitting in meditation. The issue was not so much whether meditation is necessary, but the nature of the experience and the practice leading to it. The Southern school insisted that the Northern school, in analyzing the levels or stages of the path or of meditation practice, failed to understand the nondual nature of enlightenment. To sit in meditation, "purifying" and "concentrating" the mind, expecting to attain enlightenment, is therefore, according to this view, a form of senseless passivity, the result of an erroneous perception of the nondual nature of enlightenment.

The concept of "passivity," however, is in need of clarification or qualification. The terminology itself is weakened by an inconsistency that eventually undermines most talk about "quietism." For the practice of retired contemplation, of observing the mind, is after all a form of "activity."[65] In fact, a similar objection can be raised against the doctrine of immediate (non-mediate) enlightenment. Shen-hui himself points out that the problem with "non-doing" is that conscious effort in meditation is no different from other forms of karmic construction.[66] Still, in the heat of the polemic Shen-hui seems to ignore the bind in which the subitist is necessarily trapped: if absolute (A) and relative (R) are one, any effort to bring A to R or to "change" R into A is at best unnecessary, and at worst counterproductive. This much Shen-hui concedes. But would he stay with the full implications of this position? For, it follows that anything you do—even not doing anything—is wrong. Inescapably, the moment the subitist objects to any form of spiritual exercise, "not doing" becomes intentional doing, that is, not doing becomes a means of attempting the union of A and R.

Furthermore, if A and R are one, then why is there the "illusion" of a separate A and R? What is the etiology and ontology of this error? On the theoretical or philosophical plane, Shen-hui fails to clarify his position. On the practical level, Shen-hui meets some of the objections by making concessions to the level of the relative.

In the first place, he makes allowances for some type of Buddhist institution and, therefore, for some type of Buddhist practice. This is probably the living context underlying his acceptance of "gradualism" for persons of "dull faculties."[67] In his view this is merely a concession, not a qualification of his doctrinal position; but one must question his views on the matter. For he claims that duality is delusion, yet at the same time he separates the deluded from the awakened, and the fast from the slow. But there can be no dull or sharp, slow or fast in sudden realization, since, according to Shen-hui himself, duality is delusion: only absence of distinctions can describe the fundamental reality; all marks or distinctions are illusory.[68] But this leads to a second contradiction: if duality is synonymous with delusion, then liberation or the liberated mind is defined by the absence of duality. But it is not so defined, for the no-mind of the liberated defines a new duality, that between the one and the many, the liberated and the world of duality! On the one hand, Shen-hui insists that no-mind is neither being nor not being.[69] But under pressure, when asked what is this no-mind if it cannot be named, his apophatism falls into a dualism of sorts:

> It is nothing at all. This is why no-mind *(wu-nien)* is ineffable. If one talks about it, it is only in order to reply to the questions [of others]. If one did not respond to questions, then one would have nothing to say about it. It is like a mirror: if it does not reflect an image, nothing appears on its surface. If one speaks of an image appearing in the mirror, it is [only with reference to] the object standing before the [mirror], which produced the image.[70]

Note the subtle distinction made by Shen-hui in this passage. The mirror without an image is the enlightened mind without discursive thought: if someone asks for an explanation of what this enlightened mind is, the enlightened person will have to speak up; then it is as if the mirror were reflecting an image—the image is not the mirror. Whether there is an image or not, the reflecting nature ("illuminating capacity") of the mirror remains. The metaphoric referent of the mirror's inherent capacity to reflect is the mind's innate "luminosity." Here once more Shen-hui separates the fundamental from the superficial or adventitious —mirror from image. This is subitism with dualism.

Shen-hui's inconsistencies also extend to some points of detail. First, since no-mind, though real and present from the beginning, is not obvious to most sentient beings, he must establish some kind of bridge between delusion and enlightenment. Accordingly he makes allowances, albeit reluctantly, for some form of cultivation even for those who are not of dull faculties: one must dig to reach underground water though it is already there; one must polish the *maṇi* stone to bring out its natural shine.[71] Shen-hui even concedes that certain causes and conditions are necessary for the manifestation of sudden enlightenment, only to flatly reject causes and conditions elsewhere in the *Yü-lu*.[72] Second, although he defines illusion as discrimination, he is perfectly willing to accept the scriptural conception of the afflictions *(kleśas)* as some kind of impurity that must be eliminated.[73] In other words, he accepts the *reality of impurity* and thereby opens the door to (1) a duality between the liberated and the bound, and (2) the need to exclude the world of daily preoccupations and activities from the realm of awakening.

We may say that Shen-hui is in that class of Buddhists who take literally the affirmation of nonduality, taking silence as the exclusion of all linguistic and conceptual alternatives.[74] If this is the position assumed by Shen-hui (at least implicitly), then apophasis and directness are in fact subtle forms of world-denial. This view of sudden enlightenment is not far from the definition of "suddenness" *(tun-chiao)* in the *wu chiao* section of Fa-tsang's *Golden Lion*. But, unlike Fa-tsang, Shen-hui cannot posit a stage beyond nonduality; that is, he has no way of qualifying his nonduality in order to reaffirm the world and the capacity of enlightenment to work in the world.

Any doctrine that satisfactorily "accounts" for sudden enlightenment becomes thereby a gradualist doctrine. Fa-tsang's is no exception. In the *Golden Lion* the sudden teaching is only part of a system of five different approaches to the dharma, beginning with basic Śrāvakayāna, passing through Mahāyāna, and culminating in the fourth and fifth teachings. As in Shen-hui, the sudden teaching is defined as nonduality of being and nonbeing, neither form nor emptiness, ineffable.[75] But this is a stage to be superseded by the perfect, Hua-yen, teaching of the unconfused interpenetration of all phenomena—the world of the many is one, yet each thing retains its individuality.[76] The last stage qualifies or modifies the potential radical monism implicit in a literal interpretation of the nondual stage.

We can speak therefore of suddenness implying oneness and transcendence. And we can contrast this type with suddenness leading to a doctrine of immanence. In the latter type bare facts and circumstances *(shih)* in their "facticity," that is, in their contingency and duality, are no different from the highest religious goal.[77] This conception echoes in a work of the Northern school, the *Yüan-ming lun,* in which we find a critique of the notion that eliminating deluded thoughts is synonymous with liberation. The critique is followed by an affirmation of the presence of enlightenment in the human body.[78]

In Shen-hui "sudden enlightenment" means both a condition totally distinct from all conceptual orders and a nontranscendent enlightenment immediately accessible in the world of delusion.[79] Since he makes no distinction between stages of realization, he cannot separate the apprehension of the nondual from the manifestation of enlightenment in activity. Accordingly he conceives of a state of liberation that is without duality, yet must be accessible without changing anything in the world of duality. He can only say that living beings and Buddha are at the same time different and identical.[80]

But Shen-hui's inconsistencies are best understood in his own polemical context—rather than by an abstract critique on philosophical grounds. His position is critical rather than constructive: it is formed by a set of objections to his opponents, not by a structured system. His doctrinal stance, therefore, probably derives from his perception of the gradualist as both a dualist and a "quietist." That is, in his view, "Northern" Ch'an fails, on a first count, because it does not understand fully the presence of enlightenment in sentient beings, and is confused by conceptual constructs regarding practice. Shen-hui would argue that progress and process imply distance and separation. As to method itself, Shen-hui seems to regard gradualism as contrary to fundamental Mahāyāna principles, because it turns enlightenment into a constructed, compounded, or conditioned phenomenon.[81] On a second count, Shen-hui criticizes the Northern school's meditation practice as a system of "pure *śamatha,*" that is, a meditation of quiet, the purpose of which is to isolate the mind from its content. It does not matter that he himself speaks of the mind as a mirror, because it is evident that he does not propose that one should wipe the mirror clean.

This interpretation of Shen-hui's doctrine could help us make sense of his ambivalence regarding the opposition between means and immediate enlightenment. The world of enlightenment is the world of delusion seen directly and without attachments or expectations.[82] Theoretically, there should be no reason for rejecting the world of delusion, no reason for "stopping the mind," and no reason for seeking enlightenment outside the mind's present state. In other words, it makes no sense to engage in step-by-step mental cultivation; but in practice, one must accept the distinction between the mind before and after enlightenment. Some form of spiritual discipline is necessary either as the embodiment of enlightenment or as a means to strengthen an initial, direct breakthrough into the state of no-mind.[83] This interpretation can be qualified by a hermeneutic leap with a basis in the tradition: if we grant special authority to Shen-hui's interpretation of the metaphors of purifying gold and nursing a child, taking these passages as the control texts for interpreting the rest of Shen-hui's wavering thought, we come close to Tsung-mi's distinction between enlightenment and cultivation, and perhaps also close to his definition of the Southern school—sudden enlightenment followed by gradual cultivation.

2.3 The Ambiguities of Gradualism

The subitist critique implies that those who try to conform to a plan of the path or who imitate the "forms" of enlightenment will reach only an imaginary attainment. But does this mean that nothing can or should be done about seeking enlightenment? By no means. Shen-hui himself does not deny the fact that sentient beings must cultivate specific causes and conditions to bring about the experience of enlightenment.

> It is as in the case of underground water: if one does not apply effort to drill down to it, one will never obtain water. Again, it is as in the case of the *maṇi* jewel: if one does not polish it, one will never have a clear stone, and one will have to say that it is not a valuable gem.[84]

A strange thing to say for the disciple of the Sixth Patriarch! But this is not the only concession Shen-hui will make to the gradualist. He will also admit the need for "means":

> The *Nirvāṇa Sūtra* says: "All living beings would never attain enlightenment without the assistance of Buddhas, bodhisattvas, and true spiritual friends who instruct them using skillful means." If they say they can know [enlightenment] by themselves, that is not true. It is because they do not perceive it that we may say that they do not have the Buddha-nature from the outset. . . .[85]

Among the words attributed to Shen-hui none expand on this point (with the notable exception of the *T'an-yü*). Perhaps he has no reason for elaborating—as a practitioner of the sudden path, he is committed to a thorough *apophasis*. Why should he have to say anything? Why would he want to speak at all? But, this is precisely the crux of the matter; for, if he does not speak, any doctrine can be attributed to him, yet if he proposes a method, he has abandoned strict subitism.

By leaving out the question of what are the specific causes and conditions ("means") for the attainment of enlightenment, Shen-hui has opened the way for a misunderstanding of his intentions.[86] Anything he says to assist the followers of the path is a means for the attainment of enlightenment. But saying nothing will not satisfy either his opponents or Shen-hui himself. Having committed himself to silence, could he even commit himself to his negative statements?

What is more, Shen-hui himself had already spun together a long chain of misunderstandings. Most likely he misrepresented or fabricated the teaching of the "fifth patriarch" to fit his own polemical purposes.[87] It is obvious, moreover, that he exaggerated many of the differences that separated his school from the school of Shen-hsiu.

With regard to the first of these points, we unfortunately do not have much reliable data on the fifth patriarch, Hung-jen. But the tradition attributed to him a text advocating the kind of views that Shen-hui criticized so vehemently. The document in question, the *Hsiu-hsin yao lun*, preserves the following instructions on meditation:

> Everywhere and at every moment the mind should be restrained. You should not experience the pleasures of the present, [which are] the seeds for future suffering.
>
> Continue to strive strenuously. Though this [may not seem] of much use now, it will create the [positive] causes for the future. . . .
>
> . . . sitting with the spine erect, eyes and mouth closed, visualize a sun at some distance in front of yourself, level with the heart. Hold this image with every thought, without stopping. Then you will calm the breath and stop sounds. Do not allow breathing to be heavy or light. . . .[88]

To explain the significance of these practices, the text uses to a different end the doctrines and images used elsewhere by advocates of immediate insight:

> . . . the Buddha-nature in living beings is originally pure, like the sun covered by clouds. If one strenuously guards the true mind *(shou chen-hsin),* the clouds of deluded thought will be swept away, the sun of insight will appear. . . . It is like polishing a mirror; when the dust is wiped off, the true nature appears of itself.
>
> . . . All the Buddhas of the three times are born from consciousness *(shih-hsing).* If one begins by guarding the true mind, deluded thoughts will not arise, selfish thoughts will be extinguished. Later one will become a Buddha. Therefore, we know that the practice of guarding the mind is the progenitor of the Buddhas of the three times.[89]

The *Hsiu-hsin yao lun* shares with Shen-hui the Mahāyāna conviction that Buddhas and living beings have the same nature; but the *Hsiu-hsin yao lun* does not seem to derive from this doctrine the same implications that Shen-hui has drawn.[90] The mind is innately and inherently awakened; its light will shine spontaneously—or in and of itself *(tzu-jan).* But the mind's luminosity will not be seen unless the dust of delusion is removed through the practice of sitting in meditation, guarding the true mind.

Shen-hui also gives us an inaccurate picture of the teachings of his opponents, which is not surprising since the doctrines of the Northern school approach those attributed to Hung-jen. One has only to review the many allegations made in the *Shen-hui yü-lu* against the Northern school to realize that most of them do not reflect accurately the differences that separate the two schools.[91] For one, Shen-hui himself accepts the operation of causes, conditions, and means in the realization of enlightenment, and in this context even uses the metaphor of polishing, as shown above. Moreover, although he insists on the instantaneous nature of enlightenment, he also accepts explicitly the necessity of a progressive cultivation of the "initial" instantaneous experience:

> Each of the six generations of masters of my [lineage] spoke only of penetrating directly [into the mind, as if] with a knife, of perceiving [one's

> own] nature directly and thoroughly. They did not speak of [realization occurring] by steps or gradually. . . . You must suddenly awaken [to your nature] and *then cultivate it gradually*. . . . It is like a mother giving birth to her child all at once, and then giving him her breast and gradually nourishing and raising him . . . —to awake suddenly and perceive the Buddha-nature is just like this. Wisdom naturally grows and increases gradually.[92]

Shen-hui's gradualism, however, is the opposite of Shen-hsiu's. For the latter, instantaneous enlightenment occurs after a long, arduous, and evidently gradual process of preparation or cultivation. This distinction between the two masters and their schools is recognized by Tsung-mi in his now well known typology of the Chinese systems of meditation. The contrast is clearly established by comparing the previous quotation from Shen-hui with the following passage attributed to Shen-hsiu:

> Only if you are able to collect the mind and illuminate it internally *(she hsin nei chao)* will you awaken and contemplate external clarity. You will cut off the three poisons and extinguish delusion forever, close the doors to the six thieves [—the senses—], so that they will not disturb you. Effortlessly *(tzu-jan)* you will gain hold of virtues as many as there are sands in the Ganges, and of all the adornments [of enlightenment]. You will realize each of the innumerable gates to the dharma, one after the other, and you will transcend the state of a common man and realize the condition of the saint. [Enlightenment] will be right before your eyes, not far away. Awakening will occur in an instant *(hsü-yü)*.[93]

A careful reading of the text that precedes these concluding remarks shows decidedly that his major concern is not the dialectic of instantaneous enlightenment. For him the central issue is how to get there—the means, the practices that must be cultivated in order to bring effort to fruition. These practices are all comprised by the single practice of contemplating the mind *(kuan hsin)*.[94] This primary practice does not exclude the requirement of a separate cultivation of virtue.[95]

Shen-hsiu is therefore a gradualist in another sense: he is willing to accept an order of liberation—that is, a rationalized description of the process of liberation. Examples of this abound. For instance, his anagogic interpretation of the scriptural injunction to burn incense to the Buddhas is a summary description of the classical fivefold analysis of the eightfold path:

> Furthermore, "burning incense" does not refer to the incense of the world, which has identifying characteristics *(hsiang)*. It is the incense of unconditioned dharmas. . . . It is of five kinds. First is the incense of moral practice, that is, being able to cut off all evil and cultivate the good. Second is the incense of mental concentration, that is, absolute commitment to the mind of Mahāyāna, without turning back. Third is the

> incense of insight, that is, to examine *(kuan-ch'a)* body and mind constantly, externally and internally. Fourth is the incense of liberation, that is, to cut through the bonds of all forms of ignorance. Fifth is the incense of the knowledge and vision of liberation, that is, to awaken *(chüeh)* and illuminate constantly, penetrating beyond the obstructions of ignorance.[96]

The issue, therefore, may very well be a question of emphasis, one school focusing on the goal and defining the means in terms of the goal, the other emphasizing the means and rejecting, as in the Indian traditions, the idea that the uncaused goal implies an uncaused path. Still, Shen-hui and Shen-hsiu may mean different things by the word "enlightenment" *(p'u-t'i, wu, chüeh)*. Perhaps this is what Tsung-mi means when he uses the categories "sudden" and "gradual" to distinguish types of "cultivation" as well as types of "realization." Differences in the meaning of the term "enlightenment," and therefore in the stated goals of the practice, may be as important in distinguishing sudden from gradual as differences in the conception of path and means. If this is the case, mutual criticism on the basis of a presumed shared goal, as is the case in the debates, is at best misleading, at worst meaningless.

Zeuschner has argued that gradualism arises in response to a perception of the role that means and discursive thought must have in the training of those who are unenlightened.[97] To accept the fact that most of us move only in the relative realm *(saṃvṛti)* entails accepting a form of dualism, no matter how provisional this acceptance may be. One must add, however, that there are different degrees of dualism, or varying emphases on the uses of the relative. Shen-hsiu's school seems to fall close to the extreme of dualism. In his exposition of the perfections, for instance, he gives the term *pāramitā* a peculiar sense, perhaps based on an artificial etymology associating the Chinese translation of the term, *tu,* with the Northern Ch'an concept of *li*. In this manner, the "other shore" of pāramitā takes the meaning of purification and renunciation:

> The Sanskrit term *pāramitā* means "crossing to the other shore" in Chinese. By purifying the six senses and becoming free from worldly dust, one leaves behind *(ch'u)* the perturbations *(kleśa)* and reaches the other shore of enlightenment *(p'u-t'i)*.[98]

Then further on:

> If one seeks to cultivate the six perfections one should purify the six senses; if one seeks to purify the six senses one must first subjugate the six thieves. When one is able to subjugate the thief of the eye, one abandons *(li)* all sight-objects and the mind pays no attention to them. When one is able to subjugate the thief of the ear . . .[99]

The repeated notions of purification and abandonment or relinquishment suggest that the identity of the meditator with the Buddha-nature does have a temporal dimension, and that the opposition of the impure realm ("worldly dust") to the dharmakāya is real. In other words, the "profane" ("worldly dust," the *kleśas*) and the "sacred" (enlightenment, the dharmakāya) are both real, and they contradict each other beyond conciliation.[100] The force of the affirmation of an identity between living beings and Buddha is somehow weakened by the separation that is established between delusion and enlightenment by time and means.

There is no question that this separation is not an illusion, a misapprehension of the deluded self. The world as it is for deluded beings is not the sphere of the identity of delusion and enlightenment. Accordingly, the *Kuan-hsin lun* conveys a sense of radical world denial, because the concept of the pollution of the senses is not a figure of speech used to refer to the deluded conceptual mind. The text imparts a strong sense of reality to the sphere of everyday sense impressions and desires. The realm of impurity is presented as a sphere that is to be shunned and abandoned in a very literal sense.

Accordingly, Tsung-mi's description of Northern Ch'an as "gradual cultivation followed by sudden enlightenment" would have to be qualified by underlining the dualistic flavor of Shen-hsiu's statements regarding liberation. That is to say, Shen-hsiu's sudden enlightenment is a quantum leap, not an expression of immediacy. The expression "sudden" therefore means exactly the opposite of what it means in Shen-hui.

The same sense of distance between delusion and enlightenment is found even in Northern texts with a stronger "subitist" flavor, such as the essay on "The Five Means of Approach" *(Wu fang-pien).*[101] In its discussion of contemplation, the *Wu fang-pien* describes a practice of "purifying the mind" *(ching hsin)* by "looking into the mind" *(k'an hsin),* which consists in "seeing nothing at all" during long hours of sitting in meditation.[102] Sitting in the lotus position and looking into the mind, the meditator reaches a stage in which

> body and mind become free from thought *(li nien).* [Then] one does not see the mind; the mind is just so *(ju);* the mind becomes free. One does not see the body, the body is just so; the body becomes free. One should continue to practice *(yung)* in this way for a long time without interruption. [It is like] empty space; there is not a single thing in it, perfectly pure, without marks of existence. Constantly, without interruption, continue to practice so you will be free of the veils forever. The sense organ of the eye is purified, it is free of the veils. The sense organ of the ear is purified, it is free of the veils. In the same way all the six sense organs are purified, they are free of the veils. To have no obstacles: this is liberation. Not to see the sense image *(hsiang)* of any of the six sense organs, to be pure, without a

single mark *(hsiang)* of existence, constantly, without interruption: this is [called] being a Buddha.[103]

Enlightenment is gained when neither mind nor senses move—a concept expressed with words we have seen above in Shen-hui's critique *(ch'i, tung)*.[104]

Ironically, and perhaps inconsistently, at the level of the path the differences between Shen-hui and the "Northern" Ch'an are not so clear. This is particularly notable in Shen-hsiu's doctrine of *upāya (fang-pien)*. After establishing "means" as the most essential element of the path, he fails to integrate them with the goal, and finds himself agreeing with Shen-hui on the question of the status of "means." They are, he concurs, concessions made for people of inferior capacity. Still, the mere absence of "means" does not define the true path; for the true practice is defined by one characteristic, namely, that it is an "inner," not an "outer," process. The questioner asks how one can propose a single practice if the sūtras teach the cultivation of merit, the cult of the Buddhas, and the like. To this the *Kuan-hsin lun* replies:

The sūtras taught by the Buddha contain an infinite number of means. Sentient beings, because their faculties are dull and [their aspirations] are narrow and low, cannot understand the most profound points. Accordingly, [the Buddha] teaches the unconditioned by means of the conditioned. If you do not cultivate the inner practice *(hsiu nei-hsing)*, but seek only externally, expecting to gain merit, you will not succeed.[105]

It is difficult to see why the means "taught by the Buddha" do not lead to success in the path, even if it is after a long time. But, be that as it may, the Shen-hsiu of the *Kuan-hsin lun* interprets "external" means as figures for "internal" contemplative practice. The passages that follow the above quotation in the *Kuan-hsin lun* are all devoted to the "interiorization" of Buddhist doctrine, myth, and ritual by means of anagogic interpretations. Psychologized and demythologized Buddhist doctrines are interpreted as the true or ultimate teaching; their surface meaning is only valid as expedient means to convert the persons of limited capacity. The text denies spiritual value to ceremony and ritual—they are false "means," in contrast to the true method, which is defined by a metaphoric interpretation of the paraphernalia of ritual as symbols of different aspects of spiritual cultivation.[106] For instance, temple lamps are turned into a symbol of insight:

"Lamps" refers to the correct mind of true awakening *(chüeh)*: insight and clear understanding are compared to a lamp. Therefore, those who seek liberation always make their bodies into a lamp stand, their minds into the bowl of the lamp, faith into the wick of the lamp. As oil they add moral discipline. The clear penetration of insight is compared to the flame of a

> lamp constantly shining. In this way the lamp of true awakening shines, rending the darkness of delusion and ignorance.[107]

The constant, pure mind represented by the flame of the votive lamp is a static image of both innate enlightenment and meditation practice. In the *Wu fang-pien* also, as we have seen, the theme of stopping the movement of the mind dominates, placing this text in the rhetorical, if not the practical, tradition of the *Kuan-hsin lun.* Still, although freedom from thought activities is clearly the core of the meditation practice proposed in the *Wu fang-pien,* insight and skill in means are introduced to explain the possibility of perception and action in the practice.[108] The condition in which mind and body do not stir is in fact perfect, or original, bodhi, but this does not preclude a doctrine of the function *(yung)* of the enlightened mind that brings us back to the world of action and perception.[109] The *Wu fang-pien*'s definition of skill in means is in fact orthodox: the capacity of the bodhisattva's mind to remain in the state of no-movement even when the senses are active, for he "knows that the six sense organs are from the outset unmoving." Furthermore, the text recognizes the interdependence of skill in means and insight (wisdom), acknowledging, with a somewhat clumsy exegesis, the importance of a passage from the *Vimalakīrti-nirdeśa* that will be quoted by the Indian gradualist Kamalaśīla in his attack of Mo-ho-yen's subitism: "insight without skillful means is bondage. . . ."[110] This passage is explained as follows:

> [When the sūtra] says "without skillful means, insight is bondage," [it refers to] the followers of the two [lower] vehicles. While they are in samādhi they do not hear; once they leave samādhi, they hear again. While they are in samādhi they have no insight, they are unable to explain the dharma, and they cannot take sentient beings across to safety. When they leave samādhi, they explain the dharma with a distracted mind. . . .
>
> [When the sūtra] says "with skillful means, insight is liberation," [it refers to] the bodhisattvas. They know that the mind is from the outset unmoving, whether sounds occur or occur not, cease or persist, [bodhisattvas] remain constantly in the practice of not moving. Because they are able to practice this skillful means, their correct samādhi is perfectly serene.[111]

With this passage the Northern school goes one step beyond both Shenhui and the *Kuan-hsin lun*—it seeks to account for some type of continuity or contact between the two spheres of the absolute and the relative, the liberated and the deluded, the still and the moving. Even though "skillful means" is defined as "unmoving," the originally pure is placed squarely in the world of the senses.[112]

Thus, in the *Wu fang-pien* at least, the means that are concessions to persons of limited ability are only one type of "means" in the path. There are other techniques or procedures that are necessary in the path, which we may call true, or higher, "means." Although the *Kuan-hsin lun*'s view of *upāya* is not as sophisticated as that of the *Wu fang-pien,* and the former is not as successful as the latter in accounting for sense functions, the *Kuan-hsin lun* does not neglect the question of method and process. This text's interpretation of the meaning of votive lamps as the body and mind of the seeker, which reminds us of the metaphor of the mirror and its stand, gives us a static image: sitting in meditation, manifesting the original Buddha-nature. It is almost as if the author of the *Kuan-hsin lun* in his own way suddenly sided with Shen-hui, and decided that original, self-illumination was self-sufficient. But, although it is true that the text contains no explanation of the interaction of insight and means, and no explicit gradualism of steps, the "inner practice" that serves as a hermeneutic device to reveal the true meaning of incense, lamps, and offerings of flowers is a practice of purifying the mind and the senses. Purification is unequivocally a process with distinct, if not sequential, aspects: moral discipline, mindfulness, looking into the mind, observing body and mind.[113]

In the *Kuan-hsin lun* the central practice consists of purifying the senses or abandoning thought *(li-nien).* This conception does not seem very different from the Southern school's no-thought or no-mind *(wu-nien/wu-hsin),* but the similarity is only superficial. The concept of *li-nien* implies the necessity of removing thoughts whereas *wu-nien* implies there is no need to do so.[114] This is the same distinction suggested by the poems attributed by the *Platform Sūtra* to Hui-neng and Shen-hsiu. The *Platform Sūtra,* and Shen-hui, perhaps distort these teachings by suggesting that with the doctrine of *li-nien* Northern Ch'an denies innate Buddhahood, an implication that is neither philosophically necessary nor justified by the textual evidence. The *Kuan-hsin lun,* for instance, uses a metaphor analogous to that of Shen-hui's purifying gold, suggesting immediacy while affirming gradual cultivation:

> As regards the casting of sacred images [recommended in the sūtras], it refers to living beings seeking to follow the path of the Buddhas. It means that by cultivating all the practices of enlightenment, one becomes like the Tathāgata in his wondrous appearance and features—how could this be an image made out of metal? Therefore, those who seek liberation take their body as the furnace, and the dharma as fire; wisdom becomes the skilled goldsmith; the three types of ethical practice and the six perfections become their mold.[115]

This metaphor of gradual spiritual progress is then followed immediately by an unequivocal affirmation of the innate character of enlightenment. But this is an innate enlightenment that does not contradict the concept of gradual, studied transformation:

> Within their own bodies they smelt the Buddha-nature, which is true suchness, pour it into the mold of the precepts *(chieh-lü)*, practicing according to the teaching until not a single impurity *(lou, āsrava)* remains. Then, the true appearance [of a Buddha] is completed naturally *(tzu-jan)*. The perfect, eternally abiding, subtle body of form [of a Buddha] is not a conditioned, destructible entity. If a person seeking to follow the path does not know how to cast the true form in this manner, how can that person make claims to merit?[116]

Thus, it would be a mistake to assume that innateness necessarily implies immediacy, to say nothing of suddenness. This is the mistake commonly made by Western analysts who rely more on philosophical form than on the religious interpretation of the metaphors. This possible error is corrected by Tsung-mi's "Chart," whose analysis of the verses attributed to Shen-hsiu correctly points to the tacit acceptance of Buddha-nature in the poem: "Living beings possess the nature of awakening from the outset, just as a mirror possesses the nature of illumination."[117]

The important point is that for the Northern school, at least as represented by the *Kuan-hsin lun,* fundamental or original enlightenment does not imply an instantaneous abandonment of impurity, nor even the identity of pure absolute and impure relative. The Northern school also sees the process of purification as requiring introspection and withdrawal in a manner explicitly rejected by Shen-hui. Northern meditation practice creates a gap, at least implicitly, between the world of enlightenment and the world of delusion. Under this doctrine of meditation, a critic could argue, hides a potential world-denying quietism. But the *Wu fang-pien* makes the critic's task very difficult; for in its analysis of the bodhisattva's practice, especially with reference to the doctrine of skillful means *(upāya),* the text introduces a different interpretation of the implications of its doctrine of calm and purity.

The Northern tradition, therefore, recognizes a doctrine of innate enlightenment and uses it to close the gap between the pure realm of enlightenment and the world of the senses—a gap that Shen-hui also tries to erase. Though one may argue that neither party in the dispute is wholly successful in its attempt to bridge this gap, it seems apparent that neither can be accused of turning its back on the world.[118] Although some of the technical points in the Southern school's depiction of Shen-hsiu's teachings seem to be accurate, it seems unlikely that the Northern school's position would lead to a pernicious quietism any more than Shen-hui's doctrine would lead to an unqualified rejection of means. But this is a problem for later consideration. We must now turn to the second polemic circle mentioned at the beginning of this essay, the polemics of eighth-century Tibet.

3. Second Polemic Circle: Mo-ho-yen and Kamalaśīla

The points of conflict debated in the early Ch'an school appear in other works of the period when, approximately half a century later, the Buddhism of Tun-huang was forced into the Tibetan cultural milieu. Similar issues are discussed—for instance, in documents attributed to two Tun-huang monks of the eighth century: T'an-k'uang, a gradualist of the Chinese branch of Yogācāra *(fa-hsiang),* and Mo-ho-yen, a subitist apparently associated with the Northern and Pao-t'ang lines of Ch'an.[119]

Their polemical circle is known among modern scholars as "The Council of Lhasa" or "The Councils of Tibet," following the Tibetan tradition that claims Mo-ho-yen debated the sudden-gradual polarity with a group of Indian and Tibetan monks in front of the king of Tibet, ca. 792. The issues they raised play a prominent role—sometimes in an explicitly polemical tone and form, and sometimes in a manner only implicitly polemical—in the *Bhāvanākramas* of Kamalaśīla (ca. 750–795), Mo-ho-yen's opponent at the "Council."[120] The same themes appear in other works of Kamalaśīla, such as the *Bhāvanāyogāvatāra* and the *Avikalpapraveśa-dhāraṇī-ṭīkā.*[121]

Finally, two other Tibetan sources reflecting the same polemic regarding the techniques, goals, and fruits of contemplation—a work from the Tibetan canon and a fragment from Tun-huang—stand out as being particularly pertinent. The first, a rather clumsy conflation of sudden enlightenment fragments and gradualist pieces from the *Bhāvanākramas,* is attributed to Vimalamitra and goes under the title *Cig-car 'jug-p'ai rnam-par mi-rtog-p'ai bsgom-don* (The Meaning of Cultivating the Nonconceptual By Instantaneous Access).[122] Vimalamitra's work overlaps at some points with the Tun-huang document, Pelliot tibétain 116, a catechistic manual on the doctrine of sudden enlightenment.[123]

The main figures in the debate, Kamalaśīla and Mo-ho-yen, represented two completely different cultures and religious traditions. Although the sectarian affiliation of Mo-ho-yen is still not clearly established, it appears that he belonged to a late branch of the Northern school with strong leanings toward Southern Ch'an doctrines.[124] I believe the crucial issue is not how Mo-ho-yen, his disciples, or his Tibetan admirers of later generations traced his spiritual lineage, which may be merely a matter of religious politics, but rather what his doctrinal and polemic positions were. If we ask for a typological, rather than a hereditary, affiliation, he is closer to the extreme sudden enlightenment position of Shen-hui than he is to the gradualism of Northern school works like the *Kuan-hsin lun,* or even the more radical *Wu fang-pien.*[125] This tendency set him on a collision course with the carefully intellectualized gradualism of Kamalaśīla, a scholar trained at the Indian university of Nālandā, who was a disciple of Śāntarakṣita, and therefore in the tradition of the Yogācāra-Mādhyamika. Kamalaśīla's training and doctrinal affiliation made him at the same time an expert in Indian scholastic "path theories," techniques of meditation, and Mahāyāna theory of knowledge, especially as applied to the apprehension of the ultimate goal of the contemplative path.

I shall not take any space to go into the historical details of their encounter; suffice it to say that our knowledge of their ideas stems from two very different kinds of sources. For Kamalaśīla, on the one hand, we have works of undisputed authorship preserved partly in the original Sanskrit, partly in reliable Tibetan translations. For Mo-ho-yen, on the other, we must rely on indirect sources: the *Tun-wu ta-sheng cheng-li chüeh,* a Chinese text which claims to be the minutes of his encounter with Kamalaśīla but was compiled later by Mo-ho-yen's disciple Wang-hsi, and several Tibetan translations of Chinese originals purporting to contain the words of Mo-ho-yen.[126]

3.1 The Focus of the Debate

The questions disputed in these sources can be subsumed under two headings: (1) The path to enlightenment is either a gradual process with distinct steps or stages, or it is a non-mediate, direct experience without separate components. (2) Either there are various virtues and practices that must be cultivated separately and throughout the spiritual path, or only one single practice is required to attain enlightenment.[127] These general questions, when considered in their specific details, can be expanded in the following outline:

1. Mediate access, as opposed to immediate access.
   a. Access to the nonconceptual through mental effort and cultivation, as opposed to direct access to the nonconceptual.[128]
   b. Mental cultivation involves cooperation of serenity and insight, as opposed to: serenity and insight are automatically included in nonconceptual thought.
   c. On the one hand, the state of enlightenment may be regarded as nonconceptual but not excluding conceptual knowledge. In that case, both levels of truth, absolute and relative, have a position of value in the plan of liberation. On the other hand, one may propose that only the nondual, nonconceptual realm is real or

true, and that it is directly accessible. In that case, the level of the relative is irrelevant, except as a concession to those who fail to grasp ultimate reality directly.

2. Distinct and obligatory practices, as opposed to no requirements except the nonconceptual mind itself.
   a. Cultivation of the perfections as a condition for enlightenment, as opposed to: the perfections flow naturally from the nonconceptual (or, the perfections as an optional practice).
   b. Cultivation of the perfections at all stages of the path, as opposed to: the perfections are necessary only to those who cannot enter directly into the nonconceptual realm.
   c. The theory of mediate enlightenment accepts the necessity for specific steps, methods, or strategies called "means" *(upāya).* These are the only access to higher wisdom, and include, apart from meditational practices, morality and the outward and institutional signs of religious life. Proponents of direct enlightenment argue that since higher wisdom is reached directly or immediately, "means" and methods are at best concessions to the slow-witted, at worst distractions in the way of true enlightenment.
   d. A gradualist would accept the reality of good and evil karma; one leads to enlightenment, the other does not. The subitist would respond: enlightenment is not attained, neither good nor evil means anything in the nonconceptual sphere.
   e. One theory proposes that there are two aspects to the path and enlightenment; the absolute, accessible through higher wisdom *(prajñā),* and the relative, accessible through appropriate means *(upāya.)* The other theory maintains that there is no such distinction in the nonconceptual mind, although the distinction exists for the unenlightened.
   f. One party would consider the means *(upāya)* an essential part of enlightenment, as the development of skill in means allows enlightened beings to remain in the world to manifest their compassion and assist the unenlightened. The other party would sustain a position similar to the one proposed under (d) above.

These sets of doctrinal alternatives intertwine intimately; one would be hard-pressed, therefore, to separate them into distinct categories. The participants in the polemic circles investigated here seldom made a clear-cut distinction.

3.2 Cultivation and Intuition

The first broad issue, the question of gradual *cultivation* versus direct *intuition,* can be taken as the catch-all label for the whole dispute. It is discussed in great detail in Kamalaśīla's commentary to the *Avikalpa-praveśa-dhāraṇī* and can be summarized, following this text, in this manner: although the end of the path is a state of nonconceptual awareness, before its attainment one must know how to get to it; otherwise one will follow the wrong path. Once attained, the nonconceptual is the source of activity requiring discrimination.[129] To this the follower of the sudden path responds: if the end of the path is nonconceptual knowledge, then any attempt to conceptualize, seek, or expend effort to attain it involves a distortion of the goal, and is therefore self-defeating.

The gradualist's response is unequivocal: there is no such thing as attaining the nonconceptual without first generating the determination and the energy to do so. Intuitive, experiential awareness, if it is to attain true knowledge, must be guided by specific principles and practices—that is, by Buddhist doctrine and methods of meditation. Only in this way will nondiscrimination produce accurate knowledge of a specific object and not just diffuse impressions of any object. Without guidance, in fact, intuitive awareness could confuse other objects, including illusory or deceptive ones, with the real object.[130]

Conceptual knowledge can lead to nonconceptual experience through a dialectical process cultivated in meditation but obviously based on the philosophical dialectic of Nāgārjuna: once the object of meditation appears before the serene mind clearly and constantly,

> one should investigate [asking], "Whence has this come? Whither does it go? Where does it abide?" Then one will know that it comes from nowhere, etc.
>
> The mental image is empty of self-nature, beyond being and nonbeing, beyond all discursive construction. If one investigates all dharmas in the same manner, with an understanding that is spontaneous, one will realize they are no different [from this mental image]. . . .
>
> By means of correct discernment one abandons even the thought that there is no self-existence whatsoever. Even this knowledge, whose object is beyond being and nonbeing, is itself free from all attribution of being and nonbeing. In this way one should cultivate nonapprehension *(dmigs pa med pa, anupalambha).*[131]

It is like the fire that is produced by rubbing two firesticks (the duality of conceptual knowledge): eventually the fire that these two produce will consume them (unifying nonconceptual knowledge), but without the initial friction between the two sticks, there would be no fire at all. The fire is "the true knowledge that is nonconceptual."[132]

3.2.1 Cultivation and the Direct Path

Shen-hui used the simile of firesticks in a slightly different sense—the sticks standing for the state of delusion that is to be discarded, fire representing innate Buddhahood.[133] In doing so, Shen-hui, the champion of radical nondualism, falls into a subtle, but undeniable dualism. For him, as for Kamalaśīla, the firesticks stand for the realm of duality. Following the *Mahāparinirvāṇa Sūtra,* however, he proposes a second duality: enlightenment (fire) and delusion (wood). To resolve the dilemma, he proposes both a synthesis and a denial of the ultimate value of the opposition. He proposes (1) that the duality is transcended by the suppression of one of its poles; (2) that the two poles coexist only in the realm of delusion. For Kamalaśīla the firesticks represent the gradual process of cultivation and therefore stand midway between delusion and awakening. He too sees the duality eventually transcended, but for him *both poles* dissolve when seen from the higher stages of cultivation.

Shen-hui, of course, is trying to respond to the same objection that Kamalaśīla has presented to Mo-ho-yen: how can living beings attain to the nonconceptual mind of the Buddhas if they are immersed in deluding conceptualization; and if they are already free of it, then what is the meaning of practice? The truth of the matter is that there is no way the radical "subitist" can respond adequately to this objection without qualifying his position or surrendering part of the claims he makes for his doctrine. The most a "subitist" can do to express his position is a direct command to give up duality or the conceptual mind, or a flat statement of the inherent or present reality of Buddhahood. But even illocutionary speech could be tainted with gradualism, and the true subitist must have recourse to other means of expression—perhaps Lin-chi's *kwatz,* or Chao-chou's "Go wash your bowls." Nevertheless, at the stage of development of Ch'an doctrine considered in this essay, the subitist attempts to formulate his position by one of the two types of statements mentioned above: a command to give up duality, or an assertion of the identity of the deluded and the enlightened mind.

An example of the first type of statement is the following quotation from the *Brahmaparipṛcchā* found in Vimalamitra's tract on sudden enlightenment:

> In the *Viśeṣacintibrahma-paripṛcchā* [Mañjuśrī] asked: "How do you develop the path?" [Brahmā] replied: "Dharma and adharma are both nonconceptualization. To abandon all signs is to practice the path." One meditates without apprehending any real object. Thus, samādhi should be developed by keeping in mind the fact that all dharmas, conditioned and unconditioned alike, have no reality.[134]

If we still are not convinced that this should apply to goal and path alike, our doubts are dispelled by another quotation:

> Question: But what is the cultivation of the path in the nonconceptual realm?

Reply: In the *Prajñāpāramitā* it is said: "Nonapprehension is the path, nonapprehension is the fruit."[135]

As we have seen in the Chinese controversies, especially as analyzed by Tsung-mi, the question of mediate access as opposed to immediate access is not necessarily the same as the question of gradual cultivation versus sudden enlightenment. But the opponents in the Tibetan debates do not make these distinctions. For them the controversy hinged on the question of gradual cultivation—that is, step-by-step access to the nonconceptual—in opposition to no-cultivation—that is, direct access without degrees, planning, or preparation. Mo-ho-yen was an exponent of "all-at-once" awakening or access *(tun-wu, cig-car 'jug-pa)*. Kamalaśīla proposed that awakening was attained only through a gradual process of cultivation *(bhāvanā-krama)*.

Although Kamalaśīla's conception of the highest stages of contemplation is not far from that of the subitist, he does not allow for any element of "suddenness" or "directness" in the path. Mo-ho-yen, on the other hand, accepts a schematic gradual path of five "approaches" *(fang-pien)*, but with reluctance and qualifications. One of the Tibetan fragments (Pelliot 812) summarizes Mo-ho-yen's doctrine, showing the master's acceptance of gradualism only as a second-best option for those who cannot enter into the absolute immediately and directly. To describe this immediate access to enlightenment, Mo-ho-yen uses apophatic expressions reminiscent of Shen-hui and Hui-neng. In a fragment from Tun-huang that appears to be a summary or paraphrase of Mo-ho-yen's "Essentials of Contemplation" his teachings are described as follows:

> Although there are many texts on meditation in Mahāyāna, the highest of all [the methods taught] is that of immediate access to the middle way. In the practice of this immediate access there are no means or approaches *(thabs, fang-pien)*. One meditates [directly] on the true nature of dharmas.
>
> In this connection, "dharmas" means the mind, and the mind is without origination. What has no origination is empty. It is like empty space. It is not the object of the six senses; therefore one knows emptiness [only] through awakened insight. When one practices true awakened insight, there is no insight either. Therefore, one dwells not in the knowledge of any ideas or concepts, and meditates directly on the equality of all dharmas.[136]

According to another Tibetan source, the *Bka'-thang sde lnga*, Mo-ho-yen taught the nonduality of delusion and enlightenment:

> He said that all appearances *(snang)* arise from mind, that the nature of mind is ineffable, and that the essence of mind is enlightenment itself. All beings have enlightenment as their essence; living beings and enlightenment do not constitute a duality *(gnyis su med)*.[137]

Repeatedly he describes both the experience of nonduality and the method to attain it in frankly apophatic terms: no-thought, or no-reflection *(pu-ssu, myi-bsam),* no-examination *(pu-kuan, myi-rtog).*[138] These are ideas approaching those of the Southern school. However, Mo-ho-yen accepts the language of the Northern school as well, especially in his descriptions of *practice.* He speaks, for instance, of inner illumination *(fan-chiao)* and of looking into the mind *(k'an-hsin, sems-la bltas).* Still, his view of the nature of delusion and enlightenment suggests a primarily *pāramārthika* view of practice, or at best a very half-hearted acceptance of the need to use means within the relative sphere. As is said in "The Essentials":

> The meditation taught by Master Mo-ho-yen is that of not discriminating anything, of no-thought, of abiding in the inconceivable. Only if one cannot attain this [direct insight] does [the Master offer] the teaching of the five means of approach.[139]

Mo-ho-yen's strong sudden enlightenment position comes through transparently in the *Cheng-li chüeh.* But directness is understood as resulting from a monism of sorts, for the realm of delusion, and therefore the sphere of the relative, is conceived of as pure illusion.

> Living beings cling to the false concepts of good and bad dharmas because they have been engaging in deluded discrimination since beginningless time. At times, good is on the increase, at other times it is evil that grows; accordingly, living beings turn about in the wheel of birth and death, and cannot escape. This is why the sūtras insist that all concepts of discrimination are false without exception. If one sees signs as no-signs, one sees the Tathāgata. To understand this single thought is in itself the greatest merit, surpassing by far all the merits that one could gain by cultivating good dharmas for innumerable cosmic periods.[140]

So far it seems that Mo-ho-yen is recommending the practices of no-reflection *(pu-ssu),* no-examination *(pu-kuan),* and freedom from all concepts or mental images *(wu-hsiang)* only as the *best* method; perhaps there are other, less effective, but nevertheless valid methods. Perhaps those who are less advanced in the path could benefit from other means, such as the cultivation of merit. Mo-ho-yen seems to waver on this point. Whereas his memorials to the king of Tibet accept the need for the "lower" practices, in the "debate" Mo-ho-yen declares that the method of nonconceptualization was taught as the best for all practitioners of the path:

> You claim that one should not follow this method of pure signlessness if one is still in the stage of a common person; but all Buddhas and bodhisattvas, after practicing the true dharma during innumerable cosmic periods and reaching perfect awakening, have left behind their teachings

> to be practiced and cultivated by sentient beings of future generations. . . . You claim that common persons should not follow this method. For whom, then, were these teachings left by the Buddhas? And in what sūtras is it taught that this method should not be followed by common people?[141]

Conceptual thought, in fact, is fundamentally wrong and harmful. For:

> The defect in conceptualization and discrimination is that they have the power to hinder the original omniscience of all living beings, and thus make them turn about in the endless cycle of the three evil destinies. This is their defect. It is also taught in the *Vajra[cchedikā] Sūtra* that one calls "Buddha" those who abandon all concepts.[142]

Against this point the gradualist raises an obvious objection: Mo-ho-yen seems to ignore the fact that living beings are deluded, and some of them, if not most, cannot make the leap that he would want them to make:

> Question [gradualist objection]: The point we are raising is this. There are certain occasions when one should produce and foster conceptual signs, and there are occasions when one should not produce them. In the case of those who are still in the stage of common persons, or when they are only at the beginning of their practice, they should not try to do away with conceptual signs.[143]

At this point, the subitist seems to become uncompromising, giving up even his willingness to grant some value to "means" designed for human beings of limited abilities:

> Reply: All the sūtras of the great vehicle say that all living beings are carried around by the currents of birth and death because they cling to the false concepts of birth and no-birth, on account of the false notions and distinctions they construct. They also say that living beings will be released the moment they stop clinging to the false concepts of birth and no-birth. From which sūtra text do you conclude that common living beings should not try to do away with conceptual signs?[144]

3.2.2 Calm and Insight

As the gradualist presses this point, Mo-ho-yen is forced to adopt an extreme position. When the moment comes for him to explain his method of contemplating the nonconceptual mind *(k'an-hsin),* he uses language reminiscent of the strongest of Shen-hui's statements:

> Question [by the gradualist]: What do you mean when you speak of "contemplating the mind"?

Reply: To turn the light of the mind toward the mind's source—that is contemplating the mind. This means that one does not reflect or examine whether conceptual signs are in movement or not, whether they are pure or not, whether they are empty or not. It also means not to reflect on nonreflection. This is why the *Vimalakīrti*[*-nirdeśa*] *Sūtra* explains: "Non-examination is enlightenment."[145]

Evidently Mo-ho-yen's mind contemplation is different from Shen-hsiu's.[146] One wonders, in fact, whether Mo-ho-yen, in rejecting examination *(kuan)* generally, is not criticizing Shen-hsiu as well as Indian and T'ien-t'ai concepts of meditation.[147] Be that as it may, Mo-ho-yen's opponents took the term *kuan* to mean *vipaśyanā* (as it does in the T'ien-t'ai tradition). Although Mo-ho-yen, like the *Platform Sūtra,* is seeking a definition of contemplation that will avoid the calm-insight duality, his position can be easily misinterpreted. One could accuse him, as Kamalaśīla does, of proposing a meditation practice that is pure calm—that is to say, blind mental concentration. Mo-ho-yen is partly to blame for this misinterpretation, because he uses the term *ch'an* (dhyāna) unaware of his opponent's understanding of the word, and because he hesitates too much in his treatment of the question of "means."

The gradualist is concerned, certainly, with epistemological issues and with the technical question of the stages in the path as outlined in scriptures and commentaries. But he does not stop at the theoretical level; he demands to know how one is supposed to practice meditation.

Question [by the gradualist]: By what means should one do away with false notions and habitual tendencies?

Reply: If false notions arise and one is not aware *(chüeh)* of them, that is what is called birth and death. The sphere of becoming aware, of not acting according to false notions, not grasping, not settling in any thought, this is indeed liberation, prajñā. The *Ratnakūṭa Sūtra* says: "Not to apprehend even the minutest dharma, that is the highest enlightenment."[148]

The gradualist asks, then, whether this implies that the various means taught in the sūtras are useless. Mo-ho-yen replies with an orthodox formula:

Question [by the gradualist]: The six perfections and all of the other dharma-methods, are they necessary or not?

Reply: As worldly dharmas the six perfections and the rest are means *(upāya),* because they reveal the ultimate object. [It is in this sense that] they are necessary. But, from the point of view of the ultimate object which is beyond speech, one cannot define the six

> perfections or any dharma-method as necessary or not necessary. . . .[149]

Mo-ho-yen has assumed the *pāramārthika* position that is so typical of subitism. The gradualist brings out the philosophical implications of this position:

> Question [by the gradualist]: We then ask whether worldly truth and ultimate truth are identical or different.
>
> Reply: They are neither identical nor different. In what sense are they not identical? As long as false notions have not been done away with, one holds on to the view that there is a worldly truth [separate from ultimate truth]. In what sense are they not different? When all false notions and their habitual tendencies [have been done away with], one does not distinguish identity and difference anymore.[150]

Mo-ho-yen's reply corresponds to Shen-hui's treatment of the same issue.[151] Strictly speaking, it is orthodox even by Indian standards. But in context it is clear that he does not hold the rest of the orthodox position in high regard, for he adds a few remarks that smack of arrogance and remind us of Shen-hui's rather casual interest in those who need the cooperation of "means":

> Those who have dull faculties, who have not penetrated deeply into ultimate truth, need these [means of access (*fang-pien*)]. Those whose faculties are sharp have no need to consider the question of their necessity or non-necessity.[152]

Such comments, moreover, contradict his own blank rejection of means. But, whatever the true import of these lines, Mo-ho-yen leaves no room for doubt regarding the relative importance of the two truths and, consequently, of means and wisdom. He exaggerates the latter's position of preeminence to the point that the other five perfections, which are regarded as the perfections of "means," become unnecessary:

> If one practices the six perfections, it is in order to seek the perfection of insight (*prajñāpāramitā*). Once one is in possession of the perfection of insight, one may or may not practice the other five.[153]

By subordinating the other five perfections to the perfection of prajñā (here understood as direct insight), Mo-ho-yen opens himself to the charges of antinomianism brought against him by the gradualists. It is evident that stated in such strong terms his position could only be interpreted to mean that there is in fact no need to practice any perfection except direct insight. In fact, he quotes elsewhere sūtra passages to show that there is no need for "any practice whatsoever."[154]

Relying on the centrality of insight or prajñā, Mo-ho-yen believes he can establish his doctrine on a firm scriptural footing, for he finds confirmation in selected passages from the *Prajñāpāramitā* literature. Unlike his gradualist rivals, he does not seem particularly concerned with the ethical implications of his position, or with the exegetic problems that these implications would pose. His only concern is to safeguard the preeminence of insight, even at the expense of meditation (understood as systematic mental cultivation). To protect his position he redefines dhyāna in terms that could easily be applied to nonconceptual insight:

> Regarding your claim that because we recognize the preeminence of prajñā it is not reasonable that we should practice dhyāna, it is said, for instance in the *Ratnakūṭa Sūtra:* "The son of the gods Susṭhitamati said to Mañjuśrī: 'Mahāsattva, you speak of the monk who practices dhyāna. What do you mean by a monk who practices dhyāna?' Mañjuśrī said: 'That there is not the least dharma that can be grasped, son of the gods, that is what we mean by the practice of dhyāna.' " Also in the *Ghanavyūha Sūtra* it is said:
>
> If one is able to practice
> The Tathāgata's sublime concentration,
> And knows well that there is no self in the skandhas,
> All views are completely extinguished.
>
> It is also said in the *Viśeṣacinti Sūtra*: "Not to settle anywhere in any dharma is called the perfection of dhyāna." And in the *Laṅkāvatāra Sūtra* it is said: "Not to produce discriminating thoughts *(vikalpa)* . . . this is called the perfection of dhyāna. . . ."[155]

Mo-ho-yen has mustered here irrefutable scriptural testimony proving, at the very least, that his loose use of the term dhyāna is of Indian vintage. If it raises a number of technical issues regarding the nature of meditation, it is only because it is meant to do so—even in the Indian texts this rhetoric is meant to be iconoclastic and revolutionary. By refusing to be pigeonholed, Mo-ho-yen reasserts his claim that conceptual thought is the cause of delusion and suffering. Disagreements on technical matters go hand in hand with many of the seemingly metaphysical points discussed in the debate, because methods of meditation are not merely techniques—they are ritual embodiments of religious experience and doctrine.

The Ch'an dialectic, a continuation of both Taoist and Mādhyamika rhetorical traditions, if combined with the doctrine of innate Buddhahood can produce very powerful, if not disconcerting paradoxes. But these are, for the most part, not doctrinal statements. They are a peculiarly Buddhist type of illocutionary use of language. The subitists themselves perhaps lose sight at times of this aspect of their rhetoric.

The gradualist critic for his part is prone to see in Ch'an rhetoric a direct attack at the religious foundations and goals of Buddhism.[156]

The tendency to take Ch'an rhetoric as an antinomian and iconoclastic doctrine is built into the language of the school, for Ch'an expressions are expressions of the absolute point of view. That is, they express the goal, not the means. Apart from their function as devices to force a direct entry into the inconceivable, they can only serve as embodiments of the ineffable numinous.[157] Except in the almost scholastic "kōan systems," it is difficult to see them fulfilling some of the vital functions of sacred utterances in other traditions: principles for the rationalization of human behavior. Even those who regard Ch'an turns of phrase as the highest form of religious rhetoric would have to concede that they are not too generous in explicit practical instruction. One could say that most of the objections presented by the gradualists (e.g., Kamalaśīla) are elaborations of this reservation: that statements such as Mo-ho-yen's "no reflection, no examination" do not tell the disciple what he is to do. Kamalaśīla in fact interprets the unadulterated apophatism of these statements as a sign that they must refer to a type of inactive, nonconceptual contemplation that he knows from India—the practice of pure calm *(śamatha).* He insists that the practice of mental calm and concentration for their own sake is a non-Buddhist practice that does not lead to true liberation. Withdrawing from sense objects and conceptual thoughts is only a preparatory practice; by itself it brings only an artificial and temporary peace. Like the meditation practices of Udraka Rāmaputra, the Buddha's second teacher, it does not effect liberation from the bondage of self.[158]

3.2.3 Insight and Analysis

Kamalaśīla's critique reflects both a general Indian belief in the necessity of practicing both calm and insight, and a Mahāyāna notion that the followers of the Hīnayāna do not practice the correct form of insight. Mahāyāna insight is a process of discrimination and a state of nondual knowledge. As discrimination or contemplative analysis, it is an essential aspect of meditation practice, for it guarantees both the correctness of the process (defining its object accurately) and the dialectical nature of the result. As a dialectic, insight is also the basis for generating thoughts of compassion in the calm mind of the contemplative. A doctrine proposing a direct access to liberation through the practice of sheer nondiscrimination *(nirvikalpa),* therefore, lacks in awareness and compassion.[159] One might surmise that Kamalaśīla would respond to the theory of enlightenment through direct practice of nonconceptualization by pointing out that enlightenment is nonconceptual from the point of view of the enlightened *(paramārthataḥ),* but not from the point of view of the deluded being seeking liberation—the person who is most likely to need an explanation of the meaning of the path. The texts, unfortunately, do not deal with this issue directly. Instead, Kamalaśīla finds fault in the nonconceptual approach even from the point of view of practitioners who are advanced in the path. In doing so, he brings out one of the fundamental distinctions between sudden and gradual theories of the path: insofar as they propose some type of method, sudden theories believe enlightenment is possible only by casting away, in a single blow, the veil of delusion. Gradualism is based on the conviction that this is an undesirable goal, because it is a state of mind that has nothing to do with liberation.

Thus, for Kamalaśīla supramundane knowledge *(lokottarajñāna),* the highest stage of contemplative practice, is a nondual, nonconceptual cognition, but it is not defined merely by the absence of conceptualization. In the first place, it is defined by the dialectical process that leads to it. In the second place, it is in nonbinary cognition, but cognition nonetheless.

One may be free from mental constructs, but the mere absence of mental activity or attention does not define the state sought by the Buddhist contemplative. For:

> when the *Avikalpapraveśdhāraṇī* says that [the bodhisattva] gives up the conceptual signs of form and the rest by not bringing them to mind *(amanasikārato),* it means the freedom from conscious mental acts *(amanasikāra)* that [characterizes the specific form of] nonapprehension associated with those who examine [dharmas] by means of insight *(prajñayā).* It does not refer to bare nonapprehension. For this is not like the attainment of the [temporary mental state] of unconscious concentration *(asaṃjñīsamāpatti)*—by merely casting aside mental activity *(manasikāra)* one does not become free from the obstinate mooring in [one's ideas of] material and [immaterial] entities, [habit cultivated] since beginningless time.[160]

Kamalaśīla believes that his position is supported by even those passages in the sūtras that seem to bolster the subitist's faith in the value of eliminating mental constructions:

> [To see the great vehicle (Mahāyāna) means] seeing ultimate reality. This is nothing less than the perception of ultimate reality that takes place when the vision that is right knowledge is obtained by a person who examines all things with the eye of insight *(prajñā).* Accordingly, when the [*Dharmasaṃgīti*] *Sūtra* says, "What sort of [seeing is this] seeing ultimate reality? It is not seeing any dharma," it refers only to this nonseeing [of knowing through the eye of insight], not to the nonseeing resulting from the absence of the necessary conditions or from the lack of an act of attention, as in the case of someone who is blind by birth or someone whose eyes are shut.[161]

Since he equates absence of analytic insight with sheer calm, the solution is a cooperation between calm and insight. Liberation is only possible through the cooperation of serenity and insight *(śamatha-vipaśyanā-yuganaddha),* which leads to perfect insight into the nature of all things. Calm prepares the way for the reflective process of the examination of reality *(bhūta-pratyavekṣaṇā),* but is not enough by itself.[162]

Whether or not this is a necessary implication of the doctrine of sudden enlightenment, Kamalaśīla's identification of Ch'an with pure *śamatha* derives from the perspective of only one representative of the school, Mo-ho-yen, who seems to have exaggerated the role of apophatic language to the point of overlooking what is present in his own tradition. While the "account" of the discussion in Pelliot 4646 would prove Mo-ho-yen a defender of a radical doctrine of no-thought *(pu-ssu)* and no-examination *(pu-kuan),* other documents suggest a very different view of the relative position of serenity and insight in his system, and among other followers of sudden enlightenment of the time. In the Tibetan fragments attributed to Mo-ho-yen, for instance, we find a short piece claiming to summarize the method of "immediate access." Although it is unequivocally and explicitly in the sudden enlightenment tradition, this short text instructs the practitioner to sit cross-legged in a lonely spot and collect the mind. Then, looking into the mind without examining the mind, whenever a thought arises, become aware of the thought and of its lack of substance. After "a long time," one realizes that one's own awareness is also a form of discrimination. Then one sees that "awareness itself is without name or form," and one cannot "see the place whence it originally came, nor can one discern whither it will finally go." Realizing that awareness too is without substance, one has realized the immediate path.[163]

This description of the practice of meditation in the sudden path represents a dialectic very similar to the summary of insight meditation in Kamalaśīla's *Bhāvanāyogāvatāra* that was quoted above: seeing that thoughts come from nowhere and go nowhere, one sees them as insubstantial; finally our knowledge of insubstantiality itself is seen as groundless. In this way one reaches knowledge without an object.[164]

The parallel sketched above should be enough to show that the discussion between the rivals participating in the controversy may have been more confused than we have hitherto believed. But, still another example of subitist gradualism may be of interest. Vimalamitra's tract as well recognizes the need for both serenity and insight:

> The mental concentration *(samādhi)* that does not dwell on any sign is serenity. The mental concentration that does not escape from any sign is serenity. Not to generate any sign is serenity. Not to stop any sign is

> insight. The limit of the object is serenity. Not to fall beyond the limit of the object is insight.[165]

Insight is explained in the following terms:

> One should examine accurately with the mind all the phenomena that we perceive as they are conventionally conceived, as well as those that are considered [ultimately] real. One considers then the person, the five skandhas, the sense spheres, the bases of consciousness, the bodies of the Buddha, and everything from the highest wisdom to the hells, the oceans and Mt. Meru. Then, having understood that all of this is emptiness, lacking as it does any self-existence, one thinks: "All this is completely deprived of self-existence, from the beginning empty, removed from the sphere of all thought and speech. Nirvāṇa is ungraspable, saṃsāra is unrenounceable. All is of the same nature as space." Then one should keep the mind from losing track of this thought.[166]

Such passages should not be construed as a concession to the gradualists, as they reflect, rather transparently, doctrines shared by many Ch'an proponents of sudden enlightenment and explained in the *Platform Sūtra:*

> My approach to the dharma has its basis in concentration *(ting)* and insight *(hui).* Under no circumstances should you mistakenly affirm that insight and concentration are different. They form one body *(t'i),* not two things. Concentration is the foundation *(t'i)* for insight. Wisdom is the function *(yung)* of concentration. Whenever there is insight, concentration is present in insight. Whenever there is concentration, insight is present in concentration.[167]

This passage, which is closely paralleled by a section of Shen-hui's *Yü-lu,* cannot be taken as describing a doctrinal position identical to Kamalaśīla's; the latter understands discernment, or "insight," as a process that moves from the discursive realm to the nondiscursive through various stages of *conceptual* analysis. But the passage shows that Ch'an subitists were not advocates of pure serenity or blank concentration.[168]

The Northern school perhaps could be accused of too much emphasis on the calm aspect of meditation. But the *Wu fang-pien* saw the unmoving mind as the original condition of the mind—a condition to be known, rather than to be created. Among this school, therefore, the conceptions are too complex to admit of a simple pigeonhole. A work of the Ox-head school, the *Chüeh-kuan lun,* suggests in its title (Essay on Putting an End to Examination) an attack on insight meditation, but its contents shows this interpretation to be unfounded. It is a dialectical critique of conceptual thought, and it includes, among other colorful exchanges, a critique of the practice of calm or serenity reminiscent of the legendary encounter between Bodhidharma and Hui-k'o:

> "What is mind? What is calming the mind?"
> "You should not posit a mind, nor should you endeavor to calm the mind. This is the practice of calm."[169]

In short, whenever we let the texts speak for themselves we see how inaccurate are the categories of polemicists and scholars alike—"quietism," "gradualism," "subitism," "pure calm."

To complicate the picture further, in Wang-hsi's "record of the Council," Mo-ho-yen is not accused of overemphasizing serenity. On the contrary, he is asked how it could be that his school is called the Ch'an (dhyāna) school when its primary emphasis is on insight (prajñā), not serenity! Mo-ho-yen's reply is not as felicitous as the statements of Vimalamitra and Hui-neng, but it is nevertheless worth quoting:

> What is meant by our doctrine of meditation is the meditation practice of the great vehicle, which consists in abstaining from reflection *(wu-ssu)* and is the perfection of insight *(prajñā)*. . . . The *Ratnakūṭa,* for instance, explains: "The true practice of meditation is simply this: that nothing whatsoever, no matter how insignificant, can be apprehended."[170]

Mo-ho-yen is evidently trying to establish an identity between meditation as a state of mind and insight as the type of awareness of reality that must accompany that state of mind. He comes close, therefore, to both Hui-neng and Kamalaśīla in his understanding of the Mahāyāna doctrine of meditation. But he slips badly in his choice of words, as can be seen in the statement already quoted:

> If one practices the six perfections, it is in order to seek the perfection of insight. Once one is in possession of the perfection of insight, one may or may not practice the other five.

This is precisely the position that Kamalaśīla so aptly criticizes, for it has broad implications extending beyond technical issues in the practice of meditation.

3.3 Separate Practice of the Perfections

In the quotation above Mo-ho-yen recognizes the need for the other perfections.[171] What is then the reason for the gradualist's objections? In the first place, Mo-ho-yen explicitly suggests that there is no reason why the enlightened should practice the perfections. But, secondly, he has also qualified his statements accepting the validity of the perfections as preparatory practices by making it clear that they are valuable only for those living beings whose weak spiritual faculties prevent them from making a direct leap into the nonconceptual.

This brings us to the issue of the ethical implications of the sudden enlightenment position. Pelliot 116 shows that this was a live issue in

Tun-huang at this time. Some of the questions raised in this fragment also occur in Vimalamitra's tract and reflect most of the concerns of Kamalaśīla. For instance, Kamalaśīla wonders what motivation anyone would have for practicing meditation without some understanding of the causes and effects of the path. Or, what is worse, how could one be sure that incorrect or harmful practices (for there are such) are excluded and that correct form of self-cultivation is practiced? How could human beings ever produce the desire and will to seek enlightenment, the "thought of awakening" *(bodhicitta),* if they are told at the outset not to conceptualize or discriminate in the least? This objection finds echo in Vimalamitra's tract where it receives the traditional subitist solution:

> Question: You said that when one practices nonconceptual samādhi, the higher, unconditional dharmas are grouped together with the conditioned. But in this nonconceptual practice *(dharma)* of the Mahāyāna, how is one to produce the thought of awakening?
>
> Reply: In the *Vajra*[*cchedikā*] *Sūtra* it is said: "To abandon completely all apperception is the production of the thought of unsurpassable awakening."[172]

Although one may argue, and Kamalaśīla would agree, that compassion cannot find fulfillment unless the mind is perfectly free of preconceptions, this is not what Vimalamitra or Mo-ho-yen intended. They maintain that careful cultivation—through study, ritual, meditation, and ethical practice—of the thought of enlightenment *(bodhicitta)* is not essential. Those who can take the direct road and enter the nonconceptual have fulfilled the intentions of the thought of awakening. This is different from the views expressed by Kamalaśīla, who believes that the thought of awakening as such, and in all aspects of its cultivation, is a necessary requirement for full practice of the path. The thought of awakening defines the Mahāyāna character of the path, turning practice in the right direction.

Furthermore, although the initial or "preparatory" *(prayoga)* practice leads to a state of mind that is nondual and supramundane *(lokottarajñāna),* the full meaning of this highest contemplative stage is realized only in the practice of compassion, which is in its turn the ultimate effect of the initial production of the thought of awakening and the vows of the bodhisattva.[173]

Kamalaśīla's analysis reflects, naturally, the doctrine of the two levels of truth, which is so central to Indian Buddhism. This doctrine is discussed in Wang-hsi's record in a passage we have quoted above. The concluding remarks to that passage do not seem to contradict Kamalaśīla's understanding of the two truths. The subitist claims that at the level of relative truth

> the six perfections and the rest are means *(upāya)*, because they reveal the ultimate object. [It is in this sense that] they are necessary. But, from the point of view of the ultimate object which is beyond speech, one cannot define the six perfections or any dharma-method as necessary or not necessary. . . .[174]

But the subitist does not give any hint here whether a person who has realized the absolute will practice the perfections or not.

The issue is confused even more when we read lines that are in the spirit of Shen-hui:

> Those who have dull faculties, who have not penetrated deeply into ultimate truth, need these [means of access: *fang-pien*]. Those whose faculties are sharp have no need to consider the question of their necessity or non-necessity.[175]

But immediately following this exchange Mo-ho-yen clarifies his position in terms that are indubitably orthodox by Indian Buddhist standards. Although the passage only treats the perfections in the abstract, we must interpret the discussion as a technical way of referring to the specific, fundamental issues of the debate: (1) are there or are there not any behavioral directives in Buddhism that allow the believer to map out his path; and (2) do enlightened beings follow certain behavioral standards or do they not? Mo-ho-yen responds as follows:

> The six perfections have four degrees or levels: (1) mundane perfections, (2) supramundane perfections, (3) higher supramundane perfections, and (4) inner six perfections. According to the *Laṅkāvatāra* [. . .] when one attains non-examination *(pu-kuan)* and nonreflection *(pu-ssu)* the six perfections reach their fullness naturally *(tzu-jan)*, but as long as one has not reached non-examination and nonreflection one must practice the six perfections without expecting any retribution.[176]

The passage could not be more clear: there are various levels of awareness and intentionality in the cultivation of spiritual values, from the first stages of conscious effort and motivation to the highest stage of internalized doctrine. What is more, the way the path is practiced on the first stages suggests the nature of the goal—not to expect anything.

What led then to Kamalaśīla's attacks? We can be sure that there is a good dose of *odium theologicum* in his critique, but that does not explain everything. It might be suggested that Kamalaśīla is reacting to Mo-ho-yen's Chinese ways, especially his disregard for book learning. But even this is not enough to explain their antagonism. I believe the passage above shows that inconsistency and exaggeration grow rampant in Mo-ho-yen's writings. The rhetoric of Ch'an—more concerned with impact and iconoclasm than with scholastic notions such as intellectual clarity and logical rigor—probably did not seem to an Indian from Nālandā like the most proper way of treating a subject so sacred as the word of the Buddha. Furthermore, the subitist's fixation with making statements from the point of view of ultimate truth is inherently disconcerting to anyone seeking doctrinal orientation. Among the confused issues the most important is that of the ethical directives and models that define the Buddhist path. This social and philosophical problem is not resolved satisfactorily by the subitist.

Accordingly, the gradualist presses the matter further:

Question: . . . If there is not the least dharma that can be apprehended, if there is no reflection and no examination, then one must object: is there no apprehending in working for the benefit of all living beings?

Reply: We have already replied to this question, and you come back to it! Let me repeat myself: for innumerable cosmic periods Buddhas abandon *(li)* the apprehending and the nonapprehending mind *(te pu-te hsin),* so that they have no mind *(wu-hsin)* and no reflection *(wu-ssu), like a clear mirror.* Having no mind and no reflection, they are free from apprehending or not apprehending. It is only because they conform to living beings and respond to things that they manifest forms. The metaphors of water, the jewel, the sun, the moon, and so on point to the same cardinal meaning. Moreover, the *Tathāgataguṇāvatāra Sūtra* says that not to apprehend the least dharma is to apprehend all dharmas; and this goes against your thesis. . . .[177]

Elsewhere Mo-ho-yen adds:

> The *Tathāgataguṇāvatāra Sūtra* explains in detail how one can work for the benefit of all living beings when one has no reflection and no observation: it is like the sun and the moon, whose rays illuminate all things; like the wish-gem, from which one can obtain everything; like the great earth, which [always] has the capacity to bear all fruits.[178]

These similes are in fact found in the sūtras, but unfortunately Mo-ho-yen does not follow these lines with careful and specific practical instructions on how one is to benefit beings. The reader is left, then, with doubts as to the possible "quietistic" implications of the images. The gradualist, on the other hand, cannot respond to Mo-ho-yen's criticism adequately unless he interprets the sūtra passages as figures of speech, for, if it is possible for a Buddha to assist other beings without conscious effort and planning, then it is possible to become liberated by a similar process—and perhaps even to aspire to lead a moral life by a similar mystical laissez-faire.

Kamalaśīla is a careful and consistent gradualist. Although he agrees that the highest stage of *contemplative* realization is nonconceptual *(nirvikalpa-samādhi),* this stage is preceded *and followed* by conceptual thought.[179] When Buddhas act for the sake of living beings they are free from delusions and attachments with regard to the world, but they use the tools of the world. As there are "means" for the absolute, as Buddha, to reach down to living beings, there are means for carrying out the inverse—for living beings to ascend to Buddhahood. The gradualist feels that in a world of nondiscrimination one could not speak of means, much less use them. In fact, even in the temporary condition of nondiscrimination achieved through the gradual process of cultivation, one is not able to practice means. Still,

> although it is not possible to practice means while one is in the condition of [exercising] supramundane insight, when the time comes to practice means the bodhisattva, like a magician, is in full possession of an insight *(prajñā)* that is a preparation or a consequence of supramundane knowledge. . . .[180]

This ability to practice different types of insight for different purposes corresponds to the two levels of truth *(paramārtha* and *saṃvṛti);* it embodies the nondual character of the bodhisattva's goal. Accordingly, the gradualist sees a subtle dualism in the subitist's recommendation of the exclusive practice of nonconceptual meditation.[181]

By accepting only the nonconceptual as true and worth pursuing, the subitist suggests a duality in which an important segment of reality—and ethical practice—is excluded from the Buddhist ideal. This difficulty becomes apparent in the treatment of the ethical question in the *Cheng-li chüeh* as well as in Vimalamitra and Pelliot 116. For instance, the issue of assisting living beings is treated in Vimalamitra's tract in a cryptic manner which is certainly not beyond clarification but may seem confusing to some:

> If someone were to object that [those who are] in the nonconceptual realm have no means of being of service to other living beings, one can respond with the words of the *Perfection of Wisdom:* "Subhūti, the bodhisattva mahāsattvas become established in the three samādhis [in this manner]: the concepts that are constructed by [other] living beings they place in emptiness; the signs that are used by [other] living beings they gather under the signless; the goals that living beings cherish they place in the wishless sphere. Subhūti, in this way the bodhisattva mahāsattvas, coursing in perfect wisdom, bring living beings to maturity." In this way the nonconceptual is of service to living beings. But if they use conceptual signs, teachers of dharma follow the path of Māra, and become evil friends. The **Buddhagarbha Sūtra* explains: "To teach dharma to others without knowing the true nature of things is to become the cause of their

> downfall. Why? Because to speak about dharma erroneously is to speak of signs and real entities." To benefit living beings without forming apprehensions is called the highest [dharma].[182]

It is easy to see how an opponent eager to find fault in this doctrine would suspect not only a rejection of the doctrine of means, but a certain indifference to the ethical ideals of the bodhisattva path. Kamalaśīla seems to be raising this objection when he states:

> [The statement] that there is no need to practice good actions, or to act in any other way . . . [would contradict] what the Blessed One explains everywhere in the sūtras, that the attainments of Buddhas and Bodhisattvas . . . are acquired as a result of meritorious deeds such as generosity. . . .
>
> And one who turns away from exertion in the practice of virtuous deeds will also turn away from the world of rebirth and from fulfilling the hopes of other sentient beings. This person, therefore, will be still far removed from awakening.[183]

But there is another important point at issue here. It is not only a matter of whether proponents of sudden enlightenment recognize certain ethical standards, conform to them, or merely pay them lip service. The gradualist also demands a view of ethics that presents moral growth as an integral part of the path, or at least of the theoretical system. This is a point which does not find an adequate formulation in some Buddhist traditions, especially in East Asia, but which receives special attention in Kamalaśīla's attack on sudden enlightenment.

One should note that although some of the Ch'an texts, such as the *Wu fang-pien,* incorporate the doctrine of means into their system as an integral element of the path, none gives a satisfactory account of the doctrines of skillful means and saving sentient beings in practical ethical terms. Both Kamalaśīla and the *Wu fang-pien* base their exposition of the doctrine of means on a passage from the *Vimalakīrti-nirdeśa* in which wisdom, or insight *(prajñā),* and means *(upāya)* are presented as equally important for the bodhisattva's spiritual development—one without the other becomes a bond, their cooperation is liberation.[184]

Kamalaśīla uses this passage as the central proof in his criticism of his subitist opponents. Whereas Mo-ho-yen fails to make a firm commitment to means as an integral part of the path, Kamalaśīla, following mainline Indian Mahāyāna, connects the doctrine of the cooperation of means and insight with the highest goal of the bodhisattva path, the Mahāyāna nirvāṇa, known as the "nirvāṇa on which [bodhisattvas] do not settle" *(apratiṣṭhita-nirvāṇa).*[185] This means that Kamalaśīla understands this passage (I believe, correctly) to mean that no segment of the bodhisattva practices (including the highest intuitive grasp of the truth) is sufficient in and of itself to transform a human being into a true bodhisattva; both means and wisdom are essential to all stages of the path, though one element may dominate over the other at different stages in the path.

In contrast to this view, we have seen that the Ch'an schools vacillate in their regard for the doctrine of means. With the exception of the more or less consistent assertion that means are only a concession to human beings who cannot gain direct access to enlightenment, the doctrine of means does not figure prominently in early Ch'an texts. Of the Ch'an texts considered in this essay, only the *Wu fang-pien* gives careful consideration to the doctrine of the complementarity of means and insight. Explicating the passage from the *Vimalakīrti-nirdeśa,* the *Wu fang-pien,* like the *Third Bhāvanākrama,* identifies "insight without skillful means" with Hīnayāna practice and, again in agreement with Kamalaśīla, equates "insight with skillful means" with the bodhisattva practice —in which one is in the calm of the absolute while moving freely in the relative world.[186] But it is not clear that the *Wu fang-pien* would follow Kamalaśīla on the rest of his interpretation, for the emphasis in the Indian author is on the practical application of insight rather than on the freedom of the bodhisattva. The importance of means is in their role in the performance of the activities of a Buddha. Thus Kamalaśīla quotes the *Kāśyapaparivarta:*

> As a king who is assisted by his ministers [is able to] carry out all the duties of kingship, in the same manner, O Kāśyapa, a bodhisattva's insight assisted by skillful means [is able to] carry out all the tasks of a Buddha.[187]

Kamalaśīla's explanation of means and the cooperation of means and insight is developed in his *Second* and *Third Bhāvanākramas* in the context of his doctrine of the perfections *(pāramitā).* He uses several passages from the sūtras to show that means (synonymous here with compassion) fulfill the goals of insight (synonymous with emptiness) and that the real meaning of emptiness is the practice of *all* the perfections. In fact, true emptiness is "adorned by virtue."[188]

This point is the key to the gradualist view. The integration of all aspects of the doctrine presupposes the practice of all of its elements. The defender of sudden enlightenment, on the other hand, maintains that their integration implies that distinctions among them are meaningless, and that therefore there is no sense in enjoining their separate practice.

Whereas the subitist sees the gradualist as ignoring the critical dimension of the doctrine of the perfection of wisdom (seen as a doctrine of radical insight), the gradualist sees in his opponent an excessive emphasis on one perfection at the expense of the others, a pernicious preference for emptiness at the expense of compassion and liberative technique.[189] In this sense Kamalaśīla sees Ch'an as an antinomian system.[190] In defense of the subitist, however, one could point out that a careful consideration of its position, and some help in consistency, could have produced a more sympathetic understanding among its critics. In practice most subitists exercise their iconoclasm only in the sphere of rhetoric (with the notable exception of the Szechwan schools, perhaps). Mo-ho-yen himself has filled his memoranda to the king of Tibet with protestations regarding his exemplary record as an upright man of religion.[191] In fact, the rhetoric itself often presupposes a living religion that is far from being quietistic or antinomian. For instance, it is difficult to see how the following passage could have been meaningful outside a living religion with established ethical guidelines:

> Question: What is the unsurpassable morality [practiced by one who abides] in the nonconceptual realm?
>
> Answer: The **Nāgopama Sūtra* says: "Whatever you conceive as being moral, and whatever you conceive as being immoral—these two are called distorted morality. Whatever is neither is true morality."[192]

The injunction is implicitly directed at those who are committed to moral discipline; the passage is therefore parallel to Shen-hui's sermon. Accordingly, the exegetic question is not whether these sudden enlightenment teachings are for those who are indifferent to traditional Buddhist values—this is evidently not the case. The question is whether statements such as the above undermine Buddhist ethical values. Kamalaśīla believes they do: he sees in such rhetoric a rejection of the scriptural tradition.[193]

But Kamalaśīla himself seems to be trapped in contradiction, for after all Ch'an rhetoric can find justification in a tradition of apophatism and iconoclasm that reached radical extremes even in India—as in the *Vimalakīrti-nirdeśa, Nāgaśrī-paripṛcchā,* and *Sarvadharmāpravṛtti.*[194] Kamalaśīla defends himself, however, by following a line of argument close to that of Shen-hui: passages criticizing Buddhist values are intended for those Buddhists who are attached to virtue and religious ideals; they confirm, rather than condemn, the passages enjoining moral discipline.

Is there then agreement on this point between Shen-hui, or Mo-ho-yen, and Kamalaśīla? I do not believe so; for the subitist position remains ambiguous. Although few of them would make a complete break from Buddhist institutions and ethical ideals, most fail to commit themselves explicitly to the practices they regard as "worldly" or relative. Although they insist that there is no sacred or profane, sudden or gradual in the path, someone like Mo-ho-yen tells us that means are only for the dull-witted, that ultimately means are neither necessary nor unnecessary, and that "one may or may not practice" the first five perfections.[195]

Similarly, the subitist tradition has an ambiguous relationship with Buddhist ritual—practicing it with its institutional right hand, condemning it with its doctrinal left.[196] Typical of Ch'an rhetoric on ritual is the following extract on the confession of sins from the catechism attributed to Vimalamitra:

> Some may also object that there can be no confession of sins in the nonconceptual realm. To this one should reply with the words from the *Samanta[bhadra] Sūtra*:
>
> > When one wishes to confess his sins,
> > one should sit with the back straight, looking into the real.
> > Looking correctly into the real,
> > seeing the real, one attains liberation.
>
> This is called the most excellent contrition. This means that to sit with an unmoving mind is the very best act of contrition.[197]

This passage implies that meditation is to be preferred to the ritual of confession. But there is nothing to indicate that the ritual is to be rejected altogether. A cursory glance at the documentary evidence will show how central this ritual was to Buddhist practice in Tun-huang. Furthermore, Shen-hui directs the performance of such a ritual at the beginning of his *T'an-yü*.[198] According to the *Platform Sūtra,* the sixth patriarch must have practiced at least the basic skeleton of a Mahāyāna ritual in three parts—a threefold ritual *(triskandhaka)* of sorts.[199] It goes without saying that the text offers no basis for attributing these practices to the historical person Hui-neng, but this is beside the point, since we only need to show that the Tun-huang community (whether inspired by Northern Ch'an or the Ox-head school) had a living ritual that served as the frame of reference for the subitist critique. This ritual was unquestionably very similar to the one used by Shen-hui for his own critique—which, incidentally, also served as a model for Shen-hui's own, official ritual functions.

The *Platform Sūtra* has Hui-neng explain three of the so-called precepts, here called "signless" or "formless" *(wu-hsiang)*: the three refuges, the four vows, and repentance.[200] One could argue that the "formless precepts" make sense only in the context of conventional, or literal "precepts." But this argument is unnecessary, for the *Platform Sūtra* presents two versions of the refuges, the "formless refuges" and the conventional precepts. Its version of the "confession of emptiness" is close to that of Vimalamitra but has a much stronger "antinomian" or even "quietistic" flavor: "Forever not to act is called confession."[201] Although the Kōshōji edition suggests that this statement is to be interpreted as meaning "never again to do evil," the Tun-huang text must be preferred: to be free of action is to be free of evil. This type or style of doctrinal assertion makes one wonder exactly what was the role of moral concerns in this brand of Ch'an.

But the basic idea of the awareness of emptiness taking precedence over ritual confession is not foreign to the gradualist. Kamalaśīla himself says in so many words that it is better to cultivate the thought of emptiness than to feel remorse or recite the formula of repentance.[202] It may be that the basic difficulty with the sudden enlightenment position is not so much in what it explicitly rejects as in its insensitivity to the implications of some of its more radical statements. After all, it is the gradualist, not the subitist, who has to care for logical consistency and clarity. The advocates of sudden enlightenment may claim that their critique is directed against the danger of confusing the description of a process with its realization, as well as against conceptual constructs hindering a direct apprehension of Buddha-nature. But the subitists will have to concede that a literal or unbending formulation and understanding of their own position is both a poor application of skill in means and a covert form of dualism, a subtle attachment to conceptual constructs.

4. Terminological Issues

The complex nature of the positions advocated in the polemics discussed above, as well as the inadequacy of the typology suggested by the sudden-gradual dichotomy, calls into question the accuracy of the English terminology used to describe the two ends of the polarity. But the terms themselves are inherently problematic; the terminology presents a new set of problems, different from those discussed so far. In the preceding pages I have endeavored to show how the indiscriminate use of sudden-gradual terminology can be misleading and the sense in which the identification of sudden with "quietistic" is simplistic. But one may raise other objections against the appropriateness of the two terms—for they are not always accurate representations of the terms used in the Asian debates.

Demiéville's "Miroir" is one of the earliest Western attempts at establishing a useful terminology. He briefly considered pairs of opposites such as *perfectivisme* and *imperfectivisme, totalitarisme* and *évolutionnisme,* only to adopt "provisionally" the two terms that he made current in scholarly circles: *subitisme* and *gradualisme.*[203] One could, following Stein, propose "immediatism" and "mediatism," but these terms are even less idiomatic and more cacophonous in English than Demiéville's classical pair.[204]

Another set of terms has been suggested by Broughton: "all-at-once" and "step-by-step."[205] The expression "all-at-once" has the advantage of containing some of the ambiguities of the original Chinese and Tibetan terms, perhaps more than Stein's *saisie simultanée,* which has the added disadvantage of suggesting possession or acquisition. "All-at-once" is also approximately the meaning of *cig-car* and *yugapat.*

Terminological accuracy and convenience, however, are not the real issue. The question is how much our terminological choices will affect our understanding of a given tradition. It is in this respect that researches such as the work of Stein are so valuable. Stein has shown that the terms used by the Tibetan and Chinese traditions to refer to the contrast known to us as sudden versus gradual are often ambiguous. This is beyond question correct, but he goes further to claim that the "primary," albeit not the only, meaning conveyed by the terms used for sudden enlightenment is not the instantaneousness or suddenness of the experience, but "la simultanéité (dans le temps, dans l'espace ou sur le plan de l'activité mentale)."[206] I consider this thesis to be an example of hypercorrection.

Stein claims that he will only make "quelques observations précises, purement linguistiques ou philologiques, concernant le champ semantique de terme traduit par 'subite,' " without considering "des notions philosophiques très subtiles dont la définition varie un peu selon les auteurs ou les écoles."[207] Granting that the "idiomatic usage" of the Chinese and Tibetan terms is relevant to the question, one still cannot assume thereby that "primary meanings" of non-philosophical discourse will be the central meanings of philosophical terms. I am also not persuaded by Stein's suggestion that the primary meaning of a term is easily distinguishable from any "secondary" usages, or that "secondary meanings" of the term "sudden" in English (and *subit* in French) do not include other important aspects that are covered by the concept of "immediacy," such as the unexpected and spontaneous nature of enlightenment, or the fact that it somehow occurs without previous preparation or without a transition from the previous state of delusion, and so forth.

Although Sanskrit *yugapat* means "simultaneous" and not "sudden," the Sanskrit term does not seem to play an important role in the sudden-gradual debate. The Tibetan terms, on the other hand, are of central importance, and some of them may reflect a Sanskrit model. In this connection, Gary Houston has shown that the Tibetan term *cig-car* can also mean "suddenly" or "rapidly," demonstrating the wide range of meanings and nuances in the terminology.[208]

I must express still another reservation regarding Stein's analysis of the sudden enlightenment position. I am not sure that what he sees as the philosophical foundation of this doctrine is at all present in most forms of Buddhism which I know—most certainly not in the Ch'an tradition. Strictly speaking, one can conceive of the Buddhist middle way as a *coincidentia oppositōrum* only if it is understood that the middle position is neither a "golden mean" nor a condition of literal nondifferentiation (such as Schelling's moonless night in which all cats are black). Rather, the third or middle position stands outside the plane in which the other two contrast with each other; it may even be on that same plane if one stands on it without trying to reduce one extreme to the terms of the other. In this sense, Stein's "la simultanéité de deux plans opposés, mais solidaires" falls short of being an accurate description of the doctrine in question.[209]

Finally, Stein feels that an accurate definition of subitism will immediately provide us with a definition, and an understanding, of gradualism. The data I have presented in the previous sections of this paper should suffice to show that this is not the case. I would like to mention an example of a doctrinal position in which gradualism is, at the same time, more or less the logical contrary of subitism and yet a different way of articulating the same theories that are seen by Stein and Demiéville as the basis for subitism.

Paradoxically, but indirectly confirming Stein's thesis, gradualism—which ostensively would build a bridge to span the gap between deluded beings and the perfectly enlightened—can serve as a way of maintaining and defining precisely the distinction between the transcendent state of the accomplished beings who are the object of religious awe (Buddhas and bodhisattvas) and the imperfect ones for whom enlightenment is so distant that it becomes only a hope. At this level gradualism manifests itself as the logical opposite of the thesis of innate or immediate enlightenment. But, at the same time, what makes that hope of the faithful (1) a possibility, (2) an act of will leading to effort, (3) a foreshadowing of enlightenment, and (4) enlightenment itself is the fact that liberation, as absolute emptiness, is a beginningless actuality for all entities. This is one dimension in which whatever we may learn about sudden enlightenment will not help us understand gradual enlightenment.

The importance of Stein's contribution, therefore, lies not in what he believes are the broader implications of his study. He advanced our knowledge of the problem by adding to our understanding of the range of meaning of the terms and to their documentation. But paradoxically—since he claims he did not set out to accomplish this—I find the greatest value of his piece in the way he clarifies the philosophical basis of the concepts. More specifically, he was the first to formulate in Western terms what is clearly in the texts: (1) that sudden enlightenment often implies immediate (that is, non-mediate) enlightenment; and (2) that the instantaneous character of the experience does not necessarily imply abruptness.[210]

But, in a more philosophical mood, one must clarify some of these terms by asking, "Can something occur all at once but not suddenly?" Evidently part of the confusion may be found in the term "sudden" itself, which means both "quickly" and "unexpectedly." If sudden enlightenment is abrupt enlightenment, a flash of understanding that comes without warning, it could just as well occur all at once or step by step, but presumably it could not be preceded by preparation or expectation of any kind. Similarly, sudden enlightenment could be conceived of as an event for which one could prepare, but which is nevertheless unique, whole, and direct. This second interpretation does not presuppose much about the path that leads to the experience and the consequences of the experience. For the experience to be "sudden" in this sense of the word it is sufficient that when it occurs it is not mediated by thoughts, preconceptions, or human effort. One can easily see that the distinction corresponds roughly to the difference established previously between Southern and Northern Ch'an, respectively. It also follows that in the second sense of the word "sudden," most Buddhist gradualists accepted some form of sudden enlightenment. Therefore, in spite of the doctrinal centrality of immediacy and directness, the practical distinction between abrupt and non-abrupt is still crucial to our understanding of the sudden-gradual debates.

5. The Metaphors

Underlying the terminological distinction is a set of metaphors that find interesting parallels in other religious traditions. But these are perilous analogies. The explorer of this image world is well advised to proceed with caution. One cannot assume that the occurrence of a certain simile or metaphor in different religious traditions indicates a significant connection, parallelism, or contrast in the deep structure of the religions. Perhaps a cursory examination of two of the most common metaphors of sudden enlightenment—polishing a mirror and purifying gold—will suffice to prove the point. Both metaphors are found throughout the Buddhist tradition, in very disparate contexts.[211]

The metaphor of the purification of gold is used twice by Shen-hui.[212] In the first instance it is used as an analogical argument to bolster Shen-hui's sudden enlightenment theories: innate Buddhahood (gold) is already present in all its perfection in the realm of delusion (unrefined ore). But in the second instance Shen-hui follows the analogy to its ultimate implications and is carried away from his original position. For the second use of the analogy in Shen-hui is closer to the original meaning in the scriptural source from which he borrowed it: the afflictions *(kleśa)* are like slag, because they are adventitious, merely superficial impurities. Buddhahood is like gold, it is the essential and the valuable. But innate or essential Buddhahood, like gold, has different degrees of purity: once removed from the ore it can be refined further. Thus, in the *Mahāparinirvāṇa Sūtra* and in the literature associated with it, the image of gold is a metaphor for innate Buddha-nature in a *gradualist* context.[213] The gradualist use of the metaphor is also found in the Pāli tradition, and in Kamalaśīla, who in this follows the *Sandhinirmocana.*[214] The latter two sources do not seem to imply anything regarding the innateness of Buddhahood, but the tathāgatagarbha tradition, while being frankly gradualist, is also unequivocal in its affirmation of the innateness of Buddhahood.[215]

The analogy of the mirror is equally malleable. In the *Laṅkāvatāra Sūtra* alone it occurs with at least four different meanings:[216] One can compare the activities of *vikalpa* to the unreal reflections in a mirror (20.15). Active *vijñāna* itself, therefore, is like a mirror (37.16). But, pure consciousness is also like a mirror; adventitious impurities cover it and do not allow it to manifest its clarity (327.6). The immediate or simultaneous *(yugapat)* action of the Buddha on the minds of all sentient beings and the resulting capacity of the mind to be aware, yet to be free from conceptualization, are also compared, in a mixed metaphor, to the reflecting action of a mirror (55.18):

> Just as, Mahāmati, reflections of all [sorts of] objects appear on a mirror simultaneously *(yugapat)*, without conception or distinction *(nirvikalpa)*, in the same manner, Mahāmati, the Tathāgata simultaneously purifies [the minds of] all beings [so that] the current of mental images *(svacittadṛśya-dhārā)* [becomes] free of conceptions *(nirvikalpa)*, within a domain free of mental representations *(nirābhāsagocara)*.

In the *Sandhinirmocana-sūtra,* on the other hand, the mirror stands for the unreality of the images appearing before consciousness, which is close to the abhidharmic use of the analogy, and to the one preferred by Kamalaśīla.[217] The most characteristic use of the image in the *Sandhinirmocana* is in comparing the *ādāna-vijñāna* to a mirror which suffers no alteration while manifesting (reflecting) all changes and movements that appear in front of it.[218]

As has been shown in the preceding paragraphs, metaphors in religious and philosophical language are as elusive as they are in poetry. Perhaps this is one of their major rhetorical values. One must accordingly proceed with caution in drawing any conclusions from parallels or differences in imagery. One must take into account the doctrinal context as an integral whole, as well as possible inconsistencies, contradictions, or shifts in emphasis. Cross-cultural comparisons are especially complex. In this connection, Demiéville's comments on Gregory of Nyssa can serve as a good example of the dangers of reaching conclusions only on the basis of one analogy. Demiéville has claimed that among Western masters of spirituality, Gregory of Nyssa is clearly a major representative of "subitism."[219] As a Christian, of course, Gregory has the acute sense of sin, the anxious awareness of moral disjunctives, that is considered unimportant, if not outright pernicious, in Ch'an Buddhism. Accordingly, he seeks a way to conciliate his doctrine of im-mediacy of the divine vision with the fallen state of man.[220]

Although these are not the only points that separate him from Buddhism, I would like to consider first the superficial analogies that led Demiéville to classify Gregory's mysticism as a type of "subitism." Demiéville emphasizes three points in Gregory's doctrine that seem reminiscent of "subitism": (1) innate divine nature, (2) the soul as a mirror covered by adventitious impurity, and (3) man's passivity in the task *(ergon)* of salvation. The correspondence with "subitism" could be strengthened, in fact, by adducing other concepts in Gregory's thought. For instance, the following passages from *The Life of Moses,* which are not found in Demiéville's analysis, add two more points of contact: mystical knowledge is no-knowledge, and the divine nature *cannot* be lost. In the first of these passages Gregory is simply following the tradition of the Pseudo-Dionysus:

> [The soul] thus leaves all surface appearances, not only those that can be grasped by the senses but also those which the mind itself seems to see, and it keeps on going deeper until by the operation of the spirit it penetrates the invisible and incomprehensible, and it is there that it sees God. The true vision and the true knowledge of what we seek consists precisely in not seeing, in an awareness that our goal transcends all knowledge and is everywhere cut off from us by the darkness of incomprehensibility.[221]

But this is not all. Gregory adds an explanation that immediately places him in a position very different from that of the Buddhist:

> Thus, that profound evangelist, John, who penetrated into this luminous darkness, tells us that "no man hath seen God at any time" (John 1.18), teaching us by this negation that no man—indeed, no created intellect—can attain a knowledge of God.[222]

Regarding the innate divinity of the soul, the treatise *On Virginity* adds the following comment:

> This creature man, then, did not possess as a property of his nature at the beginning any inclination to passion and mortality. For the pattern of the

image could not have been preserved if in its limitation it had in any respect contradicted its archetype.[223]

Yet, Gregory believes—unlike, say, Hui-neng—that the soul's "pollutants" are real, not a phantom of the imagination. Thus we read:

> The soul's divine beauty, that had been an imitation of its archetype, was, like a blade, darkened with the rust of sin; it no longer kept the beauty of the image it once possessed by nature, and was transformed into the ugliness of evil.[224]

For Gregory, the soul's impurities are not the result of a misapprehension, or a mistaken use of the faculty of conceptualization. Impurity and sin represent one aspect of reality—reality external to the mirror of the soul—which is categorized as that which is not the *logos*. The soul, on the other hand, is of the *logos*.

As we proceed, the differences increase. For instance, the passage quoted by Demiéville to prove the soul's absolute passivity, in its proper context says much more.

> . . . this is the image we earnestly counsel him to remove and wash away *in the purifying waters of the Christian life.* Once this earthly covering is removed, the soul's beauty will once again shine forth. Now, the removal of what is foreign is a return to what is connatural and fitting; and this we can only achieve by becoming what we once were in the beginning when we were created. Yet to achieve this likeness to God is *not within our power* nor within any human capacity. It is *a gift of God's bounty,* for He directly bestowed this divine likeness on our human nature at its creation. *By our human efforts* we can merely *clear away the accumulated filth* of sin and thus allow the hidden beauty of the soul to shine forth.[225]

Thus, notwithstanding Gregory's emphasis on grace, and his choice of the metaphor of the mirror, a path of purification and self-cultivation is prescribed. It is, therefore, difficult to imagine Gregory as a "subitist."

The suggestion of gradualism in Gregory is not only found in general statements like those above. He also sees human effort as involving a process that takes place in stages:

> Now the doctrine we are taught here is as follows. Our *initial withdrawal* from wrong and erroneous ideas of God is a *transition* from darkness to light. *Next comes a closer awareness* of hidden things, and by this the soul is guided through sense phenomena to the world of the invisible. And this awareness is a kind of cloud, which overshadows all appearances, *and slowly guides and accustoms* the soul to look towards what is hidden. *Next the soul makes progress through all these stages and goes on higher,* and as she leaves below all that human nature can attain, she enters within the secret chamber of the divine knowledge, and here she is cut off on all sides by the divine darkness. Now she leaves outside all that can be grasped by sense

> or by reason, and the only thing left for her contemplation is the invisible and the incomprehensible. And here God is, as the Scriptures tell us in connection with Moses: "But Moses went to the dark cloud wherein God was" (Exod. 20.21).[226]

Since Gregory is still hesitant to admit any direct knowledge of the divine essence, he insists that there can be no all-at-once or integral knowledge of God:

> To make this idea a little clearer, I shall illustrate it by a comparison. It is just as if you could see that spring which Scripture tells us rose from the earth at the beginning in such quantities that it watered the entire face of the earth (Gen. 2.20ff.). As you came near the spring you would marvel, seeing that the water was endless, as it constantly gushed up and poured forth. Yet you could never say that you had seen all the water. How would you see what was still hidden in the bosom of the earth? Hence no matter how long you might stay at the spring, you would always be beginning to see the water. For the water never stops flowing, and it is always beginning to bubble up again.[227]

We may regard this metaphor as the counterexample that neutralizes much of what the mirror metaphor has suggested in the way of parallelism. Gregory stands by a conviction that is totally foreign to the Buddhist tradition: the opposition between the infinite Creator and the finite, fallen creature.

Apart from all this, one cannot overlook another element in Gregory's doctrine that is unknown to the Chinese doctrine of immediate enlightenment without cultivation—the doctrine of grace. It is at this point that I would not hesitate to part ways with Demiéville's methodology. Without further words of caution Demiéville's comments on the soul's passivity in Gregory seem to me unacceptable. He says: "*Mises à part les notions de Créateur,* de *grâce,* de *resemblance,* n'est-ce pas là entre le philosophe païen et son contradicteur chrétien, le débat de Chen-sieou et de Houei-neng?"[228] I would not accept Demiéville's question as a rhetorical question, and I would reply, "It is certainly not the same." The question can be answered in the affirmative only if we ignore fundamental differences and accept the sort of facile identification that is suggested when one equates quietism and *wu-wei*—in both cases we would be guilty of misinterpretation by omission of context.

The error may be due to our natural but erroneous assumption that all humans will derive the same conclusions we do from a common set of premises—an error that is even less justifiable when the premise is clothed in religious metaphor. I will not go into this problem any further than suggesting two points that have been noted before. First, the possibility of deriving ethical propositions from religious or metaphysical propositions is not at all self-evident, and at the very least not a trivial matter. Second, the informational content and interpretation of religious propositions, especially of ultimate sacred utterances, are not always univocal. In fact ambiguity seems to be an inherent characteristic of this type of proposition. The historian must exercise great care, therefore, not to conclude that acceptance of a given religious axiom must have led necessarily to the advocacy of the implications derived from the axiom by the modern scholar.

Even granting that these last observations are open to revision, the historical evidence is unquestionable. Different religious traditions, or subsets of one particular tradition, can make different use of the same fundamental creed or symbol. One only has to bring to mind in passing a few examples from the Indian tradition, Buddhist and non-Buddhist. Śaṅkara, whom Zaehner considers a quietist and Demiéville presents as the Hindu counterpart of the Buddhist "subitist," spawned three lines of disciples—only one took a "leap-philosophy" position (to borrow K. H. Potter's terminology).[229] The mirror metaphor was rejected by none of these schools. Still, though they shared scriptural sources and the same founder, their common metaphors were interpreted in different, and often conflicting, ways.

The school of Rāmānuja, on the other hand, suffered a schism in path theory without any major split in ontology. The ontological ground could also be expressed with the mirror metaphor: the Creator's image reflected in the mirror of the creature's soul. But what corresponds here to subitism? And what holds here the gradualist position? Vedānta Deśika's theology of devotion, and the "monkey-hold" theory of grace, are, as we would expect, based on a sense of the gap that must be bridged by some form of effort. Yet the "subitist" position, that of Pillai Lokācārya's doctrine of pure surrender *(prapatti),* and the "cat-hold" doctrine of grace, claims to be based on the same assumptions about man's relationship to God.[230]

But one does not have to look outside Buddhism to find variant uses of imagery and conflicting understandings of the implications of a particular ontological position. Again, the mirror and its connection with gradual and sudden enlightenment is a case in point. Demiéville would have the gradualist and the subitist defined by their philosophical position with respect to the ontological status of the originally pure self-nature and the adventitious impurities. To this effect he quotes a passage from the *Madhyāntavibhāga* which, translated from his French version, would read:

> If there were no passions,
> All men would be liberated.

> If there were no purity,
> Their effort would be in vain.
> Emptiness has passions, yet it is without them;
> It is neither pure nor impure.
> The mind is naturally pure;
> It is soiled by adventitious passions.[231]

Demiéville then explains that the passage expresses the middle way between two extremes: "pureté et passions, absolu et rélatif. *C'est à ces deux termes que se rapportent respectivement,* dans le *Sūtra de l'Estrade,* la stance de Houei-neng et celle de Chen-sieou."[232]

Now, if this were the case, Shen-hsiu would affirm the reality of impurity and the need to produce a purity that is at present nonexistent, whereas Hui-neng would affirm the reality of original purity and deny totally the reality of impurity. But this is not an accurate description of the use of the mirror metaphor in the poems, nor is this exactly true of the doctrines found in other documents of both schools. This interpretation is in fact contradicted by Demiéville himself when he says: "Houei-neng *nie l'existence même du miroir* et de la poussière qui la souille; Chen-sieou *l'admet dans la mesure* où il est nécessaire d'en tenir compte pour purifier le miroir de la poussière."[233]

What is more, the passage quoted from the *Madhyāntavibhāga* is transparently a defense of one of the two doctrinal poles being considered in this volume: it advocates a gradual process of enlightenment. It should be of interest to offer a fragment of the relevant section in the subcommentary *(ṭīkā)* attributed to Sthiramati.

> If [emptiness] were not stained [by mental afflictions],
> All embodied beings would be free.

> Liberation is getting rid of afflictions; and this getting rid results from cultivating the path. In this connection, [the commentary says,] *if all dharmas were empty of adventitious afflictions, then even if there arose no countermeasures* [to put an end to bondage, living beings] *would not be in a state of affliction.* All living beings would be free without making any effort—in other words, without [having to develop] countermeasures. Yet, there is no liberation for breathing beings without [the practice of the necessary] countermeasures. Therefore, one must admit that when one is in the state of the common man, suchness is stained with adventitious impurities. Thus, it is established that there is a type of emptiness that is perturbed. Now, in order to establish the type that is pure, [the author] says:
>
> If [emptiness] were not pure,
> effort would be fruitless.
>
> [That is to say,] *if, on the other hand, there were no purity, then even if one produced the [appropriate] countermeasures, striving for liberation would be in vain.*[234]

The issues raised in this passage also touch on a different set of problems that relate distantly to the Chinese debate on sudden and gradual. For the question of the mind's innate nature leads to much controversy regarding the meaning of "pure consciousness"—an issue that will spill over into China through Hsüan-tsang and Bodhiruci. It is certainly no coincidence that the Chinese preferred the view that the mind is inherently pure, that there is, therefore, no such thing as an "impure aspect" of mind.

The position of Sthiramati, however, cannot be seen as the other extreme in a polarity modeled on the Buddhist "extreme positions" *(anta)*. In their ontology there is not such a great chasm between the pure mind of Shen-hsiu and the pure mind of Sthiramati. The twofold division or two conditions of emptiness do not imply separate realities. For the text adds, regarding this emptiness:

> It is not polluted [by afflictions], nor is it not polluted.
> It is not pure, nor is it impure.

> *Why is it not polluted and not impure?* Because it is in fact naturally pure from all duality. In this connection, the āgama says, "for the mind is inherently (naturally) luminous."

The last phrase echoes the next line of the stanzas:

> Because the mind is luminous.

> Here the word "mind" indicates the ultimate nature of the mind, because [the relative] mind is itself characterized by impurity.
>
> *Why is it neither unpolluted nor pure?* . . . if he said that it is perturbed, he would fall into a double contradiction, therefore, he says, "[emptiness] *is stained with adventitious affliction.*"

This is, again, the same statement as in the *kārikā:* "And because the afflictions are adventitious." To which the commentary adds: "But it is not said that it is inherently so."

Sthiramati explains that this twofold division can be further applied to the path in its mundane *(laukika)* and supramundane *(lokottara)* aspects to form a fourfold division. This second group of distinctions can be justified in a manner similar to the reasoning behind the first set, except that here it is more a question of the relative degree of purity or impurity in each stage.

At any rate, it is certain that Sthiramati is trying to define a middle way between the extremes of being and nonbeing as every serious Buddhist philosopher has done in the history of the tradition. Furthermore, with his example we see that those Indian Buddhists who believed in the inherent purity of the mind, and in its mirrorlike knowledge—that is the Yogācāra tradition—held firmly to a gradualist position. This means that the comparison between the Chinese sudden enlightenment school and Indian thought (including the putative "crypto-Buddhism" of Śaṅkara) has to be drawn with extreme caution, with so many qualifications that the "parallelism" appears less significant than it seemed on first analysis.[235]

But Sthiramati's discussion also shows that opposite interpretations of a common doctrine or symbol do not necessarily represent the two extremes in the spectrum of logical possibilities. Different varieties and degrees of opposition obtain between metaphysical and religious doctrines. Or, to express it in Buddhist terms, strong disagreement between two parties does not entail their assumption of "extreme views" and rejection of the middle way, although in the heat of debate they may accuse each other of doing just that. There is more than one approach to the middle way—more than one center, if you will. Positions may be more or less sudden or gradual, or even both at the same time.

6. Conclusions

We have examined three dimensions of the sudden-gradual controversy: (1) some of the doctrines that are usually taken to represent this duality; (2) the appropriateness of the two terms "sudden" and "gradual"; and (3) some of the analogies used by the tradition to describe different positions associated with the sudden-gradual controversies. Disparate as these three aspects may seem, their analysis points in one direction: that the sudden-gradual opposition only reflects a very general, sometimes vague, intuition of a tension or polarity between two approaches to knowledge and action. However universal the dichotomy may be, in its concrete manifestations it shows a great variety, and the vagueness of our intuition can lead to error.

One can extend the sudden-gradual polarity to include other religious phenomena besides those explicitly treated in the Chinese or Tibetan debates. For instance, it is legitimate, given the vagueness that seems inherent in the terminology, to subsume under this dichotomy religious conceptions expressing the mystery of the irruption of conversion or redemption, such as the Hindu and Christian doctrines of grace, or the Buddhist conception of *bodhicitta* as innate or uncaused seed of enlightenment. But the complexity of these doctrines and the issues that can be derived from them do not easily fit into the two simple categories of "sudden" and "gradual." The dimension of action, for instance, is treated in a variety of ways, which do not always correspond with variations in epistemology. Even figures of speech and symbols will not submit easily to this dual categorization. Even in one cultural or doctrinal context, and especially among participants in a religious controversy, the use of similar terminology may express quite different perspectives, which overlap only at very fragile points in the system. If it is not uncommon for participants in a debate to speak at cross-purposes, what could we say of religious traditions that have met only very indirectly, if at all?

A great variety of elements form the clusters or complexes that we seek to define with a simple duality. Although there does not seem to be any particular way in which these elements have to be ordered, understood, or expressed, one can easily accept the generally held view that the opposition between discursive and nondiscursive knowledge (*vikalpa/nirvikalpa,* etc.) is indicative of one important dimension in this typology. This dichotomy, however, does not seem to correspond in a necessary way to the dichotomy between activity and passivity. One would like to suggest that the various polarities associated with the sudden-gradual controversies respond somehow to one single duality, but that is not the case. Clusters of dualities, however, do overlap. There is, for instance, a certain correspondence between ineffability and nonduality in opposition to sacred word and sacred order. Yet we have seen how in Gregory of Nyssa and Rāmānuja the ineffable is not univocally nondual, and the Tantra and kōan Zen would seem to present further counterexamples. The innate seems to correspond to inner experience, in opposition to outer commitments and the life project of exertion in a spiritual path, yet we see how these categories criss-cross in the Zen tradition, and how the tathāgatagarbha tradition suggests the exact opposite.

Why so many exceptions? Are the polarities useless generalizations? I would like to suggest that, indeed, the most successful systems are the exceptions, and that religious systems often are dynamic attempts to solve all of these admittedly real and universal oppositions. The dichotomies are inherent to human thought, not constructed by philosophers or mystics, although religious effort and ideology often can be described as a resolution, or rather a balancing, of the tension between the two poles.

The distribution of religious sects along the spectrum of these dualities is unpredictable and often represents subtle differences of emphasis. However, two constants, apophatism and the middle way, seem to separate the form these tensions take in Buddhism from the form they take in other systems of thought. These constants also give some continuity to basic Buddhist attitudes, even within the diversity of positions found in the controversies considered in this paper.

One could suggest the following Buddhist commentary on the question of the duality of sudden and gradual. In the end, the variety of positions assumed with respect to this issue, and the many, often contradictory ways in which an image or metaphor can be used, suggest not only a very close connection between symbol and context, but a definite malleability of the symbol—its inherent emptiness. In this connection, one might leap to another level of discourse and consider how the images discussed above illustrate the concepts of sudden and gradual. As words they are simultaneously true and false—for all words are lies insofar as they reify the object, and true, insofar as they are empty. This is the sudden operation of words. But words also operate gradually as tools of discrimination. In the latter function one can further subdivide the sphere of language into another level of gradual and sudden distinctions. The basic building blocks of language are by themselves nonsense, yet they are grouped together in a certain order to produce signification, and when they do convey meaning the meaningless elements instantaneously become meaningful. Still at another level, words must interact with a context. The symbol reacts and conforms to its context as much as the latter responds to the former. These two simultaneous and mutual transformations I would call still another sudden dimension of language, when the symbol and the context are grasped at the same time. It is a gradual transformation when one of the two, words or context, is analyzed in terms of the other. In the first case a situation is instantaneously grasped or given form in a representation. In the second case, a given form provides the script or project for the development of a situation. These processes are inherent to language and action; they are not confined to one or another doctrinal or aesthetic conception, though different traditions may choose to emphasize one or the other.

From the point of view of Buddhist doctrine, the sudden-gradual polarity can also be understood as an expression of the Buddhist concern with the nature of change and causality. As in the case of Buddhist theories of becoming, the sudden-gradual controversy did not always lead to a satisfactory definition of the middle way. To affirm either of the two extremes is ultimately to fall into one of the two "extreme views" of "eternalism" or "nihilism."

This connection comes through transparently in the metaphor of purifying gold. Here is a figure of speech that could easily be applied to the ontological question of change, and it has, in fact, been so used (T'an-k'uang, Fa-tsang). To say that gold is not present in the ore is obviously a mistake; but to claim that they are the same thing is not only a theoretical mistake, it is a misapprehension that could have absurd consequences in the practical sphere. The translation of this ontological image to the problem of sudden versus gradual enlightenment must have occurred to some of those involved in the debates of Tibet, and is perhaps partly behind Kamalaśīla's effort to modify the Prāsaṅgika position.

An example from the history of causation theory may clarify this point. The central problem in classical ontology, Greek as well as Indian, is how to explain the fact that there is being rather than nothing, given the ever-changing state of all things. As a related question, philosophers have tried to understand the process of becoming: is it that the seed ceases to be and the sprout appears out of nothing, or is it that the sprout and the seed are mere accidents on the surface of the same, unchanging substance? Are the green apple and the ripe apple two different entities, or are they the same thing? The Buddha, according to tradition, rejected both extremes. The ripe apple is not the green apple, nor is it different from it, and so on. However, the moment one tries to explain what the Buddha meant with some kind of ontological theory, it seems one is destined to repeat one of the two extremes. Thus the Sarvāstivādin concept of dharmas and the point-instant of the Sautrāntikas —representing attempts to explain the middle way which form the two favorite ontologies of Buddhism—are only substitutions of one form of eternalism (continuous being) with another (discontinuous being). In either case the mind escapes the problem by freezing the process of change, even if it is for one indivisible instant of imaginary time.

I am, of course, expressing the views of one brand of Buddhists, with whom I must agree on this point. The Prāsaṅgika-Mādhyamika, as they are known, also insist that from the perspective of the middle way the only thing that can be affirmed is that change occurs with certain regularity and consistency *(pratītyasamutpāda)*. But they do not always follow through with the practical implications of this position.

If one assumes that the ultimate implication of this theory is the comfortable assumption that any analysis of change and causation is useless, and that to speak of the process of attainment and the consequences of attaining enlightenment is a waste of time, one is simply falling into the extreme of nihilism or discontinuity. Some advocates of sudden enlightenment tend to slip into this type of rhetoric. There is no doubt that they are, in more than one sense, heirs of the Prāsaṅgika, but like their predecessors, at times they seem to overlook a simple fact: the assertions "enlightenment is beyond causation" or "enlightenment is beyond good and evil" are statements taking place *in the conventional realm.*[236] As such they place the speaker squarely in that realm, requiring of him that he follow the rules that govern all exchanges and interactions in it.

Parting with the many-sided polemical dimension of the traditions discussed above, I would venture to say that it would be more consistent to accept both sudden and gradual, each within its range of proper application. The actual apple interacts with the concepts of green and ripe with the same flexibility and the same ontological weight that metaphors have. In both cases, the words as well as the objects manifest sudden (green is not ripe, or green ceases to be at the same time that ripe comes into existence) and gradual aspects (green becomes ripe). The process of signification and conception can be seen as an empty phenomenon—that is, a polarity in which two extremes interact in mutual dependence—without there being a third reality to which they refer. Yet emptiness does not displace the duality. The duality too is an empty metaphor; therein lies its suddenness. But the metaphor effectively brings about a transformation in both its terms, the symbol and the symbolized; this is the gradual dimension of knowledge and action. The duality remains. If it remains without conflict, it manifests the middle way.

It has been suggested that sudden represents the absolute point of view, and gradual the relative. The idea is not new; it appeared in the apocryphal *Śūraṅgama Sūtra* and was the source of much controversy and distress among the proponents of sudden enlightenment.[237] My proposal, however, is not quite the same. It is partly inspired by the statement in the *Platform Sūtra* (secs. 16, 39) to the effect that ultimately there are no gradual or sudden paths in the dharma. The absolute is that point of view from which it is possible to transcend not just the gradual (time, multiplicity, goals, and processes) but also the sudden (eternity, innate Buddhahood, oneness). But one wonders if it is not equally true, at least as an outsider's interpretation of the doctrinal statements, that in the absolute the duality remains, and words *are* different from silence, realities *always* are particulars, minutes and hours *always* occur in sequence, so that there is both sudden and gradual in the dharma. But this is a ritual song for another festival.

Notes

1. "Le miroir spirituel," *Sinologica* 1, no. 2 (1947): 112–137; reprinted in Paul Demiéville, *Choix d'études bouddhiques (1929–1970)* (Leiden: E. J. Brill, 1973), 135–156. The passage is Demiéville's conclusion—p. 137 in *Sinologica,* p. 156 in *Choix.* An English translation of Demiéville's article is included in this volume.

2. I would like to express my gratitude to Peter N. Gregory and Griffith T. Foulk for innumerable corrections and suggestions, but very specially to Peter Gregory for the invitation to participate in the conference and the subsequent advice and encouragement that made this essay possible.

3. In addition to the evidence collected below (sec. 5), as a test of Demiéville's hypothesis one should compare S. Yanagida, *Zen-shisō* (Tokyo: Chūōkōronsha, 1975), 90–95, with Alex Wayman, "Mirror-like Knowledge," *Asiatische Studien/Études asiatiques* 25 (1971): 353–363.

4. On parallels outside Buddhism, see, of course, Demiéville's "Miroir." Also of interest are his remarks in a syllabus for a course offered at the Collège

de France two years after the publication of his article on the mirror: "Le vocabulaire philosophique chinois, 3: 'subit' et 'graduel,' " *Annuaire du Collège de France* (Paris, 1949), 177–182; reprinted in Demiéville, *Choix d'études sinologiques* (Leiden: E. J. Brill, 1973), 94–99. See also his "La pénétration du bouddhisme dans la tradition philosophique chinoise," *Cahiers d'histoire mondiale* 3, no. 1 (1956): 31ff.; *Choix d'études bouddhiques,* 241ff.

5. See John R. McRae, "The Northern School of Chinese Ch'an Buddhism" (Ph.D. diss., Yale University, 1983), 387–392, where an attempt is made to establish "the original meaning" of the verses (the revised thesis, published as *The Northern School and the Formation of Early Ch'an Buddhism,* Studies in East Asian Buddhism, no. 3 [Honolulu: University of Hawaii Press, 1986] was in press at the time this essay was written). See also McRae's discussion of the mirror metaphor, 271–277.

6. It is important to keep in mind that differences in context do not necessarily mean that the phenomena are unrelated, either historically or from the point of view of the typology of religious phenomena. Cultural gaps, however, make the parallelism more problematic.

7. This is the date of the "great conference" at the Ta-yün ssu in Hua-t'ai, where Shen-hui attacked the teachings of P'u-chi. See Hu Shih, "Hsin-chiao-ting-te Tun-huang hsieh-pen Shen-hui Ho-shang i-chu liang-chung," *Chung-kuo Chung-yang yen-chiu-yüan li-shih yü-yen yen-chiu-so chi-k'an* 28, no. 2 (1958): 827–882; reprinted in Seizan Yanagida, ed., *Koteki zengaku an* (Kyoto: Chūbun shuppansha, 1975), 253–332. See also Philip B. Yampolsky, *The Platform Sutra of the Sixth Patriarch: The Text of the Tun-huang Manuscript* (New York and London: Columbia University Press, 1967), 25–45. Shen-hui and his doctrines are discussed in more detail in the chapter by McRae in the present volume.

Shen-hui's "Northern" Ch'an, it goes without saying, is a caricature of the school. See McRae, "The Northern School," 78, 387–411; also the chapters by McRae and Peter Gregory in this volume.

Shen-hui's polemics, of course, are not the only example of doctrinal controversy in the Ch'an of this age. On sectarian differences in T'ang dynasty Ch'an Buddhism, see Seizan Yanagida, ed. and trans., *Shoki no zenshi 1: Ryōgashijiki—Denbōhōki,* Zen no goroku, no. 2 (Tokyo: Chikuma shobō, 1971), and *Shoki no zenshi 2: Rekidaihōbōki,* Zen no goroku, no. 3 (Tokyo: Chikuma shobō, 1976); also Yanagida's *Shoki zenshū shisho no kenkyū* (Kyoto: Hōzōkan, 1967). See also Yampolsky, *Platform Sutra,* 1–58; McRae, "Northern School," passim; and Bernard Faure, "La volonté d'orthodoxie. Généalogie et doctrine du bouddhisme Ch'an de l'école du Nord" (Ph.D. diss., École Pratique des Hautes Études, 1984), passim.

8. Paul Demiéville, *Le concile de Lhasa: une controverse sur le quiétisme entre bouddhistes de l'Inde et de la Chine au VIIIe siècle de l'ère chrétienne,* Bibliothèque de l'Institut des Hautes Études Chinoises, 7 (Paris: Imprimerie Nationale de France, 1952), esp. 176–178; later, Giuseppe Tucci, *Minor Buddhist Texts. Part 2: First Bhāvanākrama of Kamalaśīla,* Serie Orientale Roma 9.2 (Rome: Istituto Italiano per il Medio ed Estremo Oriente, 1958), 30ff.

The dates 792–794 are those proposed by Demiéville (*Concile,* 169–178) and adopted by Tucci (loc. cit.). The date is based on the documents collected by one Wang-hsi of Tun-huang, who gives an account of the "Council" and the visit of his teacher Mo-ho-yen to Tibet. The main reference point for his account is the year of the fall of Tun-huang, which Demiéville considers to be 787. Most Chinese and Japanese historians, however, favor ca. 780–782 for both the fall of Tun-huang and the Council. The leading Japanese exponents of this theory are Akira Fujieda in "Shashū kigigun setsudoshi shimatsu," *Tōhōgakuhō* 13, no. 3, and Hisashi Satō in *Kodai Chibetto kenkyū* 2 (Kyoto, 1959). Ying-hui Su, in *Tun-huang lun-chi* (Taipei: Student Book Co., 1967), 218, 215–230, 263ff. in Chinese, 76–78 in English, favors 781 for the fall of Shachow and 785 for the fall of Tun-huang. This dating is based on Chinese documents such as the *Hsi-yü shui-tao chi* and its source, the *Yüan-ho Chün-hsien t'u-chih,* which would set the fall of Tun-huang in 781, or, at the latest, 782. These documents are discussed, and the validity of their testimony questioned, by Demiéville (*Concile,* 177–178 n. 1, and in pp. 359–360 of the addenda). The sources preferred by Demiéville, and discussed in his historical analysis, are listed in *Concile,* vi–vii.

The most important Japanese contributions after Fujieda are Daishun Ueyama, "Donkō to Tonkō no bukkyōgaku," *Tōhōgakuhō* 35 (1964): 141–214, and Zuihō Yamaguchi, review of Ueyama's piece in *Tōyōgakuhō* 47, no. 4 (1965): 333–340, the latter disagreeing with Ueyama's chronology. Both Japanese papers were reviewed by Demiéville in "Récents travaux sur Touen-houang: aperçu bibliographique et notes critiques," *T'oung Pao* 56, nos. 1–3 (1970): 29–43 and 43–44. The best summary of the discussion, however, is in a more recent article by Yamaguchi and a piece by Kikuchi in *Kōza Tonkō 2—Tonkō no rekishi* (Tokyo: Daitō shuppansha, 1980): H. Kikuchi, "Zui-tō ōchō shihai-ki no Kasai to Tonkō," 99–194, esp. 179ff.; Z. Yamaguchi, "Toban shihai jidai," 195–233.

In "Récents travaux" Demiéville challenges Ueyama's dating and discusses his own dating and account of the Council on pp. 37–42, concluding that there was not one, but several encounters: "qu'il n'y a pas eu au Tibet une ni même deux controverses sino-indiennes sur le bouddhisme, mais une série de discussions qui se sont prolongées pendant plusieurs années, en des lieux divers et sans doute par écrit comme ce fut le cas de l'intervention de T'an-k'ouang, car on ne voit pas en quelle langue Indiens et Chinois auraient pu s'entendre oralement (Ueyama, p. 169); il est hors de question que ç'ait pu être en tibétain. Il n'y a pas eu un 'concile de Lhasa,' ni un 'concile de Bsam-yas,' mais une suite de discussions formant ce qu'on peut appeler *le 'concile du Tibet'* " (p. 42). Although Demiéville expressed grave doubts regarding the value of the historical documents, he did not seem to question the value of the effort to set a date for "the debate" recorded, he believed, in Wang-hsi's Chinese "dossier."

A third setting for the controversy could be discovered in Sung China, distinguishing two doctrinal contexts: the polemics of the Neo-Confucians against the Buddhists and, slightly, but not significantly earlier, the debate regarding "silent illumination" and "word-contemplation" Zen. On possible connections between the Neo-Confucian polemic and early Ch'an conflicts, see Demiéville, "Le vocabulaire" and "La pénétration," 31ff. See also Seizan Yanagida, *Shoki no zenshi 2: Rekidaihōbōki,* 3–35; these pages were revised and published as "Mujū to Shūmitsu: Tongo shisō no keisei o megutte," in *Hanazono Daigaku kenkyū kiyō* 7 (1976): 1–36, and translated with minor additions by Carl Bielefeldt as "The *Li-tai fa-pao chi* and the Ch'an Doctrine of Sudden Awakening," in Whalen Lai and Lewis R. Lancaster, eds., *Early Ch'an in China and Tibet,* Berkeley Buddhist Studies Series, no. 5 (Berkeley, 1983), 13–49.

9. In my paper on "The Direct and the Gradual Approaches of Zen Master Mahayana: Fragments of the Teachings of Mo-ho-yen," in Robert M. Gimello and Peter N. Gregory, eds., *Studies in Ch'an and Hua-yen,* Studies in East Asian Buddhism, no. 1 (Honolulu: University of Hawaii Press, 1983), 69–168, I have raised some doubts regarding the significance of the "spiritual lineage" of the main exponent of sudden enlightenment at "The Council of Lhasa" (155 n. 58, 157 n. 7). These issues are taken up again, albeit briefly, in section 3 of this essay. I expect to present further arguments for this position in my forthcoming volume on Kamalaśīla and the polemics of eighth-century Tibet.

10. Demiéville, *Concile,* 20–22, and "Récents travaux," 41–42; also L. O. Gómez, "Indian Materials on the Doctrine of Sudden Enlightenment," in Lai and Lancaster, eds., *Early Ch'an,* 393–434. Recently Gary W. Houston, in an article he has graciously dedicated to me, argues for Chinese as the common language of the Council, which, he claims, made a significant exchange possible ("The System of Ha Shang Mahayana According to Pelliot No. 117," *The Tibet Journal* 9, no. 1 [1984]: 31–39). Thus he disagrees with my contention (in "Indian Materials") that Kamalaśīla's response to Ch'an was affected by his ignorance of the Chinese background and was heavily colored by his experiences in India. Houston unfortunately does not tell us how he intends to account for the documentary and historiographic evidence analyzed in the discussions between Ueyama and Demiéville (see references in note 8 above).

As with any other set of documents, different degrees of skepticism are possible with regard to the sources on the "Council." Even the most skeptical scholars, however, do not deny the development of a religious polemic concerning sudden and gradual enlightenment; only the historical accuracy of accounts of a meeting under the supervision of the Tibetan king is called into question. See Y. Imaeda, "Documents tibétains de Touen-huoang concernant le Concile de Tibet," *Journal Asiatique* 263 (1975): 125–146; and Herbert V. Guenther, " 'Meditation' Trends in Early Tibet," in Lai and Lancaster, eds., *Early Ch'an,* 351–366.

Although, as noted by Guenther (p. 361), some histories of the twelfth century do not mention the "Council," the earliest Tibetan account of the Council dates from precisely that period: Nyang-ral Nyi-ma-'od-zer (1124–1192), *Chos 'byung me tog snying po sbrang rtsi'i bcud* (Paro: Ugyen Tempai Gyaltsen, 1979), fol. 455–486; and *Byang chub sems dpa' sems dpa' chen po Chos rgyal mes dbon rnam gsum gyi rnam thar rin po che'i phreng ba* (Paro: Ugyen Tempai Gyaltsen, 1980), fol. 230–265. These may be the source of some of the material in Bu-ston's chronicle.

11. See André Bareau, *Les sectes du Petit Véhicule* (Saigon: École française d'Extrême-Orient, 1955), 62, 77, 78, 260, 291.

12. Vasubandhu records a scholastic debate regarding a Buddha's comprehension *(abhisamaya)* of the noble truths: the Sarvāstivādins claim that it is gradual or "by steps" *(krameṇa);* others, presumably Mahāsāṅghikas or Dharmaguptakas, affirm that it is single *(ekābhisamaya)* and undivided *(abhedena)* —*Abhidharmakośa* 6:27, *Abhidharmakośabhāṣyam of Vasubandhu,* ed. P. Pradhan

(Patna: K. P. Jayaswal Research Institute, 1975), 351ff.; see notes in Louis de la Vallée Poussin, *L'Abhidharmakośa de Vasubandhu*, tome IV, *Mélanges chinois et bouddhiques*, vol. 16 (Bruxelles: Institut Belge des Hautes Études Chinoises, 1971), 185ff. See also Bareau, *Sectes*, 62.

Recently, Brian Galloway has examined evidence for "sudden enlightenment" doctrines in the *Mahāvastu*—Galloway, "Sudden Enlightenment in Indian Buddhism," *Wiener Zeitschrift für die Kunde Südasiens und Archiv für indische Philosophie* 25 (1981): 205-211. His paper offers additional data on Indian notions of sudden and gradual; but I do not believe the evidence justifies proposing an Indian origin for the Chinese doctrine, as suggested by Galloway.

Another Indian parallel, with certain echoes in the early Chinese debates (e.g., Tao-sheng) is the question of irreversibility and instantaneous entrance into the seventh *bhūmi;* see references in R. A. Stein, "Illumination subite ou saisie simultanée: Note sur la terminologie chinoise et tibétaine," *Revue de l'histoire des religions* 179, no. 1 (1971), p. 4, n. 1. The concept of instantaneity itself presented philosophical problems to Indian Buddhists (ibid., 20-21 n. 5). An English translation of Stein's essay is included in this volume; see nn. 3 and 47, respectively, in the translation.

13. On the *Prajñāpāramitā* as a critique of gradualism, see Gómez, "Indian Materials."

14. Nathan Katz, in "An Appraisal of the Svātantrika-Prāsaṅgika Debates," *Philosophy East and West* 26, no. 3 (1976): 253-267, proposes a correspondence between the prāsaṅgika-svātantrika distinction and the sudden-gradual polarity. Alex Wayman sees a connection between the Tibetan controversies and Indian attacks on Mahāsāṅghika doctrine in his review of Tucci's *Minor Buddhist Texts* in the *Journal of the American Oriental Society* 78, no. 3 (1958): 215, and in an article titled "Doctrinal Disputes and the Debate of Bsam yas," *Central Asiatic Journal* 21, no. 2 (1977): 139-144. Again, I would caution against deriving historical connections from conceptual correlations. Not only is it a questionable, or "soft," methodology, it is also of doubtful value in light of the evidence presented later in this paper.

15. As in, e.g., *Mahāyānasūtrālaṅkāra*, chap. 9, Bodhyadhikāra.

16. *Ch'an-yüan chu-ch'üan-chi tu-hsü*, ed. Shigeo Kamata, in *Zengen shosenshū tojo*, Zen no goroku, no. 9 (Tokyo: Chikuma shobō, 1971), 29-30, 184-185. See also his "Chart," *Chung-hua ch'uan-hsin-ti Ch'an-men shih-tzu ch'eng-hsi t'u* (*ZZ* 2/15/5. 433b-438b; also in Kamata, *Zengen*, 340-341). Complete translation of the "Preface" in Jeffrey L. Broughton, "Kuei-feng Tsung-mi: The Convergence of Ch'an and the Teachings" (Ph.D. diss., Columbia University, 1975)—the most important of the above passages is translated by Broughton on 240-243.

17. On some of the parallels between Ch'an and Tantric schools (the *siddhas*, the Mahāmudrā, etc.), see note 4, pp. 5-6, in Stein, "Illumination"; note 9 in the English translation. See also Helmut Hoffmann, "Zen und später indischer Buddhismus," *Asien: Tradition und Fortschritt, Festschrift H. Hammitzsch*, ed. L. Brüll and U. Kemper (Wiesbaden: Otto Harrassowitz, 1971), 207-216. It is highly unlikely, of course, that we have here a case of influence or derivation (see Stein, "Illumination," 5-6).

18. Closely associated with the gradual path is the philosophical assumption

that the obstacles to awakening (here mostly the *kleśas*) are real entities, and not mere illusions. There is also a sense that virtues are real entities or self-existing objects or states of being that can be produced and acquired. In such systems, it is not merely as metaphor that one speaks of increasing and accumulating virtue *(sambhāra),* and of reducing gradually the strength of the *kleśas* through mental cultivation *(bhāvanā).* For, even if the system denies, strictly speaking, any reality to all entities, it does not consider the states of mind associated with virtue as more real than the states of mind that are afflicted or tainted by the *kleśas.* This does not necessarily preclude, of course, the belief in the possibility of direct mystical perception or non-mediate realization of awakening—a concept so central and characteristic to the Buddhist tradition.

As mentioned before, in the Indian tradition the metaphysical stance of a religious system does not allow us to predict its position with respect to a gradual or a sudden path. This is not to be taken as a disagreement with Potter's typology of "leap" vs. "path" philosophies; see Karl H. Potter, *Presuppositions of India's Philosophies* (Englewood Cliffs, N.J.: Prentice-Hall, 1963), passim, but esp. 1–24, 36–46, 236–256. I would argue, however, that soteriological typologies are not defined by or necessarily related to dialectic methods and ontological theory.

19. The apocryphal *Śūraṅgama Sūtra* (*T* 19.155a8–9) states: "From the perspective of the absolute *(li tse)* awakening occurs all at once *(tun).* With this awakening all is extinguished at once *(ping hsiao).* [But] in fact and in practice *(shih)* extinction is not sudden, and one accomplishes [the way] gradually *(tz'u-ti).*" But this and other passages from the sūtra have been the source of much embarrassment to the proponents of sudden enlightenment, who consider the sūtra authoritative; see Demiéville, *Concile,* 51–52n.

20. The connection between these general categories and the topics of debate as itemized by the various contending parties is not always transparent. The present essay is only a preliminary attempt at clarifying the relationship between universal dichotomies and the specific language of the debates. I present in tabular form the issues considered in the Tibetan debates in my forthcoming study of Kamalaśīla and the "Council." D. Ueyama has considered some of these problems in his "Chibetto shūron ni okeru Zen to Kamarashīra no sōten," *Nippon bukkyōgakkai nenpō* 40 (1975): 55–70 (special number, subtitled *Bukkyō ni okeru shinpi-shisō*), and in his study of T'an-k'uang, "Donkō to Tonkō," 176–188. I am inclined to agree with Ueyama and Demiéville that our sources (Kamalaśīla's works, Pelliot 116, 812, 4646, etc., the Tibetan chronicles, T'an-k'uang, etc.) share some common themes; but I do not see the issues forming a roster of the kind that would have been generated and debated in a single encounter.

21. S. Yanagida, ed. and tr., *Daruma no goroku: Ninyūshigyōron,* Zen no goroku, no. 1 (Tokyo: Chikuma shobō, 1969); studied by John Jorgensen, "The Earliest Text of Ch'an Buddhism: The Long Scroll" (M.A. thesis, Australian National University, 1979). The appellation "earliest text of Ch'an" and the attribution of this text to Bodhidharma are, of course, highly questionable; see Yanagida, *Daruma,* 2–8.

22. Yanagida, *Daruma,* 18.

23. Ibid.
24. Ibid.
25. McRae, "Northern School," 387ff., is of the opinion that the so-called Southern school is influenced by the Northern school. I think one must distinguish "influence" from the shifting of positions in the heat of debate, or the posturing against hypothetical or imagined rival opinions. Furthermore, as McRae himself has shown, the doctrines of the "Northern" school were themselves heterogeneous and fluid. In the present essay "Northern Ch'an" and "Southern Ch'an" are terms used only to designate the positions considered as the extremes in the debate. They were probably for the most part logical possibilities or straw men, not the formulations of closed dogmas or doctrinal systems.
26. Yampolsky, *Platform Sutra,* par. 4. Henceforth all references to the *Platform Sūtra* will be to page or paragraph (section) number in Yampolsky's edition and translation, unless otherwise noted. For the vulgata, references may be to *T* #2008, vol. 48, or to paragraphs in K. Itō, *Rokuso Daishi Hōbō-dankyō* (Kyoto: Kichūdō, 1967).
27. Yampolsky, *Platform Sutra,* par. 5–6.
28. Ibid., par. 6.
29. Although the metaphor of the mirror does not occupy in India the central position it occupies in China, it is not unknown—see, e.g., *Aṅguttara-Nikāya* 1:209; also see Wayman, "Mirror-like Knowledge." The Indian tradition prefers the metaphor of undisturbed clear water, or those of washing and smelting gold or silver. Well known examples of each will be found, respectively, in *Dīgha-Nikāya* 2:74–75 (cp. *Aṅguttara* 1:25–26), *Aṅguttara-Nikāya* 1:208–209 (cp. *Majjhima-Nikāya* 1:76), and *Aṅguttara* 1:210–211 and 253–255. The last of these three metaphors is taken up by the Ch'an tradition—as in Shen-hui's sayings, discussed below in this paper. More on the Indian metaphors in section 5 of this paper.
30. Yampolsky, *Platform Sutra,* par. 8.
31. Ibid. The third line in the first of the two poems attributed to Hui-neng is found in that form only in the Tun-huang Chinese version and in the Hsia-hsia translation. Other, later versions have the reading of the modern Japanese vulgata: "From the beginning there is not one thing" *(pen-lai wu i wu)*—see, e.g., Itō, *Rokuso Daishi Hōbō-dankyō,* 34, notes on 36. This variant became a famous Zen phrase, traditionally taken to represent the essence of the teaching of the sixth patriarch. It occurs elsewhere in the *yü-lu* literature—e.g., in the *Wan Ling Record;* see Yoshitaka Iriya, ed., *Denshinhōyō—Enryōroku,* Zen no goroku, no. 8 (Tokyo: Chikuma shobō, 1969), 114–117. The phrase is sometimes used as a kōan in modern Rinzai Zen.
32. All references are to paragraph numbers in Yampolsky's *Platform Sutra.*

Although the Tun-huang version and the *textus receptus* of the *Platform Sūtra* prefix the expression *nan-tsung tun-chiao* (Southern school sudden teaching) to the title of the sūtra, the *Platform* is used here as the basis for a general theoretical model of sudden enlightenment doctrines, not as the authoritative source for the doctrines of Shen-hui and his "Southern" school. Yanagida (*Shoki zenshū shisho no kenkyū,* 195–209) has argued convincingly that the "original version" of the *Platform Sūtra* was the work of a certain Fa-hai, a monk of the Ox-head school of Ch'an. Of course, this does not erase the sūtra's subsequent history as a "Southern" text. Furthermore, the Ox-head school, like Shen-hui, opposed Northern "gradualism."

Northern "influence" is also detectable in the sūtra. See John McRae, "Northern School," 391, and McRae, "The Ox-head School of Chinese Ch'an Buddhism: From Early Ch'an to the Golden Age," in Gimello and Gregory, eds., *Studies in Ch'an and Hua-yen,* 169–252. Modern scholarship from Yanagida to McRae gives us insight into the vagaries of sectarian disputes. The evidence mustered in these studies should warn us against keeping the traditional image of the schools as monolithic systems. Insofar as modern Ch'an studies undermine traditional conceptions of unbroken lines and unchanging systems, they also contradict a basic assumption of our own scholarship: that one of our tasks is to correct ancient lineages and place texts and teachers in a position consistent with their system of thought.

We must rethink our fundamental assumptions regarding systems, derivations, lineages, and influence. If, for instance, the *Platform Sūtra* was composed with Northern doctrines and images in mind, we should first assume that we have in it a living Ox-head or Southern text, not a Northern school document or a text that has been tampered with. For is it not normal in any dispute for both parties to borrow—in agreement as well as disagreement—from their rival's rhetorical or ideological arsenal? For the historian to know of the borrowing is important, and, to put it mildly, exciting, but more important than this knowledge is the understanding of the implications of such "borrowings."

The concepts of "influence," "school," and "lineage," if they are to have heuristic value, must be qualified with the following considerations: Lines between schools are seldom as sharply drawn as rival schools like to believe. Often a common ground of ideology and imagery is not only natural, but necessary. Schools have little reality apart from the individual teachers who create and maintain a myth of continuity within dynamic polemic and political contexts. Although certain fundamental texts, or "the words of the founder," are sometimes available as paradigms, these texts, or the founder's thinking, are also fluid. One should not assume that when a textual testimony appears to accept certain logical and practical constraints on its position, this proves "influence" from another school on the textual source itself.

33. See Demiéville, "Miroir," 115–117; *Choix,* 134–136. This point is taken up again in more detail in secs. 3 and 4 of the present paper.

34. *T* 12.407b9–10, 12.522c24 ff. Compare also the other classical scriptural favorite on innate Buddhahood, likewise associated with the Ch'an-Zen tradition: *Buddha-avataṃsaka, T* 10.272c5–29. Shen-hui refers to the *Mahāparinirvāṇa Sūtra's* statement on original Buddhahood when he introduces the metaphor of wood and fire (discussed below), but his exact phrasing has not been located in the sūtra.

35. Yu-lan Fung, *A History of Chinese Philosophy,* trans. Derk Bodde (Princeton: Princeton University Press, 1953), 2:390, 393ff. Noncultivation *(wu-tso)* is already used to define the "Ch'an" tradition in a work attributed to the "fourth patriarch" Tao-hsin; see David W. Chappell, "The Teachings of the Fourth

Ch'an Patriarch Tao-hsin (580–651)," in Lai and Lancaster, eds., *Early Ch'an,* 120.

36. *Shen-hui ho-shang i-chi,* ed. Hu Shih (Shanghai: Oriental Book Co., 1930). It is more convenient, however, to use the photomechanic reprint, which includes Hu's annotations (Taipei: Hu Shih chi-nien kuan, 1966; repr. 1970). All references in this paper are to the latter edition. On the above discussion, see p. 120; see also Yampolsky, *Platform Sutra,* par. 16. See also Demiéville, "Deux documents de Touen-houang sur le Dhyāna chinois," *Essays on the History of Buddhism Presented to Professor Zenryū Tsukamoto* (Kyoto, 1961), 1–14 (*Choix d'études bouddhiques,* 320–333).

37. Hu Shih, *Shen-hui,* 120–121. Here Shen-hui seems to equate *bodhicittotpāda* with bodhi, because as a subitist he cannot accept "partial" insight into reality—awakening is complete or it is not awakening. Elsewhere he claims for himself the tenth *bhūmi* (Hu Shih, 166), something that is impossible except in the most demythologized interpretation of the *bhūmi* theory. The passage may be an interpolation, however, for the *Li-tai fa-pao chi* offers a different version of the incident: Shen-hui responds by quoting the *Mahāparinirvāṇa Sūtra,* "Though his body is the same as that of common people, his mind is identical with that of a Buddha" (*T* 51.185b21–24; Yanagida, *Shoki no zenshi 2: Rekidaihōbōki,* 155; sūtra passage in *T* 12.612a21). Other Chinese traditions are not as iconoclastic; the *Mo-ho chih-kuan,* for instance, distinguishes clearly the initial breakthrough and the maturation of the experience (*T* 46.47c17 ff. and 46.55c26 ff.). Tsung-mi tries to bring Shen-hui into line with traditional Buddhist conceptions by suggesting that when he talks of sudden enlightenment he is not including the gradual cultivation that is to follow.

In the Indian context the *bodhicittotpāda* occurs at many levels, beginning by an act of will that belongs to the realm of the relative; the first *bhūmi* represents only the entrance into the path of vision *(darśana-mārga).* Although one can refer to direct and final apprehension of the absolute as a *bodhicittotpāda,* it seems unlikely that Shen-hui alludes here to the Indian concept of *pāramārthika-bodhicitta;* on which see *Second Bhāvanākrama,* fol. 44a (all references are to the folios in the Sde-dge edition of the Bstan-'gyur).

At the same time, one must note Shen-hui's treatment of the traditional theme of the life of the Buddha in his explanation of the *Vimalakīrti*'s definition of *apratiṣṭhita-nirvāṇa* (Hu Shih, *Shen-hui,* 163; *T* 14.554b3–c5): Buddhas do not reject the world of delusion because they go through all the stages of a Buddha's career, beginning with the first thought of awakening *(bodhicittotpāda)* and culminating in nirvāṇa.

38. Hu Shih, *Shen-hui,* 130–131.

39. Ibid., 105; see also 99.

The term *fan-nao (kleśa)* is usually translated "defilement." Strictly speaking, *k'uang* means "gangue" or "matrix," the mineral in which a vein of metallic ore is embedded. Technically, "slag" refers only to the mineral remaining after the ore has been smelted. Context seems to require the latter equivalent in English.

40. Ibid.

41. Compare in this regard the gradualism of Mahāmudrā practice, which

provides a conceptual and practical structure for a leap theory of enlightenment, yet shows most of the characteristics of sudden enlightenment doctrines.

42. Hu Shih, *Shen-hui,* 105. I have adopted Hu Shih's emendations to this passage. He transposes the first sentence of the original reply to the end of the question ("that the afflictions . . . no uprooting"). If this emendation is correct, then Shen-hui has not answered the second part of the question. On the other hand, if this phrase should be in the reply, then Shen-hui is simply restating his view from the higher point of view of the absolute, and Gernet's analysis is probably correct: "Si l'on tient les passions pour adventices et si l'on estime fondamentale leur destruction, c'est un moyen *(upāya)* pour mener les êtres à la *bodhi.* Mais du point de vue de la *bodhi,* toutes les dualités disparaissent, passions et *nirvāṇa* sont identiques." Jacques Gernet, *Entretiens du Maître de Dhyāna Chen-houei du Ho-tsö (668-760),* Publications de l'École française d'Extrême-Orient, vol. 31 (Hanoi: École française d'Extrême-Orient, 1949), 19 n. 13.

The last expression in the reply is highly problematic, linguistically and philosophically. It contradicts Shen-hui's own ontology of relative and absolute. The passage in fact has a strong "Northern" ring to it. It shows, however, the same ambiguities and hesitation we see in the tathāgatagarbha doctrine of the *Mahāparinirvāṇa Sūtra;* cp., e.g., *T* 12.422c, 492a, 531a. The *Mahāparinirvāṇa Sūtra,* of course, is full of strong gradualist passages, as in 546c–547b. Ironically, both subitists (Shen-hui, Huai-hai) and gradualists (Kamalaśīla) appeal to this sūtra as their authority, sometimes referring to the same passage with exactly opposite interpretations—e.g., *T* 12.547a7–16, quoted by Shen-hui, p. 138, and Huai-hai, *Tun-wu yao-men* (*Tongoyōmen,* ed. S. Hirano, Zen no goroku, no. 6 [Tokyo: Chikuma shobō, 1970]), 52, and by Kamalaśīla, *Second Bhāvanākrama,* fol. 45a.

43. Hu Shih, *Shen-hui,* 106. The first sūtra reference has not been identified. On the image of the "firesticks," see *Mahāparinirvāṇa Sūtra, T* 12.385c11, 16, 586c16–17. Two different uses of the firestick metaphor are *Avataṃsaka Sūtra, T* 10.107a2–5 (the bodhisattva's unfaltering effort) and *Third Bhāvanākrama* (Giuseppe Tucci, *Minor Buddhist Texts. Part 3: Third Bhāvanākrama,* Serie Orientale Roma, 43 [Rome: Istituto Italiano per il Medio ed Estremo Oriente, 1971]), 20 (citing *Kāśyapaparivarta* 69, on nondual knowledge arising from the duality of discerning wisdom); the same quotation is found in the *Second Bhāvanākrama* (Sde-dge Bstan-'gyur), fol. 49b. See also *Madhyāntavibhāgaṭīkā,* ed. S. Yamaguchi, in *Sthiramati, Madhyāntavibhāgaṭīkā* (Nagoya: Hajinkaku, 1934), 248, where the same sūtra passage is quoted.

44. Hu Shih, *Shen-hui,* 118; cp. 151–152.

Kamalaśīla in the *First Bhāvanākrama* (Tucci, 212–214) and *Third Bhāvanākrama* (pp. 15–17) compares a person who abstains from all mental activity to a blind man. But this is clearly a caricature, not an accurate description of the stated goals and practical paradigms of Ch'an.

45. Hu Shih, *Shen-hui,* 152.

46. Ibid., 233–234, 323–324. See the translation and notes of Walter Liebenthal in "The Sermon of Shen-hui," *Asia Major,* n.s. 3, no. 2 (1952): 132–155, to which the above translation owes much. On the phrase *yung hsin,* cp. Shen-hui's *Yü-lu* (Hu Shih, *Shen-hui,* 111, 118, 151).

47. Hu Shih, *Shen-hui,* 105.

48. See ibid., 175, for the metaphor of the mother nursing her child; the metaphor is discussed below, sec. 2.3.

49. Yampolsky, *Platform Sutra,* par. 7.

50. Ibid., 130 n. 33.

51. It would be hermeneutically legitimate—though perhaps historically questionable—to call these two levels the relative sphere of means and the absolute sphere of the goal. This is done by Jeffrey Broughton in "Kuei-feng Tsung-mi," 1-2. See my references to the *Śūraṅgama Sūtra* above, and at the conclusion of this essay.

52. Hu Shih, *Shen-hui,* 116-117; see also 97-98, 133-134, 136-137 (pp. 133f. are discussed above). The expression "thoroughly and clearly" translates *ching* in this context, but the term must evoke here its usual technical sense as well, since the clarity of the perception of the self is due to the meditator's perception of the mind's innate purity. This is therefore an instance of the teaching of "contemplating purity."

The scriptural source is the *Vimalakīrti-nirdeśa, T* 14.539c19-25. See *Platform Sutra,* par. 14, where we find the same allusion.

Regarding the problem of "sitting in meditation," see Yampolsky, *Platform Sutra,* par. 19. On the question of Ch'an as a critique and rejection of meditation, see the now classical articles by Hu Shih: "Ch'an (Zen) Buddhism in China, Its History and Method," *Philosophy East and West* 3, no. 1 (1953): 3-24; "The Development of Zen Buddhism in China," *The Chinese Social and Political Science Review* 15, no. 4 (1932): 475-505; and "Chung-kuo ch'an-hsüeh ti fa-chan," *Hu Shih chiang-i chi,* 1:87-149. These essays, and other valuable studies of Hu have been reprinted in Yanagida's *Koteki zengaku an.* See also Yampolsky, *Platform Sutra,* par. 19, and pp. 117, 135-136, 140-181; Robert B. Zeuschner, "An Analysis of the Philosophical Criticism of Northern Ch'an Buddhism" (Ph.D. diss., University of Hawaii, 1977), 15ff.; and Gómez, "Direct and Gradual Approaches," 102.

53. The Indian gradualist defines insight precisely as a form of analysis. The proponents of sudden enlightenment consider this a gross error and, furthermore, regard the purported "separation," or even the distinction, between insight and concentration as yet another duality impeding liberation (see *Platform Sutra,* par. 13; Hu Shih, *Shen-hui,* 128-129, 137-138). This criticism is directed at Northern school meditation theory, but may reflect as well a distorted view of T'ien-t'ai meditation theory. Be that as it may, what appears as a single point of disagreement has two, if not three, distinct aspects: rejection by the subitist of mental cultivation in general, especially by the use of several, distinct methodologies (calm and insight), and rejection of the definition of insight as analysis. More on this below in section 3.

54. Cp. *Platform Sutra,* par. 14. For the Northern use of *chih-kuan* theory, see McRae, "Northern School," passim. On *tso-i,* see Gómez, "Indian Materials," passim. Note the disagreement between Mo-ho-yen and the Northern school on some of these points, as well as on the matter of "viewing the mind" *(k'an-hsin).* On the latter practice, which is rejected by Shen-hui, see Hu Shih, *Shen-hui,* 133-134, 151-152, etc.

55. Hu Shih, *Shen-hui,* 133–134; see also 125–126, 175–176, and *Platform Sutra,* pars. 17–18. The vulgata of the *Platform Sūtra* also contains similar expressions, *T* 48.358b21–25 (Itō, *Rokuso Daishi,* 158; cp. 86–88). In the *Vimalakīrtinirdeśa* (*T* 14.539c20), Vimalakīrti's words are taken as a definition of *correct* "sitting." Shen-hui seems to read the passage in the same manner.

Jacques Gernet, *Entretiens,* 58 n. 34, identifies the source of the last definition in the quotation as the *Mahāparinirvāṇa Sūtra* (*T* 12.527c16–17); but the sūtra only provides the words "Not to see bodily forms is called correct concentration." It is part of a long section redefining traditional Buddhist categories, such as right effort and right mindfulness (pp. 527a23 ff.).

On the practices criticized here by Shen-hui, see also the summary attributed to Dharma Master Ch'ung Yüan in Hu Shih, *Shen-hui,* 175, where these practices are said to be the teachings of P'u-chi and Hsiang-ma, both masters of the Northern school.

The term *pu-kuan* is a standard "Southern" school term for correct contemplation, and not for abstention from contemplation. The term is meant as a criticism of the Northern school practice of *k'an-hsin* or *kuan-hsin.* The *Kuan-hsin lun,* for instance, defines wisdom *(hui)* as "the constant practice of internal and external examination *(kuan-ch'a)* of mind and body" (*T* 85.1271a5). The term *kuan-ch'a,* if borrowed from T'ien-t'ai, must stand for mental examination or *vipaśyanā.* Demiéville ("Miroir," 114–115—*Choix,* 133–134, and "Deux documents," 27 n. 103) is of the opinion that the choice of verbs is significant: the Northern school prefers verbs of imperfective aspect, "to look or observe" *(kuan/k'an),* while the Southern school chooses the perfective verb "to see" *(chien).* As I point out below, however, this distinction is not maintained consistently.

The use of the terms *k'an, kuan, kuan-ch'a,* etc., in the *Leng-ch'ieh shih-tzu chi* is problematic, especially in the description of the meditation theory of the "fourth patriarch," Tao-hsin (see Yanagida, *Shoki no zenshi 1,* 205, 210–211, 213–214, 225–226, 233–240, 248–249, 254–256). See Faure, *La volonté,* 629ff.; Chappell, "The Teachings of the Fourth Ch'an Patriarch," passim. Tao-hsin's teaching on contemplation probably played a central role in the development of Northern Ch'an meditation theory.

On the question of body and mind, see the *Yüan ming lun* in McRae, "Northern School," 449.

56. See also Yampolsky, *Platform Sutra,* 136 nn. 60–61, and 137 n. 64. It is quite evident that *san-mei* equals *ting,* which renders Shen-hui's intentions less apparent than they would otherwise be.

57. See the usage of *tung* and *ch'i* in, e.g., the *Ch'an-shih kuan-men,* attributed to Bodhidharma (*T* 2832, vol. 85).

58. Yampolsky, *Platform Sutra,* par. 17, discussed below. More on *wu-nien* in Hu Shih, *Shen-hui,* 101, 115–116 (no-thought and the mirror metaphor), 123 (no-thought is *paramārtha*), 129–130, 131, 133, 134, 136, 145, 150, 193. See Gernet, *Entretiens,* 12–13 n. 5 (translated *absence de pensée*). On *li-nien* in the Northern school, see Robert Zeuschner, "The Concept of *li nien* ("being free from thinking") in the Northern Line of Ch'an Buddhism," in Lai and Lancaster, eds., *Early Ch'an,* 131–148.

59. *Platform Sutra,* par. 14, following the Kōshōji readings. The *Vimalakīrti-nirdeśa* quotation is taken to mean that a mind of samādhi encompasses both the practice and the goal of Buddhism. The term *i-hsing san-mei* is not from the *Vimalakīrti-nirdeśa,* but from the *Saptaśātikā Prajñāpāramitā* (*T* 8.731a24 ff.). Sanskrit text, ed. G. Tucci, *Reale Accademia dei Lincei, Classe di scienze morali, etc., Memorie,* ser. 5a, vol. 17 (Rome, 1923), fol. 34a-36b, where it occurs as *eka-vyūha-samādhi.*

There is no English translation of this section of the Sanskrit version, but the relevant passage is translated from the Chinese by David Chappell in "Pure Land Responses to Ch'an Critics," in *Traditions of Meditation in Chinese Buddhism,* ed. Peter N. Gregory, Studies in East Asian Buddhism, no. 4 (Honolulu: University of Hawaii Press, 1986), 165-166. In the same volume the one-practice samādhi is discussed in T'ien-t'ai contexts by Daniel Stevenson, and in more detail with regard to Ch'an by Bernard Faure, "The Concept of One-Practice Samādhi in Early Ch'an," 99-128.

Samādhis called *ekavyūha, ekākāra,* or *ekākāra-vyūha* also appear in the samādhi lists in the *Pañcaviṁśatisāhasrikā* (p. 202), the *Śatasāhasrikā* (p. 1423) and the *Mahāvyutpatti* (pars. 592 and 594), but the Chinese equivalents do not correspond to the terms used in the *Platform Sūtra.* Yampolsky's instructive note on this point (p. 136 n. 60) is to be corrected in light of the above. In the *Pañcaviṁśati* this samādhi is defined as "seeing duality in no dharma whatsoever"; in the *Saptaśatikā* it is variously explained as the contemplation of nonproduction, as the process of not seeing, or as the visualization of the Tathāgata.

The *Saptaśatikā* is the recognized source for what must be the *Platform Sūtra*'s immediate sources, namely the *Leng-ch'ieh shih-tzu chi* (Yanagida, *Shoki no zenshi 1,* 186, 298; *T* 85.1286c23-1287a7, 1290b2-3; Chappell, "Teachings of the Fourth Patriarch," 107-108), and T'ien-t'ai doctrine (*Mo-ho chih-kuan, T* 46.11a28-12a19). On the pivotal role of the doctrine of *i-hsing san-mei* in the development of Ch'an Buddhism, see S. Yanagida's popular discussion in S. Yanagida and T. Umehara, *Mu no tankyū—Chūgoku-zen,* Bukkyō no shisō, vol. 7 (Tokyo: Kadokawa shoten, 1969), 99ff., and in K. Nishitani, ed., *Kōza Zen 3: Zen no rekishi—Chūgoku* (Tokyo: Chikuma shobō, 1967), 22ff.

The quotation attributed by the *Platform Sūtra* to the *Vimalakīrti* is from two separate passages in the original text: *T* 14.542c15 and 14.538b1; see Yampolsky, *Platform Sutra,* 136 n. 61. See also Yampolsky, 156-159, and E. Lamotte's *L'enseignement de Vimalakīrti,* Bibliothèque du Muséon, vol. 51 (Louvain: Publications Universitaires, 1962), 200 and 119, respectively. The two phrases are quoted out of context, as is often the case in Ch'an literature. The first phrase occurs as one of a long series of epithets for *bodhimaṇḍa.* The second phrase is part of a long passage in which many other states of mind or behavioral ideals of the bodhisattva are called "the pure land (i.e., the 'purified field') of the bodhisattva." In both cases the most probable Sanskrit original underlying *chih-hsin* is some form of *āśaya* (e.g., *adhyāśaya, kalyāṇāśaya*). Cp. Lamotte, *Enseignement,* 114 and 200.

Compare Hui-neng's interpretation of the concept of Pure Land in the *Platform Sutra,* par. 35; see also Tao-hsin's *Ju-tao an-hsin yao fang-pien fa-men,* in the *Leng-ch'ieh shih-tzu chi* (Yanagida, *Shoki no zenshi 1,* 192; Chappell, "Teachings of the Fourth Patriarch," 111). The "demythologization" of Buddhist doctrine is an exegetic and critical tool common to all forms of Ch'an. It is at the heart of the exegetical tracts in the *Kuan-hsin lun* and the *Wu fang-pien men,* both considered Northern Ch'an texts. In the version of the first of these texts preserved in the *Shōshitsurokumon,* for instance, we find an allusion to the *Vimalakīrti* in a definition of the bodhisattva's purification of the field that is almost a verbatim reproduction of the one offered by Hui-neng: "If you purify your own mind, then all the Buddha-fields become pure. Thus the sūtra says: 'If the mind is tainted, all living beings are tainted. If the mind is pure, all living beings are pure.' If you wish to purify your Buddha-field, you must purify the mind. As the mind is purified, the Buddha-land becomes pure. [If you can extinguish the three poisons of the mind,] the three types of ethical practice will be accomplished spontaneously" (*P'o-hsiang lun, T* 45.367c19–22). Cp. the parallel passage in the *Kuan-hsin lun* (*T* 85.1271b12–13). These parallels also foreshadow an issue to be discussed below: the proximity of Northern and Southern doctrines, including the notions of suddenness and immediacy.

60. Yampolsky, *Platform Sutra,* par. 14, p. 137; Itō, *Rokuso Daishi,* 86.

Regarding "purity" see my translation of *chien ching* above. See also Shen-hui in Hu Shih, *Shen-hui,* 125, 133, 151–152, 175–176. I translate "stirring" *(tung)* and "giving rise" *(ch'i)*—but a pun is intended, since the first word suggests (a) mental activity generally, or (b) the practice of meditation while moving in daily activities, whereas the second term could mean (a) the arising of a thought or emotion, or (b) a person arising from meditation to engage in daily activities. See the discussion above of the passage in Hu Shih, *Shen-hui,* 116–117.

61. *Platform Sutra,* par. 17. Cp. Hu Shih, *Shen-hui,* 98, 130, 132, 136–137, 146, 193.

62. *Platform Sutra,* par. 17, following the Kōshōji recension. Yampolsky, p. 138, translates freely "in all environments." But *ching* is Chinese Buddhist jargon for "sense field" (*viṣaya,* etc.). Also, his rendering of *wu-hsiang* as "nonform" is questionable; given the use of *hsiang* as equivalent of *saṃjñā* or *nimitta* in other contexts, it seems more appropriate to assume that the text refers to mental forms.

63. *Platform Sutra,* par. 17, following the Kōshōji recension.

64. On the controversy surrounding the practice of sitting meditation in T'ang dynasty Ch'an, see note 52 above.

65. On passivity and quietism, see sec. 3.3 below.

66. See Hu Shih, *Shen-hui,* 108, 136, 142, 143.

67. Ibid., 122–123.

68. Ibid., 102; see 134.

69. Ibid., 115.

70. Ibid.

71. Ibid., 108, 134–135.

72. Ibid., 108 and 143–144 in contrast to 113–114.

73. Ibid., 104, 105, 107.

74. As seems to be the case, e.g., in Vimalakīrti's *pu-erh fa-men,* which is in sharp contrast to other statements in the sūtra. See Gómez, "Words of Liberation," in J. Swearingen, ed., *The Word* (forthcoming).

75. *T* 45.664c13–23.

76. Ibid., 664c23–665a17. The doctrine is not in the least monistic, the idea being that the "absolute" does not contradict the "relative": cause and effect, distinctions and contrasts remain. For the elaboration of this doctrine in Tsung-mi, see Peter Gregory's chapter in this volume.

77. The same position is implicit in T'ien-t'ai views of suddenness, discussed under two main doctrinal categories. (1) As part of a system of "methods of conversion" *(hua-i ssu chiao),* "suddenness" refers to the manifestation of Buddhahood as one, without distinctions of doctrine or form. This is the revelation of the *Avataṃsaka.* It appears in a system of only three methods in Chih-i's *Miao-fa lien-hua ching hsüan-i* (*T* 33.806a14–807b), but it also forms part of the classical fourfold system; see *Mo-ho chih-kuan, T* 46.97c21, and Chegwan's *T'ien-t'ai ssu chiao i* (*T'ien-t'ai Buddhism: An Outline of the Fourfold Teachings,* Buddhist Translation Seminar of Hawaii, [Tokyo: Daiichi Shobō, 1983], 55–57). (2) As part of a system of three aspects of teaching *(san-chung chiao hsiang),* the sudden teaching is also the perfect or complete teaching, encompassing nonduality both as innate Buddhahood and as the presence of the sacred, soteric goal in the profane, mundane sphere of life and death (*Mo-ho chih-kuan, T* 46.1c1–3b10).

The T'ien-t'ai system, of course, cannot be understood in isolation from the school's hermeneutical theory and practice, making comparisons between its doctrines and those of Shen-hui speculative, if not problematic.

78. As edited in McRae, "Northern School," 450–452. McRae sees a connection between these passages and Shen-hui (p. 355).

79. Hu Shih, *Shen-hui,* 109, 123, 130.

80. Ibid., 140.

Shen-hui is not alone when he finds himself trapped in the inescapable quandary created by a series of ultimately unsatisfactory expressions of the doctrine of "nonduality." The alternatives are common throughout the tradition: (1) duality of delusion and enlightenment, or bondage and liberation, (2) nonduality as identity of delusion and enlightenment, (3) nonduality transcended by a stage of return to duality, and (4) nonduality defined by a dialectic. The gradualist is not less limited by these alternatives. A typology of Buddhist systems of liberation perhaps can be built on these categories. For instance, Shen-hui is defined by the first two categories, but if we take his statements as a single interconnected pedagogical text, we may see alternative 4 at work. Fa-tsang and Tsung-mi are defined more by categories 3 and 4; so is Kamalaśīla. Systems in which the dialectic dominates belong to the tradition of the *catuṣkoṭī,* represented in China by Chi-tsang's dialectic of negation and affirmation.

81. Ibid., 149–151, 151–152; also 118.

82. Thus nonduality and liberation are coterminous with the world of delusion—a point made by Tsung-mi under his definition of "sudden teaching" *(tun-chiao),* but included under the "perfect teaching" in earlier *p'an chiao* systems.

83. If we accept the available documents as reflecting his thought accurately, Shen-hui was as inconsistent on this point as he was on so many others. At times it seems that he did not reject all forms of cultivation, but the literature attributes to him some strong, unqualified statements attacking cultivation.

See, e.g., the rejection of all forms of cultivation *(hsiu-hsi)* and spiritual practices *(yung hsin)* in Hu Shih, *Shen-hui,* 148–152.

84. Hu Shih, *Shen-hui,* 108; see 136, 141, 143.

85. Loc. cit.

86. Kamalaśīla understands this to be the weakest point in the sudden enlightenment theory. He begins the second of his three *Bhāvanākramas* with a discussion of causality, and a *reductio ad absurdum* of any theory of liberation that rejects causality. One should note here in passing that the inclusion of "means" as part of the causal dimension of enlightenment does not preclude other meanings. In Kamalaśīla the term *upāya* refers to both the stage of causation (cultivation) and the stage of realization and fruition (the saving activities of Buddhas and bodhisattvas), with an emphasis on the latter. In the Northern school tradition both meanings occur, but the emphasis is on the first meaning.

Cp. also references in Stein, "Illumination," 20–21 n. 5.

87. Although we do not know much about this figure, what little we know suggests that neither Hui-neng nor Shen-hui ever met him. The only text attributed to him, the *Hsiu-hsin yao lun,* does not reveal him as a teacher of sudden enlightenment in the Southern style. The fundamental and pioneering work on this subject is Yanagida's *Shoki zenshū shisho no kenkyū* (passim). See also McRae, "Northern School," 238ff., 430ff.; Faure, *La volonté d'orthodoxie,* 724ff.; and Yanagida, *Shoki no zenshi 2,* 92ff.

88. *Hsiu-hsin yao lun,* Stein 2269, 3558, 4046, edited by D. T. Suzuki, *Zen-shisō shi kenkyū,* reprinted as vol. 2 of *Suzuki Daisetsu zenshū* (Tokyo: Iwanami shoten, 1968), 303–309; the passage quoted is from 306–307, par. 12. See also *T* 48.378a–b, under the title *Tsui-shang sheng lun*; see also McRae's edition in "Northern School," 430–449 (the quotation is from 439–440). Cp. Faure, *La volonté d'orthodoxie,* 724ff.

The third paragraph is partly inspired by the sixteen visualizations *(kuan)* of Amitāyus and his Buddha-field described in the *Wu-liang shou kuan ching* (*T* 12.342a2 ff.).

For other materials reflecting teachings of the so-called East Mountain School, see David Chappell, "Teachings of the Fourth Patriarch," 89-130.

89. *Hsiu hsin yao lun,* D. T. Suzuki, *Zen-shisō shi,* 2:306; McRae, "Northern School," 437–438; *T* 48.378a. Here I follow McRae's edition. The simile of the sun covered by clouds also occurs at the beginning of the text (McRae, 430); see Suzuki, *Zen-shisō shi,* 2:296ff.

90. Note that innate Buddhahood is expressed here as "original purity of the mind." The key metaphor is that of the sun and the clouds; see also Suzuki, *Zen-shisō shi,* 2:304, par. 2.

91. Zeuschner, *Analysis,* 23–25; also, Zeuschner, "The Understanding of Mind in the Northern Line of Ch'an (Zen)," *Philosophy East and West* 28, no. 1 (1978): 69–80.

92. Hu Shih, *Shen-hui,* 175. Other metaphors for sudden and gradual are discussed below, in section 5.

93. *P'o-hsiang lun,* in *Shōshitsu-rokumon, T* 48.369c8–11. Compare the almost identical passage in the *Kuan-hsin lun, T* 85.1273a29–b2: "Only if you are able to collect the mind and illuminate it internally will you awaken and contemplate

with constant clarity, and cut off the three poisons and extinguish delusion forever. . . . Effortlessly you will have as many virtues as there are sands in the Ganges, and all the adornments of enlightenment. All the innumerable gates to the dharma will have been realized, so you will transcend the state of a common man and realize the condition of the saint. [Enlightenment] will be right before your eyes, not far away. Awakening will occur in an instant." See Zeuschner, *Analysis*, 62–63.

94. *P'o-hsiang lun*, *T* 48.36c20 ff.; no parallel in *Kuan-hsin lun*.

95. See especially the discussion of the three types of *śīla* and the six perfections, *T* 48.367c1 ff.; parallel in *Kuan-hsin lun*, *T* 85.1271a ff. The perfections receive a very different treatment in two other texts associated with the Northern school: in Mo-ho-yen's fragments (Gómez, "Direct and Gradual Approaches," 121–123) and in the *Wu fang-pien* (D. T. Suzuki, *Zen-shisō shi kenkyū*, reprinted as vol. 3 of *Suzuki Daisetsu zenshū* [Tokyo: Iwanami shoten, 1968], 183–184).

96. *T* 85.1272a1-7. McRae ("Ox-head School," 209) states that the term *kuan-ch'a* does not refer to "the practice of *vipaśyanā* or insight meditation" (at least in his analysis of Chi-tsang). He no doubt confuses modern Burmese definitions of *vipassanā* with the type of insight meditation known to the Chinese through T'ien-t'ai and Chinese translations of Hīnayāna works. Although the exact nature of the meditation is not always transparent, this type of contemplative analysis is not substantially different from the *pratyavekṣaṇā* recommended by Kamalaśīla—a fact that contributed at the same time to some degree of communication and certain confusion during the controversies of Tibet.

97. Zeuschner, *Analysis*, 75–76, 152–161, and passim. On means and its connection to the sudden-gradual debate during the earlier period, see David C. Yu, "Skill-in-means and the Buddhism of Tao-sheng: A Study of a Chinese Reaction to Mahāyāna of the Fifth Century," *Philosophy East and West* 24, no. 4 (1974): 413–428.

98. *T* 85.1271a26–28.

99. Ibid., 1271b17–18.

100. Ibid., 1271c25–26.

101. One of its longer titles is *Ta-sheng wu-sheng fang-pien men;* Stein 2503; *T* 2834, vol. 85. It is also known from other manuscripts as the *Pei-tsung ta-sheng wu-sheng fang-pien men*, indicating its affiliation with the Northern school of Ch'an. My references are to Suzuki's edition, which contains the two main manuscripts of this work: D. T. Suzuki, *Zen-shisō shi*, 3:153–235.

The work is cited in this paper by its abbreviated title, *Wu fang-pien*.

102. Suzuki, *Zen-shisō shi*, 168–169.

103. Ibid., 168.

104. Ibid., 170–171.

105. *T* 48.368a24-b1, and *T* 85.1271c17-18. This doctrine of means, and perhaps even the meaning of the term, is different from that of the "five means." See below.

106. This is the so-called *kuan-hsin shih* or "contemplative interpretation," which is a misnomer, since contemplation is not the only value instilled by these interpretations. McRae ("Ox-head School," 231–232) calls this method "con-

templative analysis," and considers it a characteristic of the Northern school (see also "Northern School," 335–347). I do not think, however, that the exegetic strategies of the *Kuan-hsin lun* are similar to those of the *Wu fang-pien*. Nor are they accurately described with the term "extended metaphor." Furthermore, although anagoge dominates the *Kuan-hsin lun*, it is not the exclusive property of the Northern school.

The word "interiorization" I borrow from Eliade. It is to be preferred to the more natural "internalization," since the latter has a different meaning in normal English usage.

107. *T* 85.1272a20–b3.

108. Suzuki, *Zen-shisō shi*, 171–172. Note also the difference between the *Wu fang-pien*'s definition of "substance" and "function" (p. 172) and the *Platform Sūtra*'s analysis (Yampolsky, par. 13). This and other themes on which the two texts overlap, like the question of the meaning of Mahāyāna ritual formulae and the definition of the bodies of the Buddha, must have been common topics of debate at the time.

109. Suzuki, *Zen-shisō shi*, 177.

110. *T* 14.545b13–16. Quoted or alluded to in the *First Bhāvanākrama*, p. 194; *Second Bhāvanākrama*, fol. 52b; *Third Bhāvanākrama*, p. 22.

111. Suzuki, *Zen-shisō shi*, 3:178; see 178–179, 193, 197–199. My consideration of this passage here and below (sec. 3.3) overlooks the question of different recensions. Suzuki's edition consists of transcriptions of three fragmentary manuscripts, which on occasion present substantially different readings. Although I do not think the variants reflect major differences in essentials, the reader should be warned that I am conflating different manuscript traditions that may be related in origin but whose history remains obscure.

112. Ibid., 179. This is a doctrine of the *Wu fang-pien*, and represents a Northern doctrine different from that of the *Kuan-hsin lun*. It is not legitimate to try to interpret the latter text by projecting onto it the ideas expressed in the former.

113. On this point I disagree with Yanagida and McRae. The metaphor of the votive lamp by itself suggests that the practice of "guarding" or "preserving" the mind consists in "maintaining awareness of the originally pure mind," which McRae ("Ox-head School," 208 and 229) regards as a sudden enlightenment practice. But this is a "maintaining operation" different from the actual attainment of enlightenment. As I have argued in this paper, gradualism can coexist with doctrines of innate Buddhahood or even of "sudden attainment": the issue of speed or suddenness, and the question of innateness, represent only two aspects of the problem; "immediacy" and the question of method and means are a third, equally important, point of contention.

114. Zeuschner, "The Concept of *li nien*," 144ff.

115. *T* 45.368b3–12, and *T* 85.1271c22–1272a1.

116. *T* 45.368b3–12.

117. Kamata, *Zengen*, 298.

118. The *Wu fang-pien* discusses innate Buddhahood at, e.g., 178, 188–189. Contrast the clear separation this text establishes between the realm of dharma and the sphere of sentient beings (p. 170).

119. T'an-k'uang (ca. 700–788) wrote a number of works discovered in Tun-huang. Most of these were incorporated into the Chinese canon in the Taishō edition. Among them we find a piece titled *Ta-sheng ju-tao tz'u-ti k'ai chüeh* (*T* 2823, vol. 85). This is a commentary on Chih-chou's short treatise on the Yogācāra abhidharmic map of the path, titled *Ta-sheng ju-tao tz'u-ti* (*T* 1864, vol. 45). T'an-k'uang also discussed twenty-two issues of the sudden-gradual debates in a short piece preserved in Tun-huang but not included in the *Taishō Daizōkyō;* see D. Ueyama, "Donkō to Tonkō no bukkyōgaku," *Tōhōgakuhō* 35 (1964): 141–214, and W. Pachow, "A Study of the Twenty-two Dialogues on Mahāyāna Buddhism," *The Chinese Culture, A Quarterly Review* 20, no. 1 (1979): 15–64, and no. 2 (1979): 35–85.

Mo-ho-yen (ca. 720–795?) was not a scholar, and it is not known with any certainty what he wrote, if anything. His teachings are preserved in a variety of sources (see below). In Tibetan his name and title appear as Hwa-shang Ma-ha-ya-na or Ma-ha-yan. The title (from the Chinese *ho-shang,* itself a transliteration of Sanskrit *ācārya*) should not be taken as indicating any high ecclesiastic or spiritual rank; see Demiéville, *Concile,* 9–12, and notes.

120. For bibliographic references to the *Bhāvanākramas* see sec. 2.2. On the "Council" see bibliographic references in sec. 1; also K. Mimaki, "Tongo to zengo," in *Kōza daijō bukkyō: 7—Chūgan shisō,* ed. A. Hirakawa, Y. Kajiyama, and J. Takasaki (Tokyo: Shunjusha, 1982), 217–250.

121. These two works are preserved only in Tibetan translation. *Bhāvanāyogāvatāra,* ed. and trans. L. O. Gómez, *Materials for the Study of Mahāyāna Texts* (Ann Arbor: Institute for the Study of Buddhist Literature, forthcoming). I am also preparing an edition of the *Avikalpapraveśa-dhāraṇī* and its commentary, the *Avikalpapraveśa-dhāraṇī-ṭīkā*; references below are to the page and folio in the Peking edition: 5501, vol. 105, pp. 114.5–126.1.

122. Peking Tripitaka 5306, vol. 102, pp. 15.1–18.3.

123. A pericope included in this manuscript without title or introduction contains some of the questions and quotations in the text attributed to Vimalamitra (Pelliot 116, fol. 146–163). See D. Ueyama, "Tonkō shutsudo chibetto-bun zen shiryō no kenkyū—tib. 116 to sono mondai ten," *Bukkyō bunka kenkyūjo kiyō* 13 (1974): 1–11; S. Harada, "Bsam yas no shūron igo ni okeru tonmonha no ronsho," *Nihon chibetto-gakkai kaihō* 22 (1976): 8–10; R. Kimura, "Tonkō shutsudo chibetto-bun shahon: Pelliot 116 kenkyū (sono ichi)," *Indogaku bukkyōgaku kenkyū* 32, no. 2 (1975): 778–781; L. O. Gómez, "La doctrina subitista de Vimalamitra," *Estudios de Asia y Africa del Norte* 16, no. 2 (1982): 254–272.

124. Tucci, *Minor Buddhist Texts. Part 1,* 69, 82; Jeffrey L. Broughton, "Early Ch'an Schools in Tibet," in Gimello and Gregory, eds., *Studies in Ch'an and Hua-yen,* 8–9, 16, 56 n. 32; P. Yampolsky, "New Japanese Studies in Early Ch'an History," in Lai and Lancaster, eds., *Early Ch'an,* 1–11. An accommodation, compromise, or fusion of Southern and Northern elements does not seem as absurd today as it would have a few decades ago. As discussed above (sec. 2) differences between the two schools were not as sharp as was previously believed.

There is strong evidence to suggest that Mo-ho-yen was closely linked to the Pao-t'ang branch of Ch'an. Hironobu Obata has argued that Mo-ho-yen and other Tibetan Ch'an teachers cannot be considered members of either the so-called Southern or the so-called Northern traditions of Chinese Ch'an. He sees elements of both traditions and, especially, of the Pao-t'ang line in Tibetan Ch'an; see his "Kodai Chibetto ni okeru tonmonha (zenshū) no nagare," *Bukkyō shigaku kenkyū* 18 (1976): 59–80, esp. 78. The Tibetan Rnying-ma text *Blon-po bka'i thang-yig* places Mo-ho-yen at the end of a Pao-t'ang lineage that is otherwise similar to that of the *Li-tai fa-pao chi* (Tucci, *Minor Buddhist Texts. Part 1*, 68).

The evidence linking Mo-ho-yen with Northern Ch'an, however, is as strong as this sort of evidence can be: the *Tun-wu ta-sheng cheng-li chüeh,* our most reliable source on the teachings of Mo-ho-yen, ascribes to him a list of five (or six?) of his own teachers (manuscript Pelliot 4646, fol. 156b; Stein 2672, fol. 305–306). Among these, three are identified elsewhere as followers of Northern Ch'an (see P. Demiéville, "Deux documents," 24–27; *Choix d'études bouddhiques,* 343–346). At least one of them (Hsiang-mo) is the object of criticism in Shen-hui's *Yü-lu* (Hu Shih, *Shen-hui,* 175).

Obata himself seems to assume a Northern model as the basis for Mo-ho-yen's *doctrine.* Like other scholars in the field, Obata also gives considerable importance to the issues of lineage, although he would not refer to Tibetan subitism by the term *ch'an*—he prefers *tun-men p'ai.*

It is possible, however, that Tibetan subitism is an offshoot of the Szechwan schools of Ch'an (Pao-t'ang included), whereas Mo-ho-yen represents a different brand of Ch'an originating in Tun-huang. This is one case where perhaps scholars have become too attached to the traditional conception of "spiritual lineage," confusing this hagiographic device with a historically significant datum. I believe we can make more sense of Mo-ho-yen's teachings if we assume that he was not trying to conform to doctrines received by "Ch'an transmission" from Northern or Pao-t'ang masters, and that he was his own man, a moderately creative religious specialist who borrowed and innovated at will. The concepts of "teacher" and "lineage" serve a variety of ahistorical functions in his hagiography, as they do in that of so many other Buddhist masters—they are devices for recognizing or claiming inspiration, influence, and political and institutional allegiance.

More on Mo-ho-yen's thought in Mimaki, "Tongo to zengo," 228–233, and in Z. Yamaguchi, "Makaen no zen," in *Kōza Tonkō 8—Tonkō butten to zen* (Tokyo: Daitō shuppansha, 1980), 378–407. On his "works," consult Gómez, "Direct and Gradual Approaches," and K. Okimoto, "Tonkō shutsudo no chibetto-bun zenshū bunken no naiyō," in *Kōza Tonkō 8—Tonkō butten to zen,* 422–425.

125. There is no reason to assume that the "five *upāya*" discussed in the latter text represents the heart of gradualism. A close analysis shows that this doctrine is not central to the gradualist position as such—however important it may have been for other aspects of Northern school doctrine, especially for its hermeneutical tradition. It is not clear, moreover, that one can establish a historical connection between the *wu fang-pien* and Mo-ho-yen's doctrine of *upāya.* I believe the two doctrines are distinct enough so that we should argue in the opposite sense; that is, the differences between the two doctrines show that Mo-ho-yen could not have been in a direct line of descent from a Northern school branch.

The Northern school's five "approaches" *(fang-pien)* to the object of meditation (often referred to by the misnomer "five expedients") constitute a conceptual framework for explaining and defining the object of meditation in both gradual enlightenment and sudden enlightenment terms. As a gradualist doctrine, they are a description of the object of cultivation; they are "expedient means" only insofar as they serve to define what is beyond definition. As a sudden enlightenment doctrine they are statements about innate Buddhahood and are in the tradition of Tao-hsin's five "aspects" *(wu chung),* which may be interpreted as a system of reference points in the cultivation of innate Buddhahood (Yanagida, *Shoki no zenshi 1,* 225). Mo-ho-yen's five "means of approach," on the other hand, form a system of steps or degrees and, therefore, belong to the class of gradualist doctrines.

All three systems can be regarded as hermeneutical systems, insofar as they are methods of interpreting a set of religious practices and doctrines. But it seems unlikely that they were intended to play an exegetical role. Neither Tao-hsin's nor Mo-ho-yen's system is correlated with scriptural passages. The five "approaches" of the *Wu fang-pien,* although set within a textual frame of reference, are not primarily an exegetical device, and cannot be compared with *p'an-chiao* doctrines. See McRae, "Northern School," 364ff.

126. The *Tun-wu ta-sheng cheng-li chüeh* (henceforth *Cheng-li chüeh,* for short) is preserved in two manuscripts, one complete, the other almost complete. The Chinese text of the first of these manuscripts (Pelliot 4646) was reproduced and translated in Demiéville's magnum opus, *Concile.* He also published several important emendations based on the second manuscript (Stein 2672) in "Deux documents," 14–27 (*Choix d'études bouddhiques,* 333–346).

The Tibetan materials are all fragmentary. For a compilation of English translations and references to most of the Tibetan fragments, see Gómez, "Direct and Gradual Approaches." A supplement including a few additional fragments of questionable authenticity is now ready for publication, but its materials have not been considered in the present essay.

127. The same outline is followed by the Tibetan chronicles: see, e.g., Gómez, "Direct and Gradual Approaches," 144–146.

128. Note that the issue is "access"; on the nature of the goal all the disputants agree that it has to be nonconceptual.

129. *Avikalpapraveśa-dhāraṇī-ṭīkā,* Peking 5501, vol. 105, pp. 114–126.

130. *First Bhāvanākrama,* 198, 204–205.

131. *Bhāvanāyogāvatāra,* fol. 69b (references to folios in the Sde-dge version).

132. *Third Bhāvanākrama,* 20; alluding to *Kāśyapaparivarta.* See note 43 above.

133. Hu Shih, *Shen-hui,* 106; discussed above, sec. 2.2.

134. Vimalamitra, Peking 5306, 16.1. The sūtra quoted here is variously known as *Brahmā-paripṛcchā, Viśeṣacintī, Viśeṣacintā, or Viśeṣacintibrahmaparipṛcchā,* but the last seems to be the complete and correct title. The passage quoted appears in *T* 15.24a25–26, *T* 15.54b25–29, and *T* 15.87c13–15; cp. *T* 15.18b, 15.42b, 15.49b, etc.

This sūtra was a favorite among Ch'an Buddhists. See Demiéville, *Concile,* 67, 114, 143ff.

135. Peking 5306, p. 16.4. See the parallel expression from *Vajracchedikā* quoted by Vimalamitra (p. 16.4) and Pelliot 4646, fol. 129a, etc.; *Concile,* 52n.

Cp. also Vimalamitra, p. 16.4: "What is the middle way in the nonconceptual realm?" "It is said in the *Laṅkāvatāra:* 'The stopping of conceptualization which is based on abandoning the idea of an external object by the full comprehension of mind-only—this way is the middle way. This middle way which I and other Buddhas have taught does not appear as mind-only, nor is it the nonexistence of the appearing object.' " The text has been corrected by comparing Pelliot 116, fol. 148, and the Sanskrit text of the sūtra—*Laṅkāvatāra Sūtra,* ed. B. Nanjio (Kyoto: Otani University Press, 1956), p. 311.1-4; see also 25.16, 168.9, 278.5. Unfortunately all three sources represent extremely corrupt textual transmissions, and the edition of the Sanskrit text is little more than a rough guide to the text.

136. Pelliot 812. Cp. Gómez, "Direct and Gradual Approaches," 123-124.

137. Tucci, *Minor Buddhist Texts. Part 1,* 69-70.

138. Demiéville, *Concile,* 53ff., 14-15n.; Gómez, "Direct and Gradual Approaches," 133ff., glossary *sub voce.*

139. Pelliot 812. Cp. Gómez, "Direct and Gradual Approaches," 124; on his doctrine of *upāya,* see 112-113, partly discussed below.

140. *Cheng-li chüeh,* Pelliot 4646 (reproduced in Demiéville, *Concile*), fol. 134a.

141. Pelliot 4646, fol. 134a-b; reference to the memorials: fol. 155b-156b.

142. Ibid., fol. 134b.

143. Ibid.

144. Ibid., fol. 134b-135a. Exactly the same question is presented to Shen-hui (Hu Shih, *Shen-hui,* 129-130), and he avoids the issue as deftly as Mo-ho-yen.

145. Pelliot 4646, fol. 135a; cp. Peking 5306, p. 15.4, and Pelliot 116, fol. 161, where the same passage is quoted. Mo-ho-yen's hermeneutical twist in this treatment of the *Vimalakīrti* is quite obvious, and has been discussed briefly in Gómez, "Indian Materials," 432 n. 26.

Note that although Mo-ho-yen's view of enlightenment is unquestionably subitist, he uses the imperfective verb *k'an.*

146. See Zeuschner, *Analysis,* 17-20.

147. Cp. the concept of *chüeh-kuan,* central to the Ox-head school—see *Chüeh-kuan lun;* also McRae, "Ox-head School."

148. Pelliot 4646, fol. 135b-136a. This passage is also preserved in Tibetan translation with some variants (Pelliot 823; see Gómez, "Direct and Gradual," 126). The quotation is from the *Pitāputrasamāgama*; see Demiéville, *Concile,* 82 n. 8.

149. Pelliot 4646, fol. 136b.

150. Ibid.

151. Hu Shih, *Shen-hui,* 115-116, 140; discussed above, sec. 2. Cp. Shen-hui's views at 124-125, 129-130.

152. Pelliot 4646, fol. 137a. The same issue is repeated in the summary of the Tibetan controversy found in the Tibetan chronicles. See, e.g., Gómez, "Direct and Gradual Approaches," 144-146.

Cp. the discussion above regarding the same position in Shen-hui, the *Platform Sūtra,* and Shen-hsiu.

153. Pelliot 4646, fol. 141a. The same doctrine is found in Southern Ch'an

where it is explicitly connected to the teachings of the *Prajñāpāramitā* sūtras; see Hu Shih, *Shen-hui,* 180–181: "Someone who cultivates the perfection of insight is able to gather for himself all [other] dharmas. The practice of the perfection of insight is the root of all other practices. . . . If one wishes to be able to penetrate into the depths of the dharmadhātu, and enter directly into the one-practice samādhi *(i-hsing san-mei),* one should recite the *Diamond Sūtra* and cultivate the perfection of insight. . . ."

The English word "insight" is used advisedly to render *prajñā* and *hui* in some of these passages, in order to bring out the peculiar usage of the term in this branch of the Ch'an tradition. In other contexts, however, *prajñā* is translated as "wisdom" (as, e.g., in contrast to "means") or "discernment" (as, e.g., when it is the general mental function or operation accompanying insight). In the passage above "insight" translates in the first sentence the Chinese transliteration of the Sanskrit, *pan-jo po-lo-mi.* In the second sentence, the term used is the Chinese translation, *chih-hui.*

154. Pelliot 4646, fol. 144a.

155. Ibid., fol. 141a–b.

156. McRae, in "Ox-head School," 215 and 235, sees in the use of "Mādhyamika" dialectic a characteristic of the Ox-head school. I am inclined to see this trait as too general to be a useful mark for identifying the peculiarities of any school in the Buddhism of this epoch. Unfortunately, McRae's definition of "Mādhyamika dialectic" is too brief (221–222), so that I find it difficult to say whether he is referring to a specifically Ox-head turn or to Mādhyamika logic in general.

157. For an explicit recognition of this aspect of his rhetoric, see Mo-ho-yen's third memorial to the king of Tibet in *Cheng-li chüeh,* fol. 155b. It is not clear, however, that Mo-ho-yen actually sees a problem in the doctrine or in his own presentation of it.

158. *First Bhāvanākrama,* 198; *Second Bhāvanākrama,* fol. 44b.

159. E.g., *First Bhāvanākrama,* 209ff.; *Second Bhāvanākrama,* fol. 44b; *Third Bhāvanākrama,* 15ff.

160. *First Bhāvanākrama,* 212. Cp. *Avikalpapraveśa-ṭīkā,* fol. 156b–157a.

161. *First Bhāvanākrama,* 211–212; see also *Third Bhāvanākrama,* 15–17.

The source for the quotation is the *Dharmasaṃgīti,* identified by K. Mimaki in *Blo gsal grub mtha'* (Kyoto: Zinbun kagaku kenkyusho, 1982), 246 n. 602. On this issue, see Gómez, "Indian Materials," 402ff.

Note also in this passage the difference between imperfective seeing (observation) and perfective seeing (the apprehension of truth)—the latter must be what the metaphor of "not seeing" alludes to.

162. *First Bhāvanākrama,* 212–214; *Third Bhāvanākrama,* 9–10, 17ff.

163. Gómez, "Direct and Gradual Approaches," 107–109.

164. *Bhāvanāyogāvatāra,* fol. 69b.

165. Peking 5306, p. 15.2.

166. Ibid.

167. Yampolsky, *Platform Sutra,* 13. This passage may reflect Northern school influence, perhaps through Ox-head doctrine—see McRae, "Ox-head School," p. 228 and note.

168. Cp. Yampolsky, *Platform Sutra,* secs. 17–18, 26–29.

169. *Zekkanron* (Kyoto: Zenbunka kenkyūjo, 1976), 87, par. 1.1. Compare the *Wu-hsin lun, T* 2831, vol. 85.

170. Pelliot 4646, fol. 141a. Shen-hui is also accused of neglecting dhyāna and overemphasizing prajñā (Hu Shih, *Shen-hui,* 175, 180–181).

171. Also, e.g., at Pelliot 4646, fol. 137a–b. One should keep in mind, moreover, that this issue is further complicated by the fact that Mo-ho-yen, and Ch'an in general, do not always distinguish clearly between *ch'an* as dhyāna and *ch'an* as direct, intuitive knowledge. It is therefore not clear whether the preferred perfection is meditation or insight.

172. Vimalamitra, Peking 5306, 16.3–4. Cp. Pelliot 116, fol. 146, 160; Pelliot 4646, fol. 131a and passim; Demiéville, *Concile,* 62 n. 1.

173. *First Bhāvanākrama,* 221.

174. Pelliot 4646, fol. 136b.

175. Ibid., fol. 137a.

176. Ibid., fol. 138.

177. Ibid., fol. 136a–b. See *Concile,* 83–84 and notes. Also compare Vimalamitra, Peking 5306, 15.2–4, 16.3–4.

178. Pelliot 4646, fol. 140b. The doctrine of a Buddha's nonconceptual thought and effortless activity is shared by gradualists and subitists; see *Concile,* 98–99 n. 2; Sgam-po-pa, *Jewel Ornament of Liberation,* trans. Herbert V. Guenther (London: Rider & Co., 1959), 271–275. The gradualist view, however, does not exclude conceptual thought as a tool for liberation of self and others: see the objections of the gradualist in Stein 2672, Demiéville, "Deux documents," 339–342. See also the doctrine of the five *jñānas* as discussed in *Mahāyānasūtrālaṅkāra* and *Buddhabhūmi-śāstra,* and chap. 4 of the *Ratnagotravibhāga.*

179. *First Bhāvanākrama,* 218–222.

180. Ibid., 221.

181. See the gradualist position in Stein 2672, Demiéville, "Deux documents," 339.

182. Vimalamitra, Peking 5306, 18.1. The second scriptural source has not been identified; the reconstruction of the title is hypothetical *(Buddhahṛdaya?, Buddhapiṭaka).* The Tibetan original reads *sangs rgyas mdzod kyi mdo.*

183. *Third Bhāvanākrama,* 20, 21–22ff.

184. *T* 14.545b13–16; also discussed above, sec. 2.3. Quoted or alluded to in the *First Bhāvanākrama,* 194; *Second Bhāvanākrama,* fol. 52b; *Third Bhāvanākrama,* 22.

185. *First Bhāvanākrama,* 197–198; *Second Bhāvanākrama,* 52b; *Third Bhāvanākrama,* 22–29.

186. Suzuki, *Zen-shisō shi,* 3:178; quoted above, sec. 2.3, see nn. 110, 111, 112.

187. Baron A. Stäel-Holstein, *The Kāçyapaparivarta* (Shanghai: Commercial Press, 1926), par. 42; quoted in the *Third Bhāvanākrama,* 27. See also *Second Bhāvanākrama,* fol. 52a–b. On the translation of *saṃgraha* and *saṃgṛhīta,* see F. Weller's translation of pars. 25 and 42 of *Kāśyapaparivarta* (*Zum Kāśyapaparivarta,* Heft 2, Abhandlungen der Sächsischen Akademie der Wissenschaften zu Leipzig, Philologisch-historische Klasse, Band 57, Heft 3, Berlin, 1965).

188. *Second Bhāvanākrama,* fol. 51b.

189. An inconsistency in the gradualist position is evident here. For, on the

one hand, the subitist is criticized for the practice of pure calm while, on the other hand, we are told that he proposes a state of insight without means. But it seems to me clear that Kamalaśīla is in fact making a third criticism, which conciliates the other two, namely: he considers the subitist definition of insight to be equivalent to the most negative aspect of calm, sheer absence of mental activity. For Kamalaśīla true insight would imply the cooperation of calm and means.

190. *Third Bhāvanākrama,* 22ff.

191. Even Demiéville, who elsewhere cannot hide well his preferences, feels obliged to defend Mo-ho-yen on this count; *Concile,* 179.

192. Peking 5306, 16.5. The scriptural source has not been identified; the reconstruction of the title is hypothetical. The Tibetan original reads *glang bo dang mtshungs pa'i mdo.*

193. See, e.g., *First Bhāvanākrama,* 197–198, and *Third Bhāvanākrama,* 20ff.

194. Étienne Lamotte, for instance, is of the opinion that Mahāyāna undermines the foundation of morality; see "La moralité dans les deux véhicules," appendix to *L'Enseignement de Vimalakīrti,* Bibliothèque du Muséon 51 (Louvain: Publications Universitaires, Institut Orientaliste, 1962), 413-415. Although I disagree with his assessment, I mention it to prove that a person who is unquestionably a learned scholar and a careful reader can see a nihilistic streak in Mahāyāna rhetoric. (Lamotte, op. cit., 37ff., and elsewhere, hesitates on the question of ontological nihilism, mainly, I suspect, because the tradition is clear in its rejection of this type of nihilism.)

195. Pelliot 4646, fol. 137a, 141a.

196. We find notable exceptions to this phenomenon among the Szechwan schools, in which ritual was explicitly proscribed. On this topic see Tsung-mi's summary of their teachings in Y. Jan, "Tsung-mi, His Analysis of Ch'an Buddhism," *T'oung Pao* 58 (1972): 1ff.; also Yanagida, "The *Li-tai fa-pao chi* and the Ch'an Doctrine of Sudden Awakening."

197. Peking 5306, 18.2. This sūtra of course is not the same as the famous *Bhadracarī,* known in the West as "The Vows of Samantabhadra." Tao-hsin's *Ju-tao an-hsin yao fang-pien fa-men* (that is, *Leng-ch'ieh shih-tzu chi, T* 85.1287a8–10) refers to the sūtra quoted above, the *P'u-hsien kuan ching (Fo shuo kuan P'u-hsien p'u-sa hsing-fa ching), T* 9.393b11. This text is at the same time a ritual manual and an interpretation of ritual from the perspective of Mahāyāna doctrines of meditation and reality. The extant Chinese version of the sūtra, although apparently slightly different from the recension underlying Vimalamitra's quotation, provides the original context:

> If one recites the sūtras of the Mahāyāna,
> and contemplates the dharma-reality,
> one becomes forever free from all evil karma,
> and will not produce it again in future lives.
>
> . . . .
>
> The whole ocean of the impediments of karma
> arises from deluded conceptualization.
> One who wishes to confess his sins

should sit with the back straight, contemplating the real.
All sins are like dew or frost;
the sun of insight evaporates them.
Therefore, with all one's heart and mind
one should repent for his six sense organs.

The doctrine of contrition by means of contemplation is a long-standing characteristic of Ch'an. Tao-hsin's is one of the earliest statements, but the doctrine is common in the T'ang, continues in later Ch'an, and can be attested in the living oral tradition in Japan; see, e.g., *Leng-ch'ieh shih-tzu chi, T* 85.1287a8–10; Yanagida, *Shoki no zenshi 1,* 192, 249; Chappell, "Teachings," 108, 118; also the writings of Ta-hui, *T* 47.891a28ff.

The doctrine of the "higher act of contrition" is not the exclusive territory of the subitist, however; it finds a home among Mahāyāna gradualists as well. See, e.g., Sgam-po-pa, *Jewel Ornament,* 124, for an allusion to "contrition" by means of meditation on emptiness—probably inspired in part by Śāntideva's *Śikṣāsamuccaya.* For a Chinese example see Chih-i's *Shih ch'an po-lo-mi tz'u-ti famen, T* 46.486a10 ff., a long apologetic on the practice of contrition by means of contemplation, forming part of a masterful integration of Mahāyāna ritual, meditation, and ethics.

198. Hu Shih, *Shen-hui,* 227–228; also Yampolsky, *Platform Sutra,* sec. 22. See Shen-hui's *Yü-lu* in Hu Shih, *Shen-hui* 123. For standard confession formulas in the *Wu fang-pien,* see Suzuki, *Zen-shisō shi,* 3:168.

199. A Northern school fivefold ritual is described in the *Wu fang-pien,* Suzuki, *Zen-shisō shi,* 3:167–168. Total rejection of ritual practices was a characteristic of some of the Szechwan schools—see above. Tsung-mi's ritual plan, on the other hand, is close to that of the T'ien-t'ai school and conforms to Indian models.

200. Yampolsky, *Platform Sutra,* 20–24.

201. Ibid., 23.

202. *Second Bhāvanākrama,* fol. 45b–46a.

203. "Miroir," 117; *Choix,* 136. Demiéville may be referring to, among other things, the grammatical categories of the perfective and imperfective aspect of verbs. "Le miroir spirituel" was published in 1947. The following year he discussed similar issues in his course at the Collège de France—summarized in "Langue et littérature chinoises. Résumé des cours de 1948–1949. 1. Le *touen* et le *tsien* (le 'subit' et le 'graduel')," *Annuaire du Collège de France* (Paris, 1949), 177–182; *Choix d'études sinologiques,* 94–99.

204. Stein, "Illumination," 3–30.

205. J. Broughton, "Kuei-feng Tsung-mi," 1ff.

206. Stein, "Illumination," 8.

207. Ibid., 6.

208. Gary W. Houston, "Cig car, Cig Char, Ston: Note on a Tibetan Term," *Central Asiatic Journal* 20 (1976): 41–46. The Tibetan term *cig-car* also appears with the spellings *gcig-car, cig-char,* etc.

209. Stein, "Illumination," 3, and summary.

210. Ibid., 8.

211. On the mirror metaphor, see Demiéville, "Miroir"; Gernet, *Entretiens,* 32–33 n. 4. For the metaphor in non-Buddhist Chinese thought, see Fung, *History,* passim, and textual selections in Wing-tsit Chan, *A Source Book of Chinese Philosophy* (Princeton: Princeton University Press, 1963), 207, 350, 431–432, 488, 567, 601; for the metaphor in Western mysticism, see A. Daniélou, *Platonisme et théologie mystique* (Paris: F. Aubier, Éditions Montaigne, 1944), 210–222. See also: Whalen Lai, "Ch'an Metaphors: Waves, Water, Mirror, Lamp," *Philosophy East and West* 29, no. 3 (1979): 243–254. More on similar metaphors in non-Buddhist traditions in Julia Ching, "The Mirror Symbol Revisited: Confucian and Taoist Mysticism," in *Mysticism and Religious Traditions,* ed. Steven T. Katz (Oxford: Oxford University Press, 1983), 226–246. A different set of Chinese metaphors is analyzed by Donald J. Munro in "The Family Network, the Stream of Water, and the Plant: Picturing Persons in Sung Confucianism," in *Individualism and Holism: Studies in Confucian and Taoist Values,* ed. Donald J. Munro (Ann Arbor: Center for Chinese Studies, 1985), 259–292.

A detailed discussion of other metaphors and of Hindu and Christian parallels, though relevant, could not be included in this paper for reasons of space. But much of the comparative material I would have used appears in my forthcoming study of Kamalaśīla and the Sino-Tibetan controversies.

212. Hu Shih, *Shen-hui,* 99 and 105, respectively.

213. On the notion of purifying what is already pure (e.g., gold) see David S. Ruegg, *Théorie du tathāgatagarbha et du gotra: Études sur la sotériologie et la gnoséologie du bouddhisme,* Publications de l'École française d'Extrême-Orient 70 (Paris: École française d'Extrême-Orient, 1969), 425–426.

For this and other similes used in a gradualist context, see *Ratnagotravibhāga,* 1.41–45, 93–94, 96–98, 108–114; also the parable of the *maṇi* gem quoted from the *Mahāparinirvāṇa Sūtra* in the commentary to 1.153. Cf. Ruegg, *Théorie,* 79–80, 112–113, 282–286. Cf. also *Mahāparinirvāṇa Sūtra,* references in nn. 34, 37 above.

214. *Second Bhāvanākrama,* fol. 55a; *Sandhinirmocana-sūtra,* 8.36, p. 115. References to the *Sandhinirmocana-sūtra* are to the pages of the edition and to the chapter and paragraph in the translation by Étienne Lamotte, *Saṃdhinirmocana sūtra: L'Explication des mystères* (Université de Louvain, Recueil de travaux publiés par les membres des Conférences d'Histoire et de Philologie, 2e série, 34e fascicule; Louvain: Bureaux du Recueil, Paris: Librairie d'Amérique et d'Orient, 1935).

215. Cf., e.g., *Sandhinirmocana-sūtra* 3.6; T'an-k'uang, question no. 21 (cited in note 119 above); and, of course, Fa-tsang's *Golden Lion.*

216. References are to page and line numbers in B. Nanjiō's edition of the Sanskrit text (Kyoto: Otani University Press, 1956).

217. *Sandhinirmocana-sūtra* 8.7, p. 91.

218. *Sandhinirmocana-sūtra* 56–57 (5.5), 91 (8.7), 107 (8.28).

219. "Miroir," 132–134; *Choix,* 151–153.

220. *The Creation of Man,* as quoted in "Miroir," 133–134; *Choix,* 152–153.

221. Jean Daniélou, S. J., *From Glory to Glory: Texts from Gregory of Nyssa's Mystical Writings,* trans. H. Musurillo (New York: Charles Scribner's Sons, 1961), 118. See the translation from the original by A. J. Malherbe and

E. Ferguson, *Gregory of Nyssa: The Life of Moses,* Classics of Western Spirituality (New York: Paulist Press, 1978), 94–95.

At the risk of tiring my reader, I would urge him or her to explore still another contrast comparing this notion of "darkness" with the superficially similar teachings of John of the Cross, and with the Ch'an use of metaphors of darkness—e.g., Tung-shan, as quoted in Heinrich Dumoulin, *The Development of Chinese Zen after the Sixth Patriarch in the Light of Mumonkan* (New York: The First Zen Institute of America, 1953), 74.

222. Daniélou, *From Glory,* 118.

223. Ibid., 112.

224. Ibid., 113.

225. *On Virginity,* ibid., 114. The quotation in "Miroir" (p. 134; *Choix,* 153) includes only the following phrases: "Yet to achieve this likeness to God is not within our power nor within any human capacity. It is a gift of God's bounty, for He directly bestowed this divine likeness on our human nature at its creation." By overlooking the last sentence of the passage, where the role of human effort is defined, Demiéville is led to believe that effort is rejected by Gregory.

I have emphasized those parts of the passage that point to the profound difference in perspective that I believe should be highlighted more than Demiéville did.

226. Daniélou, 247. Another interesting contrast: the cloud of unknowing in Gregory compared to the image of the cloud in the Ch'an tradition.

227. Ibid., 264.

228. "Miroir," 134; *Choix,* 153 (emphasis mine).

229. Demiéville, "Miroir," 116; *Choix,* 135. See also C. Sharma, *A Critical Survey of Indian Philosophy,* reprint ed. (Delhi: Motilal Banarsidass, 1964), 290ff.

230. See, e.g., Sharma, *Critical Survey,* 338ff., 350–351.

231. "Miroir," 115–116; *Choix,* 134–135. This passage represents *kārikās* 1.21–22 of the *Madhyāntavibhāga.* Demiéville refers to the Sanskrit text edited by S. Yamaguchi in *Sthiramati, Madhyāntavibhāgaṭīkā* (Nagoya: Hajinkaku, 1934), 59–60, but this edition of the commentaries does not contain all of the verses; we must assume, therefore, that Demiéville is translating from Yamaguchi's edition of the Chinese (*Benchūbenron* [Nagoya: Hajinkaku shobō, 1937]), which comes close to Demiéville's rendering. But Demiéville only refers to the Sanskrit edition and to Stcherbatsky's English translation, *Madhyānta-vibhanga: Discourse on Discrimination between Middle and Extremes,* Bibliotheca Buddhica 30 (Moscow, 1936; reprinted Osnabrück: Biblio Verlag, 1970). See also Ruegg, *Théorie,* 426.

My translation, from Yamaguchi's original and the edition of the *bhāṣya* by G. M. Nagao (*Madhyāntavibhāga-bhāṣya: A Buddhist Philosophical Treatise* [Tokyo: Suzuki Research Foundation, 1964], 26–27), appears below, with relevant portions from the commentaries, *bhāṣya,* and *ṭīkā.*

232. "Miroir," 116; *Choix,* 135 (emphasis mine).

233. Ibid. (emphasis mine).

234. Yamaguchi, *Benchūbenron,* 59–61. In my translation the "root verse" by Maitreya-Asaṅga is quoted separately, before the commentary, even where the verses appear embedded in the original text of Sthiramati's commentary. Sthiramati's quotations from Vasubandhu's commentary are printed in italics.

235. See "Miroir," 116; *Choix,* 135.

236. To reiterate a point made earlier in this essay, correspondence in rhetorical styles does not establish a historical connection between sudden enlightenment theories and the Prāsaṅgika school.

237. See Demiéville, *Concile,* 51–52n.

Glossary

Benchūbenron 辯中邊論
ch'an 禪
Ch'an-shih kuan-men 禪師觀門
Ch'an-yüan chu-ch'üan-chi tu-hsü 禪源諸詮集都序
Ch'eng (Ch'an-shih) 澄(禪師)
cheng hui 正惠
Cheng-li chüeh 正理決
cheng ting 正定
chi (precisely) 即
chi (quickly, make haste) 疾
ch'i (arouses, giving rise) 起
Chi-tsang 吉藏
chieh-lü 戒律
chien (seeing) 見
chien (gradual) 漸
chien ching 見淨
chien hsing 見性
chien wu-nien 見無念
chih (calm, calming; *śamatha*) 止
chih (grasping) 執
Chih-chou 智周
chih-hsin 直心
chih-hui 智慧 or 智惠
Chih-i 智顗
chih-kuan 止觀
chih shih chen-ju 直示眞如
ching (sense field) 境
ching-chieh 境界
ching hsin 淨心
ching t'u 淨土
chu (fixes) 住
ch'u 出
Ch'uan fa pao chi 傳法寶紀
Ch'uan hsin fa yao 傳心法要
Chuang-tzu 莊子
chüeh 覺
chüeh-kuan 絕觀
Chüeh-kuan lun 絕觀論
[*Chung-hua ch'uan-hsin-ti*] *Ch'an-men shih-tzu ch'eng-hsi t'u* [中華傳心地]禪門師資承襲圖
Ch'ung Yüan (Fa-shih) 崇遠(法師)
Denbōhōki 傳法寶紀
Denshinhōyō 傳心法要
Dōgen 道元
Erh-ju ssu-hsing lun 二入四行論
Enryōroku 宛陵録
fa 法
fa-chieh 法界
fa-hsiang 法相
fa p'u-sa hsin 發菩薩心
fa p'u-t'i hsin 發菩提心
Fa-tsang 法藏
fan-chao (self-illumination, reflection) 返照
fan-nao 煩惱
fang-pien 方便
fen-pieh 分別
Fo shuo kuan P'u-hsien p'u-sa hsing-fa ching 佛說觀普賢菩薩行法經
gyōji 行持
Hsi-yü shui-tao chi 西域水道記
hsiang (form, mark) 相
hsiang (concept) 想
Hsiang-mo (Ch'an-shih) 降魔(禪師)
hsiang-ying 相應
Hsin-chiao-ting-te Tun-huang hsieh-pen Shen-hui Ho-shang i-chu liang-chung 新校定的敦煌寫本神會和尚遺著兩種
hsing (nature) 性
hsing (practice) 行
hsiu-hsi 脩習

Hsiu-hsin yao lun 脩心要論
hsiu nei-hsing 脩內行
Hsü kao-seng chuan 續高僧傳
hsü-yü 須臾
hsüeh 學
hua-i ssu chiao 化儀四教
Hua-t'ai 滑臺
Hua-yen 華嚴
Huai-hai 懷海
hui 慧 and 惠
Hui-kuan 慧觀
Hui-k'o 慧可
Hui-neng 慧能
Hung-jen 弘忍
huo-jan 豁然
i-chan 一斬
i-chih hsin 一直心
i-hsing san-mei 一行三昧
i-shih 一時
ju 如
Ju-tao an-hsin yao fang-pien fa-men 入道安心要方便法門
k'an 看
k'an ching 看淨
k'an-hsin 看心
k'an-hua ch'an 看話禪
kōan 公案
Kōshōji 興聖寺
kuan 觀
kuan-ch'a 觀察
kuan hsin 觀心
Kuan-hsin lun 觀心論
kuan-hsin shih 觀心釋
kuan-shih 觀釋
Kuan wu-liang shou ching 觀無量壽經
k'uang 礦 or 鑛
Leng-ch'ieh shih-tzu chi 楞伽師資記
li 離
li nien 離念
Li-tai fa-pao chi 歷代法寶記
li tse 理則
lou 漏
Miao-fa lien-hua ching hsüan-i 妙法蓮華經玄義
Mo-ho chih-kuan 摩訶止觀
Mo-ho-yen 摩訶衍
Nan T'ien-chu kuo P'u-t'i Ta-mo Ch'an-shih kuan men 南天竺國菩提達摩禪師觀門
nan-tsung tun-chiao 南宗頓教
nei chao 內照
nei cheng 內證
nei-hsing 內行
nei-wai chao 內外照
nien 念
nien-ch'i 念起
ning 凝
Ninyūshigyōron 二入四行論
p'an-chiao 判教
Pao-t'ang 保唐
Pei-tsung ta-sheng wu-sheng fang-pien men 北宗大乘無生方便門
pen 本
pen-hsing 本性
pen-lai 本來
pen-lai wu i wu 本來無一物
pen-tzu 本自
Pien-chung-pien-lun 辯中邊論
ping hsiao 併銷
P'o-hsiang lun 破相論
P'u-chi 普寂
pu-erh fa-men 不二法門
P'u-hsien kuan ching 普賢觀經
pu-i 不意
pu-kuan 不觀
pu-nien 不念
pu-ssu 不思
p'u-t'i (bodhi) 菩提
pu-tso-i 不作意
Rekidaihōbōki 歷代法寶記
Rokuso daishi hōbō-dankyō 六祖大師法寶壇經
Ryōgashijiki 楞伽師資記
san-chung chiao hsiang 三種教相
san-mei 三昧
she 攝
she hsin nei chao 攝心內照
shen hsiang 身相

Shen-hsiu 神秀
Shen-hui 神會
Shidō Bunan 至道無難
shih (facts, factual, relative; in fact, in practice) 事
shih (consciousness) 識
Shih ch'an po-lo-mi tz'u-ti fa-men 釋禪波羅密次第法門
shih-hsing 識性
shih-ting 識定
shou chen-hsin 守眞心
shou-i 守一
Ssu-ch'uan 四川
sui ching-chieh liu 隨境界流
Ta-mo yü-lu 達摩語錄
Ta pan-nieh-p'an ching 大般涅槃經
Ta-sheng ju-tao tz'u-ti 大乘入道次第
Ta-sheng ju-tao tz'u-ti k'ai chüeh 大乘入道次第開決
Ta-sheng k'ai-hsin hsien-hsing tun-wu chen-tsung lun 大乘開心顯性頓悟眞宗論
Ta-sheng wu-sheng fang-pien men 大乘無生方便門
Ta-yün ssu 大雲寺
T'an-k'uang 曇曠
T'an-yü 壇語
tao-ch'ang 道場
Tao-hsin 道心
Tao-sheng 道生
tao-t'i 道體
te-pu-te hsin 得不得心
t'i 體
T'ien-t'ai 天臺
T'ien-t'ai ssu-chiao i 天臺四教義
ting 定
tsai tso 在坐
tso-ch'an 坐禪
tso hsiu ting 坐脩定
tso-i 作意
Tsui-shang sheng lun 最上乘論
tsung 宗
Tsung-mi (Kuei-feng) 宗密(圭峯)
tu 度
tun 頓
tun-chiao 頓教
Tun-huang 敦煌
Tun-huang lun-chi 敦煌論集
tun-men p'ai 頓門派
tun-wu 頓悟
Tun-wu ta-sheng cheng-li chüeh 頓悟大乘正理決
Tun-wu yao-men 頓悟要門
tung 動
tung nien 動念
Tung-shan 洞山
tzu-jan 自然
tzu-shih (from right now) 自是
tz'u-ti 次第
wai chao 外照
wai-tao 外道
Wan-ling lu 宛陵錄
wang-hsin 妄心(亡心)
wu-chi k'ung 無旣空 or 無記空
wu chiao 五教
wu chung 五種
Wu fang-pien 五方便
Wu fang-pien men 五方便門
wu-hsiang (formless, without marks) 無相
wu-hsiang (nonconceptual) 無想
wu-hsin 無心
Wu-hsin lun 無心論
wu-i 無意
Wu-liang-shou kuan ching 無量壽觀經
wu-nien 無念
wu-ssu 無思
wu-tso 無作
wu-wei 無爲
yen tso 宴坐
yin ting fa hui 因定發惠
yü-lu 語錄
Yüan-ho chün-hsien chih 元和郡縣志
Yüan ming lun 圓明論
yung 用
yung-hsin 用心
zazen 坐禅
Zekkanron 絕觀論
Zengen shosenshū tojo 禅源諸詮集都序

II

Sudden and Gradual Enlightenment in Chinese Buddhism

Tao-sheng's Theory of Sudden Enlightenment Re-examined

WHALEN LAI

The theory of sudden enlightenment—one of the main features of the Southern school of Ch'an—was first proposed by Tao-sheng (c. 360–434), who is also remembered for asserting the doctrine of a universal Buddha-nature. Since the Ch'an school espoused seeing one's nature *(chien-hsing)* in order to be suddenly enlightened *(tun-wu)* and thus to become a Buddha *(ch'eng-fo),* it has often been thought that Tao-sheng's position anticipated the later Ch'an development. For that reason, consideration of Ch'an sudden enlightenment should take into account what Tao-sheng had to say.

The period in which Tao-sheng lived is noted for its confluence of Buddhist and Taoist traditions. It was the time of *ko-i* or concept-matching, when Buddhist concepts were understood through the lens of Neo-Taoist ideas. It was also the time when the Mahāyāna doctrine of emptiness, expounded in the Perfection of Wisdom scriptures, took root in Chinese intellectual circles. This doctrine resonated with the Neo-Taoist concern with nothingness or nonbeing *(wu),* which had been articulated by Wang Pi (226–249). Some of the early theories of prajñā were thus informed by native tendencies, and Tao-sheng's doctrine of sudden enlightenment may, in part, be traced to his Neo-Taoist background. This fusion of traditions anticipates the later Ch'an rapprochement with Taoism, although strictly speaking these two encounters were different—the Buddhist accommodation to Taoism in the earlier period being from a standpoint of weakness whereas later it was from a position of strength. Still, sufficient similarities exist to warrant our attention to possible parallels. The theory of sudden enlightenment is one of these parallels.

In this chapter I examine the evolution of Tao-sheng's theory of sudden enlightenment, tracing how what began as a Hīnayāna-inspired idea matured in time, because of certain concerns unique to early fifth-century Buddhism, to approximate the Mahāyānist position found later in Ch'an. The possibly abhidharmic origin of Tao-sheng's subitism, the centrality of the one vehicle *(ekayāna)* versus three vehicles *(triyāna)* debate in polarizing subitists and gradualists into two camps, and the rather late entry of the *Nirvāṇa Sūtra*'s doctrine of universal Buddha-nature into Tao-sheng's final theory are some of the topics treated in this investigation. Because we shall, of necessity, return to some of the forgotten detours taken by Chinese Buddhists in the intellectual upheavals of the late fourth and early fifth centuries, the present study departs from the traditional equation of Tao-sheng's position with that of later Ch'an.[1]

The Neo-Taoist Background to Early Prajñā Speculations

Neo-Taoist *hsüan-hsüeh* (dark learning) provided the basis for Chinese reflection on Buddhist mysteries. As a reaction against the tedious *ming-chiao* (teaching of names) elements in Han Confucianism, Neo-Taoism sought to discover the "dark principle" *(hsüan-li)* lying within phenomena. Thus Wang Pi in his commentary on the *I-ching* celebrated the ever-present reality of the one within the manifested function of the many. Likewise, in his commentary on the *Lao-tzu,* he emphasized the underlying substance *(t'i)* in all existents, discerning nonbeing as the basis of the myriad beings.

By so devaluating the world of forms or appearances, Wang Pi attempted to delve directly into the realm of transcendental meaning. "Upon getting the meaning *(i),*" he said, "one may forget the forms" (in this context, the emblems or *hsiang* in the *I-ching*). In this approach surface meanings are scanned in order to penetrate to the hidden principle within. This approach was also shared by the poet T'ao Ch'ien (365–427), whose autobiography, "The Life of Mr. Five Willows" *(Wu-liu hsien-sheng chuan),* plainly states how he, Five Willows, would "while reading a classic, never seek to understand the mere details." Instead, "when an insight seized him, he would so rejoice that he forgot even to sleep and neglected his meals."

Tao-sheng reflected the spirit of his time, in both thought and actions, perhaps more clearly than any other Buddhist devoted to prajñā. For that he was admired as a genius by some (and later by Ch'an enthusiasts) and also denounced as undisciplined by some of his more rule-abiding contemporaries. The monk Hui-lin's memorial essay on Tao-sheng captures his character with both economy and wit:

> Thus [Tao-sheng] put away all delusions and roamed freely at will. He found his abode in the essence, showing only its trace. In this way, he com-

prehended [the meaning of] all the sūtras and removed all his doubts. The principle of Buddhism (Śākyamuni) should be sought in ease and simplicity. What some regarded as [Tao-sheng's] "strange theories" somehow proved themselves to be timely and seasoned arguments. In this he lucidly exemplified the way of Lao-tzu and Chuang-tzu in extending the teaching of names, and the style of Hsiang Hsiu and Wang Pi in intuiting the heart of the mysteries.[2]

As Wang Pi was to the wisdom of Lao-tzu, Tao-sheng was to the prajñā of the Buddha. Tao-sheng's entry in the *Biographies of Eminent Monks (Kao-seng chuan)* describes his Neo-Taoist approach to the sūtras:

[Tao-]sheng pondered long in private until he awoke to "what is beyond words." He sighed deeply and said, "Forms exist to reveal their meaning. When the meaning is clear, forms can be discarded. Words are used to convey the principle. When the principle is clear, all words cease. Now, ever since these sūtras came east, translators have been hampered by obstacles. Most of them stick to the literal meaning, and few ever see the complete meaning. However, it is only when one can drop the trap and grab the fish that one can finally speak of the Tao."[3]

Tao-sheng's metaphor is taken from Wang Pi's *Explication of the Principle of the Chou I (Chou I lüeh-li)*, itself based on a passage from the *Chuang-tzu*:

Words exist to explicate forms. When one understands the forms, the words can be forgotten. Forms exist to embody the meaning. When one has the meaning, the forms can be forgotten. This is comparable to the snare existing for the sake of catching the rabbit. Having caught the rabbit, one can forget the snare. The trap is there to catch fish. Having caught the fish, one can forget the trap. . . . Therefore the one who can forget the words is the one who has understood the forms, and the one who can forget the forms is the one who has attained the meaning. Attaining the meaning lies in forgetting the form. Gaining the form lies in forgetting the words.[4]

In Buddhism the equivalent statement is that when one reaches the other shore, one leaves the raft behind. In the same spirit Tao-sheng applied to the sūtras the standard Buddhist hermeneutical principle: "Rely on the dharma, not the person; on the sūtra that fully exposes the meaning, not the one that does not; on the meaning, not the words; on wisdom, not [received] opinion."[5]

In his actions as well, Tao-sheng exemplified the freedom of spirit associated with Neo-Taoism. He paid no regard to the precept that monks should always sit on the ground, an Indian custom then being imposed in China, and he was not intimidated by the rule forbidding monks to eat past noon, as this passage from his biography indicates:

> Later [the Sung emperor] T'ai-tsu convened a meeting and joined the monks seated on the ground during the feast. When the monks began to be concerned about the time, the emperor remarked, "It is just starting on noon." Tao-sheng [who was present] added, "The sun adorns heaven and if heaven itself says that it's just starting on noon, who could deny it?" He then took up his bowl to eat, and all the others followed. Everyone was grateful that [Tao-sheng's] presence of mind had saved the day.[6]

It was this free thinker, then, who is credited with formulating the doctrine of sudden enlightenment. In the words of his biography:

> [Tao-sheng] then reflected on the doctrine of the highest and the mundane [truths], pondered cause and effect deeply, and came to the conclusion that "the good incurs no reward" and that "by sudden enlightenment, one becomes a Buddha."
>
> He also wrote treatises on "The Two Truths," "Buddha-nature as Future Acquisition" *(tang-yu)*, "Dharmakāya as Formless," "Buddha Has No Pure Land," "Response Requiring Condition," and so on, thus subsuming previously established items under [his own] profound principle. But as those who kept literally to the words of the scriptures were offended, contentious voices rose here and there.[7]

In the sections that follow we will seek to unravel the history of that contention.

The Basic Argument for Sudden Enlightenment

Given Tao-sheng's Neo-Taoist leanings, it may not be difficult for a historian to see how he came to the subitist position. Tao-sheng himself, however, surely regarded subitism as rooted in the words or, better, the intention of the sūtras themselves.

To Tao-sheng, Wang Pi's nonbeing was nothing other than the emptiness of all forms proclaimed in the Perfection of Wisdom sūtras, and the oneness of principle elaborated in Wang Pi's commentary on the *I-ching* was another expression of the nondual dharma at the heart of the *Vimalakīrti Sūtra*. Similarly, the discontinuity between the world of being and the domain of nonbeing recapitulated the inevitable discontinuity between saṃsāra and nirvāṇa in the Hīnayāna framework as well as the Mahāyāna distinction between the worldly and the ultimate, the discursive and the nondiscursive, truths. Tao-sheng also used the image of the mind as a mirror to argue for the totality, or suddenness, of the mind's reflection of the truth; this metaphor was common to both Buddhists and Taoists, as Demiéville has demonstrated in his essay "Le miroir spirituel."[8] Moreover, a parallel was drawn between the Buddha-nature concept and native notions of innate sagehood. To realize this a priori germ within oneself meant to awaken immediately to one's Buddhahood or sagehood. All these arguments can be found scattered here and there in Tao-sheng's writings.

Unfortunately, nothing containing a sustained argument for subitism has been preserved in Tao-sheng's writings. We have only his allusions to it and recollections by others. The most complete statement on sudden enlightenment may be the few lines in Tao-sheng's preface to the "Southern text" of the *Nirvāṇa Sūtra,* a rewording of the Dharmakṣema translation by Hui-kuan (363–443) and others some time after 430. Tao-sheng contributed the preface before his death in 434. There he states tersely:

> The true principle is *tzu-jan* [Taoist naturalness, spontaneity; Buddhist suchness]. Enlightenment occurs when one is mysteriously united with it. Since the truth allows no variance, how can enlightenment involve stages? The unchanging essence is always quiescent and shining [*chao* 'reflecting', as a mirror does]. It is only because of the delusions obscuring it that it appears to be beyond our reach.[9]

This passage affirms the indivisibility of principle, the absolute with which the enlightened mind totally fuses. The truth being indivisible, it follows that enlightenment also must occur "at once," that is, without gradations. Moreover, since the permanent essence lies within man, it is identical with the Buddha-nature.

This is perhaps the most radical part of Tao-sheng's theory, and the closest to Ch'an. The implicit connection with the doctrine of Buddha-nature was a position that Tao-sheng reached only toward the end of his life. Although it is sometimes taken by scholars to represent the basis of Tao-sheng's theory of sudden enlightenment, as if his subitism were derived primarily from the *Nirvāṇa Sūtra,* a historical reconstruction of how Tao-sheng's subitism evolved shows this not to be the case.

That the theory of sudden enlightenment did not originally involve any reference to, or require as its support, the doctrine of universal Buddha-nature is well demonstrated by Hsieh Ling-yün's (385–433) defense of Tao-sheng's subitism in his *Pien tsung lun* (On Distinguishing the Goal), composed as late as 422–423, a decade before Tao-sheng's death. Here there is no mention of the universal Buddha nature or of the eligibility of the *icchantika* (an incorrigible altogether lacking the seed of enlightenment) for eventual Buddhahood even though the shorter version of the *Nirvāṇa Sūtra* that condemned the *icchantika* to eternal ignorance had been translated by Fa-hsien and Buddhabhadra in the southern capital between 416 and 417.

That the *Nirvāṇa Sūtra* was not crucial to Tao-sheng's early subitism is also borne out in the accounts of his position by the monk Hui-ta, the layman Liu Ch'iu (438–495), and the San-lun master Chi-tsang (549–

623). The reference to subitism in Hui-ta's commentary on the *Chao-lun* underlines its connection with the prajñā tradition:

> Sudden enlightenment means that the realization of principle cannot itself be divided and that enlightenment must refer to a total illumination *(chao)*. The merging of that nondual awakening with the indivisible wisdom whereby both principle [object] and wisdom [subject] dissolve [into one] is the achievement of sudden enlightenment.[10]

Hui-ta's account makes it seem as if the doctrine of emptiness might have been an important source of Tao-sheng's early subitism. Yet this too proves not to be the case, for subitism turns out to be tangential to Tao-sheng's commentary on the *Vimalakīrti Sūtra,* the date of which, as we will see below, is fairly late.

A better indication of how the subitist-gradualist controversy began is instead found in Tao-sheng's commentary on the *Lotus Sūtra*, and Liu Ch'iu's preface to the *Wu-liang-i ching* gives oblique, but telling, mention of this more decisive connection:

> The [eightfold] noble path may arrive at nirvāṇa, but by itself does not constitute arhatship. The six perfections may reach to Buddhahood, but by themselves do not yet attain [the rank of] the king of the bodhi-tree. It is like splitting wood. As long as an inch is left, one can still halve it. Verification of the unborn depends on total cessation of being. So illumination *(chao)* cannot be piecemeal.[11]

Although the vocabulary here might still suggest ties with the prajñā tradition, the denial of stages of advancement to Buddhahood points to arguments associated specifically with the one vehicle versus three vehicles debate.

But there is a still more primitive stratum to Tao-sheng's subitism, and this is what is remembered by the San-lun master Chi-tsang in his *Erh-ti lun* (Treatise on the Two Truths):

> The first of the karmic due is in the realm of change and death (saṃsāra). Saṃsāra is the domain of the great dream. From birth through death up to the stage of the diamond-like concentration *(vajra-samādhi),* all is nothing but a dream. After [the stage of] the diamond-like concentration, there is suddenly spacious enlightenment, and nothing is left to be unveiled.[12]

Surprisingly, this passage, when subjected to scrutiny, reveals an abhidharmic origin to Tao-sheng's subitism.

Tao-sheng's Stay in Lu-shan and the *Abhidharma-hṛdaya*

There are three well-known moments in Tao-sheng's career, each associated with a key Mahāyāna corpus. The shape of his career can thus be described as a passage from the Perfection of Wisdom, through the *Lotus Sūtra*, to the *Nirvāṇa Sūtra.* Eventually Tao-sheng was to become known for fusing the three teachings of emptiness, the one vehicle, and Buddha-nature.

The emptiness philosophy came first. When Tao-sheng entered the order, he did so under a famous early exponent of prajñā, Fa-t'ai. After a first stay at Lu-shan, he studied under Kumārajīva at Ch'ang-an and acquired an appreciation of the one vehicle doctrine of the *Lotus Sūtra.* When the *Nirvāṇa Sūtra* was brought back to China by Fa-hsien, Tao-sheng embarked on the third and most famous phase of his career, espousing a doctrine of the universal Buddha-nature even before the full text of the sūtra arrived in the southern capital in 430.

Between the first and second phase, however, came the often overlooked Hīnayāna detour that Tao-sheng and his contemporaries took during his initial stay at Lu-shan with Hui-yüan (344–416). Hui-lin reminds us here:

> In his middle years, [Tao-sheng] traveled about to learn [from various masters] and widely collected new ideas from the Yang area in the south in Ch'in, ascending Mount Lu as well as the Fo ranges. He knew well the Mahāyāna principle of Kumārajīva and equally well the essentials of Deva's lesser way.[13]

"Deva" here does not refer to Aryadeva, the "lesser" Mādhyamika master, but to Saṅghadeva, a master of the "lesser way," or Hīnayāna. That Tao-sheng was at one time an abhidharmist has been confirmed by the list of Saṅghadeva's disciples in the *Ming-seng chuan chao.*[14]

Saṅghadeva introduced abhidharmic learning to the Buddhists in the south. So effective was he that for a decade or so Abhidharma was considered by many to be the higher teaching (abhi-dharma) and the Vaipulya sūtras—that is, the Mahāyāna Perfection of Wisdom tradition itself—were denounced as works of the devil.[15] That judgment was not reversed until Kumārajīva launched his counterattack.

Meanwhile, Tao-sheng was studying at Lu-shan, where in 391 Saṅghadeva had translated the *Abhidharma-hṛdaya,* to which Hui-yüan had contributed a preface. That the circle around Hui-yüan took the new teachings seriously can be seen from Hui-yüan's later exchange with Kumārajīva.[16] In 395, Hui-yüan wrote the *San-pao lun* (On the Three Kinds of Retribution), which classifies karmic retribution according to the abhidharmic scheme of recompense in the present life, in the next life, and in future lives. It also contains, I believe, the essential elements of the two theses of Tao-sheng, namely, that "doing good incurs no reward" and "by sudden enlightenment one becomes a Buddha."

Concerning the relationship between enlightenment and karmic progress, Hui-yüan writes:

> The arousal of good and evil [deeds] is due to its possession of gradual attributes. If one thoroughly analyses this gradual progress, it leads to the theory of the nine grades. Whoever attains the ninth grade suffers no further karmic retribution in the present life. How this works is not something that common men may know. The highest attainment, lying beyond all nine grades, does not admit of any of the three types of retribution.[17]

Here the discourse is on the graded nature of cause and effect. As long as we are unenlightened, we suffer grades of karmic retribution. Only the liberated one who transcends even the ninth grade is free from all karmic cause and effect. When later Tao-sheng proposed that "the good incurs no reward," he was reiterating the statement in Hui-yüan's last sentence above.

Although Hui-yüan does not use the word "sudden" in the ensuing description of a man who has attained transcendental wisdom, the sense of a "leap" is nevertheless clearly conveyed:

> The guest who abides beyond the bounds of the world *(fang-wai chih pin)* adheres closely to the wondrous dharma. He purifies his mind at the gate of mystery. In a single response, he leaps to the highest seat. For the likes of him, even if [karmic] calamities have been accumulated, no further effort is required to combat them. Somehow in principle [karma] cancels itself out—something not comprehended as part of the three kinds of retribution.[18]

This passage already contains the seed of Tao-sheng's early subitism.

That Hui-yüan's discussion is indebted to the *Abhidharma-hṛdaya* is shown by its reference to a scheme of "nine grades." This scheme has nothing to do with the nine grades in the *Kuan wu-liang ching.*[19] The "nine grades" pertains to a series of nine steps by which various mental defilements *(kleśa),* categorized with respect to the three realms *(dhātu)* of desire *(kāma),* form *(rūpa),* and formlessness *(arūpa),* are removed. In accordance with the four fruits of the stream-winner, once-returner, nonreturner, and arhat, different layers of these defilements are shed. Willeman's translation of the *Hṛdaya* offers this relevant passage:

> Not yet having renounced the desire of the realm of desires, they progress toward the first fruit [of the stream-winner]. Having abandoned six [afflictions, *kleśa*], they progress to the second one. Progress is made toward the third when the nine are pure.[20]

The nonreturner is the third fruit. He removes the ninth and final layer of defilement and suffers no more retribution in the present life. Because he is subject to birth in one of the Brahma-heavens in his next life, from where he then enters nirvāṇa, he is not totally free of all retribution (i.e., he still has a "future retribution"). Only the arhat of the fourth fruit, whose achievement transcends the nine grades, is free from all three types of retributions—those of the present life, the next life, and future lives.

When Hui-yüan speaks of the cessation of retribution as being beyond the knowledge of common men, he is referring to the discrete nature of the four fruits. At every plateau in that fourfold ascent, the afflictions associated with the prior plateau are annihilated for good. The *Hṛdaya* explains such moments of discontinuity:

> [The text reads:] That [the affliction] which is destroyed is disconnected. Its attainment is comprised within one fruit. [It means:] In the immediate path and the path of deliverance, there one obtains the destruction of the afflictions, but at the moment of attainment of a fruit, all afflictions are destroyed, and one attains one fruit which is disconnected.[21]

The removal of defilements (*kleśa;* "afflictions" in Willeman's translation) or, in Hui-yüan, the cessation of all karmic burdens culminates in the fourth and final fruit. Whereas the nonreturner of the third fruit still has to remove impure karma by cultivating pure deeds, the arhat must also remove even the pure, since nirvāṇa transcends all karmic deeds.

This abandoning of all karma, as the *Hṛdaya* clearly states, comes about suddenly:

> [The text says:] One must say that that which is not defiled is extinguished by the ninth one. [It means:] We have said that the afflictions are extinguished by a ninefold path, but that which is not defiled is abandoned by the ninth immediate path in one moment, not gradually.[22]

What the *Hṛdaya* here styles as "in one moment" Hui-yüan's *San-pao-lun* rephrases as "in a single response." Tao-sheng simply says "suddenly."

Tao-sheng's early subitism, then, was by no means Mahāyāna-inspired. Rather, his statement that "by sudden enlightenment one becomes a Buddha," because it is always associated with the statement that "the good incurs no reward," was initially a refinement of Hui-yüan's thesis on the nature of retribution. Since the ultimate good (enlightenment) is attained by a sudden cutting-off of all karma, pure as well as impure, it can incur no further karmic reward. Tao-sheng's statement that the good receives no reward is therefore not about doing good for goodness' sake. It is not, that is, a criticism of his contemporaries who did good only in hope of reward, as is sometimes argued.[23]

The *Daśabhūmika* and the Hierarchy of the Three Vehicles

Indirectly, through Hui-yüan, the Saṅghadeva-translated *Hṛdaya* might have inspired the youthful Tao-sheng to formulate a subitist position, but that "strange theory," even as it drew attention to itself, could not have triggered any heated debate. Hui-yüan would not have disagreed, and the Hui-kuan who later led the gradualist camp, himself a student of Saṅghadeva and well versed in abhidharma, could not have had any cause to have disputed it either. That being the case, what finally drove the fellow-students Tao-sheng and Hui-kuan apart?

The answer lies in the dual meaning of the word *tun* in the expression *tun-wu* as the subitists construed it—namely, that enlightenment is both sudden in approach and total in impact. The gradualist argument is not only that there is a progressive series of stages leading up to enlightenment but that enlightenment itself admits of gradations. It was this second thesis that brought the subitist-gradualist debate into the open. And at that point, more than the *Hṛdaya* was involved.

The *Hṛdaya,* even as it accepts the arhat's transcendence of the nine grades and the three realms, never says that there cannot be a deepening of understanding after attaining that immediate moment of freedom. In fact, the abhidharmic tradition maintains that the superknowledges are attained one at a time. The first such knowledge is simply the verification that indeed all the passions have been extinguished:

> [The text says:] After the diamond-like concentration, one is sure to obtain the knowledge of extinction. [It means:] Diamond-like concentration is called the last thought of one in training, the ninth immediate path at the moment of renouncing desire in the sphere of the neither-perception-nor-non-perception. There all afflictions are completely destroyed for evermore. Because all noble deeds have ended, it is called diamond-like samādhi. After this, one produces the first knowledge of one who has no more training to do: the knowledge of extinction.[24]

The diamond-like concentration *(vajra-samādhi)* is the last step in the eightfold noble path, right concentration. The attribute "diamond-like," referring to the cutting edge of this hardest of all gems, figures also in Mahāyāna and tantric meditation later. The subitist position, as recalled by Chi-tsang, admits of this diamond-like concentration: "From birth through death up to the stage of the diamond-like concentration, all is nothing but a dream. After the diamond-like concentration, there is suddenly spacious enlightenment."[25] Beyond this stage, there is indeed no more training or cultivation. On this, gradualist and subitist agreed.

However, the question remains whether there can or cannot be further enlightenment. The arhat might know he is liberated, but he has not yet acquired the full range of superknowledges. He might have knowledge of the four noble truths, but in both wisdom and status he is inferior to the pratyekabuddha, who is sometimes said to have complete cognition of the twelve-linked chain of dependent origination. And the achievements of both arhat and pratyekabuddha still fall far short of the perfection of the unexcelled, complete enlightenment attained only by the supremely enlightened Buddha. To say there is no distinction between these three types is to deny the reality of the three vehicles. Before Kumārajīva explained the implication of the one vehicle doctrine of the *Lotus Sūtra,* there was no cause even for Tao-sheng to have argued for one homogeneous and progress-free enlightenment.

What was then available as a model for classifying the achievements of the three vehicles was the ten-stage scheme proposed in the *Daśabhūmika-sūtra.* In the evolution of the bodhisattva doctrine in India, the six perfections scheme considered the sixth and final perfection, that of wisdom *(prajñā-pāramitā),* to be superior to the limited virtues of the arhat. The bodhisattva is one who can perceive in his final state of wisdom the identity of saṃsāra and nirvāṇa whereas the misguided arhat knows only of their opposition. Later, the six perfections were expanded into a set of ten, and the knowledge of emptiness at the sixth stage was surpassed by a tenth perfection that was a more intellectual wisdom known as *jñāna-pāramitā,* reserved for the tenth-stage bodhisattva.[26] This ten-stage scheme posited either the seventh or the eighth stage *(bhūmi)* as the point of demarcation between the arhat and the bodhisattva.[27] Before the time of Tao-sheng, Chih Tun (Tao-lin) (314–366) had already employed this ten-stage scheme to distinguish the Hīnayānist, who finds his liberation from saṃsāra at the sixth stage, from the Mahāyānist, who discovers that saṃsāra is nirvāṇa at the seventh stage. It is at the latter stage that the bodhisattva realizes *anupattikadharma-kṣanti,* a uniquely Mahāyāna prajñā insight, the recognition of the nonarising of all realities. Here, saṃsāra and nirvāṇa are perceived as nondual, there being neither any real arising nor any destruction of dharmas. The Chinese preferred to style this the "simultaneous perception of being and nonbeing" *(yu-wu hsiang-kuan),* an expression that reappears in later Ch'an discussions.[28]

Chih Tun was later called a "minor subitist" because he regarded this recognition of the unborn at the seventh stage to be supreme wisdom, as it already contains *in potentia* the attainments of the eighth, ninth, and tenth stages. The latter three only lend clarity to the nondual truth perceived at the seventh.

Kumārajīva used the ten-stage scheme to formulate a different categorization of the three vehicles. In his correspondence with Hui-yüan in 403, Kumārajīva considered the three vehicles to share a common career up to the seventh stage. The eighth then became the cut-off point; this is where the bodhisattva is found. The pratyekabuddha, by occupying the ninth, and the Buddha, the tenth, completed the set.[29] Although Kumārajīva's position is quite similar to Chih Tun's, later commentators deferred to Kumārajīva and classified him as a "major subitist" while crediting Hui-yüan with being a "minor subitist."[30] Historically, though, the innovation of a radical theory of sudden enlightenment that would eliminate the nine grades and the ten stages and consider enlightenment to be attained in its totality "in one step" came only with Tao-sheng.

The *Lotus Sūtra* and the Public Controversy

Tao-sheng, however, could not have advanced his subitist theory without the aid of Kumārajīva. Still, it is not the Kumārajīva who introduced the Mādhyamika philosophy who inspired subitism. Nothing in Kumārajīva's, and very little in Tao-sheng's, commentary on the *Vimalakīrti* suggests subitism.[31] Rather, Tao-sheng's subitism derives from Kumārajīva's explanation of the one vehicle doctrine of the *Lotus Sūtra* in the *Ta-chih-tu lun*.

Although the *Lotus* had already been translated in 290 by Dharmarakṣa, the implication of its position in regard to the question of one versus three vehicles went almost unnoticed by the fourth-century prajñā theorists. The *Shih-shuo hsin-yü* states that only Chih Tun understood what it meant:

> On the distinction among the "Three Vehicles" *(san-sheng)* the Buddhists are confused in their interpretation, but Chih Tun's discussion and definition made all three brilliantly distinct. . . . It appears that [others] could barely get through the first two. When they entered the third they became confused.[32]

Even Chih Tun's understanding was limited, however, for it appears that he only subsumed Hīnayāna under Mahāyāna by way of the ten stages.

In 406 Kumārajīva translated the *Lotus Sūtra,* and his version, the *Miao-fa lien-hua ching,* has been accepted as definitive by East Asian Buddhists ever since. A prologue appended to the translation by Seng-jui (Hui-jui) (352–436) notes that for the first time the true meaning of the true dharma was revealed. One of the challenges of the one vehicle doctrine involved the sūtra's claim that an arhat may become a Buddha. In other words, the *Lotus* holds that the destiny of the śrāvaka (listener) is not predetermined. Instead of mere arhatship, it is possible for him to attain Buddhahood. This idea is elaborated in the so-called parable of the prodigal son: the poor ascetic son, symbolizing the śrāvaka, has to be told that he is heir to the wealth of the Buddha, the father he could not recognize and whose wealth he dared not enjoy before.

This parable implies that the traditional distinction of the seed-lineages *(gotra)* of the three vehicles doctrine is being repealed. If the *śrāvaka-gotra* is no longer fixed and can change into *buddha-gotra,* the lineages of arhat, pratyekabuddha, and bodhisattva are not inalterably distinct. In reality, there are not even three vehicles. There is really only one vehicle, one seed-lineage, one destiny for all—what the *Nirvāṇa Sūtra* would later refer to as the universal Buddha-nature. Kumārajīva had already emphasized the *Lotus Sūtra*'s one vehicle doctrine in his translation-and-compilation, the *Ta-chih-tu lun,* the year before. There he rated the "teaching of the secret Tathāgata-store" higher than even the bodhisattva vehicle of the Perfection of Wisdom itself.[33] It was in this one vehicle doctrine, then, that Tao-sheng found a Mahāyāna principle that would eradicate the tedious nine grades and ten stages. The subitist debate became heated with Tao-sheng's commentary on the *Lotus.*

Unfortunately, Tao-sheng's commentary is not dated. We know that Tao-sheng and Hui-kuan arrived in Ch'ang-an around 405, when news of Kumārajīva's arrival was related by Yao Hsing to Hui-yüan, who dispatched the pair to study with the Kuchan monk. Tao-sheng thus could not have written his commentary until some time after. We do not know when he began work on his commentary, but in 429, when he was expelled from the Buddhist community in Ch'ang-an, he returned to Lu-shan and resumed work on this text. Although we have only this revised version, I believe that its discussion of subitism and the one vehicle doctrine remains largely unchanged from the earlier version. This is because Tao-sheng talks about sudden and gradual without explicitly referring to either sudden enlightenment *(tun-wu)* or gradual enlightenment *(chien-wu).* The subitist elements in the commentary thus remain fairly rudimentary. Tao-sheng does not use the term "Buddha-nature" even when commenting on a passage in the sūtra dealing with the Buddha's omniscience *(buddha-jñāna).* This item is singled out by Seng-jui and all subsequent authorities to justify the claim that Kumārajīva had foreknowledge of the Buddha-nature doctrine and that the *Lotus Sūtra* is consistent with the *Nirvāṇa Sūtra.*

It would thus appear that Tao-sheng only polished his earlier draft and did not substantially revise it to bring it into accord with his more recent thinking. Furthermore, there are indications that Seng-chao (374–414), defending gradualism, rebutted in 413 what Tao-sheng hinted at in this commentary. If so, we can date the core of this work between 406 and 413.

In the commentary, Tao-sheng speaks of a series of four turnings of the wheel of dharma. Often taken to be the first doctrinal classification *(p'an-chiao)* system in China, it describes the last two turnings as follows:

> The third is the dharma wheel of the true and real, aimed at the destruction of the false construct of the three vehicles and completing the beauty that is the one [vehicle]. For this reason, it is called the true and real [as opposed to the expedient and provisional]. The fourth is the dharma wheel of no residue. This is the discoursing on the return to a union, the wondrous principle of permanence. For that reason, it is called no residue.[34]

Easily mistaken as a characterization of the *Lotus* and *Nirvāṇa* sūtras, these two wheels actually refer to the second and sixteenth chapters—those on upāya and the lifespan of the Tathāgata—of the *Lotus Sūtra* itself. In one, the expediency of the three vehicles and the reality of the one vehicle are revealed. In the other, the unending life of the Buddha is proclaimed. The reference to a principle of "permanence" was probably added by Tao-sheng after 429 to make his comments consistent with the doctrine of the permanence of the Buddha-nature in the *Nirvāṇa Sūtra*. Otherwise, Tao-sheng associated the eternity of the Buddha with "nirvāṇa without karmic residue"—a Hīnayāna misnomer, the same one that appears in Seng-chao's essay *Nieh-p'an wu-ming lun* (Nirvāṇa Is Nameless), dating from the same period and concerning which more will be said in a moment.

In Tao-sheng's commentary we find the theme of the one principle that permits no piecemeal recognition.

> The sūtra has as its principle Mahāyāna. By Mahāyāna is meant the great wisdom of selfsameness. It may begin with one good [deed] but it ends in ultimate wisdom. By selfsameness is meant that principle *(li)* cannot entertain differences and that all things alike return to the one ultimate. By the great wisdom is meant the final goal.[35]

The Taoist ontological predilection for the one to which all must return reappears in Tao-sheng's subitism. But the admission of the one good deed as a means leading to the end of wisdom shows that he was still committed to the necessity of gradual cultivation.

More importantly, the words *hu* 'suddenly' and *tun* 'suddenly, all at once' appear in his description of the necessary turn from the expediency of the three vehicles to the one true vehicle. Tao-sheng was thus grafting his subitism onto the one vehicle teaching:

> The three vehicles follow external form, the manifestations of which run contrary to the essential principle. Those who are captivated with mere words and who choose to go contrary to the real, hidden intention are naturally taken aback by this Mahāyāna hymn. The Buddha, when he was about to reveal the *Lotus of the True Law,* first led people to it by a gentle discourse on its infinite meanings.[36]
>
> For those people who have long kept to outer manifestations, suddenly *(hu)* hearing that there are not in truth three vehicles all at once *(tun)* contradicts what they are fond of. Thus they are like those people [the Hīnayānists] who, though catching a glimpse of the promised shore, decide to turn back, thereby losing the great way [of Mahāyāna]. For that reason, the gradual *(chien)* [inducement by Hīnayāna] is necessary.[37]

According to Tao-sheng, Mahāyāna teaching is necessarily sudden in that it penetrates to the principle hidden within names and words.

Although Tao-sheng, in commenting on the *Lotus,* stresses the oneness of principle, he does not thereby deny the necessity of a progression by grades. In fact, the text employs the standard ten-stage scheme as its primary exegetical tool. For example, Tao-sheng locates the bodhisattva who does not backslide in the seventh stage and the bodhisattva of firm conviction in the eighth.[38] This is also how Tao-sheng explains why the future Buddha Maitreya could not recognize the superhuman bodhisattvas who welled out of the earth with promises to propagate the *Lotus Sūtra* in the evil age to come:

> Maitreya was unable to recognize any of them. This is because he did not have the insight of a bodhisattva of the tenth stage. Those who came out of the earth were still bodhisattvas and not yet Buddhas. This shows that the lot of the enlightened requires the accumulation of learning *(hsüeh)* until nonlearning *(wu-hsüeh)* is attained.[39]

Tao-sheng's belief in the possibility of pursuing learning until nonlearning is attained was a position he later repudiated.

Although he was familiar with the application of the ten stages in classifying the bodhisattvic approach to Buddhahood, Tao-sheng was not bound to any one scheme in the way his contemporaries were. Commenting on the passage in the *Lotus Sūtra* celebrating the omnipresence of the Buddha-wisdom, he writes:

> Sentient beings originally have their share of this Buddha-wisdom. However, because it is covered over by defilements, this wisdom cannot show itself. As the Buddha now helps to dispel such pollutants, it will realize itself. Some theories say that the gradual elimination of defilements occurs from the first to the seventh stage. . . . Others say that [people are awakened to wisdom] at the eighth stage when the bodhisattva, achieving samādhi, can now see the Buddha. . . . Still others say that only the ninth-stage bodhisattva has the superior wisdom to awake to the Buddha's

> omniscience, thereby entering [Buddhahood] itself. . . . There is still another theory that says only the tenth-stage bodhisattva perfects the diamond-like concentration that cuts off all defilements. . . . Broadly speaking, however, so long as the pilgrim becomes enlightened, these four theories are equally valid.[40]

But even as he accepted the need for, and even the validity of, some fixed categorization of progress such as the scheme of the ten stages, Tao-sheng ultimately believed that the one vehicle justifies only one way and one goal:

> [The sūtra], having shown the three vehicles as expedient, reveals the one vehicle [as true]. The Buddha is ultimately one. It is based on this one that [the three] appear, so how could the principle itself ever be three? Sages [Buddhas] can also appear as three [as śrāvaka, pratyekabuddha, and bodhisattva], but within principle, there cannot be three. There is only the wondrous one itself.[41]

The text goes on to note:

> The seed of Buddhahood may rise out of the conditions [of saṃsāra], but Buddhahood itself is based upon principle. As principle admits of no dualism, how could there be three [nirvāṇas]?[42]

Furthermore, the ultimate being one, the perception of the many is due to ignorance:

> Take, for example, the three thousand [world-spheres]. It is from contradicting principle that delusions arise, something that is always multiple and varying. Once this is realized, one always awakens to principle. Since the principle cannot be dual, and the Buddha discoursed only in terms of the one, it is man who has mistakenly taken it to refer to the three [vehicles]. The three are within the nature of things, but principle remains forever one. This is like the rain [in the parable of the *Lotus Sūtra*] being one while the flora [receiving it] are many. "Many" pertains to the flora; it was never intended for the rain.[43]

Tao-sheng's early reflections on the *Lotus Sūtra* left their mark on the subsequent subitist debate. The idea of "learning until nonlearning is attained" would reappear in Seng-chao's defense of gradualism. Hsieh Ling-yün would cite Tao-sheng's counterthesis in his *Pien tsung lun,* noting that "the accumulation of learning being endless, how could it be terminated by itself?" And Tao-sheng's comment that there cannot be three vehicles in the one principle would be repeated in almost identical wording in Seng-chao's 413 report on the subitist position.

The Gradualist Case: Hui-kuan's Dialectical Defense of Gradualism

Opposed to Tao-sheng was Hui-kuan, advocate of the gradualism of the three vehicles. Although the majority opinion of this time, gradualism eventually gave way to subitism when a new wave of subitist thinking surfaced in the late sixth century, and again in Ch'an. Since then, only fragments of Hui-kuan's once influential gradualist thesis survive.

That it was the one vehicle doctrine and not the philosophy of emptiness that precipitated the subitist controversy is shown by the fact that both subitists and gradualists used the dialectics of emptiness to defend their position. Tao-sheng took nonduality to mean monism, but Hui-kuan employed the neither/nor position of the Middle Path philosophy to refute monism. Since the nondual dharma *(pu-erh fa-men)* is the central theme of the *Vimalakīrti Sūtra,* the difference between a cautious and a liberal reading of the not-two position can be documented by contrasting the comments of Kumārajīva with those of Tao-sheng in the previously mentioned "joint commentary" on this sūtra.

Kumārajīva is cautious and noncommittal in this exchange found in his commentary:

> Question: Since there are also threes, fours, and so on up to an infinity of dharmas, why is there this exclusive interest in the not-two?
>
> Answer: Two is simpler and less perplexing. The [higher numbers] are extravagant and complicated. Once you negate the two, the rest can be taken care of similarly. Furthermore, all realities are born of conditions. The conditioned arisings may vary, but the least [number of] conditions that can exist is two. I have not seen any phenomenon that arises out of only a single cause. If the limiting case is two, then once the two are negated, a person can enter the realm of mystery, because all dharmas are capable of being subsumed under the dualistic mode.
>
> Question: Why not destroy the one also?
>
> Answer: If you regard [the not-two] as one, then [realize that] it is not one either. If you take it as one, then you have in fact not freed yourself from dualities [of the one and the many]. If you can [truly] abandon the two, the one disappears with it.[44]

Kumārajīva's concern here is to differentiate Mahāyāna nonduality from the Hindu belief in a single, universal substance by showing how the Buddhist notion of not-two does not entail reducing everything to one single cause.

Tao-sheng's reading, in contrast, is bold:

> As the person is awakened to its being one, all the myriad affairs can be solved. Therefore the one is the origin of all things.[45]

Less sensitive to the Hindu-Buddhist debates, Tao-sheng is concerned to align nonduality with the Neo-Taoist one principle. Yet we really cannot consider Tao-sheng to have derived his subitism from this reading of the nondual. Not only is subitism absent in his commentary on the *Vimalakīrti Sūtra,* but since the term Buddha-nature appears in one passage, this commentary must postdate the 416–417 translation of the *Nirvāṇa Sūtra.* By that time, his subitism had already been developed. That he did not even read subitism into this seemingly late commentary on the *Vimalakīrti* only shows that subitism was not perceived as being central to the nondual dharma of this sūtra.

Mādhyamika, however, could inspire a gradualist defense. Negative dialectics can justify how the same truth—form is emptiness—can be perceived differently by three parties. We see this in an essay suspected to be the *Chien-wu lun* (On Gradual Enlightenment)[46] attributed to Hui-kuan:

> Reality as it is is not to be taken as the one either. Rather, there can be three ways of different depths to understand emptiness [that is *dharmatā*]. . . . The Buddha sees fully the beginning and the end of the [conditioned, saṃsāric] chain; . . . his is the highest understanding of "form is emptiness". . . . The bodhisattva realizes the end [of the chain] but does not [have the omniscience to know] its beginning; his is the middle mode of understanding "form is emptiness." The two Hīnayāna vehicles realize only that life and death are due to the causal chain but do not know either its beginning or its end; . . . theirs is the lowest understanding of "form is emptiness." So the principle is indeed nondual, but one's ability to reflect *(chao)* it varies in degrees of keenness such that understanding of the causal chain may be complete or incomplete. Reality as it is *(dharmatā)* remains the same but the vehicles are nonetheless three.[47]

The fact that this *Chien-wu lun* fragment primarily defends the three vehicles and not gradualism per se underlines once more the centrality of the *Lotus Sūtra* in this debate. For Hui-kuan and many others, Mādhyamika supported gradualism, and the three vehicles position was entirely compatible with nondual emptiness and nondiscursive wisdom. This was a commendable solution to the problem of the one and the three.

But an even better defense of gradualism came from the master of the emptiness philosophy, Seng-chao, in his 413 essay entitled *Nieh-p'an wu-ming lun* (Nirvāṇa Is Nameless).

Seng-chao's Defense of Yao Hsing and Gradualism

Before turning to Seng-chao's essay, we must note a curious lacuna. If the subitist debate surfaced some time after 406, why was Kumārajīva never consulted? Much ink might have been saved, though possibly to the subitist's disadvantage.[48] Yet nowhere is that topic listed in the catalogues of correspondence between Kumārajīva and his various inquirers.[49] Is it possible that the controversy only arose after Kumārajīva's reported death in 412? But that seems unlikely since, when Seng-chao reported the positions of the two camps in 413, they seemed to have already had a history extending back more than a year.

If we accept Tsukamoto Zenryū's hypothesis that Kumārajīva actually died in 409, not in 412, we might then argue that the essay "Nirvāṇa Is Nameless" is a later forgery by someone borrowing Seng-chao's name. Unfortunately, both hypotheses have to be rejected. That there was a loss of momentum in the translation project after 409 can indeed be attributed to the stroke Kumārajīva suffered. Nevertheless, Tsukamoto has not yet proved that Kumārajīva did not translate (or at least preside over the translation of) Harivarman's *Ch'eng-shih lun* and other texts well into the second decade of the fifth century. Still, if we assume that Tao-sheng wrote his commentary on the *Lotus Sūtra* between 406 and 408, the year he brought Seng-chao's *Po-jo wu-chih lun* (Prajñā Is Noncognizing) back to Lu-shan, and that he refined his subitist reflections into a tract—perhaps the now lost *Tun-wu lun* (On Sudden Enlightenment)—some time after 409, it is entirely possible that Kumārajīva was not consulted because he was incapacitated.

Ōchō Einichi has refuted the claim that "Nirvāṇa Is Nameless" is a forgery.[50] And, if we understand the background to Seng-chao's pronouncements, it seems reasonable to suppose that the section on subitism and gradualism in "Nirvāṇa Is Nameless" is a later interpolation by someone else. The Later Ch'in ruler Yao Hsing had engaged Kumārajīva in an exchange on the meaning of Mahāyāna, but Kumārajīva's deteriorating health had brought it to a premature conclusion. Some years later Yao Hsing forwarded his somewhat dated thesis to his brother Yao Sung, marquis of An-yang. When Yao Sung expressed disagreement with Yao Hsing's position, Yao Hsing referred the case to Seng-chao for adjudication.[51]

Although the exchange between the two Yaos did not explicitly deal with subitism and gradualism, it did involve a subtle issue concerning the question of one versus three vehicles. Yao Hsing argued that the rays of light emitted by the Buddha in the opening chapters of many Mahāyāna sūtras are visible only to bodhisattvas of a certain level of accomplishment. Yao Hsing's theory seems to be related to a then current reading of the *Lotus Sūtra*. Tao-sheng's commentary also reports a contemporary opinion that limited the perception of the Buddha's light to bodhisattvas of the eighth bhūmi, the first stage at which their achievements are sufficiently close to the Buddha's enlightenment to permit them to see the light. Yao Sung argued to the contrary, citing sūtras, especially the *Lotus,* in which common people are also said to have witnessed the miracle. Yao Hsing countered by pointing to the Perfection of Wisdom tradition's distinction of the three vehicles. He then turned to Seng-chao for verification.

The outcome was predictable. Seng-chao was indeed no exponent of the one vehicle, and he makes scant reference to the *Lotus Sūtra* throughout the *Chao lun.* Recognizing that the Yaos were divided on the question of one versus three vehicles, Seng-chao referred to the contemporary subitist-gradualist debate to clarify his response. By showing up the folly of the subitist position, Seng-chao came to the aid of his king and patron, Yao Hsing.

Seng-chao pitted the monist argument of the subitist against the rationality of the three vehicles. He first cites the subitist claim that

> if nirvāṇa is one, then there cannot be three [vehicles]. If there are three, then they cannot have penetrated the [one] ultimate. How can there be gradations within enlightenment?[52]

"Gradations within enlightenment" (literally, "degrees of immersion")[53] is a reference to the parable of three animals crossing a river, suggesting how the three vehicles all arrive at the other shore. The śrāvaka, represented by a rabbit, swims across without touching the river bottom; his understanding is the shallowest. The pratyekabuddha, represented by a horse, bounces his way across, occasionally touching bottom; his insight is deeper. The bodhisattva has the most arduous task. Represented by the slowest animal, the elephant, he walks across, touching bottom all the way; his wisdom is the most profound. The parable thus illustrates how, although the other shore (nirvāṇa) may be the same, the depth of understanding of each of the three vehicles differs.

Seng-chao also turns the parable of the burning house in the *Lotus Sūtra* into a defense of the three vehicles.[54]

> In that [the vehicles] all deliver the sons out of saṃsāra, the vehicles are all said to be nirvāṇic. Because the riders are different, we call them three. In the end, they all meet in the one. As to your query how three could be derived from [the one] nirvāṇa, the answer lies in the riders. Three arrive at nirvāṇa. It is not that nirvāṇa itself is threefold. The *Fang-kuang* (Perfection of Wisdom in Eight Thousand Lines) denies any distinction within nirvāṇa. It is only that the Buddha has ended all the mental defilements

> whereas the śrāvaka has not. Take, for example, a man cutting wood. When he cuts off a foot, a foot is gone. When he cuts off an inch, an inch is gone. The shortening pertains to the measurement of foot and inch, but that has nothing to do with the nonbeing [at the end when all the wood is cut]. . . . [Therefore] the difference lies in the subject [i.e., in the depths of individual understanding and not in the common goal].[55]

But the subitist is not to be silenced that easily. He queries the gradualist on the relationship between rider and cart: how can there be three different types of selves walking the same nirvāṇic path?

> If [the rider and the cart are one], then you cannot argue that the distinction [of the three] lies in the selves and not in the nirvāṇic paths. If the self is not nirvāṇic, then it cannot be on the path. If [the rider and the cart are two], then it violates logic to say that a [saṃsāric] man is riding on the [nirvāṇic] path.[56]

Realizing that the point of contact between rider and vehicle is a difficulty in his argument, Seng-chao substitutes the more appropriate analogy of three birds that fly out of the same cage.

> All three [birds] are alike in escaping to where there is no more pain [of saṃsāric bondage]. Nevertheless, even as they are alike in being free, they remain different. You cannot say that just because the birds are different, their freedom is not the same, or, just because their freedom is the same, the [species of] birds are not different.[57]

As Hui-kuan had noted earlier, so now Seng-chao observes: nirvāṇa can be one without denying the not-one.[58]

The subitist then brings up the one principle that requires total, not partial, comprehension. We can almost hear Tao-sheng's voice here:

> It is said that nirvāṇa is the great way, where all things are the same and nondual. If it is nondual, it allows no variance of mind. So unless one embodies it, one cannot exhaust the most subtle of its depths. I do not see how you can propose that one can embody it without fully penetrating it.[59]

In reply, Seng-chao cites the opening chapter of the *Lao-tzu,* suggesting the perennial appropriateness of patience and humility:

> The sphere of emptiness is the realm of the mystery within the mystery *(chung-hsüan).* So boundless is its way, how is it possible to assume that it can be exhausted so quickly? Did not [Lao-tzu] say: "The man of learning increases day by day; the man of Tao decreases every day"? The student of the way is the seeker of nirvāṇa. To realize nirvāṇa, one practices daily decrease. Is that to be termed "sudden enlightenment"?[60]

Seng-chao's allusion to the *Lao-tzu* is a sobering reminder that Taoism never unambiguously supported either the subitist or the gradualist position. In fact, the *tun-chien* distinction was unknown to it.

Hsieh Ling-yün's Defense of Subitism

The subitist debate continued beyond Seng-chao. A decade later (422–423), Hsieh Ling-yün defended Tao-sheng's subitism in his *Pien tsung lun.* The following is Richard Mather's translation of the thesis.[61]

> In the discussions of the Buddhists [it is said]: "Although the way of the sage is remote, by accumulating learning one is able to attain it. Only after all bonds have been ended and illumination has been produced, ought one then gradually become enlightened." In the discussion of the Confucians, on the other hand [it is said]: "Since the way of the sage is subtle, even though [one is a] Yen [Hui], one is only 'almost' perfect. But if one embodies nonbeing and one's illumination is all-embracing, then [all] truth reveals the single ultimate."
>
> There is a monk [who has put forward] a "new thesis" which claims: "The silent illumination is extremely subtle and does not admit of any gradations. The accumulation of learning is endless, so how could it ever terminate itself?" [What I am proposing] now is to discard the "gradual enlightenment" of the Buddhists while accepting their "ability to attain," and to discard the "almost [perfect]" of the Confucians while accepting their "single ultimate." The "single ultimate" differs from "gradual enlightenment" [just as] "the ability to attain" is not the same as "almost [perfect]." Therefore, in the matter of what truth discards [of the two traditions], even though it accepts what agrees with it from each, nevertheless it departs from both the Confucians and the Buddhists. I think the pronouncements made by the two [traditions] are words with the intention of "saving beings." The claim put forward by the monk is a statement made for "getting the meaning." I would presume to permit myself to strike a compromise [between the two]. In my humble opinion, the "new theory" is the right one."[62]

What is most telling about Hsieh Ling-yün's thesis is that, in the end, "gradual enlightenment" is seen as an Indian character trait while the "sudden teaching" is claimed for the Chinese temperament:

> The Chinese find it easy to see the truth but difficult to receive instruction, so they are closed to the "repeated learning" but open to the "simple ultimate." Foreigners find it easy to receive instructions but difficult to see the truth, so they are closed to "sudden understanding" but open to "gradual enlightenment."[63]

By so construing the division along cultural lines, Hsieh in effect concedes that the subitist position has little known Indian scriptural support.

The *Pien tsung lun* deserves fuller treatment than is possible here.[64] For now, we need only note that nowhere in it do we find any mention of Buddha-nature. Since the *Nirvāṇa Sūtra* had been available since 416–417, one has to wonder why it was not cited to support the subitist argument as late as 422–423.

The Late Entry of the *Nirvāṇa Sūtra* Into the Debate

Neither Kumārajīva nor Seng-chao had any knowledge of the *Nirvāṇa Sūtra*.[65] Moreover, since the shorter version of this text brought back by Fa-hsien denied the *icchantika* any possibility of enlightenment, it is perhaps understandable that Tao-sheng and Hsieh Ling-yün did not appeal to it for support. The sūtra can only help the subitist theory if Buddha-nature is recognized as something universal and complete in itself, but as late as 426–428 Tao-sheng had not yet hit upon that idea. This can be inferred from a letter sent to Hui-kuan and Tao-sheng by Fan-t'ai, which discusses perceptual issues without ever mentioning a dispute over Buddha-nature or the fate of the *icchantika*.[66] At the time, it appears that Tao-sheng and Hui-kuan had only a friendly disagreement on sudden versus gradual enlightenment.

In 429 things changed. At the urging of Hui-kuan, Tao-sheng was expelled from the monastic community in Ch'ang-an for admitting the *icchantika* into the ranks of the enlightened in clear violation of the words of the Buddha as they were then known. Unlike the previous arguments over sudden and gradual, which could not be decided by appeal to scriptures and in which Tao-sheng found supporters, the *icchantika* controversy was one in which Tao-sheng was isolated—no one else was named in the banishment. Moreover, since the breach seems to have developed very quickly, we may infer that Tao-sheng voiced his opinion on the *icchantika* close to the year 429 itself.

I suspect that Tao-sheng initially proposed only a moderate doctrine of Buddha-nature as future acquisition *(tang-yu fo-hsing)*, that is, *icchantikas* do not have here and now the seed of enlightenment; rather, they acquire it in time as a future fruit *(tang-lai chih kuo)*.[67] That was enough to get Tao-sheng expelled. In the year 430, however, the longer version of the *Nirvāṇa Sūtra*, which had been translated in 422 by Dharmakṣema, finally reached the southern capital and the monks discovered that the sūtra had reversed itself by admitting the *icchantika* into the ranks of the enlightened. Now Tao-sheng, feeling vindicated, put forward the more radical thesis of the a priori possession of Buddha-nature *(pen-yu fo-hsing)*.[68] From this point on subitism was grounded in the doctrine of the universal Buddha-nature.

To recapitulate the evolution of this theory, we may note that previously Tao-sheng's idea of an "inner essence" had remained vague.[69] The first suggestion of it I find is in his commentary on the *Lotus Sūtra*, as related to the Buddha's omniscience:

> Sentient beings originally have their share of this Buddha-wisdom. . . . In order to show sentient beings the omniscience of the Buddha, they are

> told that they have an innate share of this wisdom. By this teaching, they achieve enlightenment. If enlightenment is due to teachings, then the sign comes from without. By that means they are awakened. Awakening, they enter the way.[70]

In this passage it is still not clear whether Tao-sheng's "wisdom" is an external means or an inner reality. A clearer statement had to await the *Pien tsung lun.*

Now it appears that the monk Hui-lin,[71] who wrote the memorial essay on Tao-sheng cited earlier, was critical of Hsieh's attempt to marry "sudden enlightenment" to the Chinese temperament and to attribute "gradual enlightenment" to India. To him, it was clear that Confucius (at least the Neo-Taoist version of him) and Śākyamuni taught both aspects:

> When Śākyamuni spoke of a gradual progression, he was taking the perspective of the mundane forms themselves [for the sake of common men]. When Confucius spoke of there being no gradual approach, he was [for the moment] assuming the standpoint of the Tao. How do I know that this is so? Because [at other times] Confucius spoke of "revering our superior nature *(hsing)* through practice." Śākyamuni spoke of the "union with enlightenment transcending even the two bhūmis." Thus, both sages alike had sudden and gradual teachings. What cause is there to charge India with only knowing [gradual] teachings and to prize China alone for having the [sudden] principle?[72]

Hsieh Ling-yün's response was to invoke the doctrine of Buddha-nature.

> Although Confucius did speak of "revealing the superior path" [to the above average], he still stressed "ungraded sagehood" more. Although Śākyamuni endorsed the "one unity" [beyond the bhūmis], he still stressed "sentient possession of Buddha-nature" more. Beings with Buddha-nature are destined [eventually] to return to the one refuge [of Buddhahood].[73]

Here it is clear that the possession of Buddha-nature, understood as the seed of enlightenment requiring time and effort to bear fruit, was thought to support gradualism. Only the last line, which affirms the growth of this seed into the fruit of Buddhahood, suggests a possible link with sudden enlightenment.

For the most part, Hsieh Ling-yün's advocacy of Tao-sheng's subitism did not rely on any doctrine of an "inner essence." In fact, he was so interested in distinguishing practice from enlightenment that Tao-sheng had to intervene at one point. It seems that one of the contenders in the controversy, Wang Wei-chün, was so dissatisfied with Hsieh's rebuttal of his position that he forwarded their exchange to Tao-sheng.[74]

Hsieh had followed the *Hṛdaya* in making too sharp a distinction between dark (or blind) faith and bright (or luminous) enlightenment:[75]

> No, enlightenment cannot be arrived at gradually. Faith is aroused by the teachings. How? As there is teaching, there is faith and daily merit. However, enlightenment itself cannot be piecemeal, because illumination *(chao)* cannot be gained in that fashion. The aspiration for the Tao begins with the one good [thought]. Then with the suppression of defilements, there is the elimination of evil. Still, even as that approximates nonbeing, even as the pure counters the impure, such actions are not sufficient. They are not the same as having an undefiled mind.[76]

Concerned that Hsieh might have separated faith from wisdom, Tao-sheng added this rider:

> The [dark] faith that is based on the teaching is not totally unknowing. Rather, it is that the aid to knowledge is in principle something lying beyond me[77] and leads to the discovery of the [true] self of man. Thus, how can it be said that there is no merit in daily progress? Yet even that [formulation] may not pertain to true self-knowing. How can it claim to have a role in illumination *(chao)*? Now, is that not equivalent to saying that since a person still regards the principle to be beyond him, he cannot be considered to be fully enlightened? If knowledge is not derived [ultimately] from one's center, one cannot be said to have attained illumination.[78]

Although Tao-sheng did not yet identify this principle within as the Buddha-nature, this passage might mark his hesitant move toward that conclusion.

Some time between writing that comment and the year 429, when Tao-sheng argued that the *icchantika* was included in the ranks of the enlightened, Tao-sheng spelled out his doctrine of Buddha-nature, and Seng-jui in his *Yü i lun* echoed that position:

> The *Lotus Sūtra* recognizes the [one] Buddha vehicle and shows how there cannot be a second or a third [vehicle]. However, it never openly admits that all sentient beings have Buddha-nature [as does the *Nirvāṇa Sūtra*]. Yet even though that teaching is absent, it does not mean that it was not implied [in the *Lotus'* doctrine of the all-pervasive Buddha-jñāna]. Now, Fa-hsien had traveled far to India to find and bring back to the capital this true scripture [the *Nirvāṇa Sūtra*]. It was then translated with the help of Dhyāna Master Buddhabhadra and more than a hundred monks. The sūtra states that nirvāṇa means nonextinction [instead of extinction], that Buddhas have a true self, that all sentient beings have Buddha-nature, and that they will become Buddhas upon the completion of learning. As the Buddha is said to have a true self, the sūtra is called the special teaching of the sage mirror *(sheng-chao)* and the crown of all sūtras. As nirvāṇa is nonextinction, the sūtra affirms a true basis. However, there are still those

> who are satisfied with gradual enlightenment and who deride stubbornly this true teaching. How foolish are these deluded ones who do not care to save themselves . . . and how much they are like the *icchantika* mentioned by the sūtra [who denied the same doctrine]![79]

The last sentence condemning the *icchantika* would date the *Yü i lun* before 429 when Tao-sheng repudiated their condemnation.

The Aftermath

In this chapter I have tried to reconstruct the development of Tao-sheng's reflections on the rationale for sudden enlightenment. I have argued that his subitism had an innocuous abhidharmic beginning; that it did not become a matter of debate until it was aligned with the one vehicle doctrine of the *Lotus Sūtra;* that Seng-chao defended gradualism in terms of his understanding of the three vehicle teaching of the Perfection of Wisdom tradition; that the concept of universal Buddha-nature was not connected with the sudden-gradual debate as late as Hsieh Ling-yün's *Pien tsung lun;* that this connection was probably first made only shortly before Tao-sheng formulated his thesis that even *icchantika* have Buddha-nature; and that Tao-sheng's final theory, in which the two theses were fused, came only after 430.

Tao-sheng's subitist triumph was short-lived. For a century, the gradualist teaching held sway, and it was not until the Ch'en dynasty (557–589) that subitism was revived. That was also the time when the *Awakening of Faith in Mahāyāna* appeared. This text was influential in recasting the issue in terms of *pen-chüeh* (a priori enlightenment) versus *shih-chüeh* (incipient enlightenment), whereby the latter presupposes the former. With the development of the more totalistic T'ien-t'ai understanding of Mahāyāna based on the one vehicle doctrine and the new idealism of the *Laṅkāvatāra Sūtra,* the old debate was also being redefined. Whereas Tao-sheng had spoken of gradual practice as a prerequisite for sudden enlightenment, Tsung-mi (780–841), representing the later Ch'an position, would take enlightenment to be a priori *(pen-chüeh)* and accordingly deem practice to be its derived function—a gradual cultivation based on sudden enlightenment.

Notes

I would like to thank Richard Lynn for his stylistic revisions of an earlier draft and Peter Gregory for his comments and suggestions. Any errors of fact or interpretation that remain are, of course, my own responsibility.

1. A continuity between Tao-sheng's subitism and that of Ch'an is assumed by Heinrich Dumoulin in his *History of Zen Buddhism* (New York: Random

House, 1963) as well as by a number of other scholars. Previous studies in English on Tao-sheng are those of Walter Liebenthal: "A Biography of Chu Tao-sheng," *Monumenta Nipponica* 11 (1955): 284–316, and "The World Conception of Chu Tao-sheng," *Monumenta Nipponica* 12 (1956): 66–103 and 241–268. I have relied principally on T'ang Yung-t'ung's study of Tao-sheng, which has been incorporated in his *Han-Wei liang-Chin Nan-pei-ch'ao Fo-chiao shih* (Peking: Chung-hua shu-chu, 1958; reprint of the 1938 ed.), 601–676.

2. From Tao-hsüan's *Kuang hung-ming chi, T* 52.265c–266a.

3. *T* 50.366c.

4. Cf. Derk Bodde's translation in Fung Yu-lan's *A History of Chinese Philosophy*, vol. 2 (Princeton: Princeton University Press, 1963), 184. For the *Chuang-tzu* passage from which Wang Pi's derives, see Burton Watson, trans., *The Complete Works of Chuang Tzu* (New York: Columbia University Press, 1968), 302. Note, however, the change in logic wrought by Wang Pi. Whereas the *I-ching* accepts means to an end, Wang Pi insists on forsaking the means to attain the end. Tao-sheng again emulates Wang Pi in his commentary on the *Lotus Sūtra* (*HTC* 150:828a–b): "One speaks quite naturally of limits but that is only when one has not yet seen the principle. Once the principle is seen, what use is there for words? This is comparable to the trap and the snare: once the fish or rabbit is caught, what use is there for trap and snare? [One may say] that upon hearing the sūtra, a person gains the [Hīnayāna] status of nonreturner or the [Mahāyāna] state of the certainty of the nonarising of dharmas *(anupattikadharma-kṣānti)*. However, this is truly not how the principle operates, and such explanations are [ultimately] beside the point. What can words add [to the experience] wherein there is neither advancement nor backsliding? And why do we still use metaphors? It is as the sūtra says, to defend the bhūmi theory. Although free of mundane falsehoods, the sage still abides among the ranks of the expedient, and, although in the realm of the useless, he still makes use of it."

5. See *Vimalakīrti Sūtra, T* 14.556c. See also Étienne Lamotte, trans., *L'Enseignement de Vimalakīrti* (Louvain: Publications Universitaires, 1962), 380–382 n. 23 for references. Lamotte includes a translation of Kumārajīva's explication of "the four refuges" *(catuṣpratisaraṇa)*.

6. *T* 50.366c. Cf. Kenneth Ch'en, *Buddhism in China* (Princeton: Princeton University Press, 1964), 113.

7. *T* 50.366c.

8. See the translation of this essay, "The Mirror of the Mind," earlier in this volume.

9. *T* 37.377b. For a full translation and analysis, see my essay "The *Mahāparinirvāṇa Sūtra* and Its Earliest Interpreters in China," *Journal of the American Oriental Society* 102 (1982): 99–103.

10. *T* 55.66c. Hui-ta remembered Tao-sheng as someone who dismissed the gradations of the Hīnayāna four fruits and the Mahāyāna ten stages.

11. *Ch'u-san-tsang chi-chi, T* 55.68c.

12. *T* 45.111b.

13. *T* 52.265c. I am following T'ang's reading below.

14. Cited by T'ang, *Fo-chiao shih*, 612–613.

15. See the letter of Fan-t'ai to Tao-sheng and Hui-kuan as preserved in the *Hung-ming chi, T* 52.78b–c; for dating, see T'ang, *Fo-chiao shih,* 619–620.

16. In the *Ta-sheng ta-i chang,* many questions posed by Hui-yüan were from the abhidharmic perspective. These Kumārajīva had to disown.

17. *T* 52.34b.

18. *T* 52.34c.

19. The Japanese translation of this text in *Gumyōshū kenkyū,* vol. 2 (Kyoto: Kyōtō daigaku jinbun kagaku kenkyūjo, 1974), 323, has erred in assuming that it does (see notes 12 and 13 on p. 326). T'ang, *Fo-chiao shih,* 645 and 657, has correctly identified the source.

20. Charles Willeman, trans., *The Essence of Metaphysics: Abhidharmahṛdaya* (Brussels: Publication de L'Institut Belge des Hautes Études Bouddhiques, 1975), 74.

21. Ibid., 82.

22. Ibid.

23. Ch'en, *Buddhism in China,* 118; T'ang, *Fo-chiao shih,* 643–647.

24. Willeman, *Essence of Metaphysics,* 78.

25. *T* 45.111b.

26. See Har Dayal, *The Bodhisattva Doctrine in Buddhist Sanskrit Literature* (London: Routledge & Kegan Paul, 1932), 271ff.

27. A more primitive scheme used the seventh stage to designate the bodhisattva's superiority to the arhat arrested at the sixth, but when the scheme was expanded to a full ten stages, the break was shifted to the eighth.

28. See the clarification of this rather obscure thesis in T'ang, *Fo-chiao shih,* 652–653; see also Hui-ta's summation in *HTC* 150.858b.

29. On this rather involved discussion, see Leon Hurvitz, "*Daijō daigishō* ni okeru ichijō sanjō no mondai ni tsuite," in Kimura E'ichi et al., eds., *Eon kenkyū,* vol. 2 (Kyoto: Kyōtō daigaku jinbun kagaku kenkyūjo, 1962), 169–193.

30. Hui-ta says: "Kumārajīva says that the king of the bodhi tree attained the way. In Hīnayāna, there are forty-three degrees of mind, but in Mahāyāna one is surely enlightened in one thought-moment *(nien, kṣana),* attaining omniscience" (*HTC* 150.858b). This argument seems to be based on a contrast of the Hīnayāna concept of mind (all forty-three are saṃsāric) with the Buddha's instant (i.e., single-minded and pure) knowledge of all. This mode of argument is also adopted by Fuse Kōgaku in his study of the antecedents of the subitist and gradualist debate. He gives credit to Kumārajīva for inspiring subitism. See his *Nehanshū no kenkyū,* vol. 2 (Tokyo: Sobun, 1942), 139–196, esp. 153–155.

31. Their commentaries, along with Seng-chao's, are found jointly in the commentary now listed in the Taishō canon under Seng-chao's name. See note 30 above and citations from this commentary below.

32. Richard B. Mather, trans., *Shih-shuo hsin-yü: A New Account of the Tales of the World* (Minneapolis: University of Minnesota Press, 1976), 112. This passage poses some problems. Ōchō Enichi, in his *Hokke shisō no kenkyū* (Kyoto: Heirakuji, 1971), 139, punctuated the last two lines in such a way that it reads: "When [others] were just about to subsume the two [lesser vehicles] into the third [great vehicle], they became confused." Though grammatically flawed, Ōchō's reading makes more sense doctrinally. The point of the passage has to

do with how the first two Hīnayāna vehicles can be subsumed into the third Mahāyāna vehicle, not with the identity of the three vehicles. In the same piece, Ōchō cites Chih Tun's "Preface to the Parallel Text of the Perfection of Wisdom," *T* 55.55b, to show how Chih Tun understood that natural unity: "Exhausting nonbeing, one forgets even the mystery itself, thereupon attaining no-mind. Then the two traces [two vehicles] are baseless, and nonbeing and being totally cease. The Buddha, understanding the beginningless wisdom [one vehicle], reckons the naturalness of all things."

33. See chaps. 3, 4, and 10 of the *Ta-chih-tu lun*. For the changes in the intellectual climate during this time, see Ōchō Enichi, *Chūgoku bukkyō no kenkyū*, vol. 3 (Kyoto: Hōzōkan, 1971), 145–161; translated by Robert Rhodes as "The Beginning of the Buddhist Classification in China," *The Eastern Buddhist*, n.s. 14, no. 2 (1981): 71–94.

34. Ōchō, *Chūgoku bukkyō*, vol.2 (Kyoto: Hōzōkan, 1971), 159.

35. *HTC* 150.800b.

36. This will become the pretext for the Chinese to prefix the *Wu-liang-i ching* to the *Lotus Sūtra* to produce the *Threefold Lotus Sūtra*.

37. *HTC* 150.803a.

38. Ibid., 806b. Conviction here is not the elementary faith of *sraddha*.

39. Ibid., 807b.

40. Ibid.

41. Ibid.

42. Ibid., 808b.

43. Ibid., 818b.

44. *T* 38.396c.

45. Ibid.

46. From the *Ming-seng chuan ch'ao*, as cited by T'ang, *Fo-chiao shih*, 671.

47. *HTC* 134.16a–b.

48. As Gómez points out in the preceding chapter, gradualism was the predominant assumption in India, and Kumārajīva accepted the ten-stage scheme.

49. See the list in the *Ch'u-san-tsang chi-chi*, *T* 55.57b–c. Hui-yüan (and others) did inquire about the one vehicle and the three vehicles, but subitism and gradualism does not yet appear as a necessary corollary to that issue.

50. Ōchō Enichi, "*Nehan mumyōron* to sono haikei," in Tsukamoto Zenryū et al., eds., *Jōron kenkyū* (Kyoto: Kyōtō daigaku jinbun kagaku kenkyūjo, 1955), 190–199. This essay includes a review of the traditional dating of Kumārajīva's death, Tsukamoto's revision of it, and previous allegations of the forgery of Seng-chao's essay (including Walter Liebenthal's view). The charge that the essay is a forgery seems to have been founded on the assumption that Seng-chao could not possibly have sided with gradualism.

51. See *Kuang Hung-ming-chi*, *T* 52.228a–230a. For a translation of the exchanges between the Yaos and an analysis of the issues involved, see my essay "Yao Hsing's Discourse on Mahāyāna," *Religious Traditions* 4, no. 2 (1981): 35–58.

52. My translation; see *T* 45.159c.

53. Walter Liebenthal, *Chao Lun: The Treatises of Seng-chao*, 2d revised ed. (Hong Kong: Hong Kong University Press, 1968), 119, n. 619.

54. Seng-chao seems to have in mind Tao-sheng's interpretation of this in the latter's commentary on the *Lotus Sūtra*.

55. *T* 45.159c–160a.

56. *T* 45.160a.

57. Ibid.

58. The nondual (i.e., the three) can well coexist with the one.

59. *T* 45.160b.

60. Ibid. Note that this is similar to Tao-sheng's argument about "learning until nonlearning is attained" in his commentary on the *Lotus Sūtra*.

61. I am grateful for Professor Mather's counsel on many parts of the translation, interpretation, and analysis here. I adhere to his use of "goal" for *tsung* in the title.

62. *T* 52.224c–225a.

63. *T* 52.225a–b.

64. See my essay "Yao Hsing's Discourse on Mahāyāna," cited in note 51 above.

65. The claim that the "Nirvāṇa Is Nameless" essay cites the *Nirvāṇa Sūtra* has been proven spurious by Ōchō Enichi in the essay "*Nehan mumyōron* to sono haikei," cited in note 50 above.

66. *T* 52.78b–c. On dating, see T'ang, *Fo-chiao shih*, 637–638.

67. Whether Tao-sheng argued for *pen-yu fo-hsing* (original possession of the Buddha-nature) before 430 is open to question. T'ang, in his *Fo-chiao shih*, 633–643, has established that Tao-sheng was not an incipientist *(shih-yu)*. Though that may be correct, I still believe that Tao-sheng initially proposed only a *tang-yu fo-hsing* thesis, following a clue in the sūtra passage that says the *icchantika* cannot be enlightened because all his good roots *(kuśalamūla)* have been burnt out. Tao-sheng saw that these good roots could be restored by the cultivation of good karma.

68. That is, Tao-sheng's position shifted from a causative analysis of Buddha-nature to one asserting a priori possession of this essence.

69. The concept of "innately pure mind" did not figure in the subitist-gradualist debate, perhaps owing to the legacy of Abhidharma, which considers all *citta-dharmas* (even the diamond-like concentration) as saṃsāric. The *Yü i lun*, however, might have incorporated the tradition of the tathāgatagarbha.

70. *HTC* 150.807b.

71. Hui-lin later wrote the *Ho-pai lun* (On Black and White), which was to inspire Tsung Ping's *Ming fo lun*. A critic of monastic wealth, he was turned out from the community for his disrespect.

72. *T* 85.226b–c.

73. *T* 52.227a. Text corrupted.

74. See the appended exchange to the *Pien tsung lun*, *T* 52.228a.

75. The expression *an-hsin* (dark trust) was used by Hui-yüan. Cf. T'ang, *Fo-chiao shih*, 657: "It seems that Saṅghadeva's *Hṛdaya* made this distinction and Tao-sheng might have gotten the idea from it."

76. The pure mind as the last step in the nine grades still needs sudden cutting off. See *T* 52.225b.

77. "Beyond" or "behind" is used to describe the location of nonbeing rela-

tive to being, in contrast to the immanence of something in "one's center." Tao-sheng here seems to be moving beyond *tang-yu* to *pen-yu*.

78. *T* 52.228a.

79. *T* 55.41c. Seng-jui aligns the Buddha-jñāna of the *Lotus Sūtra* with the Buddha-nature doctrine of the *Nirvāṇa Sūtra*, arguing for Kumārajīva's foreknowledge of the new doctrine. That portion is omitted in the translation above.

Glossary

an-hsin 暗信
Ch'an 禪
chao 照
Chao lun 肇論
ch'eng-fo 成佛
Ch'eng-shih lun 成實論
Chi-tsang 吉藏
chien 漸
chien-hsing 見性
chien-wu 漸悟
Chien-wu lun 漸悟論
Chih Tun 支遁
Chou-i lüeh-li 周易略例
Chuang-tzu 莊子
chung-hsüan 重玄
Erh-ti lun 二諦論
Fa-hsien 法顯
Fa-t'ai 法汰
Fan-t'ai 范泰
Fang-kuang 放光
fang-wai chih pin 方外之賓
Ho-pai lun 黑白論
hsiang 象
Hsiang Hsiu 向秀
Hsieh Ling-yün 謝靈運
hsing 性
hsüan-hsüeh 玄學
hsüan-li 玄理
hsüeh 學
hu 忽
Hui-jui 慧叡
Hui-kuan 慧觀
Hui-lin 慧琳
Hui-ta 慧達
Hui-yüan 慧遠
i 意
I-ching 易經
Kao-seng chuan 高僧傳
ko-i 格義
Kuan wu-liang ching 觀無量經
Lao-tzu 老子
li 理
Liu Ch'iu 劉虬
Miao-fa lien-hua ching 妙法蓮華經
ming-chaio 名教
Ming fo lun 明佛論
Ming-seng chuan ch'ao 名僧傳鈔
Nieh-p'an wu-ming lun 涅槃無名論
p'an-chiao 判教
pen-chüeh 本覺
pen-yu fo-hsing 本有佛性
Pien tsung lun 辯宗論
Po-jo wu-chih lun 般若無知論
pu-erh fa-men 不二法門
San-lun 三論
San-pao lun 三報論
san-sheng 三乘
Seng-chao 僧肇
Seng-jui 僧叡
sheng-chao 聖照
shih-chüeh 始覺
Shih-shuo hsin-yü 世說新語
shih-yu 始有
Ta-chih-tu lun 大智度論
tang-lai chih kuo 當來之果
tang-yu 當有

tang-yu fo-hsing 當有佛性
T'ao Ch'ien 陶潛
Tao-lin 道林
Tao-sheng 道生
t'i 體
T'ien-t'ai 天臺
Tsung-mi 宗密
Tsung Ping 宗炳
tun 頓
tun-chien 頓漸
tun-wu 頓悟
Tun-wu lun 頓悟論
tzu-jan 自然
Yao Hsing 姚興
Yao Sung 姚嵩
yu-wu hsiang-kuan 有無相觀
Yü i lun 喻疑論
Wang Pi 王弼
Wang Wei-chün 王衛軍
wu (nonbeing) 無
wu-hsüeh 無學
Wu-liang-i ching 無量義經
Wu-liu hsien-sheng chuan 五柳先生傳

Sudden and Gradual Intimately Conjoined: Chih-i's T'ien-t'ai View

NEAL DONNER

Paul Demiéville may be credited with first bringing to the notice of Western Buddhologists the Chinese debate on sudden versus gradual enlightenment.[1] At the same time, we cannot deny the influence of D. T. Suzuki in focusing our attention on the rival poems of Hui-neng and Shen-hsiu in the *Platform Sūtra.*[2] But there is a second strain of modern Buddhology that, practically independent of the above, has used the sudden-gradual pair of antonyms to clarify the phenomenon of doctrinal classification *(p'an-chiao)*. Here the use of the two terms is rather distant from the controversy over "how quickly enlightenment is obtained."

Such a bifurcation of scholarly attention oddly parallels the nonintegration of teaching and practice deplored and strenuously combatted in his day by Chih-i (538–597), the scholar-monk from whom emanated the great T'ien-t'ai school of Chinese (and later, under the name of Tendai, Japanese) Buddhism. One may, in fact, view Chih-i's entire life and teachings as an effort to restore to a proper harmonious unity the pursuit of wisdom in its two forms, intellectual and experiential. Since he made liberal use of the sudden-gradual terminology in both his doctrinal and his practical works, we can gain useful insight into the debate by examining his use of the terms and their place in his thought. Moreover, his influence on Chinese Ch'an and on the Japanese Tendai and Nichiren sects was so pronounced that a correct understanding of Chih-i's thought is indispensable to an accurate assessment of many later developments in East Asian Buddhism. This chapter will deal with Chih-i's understanding of "sudden" and "gradual" in the context of his thought on teaching and practice.

Chih-i's Double Emphasis: Teaching and Practice

Although the T'ien-t'ai school is named after the mountain where Chih-i's monastery stood, he was certainly not the only prominent teacher in his line. Several important texts by his teacher, Hui-ssu (515–577), have been preserved in the Chinese Buddhist canon, and this man clearly influenced Chih-i profoundly, especially in the latter's early years. Several generations later, in the middle of the T'ang dynasty, the scholar-monk Chan-jan (711–782) was able to revive this tradition after a period of eclipse. Many of his voluminous works, prominently including the standard commentaries to Chih-i's *Fa-hua hsüan-i* (Profound Meaning of the Lotus Sūtra; henceforth referred to as the *Hsüan-i*) and *Mo-ho chih-kuan* (The Great Calming and Contemplation), may be found in the canon. Chan-jan's debates with scholars of the Hua-yen school are a fascinating episode in T'ang Buddhism, as yet unmined by Western scholars. It was at this point, and through this process, that both T'ien-t'ai and Hua-yen became self-conscious as separate traditions or schools *(tsung)*. Further important developments in the T'ien-t'ai lineage occurred in the Sung dynasty, while in Japan the school had been reborn under Saichō (767–822) as Tendai, carving out for itself a preeminent position in the world of Japanese Buddhism.

The other luminaries in the tradition notwithstanding, it remains true that "T'ien-t'ai thought" means, above all, the thought of Chih-i himself, the "great teacher of T'ien-t'ai," intellectual founder of the tradition, and, according to the derivative Nichiren school in Japan, the Buddha of the period of the Reflected Dharma. The noted Ch'an historian Yanagida Seizan has argued that the history of the Ch'an movement really begins when, at the time of the fourth and fifth patriarchs, Tao-hsin (580–651) and Hung-jen (610–675), an effort was made to find in Bodhidharma a source of authority older than Chih-i that could be used to establish Ch'an as a tradition in its own right, separate from T'ien-t'ai.[3] Traces of Chih-i's thought are evident in the *Platform Sūtra*, and it seems that when Tsung-mi (780–841) bent his efforts toward strengthening a rather deteriorated tradition of sitting meditation in the Ch'an school, he found it necessary virtually to copy a minor, but popular meditation text by Chih-i, the *Hsiao-chih-kuan* (Lesser Calming and Contemplation).[4] Sekiguchi holds that this work of Tsung-mi became the basis for all Ch'an and Zen meditation manuals thereafter, its influence discoverable even in the meditation manuals of the great Japanese monk Dōgen (1200–1253).[5] Granted the possibility that Sekiguchi overstates his point, the fact remains that T'ien-t'ai meditation was a tradition that it was impossible for the Ch'an movement to ignore (though T'ien-t'ai *doctrine* was more easily avoided, at least by Ch'an). Whether reacting against or borrowing from T'ien-t'ai, Ch'an was forced to grow in the shadow of Chih-i's stupendous systematization of Mahāyāna methods of meditation and cannot be fully understood without reference to his work.

The works attributed to Chih-i fall, for the most part, into the category of either doctrine (teaching) or practice (meditation), the *chiao-men* and the *kuan-men*. Throughout his life he continued to lecture in both areas, until in maturity he produced the *Hsüan-i* (593) and the *Mo-ho chih-kuan* (594), the former being his crowning achievement in the realm of doctrine, the latter occupying the same position in the realm of practice.

The twofold nature of his works reflects the double emphasis in Chih-i's thought. Throughout his career he insisted tirelessly that *both* doctrinal and practical (contemplative) training are essential for the aspirant seeking an enlightened life. On the one hand, he said, the study of doctrine as set forth in the scriptures and commentaries is indispensable. Why? Because practice or meditation without study leaves us open to false arrogance.[6] Without proper doctrinal study, we fall prey to the conceit that we are equal to the Buddha (a conceit that recurs frequently in the course of Mahāyāna history). To meditate while remaining innocent of the teachings is likened to grasping a torch (symbolizing the searing flame of samādhi) improperly and hence burning ourselves. On the other hand, to restrict ourselves to doctrinal study, never getting authentic experience of our own "dharma-treasure," is comparable to a pauper counting other people's money. Ideas "enter our ears and exit from our mouths, yet the mind remains undisciplined," with the result that our opinions multiply and once again we develop arrogance. Study of the teachings in the absence of contemplation is likened to grasping a knife (symbolizing the cutting edge of the intellect) improperly and hence cutting ourselves.

There are four permutations of study with meditation: little study with little meditation, little study with much meditation, much study with little meditation, and finally, much study with much meditation. Only the last group of aspirants really succeed, in Chih-i's view. Once one has trained the wisdom-eye through meditation, and has allowed (through study) the outer light to shine, it is possible to see clearly the "object" perceived by subjective enlightened intuition (though it must be understood that at such a stage the subject-object dichotomy is no longer in effect). One can then take real possession of the dharma-treasure yet harbor no conceit.

In the *Hsüan-i* passage from which the above comments are taken,[7] Chih-i goes on to specify under meditation the so-called three views *(san-kuan)*, designed to correct the tendency toward uncentered thinking; and under study he specifies the doctrine of the six identities *(liu-chi)*, used to correct the arrogance of unstudied meditation.

The six identities are a marvelously concise and clear rubric, well suited to elucidate the relationship between doctrine and practice, as well as between identity and difference, in Chih-i's thought. They reveal the structures of his thought with greater clarity than any of his other doctrines, with the exception of the three views. The six identities are:[8]

1. Identity in principle. This affirms inherent Buddhahood.
2. Verbal identity. Here intellectual understanding that we are Buddhas is gained.
3. Identity of religious practice. Here behavior and mental state are brought into correspondence with the prior verbal formulations. The *Mo-ho chih-kuan* compares this to the practice of archery, in which one begins by aiming at large targets, then gradually reduces the target size until finally one can hit the hundredth part of a hair.[9]
4. Identity of resemblance. One's "thoughts and evaluations approach what has been expounded in the sūtras of previous Buddhas."[10]
5. Identity of partial truth. "Ignorance weakens and wisdom becomes increasingly prominent."
6. Ultimate identity. Buddhahood, the final fruit.

The T'ien-t'ai tradition correlates these six identities with the fifty-two stages, an expansion of the ten stages expounded in the *Daśabhūmika-sūtra*, but the six nevertheless differ critically from the ten or the fifty-two in their assertion of identity with the highest reality at every level. For according to this doctrine, even before we have begun to tread the path toward final realization, we are already identical, in a certain sense, to Buddha, and we thus partake of the ultimate reality without even trying to do so. Yet as we advance in our practice, over time, the nature of the identity changes: we become increasingly aware of that truth-in-ourselves, until ultimately the inherent identity has become completely realized. Chih-i has creatively adapted a parable from the *Nirvāṇa Sūtra* to illustrate this interpenetration of inherent Buddhahood with progress in realization: (1) Suppose there is a pauper with a cache of treasure around his house that he is not aware of. (2) A friend shows him where it is buried. (3) He clears away the weeds and begins to dig it out, (4) gradually getting closer and closer. (5) He reaches and opens the cache, (6) empties it and puts the treasure to use.[11]

The endpoint of practice, fully realized Buddhahood, is a distant goal that Chih-i never claimed to have reached. Tradition has it that in his own opinion he never passed beyond the third identity, as he had expended so much of his efforts on behalf of his students rather than on himself.[12]

The relationship between identity and difference in this doctrine is analogous to the relationship between study and meditation, doctrine and practice, alluded to above. The existence of identity erases self-depreciation and doubt while the existence of six gradations erases arrogance. Among Buddhists, those who exaggerate identity fall prey to arrogance while those who overemphasize differentiation (i.e., the six) are subject to a loss of faith in themselves.[13] Even at the outset we are truly, already Buddhas, even without having heard the first suggestion that this is so. One of the senses of "sudden" in the later sudden-gradual controversies is equivalent to this first identity: that even in our totally naive state we are already Buddhas in the full sense, with no practice or study whatever required. Taken out of context, even Chih-i can be cited to support such an interpretation: "If living beings are already identical with enlightenment, then they cannot attain anything further."[14] Another sense of "sudden" in the later controversies is equivalent to verbal identity, the second identity as equated with the sixth. According to this interpretation, all we need do is give intellectual assent to the proposition that we are Buddhas, and we have attained Buddhahood in the full sense.

As for the three views, these are the subjective aspect of the three truths. The latter should not be confused with the venerable four noble truths, being instead an expansion of the Mādhyamika two truths doctrine (*saṃvṛti* and *paramārtha,* provisional and ultimate). Briefly, the third truth is generated from the other two by viewing them as extremes, dialectically reconciled in the middle truth. That things *are* is the first truth (provisional); that they are *not* is the second (ultimate); and that they *both* are and are not, as well as *neither* are nor are not, is the third truth, considered necessary by Chih-i in order to avoid the extreme of negation into which he perceived many of those falling who clung to the doctrine of emptiness as an ultimate. Nāgārjuna himself had warned of this danger, and in India the Yogācāra philosophy developed a parallel, but different reconciliation of the extremes of "being" and "nonbeing." The third or middle truth, expressible as above in two equivalent ways ("both" and "neither") is not truly a compromise, a "middle way" between extremes as we might first think, but instead emphasizes the paradoxical nature of reality: that the truth cannot be reduced to a single formulation.

Here is a recurrence of Chih-i's "binocular vision," the double emphasis which is a leitmotiv of his thought. It is necessary, according to Chih-i, to phrase the truth in opposite ways *and* to understand that the opposite formulations are finally (in an expressible sense) pointing to the same "thing." At the level of the perfect or actionless teaching, which we shall touch upon later, each moment of thought

> is identical with emptiness, with the provisional, and with the middle. All [three] are ultimate emptiness, all are the tathāgatagarbha, all are the ultimate reality. Though they are not three, yet they are three; though they are three, they are not three. . . . They are neither the same nor different, yet they *are* the same and they *are* different.[15]

Restating the argument, we may say that the truth is for Chih-i on the one hand differentiable, on the other hand undifferentiable, and finally something that neither of these opposites can convey. Similarly, light is conceived of today as consisting of (differentiated) particles, or alternatively of (undifferentiated) waves, or as something which cannot ultimately be caught in this conceptual net. To complete the analogy with Chih-i's thought, we must add that these three ways to conceive of light can both be completely identified with and completely distinguished from one other.

At every stage along the path there is the temptation to claim final attainment, particularly when one's attainment is already profound (following identity 2). The nondualism of the Perfection of Wisdom sūtras, upon which Chih-i and the whole Ch'an tradition based their thought, is not hard to construe with such a one-sided emphasis. Chih-i's nondualism contained an added sophistication, however, in that he shrank from claiming to have found the one principle, preferring instead to leave us ambiguously with the challenge of the coexistence of apparently contradictory propositions: that nothing is excluded from perfection, yet serious training is required to perfect oneself nevertheless; that both being and nothingness are equally valid, and equally invalid, characterizations of the nature of reality. We see this double emphasis throughout Chih-i's work, bearing on a multitude of doctrines, and consistently viewing the world with "binocular" vision.

The union of doctrine and practice, of teaching and meditation, must be kept in mind whenever either aspect is under discussion. This has regrettably not always been the case when scholars both past and present, oriental and occidental, have dealt with T'ien-t'ai *doctrine* in particular, with the result that Chih-i's doctrinal classification *(p'an-chiao)* scheme has over centuries come to be treated in virtual isolation from considerations of practice. In recent years this one-sided understanding of his thought has begun to be rectified,[16] and an effort will be made here to keep both aspects in balance.

We find a tripartite division in both teaching and meditation in Chih-i. Or put another way, there is a tripartite division—namely sudden, gradual, and variable[17]—in which each term can be interpreted from two points of view,[18] teaching and meditation (the *chiao-men* and the *kuan-men*), making six possibilities in all. Everything written or dictated by Chih-i can be approached with reference to this basic hexapartite pattern. We must be careful to observe, however, that in accordance with the general principle of his thought, Chih-i clearly viewed this (and every other) classification as provisional, not a representation of ultimate truth, and conceived of each member of the six as present in all the others.[19]

Chih-i uses "sudden," in regard to teaching, to refer to the *Avataṃsaka-sūtra,* believed to have been expounded by the Buddha to mostly uncomprehending listeners immediately after his enlightenment. "Sudden" here means for Chih-i that the Buddha, making no concessions to the intellectual or spiritual capacities of the individuals in his audience, elucidated the highest truth and nothing else. Having just emerged from his enlightenment experience, he was concerned to characterize as accurately as possible the content of his vision. To a certain extent, the *Lotus* and the *Nirvāṇa* sūtras may also be considered sudden—for though they were supposedly expounded at the end, rather than the beginning, of the Buddha's teaching career, they likewise embody the highest truth. As regards meditation, "sudden" refers to the type of meditation outlined in the *Mo-ho chih-kuan,*[20] in which "ultimate reality is taken as the object of meditation from the very beginning."[21] This meditation is often called the "perfect and sudden" rather than merely "the sudden," and its scriptural substantiations are by no means limited to the three "sudden" sūtras just mentioned.

Chih-i used "gradual," in regard to teaching, to refer to all the other sūtras expounded by the Buddha. That is, once the Buddha had delivered the *Avataṃsaka-sūtra* and realized how unsuccessful he had been at conveying the highest truth to his listeners, he decided that it was necessary to simplify his teaching and begin at an elementary level. Then he could lead them by degrees to the highest truth. Even the *Lotus* and the *Nirvāṇa* may sometimes be considered gradual, merely because they were not the first to be delivered (though this does not mean they are not "perfect"). As for meditation, the gradual refers to the types of meditation outlined in the *Tz'u-ti ch'an-men* (The Graduated Teaching of Meditation), the unprecedented systematization of Hīnayānistic meditation methods that was Chih-i's first work (571) and that by itself would have assured his immortality.[22] The above-mentioned *Hsiao-chih-kuan* is a synopsis of this greater work.[23]

The "variable" for Chih-i does not refer to any teaching of meditation separate from the sudden and the gradual but to the various combinations of levels of teaching and meditation that are possible. Thus one may pick whichever is most appropriate in one's own case and apply it. The metaphor used by Chih-i to elucidate both aspects is from the *Nirvāṇa Sūtra* (whence he derived so many of his metaphors): poison in milk.[24] No matter what the successive states in the processing of milk—whether it curdles, becomes cheese, butter, or ghee—once the poison is present, it remains there and has the capacity to kill whoever consumes the medium in which it dwells. Just so is the perfect teaching embedded in every lesser teaching of the Buddha, and the perfect meditation embedded in every lesser meditation.[25]

We now take a closer look at first the teaching aspect of Chih-i's thought, then the meditation aspect, with a view to clarifying in both cases more precisely just what he meant by "sudden" and by "gradual."

The Teaching Aspect of Chih-i's Buddhism

Here we come face-to-face with Chih-i's *p'an-chiao* system, in which he distilled the best elements from virtually every scheme that preceded him and influenced many of those which followed (the *Mo-ho chih-kuan* performed a similar function for meditation in the history of Chinese Buddhism). Although the slogan of the "five periods and eight teachings" has been used for centuries to characterize his *p'an-chiao* system,[26] it has recently become apparent that this formula was a later development and does not fairly represent Chih-i's own thought, as contained in the *Hsüan-i* for example.[27] Without digressing into a detailed criticism of the "five periods and eight teachings" slogan, we shall start instead with the well-known metaphor of the five flavors that Chih-i borrowed from the *Nirvāṇa Sūtra.* Then instead of the "eight teachings," we will elaborate "four teachings," bearing in mind that even the resulting formula ("the five flavors and the four teachings") falls far short of indicating the breadth or the heart of Chih-i's thoughts on teaching.

Chih-i did not have a fixed *p'an-chiao* scheme but used a wide variety of rubrics in different contexts and for different purposes throughout his vast oeuvre. We find that the *p'an-chiao* framework used in the *Mo-ho chih-kuan* differs from that in the *Hsüan-i,* and again from that in the *Ssu-chiao-i.* A definitive statement on this topic must await translation and analysis of a greater portion of Chih-i's works than has so far been attempted. We can recognize, however, that the general structures of Chih-i's thought, as revealed in his *p'an-chiao* categories among other places, merit more attention than has been given them in the cut-and-dried doctrinal analysis that medieval scholiasts found so attractive.

The *locus classicus* of the five flavors metaphor appears in the *Nirvāṇa Sūtra*:

> From the cow there comes milk, from milk comes cream, from cream come butter curds, from butter curds comes butter, and from butter comes ghee. . . . Oh sons of good family, it is also thus with the Buddha [and his teaching]. From the Buddha come the twelve divisions of scripture, from the twelve divisions of scripture come the sūtras, from the sūtras come the *vaipulya* [Mahāyāna] sūtras, from the *vaipulya* sūtras comes Perfection of Wisdom, and from Perfection of Wisdom comes *Mahāparinirvāṇa,* which is to be compared to ghee. Ghee is analogous to the Buddha-nature.[28]

This metaphor had already been used before Chih-i's time in a *p'an-chiao* scheme that he criticized in the *Hsüan-i.*[29] He also shared with earlier schemes the supposition that the *Avataṃsaka-sūtra* was a "sudden" teaching that preceded all the rest, although this aspect does not appear in the *Nirvāṇa Sūtra* passage quoted above. In fact, it is not clear that the passage refers to individual scriptures at all, despite the use of the terms Perfection of Wisdom and *Mahāparinirvāṇa,* nor that a chronological sequence of teaching is necessarily implied. Mochizuki in his encyclopedia states that in his opinion the *Nirvāṇa Sūtra* is *not* referring to a chronological sequence of teachings, but to progressive refinements down to the purest essence.[30] Nevertheless, it seems undeniable that not only his predecessors, but also Chih-i himself, used the passage to arrange the scriptures in a chronological sequence supposed to match their order of exposition in the Buddha's actual life. We find, therefore, a certain ambiguity in the uses of the symbolism: milk can symbolize both the coarsest and the earliest version of the teachings, while ghee corresponds to both the purest and the latest teaching.

Chih-i's central interest here was not, however, a chronological arrangement of the scriptures, with the more profound ones (except for the *Avataṃsaka*) coming later, but to determine the relationship between ultimate and provisional truth as revealed in the teachings of the Buddha. In pursuit of this goal he employed a variety of doctrinal categories quite freely, commenting frequently that the truth lay quite beyond the doctrine. The five flavors and the sudden-gradual distinction are examples of such categories, whose ultimacy he undercut by a number of devices, including the notion of interpenetration. The poison-in-milk metaphor mentioned above was thus used to illustrate his contention that even the lowest-category teaching has the capacity to liberate suffering living beings.

Therefore it is true, says Chih-i, that the *Avataṃsaka-sūtra* is sudden. Yet it (or the time when it was preached) can be both "milk" and "ghee."[31] In depth of teaching it is ghee, while in terms of when the Buddha expounded it, it is milk. Moreover, the listeners to that sūtra included both "ghee-listeners" (indicating those few "sudden" bodhisattvas who were able to understand and thereby gain liberation immediately) and "milk-listeners" (those who were "as if deaf and dumb," failing to understand the purport of what was being said).[32] Hence we find that not only can "ghee" listeners obtain liberation when "milk" is preached, but also that "milk" listeners may be present when "ghee" is preached.

The five flavors may be contrasted with the very simple "half/full" hermeneutic, attributed to Bodhiruci. This teaching, as presented in the *Hsüan-i*,[33] had defects that Chih-i was concerned to correct. It held that the Buddha first preached the Hīnayāna ("half-word") and afterwards the Mahāyāna ("full-word").[34] On the contrary, says Chih-i, the Buddha expounded prajñā, the full teaching, from the very moment of his enlightenment and throughout his career. Moreover, the "half-word" is not to be denigrated, for the Buddha praised such means precisely because of their power to bring about the "full-word" (perfect, *paramārtha*) teaching.[35] In fact, it was precisely because it lacked upāya that the *Avataṃsaka-sūtra* failed to bring about the enlightenment of more beings than it did, despite its status as an ultimate teaching. But the *Lotus* and *Nirvāṇa* sūtras, coming at the end of the Buddha's teaching career, do not lack upāya. In these, prajñā and upāya, the ultimate and the provisional, function together, "like the two wings of a bird." Put another way, it is the great virtue of the *Lotus* in particular that it is "gradual-sudden,"[36] for this completes its capacity to save living beings. Being purely "sudden," the *Avataṃsaka* lacks this virtue.[37]

Along similar lines Chih-i criticizes an earlier scholar's distinction between the two kinds of Mahāyāna: the teaching "with features" (*yu-hsiang*, i.e., involving graduated stages), and the teaching "without features" (*wu-hsiang*, i.e., without stages or "sudden").[38] Not only is it the case that "from the night he gained enlightenment [the Buddha] consistently expounded prajñā"[39] but even within Mahāyāna the Buddha did not ever rely solely on either the teaching with or the teaching without features:

> If [the Buddha] had used only [the teaching] with features, then—since such features would lack any [corresponding] referent—to what could the teaching refer? The way could not then be achieved. But if he had used only [the teaching] without features, then—since the featureless is true quiescence, ineffable, and separate from features, with mental processes extinguished—in such a case even this [featureless] teaching would not be [what is meant by "featureless"], for how could it be expounded at all? If we speak of "this teaching," the teaching so indicated does have features. How could it be called "featureless"? In the *Perfection of Wisdom in Twenty-five Thousand Lines*, Subhuti asked, "If all dharmas are ultimately without substance, why then do you say there are the ten stages?" The Buddha answered, "It is precisely because there is ultimately no substance to the

> dharmas that the ten stages of bodhisattva exist. If dharmas had a fixed nature, there could be no ten stages." Know therefore that to speak of two kinds of Mahāyāna as separate from each other is to contradict the sūtras.[40]

Here we are very near the core of Chih-i's thought. In his vocabulary, though there are no distinctions, yet there are distinctions; and though there are distinctions, yet there are no distinctions. Specifically regarding progress along the path, the statement becomes: though there are no stages, yet there are stages; and though there are stages, yet there are no stages. Wherever words are used, we find the gradual teaching; hence this is present in *all* the sūtras. Yet the "sudden" ultimate truth is also present, at least implicitly, in *all* the sūtras. The sudden and the gradual both completely permeate the teachings of the Buddha. The coexistence of equal and opposite imperatives is not only permitted but required if we are to penetrate closer to ultimate truth.

We cannot leave the subject of the teaching aspect of Chih-i's Buddhism without touching upon the so-called four teachings: (1) tripiṭaka, (2) shared, (3) separate, and (4) perfect. These are relevant for our discussion mainly because the fourth of these, the perfect teaching, may often be taken as the sudden teaching by another name. The two expressions are frequently combined into one: the perfect-and-sudden teaching (or meditation). Although this latter term is frequently used in the texts attributed to Chih-i, he seldom makes reference to the "four teachings" as a group or principle of classification in either the *Hsüan-i* or *Mo-ho chih-kuan.*[41] Instead, the *Hsüan-i* analysis is based mainly on the five flavors and the three modes of teaching (sudden, gradual, variable), while the *Mo-ho chih-kuan* employs a different group of four: arising, arising-and-perishing, innumerable, and actionless. Chih-i used categories freely in his effort to expound the dharma, shifting between them whenever it seemed convenient. If later generations (especially Chan-jan, his principal commentator) developed the habit of summarizing his far-ranging and subtle thought in a few pithy slogans, modern scholars must all the more resist the temptation to view his thought through their eyes.

What is the perfect teaching? In Chih-i's words:

> To seek ultimate reality apart from mundane dharmas is like departing empty space in one place to look for it in another. . . . There is no need to reject the mundane to turn toward the saintly. . . . Even though we make fine distinctions between shallow and profound, . . . nevertheless the provisional and the ultimate are universally coextensive.[42]

Elsewhere he calls this same teaching the actionless *(wu-tso).* Contained in various places throughout the Mahāyāna (and implicitly even the

Hīnayāna sūtras), the perfect teaching can serve as a point of reference when one considers the later doctrine of sudden enlightenment as presented in the *Platform Sūtra.* According to the perfect teaching, "there is not a single shape or smell that is not the middle way, . . . and the defilements are identical to enlightenment."[43] The entire universe is immanent in a moment of thought *(i-nien san-ch'ien)* and is perceived (by the enlightened mind) simultaneously as empty, as substantial, and as both and neither.

The Practice Aspect of Chih-i's Buddhism

Chih-i's thoughts and texts on practice can be arranged according to the same sudden-gradual-variable classification that furnishes the framework for the discussion on teaching. As in the previous section, the variable practice cannot be discussed apart from the other two on the grounds that it does not constitute a separate practice.[44] We are left then with the gradual practice and the sudden practice.

Chih-i's massive and influential early work, the *Tz'u-ti ch'an-men,*[45] is considered to be his definitive statement of the gradual, or graduated, meditation practice. It moves from the elementary to the profound, step by step, with its core chapter based on the progression from "mundane" meditations to "both mundane and supramundane," to "supramundane," to "neither mundane nor supramundane." Though the methods are for the most part borrowed from Hīnayāna meditation manuals, their doctrinal basis is set firmly in Mahāyāna thought. At this point in Chinese Buddhism, there was not yet a stigma attached to "gradualistic" teachings or methods of contemplation. By the end of the next century, however, "gradual" had become a term of revilement, functionally equivalent to the word "Hīnayāna" as used in many Indian Mahāyāna texts.

Though eminently a meditation text, the *Tz'u-ti ch'an-men* uses the word *ch'an* (dhyāna) to sum up all religious practice, its meaning extending beyond meditation to include discipline and insight—all of the three disciplines (śīla, samādhi, prajñā) of which Buddhism is said to be composed. This is the same sense in which the term *ch'an* is later used by the (as yet nonexistent) Ch'an school itself. Although the term had already been in use for centuries (even in the titles of translated Hīnayānist meditation manuals), it did not assume this comprehensive sense until Chih-i's *Tz'u-ti ch'an-men.* It is therefore a matter of more than casual interest that toward the end of his life, Chih-i substituted for *ch'an* the expression *chih-kuan* (calming and contemplation, concentration and insight, *śamatha-vipaśyanā*). *Ch'an* thus belongs to his early "gradualist" period while *chih-kuan* belongs to his later "perfect-and-sudden" period. This fact did not prevent the Ch'an school from later criticizing T'ien-t'ai and the *chih-kuan* practice as "gradualistic."

The reason the *Mo-ho chih-kuan* prefers the term *chih-kuan* is that *ch'an*, in its more restricted meaning of dhyāna, is skewed toward the negative side of the static-dynamic polarity, connoting only the quiescent aspect of meditation. Here, as always, Chih-i emphasized the unity of opposites, being concerned to show that meditation involves more than cessation of thought and motion. The latter corresponds to *śamatha,* but not *vipaśyanā*. The relation between the two is just as intimate as the relation between meditation as a whole and teaching (in fact, *vipaśyanā* may be understood as the teaching aspect brought into the practice of meditation): like two wheels of a cart or two wings of a bird. In Chih-i's words, *śamatha* (or *chih*) is the hand that holds the clump of grass, *vipaśyanā* (or *kuan*) the sickle that cuts it down. The first is also likened to a closed and windless room, the second to a lamp that burns brightest when the air is still; or the first is the soap that loosens the dirt, the second the clear water that rinses it away. The point needs emphasis because of the great care that Chih-i took to avoid extremes in his teaching and practice. Although these two aspects of meditation are not strictly parallel to the sudden-gradual dichotomy, there is still a deep relationship between the two pairs. The relationship can be more easily seen as soon as we replace *śamatha-vipaśyanā* with the often synonymous samādhi-prajñā (meditation and wisdom). We may then observe that prajñā is what both Tao-sheng and the Ch'an school understood to be instantly attained—while samādhi has a ring of gradualism to it.

The meditation methods elaborated in the *Mo-ho chih-kuan* include (1) the four samādhis and (2) the ten modes and ten object-fields of meditation. While the discourse on the latter occupies six of the ten fascicles of the text, and may therefore be considered the main topic of the work, we will not discuss them here[46] because of the length such a discussion would require, and because they have yet to be given close study and analysis based on an annotated Western-language translation. Moreover, their influence on later generations (both within and outside T'ien-t'ai) does not approach that of the four samādhis, which Chih-i himself presents as a summation of the whole of religious practice.[47]

The four samādhis—here the word "samādhi" primarily means "mode of religious practice"—are classified according to the physical posture of the practitioner: (1) the constantly sitting, (2) the constantly walking, (3) the half-walking and half-sitting, and (4) the neither walking nor sitting. Of these, the first refers simply to the practice of sitting meditation, the second to reciting the name of Amitābha Buddha (as in the Pure Land tradition), the third to two complex visualizations (as in the tantric tradition),[48] and the fourth to the practice of meditation in all aspects of daily life ("walking, standing, sitting, and lying down," as well as when "speaking and being silent"). To the discussions on the first three are appended strong exhortations to engage zealously in the practice, but the section on the fourth "samādhi" is followed by a detailed and significant caveat advising restraint, for reasons that we shall see.

The constantly sitting samādhi makes use of the venerable lotus posture, *padmāsana,* in which the Buddha is often portrayed. Like the other three, the constantly sitting samādhi is a "perfect and sudden" practice. In what sense is this so? It is not simply breath-counting, nor does it involve focusing the attention on a single point in the visual field (such as the tip of the nose, the navel, or a candle flame). Certainly no discursive contemplation of the categories of Buddhist doctrine (such as the four noble truths, the chain of dependent origination, etc.) is involved.[49] While certain doctrinal categories are brought into the meditation—for example, the three truths (empty, provisional, and middle) and the three obstacles (suffering, defilements, and karma)—the sole purpose of this effort is to identify them, one after the other, with ultimate reality. Thus one contemplates the Tathāgata, symbolizing ultimate reality, as beyond time and space (empty), as omnipresent in multiplicity (provisional), and as beyond, yet present in, each aspect of form (middle). Similarly, suffering, the defilements, and karma itself are all to be identified with the dharmadhātu, or ultimate reality. Yet even this meditation is derivative.

The main practice, including the prescriptions for body, voice, and mind, is described under the heading of the constantly sitting samādhi:

> Sit constantly, without walking, standing, or lying down. One may be in a group, but it is better to be alone. Sit in a quiet room or out of doors in a peaceful place, apart from all clamor. . . . For a period of ninety days sit in the proper position, legs crossed, the neck and backbone perfectly straight, neither moving nor wavering, not drooping nor leaning on anything. . . . Except for brief periods of walking meditation, eating, and relieving yourself, just sit, properly facing the direction of a Buddha, and as time passes do not falter for even a moment. What is permitted is just sitting. . . . If very tired, ill, overcome with sleepiness, or subject to unregulated thinking, then recite intently the name of a Buddha. . . . Just sit and rectify your thought. Dispel evil thoughts and discard disordered fantasies. Mix in no mental activity and do not grasp mentally at forms. Just identify the objects of cognition with the dharmadhātu and rest your thought in the dharmadhātu alone. . . . If you are confident there is nothing that is not the Buddha's teaching, then there is no earlier and no later, no knower or expounder of the teaching. . . . Neither existent nor inexistent, neither knower nor nonknower, dwell then where no dwelling is pos-

> sible, . . . in the perfectly quiescent dharmadhātu where all the Buddhas dwell.[50]

Following this prescription for practice, Chih-i encourages us to engage in it:

> By practicing diligently without shirking, one will be able to enter this one-practice samādhi. It is like caring for a jewel: the more it is polished, the more it shines. . . . If a bodhisattva is able to learn it, he will quickly gain enlightenment. If monks and nuns hear it [being expounded] without being alarmed, their abandonment of the secular life will accord with that of the Buddha. If laypeople listen without being alarmed, they will truly take refuge.[51]

Notice here the use of the term *i-hsing,* translated as "one-practice." While the term has been variously interpreted in other contexts, within the *Mo-ho chih-kuan* it is clearly used as a synonym for the constantly sitting samādhi.[52]

The second samādhi involves mindfulness of the Buddha *(nien-fo, buddhānusmṛti)* while walking. The practitioner is directed to circumambulate the meditation hall while reciting the name of Amitābha Buddha and thinking of him in all his magnificence. Care must be taken in this, as in other meditations, to maintain awareness of this vision as fundamentally empty and a creation of the mind.

The third samādhi is divided into the Vaipulya samādhi and the Lotus samādhi, named after the two sūtras that set forth many of the details of the practice. The Vaipulya samādhi involves a complex identification of ritual objects and doctrinal notions, together with continual recitation of *dhāraṇīs* from the sūtra (i.e., the third fascicle of the *Mahāsamnipāta-sūtra*), while the Lotus samādhi centers on an elaborate visualization of the bodhisattva Samantabhadra (as described in the last chapter of the *Lotus Sūtra* and another short related scripture).

The fourth samādhi is called both the samādhi of following one's own thought and the samādhi of awakening to (the nature of) thought.[53] Whereas in the first samādhi the practice of meditation while sitting is expounded, this fourth samādhi is the meditation that can be accomplished in all aspects of one's daily life, all modes of conduct. Its mere presence among the four samādhis is a sufficient demonstration that Chih-i's recommended meditation practice is not merely "quietistic." The great advantage of this practice, as stated in the *Mo-ho chih-kuan,* is that

> if one practices the way at the level of provisional forms, then one is able to achieve mental control upon entering the meditation chamber but unable to do so after leaving. There is, however, no break (in contemplation) in the case of "following one's own thought."[54]

More attention is devoted to this practice than to any of the other three, as Chih-i discusses in some detail good, evil, and morally neutral thoughts, their arising and their perishing (particularly in reference to his doctrine of the four phases of thought), the functioning of the five senses and the mind, the six modes of conduct (walking, sitting, etc.), and the six perfections—in short, the emphasis throughout is on "viewing the mind" *(kuan-hsin),* a term that Chih-i uses to denote meditation as a whole but that here applies in a stricter sense. It is clear that there is no situation in human life to which this meditation cannot be applied—for the only prop necessary to engage in it is the very mind that a human being is never without wherever he goes.

Alone of the four samādhis, this one has a warning appended to it rather than an exhortation to practice diligently. It is not a practice for the untrained except when no other practice is possible. We may here recall the statement in the *Hsüan-i* that practice (meditation) without study produces arrogance.[55] The danger that accompanies the practice of this samādhi is the breakdown of moral standards. Chih-i, while uncompromising in his nondual assertion of the identity of good and evil, is equally uncompromising in upholding the necessity of moral restraints. He echoes conventional Confucian historians, for example, in suggesting that it was the licentiousness of certain Neo-Taoists that caused the tragic loss of northern China to the barbarians in the early fourth century, and further that the Northern Chou dynasty's persecution of Buddhism (574–577) was brought on by immoral members of the saṅgha. It was their failure to understand the six identities that lay at the root of this event[56]—meaning that in their embrace of identity (oneness) they forgot the need for differentiation. Rephrasing, we could say that their "suddenness" overcame their "gradualness."

All of the four samādhis are variations on the central practice of viewing the mind *(kuan-hsin).* As Chih-i clearly states, "Your own mind contains the whole of the Buddha's teachings."[57] He also says, "It is via the mind that Buddhas attain liberation,"[58] and further that "when mind sees itself, it is the Buddha; mind is the Buddha mind, it is my own self."[59] The mind in question is by no means the *manas,* or mind taken as controller and organizer of the data from the five senses (though the Chinese word *hsin* obscures this fact); it is none other than the dharmadhātu, or ultimate reality, so that in viewing this mind, one thereby views the nature of the Buddha, "sees the Buddha-nature" *(chien fo-hsing).*[60]

We come now to the point where it is necessary to consider in some detail just what Chih-i means by the expression "perfect and sudden" practice. In the course of this chapter we have come across some useful indications as we approached the question indirectly and from various points of view. Here we encounter it directly.

While it is true that the ten modes and ten object-fields, the exposition of which occupies the bulk of the *Mo-ho chih-kuan,* constitute an unwieldy and intricate system, still they are organized according to a single clear and simple principle that can be taken as the definition of the perfect and sudden practice:

> In the perfect and sudden meditation *(yüan tun kuan)* one takes ultimate reality *(shih-hsiang)* as the object of contemplation even from the time that the thought of enlightenment makes its first appearance. When one practices the four samādhis and the eightfold path, then the wisdom and vision of the Buddha open in that place of enlightenment, and one attains acceptance of the nonarising [of dharmas]. It is like the cow [in the *Nirvāṇa Sūtra*] that eats the *kṣānti* grass: one gets ghee from it immediately. The meaning of this is [expounded] in the *Mo-ho chih-kuan.*[61]

Appropriately enough, we find reference to the perfect and sudden practice as such only outside the *Mo-ho chih-kuan* itself, in a passage where we are referred *to* the latter text.[62] This is because the *Mo-ho chih-kuan* in its entirety deals with the perfect and sudden practice.

The ten modes and ten object-fields *begin* with the highest contemplation of all: the mode of "viewing the object as inconceivable" *(acintya)* is a contemplation of the realm of *skandhas-āyatanas-dhātus*—that is, the realm of phenomenal reality. Although ninety-nine more combinations of mode with realm are possible, this pair ("vehicle") alone is sufficient for the practitioner of great capacity to attain the goal immediately. We see that the usual sequence in which the practitioner is led from shallow to profound (found, for example, in Chih-i's text on "gradualist" practice, the *Tz'u-ti ch'an-men*) is inverted. It is only the least talented meditators who need to work their way through the whole system in reverse, stage by stage—for them, it is undeniable that the text may be understood as "gradualistic." "Perfect and sudden" means here that the "perfect" truth is presented "suddenly," immediately, directly to the awareness of the practitioner.

We may recall Chih-i's *p'an-chiao* at this point, according to which the perfect or highest teaching, in the form of the *Avataṃsaka-sūtra,* was the very first propounded by Śākyamuni after his enlightenment. For Chih-i, however, the perfect teaching is found throughout the Mahāyāna sūtras, and even implicitly in those of the Hīnayāna. We find, accordingly, that the *Mo-ho chih-kuan* draws from a tremendous range of Buddhist literature, very prominently citing the *Ta-chih-tu lun* (Great Perfection of Wisdom Treatise) and the *Śūraṅgama, Nirvāṇa, Pratyutpanna-samā-*

dhi, Mañjuśrī-nirdeśa, and *Lotus* sūtras (though the last is less prominent than one might think in a work that has traditionally been classified in T'ien-t'ai and Tendai as one of the "three great *Lotus* commentaries" of Chih-i).[63]

As we have seen in Chih-i's criticism of Bodhiruci's *p'an-chiao*, a perfect teaching that is completely unadulterated with the provisional, or upāya, cannot even be spoken. Similarly, the highest reality cannot be taken as an object at all, because this reality transcends the subject-object dualism. But when words are used and objects perceived, it is precisely the so-called perfect teaching (or truth) that represents the limit they can attain. In the last analysis it can have no "marks" or features *(hsiang)* at all. This is what is meant by the "featureless" Lotus samādhi (one of the two "half-walking and half-sitting" samādhis in the *Mo-ho chih-kuan*). It is "the expedient consisting of directly contemplating the emptiness of all dharmas."[64] The "featureless repentance," a term whose significance is magnified by its later mention in the *Platform Sūtra*, implies this same perfect teaching wherein every category of analysis and every assumed dualism is finally shown to be "empty." The perfect or "featureless" repentance is one that recognizes that "since one's own mind is void of itself, there is no subject in whom sin or merit [could inhere]."[65]

Kuan-ting's introduction to the *Mo-ho chih-kuan* includes his summation of the perfect and sudden "calming and contemplation" (i.e., meditation), whose authority is so great that monks in the T'ien-t'ai school still chant it daily:

> The perfect and sudden from the very beginning takes ultimate reality as its object. No matter what the object of contemplation might be, it is seen to be identical to the middle. There is nothing that is not the ultimate reality *(chen-shih)*. When the objects of cognition are identified with the dharmadhātu, and when thought rests in the dharmadhātu alone, then there is not a single shape or smell that is not the middle way. The same goes for the realm of self, the realm of Buddha, and the realm of living beings. Since all aspects of the phenomenal world are thus, there is no suffering to be cast away. Since ignorance and defilements are identical with enlightenment, there is no cause of suffering to be eradicated. Since extremes are the middle and false views are the right view, there is no way to be cultivated. Since saṃsāra is identical to nirvāṇa, there is no annihilation to be achieved. Because of the nonexistence of suffering and of the cause of suffering, the mundane does not exist; because of the nonexistence of the way and of annihilation, the supramundane does not exist. The single, unalloyed ultimate reality *(shih-hsiang)* is all there is—no entities whatever exist outside it. That entities are by nature quiescent is called "calming" *(chih, śamatha)*; that, though quiescent, they are ever lustrous is called "contemplation" *(kuan, vipaśyanā)*. Though a verbal distinction is made between

earlier and later [stages of practice], there is no duality, no distinction between them. This is what is called the perfect and sudden calming and contemplation.[66]

This summation denies ultimacy to the four noble truths in a manner very similar to the *Heart Sūtra,* so essential a text to the practice of Ch'an and Zen. We are presented here with the four noble truths at their highest level, the actionless, fourth of Chih-i's four kinds of four noble truths. The actionless is synonymous with the perfect teaching in the more widely known arrangement of the four teachings according to content (tripiṭaka, shared, separate, perfect) which occurs prominently in Chih-i's *Ssu-chiao-i* (and Chegwan's *Ssu-chiao-i*) but does not play much of a role in the *Hsüan-i* or *Mo-ho chih-kuan.* Now it is clear that even at the level of the actionless, *effort* remains essential. The perfect practice, to quote Kuan-ting again, means to practice

the middle even while adhering to the extremes; to cultivate the three truths perfectly without being distracted; to be neither rendered quiescent by the infinite nor agitated by the finite, but, neither agitated nor quiescent, to enter the middle way directly.[67]

On the other hand, the sudden aspect of this practice is "like a magician mounting into space,"[68] since "space is of the same essence whether close to or far from the ground."[69]

Closely associated as they may be, the perfect and the sudden may also be provisionally distinguished, as in the phrase "the perfect truth is presented suddenly to the awareness of the practitioner." The aspirant is thus made aware of the same perfect teaching, as far as the latter can be verbalized, which is elucidated in Chih-i's *p'an-chiao* system. The perfect teaching, moreover, is merely another name for the highest of the three truths, that which is called the middle.

We turn now to the question of "temporal" subitism in Chih-i's thought. That is, does he or does he not hold that "enlightenment" occurs "suddenly"? Put another way, how does his position compare to that which Hui-neng seems to assert in the *Platform Sūtra?*

It is apparent that this issue, as it is usually understood, was fundamentally uninteresting to Chih-i. We know that he himself had at least two "enlightenment" experiences, the first at Mt. Ta-su under his great teacher Hui-ssu, the second not long after moving to Mt. T'ien-t'ai in 575. Clearly he was aware of the fact that there can be a sudden access of insight. But for all the stress on "perfect and sudden" in his writings on teaching and meditation, he consistently takes care *not* to suggest that the final fruit, the sixth of the six identities, is easily and quickly attained by the average person. To be sure, he theoretically admits the existence of those whose capacity is so great that a single hearing of the perfect teaching suffices to catapult them into supreme Buddhahood. These bodhisattvas, presented "suddenly" with the "perfect" truth, also attain it "suddenly." Moreover, since the perfect teaching is present in some sense throughout the scriptures, the most perspicacious bodhisattvas may attain supreme truth upon hearing only the slightest hint of it, just as the finest horse "responds to the mere shadow of the whip." Yet this kind of instant attainment remains theoretical. Even his own powerful enlightenment experiences did not move Chih-i to claim Buddhahood. On the contrary, he felt his attainment to be comparatively modest.

The word *tun,* which we are accustomed to translating as "sudden," is not, so far as I have found, applied adjectivally by Chih-i to the word *wu,* which we usually translate as "enlightenment." Only an exhaustive exploration of his entire corpus will disclose whether this preliminary observation can stand as a final datum. But it is not too early to suggest that *tun-wu,* if it appears, was not an especially meaningful term of discourse for Chih-i, even though Tao-sheng had already employed it in his own discussions and the terms "sudden" and "enlightenment" had been used to express critical concepts in Chih-i's thought.

Although *tun* and *wu* do not appear in tandem, one can find a passage in his *Hsüan-i*[70] where the apparently subitistic term *huo-jan* (often translated as "sudden"), used by Kumārajīva in the *Vimalakīrti Sūtra* commentary,[71] is applied several times adjectivally to other binomes that all mean "enlightenment": *k'ai-wu, wu-chieh, hsin-wu,* and *hsin-k'ai.* Several points can be made about this. First, it is by no means certain that *huo-jan* means "sudden" either to Kumārajīva or to Chih-i, although the term did eventually acquire this sense.[72] Second, these terms occur in a brief passage dealing not with the "sudden" but with the "variable" meditation, and while there are four different binomes meaning "enlightenment," none of them suggests the "supreme enlightenment" of Buddhahood, or "Buddha's wisdom." To attribute the latter sense to terms capable of a much less exalted interpretation, especially when used casually, would posit an extreme subtlety in a text that is otherwise concerned to point out the fallibility in the notion of an easy attainment of the goal, despite its inherence in us.

In the whole sweep of Chih-i's thought, there is very little of the quick and easy in his expositions of the concept of suddenness. Yet at the same time he cannot fairly be charged with the gradualism that later commentators have found in T'ien-t'ai. In the three truths and the four teachings, the five flavors and the six identities, Chih-i consistently points out that the terms in these sets of oppositions cannot be regarded as mutually exclusive. Assuredly, the sudden teaching exists because the highest truth cannot be expounded over time; and the sudden practice exists because some practitioners of great capacity may, upon directly encountering the highest teaching, attain much in a short space of time. Nevertheless it is precisely the "constant practice of meditation that will make the capacities keen," whereupon the goal can be attained in the next life if not in this.[73]

Conclusion

Chih-i, several generations before the appearance of the Ch'an school, found a place for both "sudden" and "gradual" in his massive syntheses of teaching and practice, avoiding the later tendency of emphasizing suddenness to the detriment of gradualness, whether in meditation or in the exposition of the Buddha's word. What seems most characteristic of his thought is the effort to bring such opposite poles into harmony with each other.

So far as teaching (doctrine) is concerned, Chih-i regarded the *Lotus Sūtra* as the paradigmatic integration of the highest or perfect truth with the skillful means that enable living beings to apprehend it. The *Lotus* thus represented the interfusion of the perfect and sudden teaching with numerous gradualist subdoctrines, without implying a denigration of those teachings (sūtras) that the Buddha expounded prior to the *Lotus*. The perfect teaching inhered for Chih-i in every sūtra that the Buddha spoke, just as the entire cosmos was contained in every thought of all living beings.

In his exposition of practice (meditation), Chih-i carved a similar template for the T'ien-t'ai school. A "perfect and sudden" meditation signified the direct apprehension of ultimate reality from the first moment of practice. Inverting the traditional sequence that led from shallow to profound, Chih-i near the end of his life set forth a form of contemplation in which the practitioner, at the outset of his practice, apprehends the nonduality of self and contemplative object, good and evil, bondage and liberation. Yet while expounding the perfect and sudden meditation, Chih-i did not feel it necessary to censure the gradual path. His principal meditation treatises bristle with a panoply of contemplative techniques inherited from earlier gradualist sources, but each is reinterpreted in the context of the perfect nondual teaching—each is sudden in its gradualness.

The sudden and gradual relationship in Chih-i's thought is thus precisely analogous to the relationship between identity and difference in his doctrine of the six identities. The fact that the practitioner is identical with Buddha at every stage of the path does not mitigate the fact that there are stages—to think otherwise exposes us to arrogance. And the strenuous effort necessary for deepening one's insight never contradicts inherent Buddhahood—failing to grasp this, a practitioner is apt to slip into morbid self-depreciation. As he progresses in his practice, the attentive meditator keeps equally distant from either extreme, intuiting new and deeper nuances in his already attained inseparability from the perfect truth.

Notes

1. In his two seminal articles, "La pénétration du Bouddhisme dans la tradition philosophique chinoise," *Cahiers d'Histoire Mondiale* 3, no. 1 (1956): 19–38, and "Le miroir spirituel," *Sinologica* 1, no. 2 (1947): 112–137 (an English translation of which is included in this volume), as well as in his book, *Le concile de Lhasa: une controverse sur le quiétisme entre bouddhistes de l'Inde et de la Chine au VIIIe siécle de l'ère chrétienne, Bibliothèque de l'Institut des Hautes Études Chinoises,* vol. 7 (Paris: Imprimerie Nationale de France, 1952).

2. Especially in his *The Zen Doctrine of No-Mind* (London: Rider & Co., 1949).

3. *Mu no tankyū: Chūgoku Zen* (Tokyo: Kadokawa shoten, 1969), 102.

4. *T* 46.462–475. Andō Toshio, in his *Tendai-gaku* (Kyoto: Heirakuji shoten, 1968), 300, states his belief that this text also influenced the thought of the fourth Ch'an patriarch. The *Hsiao-chih-kuan* has been translated by Wai-tao in Dwight Goddard, ed., *A Buddhist Bible* (New York: E. P. Dutton, 1938) and by Charles Luk in *The Secrets of Chinese Meditation* (London: Rider & Co., 1964). For a reappraisal of this text's influence on Ch'an meditation manuals, see Carl Bielefeldt, "Ch'ang-lu Tsung-tse's *Tso-ch'an i* and the 'Secret' of Zen meditation," in Peter N. Gregory, ed., *Traditions of Meditation in Chinese Buddhism,* Studies in East Asian Buddhism, no. 4 (Honolulu: University of Hawaii Press, 1986).

5. Sekiguchi Shindai, *Tendai shikan no kenkyū* (Tokyo: Iwanami shoten, 1969), 272.

6. *Hsüan-i, T* 33.686a, 806a–c.

7. *T* 33.686a.

8. *MHCK, T* 46.10b–c.

9. The metaphor is borrowed from the *Śūraṅgama-samādhi-sūtra,* see *T* 15.633c–634a.

10. Chan-jan's comment here is helpful: " 'But their words cannot yet be called sūtras.' This is because the pronouncements of aspirants at this level are not original with them, but as yet merely resemble, or are imitative of, what has been said before. We might liken this to the art of an apprentice painter, who becomes skilled in copying the great masters but is still unable to produce original masterpieces."

11. *T* 12.407b.

12. Leon Hurvitz, *Chih-i (538–595): An Introduction to the Life and Ideas of a Chinese Buddhist Monk, Mélanges Chinois et Bouddhiques* 12 (1960–1962), 172.

13. Following Chan-jan's comments to this passage in the *MHCK.*

14. *MHCK, T* 46.9a.

15. *MHCK, T* 26.8c–9a.

16. See the various works of Sekiguchi Shindai, especially his *Tendai shikan no kenkyū*, and David Chappell's "Introduction to the *T'ien-t'ai ssu-chiao-i*," *Eastern Buddhist*, n.s. 9, no. 1 (1976): 72–86.

17. This set of three terms was borrowed from earlier scholars mentioned in the *Hsüan-i* (*T* 33.801), but Chih-i's use of the terms is his own.

18. *Hsüan-i*, *T* 33.806a.

19. Two further doctrinal expressions of the all-in-each/each-in-all principle are (1) the trichiliocosm in each moment of consciousness and (2) each of the ten destinies present in all of the others (implied in the previous expression). The latter result allows for Buddha-nature in hell and hell in Buddha-nature, a question that became quite controversial during the T'ang dynasty and later.

20. My doctoral dissertation consists of a carefully annotated translation of the important first chapter of this work. See "*The Great Calming and Contemplation* of Chih-i. Chapter One: The Synopsis" (Ph.D. diss., University of British Columbia, 1976).

21. *MHCK*, *T* 46.1c.

22. *T* 46.475–548.

23. Since the *Hsiao-chih-kuan* turned out to be the standard for later meditation manuals in the Ch'an tradition, it is ironic that Ch'an thus used a "gradualistic" text as a partial foundation for its own supposedly "sudden" practice, and doubly ironic because Ch'an liked to criticize T'ien-t'ai itself as "gradual."

24. *T* 12.784c.

25. *Hsüan-i*, *T* 33.806b–c.

26. This formula, as set forth in the Korean monk Chegwan's *Ssu-chiao-i*, was still accepted by Leon Hurvitz in his important *Chih-i*.

27. See Sekiguchi, *Tendai shikan no kenkyū;* Chappell, "Introduction to the *T'ien-t'ai ssu-chiao-i*"; and John McRae, *The Northern School and the Formation of Early Ch'an Buddhism*, Studies in East Asian Buddhism, no. 3 (Honolulu: University of Hawaii Press, 1986).

28. *T* 12.690c–691a.

29. *T* 33.803b.

30. *Bukkyō daijiten*, vol. 2 (Tokyo: Sekai seiten kankō kyōkai, 1933–1936), 1300b.

31. Unlike his predecessors, Chih-i included the *Avataṃsaka* within the five flavors. Earlier exegetes had begun the five flavors with the Hīnayāna teachings, that is, after the *Avataṃsaka*.

32. *Hsüan-i*, *T* 33.807a.

33. *T* 33.804a–b.

34. This seems to be a pair of Chinese terms for *neyārtha* and *nītārtha*.

35. *Hsüan-i*, *T* 33.809a.

36. *Hsüan-i*, *T* 33.683c.

37. Such considerations formed the basis for the later position of the T'ien-t'ai school in its controversies with Hua-yen over the nature of the absolute, during the T'ang dynasty. The two schools were represented respectively by Chan-jan and Ch'eng-kuan (738–839). While the absolute or the one was for both thinkers identical in some sense with the relative or the many, Chan-jan

criticized Ch'eng-kuan and implicitly the whole school of thought that the latter represented for tending toward excessive transcendence, unalloyed purity, and a monistic absolute (just as the *Avataṃsaka-sūtra,* according to Chih-i, lacks upāya). See Tamura Yoshirō, *Zettai no shinri: Tendai* (Tokyo: Kadokawa shoten, 1960), 181–183.

38. *Hsüan-i, T* 33.801b.

39. *Hsüan-i, T* 33.804a.

40. *Hsüan-i, T* 33.805a.

41. These four teachings are the basis for the exposition in Chih-i's *Ssu-chiao-i, T* 46.721–769; the title of this work is homophonous with the title of the now-notorious precis of the medieval Korean monk Chegwan (fl. late tenth century), the *Ssu-chiao-i, T* 46.773–781. The latter, a completely different work from that by Chih-i, purports to summarize Chih-i's doctrine but errs in numerous places. For a translation of Chegwan's work see David Chappell, *T'ien-t'ai Buddhism: An Outline of the Fourfold Teachings* (Tokyo: Daiichi shobō, 1983).

42. *MHCK, T* 46.6a–b.

43. *MHCK, T* 46.1c. Less well known but equivalent in meaning is a dictum occurring later in the same text: "the defilements are identical to the dharmadhātu" (*T* 46.49c).

44. Still, one of Chih-i's works is traditionally associated with the variable practice, namely the *Liu-miao-fa-men* (*T* #1917), the "Six Wondrous Teachings." This text elucidates the same three stages of *śamatha* and three of *vispaśyanā* upon which the second-century translation (by An Shih-kao) of the *Ānāpānasmṛti-sūtra* bases its own exposition. While it is among his early works, it is of great interest because of Chih-i's use here of the *śamatha-vipaśyanā* terminology.

45. *T* 46.475–548.

46. Summaries and short discussions of them may be found in Hurvitz's *Chih-i* and in my own dissertation.

47. *MHCK, T* 46.11a. Also in the *Hsüan-i, T* 33.806b, where Chih-i makes reference to the perfect and sudden practice, he speaks of the four samādhis rather than the ten modes and ten object-fields. See Daniel Stevenson, "The Four Kinds of Samādhi in Early T'ien-t'ai Buddhism" in Gregory, *Traditions of Meditation in Chinese Buddhism.*

48. One of these, the "Lotus samādhi," was of great importance in the development of Chih-i's thought but turned out to have little influence in later generations, at least so far as the specific details of the practice were concerned.

49. All the preceding techniques may be considered "gradualistic."

50. *MHCK, T* 46.11b.

51. *T* 46.12a.

52. *MHCK, T* 46.11b: "constantly sitting . . . is also called the one-practice samādhi." See Bernard Faure, "The Concept of One-Practice Samādhi in Early Ch'an" in Gregory, *Traditions of Meditation in Chinese Buddhism.*

53. For details, see my paper, "Chih-i's Contemplation of Evil," in David W. Chappell, ed., *Buddhist and Taoist Practice in Medieval Chinese Society* (Honolulu: University of Hawaii Press, 1987).

54. *T* 46.18c.

55. *T* 33.686a.

56. *T* 46.19b.
57. *MHCK, T* 46.9a.
58. *MHCK, T* 46.12c, quoted from the *Pratyutpanna-sūtra* at *T* 13.909a.
59. *MHCK, T* 46.12c, quoted from the *Pratyutpanna-sūtra* at *T* 13.905c–906a.
60. *Hsüan-i, T* 33.806b.
61. *Hsüan-i, T* 33.806b.
62. Kuan-ting's preface to the *MHCK,* also outside the text proper, contains a nearly identical definition of the perfect and sudden practice, and his formulation is the one usually referred to. See *MHCK, T* 461c (quoted below). Since he was Chih-i's scribe and dharmic successor, Kuan-ting's formulations carry an authority nearly equal to that of his teacher.
63. The *Hsüan-i* and *Fa-hua wen-chü* being the other two. Only the latter is a true commentary in the usual sense of a passage-by-passage elucidation of the meaning of the main text.
64. *MHCK, T* 46.14a.
65. Quoted in *MHCK, T* 46.14a, from the *Kuan p'u-hsien ching* at *T* 9.392c. The passage, which is a famous one, reads in full:

> What is sin, what is merit? Since one's own mind is void of itself, there is no subject in which sin and merit [could inhere]. Similarly with all [other] dharmas: they lack both abiding and perishing. Such a repentance—in which one contemplates the mind as lacking [the nature of] mind, and the other dharmas as not abiding in themselves, but [sees them] all as liberated, as the noble truth of annihilation, and as quiescent—is called the great repentance, the adorned repentance, the sinless repentance, the destroyer-of-mind-and-consciousness repentance.

66. *T* 46.1c–2a. Kuan-ting borrowed all the phrases in this summation from Chih-i himself.
67. *MHCK, T* 46.2a.
68. *T* 46.1c.
69. Chan-jan furnishes us with the latter comment.
70. *T* 33.806c.
71. *T* 38.365a–b.
72. It is so used in later Chinese Buddhist literature such as the *Platform Sūtra* and in Tsung-mi (780–841), where it is understood as a synonym for *tun,* but such a construction is hardly necessary here. The initial character of the binome carries the weight of meaning, which is hinted at by the "valley" radical on the right: "vast, deep, broad, open"—i.e., no sense of instantaneousness or temporal subitism is implied.
73. *MHCK, T* 46.19c–20a.

Glossary

Ch'an 禪
Chan-jan 湛然
Chegwan 諦觀
chen-shih 眞實
Ch'eng-kuan 澄觀
chiao-men 教門

chien 漸
chien fo-hsing 見佛性
chih 止
Chih-i 智顗
chih-kuan 止觀
Dōgen 道元
Fa-hua hsüan-i 法華玄義
Fa-hua wen-chu 法華文句
hsiang 相
Hsiao chih-kuan 小止觀
hsin 心
hsin-k'ai 心開
hsin-wu 心悟
Hsüan-i 玄義
Hua-yen 華嚴
Hui-neng 慧能
Hui-ssu 慧思
Hung-jen 弘忍
huo-jan 豁然
i-hsing 一行
i-nien san-ch'ien 一念三千
k'ai-wu 開悟
kuan 觀
kuan-men 觀門
kuan-hsin 觀心
Kuan p'u-hsien ching 觀普賢經
Kuan-ting 灌頂
liu-chi 六即
Mo-ho chih-kuan 摩訶止觀
Nichiren 日蓮
nien-fo 念佛
p'an-chiao 判教
Saichō 最澄
san-kuan 三觀
Shen-hsiu 神秀
shih-hsiang 實相
Ssu-chiao-i (by Chih-i) 四教義
Ssu-chiao-i (by Chegwan) 四教儀
Ta-chih-tu lun 大智度論
Tao-hsin 道信
Tao-sheng 道生
Tendai 天臺
T'ien-t'ai 天臺
tsung 宗
Tsung-mi 宗密
tun 頓
tun-wu 頓悟
Tz'u-ti ch'an-men 次第禪門
wu 悟
wu-chieh 悟解
wu-hsiang 無相
wu-tso 無作
yu-hsiang 有相
yüan tun kuan 圓頓觀
Zen 禪

Shen-hui and the Teaching of Sudden Enlightenment in Early Ch'an Buddhism

John R. McRae

I. Introduction

A. The Understanding of Suddenness in Modern Ch'an Studies

The field of Ch'an studies has seen some very lively disputes over the course of the twentieth century, but there has been general agreement on the proposition that the doctrine of sudden enlightenment represents the highest expression of the doctrinal mainstream of early Chinese Ch'an Buddhism. Although there is some quibbling regarding details and specific interpretations, scholars working in this field often describe the history of the doctrine of sudden enlightenment within Ch'an in terms of three subjects: (1) Hui-neng's doctrine of sudden enlightenment as shown in his "mind verse" *(hsin-chieh)* in the *Platform Sūtra of the Sixth Patriarch (Liu-tsu t'an-ching);* (2) Shen-hui's campaign in opposition to the gradual teaching of the Northern school and in support of the public recognition of Hui-neng as sixth patriarch; and (3) the continuation of the spirit of Hui-neng in the teachings and religious practice of Ma-tsu, Shih-t'ou, and the later Ch'an tradition.

Research done in recent years has shown that the traditional interpretations of these three subjects are all substantially incorrect, although the implications of these findings have not yet been fully realized. The history of early Ch'an is in the process of being thoroughly rewritten, but it is already clear that the doctrine of sudden enlightenment and the dispute between the sudden and gradual teachings should no longer be used as yardsticks by which the religious message of Ch'an and its widespread acceptance in T'ang dynasty China are understood.

In the first place, we know now that it is impossible to describe the teachings of the historical figure Hui-neng (638–713) with any certainty whatsoever. The rather extensive works of Hui-neng's most active disciple Shen-hui[1] (684–758) never quote his master's sayings. Since Shen-hui could have bolstered the legitimacy of his doctrinal claims by quoting Hui-neng, we may infer that Shen-hui did not possess any record of Hui-neng's teachings.[2] An epitaph for Hui-neng written by the poet Wang Wei and commissioned by Shen-hui or one of his followers contains a biographical statement but only vague allusions to his teachings.[3] Hence it is most reasonable to assume that Shen-hui was guided only by his memory and not by any written transcript of Hui-neng's teachings, and that Shen-hui's recollections regarding Hui-neng's teachings were not sharply distinguished from Shen-hui's own teachings. The *Platform Sūtra,* which purports to record one of Hui-neng's sermons, is now known to have been written about the year 780 by a member of an early Ch'an faction known as the Ox-head school. The possibility that this text contains at least some kernel of Hui-neng's teachings is undercut both by the differences between the contents of this text and the doctrines of Shen-hui and by the similarity between those contents and the known doctrines of the Ox-head school.[4] Hui-neng is extremely important as a legendary image, but the indications of any historical contributions by him are irretrievably lost.[5]

Thus the *Platform Sūtra*'s account of the exchange of "mind verses" between Hui-neng and Shen-hsiu (606?–706) of the Northern school, perhaps the most famous anecdote in Ch'an history, has been discovered to be a creative legend rather than a factual account. Although this is not to say that the legend was unimportant—far from it!—the ideas contained in these two verses should not be understood in terms of a simple opposition between the "gradual teaching" of Shen-hsiu and the "sudden teaching" of Hui-neng. Rather, the two verses constitute a single unit expressing a rarified understanding of the "perfect teaching" of constant bodhisattvic practice. That is, one should labor unceasingly to save all other sentient beings from suffering even as one remained constantly in meditation, but without ever conceptualizing sentient beings, salvific action, or meditation.[6]

In fact, in direct contrast to the traditional interpretation, Northern school ideas and terminology were used in the compilation of these famous verses. This is true not only of the basic metaphors, such as the mirror stand, the bodhi tree, and polishing, which one would expect to have had some association with Shen-hsiu. The most intriguing aspect of the verses is that the line "Fundamentally there is not a single thing," which occurs as the third line of "Hui-neng's" verse in all but the Tun-huang version of the text, itself is presaged by a line in a Northern school text. Perhaps more important, Northern school texts contain numerous discussions of the nonexistence of a "single thing." Therefore, we must conclude that Northern school ideas were used in the compilation of the *Platform Sūtra* mind verses.[7]

As a result, what was once introduced as a very simple rubric for explaining the origins of the doctrine of sudden enlightenment in the Ch'an school must now be explained as the result of an extensive and even convoluted doctrinal progression. The traditional interpretation of the anecdote and verses as representing gradualist versus subitist positions must be discussed in the context of the mid-ninth century and beyond and should not be used to describe either the historical or doctrinal development of early Ch'an Buddhism.

The third subject listed above, the continuation of the early Ch'an doctrine of sudden enlightenment by Ma-tsu Tao-i (709–788), Shih-t'ou Hsi-ch'ien (700–790), and the later Ch'an tradition, also involves unsupportable assumptions. The relatively late provenance and the Ox-head school authorship of the *Platform Sūtra* clearly obviates the possibility of any direct succession from Hui-neng and/or Shen-hui to Ma-tsu, et al., and the fictive nature of such a succession is corroborated by the biographical evidence.[8] Moreover, we should not be misled by the fact that the later Ch'an school adopted the name "Southern school," which was Shen-hui's battle standard against the gradualists of the so-called Northern school. In fact, this continuity of sectarian label obscures the single most important distinction in eighth- and ninth-century Ch'an: that between the "early Ch'an" factions (the Northern, Southern, and Ox-head schools) and the "classical Ch'an" beginning with Ma-tsu's Hung-chou school.

Indeed, understanding the dynamics of the early-to-classical transition is one of the most important issues now facing Ch'an studies. This is because of the very distinct nature of the disconformity between the two, which is manifested in the marked differences in the textual legacies of early and classical Ch'an: classical Ch'an is distinguished by its almost total dedication to the practice of "encounter dialogue," the spontaneous and unstructured repartee between masters and students. Where early Ch'an texts contain a wide variety of doctrinal formulations, practical exhortations, and ritual procedures, the texts of classical Ch'an are more uniform in their dedication to the transcription of encounter dialogue incidents, and they delight in baffling paradoxes, patent absurdities, and instructive vignettes of nonconformist behavior. Where early Ch'an texts attempt to infuse new meanings and a new spirit of dedication into conventional Buddhist doctrines and practices, classical Ch'an texts reject or simply ignore traditional activities completely. And where early Ch'an texts are alternately charming, informative, and baffling in their varied attempts to enunciate the new message, classical Ch'an texts derive their power from vivid portrayals of specific living masters and students grappling with real spiritual problems.

For better or worse, the elucidation of the early-to-classical transition also involves some very difficult problems regarding the primary sources. Perhaps the most remarkable indication of the very existence of the discontinuity between early and classical Ch'an is that the texts of the classical phase—or at least the most distinctive texts, those containing transcripts of encounter dialogue—are uniformly absent from the finds at Tun-huang.[9] One reason for this absence, of course, is the great geographical distance between Tun-huang and south-central China, where Ma-tsu and his Hung-chou school flourished. Also, the very close relationship between the encounter-dialogue practice of classical Ch'an and word play in oral Chinese must have left the Tibetans in Tun-huang and Tibet proper very much unmoved. It would be many years before Ch'an was transmitted (to any substantial degree) even to Korea and Japan, which imbibed much more heavily of Chinese language and culture. Either classical Ch'an was not considered an appropriate model for export to Tun-huang and Tibet, or the Buddhist community in Tun-huang was neither ready nor able to consider such a new type of religious practice.

The absence of classical texts from Tun-huang is not merely an indication of cultural and chronological disparity, for it means that we are left without any independent scale by which to understand the textual development of classical Ch'an. We simply do not have any texts relevant to the earliest period of classical Ch'an that did not pass through the hands of Sung dynasty editors, who either knowingly or unknowingly homogenized the editions they produced. Such problems are beyond the scope of this paper.[10]

What is striking about the emergence of encounter dialogue in south-central China is not merely that it occurred, but that it seems to have been the total focus of attention by the members of the Hung-chou school and the subsequent Ch'an tradition. In other words, although we can perceive in early Ch'an prototypic forms of encounter dialogue,[11] this was but one aspect of early Ch'an religious practice. On the other hand, although encounter dialogue may be interpreted in terms of doctrines and practices developed by the Northern, Southern, and Ox-head schools and the Szechwan factions, it received such a single-minded emphasis in the Hung-chou school and other classical Ch'an factions that their religious practice was fundamentally different from the pluralistic endeavors of early Ch'an. Hence the differences between early and classical Ch'an are both qualitative and quantitative, and at the very least it should be clear that we cannot march directly from Hui-neng to Ma-tsu.[12]

So what, then, was the real impact of Shen-hui and his doctrine of sudden enlightenment?

B. Shen-hui and Modern Ch'an Studies

For a variety of reasons, it is perfectly understandable that Shen-hui's life and teachings became a cynosure of scholarly interest during the twentieth century. Transcripts of his oral and written teachings are among the most interesting and thought-provoking of the many early Ch'an texts discovered at Tun-huang. Not only is it unusual for such texts to be specifically attributable to a single historical personage, but they seem to derive from different points throughout Shen-hui's career and thus to allow consideration of the evolution of his positions, a unique opportunity within the context of early Ch'an studies. Even granting the apparent discontinuity between early and classical Ch'an, it is still the case that the labels "Southern school" and "sudden teaching" were accepted by the orthodox tradition as descriptions of the mainstream of Chinese Ch'an. Since it was indeed Shen-hui who first championed the doctrine of sudden enlightenment and the cause of the Southern school, his career did have a much greater impact on the development of Ch'an than is apparent in the traditional literature.

In spite of this, I believe that modern scholarship overestimates Shen-hui's significance and distorts the nature of his contributions. This misinterpretation of Shen-hui's teachings and historical role devolves initially from the work of the noted Chinese scholar Hu Shih (1891–1962), who was the first to discover and study the Tun-huang manuscripts of Shen-hui's teachings.[13] Briefly put, Hu Shih believed that Shen-hui's career signaled the beginning of a major transformation, not only in Chinese Buddhism, but in Chinese intellectual and cultural history in general. Hu defined this transformation as the reassertion of native Chinese values and the rejection of the Buddhist ideas that were so popular during the Six Dynasties and early T'ang dynasty periods. The mechanism by which Shen-hui initiated this transformation was the teaching of sudden enlightenment, which Hu believed to be inherently Chinese in its essentially simple approach to the problem of religious cultivation.[14]

Hu Shih's basic work on Shen-hui was widely accepted by other authorities, although usually without reference to his larger interpretive scheme. Not the least significant of these other scholars was D. T. Suzuki, whose distinctive interpretation of Chinese and Japanese Zen, especially Rinzai, inspired great interest in and significantly informed the modern understanding of the Ch'an/Zen tradition. Suzuki sharply criticized Hu's overly historical approach to Ch'an studies but did not fault his findings.[15] Suzuki agreed that Shen-hui was responsible for the eventual success of the sudden teaching, but he tended to ignore the subject of Shen-hui's historical contributions—in his interest to get at the heart of the Ch'an message, Suzuki was much more attracted to discussion of the original creative insight of Ch'an, which he attributed to Bodhidharma and Hui-neng. Suzuki did feel that the triumph of the message taught first by Bodhidharma and Hui-neng and later by Shen-hui represented a major transformation in Chinese Buddhism, although in his mind this transformation was not the reemergence of native Chinese culture but rather the final elimination of extraneous intellectual baggage from a tradition destined to become the unalloyed expression of the "enlightenment experience."

Indeed, Shen-hui *was* a major figure in the development of Chinese Ch'an Buddhism, although his contributions were quantitatively less significant and qualitatively different from the manner in which they are described in most modern writings on Ch'an. Ch'an Buddhism did undergo a major transformation in the latter part of the eighth century (this is not quite the same as saying that the emergence of Ch'an per se represented a transformation in Chinese Buddhism or in Chinese intellectual history), but Shen-hui was only one of a number of individuals involved in the process. The emergence of Ch'an was a major event in Chinese religious and intellectual history—an event that must be considered within the larger context of the transition from the medieval society of the T'ang to the premodern society of the Sung—but the teaching of sudden enlightenment was only one of the many relevant doctrinal and practical factors involved.

In the pages that follow I offer a preliminary re-evaluation of Shen-hui's life and basic doctrines, especially his doctrine of sudden enlightenment, based in part on new epigraphic and textual evidence. This material has allowed me to develop a new chronology for Shen-hui's life and a new interpretation of his early doctrinal development, both of which imply a much closer relationship between him and the Northern school than has previously been thought to have existed. The analysis of this relationship provides the basis for a hypothesis concerning the role of the doctrine of sudden enlightenment in Shen-hui's life and thought and, to a lesser extent, in the subsequent Ch'an tradition.

II. Shen-hui's Biography

Very recently, the study of Shen-hui's biography[16] has been aided by the discovery of his stele and ritual implements at Lung-men. Although the stele in question was crudely done and is very simple in content, it was erected in 765 and thus represents the earliest source for the dates of Shen-hui's life. The major contribution of this new discovery is its statement that Shen-hui died in 758 at the age of seventy-five and after fifty-four years as a monk. The revision of Shen-hui's dates to 684–758 (the dates given previously were 670–762) clears up a controversy about his age at the time of his commencement of training under Hui-neng, although it makes his period of service to the T'ang ruling house after the An Lu-shan rebellion remarkably brief. The newly discovered stele is also the earliest source to refer explicitly to Shen-hui as the seventh patriarch of Ch'an. Along with the stele were discovered four artifacts connected with Shen-hui that are exquisite examples of T'ang craftsmanship: a reliquary bowl with cover in the shape of a stūpa (which contained ashes—probably Shen-hui's—when it was discovered), a *kuṇḍika* water vessel, a long-handled censer, and a begging bowl. The first three items are of gilt bronze, and the last was of very lightweight pottery lacquered to a highly reflective gloss.[17]

A. Shen-hui's Early Training

Shen-hui was born in 684 as a member of the Kao family of Hsiang-yang.[18] His biography in the *Sung kao-seng chuan* (Biographies of Eminent Monks [Compiled during the] Sung [Dynasty]; hereafter cited as *SKSC*) describes him in typical fashion as a gifted youth conversant in the *Lao-tzu* and *Chuang-tzu* who discovered Buddhism while reading the *Hou Han shu* (Book of the Later Han [Dynasty]). He left home to become a monk under Dharma Master Hao-yüan of Kuo-ch'ang ssu in Hsiang-yang, a figure who is otherwise unknown.[19] According to Tsung-mi and the *Ching-te ch'üan-teng lu* (Records of the Transmission of the Lamp [Compiled during the] Ching-te [Period]; hereafter cited as *CTL*), Shen-hui first traveled to Ts'ao-ch'i (in modern Kwangtung province) to study under Hui-neng at the age of 14.[20] Using the dates given in the newly discovered stele inscription, this would have been in 697. It is not known exactly how long Shen-hui stayed in Ts'ao-ch'i. Eventually, he traveled north and in 704 took the full ordination in Ch'ang-an.[21] He must have continued his religious training under northern master(s) at this time; Tsung-mi actually says that he studied under Shen-hsiu himself for three years.[22] In any case, according to Tsung-mi, after Shen-hui returned to Ts'ao-ch'i sometime during the years 707–709, Hui-neng "recognized his pure maturity and silently transmitted the secret words" to him.[23] Shen-hui no doubt stayed with Hui-neng until the latter's death in 713.

B. Shen-hui's Teaching Career

It would be very interesting to know of Shen-hui's activities during the years 713–720, immediately after Hui-neng's death. Although I will make some inferences regarding this period below, virtually no specific biographical data is available.[24] The *SKSC* says very tersely that after

Hui-neng's death Shen-hui "wandered about to famous sites." In 720 he took up residence at the Lung-hsing ssu in Nan-yang, which was only a short distance north of Hsiang-yang, his native place, and not very far from the eastern capital of Lo-yang. Shen-hui apparently began to focus his attentions on Lo-yang during this period; the *SKSC* claims that his teachings started to become known during this period, even though the school of P'u-chi was still predominant.[25] Shen-hui's works contain dialogues with prominent individuals identified with Nan-yang, some of which may derive from this period.[26] Shen-hui's *Platform Sermon* probably also dates from this period, although the dating is uncertain.[27]

In 730, 731, and 732, Shen-hui lectured before public audiences of monks and laymen, openly and vociferously attacking the teachings and religious genealogy of P'u-chi (651–739) and Hsiang-mo Tsang of the Northern school. The best-known of these public lectures occurred at the Ta-yün ssu in Hua-t'ai (Hua hsien, Honan) on the fifteenth day of the first month of 732, the date that is often mistakenly given (rather than 730) for the initiation of Shen-hui's anti-Northern school campaign. Tsung-mi states that Shen-hui criticized the Northern school with regard to the transmission of Bodhidharma's robe in Lo-yang while he was in Lo-yang prior to 732, but this statement may not be chronologically rigorous.[28] Since dharma masters from Fu-hsien ssu and Ho-tse ssu in Lo-yang supposedly took part in the 732 meeting, we may infer that Shen-hui had already developed special relationships with these monasteries.[29] The location of the other meetings is not known. (I will discuss the possible reasons for Shen-hui's choice of Hua-t'ai in section A of the conclusion to this essay.)

In 745 Shen-hui formally took up residence at Ho-tse ssu in Lo-yang, which is the location with which he is most closely associated. The *CTL* actually states that it was only after his move to Lo-yang in 745 that Shen-hui wrote the *Hsien-tsung chi* (Record of the Manifestation of the Truth) and "defined the two schools," i.e., the "southern [Hui]-neng sudden school and northern [Shen]-hsiu gradual teaching."[30] The *Definition of the Truth* (*P'u-t'i-to-ma nan-tsung ting shih-fei lun,* Definition of the Truth [Regarding] Bodhidharma's Southern School), which was based primarily on the 732 Ta-yün ssu lecture, was also edited sometime during the years 744–749, probably shortly after Shen-hui's move to Ho-tse ssu in 745.[31] Tacitly admitting that Shen-hui's activities at Hua-t'ai had not had much of an impact, Tsung-mi suggests that it was from the time of his move to Lo-yang that the differences between the Northern and Southern schools became widely known.[32] The *SKSC* says that Shen-hui established a hall at Ho-tse ssu containing a likeness of Hui-neng, for which a layman named Sung Ting erected a stele. The newly discovered stele for Shen-hui corroborates this in its vague statement that Sung Ting (whom the stele identifies as a *ping-pu shih-lang* or vice minister of the ministry of war) "extended an invitation [to Shen-hui to come to] Lo-yang to expansively open the dharma eye, erected an epitaph and established a likeness."[33] Presumably both the epitaph and the likeness were Hui-neng's, the former probably being that written by Wang Wei.[34] The *SKSC,* again, reports that Shen-hui also taught about the succession from Śākyamuni and the six Chinese patriarchs and had pictures painted of the latter, to which Fang Kuan added a preface.[35] About this time Shen-hui was also involved in efforts to provide the third patriarch, Seng-ts'an, with a suitable biography.[36] (Seng-ts'an had been the most obscure of the Chinese patriarchs ever since the formation of the theory of the transmission from Bodhidharma around the turn of the eighth century.)

Although Shen-hui openly criticized the heterodox transmission and faulty teachings of the Northern school after his move to Ho-tse ssu in 745, there is no specific record of any public lecturing by him there until 749. According to one sometimes unreliable text, beginning in this year Shen-hui continued his public attack on the Northern school from the ordination platform every month.[37] However, the variety of subjects discussed in Shen-hui's *Miscellaneous Dialogues,* which contains exchanges with monks and laymen primarily from the Nan-yang period of Shen-hui's life, suggests that the anti-Northern school campaign was not his only concern.[38]

C. *Shen-hui's Banishment and Reinstatement*

In 753 Shen-hui was banished from the capital at the instigation of a military official named Lu I, who memorialized against the possible problems involved with Shen-hui's large audiences. Lu I is said to have been guided in this matter by P'u-chi, even though this influential Northern school monk had died almost a decade and a half earlier.[39] Tsung-mi points out that the religious leadership of the Northern school did not agree with Shen-hui's banishment, which was the work of ignorant followers more given to a sense of competition. Actually, given the political climate in Ch'ang-an in 753, it is quite possible that the mere fact of Shen-hui's large audiences might have been as important in Shen-hui's removal from the capital as any factional aggressiveness.[40]

In any case, Shen-hui's banishment seems to have been anything but severe. On the basis of Lu I's accusation, Shen-hui was taken by two high-ranking ministers to meet Emperor Hsüan-tsung. A conversation in the emperor's bath house was followed by an edict " 'demoting' Shen-hui and relocating him to the provinces,"[41] first to I-yang (I-yang, Kiangsi) and then to Wu-t'ang (Chin hsien, Hupeh). In 754 Shen-hui was transferred by imperial order to Hsiang-yang. Finally, in the seventh month of 754, an imperial proclamation had him take up residence at the K'ai-yüan ssu in Ching-chou. Of these locations, Hsiang-chou was Shen-hui's native place and Ching-chou was one of the most important centers of Buddhist activity in south-central China. In addition, Wu-t'ang was then the residence of Nan-yang Hui-chung (d. 775), who was to become famous after Shen-hui's death. The two men must have met during this time, if not before, and it is my impression that Hui-chung's later activities were in some sense a continuation of Shen-hui's.[42] Tsung-mi, who is our source for the details of Shen-hui's movements, says that the Northern school was present at all four locations. Far from being a "banishment," the impression given by the description of Shen-hui's movements is that of an imperially sponsored regional lecture tour.

After the beginning of the An Lu-shan rebellion in 755, the central government found itself very short of funds, and it was soon suggested that ordination platforms be established in the major prefectures and aspirants allowed to become monks after the payment of "incense money" *(hsiang-shui ch'ien).* Theoretically, the ordinands had to be able to recite five hundred pages of scripture in order to be ordained; in fact, anyone willing to pay one hundred strings of cash was accepted.[43] The reason for paying such sums, of course, was that monks were exempt from further taxation. After two abortive attempts—in which Shen-hui presumably did not participate[44]—in the fifth month of 757 an order was promulgated to carry out the plan throughout the entire country, beginning in Lo-yang.[45]

Shen-hui's former accuser Lu I had been killed by the rebels in the twelfth month of 755, so there was nothing to prevent Shen-hui from being summoned back to the eastern capital to lead the sale of ordinations. Specifically, we are told that he built a temporary chapel and established a square ordination platform among the ruins of burned Buddhist monasteries. Shen-hui seems to have begun his fundraising activities while the rebels were still in at least nominal control of the two capitals, since the *SKSC* says that he was greatly beneficial to the future emperor Tai-tsung (r. 762–779) and his general Kuo Tzu-i when they retook Ch'ang-an and Lo-yang in the ninth and tenth months of 757, respectively. Because he was able to raise a great deal of money for the T'ang government, Shen-hui was summoned to the palace to receive offerings sometime after Emperor Su-tsung (r. 756–762) returned to Ch'ang-an. The emperor also built a "Ch'an building" *(ch'an-yü)* for Shen-hui at Ho-tse ssu in recognition of his services to the state. It is interesting to note how brief was Shen-hui's participation in this fund-raising endeavor: from the promulgation of the order in the fifth month of 757 at the earliest until his death in the same month of the following year.[46]

D. *Shen-hui's Death and Official Recognition*

Shen-hui died at the K'ai-yüan ssu in Ching-chou on the thirteenth day of the fifth month of 758.[47] His death is described in typical Ch'an fashion: after commanding his students to ask him for the last time about the dharma and repeatedly praising the "single unconditioned (or, inactive) dharma" *(wu-wei i fa),* he passed away in the middle of the night. According to Tsung-mi, that night the military governor of Shan-nan-tung tao, Li Kuang-chu,[48] supposedly saw him passing through the air on his lecture seat. When Li went to inquire at Shen-hui's monastery, it was discovered that the elderly monk had died.

There are minor discrepancies regarding Shen-hui's stūpas. According to Tsung-mi, in 759 a stūpa was erected at Lung-men, and in 763 the location of the stūpa was named Pao-ying ssu. The *SKSC,* on the other hand, suggests that the stūpa was moved to Pao-ying ssu in Lo-yang in 763.[49] For whatever reason, in 765 the stūpa at Lung-men was rebuilt and the newly discovered stele added. The relationship between this and the previous stūpa or stūpas is uncertain. However, the stele inscription does say that Li Ssu, or Li Wang-tsai, probably the same individual who appears in the *Definition of the Truth* as Ssu Tao-wang, received Shen-hui's remains for interment into the new stūpa.[50]

The stele inscription of 765 refers to Shen-hui as "Seventh Patriarch and National Teacher," which were unofficial appellations used out of respect for a departed master.[51] In 770 there was an imperial bequest of a name tablet for his "patriarchal hall" *(tsu-t'ang),* which was called "Hall of the Transmission of the Dharma of the True School of Prajñā" *(chen-tsung po-jo ch'üan-fa chih t'ang).* In 772 a similar bequest included a name tablet for his stūpa, which bore the title "Stūpa of the Great Master of Prajñā" *(Po-jo ta-shih chih t'a).*[52] Hence Shen-hui is known by the posthumous titles "True School" and "Prajñā." In 796, according to Tsung-mi, Emperor Te-tsung ordered his crown prince to call an assembly of Ch'an masters, after which Shen-hui was formally recognized as the seventh patriarch of Ch'an.[53]

III. Traces of Shen-hui's Influence in Northern School Literature

A. *The Problem of Shen-hui's Early Teaching Career*

Ironically, decades of study of the Ch'an materials from Tun-huang has resulted in the increased obscurity of an important part of Shen-hui's religious development. Formerly, anyone interested in the early formation of Shen-hui's personal philosophy could simply point to the teachings of his master Hui-neng as known through the *Platform Sūtra* and other works. However, the specific teachings of the historical Hui-neng —as opposed to the legendary personality depicted in the *Platform Sūtra* and elsewhere—are completely unknown. On the other hand, Tsung-mi explicitly refers to Shen-hui's spiritual maturation around the time of his ordination in Ch'ang-an, which implies that Shen-hui was influenced by other teachers in addition to Hui-neng.

And what about the period after Hui-neng's death, when Shen-hui supposedly traveled about to religious sites in different parts of China? Why did Shen-hui wait for almost two decades after his master's death in 713 to initiate his campaign on behalf of Hui-neng's recognition as sixth patriarch and against the supposed errors of the Northern school? Once again, the absence of any direct quotations from Hui-neng's teachings in Shen-hui's works renders uncertain the substance and extent of Shen-hui's religious inheritance from his southern master, but it seems reasonable to suppose that Shen-hui's ideas developed substantially in the north both at the time of his ordination and after Hui-neng's death.

In fact, it is not difficult to imagine that Shen-hui's experience in the north was quite positive both before and after Hui-neng's death. As far as we can tell, cordial relations prevailed between Hui-neng and the members of what is now called the Northern school during the first two decades of the eighth century. During this time Hui-neng was perceived as a member in good standing, albeit far removed, of that loosely knit confraternity: he is included along with Shen-hsiu, Lao-an, and others in the well-known list of Hung-jen's ten disciples that first occurs in Northern school texts, and his name also occurs in an obscure work found in one of the most important of Northern school Tun-huang manuscripts, in this case accompanied by such well-known names as Aśvaghoṣa, Hui-k'o, and Shen-hsiu.[54]

Moreover, at least three students are known to have studied under Hui-neng and other Northern school masters. Other than Shen-hui himself, the most interesting of these was a monk named Ching-tsang (675–746), who studied under the Northern school master Lao-an, then traveled south to meet Hui-neng, and ultimately returned to the north to maintain his first teacher's stūpa.[55] Although Shen-hui's example should perhaps be excluded from consideration here on logical grounds (since the issue is the believability of his studies under Shen-hsiu), there is no a priori reason to reject the possibility that Shen-hsiu directed him to go to Ts'ao-ch'i to study under Hui-neng at the time of the former master's invitation to the imperial court. Although no one else is known to have accompanied Shen-hui to Ts'ao-ch'i, the suggestion itself would not have been out of character for Shen-hsiu, who left other students behind in Ching-chou in an atmosphere more conducive to meditation than that at Lo-yang and Ch'ang-an.[56] The implication is that there is no reason to distinguish Hui-neng and his teachings from the rest of early Ch'an until the onset of Shen-hui's propaganda drive.

B. The Texts

I will introduce below a partial translation of an early Ch'an text that sheds light on Shen-hui's ideas and associations at a time when he was cooperating with Northern school figures, prior to the initiation of his anti-Northern school campaign. The text is known as the *Treatise on the True Principle,* (*Ta-sheng k'ai-hsin hsien-hsing tun-wu chen-tsung lun,* Treatise on the True Principle of Opening the Mind and Manifesting the [Buddha]-nature in Sudden Enlightenment [according to] the Mahāyāna).[57]

Although Shen-hui had some influence on the *Treatise on the True Principle,* the most intriguing aspect of the text is its obvious Northern school origin. First, both Shen-hui and the Northern school master Lao-an are listed as the teachers of the text's author Hui-kuang, who may have also studied under P'u-chi.[58] Second, the very structure of the text is closely modeled on a Northern school text known as the *Essential Determination* (*Tun-wu chen-tsung chin-kang po-jo hsiu-hsing ta pi-an fa-men yao-chüeh,* Essential Determination of the Doctrine of Attaining the Other Shore [of Nirvāṇa] by the Practice of Adamantine Wisdom [According to] the True Teaching of Sudden Enlightenment).[59]

The author of the *Essential Determination* was Chih-ta (d. 714), who is identified in the preface as a student of Lao-an and Shen-hsiu (as compared to Lao-an and Shen-hui for the author of the *Treatise on the True Principle*). An epitaph discovered recently by Bernard Faure indicates that this monk (also known by the rare three-character surname and given name Hou-mo-ch'en Yen-chih) was a native of Ch'ang-an who became a monk at age twenty, entered Mount Sung and studied first under Lao-an (given here as Ācārya An) and later under Shen-hsiu (Hsiu ho-shang). After more than twenty years of training he attained enlightenment, after which he changed his name to Chih-ta on the basis of Shen-hsiu's comment that his "wisdom and discrimination [were] unhindered" *(chih-ta pien-ts'ai wu-ai).* Afterwards he traveled about the Lo-yang and Ho-pei areas teaching. He died on the tenth day of the sixth month of 714, although his age is not given. In addition to some interesting dialogue, Chih-ta's epitaph is notable for including the phrase "broadly opening (i.e., disseminating) the teaching of sudden enlightenment" *(tun-wu chih tsung)* and references to "expedient means" *(fang-pien)* and "transmitting the lamp" *(ch'üan-teng).* Although this is substantially more detail than is given in the *Essential Determination,* text and epitaph are in complete agreement.[60]

The *Essential Determination* and the *Treatise on the True Principle* are both presented as oral dialogues between a Ch'an master and a layman—but a close reading of the preface of each text reveals that teacher and interrogator are one and the same individual! Since the *Essential Determination* was written in 712 (while Shen-hui was still with Hui-neng in Ts'ao-ch'i) and since it betrays no influence by Shen-hui, we may infer that it was the model for the *Treatise on the True Principle,* rather than vice versa. This is in accord with the probable post-720 date of composition of the *Treatise on the True Principle.*[61] The efforts taken in these two texts to present their messages in dramatic form is a delightful innovation in the history of Ch'an literature, the power of which is only confirmed by its duplication.[62]

The modeling of one text on the other is not limited to overall structure, since a considerable portion of the prefaces of the two texts are identical. In the partial translation below, identical or closely similar passages are printed in italics. In addition, omissions (relative to the *Treatise on the True Principle*) are indicated by ellipses enclosed in square brackets. Finally, I have numbered the questions for the reader's convenience.

Treatise on the True Principle

Compiled and Explained by the Śramaṇa Ta-chao and the Layman Hui-kuang[63]

[Preface]

In the melding of the mind in the great enlightenment *(ta tao),* it is the one true principle that is manifested. The former and later sages proceed only according to this teaching. To the enlightened, the triple realm is only the mind; the unenlightened are asleep within the false and the correct. The doctrine *(tsung)* of the Mahāyāna must manifest the true in relation to characteristics.[64] To comprehend the [Buddha]-nature *(liao-hsing)*[65] is to know the quiescence of all the dharmas: Phenomena are based on causes and conditions, and names (i.e., perceived identities) are created through the provisional conjunction [of individual elements]. To not comprehend [the Buddha-nature] is to be attached to names and fixated on words, to grasp at one's thoughts and [for one's mind] to race among the false.

If you wish to control the false and return to the true, making both defiled and pure universally same *(p'ing-teng)*, you must concentrate the will and contemplate the mind *(chu-i kuan-hsin)*. Fundamental enlightenment will appear of itself. You should practice your mental contemplation *(i-kuan)* with energy, but without interrupting your concentration[66] to think about reaching the "other shore" [of nirvāṇa]. Remain constantly immersed in profoundly deep meditation. Practice long, without cease, and matters will all come to their own natural conclusion (i.e., spiritual progress will occur automatically). If you persevere in contemplation, you will gradually progress toward the true.

If you let go of body and mind, their defects will be evaporated.[67] Your willful functions *(ch'i-tso)* are permanently serene; [your mind] illuminates without being conditioned[68] [by its objects]. Consign yourself freely to samādhi, [so that you may] incubate the way *(tao)* and nurture virtue *(te)*, thus helping to create *(tzu-ch'eng)* the dharmakāya. Being enlightened to the mind-source, one is without obstruction and without hindrance, one is in essence like space: this is called the limitless samādhi. The mind is without exit and entrance (i.e., it does not enter and leave meditative or perceptual states): this is called the samādhi of no quiescence. To be pure and without seeking with respect to all the loci of being *(yu-so)*[69] is called the inconceivable samādhi. For one's samādhi to be unobscured *(san-mei pu mei)* and to not derive from conditions is called the samādhi of the dharma-nature.

All the students [nowadays] seek just for understanding, not for their own realization. You should definitely understand that it would be mistaken to attempt to cultivate the Mahāyāna without understanding pacification of the mind *(an-hsin)*.

At the time, there was a *layman of the surname* Li *and name* Hui-kuang. *He was from Ch'ang-an in Yung-chou. His religious name was* Ta-chao.[70] *Unconcerned with fame and profit but wishing to seek bodhi,* [. . .][71] *he first studied under Ācārya* [*Lao*]*-an and later under Preceptor* [Shen]-hui.[72] *He intimately received oral determinations* [*of the teachings*] *from both of them; the doctrines* [*of Ch'an*] *were secretly transmitted to him. He thoroughly penetrated the fundamental source of the wondrous principle of the vital doctrine, and his exit from being and entrance into nonbeing were perfectly coalescent and free.*[73] [. . .][74]

During his time off from meditation, the layman lamented the [*plight of*] *deluded* [*sentient beings*] *and has accordingly* manifested [. . .] the abstruse teaching of phenomena and principle. He explained the wondrous meaning and *revealed the essentials of the dharma.* [. . .] [His teachings] *may be called a ship for crossing the ocean, by which one can "proceed directly to bodhi." These words are worthy of trust.* Hopefully, those who are not now enlightened will become enlightened, those whose [minds] are not now pacified will become pacified, and those who are not emancipated will become emancipated.[75]

[Text]

1. The layman asked: *"Buddhism is abstruse and mysterious, so that it is incomprehensible for the ordinary person. Its literature is vast and its doctrines difficult to understand. I [would now] inquire of the dhyāna master [regarding] the essentials of the teaching.* [. . .] Temporarily cease with expedient means and speak directly.[76] Do not forsake the common sort [of ignorant person such as myself], and please have no secrets."[77]

Dhyāna Master Ta-chao answered: "Excellent! Excellent! From your question, I can see that you have the aptitude of a bodhisattva and wish to purify and develop yourself. *In my forty-five years of life and over twenty years as a monk,*[78] *never has anyone asked me about this meaning (i.e., about the ultimate message of Buddhism). What problems do you have? What doubts can I settle? Ask directly and I will explain directly—do not bother with elaborate speech."*

2. Question: "If one wishes to enter into enlightenment *(ju-tao),* what dharma should one cultivate? What dharma should one view? What dharma should one realize? What dharma should one seek? To what dharma should one become enlightened? And what dharma should one attain, so as to proceed to bodhi?"

Answer: "You should not view a single dharma, and neither should you have any seeking. You should not realize a single dharma, and neither should you have any subsequent [attainment]. You should not become enlightened to a single dharma, and neither is there any enlightenment *(tao)* that can be cultivated. This is bodhi."

3. Question: "Since beginningless time this disciple has been floating along in the waves of saṃsāra, at odds with the [true] principle. Although I have heard the teaching of suddenness *(tun-shuo),* I have been stupid and have not understood. My spirit *(shen-shih)* is obscured and I know not where it is—I am like a drunken man who cannot sober up. On behalf of deluded sentient beings, I beseech you to bestow the expedient means that are in accord with the truth [regarding] a few questions."

Question: "What is the true nature *(chen-hsing)*?"

Answer: "The nonactivated mind *(pu-ch'i hsin),* which is constantly without characteristics and pure."

4. Question: "What are the self-natures *(tzu-hsing)*?"

Answer: "The perceptive capacities *(chien-wen chüeh-chih),* the four elements, and all dharmas each have their own self-natures."

5. Question: "From what are these self-natures generated?"
   Answer: "They are generated from the false (i.e., the deluded) mind."
6. Question: "How can the self-natures be transcended *(li)*?"
   Answer: "When the mind is not activated, they are transcended."
7. Question: "What is enlightenment *(tao)*? What is the principle *(li)*? What is the mind *(hsin)*?"
   Answer: "The mind is enlightenment. The mind is the principle. The principle[79] is the mind. Outside the mind there is no principle; outside the principle there is no mind. The capability of the mind to be universally same *(p'ing-teng)* is called the principle; the capability of the principle to illuminate brightly is called the mind. When mind and principle are universally same, they are called the Buddha-mind. He who attains this principle does not perceive [that there is any] saṃsāra.

   There is no difference between ordinary people and sages; [perceptual] realm and wisdom are not distinct. Phenomena and principle are both melded [together]; defiled and pure are as one. That which illuminates truthfully as the principle cannot be other than enlightenment *(tao)*. Self- and other- [natures] are both transcended—in all activities and at all times, there is neither any before or after, nor any intermediate. Bondage and emancipation [occur] spontaneously. This is called enlightenment."

1. The Northern School Character of the Essential Determination *and* Treatise on the True Principle

I have already mentioned the specific attribution of the *Essential Determination* to a Northern school figure, but it is still important to consider the doctrinal character of this text in order to gauge the nature of Shen-hui's influence on the *Treatise on the True Principle*.

The Northern school character of the *Essential Determination* is apparent in several ways. First, the text pays attention to the "nonactivation" *(pu-ch'i)* of the mind, which was a well-known catchword for Ch'an practitioners in the second decade of the eighth century.[80] Second, many of the doctrinal formulations found in the *Essential Determination* are done in a style known as "contemplative analysis" (*kuan-hsin shih,* or *kanjin shaku* in Japanese) that typifies Northern school texts.[81] Third, the use of terms such as *shou-hsin* 'to maintain [awareness of] the mind', which is the key doctrine of an important text attributed to Hung-jen, indicates a close relationship with the Northern school.[82] Fourth, the text was circulated within the late Northern school corpus of material.[83]

One interesting feature of the *Essential Determination* is the manner in which it combines the rhetoric of "viewing the mind" with that of "seeing the [Buddha]-nature." The latter concept is in fact the very heart of one of the most important motifs of early Ch'an doctrine, but it was only with Shen-hui that it became a well-known slogan. In fact, the *Essential Determination* cites the *Nirvāṇa Sūtra,* just as Shen-hui was to do a few years later: "See the [Buddha]-nature and achieve the enlightenment of Buddhahood."[84]

Perhaps even more than the *Essential Determination,* the *Treatise on the True Principle* is clearly a Northern school text. The central theme is once again the contemplation of the mind, which this text also explicates in terms of "nonactivation" or *pu-ch'i.* The text uses the term *li* 'to transcend' in a fashion similar to Northern school usage. Other similarities with known Northern school literature are the use of the distinction between inner-directed and outer-directed wisdom and the use of a distinctive "contemplative analysis" style of doctrinal reinterpretation.[85] Also, the pairing of *shun* 'direct' and *wang* 'false' is similar to the *shun-kuan* 'direct contemplation' and *ni-kuan* 'reverse contemplation' of the Northern school's *Yüan-ming lun* (Treatise on Perfect Enlightenment), and the description of the *tzu-hsin* 'self-mind' and *wang-hsin* 'false mind' resembles the dualism of Shen-hsiu's *Kuan-hsin lun* (Treatise on the Contemplation of the Mind).[86] Finally, at one point the *Treatise on the True Principle* shares a passage with the Northern school's *Leng-ch'ieh shih-tzu chi* (Records of the Masters and Disciples of the Laṅkā[vatāra]), which was written sometime during the years 713–716, and at another point discusses an obscure scripture in a fashion similar to that in the *Kuan-hsin lun.*[87]

For the purposes of this discussion, however, it is also important to note the apparent indications of Shen-hui's presence within the doctrines of the *Treatise on the True Principle.* The points that most clearly parallel his later doctrinal inclinations are the apophatic mood of some of the statements regarding the contemplation of the mind (evident to a certain extent in section 2 of the translation), occasional references to the doctrine of suddenness, and the use of the phrase "truly comprehend the [Buddha]-nature" *(chen liao-hsing).* This terminology figures prominently in the title of Shen-hui's *Platform Sermon.*[88]

Before drawing any conclusions from this evidence, let me briefly discuss another relevant text.

2. *The Evidence of the* Treatise on the Dharma-nature

The *Essential Determination* and *Treatise on the True Principle* are not the only sources of evidence for Shen-hui's early membership in the Northern school doctrinal community. Another interesting text found among the Tun-huang treasures is a short essay provisionally titled the *Treatise on the Dharma-nature (Fa-hsing lun),* which contains terminology reminiscent of Shen-hui's *Platform Sermon.* This treatise occurs in two out of eight or nine manuscripts devoted to a set anthology of Northern Ch'an material. The two manuscripts in question are the longest and most complete of the entire set, which includes the very important *Treatise on the Essentials of the Cultivation of the Mind (Hsiu-hsin yao lun)* attributed to Hung-jen, Shen-hsiu's *Treatise on the Contemplation of the Mind (Kuan-hsin lun),* and other less well known East Mountain teaching and Northern school texts.[89] Another interesting detail is that the last few lines of this treatise occur in one Tun-huang manuscript in conjunction with a verse by a Reverend Chi, presumably P'u-chi of the Northern school.[90] Although it is impossible to identify the specific author of the *Treatise on the Dharma-nature,* the text obviously derives from an era when there was no explicit animosity between the groups now known as the Northern and Southern schools and when the teachings of Hui-neng and Shen-hui were accepted as variations on the East Mountain teaching.

The *Treatise on the Dharma-nature*[91] exhibits a number of similarities with Shen-hui's thought. First of all, of course, is the attention to the concept of "seeing the nature" or *chien-hsing* (*kenshō* in Japanese). Although both the concept and the specific terminology do occur in pre-Shen-hui Northern school literature,[92] the term occurs in both the title and text of Shen-hui's *Platform Sermon.* Hence it seems safe to suggest that this terminology and the associated ideas constitute an early trademark of Shen-hui's religious philosophy. In addition, the *Treatise on the Dharma-nature* quotes a line from the *Vimalakīrti Sūtra* that also occurs in Shen-hui's works—and in the *Treatise on the True Principle.*[93] Both Shen-hui and the *Treatise on the Dharma-nature* make use of a metaphor involving gold and gangue in order to explain the existence of the Buddha-nature within sentient beings.[94] In a passage already mentioned above, both describe the relationship between meditation and wisdom as one of "equivalent functioning" *(ting hui teng yung),* and the character *chia,* normally meaning "house," occurs in this text exactly as it does in Shen-hui's *Platform Sermon* as a substitute for the grammatical particle *chih* (e.g., *kuang chih shih teng chia yung*).[95] Moreover, the text uses the terms *wu-hsiang* and *wu-nien,* both of which may be translated as "non-thought." This is significant because Shen-hui laid great emphasis on *wu-nien,* which he contrasted with the *li-nien* or "transcending thoughts" of the Northern school. Taken collectively, these correspondences suggest a close relationship between the *Treatise on the Dharma-nature* and Shen-hui's teachings as seen in his *Platform Sermon.*[96]

The doctrinal presence of Shen-hui, and behind him Hui-neng, in the *Treatise on the True Principle* and the *Treatise on the Dharma-nature* seems to me to be beyond question. This doctrinal presence and the identification of the *Treatise on the Dharma-nature* with Ts'ao-ch'i would have been appropriate for an early stage in Shen-hui's teaching career, when he wished to attribute his doctrines retrospectively to his master Hui-neng. At the stage when both this text and the *Treatise on the True Principle* were produced, probably during the 720s, Shen-hui would still have perceived himself and would have been perceived as a member of the religious community that we now refer to as the "Northern school." At this point Shen-hui's ideas were in perfect harmony with the overall framework of early Ch'an doctrine.[97]

IV. Shen-hui's Teachings and the Doctrines of the Northern School

Actually, the close relationship between Shen-hui's teachings and the doctrines of the Northern school does not end with these very early works. Professor Yanagida has suggested that the "Southern school" was predicated on the "Northern school," and indeed we can find evidence of this in Shen-hui's writings.[98]

Our focus here will be on two texts, the *Platform Sermon* and the *Definition of the Truth*. Certain of Shen-hui's other writings may contain passages representing his earlier teachings, but the identification of these passages depends on complex and sometimes subjective arguments. Actually, even the dates of these two texts are not certain: the *Platform Sermon* is generally considered to have been written sometime during the 720s, but there is no specific textual evidence to support this supposition. True, it does lack the polemical vitriol of the *Definition of the Truth,* but it would be unreasonable to assume that Shen-hui never abandoned his campaign against the Northern school, even temporarily. Close attention to the content and dating of Shen-hui's dialogues with laymen whose biographies are known may eventually help us specify the date of composition of the *Platform Sermon,* but this is a task for the future. On the other hand, the *Definition of the Truth* may have undergone considerable editing between the public lecture of 732 on which it is primarily based and the final redaction of the text during 745–749. However, although the *Definition of the Truth* is more primitive doctrinally than the *Platform Sermon,* there is no sharp divergence between the two. Given these uncertainties, at this stage we may consider evidence from both these texts at once.

First, it is relatively simple to identify Shen-hui's criticisms of Northern school doctrines in these texts. The most obvious of these, of course, are the references to specific approaches to meditation, especially his well-known "four pronouncements" criticizing "freezing the mind to enter samādhi, stopping the mind to view purity, activating the mind for outward illumination, and concentrating the mind for inner realization." These occur in both the *Platform Sermon* and *Definition of the Truth,* although it is only in the latter text that they are specifically directed at the teachings of the Northern school.[99] There are also other less well known comments in a similar vein: the rejection of the "viewing afar" practices (found in the *Wu fang-pien* [Five Expedient Means] of the Northern school) and criticism of the tendency to "grasp purity."[100] The contention that one must actually perceive or "see" the Buddha-nature rather than simply accept its presence within oneself may also be an implicit criticism of the *Hsiu-hsin yao lun* attributed to Hung-jen.[101] I have detected at least two other implicit criticisms of Northern school doctrines, one a reference to realizing the dharmadhātu with the dharmadhātu and the other a denigration of the use of expedient means rather than the doctrine of suddenness.[102]

But Northern school texts also contain numerous warnings against meditative abuses. The most common such warning is against "blankness of mind" *(wu-chi),* a dull state of consciousness in which the practitioner is entranced by or attached to his objects of perception. Such warnings occur in several Northern school texts.[103] The description found in the *Wu fang-pien* of Hīnayānists as being unable to hear while in meditation is in effect a criticism of "freezing the mind to enter samādhi," to borrow Shen-hui's phrasing.[104] Also, a statement on meditation by Shen-hsiu exhibits a sharp awareness of the problems of mental blankness, dualistic conceptualization, and grasping for the fruit of enlightenment.[105]

The Northern school passage that contains sentiments most similar to Shen-hui's criticisms, however, is found in the *Essential Determination:*[106]

> The minds of all sentient beings are all generated from the storehouse of the Tathāgatas.
> If you wish to save the myriad living beings[107]
> you should clearly contemplate the recollections of the lion (i.e., the Tathāgata).[108]
>
> The mind comes from the locus of nonbeing.
> You must vow to forsake the myriad conditions—
> if they occur (*lai* 'come') then view them with complete attention.[109]
> This is called the "uninterrupted dharma."
>
> The mind comes from the locus of nonbeing.
> With complete attention one views, and views again.
> Viewing, viewing, viewing without interruption.
> This is called "wisdom without impurity."

The mind comes from the locus of nonbeing.
When one craves understanding of the scriptures,
one considers them occasionally and does not view everlastingly.
This is called "craving worldly wisdom."

The mind comes from the locus of nonbeing.
When one craves the development of conditioned [abilities]
one recollects emptily rather than viewing determinedly.
This is called the "heretical teaching."

The mind comes from the locus of nonbeing.
When one craves entry into the trance of empty tranquility,
one's mind is tranquil but one's consciousness sinks[110] into emptiness.
This is called the "difficulty of the auditor *(śrāvaka)*."[111]

The mind comes from the locus of nonbeing.
When one is constantly immersed in the purity of the locus of nonbeing
and does not emerge into the [phenomenal] world
this is called the "fetters of the bodhisattva."

The mind comes from the locus of nonbeing.
When, in the locus of nonbeing, one is constantly pure
and emerges into the world with champaign sameness
this is called the "emancipation of the bodhisattva."

The mind comes from the locus of nonbeing.
When purity is constantly immediately manifest
and one is unattached to all characteristics
this is called the "realm of the Buddhas."[112]

The mind comes from the locus of nonbeing.
The eastern quarter cannot be calculated,
and the four directions are likewise.
This is called "returning to the great house."[113]

It should be obvious that the "viewing the mind" practices of the Northern school were not exactly as Shen-hui described them, but were instead free and easy exercises in the emulation of the expansive mind of the sage. More important in the present context, however, is the observation that the descriptions of these practices contained warnings against the same abuses Shen-hui later descried so strongly.

In addition, the following statement attributed (no doubt falsely) to Tao-hsin indicates that the Northern school masters also instructed their students to refrain from "activating the mind for outward illumination": "If the mind activates *(ch'i)* its cognitive [functions] *(chüeh)* in connection with some sense realm separate from itself, then contemplate the locus of that activation as ultimately nonactivating *(pu-ch'i)*."[114] "Tao-hsin" also describes meditation practice in an apophatic mode similar to that favored by Shen-hui:

> Do not [practice] mindfulness of the Buddha, do not grasp the mind, do not view the mind, do not measure the mind, do not meditate, do not contemplate, and do not disrupt [the mind]. Just let it flow. Do not make it go and do not make it stay. Alone in a pure and ultimate location (i.e., the absolute), the mind will be naturally bright and pure.[115]

Although I could provide additional documentation to show that Shen-hui's criticisms failed to portray the meditation practices of the Northern school fairly, accurately, or completely, his reportage is not really at issue here. It is possible, of course, that some of the members of the Northern school undertook practices that were not in accord with the highest understanding of their teachers' guidance, but this possibility too is beside the point at the moment. Instead, the present concern is the lack of absolute originality of Shen-hui's criticisms themselves within the context of the Ch'an tradition. The passages cited above indicate that there are numerous precedents within Northern school texts for those criticisms.

There are two differences between the uses of such criticisms in Northern school works and by Shen-hui. First, the Northern school texts address their comments to meditation practitioners in order that they might refine their spiritual endeavors to the highest possible degree. In the context of Shen-hui's overall message, on the other hand, the criticisms seem to be used as a justification for the rejection of a certain approach to meditation, or even a total repudiation of meditation practice per se. Second, in the *Definition of the Truth,* of course, Shen-hui applied his criticisms to the teachings of specifically named masters. Thus his innovative use of these criticisms involved not only the precipitation of these critical sentiments into a concise set of slogans but also the radical expansion of their interpretation and their use within a polemical context.

Shen-hui's doctrines were of course not limited to the criticism of the Northern school. The following similarities between his doctrines and the ideas of that school have generally not been appreciated, however: Shen-hui's redefinition of *tso-ch'an* or "seated meditation" is cast in the "contemplative analysis" style, in which nominally unacceptable correlations are made in order to jar the reader or listener to a new religious perspective. Thus the character *tso* 'to sit' becomes the "nonactivation of thoughts," while *ch'an* 'meditation' becomes "seeing the original nature."[116] Although "seeing the nature" was one of Shen-hui's most characteristic doctrines and was used without particular emphasis in earlier texts, the concept of "nonactivation" was a very central concept in the teachings of the Northern school, as we have seen above. This term occurs repeatedly throughout Shen-hui's writings.[117]

There are references in Shen-hui's writings to the transcendence of the body, ego, and consciousness, and to the autonomy attained in the various sense capabilities and types of sensory data.[118] Exactly the same type of assertions vis-à-vis individual components of human existence are made almost ad nauseum in the *Wu fang-pien*. Shen-hui also posits some distinctions very similar to the concepts of inner sageliness and outer wisdom, as well as those of fundamental and successive wisdom.[119] In addition, he makes references to space very similar to those in the *Wu fang-pien* and the *Yüan-ming lun.*[120] Finally, the very use of the concept of the Buddha-nature obscured by illusions harks back to Hung-jen's *Essential Treatise,* even though the interpretation differs.[121]

V. Shen-hui's Emphasis on Sudden Enlightenment

Although there is evidence of a core of shared ideas in the works I have discussed thus far, we should not lose sight of an important distinction. In the *Treatise on the True Principle* and the *Treatise on the Dharma-nature,* Shen-hui's ideas appear to have been inserted into an identifiably Northern school message. In Shen-hui's own works, however, the message is different, even though we can detect numerous similarities with earlier Northern school ideas.

The major impression one gets from reading Shen-hui's works, of course, is the very concrete sense of his doctrine of sudden enlightenment. This impression holds even in the case of the *Platform Sermon,* in which he hardly uses the term "sudden" *(tun)* at all. It is abundantly clear in this text that Shen-hui's intent was that those listening to him should generate *bodhicitta,* the aspiration to achieve enlightenment, even as they listened to his sermon. He appears to have been a consummate evangelist: although the ethical vows found at the beginning of the text were no doubt part of the conventional liturgical repertoire, Shen-hui must have used them in order to lead his congregation to a more exalted frame of mind in which they would be more open to moments of inspiration. There is not however any real consideration of the practice of meditation after that first generation of *bodhicitta,* a term which he uses in a manner that is virtually tantamount to the final achievement of enlightenment. For example, Shen-hui's *Platform Sermon* contains the following verse in adulation of *bodhicitta:*

> Although *bodhicitta* and the ultimate [realization] are no different.
> Of these two [states of] mind, it is difficult to say which is more important
> With oneself still unsaved, to first save others—thus do we reverence the
> initial [achievement of] *bodhicitta.*
>
> By this initial *bodhicitta* one becomes a teacher of men and gods,
> superior to the auditors and solitary Buddhas.

> With such a *bodhicitta,* one transcends the triple realm,
> hence this is called the most insurpassable.[122]

Shen-hui does not hedge on the issue of immediate inspiration by specifying some preliminary period of religious practice, however brief. His most well known metaphor for the relationship between the initial moment of enlightenment and the subsequent course of self-cultivation is that of childbirth, in which a baby is born suddenly but must mature gradually.[123] (I am always astounded by the monkish oversimplification of this metaphor!) Shen-hui's prescriptions to be followed during the period of maturation are very general, however, and it seems likely that he was more adept at inspiring his listeners to that first moment of inspiration than at guiding practitioners throughout their careers.

The strongly propagandistic flavor of the *Definition of the Truth* leaves the very palpable sense that, in this case, Shen-hui is more interested in winning converts to his faction—or at least in winning agreement with his positions—than in actually inspiring spiritual experiences in his listeners. We should not overlook the correlation with this more contentious atmosphere and the much more numerous, if frequently unexplained, explicit references to suddenness. Nor should we overlook the fact that the only practical injunctions found in the *Definition of the Truth* enjoin the congregation to recite the *Diamond Sūtra* in order to achieve their first moment of insight. In the context of the developing Ch'an tradition, this was definitely a retrograde position.[124] In other words, Shen-hui's polemical fervor correlates with doctrinal and practical superficiality.

VI. Conclusion

A. The Religious Context of Shen-hui's Training

It is clear from the evidence that Shen-hui began his religious career in a presectarian Northern school milieu. Please note that I use the term "Northern school" in a different manner than did Shen-hui: for him, the term was polemical, an intentionally critical epithet applied to men who he felt were not privy to the spirit of Bodhidharma's teachings and hence should not be allowed to appropriate the term "Southern school." In my usage, on the other hand, the term "Northern school" refers to the informally organized group of masters and disciples who enunciated and disseminated the new message of Ch'an in the two capitals of Loyang and Ch'ang-an during the early decades of the eighth century. These men referred to their own teachings as the "East Mountain teaching," the "Laṅkāvatāra school," and even as the "Southern school," so that it is only out of deference to the conventions of the later Ch'an tradition that I use the originally pejorative term "Northern school" in this regard.

It is important to keep in mind the presectarian nature of this school; the Northern school masters represent the entirety of early Ch'an at the beginning of the eighth century. They were no doubt a diverse lot, with a multiplicity of interests and spheres of activity, but the extant sources allow us to detect only minor differences of style between specific historical figures. There were several attempts to formulate coherent and comprehensive expressions of the religious message of Ch'an, but it is difficult if not impossible from this vantage point to correlate these formulations with specific lineages. The overwhelming impression one gets from this early literature is that of an abundant religious vitality, the energy with which the growing Ch'an movement was striving to recognize and articulate its own self-understanding. Hui-neng was certainly a member of this somewhat amorphous religious community, as was Shen-hui before—and perhaps even after—the initiation of his anti-Northern school campaign.

There is no doubt that Shen-hui was motivated at least in part by a sincere disaffection with contemporary developments in the realm of Ch'an. He was not, in fact, the first to offer such criticisms. Paradoxically, the very text that Shen-hui cites in his criticism of P'u-chi, the *Ch'üan fa-pao chi* (Annals of the Transmission of the Dharma-treasure), sharply criticizes Hung-jen, Shen-hsiu, and, implicitly, even P'u-chi for popularizing Ch'an among large numbers of persons unready or unable to comprehend its deeper meaning.[125] These criticisms were clearly elitist and in some ways diametrically opposed to those of Shen-hui, who went further than anyone else to simplify his teachings for public consumption. Nevertheless, we can easily imagine that there were wide variations in how both masters and students interpreted the spiritual enterprise embodied in the new religious movement known as Ch'an. Since we are limited to textual archives preserved for the most part at Tun-huang on the outskirts of the Chinese cultural realm, it is quite reasonable that these texts do not provide specific details of any such excesses, distortions, or facile interpretations. It has already been shown that Shen-hui's criticisms of Northern school doctrine are off the mark, but they may have been valid with regard to non-mainstream tendencies.[126] Nevertheless, Shen-hui's delineation of a Northern school defined entirely in terms of these non-mainstream tendencies was an intentional polemical trope.

The specific catalyst that led Shen-hui to initiate his anti-Northern school campaign remains obscure. Given the partisan vigor with which he carried out his chosen mission, it is likely that his own personal temperament had a great deal to do with the matter, but there are also some indications that his religious lineage may have been a factor. I am not thinking of Hui-neng, but rather of Lao-an, the Northern school figure most closely associated with Hui-neng and Shen-hui. We have the names of two monks who studied under both Hui-neng and Lao-an, and we should not forget that Lao-an's name is listed in both the *Essential Determination* and the *Treatise on the True Principle*. In addition, the very choice of Hua-t'ai as the scene of Shen-hui's early attack on the Northern school may be related to the fact that it was Lao-an's birthplace.[127] Most intriguing is the observation that Lao-an's biography shows a definite tendency to one-upmanship with regard to the charismatic centenarian Shen-hsiu: according to his epitaph, Lao-an is supposed to have begun his studies under Hung-jen earlier, to have cut a more exotic figure, and to have lived even longer than Shen-hsiu.[128] It may be this tendency to one-upmanship in Lao-an that was translated into a spirit of factional competitiveness in Shen-hui.

B. Shen-hui's Doctrine of Sudden Enlightenment

Judging from the evidence introduced here, it seems reasonable to accept the traditional interpretation that Shen-hui inherited his emphasis on sudden enlightenment from Hui-neng. However, we lack any reliable description of Hui-neng's teachings and thus cannot tell whether his instructions on the matter of sudden enlightenment remained consistent in both nature and emphasis before and after Shen-hui's trip north. The most likely alternatives are as follows: if Shen-hui had achieved his own moment of sudden inspiration prior to his ordination and further training in Ch'ang-an, Hui-neng's remarks on his return might refer to Shen-hui's greater appreciation of the wider spiritual ramifications of that experience. Or, Shen-hui's wider understanding after several years in the north might have finally made it possible for him to achieve that sudden enlightenment after his return to Ts'ao-ch'i for further instruction under Hui-neng.

Although it is impossible to tell which, if either, of these scenarios is correct, we can safely infer that during this very early period there was no apprehension of any conflict or incompatibility between the doctrine of sudden enlightenment and the teachings of the Northern school. There is certainly no indication in any of the texts discussed above in conjunction with Shen-hui's early career of any internal conflict or tension between sudden enlightenment and the surrounding doctrinal framework. On the contrary, the real difficulty is ascertaining where Shen-hui's ideas begin and where they leave off. And this shared doctrinal foundation is apparent throughout Shen-hui's works.

The notion of sudden enlightenment was absolutely central to Shen-hui's religious philosophy. In one sense, this was a direct continuation of the Northern school mission of eliciting conversions to its own interpretation of Buddhism, as demonstrated in such works as the *Hsiu-hsin yao lun* attributed to Hung-jen and the *Kuan-hsin lun* by Shen-hsiu. These texts urged their readers to give up formalistic practices justified on the basis of the accrual of religious merit and to turn immediately to the practice of meditation and the pursuit of enlightenment in this very life. Shen-hui made this message even more immediate in his public sermons by attempting to inspire his audiences to make this decision even as they listened to him—to have them achieve a state of religious exaltation through the power of his own charismatic delivery.

In a more immediate sense, though, Shen-hui's single-minded emphasis on sudden enlightenment represented a qualitative change from the positions of earlier Northern school texts.[129] This is true not because his message differed in any major way, but rather because of his chosen medium. The central thread that unites all of Shen-hui's ideas and activities was his vocation of lecturing from the ordination platform,[130] and it is thoroughly understandable that his chosen role of inspiring conversion to the Buddhist spiritual quest was combined with an overriding concern with the initial moment of religious inspiration. To put it in the simplest of terms, there is an inextricable relationship between Shen-hui's emphasis on sudden enlightenment and his proselytic, evangelical role, so much so that it is impossible to tell which was cause and which was effect. Shen-hui espoused the doctrine of sudden enlightenment because he taught from the ordination platform, and he taught from the ordination platform because he espoused the doctrine of sudden enlightenment.

This interpretation helps us understand one of the more curious aspects of Shen-hui's doctrines: his failure to consider post-inspiration cultivation in any serious fashion. Although he did grant that gradual cultivation would be required after the initial experience of awakening, much as a child is complete at birth but must grow into an adult, Shen-hui was apparently totally unconcerned with the details and dynamics of this process of spiritual maturation. This is the reason Hu Shih was able to refer to Shen-hui's teachings as a "new Ch'an which renounces *ch'an* itself and is therefore no *ch'an* at all."[131] As a missionary concerned only with increasing the size of the flock, Shen-hui was probably not directly involved in the ongoing instruction of trainees engaged in meditation and the other activities of the Buddhist spiritual path. At least, there are no indications in any of the doctrinal and biographical sources pertaining to Shen-hui and his disciples that suggest any ongoing regimen of training. This supposition is also corroborated by the relatively early demise of Shen-hui's lineage, which was superseded in size, vitality, and longevity by that of P'u-chi.[132] P'u-chi was able to inspire greater personal loyalty because he participated actively in the training of his successors, rather than merely starting them off on their religious careers as Shen-hui did.

This lack of involvement in meditation practice may be another reason why Shen-hui could distort the Northern school doctrine of constant practice into gradualism—he did not really understand the kind of sensitivity that was needed in the context of ongoing spiritual training. The doctrine of *shou-hsin* (maintaining [awareness of] the mind) attributed to Hung-jen is a good example of an approach to meditation whose practical multivalence is very easily overlooked. In the *Hsiu-hsin yao lun* there is a palpable sense that this formulation is used simultaneously to induce trainees to vigorous effort and to restrain them from grasping for the fruit of enlightenment.[133] This is a type of subtle formulation that is entirely absent from Shen-hui's writings.

To go one step further, it may well be the case that Shen-hui emphasized the doctrine of the equivalence of the "three learnings" of morality, meditation, and wisdom precisely because it undercut the rationale for extended meditation practice and, by implication, the traditional monastic regimen of self-control and spiritual cultivation. Certainly the caricatures of Northern school monks in Shen-hui's texts and their emphasis on the primacy of meditation practice imply that hard work was not required, only the inspiration that Shen-hui set out to provide.[134] Although Shen-hui's life work was carried out on the ordination platform, his teachings lightened the burden of being a Buddhist monk and removed the distinction between monks and laymen, thereby aiding the dissemination of Ch'an among the unordained. In this sense there is a direct continuity between Shen-hui's teachings and the *Platform Sūtra,* as well as one of the keys to the subsequent popularity of Chinese Ch'an.

C. The Acceptance of the Doctrine of Sudden Enlightenment within the Ch'an School

Paradoxically, although Shen-hui was unconcerned with the problems of ongoing spiritual cultivation, his doctrine of sudden enlightenment was accepted because it was very useful in this regard. This point requires careful explanation.

In espousing subitism and rejecting gradualism, Shen-hui explicitly selected a doctrine that disallowed dualistic formulations. The very problem with the gradualistic approach (other than the superficial but unforgettable implication that it was incredibly time-consuming) was that it postulated both a difference between ignorance and enlightenment and the possibility of transporting oneself from one state to the other. There was no difference, according to this approach, between meditation undertaken for spiritual self-improvement and the performance of good works undertaken for the accrual of religious merit. For example, Shen-hui criticized the Northern school use of the term *li-nien,* the "transcendence of thoughts," which he felt implied a purposive or intentional effort to achieve a state of liberation—which would be a contradiction in terms. His alternative was *wu-nien* or "nonthought," by which he meant a level of consciousness ontologically prior to the discrimination of individual thoughts, or the source of liberation already immanent in sentient beings. Although the terms *li-nien* and *wu-nien* differ very little in their original meanings, Shen-hui favored the latter because it had the appearance of being less dualistic.

Now, the experience of nondualism may be an important psychological feature of sudden enlightenment, but it was also something more than this. In combination with his doctrine of subitism, the very heat of Shen-hui's criticism of gradualism had a rhetorical impact of the highest significance: by publicly criticizing one faction's meditation teachings he made all the members of the growing Ch'an school more aware of the external expression—the packaging, if you will—of their ideas and modes of practice. After Shen-hui, Ch'an masters learned to protect themselves from criticism by avoiding dualistic formulations. His campaign worried subsequent masters into avoiding even the hint of gradualism and the spectre of unilinear, goal-oriented logic in the presentation of their own ideas. This is obvious in the ploy taken in the *Platform Sūtra* and other Ox-head school works, which define an ideal of spiritual training only to follow it with an immediate rejection of that ideal on the basis of its underlying dualism, resulting in the specification of a higher and more subtly defined religious ideal. (This process is known as *chih-yang* 'stopping and lifting' in a Buddhist context, or *aufheben* in Western philosophy.) The imposition of this avoidance of dualistic formulations, which I call the rule of rhetorical purity, was one of Shen-hui's most important areas of impact on Chinese Ch'an.

The doctrine of sudden enlightenment was universally accepted by the Ch'an tradition after Shen-hui, but how significant was this contribution in doctrinal terms? The terms "sudden teaching" and "sudden enlightenment" had at least as much value as slogans or labels as they did as substantive doctrinal positions. This was certainly true in the case of Shen-hui, whose emphasis on the idea of sudden enlightenment is greatest where his polemical tone is most strident and his overall practical and theoretical framework is most backward. We often see the term used in the titles of other, nonpolemical texts, even where the doctrine is hardly considered in any explicit fashion in the body of the text itself—examples include both the *Essential Determination* and *Treatise on the True Principle* discussed above and the well-known *Tun-wu yao men* (Essential

Teaching of Sudden Enlightenment) attributed to Ta-chu Hui-hai.[135] My impression, in fact, is that the term occurs much more frequently as an identifying slogan than as a doctrine with explicit content. I believe that the concept of sudden enlightenment became widely accepted in part because it was attractive, flexible, and inoffensive as a slogan.

No doubt the ontological and practical implications of the idea of suddenness were momentous, but they were also malleable. In its most simple sense, the term denotes nothing more than a nondualistic realization of religious truth achieved in a single moment of insight. On this level, the term was attractive in two ways at once: first, it at least appeared to offer religious aspirants a key to quick and easy achievement of the ultimate goal (in contrast to lifetimes of self-cultivation), and second, its use allowed one to assume a posture of accordance with the post-Shen-hui requirement of rhetorical purity. Since Ch'an masters were not inclined to a more profound specification of both the ontological and practical implications of the idea—this would have been to engage in pointless doctrinal speculation—they could and did describe any number of teachings as being "sudden," without being bound to uphold the doctrine in absolute terms. Even Shen-hui mitigated the impact of his own teaching of suddenness by requiring (or allowing) a subsequent period of gradual cultivation.

The slogan of suddenness is bandied about rather freely in the titles of Ch'an texts, and its specific doctrinal implications were not of primary importance. However, this was not just an empty slogan. On the contrary, I believe that the most important aspect of this slogan was that it combined within a single term the very kind of sensitivity toward meditation practice mentioned above. That is, where meditation texts and instructors once had to concatenate exhortations to energetic endeavor and injunctions against grasping for the goal, the doctrine (or slogan) of sudden enlightenment incorporated this practical sensitivity within itself. The appeal of a rapid and complete transformation into the enlightened state worked as a carrot to induce students to energetic endeavor, while the explicit caution against gradualistic approaches worked as a brake against dualistic conceptualization of the goal. Since the slogan "sudden enlightenment" could be appended quite easily to any text or doctrine to communicate the importance of this sensitivity but without making any great demands on the specific content of the texts or doctrines themselves, it should not be surprising that suddenness should have been accepted as a slogan. Thus it was that sudden enlightenment became the watchword of the Ch'an tradition.

D. Shen-hui's Historical Impact on Ch'an

Just because Ch'an enthusiastically embraced Shen-hui's slogan of sudden enlightenment, we should not conclude that the same was true of his other positions. In fact, Shen-hui's contributions to Ch'an were generally achieved through a process of negative impact. Shen-hui created a crisis in early Ch'an with his factionalist anti-Northern school campaign, which led to creative growth in Ch'an only because of the efforts taken by the tradition to overcome the divisiveness of his attack. It is not even accurate to say that he caused the disappearance of the Northern school, since it never existed as an institutional entity to begin with, or the supersedure of the sudden teaching over the gradual teaching, since no one ever advocated the doctrinally backward position that he described and criticized. In fact, many of the contributions of the "Northern school" were maintained by the later Ch'an tradition, even though they were presented under the aegis of the Ox-head and Hung-chou schools. The Ox-head school, with the *Platform Sūtra,* and the Szechwan factions, with the *Li-tai fa-pao chi,* collectively installed many of Shen-hui's innovations into the Ch'an tradition—with his authorship neatly obscured.[136] Certain sayings of Ma-tsu and Hui-chung also appear to criticize ideas of Shen-hui's.[137]

Just as Shen-hui's major effort was propagandistic, his major impact lay in the realm of rhetoric and mythopoeia. In addition to establishing a standard of rhetorical purity, he is responsible for the addition of many new anecdotes regarding Bodhidharma and the early patriarchs to the early Ch'an library. In the process Shen-hui helped make the theory of the transmission of the dharma much more concrete and precise, even though he did not significantly alter the conceptual basis of the theory.[138] Coupled with his penchant for story-telling, this new attention to the form rather than only the substance of religious pronouncements may have helped bring about the emergence of encounter dialogue and the "recorded sayings" genre of Ch'an literature.[139] These changes may be formalistic, but they were of the highest significance to the development of the Ch'an tradition.

The real transformation that took place in Ch'an during the eighth century was the emergence of the practice of "encounter dialogue" in the Hung-chou school of Ma-tsu Tao-i, which is the earliest faction of the classical phase of Chinese Ch'an Buddhism. The literature of encounter dialogue may be placed under the rubric of the sudden teaching, in the sense that it satisfies the twofold criteria mentioned above. Since the practitioners of encounter dialogue relentlessly attacked gradualistic formulations and exhorted students on to diligent endeavor, they could make effective use of the slogan of sudden enlightenment. In addition, since Shen-hui's anti-Northern school campaign and the appearance of the *Platform Sūtra* had provided a legendary explanation of the sudden-gradual dichotomy that was convenient, instructive (in a very profound sense), and entertaining, the later Ch'an school adopted this legend as part of its own historical self-understanding. In contrast to the image presented in this legend, however, the sudden-gradual dichotomy was something of a false issue in the development of Ch'an. Although Shen-hui contributed to the increasingly clear crystallization of Ch'an ideas and to the elaboration of its iconoclastic spirit, his career did not represent a fundamental break in the course of the school's development. Shen-hui's teachings were extensions of, rather than radical alternatives to, Northern school doctrine, and his innovations only contributed to the emergence of classical Ch'an within the overall context of early Ch'an in general.

Notes

1. This chapter is the first in a set of studies on Shen-hui. Also planned are an examination of Hu Shih's interpretation of Shen-hui's historical significance, an investigation of the possible relationship between Nan-yang Hui-chung and Shen-hui's lineage, and, ultimately, an annotated and copiously cross-referenced translation of the entire corpus of Shen-hui's known works.

2. This point is made by Philip B. Yampolsky, *The Platform Sutra of the Sixth Patriarch: The Text of the Tun-huang Manuscript, with Translation, Introduction, and Notes* (New York and London: Columbia University Press, 1967), 32. There is one possible exception, however: the sermon attributed to Shen-hui in the *Ching-te ch'üan-teng lu* (Records of the Transmission of the Lamp [Compiled during the] Ching-te [Period], hereafter cited as *CTL*), fasc. 28, *T* 51.439b–440a, includes six questions and answers between Shen-hui and the "sixth patriarch" *(liu-tsu).* Yanagida Seizan, "Goroku no rekishi," *Tōhō gakuhō* 57 (March 1985): 395, suggests that this is an excerpt from a very early text of Shen-hui's, which does seem plausible from the contents. However, he also suggests that the term *liu-tsu* does not necessarily refer to Hui-neng. His point, I believe, is that the passage is so early that the teacher involved may have been Shen-hsiu, under whom Shen-hui also studied. I can see no reason to disagree with Professor Yanagida's point, and a presentation of the contents of this text would add substance to my argument below regarding Shen-hui's early teaching career. However, since doing so would be based solely on doctrinal grounds and would involve a considerable amount of supporting analysis, I have decided to keep to the general practice of using only contemporary materials. Incidentally, Robert B. Zeuschner has published a translation of the other material included here (i.e., Shen-hui's address and not the dialogues) in "A Sermon by the Ch'an Master Ho-tse Shen-hui," *Middle Way* 49, no. 3 (November 1974): 45–47.

3. This epitaph is discussed in Yampolsky, 66–69. A liberally annotated edition may be found in Yanagida Seizan, *Shoki Zenshū shisho no kenkyū* (Kyoto: Hōzōkan, 1967), 539–558.

4. The Ox-head school authorship of the *Platform Sūtra* was the subject of an

extensive argument in Yanagida, *Shoki Zenshū shisho,* 181–212. Although this argument is based largely on circumstantial evidence, to my knowledge it has not been challenged. In addition, I have found Yanagida's theory to conform well with other information regarding the Ox-head school. See John R. McRae, "The Ox-head School of Chinese Buddhism: From Early Ch'an to the Golden Age," in Robert M. Gimello and Peter N. Gregory, eds., *Studies in Ch'an and Hua-yen,* Studies in East Asian Buddhism, no. 1 (Honolulu: University of Hawaii Press, 1983), 218–232.

5. On the development of the legend of Hui-neng, see Yampolsky, especially 58–88.

6. See John R. McRae, *The Northern School and the Formation of Early Ch'an Buddhism,* Studies in East Asian Buddhism, no. 3 (Honolulu: University of Hawaii Press, 1986), 1–7 and 235–238, for a more extensive discussion of the mind verses of the *Platform Sūtra.*

7. See McRae, *Northern School,* 237–238, for the specific references underlying this assertion. An additional supporting reference is mentioned in note 80 below.

8. Judging from the biographical data, Ma-tsu was most greatly indebted to masters of the Northern school and Szechwan faction lineages. See Nishiguchi Yoshio, "Baso no denki," *Zengaku kenkyū* 63 (1984): 123–124.

9. There are one or two texts attributed to classical Ch'an figures found at Tun-huang, but the texts themselves manifest none of the distinctive characteristics of classical Ch'an texts. The most prominent example is the *Kuei-shan ching-ts'e* (Kuei-shan's Wakening Stick) attributed to Kuei-shan Ling-yu (771–853), which occurs in a Tun-huang manuscript under the title *Ta-kuei ching-ts'e.* This text, which is discussed by Tanaka Ryōshō in his *Tonkō Zenshū bunken no kenkyū* (Tokyo: Daitō shuppan sha, 1983), 335–342, contains a very conventional message on monastic discipline. This work has been translated by Melvin Masa Takemoto, "The *Kuei-shan ching-ts'e:* Morality and the Hung-chou School of Ch'an" (M.A. thesis, University of Hawaii, 1983).

10. Professor Yanagida's recent "Goroku no rekishi" is a grand summation of his work on the history of Ch'an recorded sayings literature, from its beginnings up to Lin-chi I-hsüan.

11. See McRae, *Northern School,* 91–97.

12. My primary research at present concerns the Hung-chou school of Ma-tsu and its relationship to early Ch'an.

13. Hu Shih's biographical study of Shen-hui was published in 1930. It is reprinted in his *Shen-hui ho-shang i-chi—fu Hu hsien-sheng tsui-hou-te yen-chiu,* ed. Ma Chün-wu (Taipei: Hu Shih chi-nien kuan, 1966; repr. 1968), 3–90, as well as in Yanagida Seizan, ed., *Ko Teki Zengaku an* (Kyoto: Chūbun shuppan sha, 1975), 99–142. The latter volume contains all of Hu Shih's published writings on Ch'an Buddhism, most of which concern Shen-hui either directly or indirectly.

14. Hu Shih's comprehensive theory of Chinese history is stated in a number of works, the most concise statements occurring in his articles "Chinese Thought" in *China,* ed. Harley Farnsworth MacNair (Berkeley and Los

Angeles: University of California Press, 1951), 221–230, and "Religion and Philosophy in Chinese History," in *A Symposium on Chinese Culture,* ed. Sophia Heng-che (Chen) Zen (Shanghai: China Institute of Pacific Relations, 1931), 32.

15. The disagreement between Hu and Suzuki, which led to a well-known exchange of articles in *Philosophy East and West,* is without question the most celebrated mismatch of modern Ch'an studies. Unfortunately, this exchange of articles occurred virtually at the end of their respective academic careers, decades after their most creative periods. Perhaps as a result of this, neither man seems to have had the interest or capacity to really consider the other's position, and no one since then has chosen to redefine and carry on their dialogue. See Hu's "Ch'an (Zen) Buddhism in China: Its History and Method," *Philosophy East and West* 3, no. 1 (April 1953): 3–24, and Suzuki's rejoinder, "Zen: A Reply to Hu Shih," 25–46 of the same issue.

16. The first modern study of Shen-hui's biography was that published in 1930 by Hu Shih, cited in note 13 above. Hu's findings, including his more recent conclusions, are summarized by Philip Yampolsky in his introduction to *The Platform Sutra,* 23–38.

17. The discovery of Shen-hui's stele was announced by Wen Yü-ch'eng (Wen Yucheng in Pinyin), a member of the Lung-men museum staff in Honan. Wen's article, "Chi hsin ch'u-t'u-te Ho-tse ta-shih Shen-hui t'a-ming," *Shih-chieh tsung-chiao yen-chiu,* no. 2 (1984), 78–79, describes the inscription and analyzes its historical significance. This article was subsequently summarized in Japanese, with substantial additional analysis and a transcription and Japanese translation of the inscription, in Takeuchi Kōdō, "Shinshutsu no Kataku Jinne tōmei ni tsuite," *Shūgaku kenkyū* 27 (March 1985): 313–325. Shen-hui's ritual implements appeared in an exhibition of artifacts from China that toured Japan in the summer of 1986; see *Kōga bunmei ten,* Tōkyō Kokuritsu Hakubutsukan (Tokyo: Chūnichi shimbun sha, 1986), plates 110–113 and explanation, pp. 185–186 (Japanese) and 201 (English). Professor Yanagida informed me in a personal communication shortly after the exhibition of its inclusion of Shen-hui's bowl and other artifacts; he seems willing to accept them as authentic. The occurrence of the begging bowl in Shen-hui's grave corroborates the implication of written sources that he did not possess the legendary bowl of Bodhidharma—or at least that he did not pass it along to a disciple. The exhibition catalogue describes the bowl simply as a gilt bronze bowl with cover in the shape of a stūpa; the ash found within it is said to be from incense.

18. Shen-hui's family name and place of birth are given in his biographies in both the *SKSC, T* 50.756c–757a, and *CTL, T* 51.245a–b. Hu, *I-chi,* 5, corrects the two variants given in Tsung-mi's works to Kao. Three of Tsung-mi's works contain biographical statements for Shen-hui: the *Yüan-chüeh ching ta-shu ch'ao,* fasc. 3B, *ZZ* 1/14/3.277a–d; the *Yüan-chüeh ching lüeh-shu ch'ao,* fasc. 4, *ZZ* 1/15/2.131a–d; and the *Chung-hua ch'üan hsin-ti ch'an-men shih-tzu ch'eng-hsi t'u* or "Ch'an Chart," *ZZ* 2A/15/5.433d–434a, or Kamata Shigeo, *Zengen shosenshū tojo,* Zen no goroku, no. 9 (Tokyo: Chikuma shobō, 1971), 277. The *Ta-shu ch'ao* and *Lüeh-shu ch'ao* accounts are identical, except that the former contains addi-

tional information given under Hui-neng's name. Below I will cite the *Lüeh-shu ch'ao* only where it differs from the other text. Part of the "Ch'an Chart" account is taken verbatim from the *Ta-shu ch'ao.*

19. The *Hsü kao-seng chuan* (Continued Lives of Eminent Monks), *T* 50.587a, mentions a Dhyāna Master Hao from Hsiang-yang who was the teacher of a monk who died in 632 at the age of 61. Although this is considerably before Shen-hui was born, the coincidence of place and personal names suggests some kind of relationship between the two individuals.

20. Wang Wei's epitaph for Hui-neng states that Shen-hui began his studies under Hui-neng when he (Shen-hui, that is) was "middle-aged" *(chung-nien).* Hu Shih and others have taken this to be more authoritative than the age followed here (see Yampolsky, 26n), but Takeuchi, 317, argues forcefully that the character *chung* 'middle' should be read as *ch'ung* (the same character with the water radical added), meaning adolescence. The *Ts'ao-ch'i ta-shih chuan,* a biography of Hui-neng written about the same time as (but independently of) the *Platform Sūtra,* has the event occurring at Shen-hui's age 13. See *ZZ* 2B/19/5.485b, or *Enō kenkyū—Enō no denki to shiryō ni kan suru kisoteki kenkyū—,* comp. Komazawa Daigaku Zenshūshi kenkyūkai (Tokyo: Daishukan shoten, 1978), 42. Tsung-mi's *Ta-shu ch'ao* gives his age as fourteen. Also, in the *Platform Sūtra* Hui-neng addresses Shen-hui as a "young monk." These details would seem to corroborate Takeuchi's interpretation.

21. The fact that Shen-hui took his full ordination in Ch'ang-an is stated in Tsung-mi's *Yüan-chüeh ching ta-shu ch'ao* and in the *CTL,* which also states that he returned to Ts'ao-ch'i in 707–709. The date 704 for Shen-hui's ordination was determined by subtracting the length of Shen-hui's career as a monk from his age at death as given in the stele.

22. This subject is discussed in Hu, *Shen-hui ho-shang i-chi,* 7–8.

23. See the discussion in Takeuchi, 316–317.

24. Shen-hui did have contact with a student named Shen-ying in the sixth month of 716, but only to suggest that the student go to Mount Wu-t'ai. Their meeting may have taken place at Nan-yüeh, but this is uncertain. See Ui Hakuju, *Zenshūshi kenkyū,* vol. 1 (Tokyo: Iwanami shoten, 1939), 207 and 248–249. Ui, 207–208, criticizes Shen-hui for taking a student so early in his career, but there is no evidence that the contact between the two was anything more than incidental. For a comprehensive treatment of Shen-ying, see Raoul Birnbaum, "The Manifestation of a Monastery: Shen-ying's Experiences on Mount Wu-t'ai in T'ang Context," *Journal of the American Oriental Society* 106, no. 1 (1986): 119–137. The encounter with Shen-hui is mentioned on p. 121.

25. *T* 50.756c.

26. See Hu, *Shen-hui ho-shang i-chi,* 13–14. Yampolsky, 24–25n, gives a very convenient résumé of the various manuscripts (and most of the editions) of Shen-hui's various works. There are several manuscripts of the text containing Shen-hui's miscellaneous dialogues. Two of these were circulated under the provisional title "Shen-hui's Recorded Sayings" *(Shen-hui yü-lu* or *Shen-hui lu),* i.e., a fragment published by Hu Shih (Pelliot 3047 [part 1]; see the *I-chi,* 91–158, for Hu's editions, annotation, and commentary) and another owned by Ishii Mitsuo in Japan and published in facsimile in 1932 under the title *Tonkō shutsudo*

Jinne roku and two years later in an edited version by D. T. Suzuki and Kuda Rentarō, *Tonkō shutsudo Kataku Jinne zenji goroku* (Tokyo: Morie shoten, 1934). In 1956, however, Iriya Yoshitaka discovered a third manuscript (Stein 6557) during an examination of Stein collection microfilms, which was published with an introduction and annotation by Hu Shih in 1960. (Hu's work was published in the *Chung-kuo Chung-yang Yen-chiu-yüan Li-shih Yü-yen Yen-chiu-so chi-k'an*, extra vol. 4, no. 1 [September 1960]: 1–31; I have consulted the reprinted version in Hu's *Shen-hui ho-shang i-chi*, 401–452.) This third version bears the title *Nan-yang ho-shang wen-ta tsa ch'eng-i*, or "Dialogues on Miscellaneous Inquiries of the Preceptor [Shen-hui] of Nan-yang." (Yanagida, "Goroku no rekishi," 367–369, suggests that the character *ch'eng* refers to questions placed by a teacher to students, rather than vice versa; the interpretation is a problem because the character does not occur in the body of the text. I will cite the text below by the abbreviated title *Miscellaneous Dialogues*.) It includes a preface by one Liu Ch'eng, who is identified in Ennin's catalogue as the compiler of the text. See Yanagida's "Zenseki kaidai," ed. Nishitani Keiji and Yanagida Seizan, *Zenke goroku*, vol. 2, Sekai koten bungaku zenshū, no. 36B (Tokyo: Chikuma shobō, 1974), 461. Paul Demiéville's "Deux documents de Touen-houang sur le Dhyāna chinois," *Essays on the History of Buddhism Presented to Professor Tsukamoto Zenryū* (Kyoto, 1961), 1–14 (from the back), contains a discussion of Stein 6557.

In addition to the text in the *I-chi*, the *Suzuki Daisetsu zenshū*, vol. 3 (Tokyo: Iwanami shoten, 1968), 236–288, contains a synoptic edition of Pelliot 3047 and the Ishii manuscript. Jacques Gernet, *Entretiens du Maître de Dhyāna Chen-houei de Ho-tsö (668–760)*, Publications de l'école française d'Extrême-Orient, vol. 31 (Hanoi, 1949), contains translations of all of Shen-hui's works found in the first edition of Hu Shih's *I-chi*, including the *Miscellaneous Dialogues*. Gernet's "Complément aux entretiens du Maître de Dhyāna Chen-houei," *Bulletin de l'Ecole française d'Extrême-Orient* 44, no. 2 (1954): 453–466, contains the balance from the Suzuki and Kuda edition of the Ishii manuscript.

No doubt drawing from Hu's analysis (*I-chi*, 415–421), Yanagida, "Goroku no rekishi," 367 and 370–372, suggests that the different manuscripts for the *Miscellaneous Dialogues* derive from different points in Shen-hui's career, with the manuscript bearing Liu Ch'eng's preface being the earliest and only containing material antedating Shen-hui's move to Lo-yang in 745. Pelliot 3047, however, includes some additional dialogues and refers to Shen-hui as Ho-tse ho-shang (Preceptor of Ho-tse [ssu]), so it was compiled after 745. The Ishii manuscript is the latest of the three, since it manifests significant editing and contains material not found in the other two versions (some of the most interesting of which—biographies of the patriarchs, etc.—is omitted from the *Suzuki Daisetsu zenshū* edition and must be sought in Suzuki's 1934 publication of the text, a rare volume). The compiler Liu Ch'eng, incidentally, may have been related to several other men bearing the same surname known to have been close to various early Ch'an figures. See Yanagida, "Goroku no rekishi," 377.

27. The full title of this work is *Nan-yang ho-shang tun-chiao chieh-t'o ch'an-men chih liao-hsing t'an-yü* (Platform Sermon by the Preceptor of Nan-yang on Directly Comprehending the Nature According to the Ch'an Doctrine of the

Sudden Teaching and Emancipation). This is generally considered to be Shen-hui's earliest extant work, dating from his residence at Nan-yang beginning in 720, although there is no specific evidence pertaining to its date. Professor Tanaka, *Tonkō Zenshū bunken,* 254, dates the *Platform Sermon* as post-718. This is no doubt correct, but I have been unable to trace the reasoning or evidence involved. See Yanagida's characterization of this work summarized in note 139 below.

The first manuscript of this work (Peking han-81) was discovered and published by Suzuki; see his "Jinne oshō no dango to kangaubeki Tonkō shutsudo bon ni tsukite," *Ōtani gakuhō* 16, no. 4 (December 1935): 1–30; *Shōshitsu issho* (Osaka: Ataka Bukkyō bunko, 1935), 37–55; and *Kōkan Shōshitsu issho oyobi kaisetsu* (Osaka: Ataka Bukkyō bunko, 1936), 57–71 (text) and 50–68 (commentary). This material is reproduced in *Suzuki Daisetsu zenshū,* 3:290–317, with the commentary preceding the edited text. (There seem to have been only the most minor modifications to the *zenshū* version.) The existence of another manuscript (Pelliot 2045 [part 2]) was first discovered by Wang Chung-min and announced in Hu Shih's "Hsin chiao-ting te Tun-huang hsieh-pen Shen-hui ho-shang i-chu liang-chung," *Chung-kuo Chung-yang Yen-chiu-yüan Li-shih Yü-yen Yen-chiu-so chi-k'an* 29, no. 2 (February 1958): 827–882. (Also included in this manuscript [referred to as part 1] was Shen-hui's *Definition of the Truth.*) This version is republished in Hu's *I-chi,* 225–252. Professor Iriya has also discovered two additional fragments (Stein 2492 and 6977).

Shinohara Toshio used all the available versions of the text in preparing his edition and translation, "Kataku Jinne no kotoba—Yakuchū *Nan'yō wajō tonkyō gedatsu zenmon jiki ryōshō dango,*" *Komazawa Daigaku Bungakubu kenkyū kiyō* 31 (March 1973): 1–33. Certain errors in Shinohara's work were revised in Nakamura Shinkō's "*Nan'yō wajō tonkyō gedatsu zenmon jiki ryōshō dango* hon'yaku," *Komazawa Daigaku Bukkyōgaku Kenkyūkai nenpō* 8 (1974): 137–146.

The *Platform Sermon* has been translated into English by Walter Liebenthal as "The Sermon of Shen-hui," *Asia Major,* n.s. 3, no. 2 (1952): 132–155. Liebenthal used only one manuscript, Pelliot 2045, although he was able to refer to Gernet's *Entretiens.*

28. See Ui, 212.

29. See Suzuki Tetsuo, "Kataku Jinne ron," *Bukkyō shigakkai* 14, no. 4 (November 1969): 226.

30. *T* 51.245a. The title *Hsien-tsung chi* is used for the text in the *CTL,* fasc. 30, 458c–459b. A similar title, *Hsien-tsung lun,* is used for the excerpt (matching the Tun-huang text) found in the *Tsung-ching lu* (Records of the Mirror of Truth), fasc. 99, *T* 48.949a–b. The original title is *Tun-wu wu-sheng po-jo sung* (Verses on Sudden Enlightenment, the Birthless, and Prajñā). This title occurs in Stein 468, an annotated edition of which may be found in Hu, *I-chi,* 193–199, with Hu's commentary following on 200–208. The Tun-huang version is said to be simpler than the text found in the *CTL,* and lacks the statement of twenty-eight patriarchs attached to the latter. (Yanagida, *Shoki Zenshū shisho,* 124, 324, and 365–380, has argued that the scheme of twenty-eight patriarchs was an innovation of the *Pao-lin chuan* and never suggested by Shen-hui.) There is a second Tun-huang manuscript (Stein 296) of unknown length. The earliest

notice of the Tun-huang version of this text (Stein 468) was in Yabuki Keiki, *Meisha yoin—Tonkō shutsudo miden koitsu Butten kaihō* [English subtitle: *Rare and Unkown Chinese Manuscript Remains of Buddhist Literature Discovered in Tun-huang Collected by Sir Aurel Stein and Preserved in the British Museum*] (Tokyo: Iwanami shoten, 1930). Robert B. Zeuschner has translated the text in "The *Hsien-tsung chi*: An Early Ch'an Text," *Journal of Chinese Philosophy* 3 (1976): 253–268. This text is written in polished form and lacks the evangelical immediacy and polemical fire of the *Definition of the Truth*.

31. Suzuki Tetsuo has noticed that the text's reference to the date of the original Hua-t'ai debate is couched in terms of a usage that was instituted in 744. He also suggests that 749 is the terminus ad quem for the text since it does not mention the debate that occurred in that year, according to the *Li-tai fa-pao chi* (Record of the [Transmission of the] Dharma-treasure through the Generations, or *LTFPC*). See "Kataku Jinne ron," *Bukkyō shigaku* 14, no. 4 (November 1969): 225–226 and 238 nn. 8–9. The *LTFPC* citation occurs at *T* 51.185b, or see Yanagida Seizan, *Shoki no Zenshi 2—Rekidai hōbō ki—*, Zen no goroku, no. 3 (Tokyo: Chikuma shobō, 1976), 155.

There are three Tun-huang manuscripts for the *Definition of the Truth*: Pelliot 2045 (part 1), 3047 (part 2), and 3488 (part 1). The text occurs in Hu, *I-chi*, 260–314. The discovery of the manuscripts of this text by Hu in Paris was the catalyst for his biographical study of Shen-hui and, indeed, all of his subsequent work on Chinese Ch'an. Yanagida, "Goroku no rekishi," 376, suggests that this text stands midway between the first and third versions of the *Miscellaneous Dialogues* in the development of Shen-hui's teachings.

32. This comment is in all three of Tsung-mi's texts, as mentioned in Ui, 231. In the preceding pages, Ui emphasizes the lack of impact of Shen-hui's campaign.

33. Takeuchi, 324.

34. As mentioned in Yampolsky, 66n, Jacques Gernet, "Biographie du Maître Chen-houei du Ho-tsö," *Journal Asiatique* 249 (1951): 48, has suggested on the basis of the title used to identify Wang Wei that the epitaph for Hui-neng was written after 739.

35. Ui, 210–211, points out that these refer to the material found only in the Suzuki/Kuda edition of the Ishii manuscript of the *Miscellaneous Dialogues*.

36. This is discussed in Matsuda Fumio, "Jinne no hōtōsetsu ni tsuite—toku ni sanzo kenshō mondai—," *IBK* 6, no. 2 (12; March 1958): 221–224 (532–535).

37. This is according to the sometimes unreliable *LTFPC*, as mentioned in note 130 below.

38. A reference in Tsung-mi's writings suggests that Shen-hui also gained prominence through his explanation of the metaphor of the three carts in the *Lotus Sūtra;* Hu infers from the biography of the individual mentioned that this occurred around the end of the K'ai-yüan period (713–741). The wording also implies that Shen-hui was residing at the Lung-hsing ssu in Nan-yang at the time. See Ui, 209, citing Hu, 14 and the text on 110–111. The inference regarding Shen-hui's residence is from Ui, 230.

39. Actually, given the anachronistic references to P'u-chi and Shen-hsiu in

the biographies of late eighth-century figures, this may not be that great a problem; Lu I's guidance from P'u-chi could have been through his own memory of the master or through some contemporaneous successor. See McRae, *Northern School,* 71 and 293–294n. The phrasing of the *SKSC* reference is also somewhat vague in saying that Lu I falsely memorialized against Shen-hui to "curry favor" with (*o,* also meaning to "fawn on" or "flatter") P'u-chi.

40. Whatever the degree of Northern school involvement in Shen-hui's removal from the capital, it is possible that he exaggerated the entire incident so as to incite his followers against the Northern school. In this case, there would be no reason to suppose that all of Shen-hui's public lectures were virulent attacks on the Northern school; the polemical maneuver would have occurred after his expulsion from Lo-yang.

41. This and the following information is according to Tsung-mi's *Ta-shu ch'ao.* The term used is *ch'u,* which refers to a demotion and/or relocation.

42. I will document the reasons for this impression on a later occasion, but see note 137 below.

43. Ui, 234.

44. According to Yamazaki Hiroshi, "Kataku Jinne zenji," *Zuitō Bukkyō no kenkyū* (Kyoto: Hōzōkan, 1967), 211–214 (with a summary on 213–214), this plan was first carried out by the infamous Yang Kuo-chung in either T'ai-yüan or Ho-tung. The same scheme was used after Yang's death, this time in P'eng-yüan.

45. The plan was initiated by an order issued from Emperor Su-tsung's camp at Feng-hsiang (in modern Shensi) at the instigation of P'ei Wan (d. 769).

46. C. A. Peterson, "Court and Province in Mid- and Late T'ang," in *Sui and T'ang China, 589–906,* Part 1, ed. Denis Twitchett, vol. 3 of *The Cambridge History of China* (Cambridge: Cambridge University Press, 1979), 474, describes this year as being toward the end of a period of rebel ascendancy (July 756 to November 757) and immediately preceding a period of relative military inactivity (autumn 757 to autumn 758).

47. The specific date used here is that given in Shen-hui's stele inscription. The *Ta-shu ch'ao, SKSC,* and *CTL* place Shen-hui's death at the thirteenth day of the fifth month, although the years differ. Tsung-mi's text agrees with the stele in assigning the year 758 to Shen-hui's death. The *SKSC* specifies a year in terms that do not match any legitimate year, although Hu Shih thought the year intended was 762. See Hu Shih, "Hsin chiao-ting te Tun-huang hsieh-pen," 875. The *SKSC* states that Shen-hui lived to be 93 whereas the *CTL* agrees with the stele in reporting his age at death to be 75. Takeuchi reviews these discrepancies on pp. 315–316. Ui, 235–236, notes that there is a discrepancy about the location where Shen-hui died, either K'ai-yüan ssu or Ho-tse ssu. I have followed the stele and *Ta-shu ch'ao* (see the following anecdote, which refers to K'ai-yüan ssu), but note that this further reduces the length of time he was involved in fundraising on behalf of the government.

48. Biography unknown.

49. *T* 50.757a.

50. See Takeuchi, 324, and Suzuki Tetsuo, "Kataku Jinne ron," 320.

51. Takeuchi, 320, adduces evidence to show that "national teacher" was not used as an official title at the time, but rather as a generic term of reference for masters of great standing or national prominence.

52. See Takeuchi, 320.

53. Tsung-mi mentions this in his *Ch'an Chart.* See *ZZ* 2A/15/5.434b, or Kamata, 277. Ui, 237, points out that a similar resolution of conflict in the Vinaya school took place in 778.

54. The earliest work in which the list of Hung-jen's students occurs is the *Leng-ch'ieh shih-tzu chi* (Records of the Masters and Disciples of the Laṅkā[vatāra]), which was composed in 713–716. The provenance of the second text is probably similar. See McRae, *Northern School,* 38–39 and 84.

55. See McRae, *Northern School,* 58–59 and 291n.

56. This is known through a letter written by Shen-hsiu's sometime student I-hsing. See McRae, *Northern School,* 51 and 289n.

57. This text, the complete Tun-huang manuscript for which is Pelliot 2162, was first described in Yabuki's *Meisha yoin,* 538–540. The text may be found in *T* 85.1278a–1281c or the *Suzuki Daisetsu zenshū,* 3:318–330. (Photocopies of a fragment, Stein 4286, which includes approximately the first third of the text but in a most disordered fashion, are reproduced at the end of Jao Tsung-i, "Shen-hui men-hsia Mo-ho-yen chih ju-Tsang, chien lun Ch'an-men nan-pei tsung chih t'iao-ho wen-t'i," *Hsiang-kang Ta-hsüeh wu-shih chou-nien chi-nien lun-wen chi,* vol. 1 (Hong Kong: Hsiang-kang Ta-hsüeh, 1964), following 178. Another printed version (based on the *Taishō* edition) occurs in Kim Kugyŏng (Chin Chiu-ching), *Chiang-yüan ts'ung-shu* (Shen-yang, 1934). For an analysis of the authorship and contents of this text, including the relationship between it and other Northern school literature, plus a comparison with the *Essential Determination,* see Tanaka Ryōshō, *Tonkō Zenshū bunken no kenkyū* (Tokyo: Daitō shuppan sha, 1983), 237–259. The partial translation included in this paper is based on the Suzuki edition, which I have checked against the photographs of Stein 4286, with reference to Tanaka, *Tonkō Zenshū bunken,* 253–254, for comparison with the *Essential Determination.* Recently, J. C. Cleary has published a translation of the entire *Treatise on the True Principle* in *Zen Dawn: Early Zen Texts from Tun Huang* (Boston and London: Shambhala, 1986), 103–130. Cleary's translation is uneven in style but generally accurate, and his reading occasionally implies punctuation superior to that of the Suzuki edition. Unfortunately, he refrained from including any annotation or interpretation of the text, and he apparently used the outdated *Chiang-yüan ts'ung-shu* edition. See my review of *Zen Dawn* in *The Eastern Buddhist* 19, no. 2 (1986): 138–146.

58. A monk named Hui-kuang who studied under P'u-chi is known as the man who "discovered" the *Ch'an-men ching* or *Sūtra of Ch'an* around the year 720. See Yanagida Seizan, "Zenseki kaidai," 462, and Yanagida, "*Zenmonkyō* ni tsuite," *Tsukamoto hakase shōju kinen Bukkyō shigaku ronshū* (Tokyo: Tsukamoto hakase shōju kinen kai, 1961), 869–882. Both Yanagida and Tanaka, *Tonkō Zenshū bunken,* 243–246, infer that these were two separate individuals. Tanaka, in fact, goes on to note the structual similarities between the *Treatise on the True Principle* and certain other early Ch'an texts and concludes by suggesting that the Hui-kuang of this text was a fictional personality. If he were a real individual,

and taking the year 725 as a rough date for the composition of the *Treatise on the True Principle,* Hui-kuang would have been born around 680.

59. For a discussion and edition of this text, including a translation of the Tibetan version, see Ueyama Daishun, "Chibetto-yaku *Tongo shinshū yōketsu* no kenkyū," *Zenbunka Kenkyūjo kiyō* 8 (1976): 33–103. Ueyama argues convincingly that the Tibetan translation of this text is more reliable than any of the Chinese manuscripts. Yanagida, "Zenseki kaidai," 458–459; Yanagida, "Hokushū-Zen no shisō," *Zenbunka Kenkyūjo kiyō* 6 (1974): 80; and Tanaka, *Tonkō Zenshū bunken,* 251–256, describe this text as a later Northern school product.

60. See the *Liu-tu ssu Hou-mo-ch'en ta-shih shou-t'a ming wen ping hsü* by Ts'ui Kuan, which occurs in the *Mang-lo chung-mo i-wen ssu-pien,* comp. Lo Chen-yü, *Shih-k'e shih-liao hsin-pien,* series 1 (Taipei: Hsin wen-feng ch'u-pan kung-ssu, 1977), 19:14263b–14264b. Faure has reported his findings in the forthcoming "Le maître de dhyāna Chih-ta et le 'subitisme' de l'école du Nord," *Cahiers d'Extrême-Asie* 2, Kyoto (1986). In addition to the information mentioned, the names of the half-dozen disciples responsible for constructing his stūpa are given, although none of them is immediately recognizable to me. According to the figures given in the epitaph, Chih-ta was at least forty years of age during Shen-hsiu's lifetime. Hence he must have been born sometime around or before (perhaps well before) 660. The epigrapher is mentioned briefly in the *T'ang shu, Erh-shih-wu shih,* K'ai-ming shu-tien ed., 3411c, in the context of his older brother Ts'ui Ning's biography and with regard to an incident in 767. Thus either the stele was erected quite some time after Chih-ta's death in 714 or the elaborate prestige titles by which Ts'ui Kuan is identified (which identify him as rank 5a1 by Hucker's scheme) were added by the recorder of the epitaph. If the former alternative is the case, it is possible that the epitaph was written to corroborate the *Essential Determination.*

61. The *Treatise on the True Principle* shares a passage with the Northern school's *Leng-ch'ieh shih-tzu chi,* which was composed sometime during the years 713–716 far away from the two capitals. I suspect that the direction of borrowing was from this text to the *Treatise on the True Principle,* rather than vice versa. See sec. III.B.1 below. Also, the borrowing of the name of Hui-kuang (which even in the case of the *Ch'an-men ching* may be fictional) implies that the *Treatise on the True Principle* derives from sometime after 720, although once again the borrowing could have gone the other way.

62. The close relationship between these two texts has also been the subject of comments in Yanagida, "Hokushū-zen no shisō," 80. Both Ueyama, "*Tongo shinshū yōketsu,* 67–68, and Tanaka, 253–254, include synoptic presentations of the two prefaces.

63. The colophon of the *Essential Determination* reads "Ch'an Master Chih-ta's oral determination of the questions of Hou-mo-ch'en Yen, transcribed by the scribe Ying."

64. Following Cleary, 105, I repunctuate Suzuki's edition to end the sentence after *chen* 'true'. Suzuki shows three missing characters just prior to *sheng* 'vehicle', for which Stein 4286 has *hsieh cheng ta* 'false (heterodox), correct, great'. An attempt seems to have been made to delete the character *ting,* which I have interpreted as having the force of "must," from Stein 4286.

65. Stein 4286 has *hsing* 'nature' instead of Suzuki's *wu* 'enlightenment'.

66. The character *i* is difficult to translate consistently. In Indian Buddhist philosophy it refers to *manas* and may be used as a synonym for consciousness in general, as a term for the sixth sensory faculty (the mind as the processor of data from the other senses), or, in Yogācāra, as the name of the seventh *vijñāna*. In Chinese the character also has the meaning of "will" or "intention." Hence the different translations here as "will," "mental," and "concentration."

67. "Evaporated" is a translation of *hsü-huo* '[made] empty and expansive'.

68. Stein 4286 has *yüan* 'conditioned' rather than Suzuki's *hsiang* 'modelled on'.

69. "Realms of existence" might be a better translation here, except for the need for parallelism with *wu-so,* which occurs in the *Treatise on the True Principle.* See note 81 below.

70. The *Essential Determination* identifies Hou-mo-ch'en's lay name as Yen (the epitaph has Yen-chih) and his religious title as Chih-ta.

71. These periods enclosed in brackets indicate the occurrence of material in the *Essential Determination* that is not found in the *Treatise on the True Principle.* Here the former text states that Chih-ta stayed on Mount Sung for more than twenty years.

72. Chih-ta, of course, was a student of Lao-an and Shen-hsiu.

73. I wonder if the phrase "exit from being and entrance into nonbeing" *(ch'u-yu ju-wu)* is similar to the reflexive literary form known as *hu-wen,* so that Hui-kuang was able to enter and exit both being and nonbeing.

74. Here the *Essential Determination* reads: "His accordance with the mysterious wisdom within the house (i.e., immanent in sentient beings) and attainment of the correct realization of cultivating the mind *(hsiu-hsin)* were incomparable." The term *hsiu-hsin,* of course, recalls the title of the *Hsiu-hsin yao lun* (Treatise on the Essentials of Cultivating the Mind) attributed to Hung-jen.

75. For this paragraph, the *Essential Determination* has: "In his time off from contemplation, the layman lamented the [plight of] deluded [sentient beings] and eventually utilized their [errors] to formulate a dialogue whereby he could reveal the essentials of the dharma. He may be called the 'dragon-and-elephant of the house of Śākya, the boat across the ocean [of ignorance].' A sūtra says: 'Go directly to bodhi.' These words are worthy of trust. Future students are thus fortunate to be able to maintain [awareness of the] mind *(shou-hsin)* according to the text." Following this, the *Essential Determination* has: "Recorded by the Prefect *(tz'u-shih)* of Ti-chou (Yang-hsin hsien, Shantung) Liu Wu-te on the fifth day of the eleventh month of the first year of Hsien-t'ien (= December 8, 712)."

76. Stein 4286 has *chen-yen* 'true words' instead of Suzuki's *chih-yen* 'direct words', but note the *chih-wen chih-shuo* 'ask directly and I will explain directly' just below.

77. For this paragraph the *Essential Determination* has: "Yen inquired of Dhyāna Master Chih-ta, 'Buddhism is abstruse and . . . difficult to understand. I would like to inquire of the essential teaching of Ch'an—not in order to gain rebirth as a man or god, but to proceed directly to the 'other shore' of bodhi. I request that in your compassion, you will not forsake the common sort . . . and

please have no secrets. Refrain from discussing mundane paths. Please do not belabor your wisdom in regard to the conditioned [matters of] this world; I request that you favor me with the essential teaching of the unconditioned [matters of the] supramundane.' " (Elisions mark language identical to that in the *Treatise on the True Principle*.)

78. The *Essential Determination* has Chih-ta say he is fifty-three years old and had been a monk for thirty-two years.

79. Stein 4286 has the character *li* here twice.

80. Sometime after his entry into Ch'ang-an in 716, the esoteric master Śubhākarasiṃha criticized Shen-hsiu's student Ching-hsien (660–723) and other devotees of Ch'an for what he thought was self-defeating single-mindedness: "You beginners are [in such] great fear of activating the mind and mobilizing thoughts *(ch'i-hsin tung-nien)* that you cease to make spiritual progress. In single-mindedly maintaining nonthought *(wu-nien)* as the ultimate, the [longer you] search, the more unattainable [is your goal]" (*T* 18.945a). Hence *pu-ch'i, wu-nien,* and, incidentally, *wu i wu* 'not a single thing', which occurs on 945b, were well-known terms at the time.

81. The term "contemplative analysis" derives from the writings of Chih-i and refers to the explication of Buddhist terms and ideas by recourse to insights gained during meditation. Applied to early Ch'an texts it refers to the sometimes bizarre and almost always forced reinterpretations of standard terminology in terms of the contemplation of the mind. Both the Northern and Ox-head schools are known for this practice. For a longer discussion of this practice, see McRae, *Northern School,* 198–207. The *Essential Determination* applies this style of interpretation to a famous line from the *Diamond Sūtra: ying wo-so-chu erh sheng ch'i hsin:*

> "For all [moments of] consciousness to be nonexistent is called the 'locus of nonbeing' *(wu-so)*. To refrain from any further activation of consciousness *(pu ch'i-hsin)* is called 'residing' *(chu)*. [In the phrase] 'generating consciousness' *(erh sheng ch'i hsin)*, 'should' *(ying)* means 'should' *(tang)* and to 'generate' *(sheng)* means to 'view' *(k'an)*. Thus 'should view the locus of nonbeing' is equivalent to [the phrase] 'generating consciousness. . . .' "
>
> Question: "What thing does one see?"
> Answer: "The [*Nirvāṇa*] *Sūtra* says: 'See the [Buddha]-nature and achieve the enlightenment of Buddhahood.' " (Ueyama, 96–97)

The *Nirvāṇa Sūtra* citation is actually a modified summary of material at *T* 12.547a. For early occurrences of the term *wu-so,* see Yanagida Seizan, *Daruma no goroku—Ninyū shigyō ron,* Zen no goroku, no. 1 (Tokyo: Chikuma shobō, 1969), 158n; Ogawa Kan'ichi, "*Hannya haramitta shingyō* kaidai," *Seiiki bunka kenkyū,* vol. 1, *Tonkō Bukkyō shiryō* (Kyoto: Hōzōkan, 1958), 83b; and Iriya Yoshitaka, *Denshin hōyō—Enryōroku,* Zen no goroku, no. 8 (Tokyo: Chikuma shobō, 1969), 124n. Since the *Diamond Sūtra* line is quoted in at least one other text by a Northern school figure, its presence here cannot be used as evidence of influence from Hui-neng; see I-hsing's (685–727) commentary on the *Ta-jih ching (Mahāvairocana Sūtra), T* 39.579b.

82. For two occurrences of *shou-hsin* in the *Essential Determination,* see notes 74 and 75 above. For a discussion of the doctrine of *shou-hsin* in the *Hsiu-hsin yao lun,* see McRae, *Northern School,* 136–138.

83. See Ueyama's description of the manuscripts for this text, "*Tongo shinshū yōketsu,* 34–36.

84. See note 81 above.

85. See the *Suzuki Daisetsu zenshū,* 3:327, 326–327, and 329, respectively.

86. See ibid., 320. (*Tzu-hsin* is, however, an unusual term.)

87. See Tanaka, *Tonkō Zenshū bunken,* 247–250.

88. One apparently Northern school text bears the title *Liao-hsing chü* (Stanzas on Comprehending the Nature), but it does not contain the three-character phrase so characteristic of Shen-hui. See *Suzuki Daisetsu zenshū,* 2:450–452.

89. I use the terms "East Mountain teaching" and "Northern school" to represent (1) the basic doctrines of early Ch'an generally attributed to Hung-jen and Tao-hsin, and (2) the more complex ideas formulated by Shen-hsiu and his disciples. See McRae, *Northern School,* 8–10, for an explanation of this somewhat arbitrary but useful distinction. (Where the term Northern school occurs independently it may be used inclusive of the other term.) The anthology referred to here is described in ibid., 311–312n.

90. See *Suzuki Daisetsu zenshū,* 3:445 and *Kōkan Shōshitsu issho,* 89. The shared passage begins with a quotation from the *Nirvāna Sūtra* (actually a paraphrase of *T* 12.547a) and continues in language that is very similar to that in the *Platform Sermon;* Hu, *I-chi,* 243. (See note 81 above, and compare a passage attributed falsely to Nan-yüeh Hui-ssu in the *Tsung-ching lu, T* 48.941a.) Taken by itself, this set of coincidences would not be particularly meaningful because of the haphazard nature of the Tun-huang manuscript transcriptions.

91. "Treatise on the Dharma-nature" is Suzuki's provisional title; the text itself does begin with a reference to *fa-hsing* but later on reads: "Now, according to the true and comprehensive manifestations of the nature in the gateway of principle of the sudden teaching, the reference to 'seeing the nature' is to the Buddha-nature *(fo-hsing).*" See the *Suzuki Daisetsu zenshū,* 2:444.

92. See the *Hsiu-hsin yao lun* in McRae, *Northern School,* 125 and 317 n. 79.

93. See *T* 14.554b; *Suzuki Daisetsu zenshū,* 2:445 and 3:322; and Hu, *I-chi,* 236. The implications of this coincidence need to be studied further. The line itself reads: "Constantly seek the practice of wisdom of the true characteristic of nonthought," but the Ch'an texts omit "practice."

94. *Suzuki Daisetsu zenshū,* 3:444 and 2:237 *(Miscellaneous Dialogues).*

95. See the passage that occurs in conjunction with the verse by P'u-chi.

96. However, note that the *Treatise on the Dharma-nature* points out that attachment to *wu-nien* can also represent a serious spiritual problem, an awareness that seems to have escaped Shen-hui.

97. This analysis differs from that of Yanagida and Tanaka, who feel that the *Essential Determination* is more advanced doctrinally than the *Treatise on the True Principle* and that both texts represent a Northern school response to Shen-hui's doctrines. (See Tanaka's summary, 255–256.) I believe that the revision offered here is a more reasonable interpretation of the evidence, not all of which was available when they were writing on the subject.

98. See Yanagida, *Shoki Zenshū shisho,* 101.

99. Hu, *I-chi,* 287.

100. Ibid., 247 and 249.

101. Ibid., 246.

102. Ibid., 236 and 252.

103. See, for example, the *Hsiu-hsin yao lun* in McRae, *Northern School,* 128.

104. McRae, *Northern School,* 181–183. The *Yüan-ming lun* contains a critique of what it calls "reverse contemplation" *(ni-kuan),* in which objects are analyzed down to their smallest constituent particles and then into nothingness. This seems to be directed at an older and already outmoded doctrinal position; whether or not anyone actually practiced according to this approach in the early eighth century is dubious. See McRae, *Northern School,* 213–215.

105. McRae, *Northern School,* 215–217.

106. The Chinese version used here is that which was first presented in Suzuki's *Shōshitsu issho,* but I have used Ueyama's edition, 102–103. His translation of the corresponding Tibetan is on p. 88.

107. The term *yu-ch'ing* here is synonymous with *chung-sheng* 'sentient beings'.

108. Where the Chinese has *i* 'recollection', Ueyama translates the Tibetan as *jūsho* 'residence'.

109. The Tibetan for the middle two lines of this stanza are somewhat different: "Other elements come in [each] moment. / When they come fix the mind and attention *(hsin* and *i)* [on them] and view."

110. The character *fan* 'float' is presumably a mistake for *mo* 'sink'.

111. The Tibetan stanza reads:

The mind comes from the locus of nonbeing.
If one is attached to the attainment of empty immobility,
then understanding it by fixing the mind on it to understand it is an attachment to emptiness.
This is called the "teaching of the auditors."

112. The Tibetan version lacks this and the previous stanza.

113. The Tibetan has "returning to [one's] original house." The Chinese has the concluding line: "The other teachings also have four-line [verses], but they cannot be connected with (lit., "attached" to) the larger topic of the treatise."

114. See Yanagida, *Shoki no Zenshi 1,* 249, or *T* 85.1288a.

115. See Yanagida, *Shoki no Zenshi 1,* 205, or *T* 85.1287b.

116. See the *Definition of the Truth* in Hu, *I-chi,* 287–288. Shen-hui's formulation is carried a step further in the *Platform Sūtra;* see Yampolsky, 140.

117. Suzuki Tetsuo has pointed out a subtle difference in terminology between Shen-hui's writings and the *Platform Sūtra,* in that the former exhort the reader to "see the [Buddha]-nature" *(busshō o miyo)* where the latter refers to "seeing the nature" *(kenshō)* as a bound form. See his "Kataku Jinne no ken no shisō, *IBK* 16, no. 1 (31; December 1967): 132–133, and "Kataku Jinne yori Dankyō ni itaru kenshō no tenkai," *IBK* 17, no. 1 (33; December 1968): 302–304.

118. Hu, *I-chi,* 232 and 241–242.

119. Ibid., 237, 239, and 241.

120. Ibid., 240 and 244.

121. Ibid., 233.

122. See ibid., 250–251. It is also possible that Shen-hui purposely avoided specific statements regarding meditation practice so as not to invite criticisms of the type he addressed to the Northern school. See the conclusion of this article.

123. Ibid., 287.

124. See ibid., 299–304. The *Yüan-ming lun* contains the line "You cannot understand the principle of this through an [insight] into a text [gained] through recitation." See McRae, *Northern School,* 159.

125. See McRae, *Northern School,* 268–269. Fa-ju (638–689), an important figure not relevant to the present discussion, is also among those listed for criticism.

126. See Robert Zeuschner's "An Analysis of the Philosophical Criticisms of Northern Ch'an Buddhism" (Ph.D. diss., University of Hawaii, 1977). Although the Tun-huang texts do not explicitly describe the possible excesses, etc., of early Ch'an, some of the texts may provide examples of simplistic approaches. One such example might be the *Nan T'ien-chu-kuo P'u-t'i-ta-ma ch'an-shih kuan-men* (The Contemplation Teaching of Meditation Master Bodhidharma from South India), *T* 85.1270b–c or *Suzuki Daisetsu zenshū,* 2:219–221.

127. It may have been at least equally important that the magistrate at the time was Li Yung, a layman usually associated with P'u-chi.

128. See McRae, *Northern School,* 57–58. If we are to believe the epitaph, Lao-an began his studies under Hung-jen even before Tao-hsin's death, was singled out by Empress Wu for his composure (during an incident that occurred in the company of Shen-hsiu, who goes unmentioned), and lived to the age of 128!

129. Yanagida, "Goroku no rekishi," 392–393, describes Shen-hui's philosophy as a doctrine of *tun-chiao* or the "sudden teaching," whereas the Northern school described a doctrine of *tun-wu* or "sudden enlightenment." Although we take different views regarding the provenance of the *Treatise on the True Principle,* the distinction still holds.

130. The *LTFPC* says that Shen-hui preached from the ordination platform every month, "destroying the Ch'an of purity and establishing the Ch'an of the Tathāgatas." This seems to be a general statement about Shen-hui's career, but it probably applies mainly to his later years. See *T* 51.185b or Yanagida, *Shoki no Zenshi 2,* 155. In "Goroku no rekishi," 404–409, Yanagida discusses the sequence of developments regarding ordination platforms in China from Tao-hsüan to Hui-chung.

131. "Ch'an (Zen) Buddhism in China," 7.

132. Shen-hui's lineage is considered to have lasted for five generations, until the great Kuei-feng Tsung-mi (780–841), but the linkage between the third through fifth generations is suspect. Ui, 255–256, points out that Shen-hui had about half as many (33) known students as P'u-chi, and that the ages of the students in the two lineages were about the same (only three of Shen-hui's lived past 800). The geographical distribution of the two groups was also about the same. But in the next period, Shen-hui's Southern school faction becomes so

small as not even to be comparable to the Northern school. On p. 258, Ui notes that Shen-hui's lineage includes only 12–15 individuals in the second generation. (Of these, I accept only nine as legitimate students of Shen-hui. The biographies of all these figures are unknown.) Hence at this point (the third generation of the Ho-tse school, beginning with Shen-hui) the strength of the faction suddenly dissipated. After the year 800, only Yün-t'an (d. 816) and Fa-ju (d. 811) continued on. Fa-ju's successor Nan-yin continued on only ten years after this, and this was in far-off Szechwan (and I do not accept Nan-yin as a legitimate successor to Shen-hui).

Judging from the biographies, only two of Shen-hui's students stayed with him for any length of time. The biographies are strikingly uniform in their lack of detail regarding the students' activities before and after meeting Shen-hui. For several of them, the characteristic profile is as follows: the encounter with Shen-hui occurred early in the student's career and was followed by the student's retreat to some remote location, often a return to the student's original temple or native place. At this remote location, the student took up residence in a rude hut—his presence there sometimes being credited with the subjugation of wild beasts in the area—and the hut was eventually transformed into an active training center by dint of the student's abilities. The locations mentioned in this regard include Nan-yang and Ch'ang-an, as well as references (for two students) to Mount Yang-chih, a place name associated in later years with a faction of the Lin-chi school, and other locations around Lake Tung-t'ing.

133. See McRae, *Northern School,* 136–137.

134. Yamazaki, "Kataku Jinne zenji," 208–211, characterizes Shen-hui's lay followers as being predominantly ambitious self-made men rather than members of old elite families. Although these men succeeded through their own efforts, the secular correlation with the religious work versus inspiration dichotomy would be that of aristocratic privilege versus success in civil service examinations or on the battlefield.

135. This text has been translated into modern Japanese by Hirano Sōjō, *Tongo yōmon,* Zen no goroku, no. 6 (Tokyo: Chikuma shobō, 1969). There are also two unsatisfactory English translations: John Blofeld, *The Zen Teaching of Hui Hai on Sudden Illumination* (London: Rider & Company, 1962) and Thomas F. Cleary, *Sayings and Doings of Pai-chang, Ch'an Master of Great Wisdom* (Los Angeles: Center Publications, 1978).

136. On the *Li-tai fa-pao chi,* see Yanagida, *Shoki no Zenshi 2,* 3–35, or "The *Li-tai fa-pao chi* and the Ch'an Doctrine of Sudden Awakening," tr. Carl Bielefeldt, in Whalen Lai and Lewis R. Lancaster, eds., *Early Ch'an in China and Tibet,* Berkeley Buddhist Studies Series, no. 5 (Berkeley: Asian Humanities Press, 1983), 13–49.

137. See Yanagida, "Goroku no rekishi," 388, 393, 402, and 407–408. On 410, he suggests that the *Platform Sūtra* then in turn criticized Hui-chung's ideas. (Yanagida also mentions criticisms by members of the Ox-head school and other figures.)

138. Professor Yanagida feels that throughout his life Shen-hui maintained a chronologically absurd theory of eight Indian patriarchs between the Buddha and Bodhidharma. See *Shoki Zenshū shisho,* 124.

139. In fact, Professor Yanagida describes Shen-hui's *Platform Sermon* as having all the basic elements of the genre: it was compiled by a named individual, rather than anonymously; circulation was intended to be limited to those with affinities for Shen-hui's teachings; Shen-hui is treated with the respect due one's personal master; and, most important, the emphasis of the text is on the instruction of the people actually in Shen-hui's audience at one specific time. See "Goroku no rekishi," 391–392 and 399, plus the related comments regarding the *Miscellaneous Dialogues* on 369 and 376.

Glossary

an-hsin 安心
busshō o miyo 佛性を見よ
ch'an 禪
Ch'an-men ching 禪門經
ch'an-yü 禪宇
chen 眞
chen-hsing 眞性
chen liao-hsing 眞了性
chen-tsung po-jo ch'üan-fa chih t'ang 眞宗般若傳法之堂
chen-yen 眞言
ch'eng 徵
Cheng Shu-ch'ing 鄭叔清
ch'i 起
ch'i-hsin tung-nien 起心動念
ch'i-tso 起作
chia 家
chien-hsing 見性
chien-wen chüeh-chih 見聞覺知
chih 之
Chih-i 智顗
Chih-ta 智達
chih-ta pien-ts'ai wu-ai 智達辯才無礙
chih-wen chih-shuo 直問直說
chih-yang 止揚
chih-yen 直言
Ching-chou 荊州
Ching-hsien 景賢
Ching-te ch'üan-teng lu 景德傳燈錄
Ching-tsang 淨藏
chu 住
ch'u 處
chu-i kuan-hsin 注意觀心
ch'u-yu ju-wu 出有入無
Ch'üan fa-pao chi 傳法寶紀
ch'üan-teng 傳燈
chüeh 覺
chung 中
ch'ung 沖
Chung-hua ch'üan hsin-ti ch'an-men shih-tzu ch'eng-hsi t'u 中華傳心地禪門師資承襲圖
chung-nien 中年
chung-sheng 衆生
fa-hsing 法性
Fa-hsing lun 法性論
Fa-ju 法如
fan 汎
Fang Kuan 房琯
fang-pien 方便
Feng-hsiang 鳳翔
fo-hsing 佛性
Fu-hsien ssu 福先寺
han 寒
Hao-yüan 顥元
Ho-pei 河北
Ho-tse ho-shang 荷澤和尚
Ho-tse ssu 荷澤寺
Ho-tung 河東
Hou-mo-ch'en Yen-chih 侯莫陳琰之
hsiang 像
Hsiang-mo Tsang 降魔藏
hsiang-shui ch'ien 香水錢
Hsiang-yang 襄陽
hsieh cheng ta 耶正大
Hsien-tsung chi 顯宗記

Hsien-tsung lun 顯宗論
hsin 心
hsin-chieh 心偈
hsing 性
hsiu-hsin 修心
Hsiu-hsin yao lun 修心要論
hsü-huo 虛豁
Hsü kao-seng chuan 續高僧傳
hu-wen 互文
Hua-t'ai 滑臺
Hui-chung (*see* Nan-yang Hui-chung)
Hui-k'o 慧可
Hui-kuang 慧光
Hui-neng 慧能
Hung-chou school 洪州宗
Hung-jen 弘忍
i (will, etc.) 意
i (recollection) 憶
I-hsing 一行
i-kuan 意觀
I-yang 弋陽
jūsho 住處
ju-tao 入道
K'ai-yüan ssu 開元寺
k'an 看
kanjin shaku 観心釈
Kao 高
kenshō 見性
Kuan-hsin lun 觀心論
kuan-hsin shih 觀心釋
kuang chih shih teng chia yung 光之時燈家用
Kuei-feng Tsung-mi 圭峯宗密
Kuei-shan ching-ts'e 潙山警策
Kuei-shan Ling-yu 潙山靈祐
Kuo-ch'ang ssu 國昌寺
Kuo Tzu-i 郭子儀
Lao-an 老安
lai 来
Leng-ch'ieh shih-tzu chi 楞伽師資記
Li 李
li (transcend) 離
li (principle) 理
Li Kuang-chu 李廣珠
li-nien 離念
Li Ssu 李嗣
Li-tai fa-pao chi 歷代法寶記
Li Wang-tsai 李王侮
Li Yung 李邕
liao-hsing 了性
Liao-hsing chü 了性句
Lin-chi I-hsüan 臨濟義玄
Liu Ch'eng 劉澄
Liu Wu-te 劉無得
liu-tsu 六祖
Liu-tsu t'an-ching 六祖壇經
Liu-tu ssu Hou-mo-ch'en ta-shih shou-t'a ming-wen ping hsü 六度寺侯莫陳大師壽塔銘文並序
Lo-yang 洛陽
Lu I 盧奕
Lüeh-shu ch'ao 略疏鈔
Lung-hsing ssu 龍興寺
Ma-tsu Tao-i 馬祖道一
mo 没
Mount Wu-t'ai 五臺山
Mount Yang-chih 楊岐山
Nan T'ien-chu-kuo P'u-t'i-ta-mo ch'an-shih kuan-men 南天竺國菩提達摩禪師觀門
Nan-yang 南陽
Nan-yang ho-shang tun-chiao chieh-t'o ch'an-men chih liao-hsing t'an-yü 南陽和上頓教解脱禪門直了性壇語
Nan-yang ho-shang wen-ta tsa ch'eng-i 南陽和尙文答雜徵義
Nan-yang Hui-chung 南陽慧忠
Nan-yin 南印
Nan-yüeh 南嶽
Nan-yüeh Hui-ssu 南嶽慧思
ni-kuan 逆觀
o 阿
Ox-head school 牛頭宗
Pao-lin chuan 寶林傳

Pao-ying ssu 寶應寺
P'ei Wan 裴晁
P'eng-yüan 彭原
ping-pu shih-lang 兵部侍郎
p'ing-teng 平等
Po-jo ta-shih chih t'a 般若大師之塔
pu-ch'i 不起
pu-ch'i hsin 不起心
P'u-chi 普寂
P'u-t'i-to-mo nan-tsung ting shih-fei lun 菩提達摩南宗定是非論
san-mei pu mei 三昧不昧
shen-shih 神識
Seng-ts'an 僧璨
Shan-nan-tung tao 山南東道
Shen-hsiu 神秀
Shen-hui 神會
Shen-hui yü-lu 神會語錄
Shen-ying 神英
sheng 乘
Shih-t'ou Hsi-ch'üan 石頭希遷
shou-hsin 守心
shun 順
shun-kuan 順觀
Ssu Tao-wang 嗣道王
Sung Kao-seng chuan 宋高僧傳
Sung Ting 宋鼎
Ta-chao 大照
Ta-jih ching 大日經
Ta-kuei ching-ts'e 大潙警策
Ta-sheng k'ai-hsin hsien-hsing tun-wu chen-tsung lun 大乘開心顯性頓悟眞宗論
Ta-shu ch'ao 大疏鈔
Ta-yün ssu 大雲寺
T'ai-yüan 太原
tang 當
tao 道
Tao-hsin 道信
Tao-hsüan 道宣
te 德
Ti-chou 棣州
ting 定
ting hui teng yung 定慧等用
Ts'ao-ch'i 曹溪
Ts'ao-ch'i ta-shih chuan 曹溪大師傳
tso 坐
tso-ch'an 坐禪
tsu-t'ang 祖堂
Ts'ui Kuan 崔寬
Ts'ui Ning 崔寧
tsung 宗
Tsung-ching lu 宗鏡錄
Tsung-mi (*see* Kuei-feng Tsung-mi)
tun 頓
tun-chiao 頓教
tun-shuo 頓說
tun-wu 頓悟
Tun-wu chen-tsung chin-kang po-jo hsiu-hsing ta pi-an fa-men yao-chüeh 頓悟眞宗金剛般若修行達彼岸法門要決
tun-wu chih tsung 頓悟之宗
Tun-wu wu-sheng po-jo sung 頓悟無生般若頌
tzu-ch'eng 資成
tzu-hsin 自心
tzu-hsing 自性
tz'u-shih 刺史
wang 妄
wang-hsin 妄心
Wang Wei 王維
wu 悟
wu-chi 無記
wu-ch'u 無處
wu-hsiang 無想
wu i wu 無一物
wu-nien 無念
Wu-t'ang 武當
wu-wei i fa 無為一法
Yang Kuo-chung 楊國忠
Yen 琰
Yen-chih 琰之
Ying 榮
ying wo-so-chu erh sheng ch'i hsin 應無所住而生其心

yu-ch'ing 有清
yu-ch'u 有處
yüan 緣
Yüan-chüeh ching lüeh-shu ch'ao 圓覺經略疏鈔
Yüan-chüeh ching ta-shu ch'ao 圓覺經大疏鈔
Yüan-ming lun 圓明論
Yün-t'an 雲坦
Yung-chou 雍州

Sudden Enlightenment Followed by Gradual Cultivation: Tsung-mi's Analysis of Mind

PETER N. GREGORY

As a Ch'an historian and later exponent of Shen-hui's teaching line, Kuei-feng Tsung-mi (780–841) upheld Shen-hui's claim that the Southern line of Ch'an founded by Hui-neng was the authentic line of Ch'an transmission. According to his account contained in the *Ch'an Chart:*[1]

> The Southern line is the true line in which the robe and dharma have been uninterruptedly transmitted over successive generations from the time when the great master Hui-neng of Ts'ao-ch'i received the essence of Bodhidharma's teaching. Later, because Shen-hsiu widely spread the gradual teaching in the north, it was called the Southern line to distinguish it [from the Northern line of Shen-hsiu].[2]
>
> After the priest Hui-neng died, the gradual teaching of the Northern line was greatly practiced and thus became an obstacle to the widespread transmission of the sudden teaching. . . . In the beginning of the T'ien-pao era [742–756] Ho-tse [Shen-hui] entered Loyang and, as soon as he proclaimed this teaching, made it known that the descendents of Shen-hsiu were collateral and that their teaching was gradual. Since the two lines were being practiced side by side, people of the time wanted to distinguish between them; the use of the names "Northern" and "Southern" thus came about.[3]

Tsung-mi goes on to report that in 796 an imperial commission determined that the Southern line of Ch'an represented the orthodox transmission and established Shen-hui as the seventh patriarch, placing an inscription to that effect in the Shen-lung temple.[4]

Tsung-mi followed Shen-hui in criticizing the Northern line for its sole emphasis on a graduated meditative regimen to the neglect of sudden enlightenment altogether.[5] Yet, while he maintained that Shen-hui's teaching was "sudden," he held that it contained a gradual component as well. In fact, he described Shen-hui's teaching in regard to practice and enlightenment as advocating the necessity of a sudden experience of enlightenment to be followed by a gradual process of cultivation, in which the practitioner's initial insight into his true nature is systematically deepened until it becomes integrated into every aspect of his life. In this chapter I examine the context, content, and doctrinal basis of Tsung-mi's theory of sudden enlightenment followed by gradual cultivation.

1. Tsung-mi's Explication of "Sudden" and "Gradual"

Shen-hui's attack on the Northern line of Ch'an issued in a period of intense and often bitter sectarian rivalry among the proponents of the different Ch'an lineages. In Tsung-mi's day the words "sudden" *(tun)* and "gradual" *(chien)* had become shibboleths of contending factions, whose mutual antagonism he described in martial imagery.[6] Not only were Ch'an Buddhists divided against themselves, but, according to Tsung-mi, the Chinese Buddhist world as a whole was split between those who identified themselves with the scholastic traditions—such as Hua-yen and T'ien-t'ai—and those who identified themselves with the practice-oriented tradition of Ch'an.

Tsung-mi was gravely distressed by the rivalry that divided Chinese Buddhists into contending camps, describing it as a situation in which Buddhist teachings had become a disease that often impaired the progress of the very people they purported to help.[7] He perceived the primary split as lying between the scholastic traditions of Buddhist learning *(chiao)* and the more practice-oriented tradition of Ch'an, which emphasized the necessity of the actualization of enlightenment in this very life. It was in an effort to resolve this division that Tsung-mi wrote his *Ch'an Preface,* a work whose overall intent was to unify *chiao* and *ch'an (chiao-ch'an i-chih).* As someone who had a foot in both camps—being traditionally reckoned as the fifth patriarch in both the Hua-yen tradition and the Ho-tse line of Southern Ch'an—he was eminently qualified to undertake such a task.

Tsung-mi viewed the seemingly irreconcilable opposition between subitism and gradualism as one of the major issues dividing Buddhists whose primary focus lay in the study and interpretation of the teachings *(chiao)* from those whose primary focus lay in the personal realization of those teachings in practice *(ch'an),* as well as pitting followers of the various Ch'an lineages against one another. As he makes clear at the outset, this is one of the main issues that he seeks to address in the *Ch'an Preface.*

Although, as a successor in the Ho-tse line of Southern Ch'an, Tsung-mi must be regarded as a partisan on the issue, his ecumenical approach stands in sharp contrast to the polemical style of Shen-hui. He cites the famous parable of the blind men and the elephant to characterize the situation in which the proponents of the various positions argue with one another, suggesting that the problem is really one of perspective.[8] He contends that "sudden" *(tun)* and "gradual" *(chien)* are complementary rather than mutually exclusive terms. After making the further point that the terms have a broad range of meaning that varies according to context, he goes on to enumerate a number of different contexts in which they are used.[9] Tsung-mi's standpoint in explicating the different meanings of *tun* and *chien* is broad and inclusive, seeking to establish a larger context in which the various and seemingly contradictory positions in regard to the meaning of these terms can be validated as integral parts of a manifold whole—in which the trunk, tail, leg, side, and so forth are all seen as belonging to the same elephant. In doing so, he maintains that no one position has an exclusive claim to the truth, but that it is only when all of them are taken together that we can arrive at a true understanding of something as complex as the nature of religious experience. Any one position taken up to the exclusion of the others is, *by that very fact,* invalid. When that position is understood within a context that includes the others, however, it will be seen to offer its own unique perspective, wherein lies its own particular validity.[10]

Tsung-mi remarks that he has encountered many Buddhists who use the terms "sudden" and "gradual" in a thoroughly uncritical and indiscriminate way,[11] and his analysis is based on the assumption that much of the emotional intensity that enveloped the controversy could be dispelled by clarifying the different meanings that the terms have in different contexts. Then it would be seen that the various sides in the controversy are, in fact, talking about different things.

Tsung-mi says that we should first differentiate between how these terms are used in doctrinal discussions of the Buddha's teaching and how they are used in discussions of the practice and realization of the Buddha's teaching as it is carried out by Buddhists.[12] Tsung-mi is here making the point that to claim that the *Avataṃsaka-sūtra,* for example, represents the "sudden teaching" *(tun-chiao)* is to use the word "sudden" in a way quite different from saying that Shen-hui's teaching emphasized the experience of "sudden enlightenment" *(tun-wu).*

In contrast to his predecessors in the Hua-yen tradition—Chih-yen, Fa-tsang, and Ch'eng-kuan—Tsung-mi does not establish the sudden teaching as a separate category in his system of doctrinal classification *(p'an-chiao).*[13] Rather, like the eighth-century reviver of the T'ien-t'ai tradition, Chan-jan (711–782), he maintains that in a doctrinal context the terms "sudden" and "gradual" refer to methods by which the Buddha taught, not to separate teachings.[14] He says that the term "sudden teaching" refers to the fact that "whenever [the Buddha] encountered a person of superior capacity and insight, he would directly reveal the true dharma to him," enabling him to become suddenly awakened *(tun-wu)* to the fact that his true nature *(chen-hsing)* is wholly identical with that of all Buddhas. "Sudden" thus refers to the method by which the Buddha directly revealed the truth to persons of the highest spiritual aptitude. Tsung-mi identifies the sudden teaching with the teaching of those sūtras that expound the tathāgatagarbha doctrine, such as the *Avataṃsaka, Yüan-chüeh* (Perfect Enlightenment), *Śūraṅgama, Ghanavyūha, Śrīmālā,* and *Tathāgatagarbha.* He adds that this teaching is identical with the highest form of Ch'an teaching—that of the Ho-tse line founded by Shen-hui.[15]

The gradual teachings, on the other hand, refer to those teachings that the Buddha addressed to persons of average or inferior capacity. The term "gradual" thus refers to the method by which the Buddha made skillful use of expedient means to lead these people through a graduated series of teachings, beginning with the most elementary and culminating in the most profound.[16]

Tsung-mi goes on to point out that within the context of Buddhist practice the terms "sudden" and "gradual" are used in a variety of ways. He then enumerates five different ways in which these terms are used in regard to practice and enlightenment.[17]

1. GRADUAL CULTIVATION FOLLOWED BY SUDDEN ENLIGHTENMENT *(chien-hsiu tun-wu).* Tsung-mi illustrates this position by recourse to two analogies: (1) it is like chopping down a tree: one gradually cuts away at it until it suddenly falls; (2) it is like traveling to a distant city: one gradually approaches it with each step until one day one suddenly arrives. As the analogies make clear, "gradual cultivation" refers to the *process* by which one moves towards the ultimate goal of enlightenment, while "sudden enlightenment" refers to the moment of *experience* in which that goal is realized.
2. SUDDEN CULTIVATION FOLLOWED BY GRADUAL ENLIGHTENMENT *(tun-hsiu chien-wu).* The analogy that Tsung-mi uses to illustrate this position is that of someone learning archery. He says that "sudden" refers to the act of aiming directly at the bull's eye (which he says is used as a metaphor for resolving to attain supreme enlightenment) while "gradual" refers to the process by which one's aim gradually becomes perfected until one can hit the bull's eye consistently without missing. Tsung-mi further explains that "sudden" here has to do with the intentionality *(yün-hsin)* of one's practice, not with the sudden perfection of meritori-

ous practices. In this context, *tun* could be better rendered as "direct" or "immediate." The use of the word *tun* in this case corresponds to its use within the system of T'ien-t'ai meditation, where it was classically defined by Kuan-ting in his preface to the *Mo-ho chih-kuan* (The Great Calming and Contemplation): "The sudden-perfect [calming and contemplation] from the very beginning takes ultimate reality as its object."[18]

3. GRADUAL CULTIVATION AND GRADUAL ENLIGHTENMENT *(chien-hsiu chien-wu).* Here Tsung-mi uses the analogy of climbing a nine-story tower: with each story that one mounts one's gaze extends further. This position emphasizes the fact that not only is the process that leads to enlightenment graduated, but enlightenment itself is also subject to gradation.

Tsung-mi points out that in the first three cases the term "enlightenment" refers to the enlightenment of complete realization *(cheng-wu),* in contradistinction to the enlightenment of initial insight *(chieh-wu).* He explains these terms in his subcommentary to the *Scripture of Perfect Enlightenment (Yüan-chüeh ching ta-shu ch'ao):* "Because one first has an initial experience of enlightenment *(ch'u yin chieh-wu),* one engages in religious practice based on that experience *(i wu hsiu hsing),* and, as soon as one's practice is completed and one's task perfected *(hsing man kung yüan),* one realizes the fulfilment of enlightenment *(chi te cheng-wu).*"[19] Tsung-mi's explanation of these qualitatively different kinds of enlightenment presupposes a three-staged model of the path: (1) initial insight *(chieh-wu),* (2) gradual cultivation *(chien-hsiu),* and (3) final enlightenment *(cheng-wu).*

4. SUDDEN ENLIGHTENMENT FOLLOWED BY GRADUAL CULTIVATION *(tun-wu chien-hsiu).* This is the position that Tsung-mi identifies with Shen-hui, and it will be treated in detail below. Here "enlightenment" refers to initial experience of insight *(chieh-wu).*
5. SUDDEN ENLIGHTENMENT AND SUDDEN CULTIVATION *(tun-wu tun-hsiu).* This position applies only to those of the highest capacity and aspiration whose initial insight *(chieh-wu)* is so penetrating and profound as to at once be equal to fully realized enlightenment *(cheng-wu),* thus making any further cultivation unnecessary.[20] Tsung-mi points out, however, that this is only possible because such persons have already engaged in a long process of spiritual cultivation in past lives—hence there is a gradual component in this position as well. Tsung-mi says that in this case obstructions are "suddenly" cut off just as myriad strands of silk are "suddenly" severed when cutting a piece of silk cloth[21] and that

> virtuous practices are "suddenly" perfected just as myriad strands of silk are "suddenly" dyed with color when a piece of silk cloth is submerged in dye. He then quotes Shen-hui twice: "When one sees the essence that is without thoughts, one will not follow the arising of things." "If, in a single moment of thought, one becomes one with one's intrinsic nature, then the practice of the eighty thousand perfections will all simultaneously come into effect."[22]

Tsung-mi's analysis is useful for providing a conceptual framework for making sense out of the confusion that has often marked discussions of the sudden-gradual controversy; it does so by distinguishing the variety of ways in which the terms "sudden" and "gradual" can be applied to cultivation and enlightenment, making it clear that *tun* and *chien* have entirely different meanings when used in different contexts. In the first three cases—all examples of *cheng-wu*—"enlightenment" can refer to both the *process* of its actualization as well as the *experience* in which it is finally consummated. In the first case, that of gradual cultivation followed by sudden enlightenment, "enlightenment" clearly refers to the final goal that is suddenly attained only after the consummation of a long process of cultivation. However, in the second and third cases—sudden cultivation followed by gradual enlightenment, and gradual cultivation and gradual enlightenment—"enlightenment" refers to the process by which enlightenment is consummated and accordingly corresponds to what Tsung-mi refers to as "gradual cultivation" in the first case. The meaning of "cultivation" also varies with context. Whereas in the first and third cases it refers to the process of the actualization of enlightenment, in the second it refers to the intentionality informing that process.

Moreover, as Tsung-mi points out, the enlightenment in question in the first three cases is what he calls *cheng-wu,* the enlightenment of complete realization. This term is contrasted with *chieh-wu,* the enlightenment of initial insight, the kind of enlightenment that is instanced in the fourth and fifth cases, those of sudden enlightenment followed by gradual cultivation and sudden enlightenment and sudden cultivation. Whereas *chieh-wu* is always a sudden experience of insight, *cheng-wu* can be either gradual or sudden depending on whether it is regarded from the standpoint of the process of the actualization of final enlightenment or the actual experience of that enlightenment. In the cases in which *cheng-wu* is regarded as gradual, it is synonymous with gradual cultivation *(chien-hsiu).* Tsung-mi's distinction between these two types of enlightenment posits three stages in the course of religious practice: (1) initial awakening, (2) gradual cultivation, and (3) fully realized enlightenment. In the fifth case, that of sudden enlightenment and sudden cultivation, the first and third stage are collapsed together, obviating the necessity of stage two as a discrete stage of practice.

Although he makes no reference to classical Buddhist divisions of the path, the distinctions Tsung-mi introduces correspond (in structure if not in content) to the traditional threefold division of the path into *darśana-*, *bhāvanā-*, and *aśaikṣa-mārga*. For all his emphasis on the importance of the experience of sudden enlightenment, Tsung-mi here articulates a position that has more in common with that of Kamalaśīla than with that of Mo-ho-yen, that is, with the gradualist rather than the subitist camp in the Tibetan controversy.

It is also worth noting that Tsung-mi does not mention a stage of prepatory practice *(prayoga-mārga)* prior to the initial insight *(chieh-wu)*. Although he does not discuss his reasons, it is clear that he felt that such practices were not necessary for the experience of sudden enlightenment to occur—which, of course, is not to say that he advocated that they should therefore be discarded. There were ample examples in Ch'an literature of persons who had been suddenly enlightened without first having engaged in prepatory practices, the most notable being that of Hui-neng, the archetype for Ch'an religious experience, at least within the Southern line. Tsung-mi cautioned to add, however, that such cases were only possible because such people had cultivated good roots in past lives.

More important, the fact that Tsung-mi does not mention prepatory practices in his analysis of the stages of the path emphasizes the radical transformation that he believes takes place upon the experience of sudden enlightenment. For Tsung-mi it is only after such an experience that true Buddhist practice can begin. There is thus a fundamental difference between practices engaged in prior to this experience and those engaged in after it. And it is based on the transformative power of the initial insight of *chieh-wu* and the qualitative difference that it effects in one's practice that Tsung-mi criticizes the practice followed in the Northern line of Ch'an as inauthentic.

Finally, although Tsung-mi is careful to distinguish between the uses of the term *tun* in its scholastic and practical contexts, there is still a connection between the two usages that needs to be brought out. That is, the sudden teaching for Tsung-mi is the teaching that does not rely upon any expedients but directly reveals the true nature, which is the content of the Buddha's enlightenment as well as that into which the Buddhist practitioner has insight when he experiences *chieh-wu*. The sudden teaching is thus the teaching that enables one to experience sudden enlightenment.[23]

2. Sudden Enlightenment Followed by Gradual Cultivation

For Tsung-mi sudden enlightenment did not obviate the need for the cultivation of a graduated series of stages of religious practice. In fact, according to him, the experience of sudden enlightenment is the indispensable foundation upon which such practice has to be carried out. As he says in the *Ch'an Preface,* "If one engages in spiritual cultivation without having first experienced enlightenment, then it is not authentic practice."[24] In other words, it is the experience of sudden enlightenment (i.e., *chieh-wu*) that authenticates Buddhist practice. But this experience is identified by Tsung-mi as being only the first stage in a ten-stage process culminating in the attainment of Buddhahood.

Tsung-mi uses three analogies in the *Ch'an Chart* to illustrate what he means by "sudden enlightenment followed by gradual cultivation." The first, adapted from the *Awakening of Faith,*[25] is that even though the wind that has stirred the originally tranquil surface of the ocean into movement ceases suddenly, the motion of its waves only subsides gradually.[26] The second is that even though the sun appears suddenly, the morning frost only melts gradually.[27] The last, which Tsung-mi borrows from Shen-hui,[28] is that even though an infant possesses all of its limbs and faculties intact the moment it is born, it only learns to master their use gradually.[29] Doctrinally, Tsung-mi claims that the teaching of sudden enlightenment followed by gradual cultivation is based on the *Awakening of Faith, Scripture of Perfect Enlightenment,* and *Avataṃsaka-sūtra.*[30]

Tsung-mi's fullest description of sudden enlightenment occurs in the *Ch'an Chart,* where he says:

> While awakening from delusion is sudden, the transformation of an unenlightened person *(fan)* into an enlightened person *(sheng)* is gradual.[31] Sudden enlightenment means that although [beings] have been deluded from [time] without beginning, recognizing the four elements as their body and deluded thoughts as their mind and taking them both together as constituting their self, when they meet a good friend *(kalyāṇamitra)* who explains to them the meaning of the absolute and conditioned [aspects of suchness], the nature and its phenomenal appearance, the essence and its functioning . . . , then they at once realize that [their own] marvelous knowing and seeing is the true mind, that the mind—which is from the beginning empty and tranquil, boundless and formless—is the dharmakāya, that the nonduality of body and mind is the true self, and that they are no different from all Buddhas by even a hair.[32]

Thus, for Tsung-mi, sudden enlightenment is the experience in which one sees that one's true nature is, and always has been, wholly identical with that of all Buddhas. The paradigm for this experience is, of course, the Buddha's own enlightenment. The passage that Tsung-mi cites in both the *Ch'an Preface* and the *Inquiry into the Origin of Man (Yüan-jen lun)* as canonical authority for his description of the highest teaching of the Buddha comes from the *Avataṃsaka* and was especially valued in the Ch'an tradition,[33] as it was believed to contain the first words uttered by the Buddha after his enlightenment:

> O Sons of Buddha, there is no place where the wisdom of the Tathāgata does not reach. Why? Because there is not a single sentient being that is not fully endowed with the wisdom of the Tathāgata. It is only on account of their deluded thinking, erroneous views, and attachments that they do not succeed in realizing it. When they become free from deluded thinking, the all-comprehending wisdom, the spontaneous wisdom, and the unobstructed wisdom will then be manifest before them. . . . At that time the Tathāgata with his unobstructed pure eye of wisdom universally beheld all sentient beings throughout the universe and said, "How amazing! How amazing! How can it be that these sentient beings are fully endowed with the wisdom of the Tathāgata and yet, being ignorant and confused, do not know it and do not see it? I must teach them the noble path, enabling them to be forever free from deluded thinking and to achieve for themselves the seeing of the broad and vast wisdom of the Tathāgata within themselves, and so to be no different from the Buddhas.[34]

The significance of this passage for Tsung-mi lay in the fact that it establishes that the content of the Buddha's enlightenment consisted in his realization that all sentient beings already fully possess the enlightened wisdom of the Buddha within themselves and are therefore fundamentally identical with all Buddhas. Sentient beings' enlightenment thus lies in their awakening of this intrinsic Buddha-wisdom within themselves.

Although the Buddha's enlightenment is the paradigm for sentient beings' experience of enlightenment, it must also be pointed out that what Tsung-mi means by sudden enlightenment differs significantly from the enlightenment experienced by the Buddha, which all Buddhist traditions have characterized as supreme, perfect enlightenment *(anuttarāsamyaksaṃbodhi)*. As we have noted, "sudden enlightenment" in the context of Tsung-mi's theory of sudden enlightenment followed by gradual cultivation refers to *chieh-wu,* initial awakening, only the first stage in Tsung-mi's ten-stage process of spiritual cultivation. The Buddha's enlightenment, on the other hand, corresponds to *cheng-wu,* the final culmination of enlightenment.

For Tsung-mi the necessity of commencing a process of gradual cultivation following the initial experience of enlightenment *(chieh-wu)* is based on the sheer tenacity of the karmic residue of past actions, the *vāsanā* or *hsün-hsi* which have thoroughly permeated the *ālayavijñāna* or store-consciousness over the course of innumerable lifetimes. Thus, although the initial experience of enlightenment is sudden, one must still engage in a long process of cultivation in order to extirpate the deeply rooted seeds of the false view of a substantial self that have become ingrained in our mentality. As Tsung-mi says in the *Ch'an Chart:*

> Even though one suddenly realizes that the dharmakāya, the true mind, is wholly identical with Buddha, still, since for numerous kalpas one has deludedly clung to the four elements as constituting one's self [so that this view] has become second nature and is difficult to do away with all at once, one must cultivate oneself on the basis of [this experience of] enlightenment. When one has reduced it and further reduced it until there is nothing left to reduce, then it is called attaining Buddhahood.[35]

Even though the practitioner has gained an insight into his own true nature, realizing his identity with all Buddhas, he is still not fully liberated, for he has yet to root out the seeds of his misperception of himself as a separate and self-existing entity. Although he has seen that this view is illusory, his behavior and entire mode of being in the world are still predicated on this false view of the self, to which he has become habituated by a long process of conditioning. It is therefore necessary to embark upon a program of gradual cultivation that will eliminate the seeds of this misconception so that his original insight into his true nature can be fully and freely manifested in his every action. Gradual cultivation is thus the process by which one's initial insight is integrated into one's personality.

3. The Doctrinal Basis of Tsung-mi's Theory

Doctrinally, Tsung-mi's explanation of sudden enlightenment is based on the tathāgatagarbha whereas his explanation of gradual cultivation is based on the ālayavijñāna. Although these two cardinal Mahāyāna doctrines seem to have originated independently and their relationship can be described as being diametrical, they were nevertheless combined together into a unified doctrinal framework in the *Awakening of Faith,* the text that forms the basis for Tsung-mi's theory of sudden enlightenment followed by gradual cultivation. In order to understand why this text was of such importance for Tsung-mi, we must first consider these two different conceptions of the mind separately.[36]

As is generally acknowledged by modern Buddhologists, the tathāgatagarbha doctrine can ultimately be traced back to the early pre-Mahāyāna teaching of an innately pure luminous mind *(prabhāsvara citta)* which is only adventitiously covered over by defilements *(āgantukakleśa).*[37] The term *tathāgatagarbha* means both the embryo and the womb of the Tathāgata—the first sense of the term emphasizing the potentiality for Buddhahood, which exists embryonically within all sentient beings, while the second emphasizes the fact that the pure dharmakāya lies hidden within the defiled condition. The implication of this doctrine as it was elaborated in tathāgatagarbha texts such as the *Tathāgatagarbha* and *Śrīmālā* scriptures and the *Ratnagotravibhāga* is that enlightenment is the natural and true state of the mind. The basis for enlightenment thus exists within the mind of all sentient beings. This means that enlightenment does not represent an overcoming of, or triumph over, the mind so much as a realization of its own inherent potential.

Whereas the tathāgatagarbha doctrine provides an answer to the question of how enlightenment is possible, it does so by side-stepping the equally vexing problem of the origin of ignorance. That is, if the fundamental nature of the mind is intrinsically pure (i.e., enlightened), how, or from where, do the impurities that obscure it (i.e., ignorance) arise? If they arise from the mind itself, how can the nature of the mind be considered intrinsically pure? If, on the other hand, they arise from somewhere outside the mind, then how can the mind be considered the fundamental ground of both saṃsāra and nirvāṇa? Moreover, if we posit a separate origin for ignorance (or the impurities), that would lead to the untoward consequence of a dualism in which enlightenment and ignorance function together as ontological principles in the soteriological drama of saṃsāra and nirvāṇa.

The particular weakness of tathāgatagarbha thought—its shunting of the problem of the origin of ignorance—is systematically dealt with in the Yogācāra analysis of the mind and mental processes. Here the ālayavijñāna is posited as the repository or seedbed out of which impurities arise, and the impure seeds from which they originate are said to exist innately within the ālayavijñāna *ab aeterno*. Futhermore, the impurities that are manifested from out of the ālayavijñāna in turn condition the ālayavijñāna, forming new seeds from which further impurities are generated. Thus, according to the Yogācāra analysis, the ālayavijñāna is the source and support of all impure dharmas. Whence, then, do pure dharmas, those which have the power to reverse the self-perpetuating process of conditioning by which impure dharmas are produced, arise?

According to the *Mahāyānasaṃgraha (She ta-sheng lun)*, one of the principal texts regarded as authoritative for the Yogācāra tradition, the supramundane pure mind is born from seeds sown by the correct hearing of the dharma.[38] In other words, the process by which the mind becomes purified has its inception outside the mind. The mind does not contain the seeds of its own transformation; these, rather, are extrinsic to it. Enlightenment is thus characterized as a revolution of the support *(chuan-i, āśrayaparāvṛtti)*: the nature of the mind must undergo a fundamental and radical transformation before enlightenment can take place, and the mind of one who has undergone such a transformation can no longer be spoken of as the ālayavijñāna—it must be referred to as the *amalavijñāna (a-mo-lo-shih)* or "undefiled consciousness" instead. Hence, although the Yogācāra tradition can be seen as giving a successful and cogent account of the origin of ignorance in its doctrine of the ālayavijñāna and the process of mental conditioning *(vāsanā),* it does so by making the basis of enlightenment extraneous to the mind, thus implying that enlightenment is fortuitous.

The fact that the tathāgatagarbha and ālayavijñāna doctrines can be seen as complementing one another in such a way that each compensates for the shortcoming of the other made some kind of synthesis of the two inevitable, as seems to have happened for the first time with the *Laṅkāvatāra-sūtra.* This synthesis was carried further, and pursued more systematically, in the *Awakening of Faith.* This work, whose provenance is still controversial, seems to have been composed in China sometime during the third quarter of the sixth century. It defines the tathāgatagarbha as the absolute mind of suchness *(chen-ju i-hsin),* which it analyzes as having two aspects: the absolute *(pu-pien),* which it refers to as the "mind as suchness" *(hsin chen-ju),* and the conditioned *(sui-yüan),* which it refers to as the "mind that is subject to birth-and-death" *(hsin sheng-mieh).* The first aspect corresponds to the tathāgatagarbha as it truly is—that is, the dharmakāya—while the second aspect corresponds to the tathāgatagarbha as the dharmakāya covered over by defilements. Moreover, the conditioned aspect of the tathāgatagarbha, the mind that is subject to birth-and-death, is identified with the ālayavijñāna, which is defined as the "interfusion of that which is not subject to birth-and-death with that which is subject to birth-and-death in such a way that they are neither one nor different."[39] Because the ālayavijñāna is defined as the point where these two aspects of the mind interact, it thus functions as the dynamic factor in the equation of mind by containing within itself the potential for both enlightenment *(chüeh)* and non-enlightenment *(pu-chüeh).*

4. Tsung-mi's Analysis of Mind

As graphically illustrated in the diagram that occurs at the end of the *Ch'an Preface,* both the process of delusion and that of enlightenment are based on the dynamic ambivalence of the ālayavijñāna, which contains both an enlightened and an unenlightened aspect. Tsung-mi, furthermore, breaks down both of these processes into ten symmetrical stages, which can best be represented by reproducing the relevant portion of his diagram.

Tsung-mi's Diagram of the Process of Enlightenment and Delusion

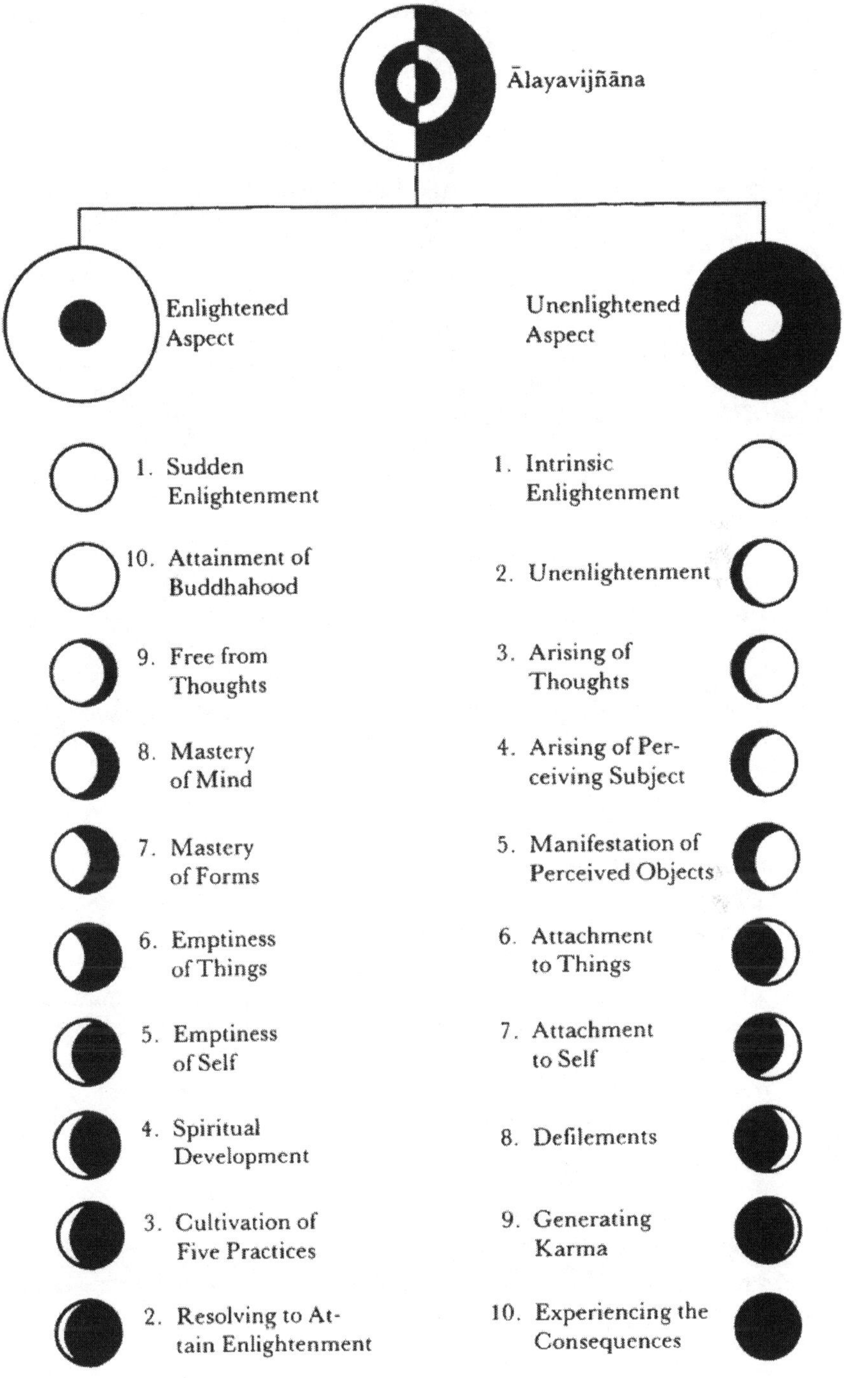

Enlightened Aspect

1. Sudden Enlightenment
10. Attainment of Buddhahood
9. Free from Thoughts
8. Mastery of Mind
7. Mastery of Forms
6. Emptiness of Things
5. Emptiness of Self
4. Spiritual Development
3. Cultivation of Five Practices
2. Resolving to Attain Enlightenment

Unenlightened Aspect

1. Intrinsic Enlightenment
2. Unenlightenment
3. Arising of Thoughts
4. Arising of Perceiving Subject
5. Manifestation of Perceived Objects
6. Attachment to Things
7. Attachment to Self
8. Defilements
9. Generating Karma
10. Experiencing the Consequences

The ten stages in the genesis and development of delusion answer the question of how sentient beings come to assume a human form. Basing his theory on the *Awakening of Faith,* Tsung-mi gives an account of how this process begins in his *Inquiry into the Origin of Man:*

> At first there is only the one true numinous nature *(i-chen-ling-hsing),* which is neither born nor destroyed, neither increases nor decreases, and neither changes nor alters. [Nevertheless,] sentient beings are from [time] without beginning asleep in delusion and are not themselves aware of it. Because it is covered over, it is called the tathāgatagarbha, and the phenomenal appearance of the mind that is subject to birth-and-death comes into existence based on the tathāgatagarbha. The interfusion of the true mind that is not subject to birth-and-death and deluded thoughts that are subject to birth-and-death in such a way that they are neither one nor different is referred to as the ālayavijñāna. This consciousness has the two modes of enlightenment and unenlightenment.[40]

The aetiology of delusion, as it is schematically laid out in the *Ch'an Preface,*[41] can be outlined as follows:

1. INTRINSIC ENLIGHTENMENT *(pen-chüeh).* This is the ontological ground from which the process evolves. The *Awakening of Faith* defines intrinsic enlightenment as follows: " 'Enlightenment' means that the essence of the mind is free from thoughts. The characteristic of being free from thoughts is like the realm of empty space that pervades everywhere. As the single characteristic of the dharmadhātu, it is the undifferentiated dharmakāya of the Tathāgata. Since it is based on the dharmakāya, when it is spoken of it is referred to as 'intrinsic enlightenment.' "[42] Tsung-mi compares intrinsic enlightenment to a wealthy and respected man, upright and wise, living in his own home.
2. UNENLIGHTENMENT *(pu-chüeh).* This refers to the unenlightened aspect of the ālayavijñāna. Tsung-mi compares it to the wealthy and respected man falling asleep and forgetting who he is. The metaphor of delusion as a state of being asleep is naturally suggested by the term for enlightenment, *chüeh,* which literally means "to awaken." This stage is what in other contexts Tsung-mi refers to as primordial ignorance *(ken-pen wu-ming)* or autonomous ignorance *(tu-t'ou wu-ming).* It is the "root" *(pen)* of the remaining stages in the process of the evolution of delusion, which, accordingly, are its "branches" *(mo).*
3. ARISING OF THOUGHT *(nien-ch'i).* This is the first subtle movement of thought, which initiates the process of phenomenal evolution by giving rise to the bifurcation of consciousness into subject and object. It corresponds to the first of the three subtle

phenomenal appearances *(san hsi-hsiang)* enumerated in the *Awakening of Faith,* that of activity *(yeh)* or, more fully, the activity of ignorance *(wu-ming yeh).*[43] Tsung-mi compares it to the dreams that naturally arise in the mind of the sleeping man.

4. ARISING OF THE PERCEIVING SUBJECT *(chien-ch'i).* This corresponds to the second subtle phenomenal appearance of the *Awakening of Faith,* that of perceiving subject *(neng-chien).*[44] Tsung-mi compares it to the dreaming consciousness.
5. MANIFESTATION OF PERCEIVED OBJECTS *(ching-ch'i).* This refers to the manifestation of the body of the senses and the receptacle world. It corresponds to the third subtle phenomenal appearance of the *Awakening of Faith,* that of objects of perception *(ching-chiai).*[45] Tsung-mi compares it to the wealthy and respected man who, within his dream, sees himself dwelling in squalor and misery and perceives things that he likes and dislikes.
6. ATTACHMENT TO THINGS *(fa-chih).* This corrsponds to the first and second of the six coarse phenomenal appearances *(liu ts'u-hsiang)* enumerated in the *Awakening of Faith,* those of discrimination *(chih)* and continuation *(hsiang-hsü).*[46] Tsung-mi compares this stage to the man clinging to the things that he sees in his dream as real.
7. ATTACHMENT TO SELF *(wo-chih).* This corresponds to the third and fourth coarse phenomenal appearances in the *Awakening of Faith,* that of attachment *(chih-ch'ü)*[47] and symbolic representation *(chi-ming-tzu).*[48] Tsung-mi compares it to the man identifying himself with the person in the dream.
8. DEFILEMENTS *(fan-nao).* This refers to the three poisons of greed, anger, and folly. Tsung-mi compares it to the man hankering after those things in the dream that accord with his feelings and forming an aversion to those things in the dream that go against his feelings.
9. GENERATING KARMA *(tsao-yeh).* This corresponds to the fifth coarse phenomenal appearance in the *Awakening of Faith,* that of giving rise to karma *(ch'i-yeh).*[49] The dreaming man commits various good and bad deeds on the basis of his likes and dislikes.
10. EXPERIENCING THE CONSEQUENCES *(shou-pao).* This corresponds to the sixth coarse phenomenal appearance in the *Awakening of Faith,* that of the suffering connected with karma *(yeh-hsi-ku).*[50] The dreaming man thus experiences various good and bad consequences.

The ten stages in the process of phenomenal evolution function in the same way as the classical twelve-linked chain of conditioned origination *(pratītyasamutpāda)*. According to Aśvaghoṣa's account of the Buddha's enlightenment in the *Buddhacarita,* for example, it was by understanding the chain of conditions upon which the whole mass of suffering attendant upon the cycle of birth-and-death depended that the Buddha was thereby able to reverse the process by successively eliminating each stage.[51] The ten stages of phenomenal evolution that Tsung-mi enumerates in the *Ch'an Preface* likewise serve as a map for liberation. Accordingly, each stage in the process of enlightenment counteracts *(fan)* the corresponding stage in the process of delusion.

1. SUDDEN ENLIGHTENMENT *(tun-wu)*. In this stage one meets a good friend *(kalyāṇamitra)* whose guidance enables him to gain an insight into the intrinsically enlightened true nature of the mind. This stage counteracts the second stage in the process of delusion, that of *unenlightenment.*
2. RESOLVING TO ATTAIN ENLIGHTENMENT *(fa-hsin)*. In this stage one generates compassion, wisdom, and vows, resolving to attain supreme enlightenment. This stage counteracts the tenth stage in the process of delusion, that of *experiencing the consequences* of one's actions, according to which one is born in one of the six destinies.
3. CULTIVATING THE FIVE PRACTICES *(hsiu wu-hsing)*. In this stage one cultivates giving *(dāna)*, morality *(śīla)*, patience *(kṣānti)*, striving *(vīrya)*, and meditative insight *(śamatha-vipaśyanā)*. These are the five practices enumerated in the *Awakening of Faith,*[52] according to which the fifth and sixth perfections *(pāramitā)*—those of dhyāna and prajñā—in the standard scheme of six perfections have been collapsed into one, that of meditative insight. The fifth practice, however, consists of two elements, corresponding to dhyāna and prajñā, which are subsequently treated separately in the *Awakening of Faith.*[53] This stage counteracts the ninth stage in the process of delusion, that of *generating karma.*
4. SPIRITUAL DEVELOPMENT *(k'ai-fa)*. This stage entails the development of the compassion, wisdom, and vows previously generated in the second stage and counteracts the eighth stage in the process of delusion, that of *defilements.*
5. EMPTINESS OF SELF *(wo-k'ung)*. In this stage one realizes that there is no substantially existing autonomous self. This stage counteracts the ninth stage in the process of delusion, that of *attachment to self.*
6. EMPTINESS OF THINGS *(fa-k'ung)*. In this stage one realizes that all things are devoid of a self-nature. This stage counteracts the sixth stage in the process of delusion, that of *attachment to things.*

7. MASTERY OF FORM *(se-tzu-tsai).* Having realized that the objects of perception are nothing but manifestations of one's own mind, one gains mastery over them in this stage. This stage counteracts the fifth stage in the process of delusion, that of the *manifestation of perceived objects.*
8. MASTERY OF MIND *(hsin-tzu-tsai).* In this stage one gains mastery over the perceiving subject. This stage counteracts the fourth stage in the process of delusion, that of the *arising of the perceiving subject.*
9. FREEDOM FROM THOUGHT *(li-nien).* In this stage one becomes fully aware of the ultimate origin of deluded thoughts and sees that the true nature of the mind is eternal. This is the stage of ultimate awakening *(chiu-ching chüeh)* described in the *Awakening of Faith*[54] and counteracts the third stage in the process of delusion, that of the *arising of thoughts.*
10. ATTAINMENT OF BUDDHAHOOD *(ch'eng-fo).* In this stage one returns to the ultimate source of the mind, realizing that, since the mind is of its very essence free from thoughts, there is ultimately no distinction between the various stages in the process of the realization of enlightenment, all of which were from the very beginning undifferentiated and identical with *intrinsic enlightenment,* which is one and indivisible.

When this process of the realization of enlightenment is completed and one has attained Buddhahood, it is seen that the genesis and unfolding of delusion and the realization of enlightenment are not two separate, parallel, linear processes moving in opposite directions. Rather, one realizes that the two form a continuum. The final stage in the process of enlightenment brings one back to the fundamental basis from which the process of delusion unfolded. The process taken as a whole thus forms a circle in which *intrinsic enlightenment* would be represented by zero degrees and *attainment of Buddhahood,* by three hundred sixty degrees. The circularity of the process is symbolized by the circles that correspond to each stage, the relative degree of enlightenment and delusion of which is represented by the relative degree of white and black, suggesting that the phases of delusion and enlightenment evolve and change like the waxing and waning of the moon. The points between zero and one hundred eighty degrees—that is, the nine stages in the process of the unfolding of delusion beginning with *unenlightenment* and ending with *experiencing the consequences*—all involve a movement away from enlightenment, what Tsung-mi refers to as the process of conforming to the flow of birth-and-death *(shun, anuloma).* It is during this phase of the process that one gains a human body and, because of

Rearrangement of Tsung-mi's Diagram in the Form of a Circle

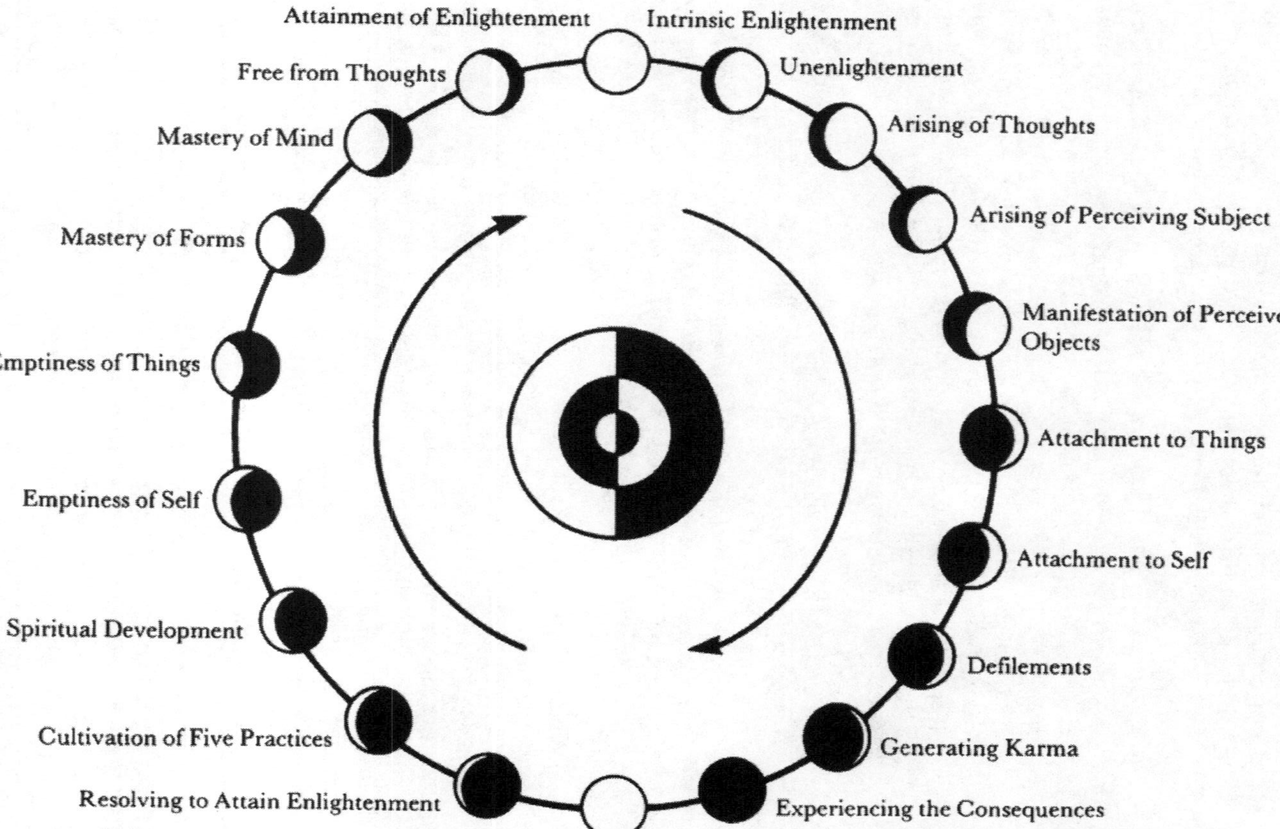

good karma generated in previous existences, finally comes to the turning point in the process, located at one hundred eighty degrees, when one meets a good friend whose guidance enables one to gain a sudden insight into one's true nature. This is what Tsung-mi refers to as *sudden enlightenment* (i.e, *chieh-wu*), an experience that reverses the direction of one's karma—what Tsung-mi refers to as the process of going against the flow of birth-and-death *(ni, pratiloma)*—and begins one's return back to one's original enlightened nature. The eight stages in the process of the realization of enlightenment—that is, those beginning with *resolving to attain enlightenment* and ending with *freedom from thoughts*—describe the process of gradual cultivation (or what the *Awakening of Faith* refers to as *shih-chüeh*). With the *attainment of Buddhahood* (i.e., *cheng-wu*), one returns to the ultimate point of origin, beginning and end are one, the circle is completed, and the process is brought to its natural conclusion. Tsung-mi's diagram can thus be rearranged in the form of a circle.

Moreover, when one has attained Buddhahood, one realizes that all the stages in the process are equally nothing but a manifestation of the absolute mind *(i-hsin)*, whose fundamental nature is eternally pure and enlightened and can never be tainted by the defilements that appear to obscure it. The defilements are accidental, being only the result of sentient beings' delusion. But the true nature of reality is unaffected by the failure of sentient beings to see it as it really is. Thus, even though the tathāgatagarbha appears to be defiled, it is forever immaculate and inviolate. When one attains enlightenment, one realizes that *intrinsic enlightenment* is more than a stage in the process of delusion and enlightenment, it is also the fundamental ground upon which the entire process is based. The *pen* in the term *pen-chüeh* thus indicates that *intrinsic enlightenment* is not only ontologically prior to the other phases of the process, which are only epiphenomena (*mo* or *hsiang*), but that it is also the ontological ground (*pen* or *hsing*) that underlies all of them equally.

The relationship between *intrinsic enlightenment* and the other phases of the process of delusion and enlightenment can best be illustrated by making use of Tsung-mi's adaptation of the famous metaphor of water and waves from the *Awakening of Faith*. The originally tranquil surface of the water in which all things are reflected clearly *(intrinsic enlightenment)* becomes stirred up by the action of the wind of ignorance *(unenlightenment)* to form waves (i.e., the process of delusion). Even though the wind ceases suddenly *(sudden enlightenment, chieh-wu)*, the motion of the waves only subsides gradually (i.e, the process of the realization of enlightenment, gradual cultivation, *shih-chüeh*) until all movement has stopped and the surface of the water is once again tranquil *(attainment of Buddhahood, cheng-wu)*. Nevertheless, whether the surface of the water is tranquil or agitated, whether its waves are large or small, it is all equally water (i.e., the absolute mind). Moreover, the changing condition of the surface of the water does not affect its fundamental nature of being able to reflect all things *(intrinsic enlightenment)*.

5. Tsung-mi's Criticism of the Northern and Hung-chou Lines

In order to assess Tsung-mi's position with respect to the larger historical context of the sudden-gradual polarity, it is first necessary to analyze his criticisms of some of the other Ch'an approaches to religious cultivation. As his criticisms of these other approaches turn on his understanding of the fundamental nature of mind, the analysis will further clarify the deep structure of his thought as well as highlight what was at stake for him in his characterization of the Ho-tse teaching as sudden enlightenment followed by gradual cultivation. The two Ch'an traditions whose critiques are most pertinent in this regard are the Northern and Hung-chou lineages.

A. *Tsung-mi's Critique of the Northern Line*

Within his scheme of the various permutations of the terms "sudden" and "gradual" as they apply to enlightenment and cultivation, Tsung-mi identifies the teaching and practice of the Northern line as falling under the category of gradual cultivation followed by sudden enlightenment. In both his subcommentary to his commentary and his abridged commentary to the *Scripture of Perfect Enlightenment (Yüan-chüeh ching ta-shu ch'ao* and *Lüeh-shu ch'ao)*, he points out that this case can be interpreted in two ways.[55] The first presumes a prior sudden insight (i.e., *chieh-wu*), thus conforming to his threefold model of religious practice and so differing only in emphasis, but not substance, from the case of sudden enlightenment followed by gradual cultivation, which presumes a subsequent realization of enlightenment *(cheng-wu)* as its unstated third term. The second interpretation of gradual cultivation followed by sudden enlightenment does not presume a prior experience of insight, and it is within this framework that Tsung-mi places, and criticizes, Northern Ch'an.

Tsung-mi's clearest criticism of Northern Ch'an occurs in his *Ch'an Chart*, where he gives the following characterization of its major tenets:

> Sentient beings originally have an enlightened nature just as a mirror has a luminous nature, but defilements cover it from view just as a mirror is darkened by dust. If we rely on the teachings of a master and extinguish our deluded thoughts, then, when those thoughts are eliminated, the nature of the mind will be enlightened and there will be nothing that is not known. It is like wiping away dust: when the dust is eliminated, the

essence of the mirror is luminous and clear and there is nothing that is not reflected in it. Therefore, the founder of this lineage, Shen-hsiu, presented the following verse to the fifth patriarch:

> The body is the bodhi tree,
> The mind is like a luminous mirror.
> We must always wipe it clean
> And never let dust collect.[56]

Tsung-mi then goes on to give the following critique:

> This [teaching] merely consists in the method of going against the flow [of birth-and-death] and opposing residual conditioning *(hsi, vāsanā)* [based on] the phenomenal appearances of impure and pure conditioned origination *(jan ching yüan-ch'i chih hsiang)* and has not yet awakened to the fact that deluded thoughts are intrinsically empty and that the nature of the mind is intrinsically pure. When enlightenment is not yet deeply penetrating, how can cultivation be in conformity with the true?[57]

Tsung-mi's characterization of Northern Ch'an emphasizes the importance of the tathāgatagarbha, the intrisically enlightened nature possessed by all sentient beings. His criticism also shows that he sees its understanding of the tathāgatagarbha as being different from his own in a profoundly significant way. In order to see precisely wherein this difference lies, and what it means for Tsung-mi, it is necessary to place Tsung-mi's critique of Northern Ch'an into the larger doctrinal context that he articulates in his *Ch'an Preface,* where he identifies its teaching with that of the Fa-hsiang brand of Yogācāra. Tsung-mi's major critique of Fa-hsiang is that there is an unbridgeable gap between the ālayavijñāna and suchness *(chen-ju, tathatā).* He charges that in the Fa-hsiang teaching "dharmas subject to birth-and-death are not connected with suchness" *(sheng-mieh teng fa pu-kuan chen-ju).*[58] In terms of the two aspects of the mind outlined in the *Awakening of Faith,* this means that there is no connection between the mind as suchness *(hsin chen-ju)* and the mind that is subject to birth-and-death *(hsin sheng-mieh);* in other words, there is no connection between the tathāgatagarbha and ālayavijñāna. Suchness is seen to be static (*ning-jan* 'inert' and *pu-pien* 'unchanging')—that is, it is not involved in the production of pure and impure phenomenal appearances *(hsiang).* Where the Fa-hsiang teaching falls short is in its recognition of only one aspect of the absolute mind *(i-hsin):* while it acknowledges its "unchanging" *(pu-pien)* character, it wholly ignores its "conditioned" *(sui-yüan)* character. In other words, it does not realize that the phenomenal appearances it purports to analyze are the functioning *(yung)* of the mind as suchness as it accords with conditions *(sui-yüan).* But it is precisely the conditioned aspect of suchness that is of vital importance for Tsung-mi, because it links the tathāgatagarbha with the ālayavijñāna and thereby accounts for how suchness accords with conditions to form all pure and impure states. It is this conditioned aspect of suchness that Tsung-mi refers to as nature origination *(hsing-ch'i),* a term that emphasizes the dynamic quality of his understanding of the fundamental nature of the mind.

In Tsung-mi's view, it is because the Fa-hsiang teaching lacks the principle of nature origination that there is nothing to mediate between the ālayavijñāna and suchness, the realm of defiled activity and that of unconditioned purity. It is thus guilty of a fundamental dualism. Nature origination, on the other hand, bridges this gap by affirming that all phenomenal appearances *(hsiang)* are nothing but a manifestation *(yung)* of the nature *(hsing)* that is their very essence *(t'i).* Nature origination overcomes this dualism by making use of the paradigm of essence and function *(t'i-yung).* This conceptual paradigm, which had played a dominant role in Chinese metaphysical vocabulary since at least the "Neo-Taoist" speculations of the third century, provides the basic conceptual framework in terms of which Tsung-mi structures his thought. The various polarities that Tsung-mi employs—such as nature and phenomenal appearances, or root *(pen)* and branch *(mo)*—all conform to this paradigm. Essence, nature, and root, on the one hand, and function, phenomenal appearance(s), and branch, on the other, are all interchangeable. The equation of the essence and function paradigm with that of root and branch also reveals toward which side the polarity is weighted in value.

Tsung-mi's criticism of Fa-hsiang applies to Northern Ch'an as well, whose practice is directed toward removing the impurities that obscure the intrinsic purity of the mind. Such a practice is based on a fundamental misconception because it does not realize that the impurities themselves are empty *(k'ung, śūnya)*—and by "empty" Tsung-mi means that they lack any independent reality of their own, because they are nothing but a manifestation of the intrinsically pure mind as it accords with conditions. The "impurities" are thus not impure in themselves. Rather, their impurity lies in the dualistic misapprehension of them as impure—in other words, the failure to see through them to the intrinsically pure nature that is their essence and of which they are an expression.

This dualism, or fundamental misconception, which Tsung-mi sees as informing Northern Ch'an teaching is based on the absence of *chieh-wu,* the initial, sudden experience of insight. Such an insight consists in recognizing the fundamental identity of sentient beings and Buddhas, saṃsāra and nirvāṇa, hence it also entails the recognition that deluded thoughts (i.e., dust) lack any reality of their own *(wang-nien pen wu)* because they are merely the functioning of the essence of the mind as it accords with conditions. In other words, *chieh-wu* is an insight into nature origination as the fundamental unifying principle behind the apparent multiplicity of phenomenal appearances. This insight validates the mundane world of phenomenal appearances as the manifestation of our nature. Phenomenal appearances are therefore "empty" and so are not really impure.

Tsung-mi's most comprehensive discussion of nature origination occurs in a passage in his subcommentary to Ch'eng-kuan's commentary to the chapter on the practice and vows of Samantabhadra from Prajña's translation of the *Gaṇḍavyūha*. There he connects it to conditioned origination *(yüan-ch'i, pratītyasamutpāda)* and shows how it is related to the processes of delusion and enlightenment. Nature origination and conditioned origination present two different causal models offering different levels of explanation. Conditioned origination explains how different phenomenal appearances condition one another, while nature origination explains how all phenomenal appearances are ultimately based upon the nature. In his discussion of conditioned origination, Tsung-mi first distinguishes between two modes: what he calls "defiled conditioned origination" *(jan-yüan-ch'i)* and "pure conditioned origination" *(ching-yüan-ch'i)*.[59] These two modes correspond to the parallel processes of delusion and enlightenment discussed above. He then goes on to make the further crucial distinction between two different levels of defiled conditioning, which he refers to as (1) its "beginningless root" *(wu-shih ken-pen)* and (2) its "evolved branches" *(chan-chuan chih-mo)*. The first refers to autonomous ignorance *(tu-t'ou wu-ming;* var. *tu-hsing wu-ming, pu-kung wu-ming; avidyā-aveṇikī)*[60] or what he later refers to as primordial ignorance *(ken-pen wu-ming)*.[61] This is an ignorance that exists prior to (at least logically if not also temporally) and independently of the defilements *(kleśa)*. It is the root *(pen)* of the later "evolved branches" (i.e., the last eight stages in the process of delusion). Sudden enlightenment *(chieh-wu)* counteracts this primordial ignorance.[62] Once the process of delusion has been set in motion, however, it becomes self-perpetuating. Gradual cultivation is therefore necessary to counteract its "evolved branches."

Since, according to Tsung-mi's analysis, the Northern line lacks sudden enlightenment *(chieh-wu)*, its "gradual cultivation" is qualitatively different from the gradual cultivation that follows *chieh-wu*. Nature is not only the basis of phenomenal appearances, but also the ground of practice. This failure to recognize the essential nature of all phenomenal appearances is implicit in Tsung-mi's charge that the practice taught by Northern Ch'an is "inauthentic" *(fei-chen)*. As Tsung-mi adds in his account of this teaching in his subcommentary to the *Scripture of Perfect Enlightenment*, "If cultivation is not in conformity with the true, how can one attain realization even after many kalpas?"[63] Thus when Tsung-mi says that Northern Ch'an "merely consists in the method of going against the flow and opposing residual conditioning [based on] the phenomenal appearances of impure and pure conditioned origination," he is implicitly criticizing it for not understanding nature origination.

B. Tsung-mi's Critique of the Hung-chou Line

Tsung-mi characterizes the teaching of the Hung-chou line as being diametrically opposed to that of the Northern line. He contrasts the two by remarking that the Northern line regards "everything as altogether false" *(wang)* whereas the Hung-chou line regards "everything as altogether true" *(chen).* Their approaches to cultivation are accordingly opposite: the Northern line advocates "subjugating the mind so as to extinguish the false" *(fu-hsin mieh-wang)* whereas the Hung-chou line advocates "entrusting oneself to act freely according to the nature of one's feelings" *(hsin-jen ch'ing-hsing).*[64] Where the Northern line falls into dualism, the position of the Hung-chou line leads to a radical nondualism by collapsing essence *(t'i)* into function *(yung).* Tsung-mi characterizes its stance in the *Ch'an Chart:*

> The arising of mental activity, the movement of thought, even snapping the fingers or moving the eyes—all actions and activities are the functioning of the entire essence of the Buddha-nature. Since there is no other kind of functioning, greed, anger, and folly, the performance of good and bad actions and the experiencing of their pleasurable and painful consequences are all, in their entirety, Buddha-nature.[65]

Because all activities—whether good or bad, enlightened or deluded—are "the functioning of the entire essence of the Buddha-nature," there is no essence outside of its functioning.

> If one examines the nature of its essence thoroughly, one will see that ultimately it can neither be perceived nor be realized, just as the eye cannot see itself, and so on. If one considers its responsive functioning, one will see that everything that one does is the Buddha-nature and that there is nothing else that can either realize it or be realized.[66]

The ethically dangerous implication of this teaching for Tsung-mi is that, if the essence can only be perceived through its functioning and, moreover, everything is equally the functioning of the essence in its entirety, then the essence becomes totally eclipsed by its functioning. Tsung-mi, however, insists that while the essence and its functioning are different aspects of the same reality, they are nevertheless still different and that their difference is important because the essence, as what is most fundamental *(pen),* is the source of value. His assimilation of the essence-function *(t'i-yung)* paradigm into that of root and branch *(pen-*

mo) entails a notion of religious practice as a return to a more basic state, the primordial condition of the mind before its bifurcation into subject and object, attendant upon the first subtle movement of thought. It is only through a direct experience of the essence that its functioning can be validated as true.

It is because the Hung-chou line collapses essence into function that Tsung-mi regards its attitude towards cultivation as antinomian. He holds that its proponents maintain that

> one should neither rouse the mind to cut off evil nor cultivate the way. Since the way itself is the mind, one cannot use the mind to cultivate the mind. Since evil is also the mind, one cannot use the mind to cut off the mind. One who neither cuts off [evil] nor does [good] but freely accepts things as they are is called a liberated person. There is no dharma that can be clung to or any Buddhahood that can be attained. . . . Simply allowing the mind to act spontaneously is cultivation.[67]

Although on one level Tsung-mi would not gainsay the Hung-chou assertion that ultimately there is no Buddhahood to attain, he would also insist that that realization is precisely what Buddhahood consists in and that such a statement can only be meaningfully made from the standpoint of one who has attained Buddhahood. It would be a grave error for one who has not yet realized that state to conclude facilely that there is therefore no reason to cultivate Buddhahood. Tsung-mi insists that while ultimately the nature transcends all dualistic categories, yet there is still a difference between enlightenment and delusion as far as sentient beings are concerned. And it is the tension created by the difference between enlightenment and delusion that vivifies practice.

> Hung-chou constantly says: "Since greed, anger, compassion, and good deeds are all the Buddha-nature, how can there be any difference between them?" This is like someone who sees that there is never any difference in the wetness [of the water] not realizing that there is an enormous difference between the success of a boat that crosses over it and the failure of a boat that capsizes in it. Therefore, as far as this line's approach toward sudden enlightenment is concerned, even though it comes close, it still does not hit the mark, and, as far as its approach toward gradual cultivation is concerned, it is mistaken and completely backwards.[68]

Tsung-mi's criticism of the Hung-chou line reveals that his use of the essence-function paradigm is more complex than might at first be apparent. While he emphasizes the inseparability of essence and function as different aspects of the same reality, he also stresses their difference: they are neither one nor different *(pu-i pu-i),* just as the true mind that is not subject to birth-and-death interfuses with deluded thoughts in such a way that they are neither one nor different. Their inseparability is what makes religious cultivation possible and their difference is what makes religious cultivation necessary. Tsung-mi thus uses the essence-function paradigm to preserve an ethically critical duality within a larger ontological unity. While this paradigm overcomes the dualism of Northern Ch'an on the one hand, it also serves to avoid the radical nondualism of Hung-chou on the other.

As part of his criticism of the Hung-chou line, Tsung-mi uses the analogy of a bronze mirror to illustrate the difference between its teaching and that of his own Ho-tse line. He does so by introducing a critical distinction between two levels of functioning: what he calls the "intrinsic functioning of the self-nature" *(tzu-hsing pen-yung)* and its "responsive functioning in accord with conditions" *(sui-yüan ying-yung).*

> The material substance of the bronze [mirror] is the essence of self-nature; the luminous reflectivity *(ming)* of the bronze is the functioning of the self-nature; and the images reflected by its luminous reflectivity are its functioning in accord with conditions. The images are reflected in direct response to conditions. While the reflections may have thousands of variations, the luminous reflectivity is the ever-present luminous reflectivity of the self-nature.[69]

The functioning of self-nature is synonymous with intrinsic enlightenment. The functioning in accord with conditions refers to the psychophysical functions of "speech, discrimination, bodily movement, and the like."[70] The relationship between these two orders of functioning can be characterized in terms of the essence and function, or root and branch, paradigm: the functioning of the self-nature is the essence or root of the functioning in accord with conditions. Tsung-mi uses this distinction to point out that the Hung-chou line, in overemphasizing the "responsive functioning" of the Buddha-nature, altogether misses the functioning of its self-nature. Its practice therefore lacks ontological grounding and is apt to veer off in ethically dangerous directions. By making this distinction crucial for differentiating between the Hung-chou and Ho-tse teachings, Tsung-mi reaffirms his emphasis on essence in contradistinction to function. By calling attention to the importance of the intrinsic functioning of the self-nature, Tsung-mi effectively drives a wedge between essence and function to insure that they cannot be collapsed in the way he understands the Hung-chou teaching to have done.

6. Tsung-mi's Theory and Shen-hui

Tsung-mi's characteristic tendency to find the most comprehensive framework into which all other perspectives can be subsumed must be taken into consideration when evaluating his accounts of the various Ch'an traditions. That is to say, his characterizations are schematic rather than descriptive: locating a tradition within a larger conceptual scheme often seems to be more important than giving a textured description of it. And that larger conceptual scheme is the particular vision of Hua-yen teaching that Tsung-mi espoused and identified with the teaching of Ho-tse Shen-hui. It could be objected that his identification of the teaching of the Northern line of Ch'an with that of Fa-hsiang, for example, is reductive and forces the complexity of its teaching into a prefabricated mold (equipped with its own built-in doctrinal critique). All the same, Tsung-mi was thoroughly acquainted with much of the Ch'an literature of his time, having devoted himself to collecting the extant writings of the various Ch'an traditions into a separate "basket" *(piṭaka)* to which his *Ch'an Preface* was to serve as a general introduction. His opinions on the various traditions were thus based on a broad knowledge of their teachings and therefore merit our careful attention. Nevertheless, we must also bear in mind that his understanding and portrayal of them were framed by his own doctrinal orientation, which, in turn, was shaped by his reaction to the more radical interpretations of Ch'an practice that he encountered during his formative period of Ch'an training in Szechwan. As Yanagida Seizan has shown, the most extreme of these, the Pao-t'ang, had extended Shen-hui's teaching of no-thought *(wu-nien)* to entail a rejection of all forms of traditional Buddhist ethical practice and ritual observance.[71]

Tsung-mi's reaction against radical forms of Ch'an, seen in his critique of the Hung-chou line, calls into question the degree to which his teachings authentically represent those of Shen-hui. Evidence can be found in the extant fragments of Shen-hui's teachings to support Tsung-mi's claim that his position can be characterized as advocating sudden enlightenment followed by gradual cultivation. As we have seen, one of the analogies that Tsung-mi uses to illustrate this position is that of an infant who possesses all of its limbs and faculties intact the moment it is born but only learns to master their use gradually. This analogy was very likely drawn from Shen-hui, as the following passage from his *Recorded Sayings* suggests.

> Each one of the great masters of my [lineage] for the [last] six generations spoke of piercing through [the heart of the matter] with a single thrust of the sword *(tan-tao chih-ju)* and directly seeing the nature *(chih-liao chien-hsing)*; they didn't say anything about a gradual progression *(chiai-chien)*. Followers of the way, you should suddenly see your Buddha-nature *(tun-chien fo-hsing)* and then gradually cultivate causal conditions *(chien-hsiu yin-yüan)*. . . . It is like a mother suddenly giving birth to a child, giving him her breast, and gradually nurturing and rearing him. . . . Suddenly

awakening and seeing one's Buddha-nature *(tun-wu chien-fo-hsing)* is also like this—wisdom naturally increases gradually *(chih-hui tzu-jan chien-chien tseng-chang)*.[72]

Yet Tsung-mi also uses an analogy from Shen-hui to illustrate sudden enlightenment and sudden cultivation—the position in which obstructions are suddenly cut off just as myriad strands of silk are severed with a single stroke when cutting a piece of silk cloth. Compare Tsung-mi's use of this analogy with the following passage from Shen-hui's *Recorded Sayings*.

> [Wu-hsing] further asked: "If the defilements are so innumerable and limitless that Buddhas and bodhisattvas pass through eons and still have not been able to succeed [in eliminating them], how could the dragon girl [in the story from the *Lotus Sūtra*] have been able to give rise to her aspiration for enlightenment in an instant *(ch'a-na fa-hsin)* and immediately have attained true enlightenment *(pien ch'eng cheng-chüeh)*?"
>
> The Ho-shang [Shen-hui] replied: "Raising the aspiration for enlightenment can be either sudden or gradual *(fa-hsin yu tun chien)* and delusion and enlightenment can be either slow or quick *(mi wu yu ch'ih chi)*. Delusion lasts for repeated eons *(mi chi lei-chieh)*, but enlightenment takes place instantaneously *(wu chi hsü-yü)*. . . . For example, even though the number of strands in a roll of silk is incalculable, if one gathers them together into a rope, puts them on a board, and severs them with a sharp sword, then at once they will all be cut in two. Although the strands are numerous, they do not take more then a single stroke of a sword. A person who gives rise to the aspiration for enlightenment is also like this. If he meets a true good friend who skillfully uses expedients to reveal suchness directly, then with his diamondlike wisdom he will cut through the defilements belonging to the various stages [of the bodhisattva], be immediately enlightened *(huo-jan hsiao-wu)*, and see for himself that the nature of reality *(fa-hsing)* is originally empty and tranquil. His wisdom will then be sharp, bright, and clear and will penetrate [everywhere] without obstruction. When he realizes this, his myriad [karmic] conditions will be simultaneously severed and his deluded thoughts, which are more numerous than the sands of the Ganges, will be suddenly done away with all at once. The limitless excellent virtues [of a Buddha] will be fully ready to be used according to circumstances.[73]

As already noted, Tsung-mi also quotes twice from Shen-hui in his explanation of the case of sudden enlightenment and sudden cultivation in the *Ch'an Preface*. The fact that Tsung-mi can draw from Shen-hui to illustrate two contrasting positions suggests, at the very least, that there are divergent tendencies intermixed within Shen-hui's thought. However we assess Shen-hui as a personality, he was certainly not a systematic thinker. Whatever his motivation, he seems to have put forward different positions in response to different questions and never seems to have felt a need to integrate them into a comprehensive doctrinal framework.

The position that Tsung-mi upholds as the orthodox one, that of sudden enlightenment followed by gradual cultivation, could be characterized as conservative in contrast to that of sudden enlightenment and sudden cultivation, which could accordingly be characterized as radical. While we can find evidence for both positions within the Shen-hui fragments, that of sudden enlightenment followed by gradual cultivation generally seems to be a fallback position to which Shen-hui retreats under the brunt of a certain line of questioning—it does not seem to be the position that he puts forward as his own when he is on the offensive.[74] In any case, Tsung-mi, in his characterization of Shen-hui's teaching, seems to have identified the more conservative strand of his thought as orthodox and suppressed the more radical one. That is, he plays down the strong *prajñā-pāramitā* thrust in Shen-hui's teaching while emphasizing a Yogācāra understanding of the obduracy of the defilements. This emphasis no doubt reflects Tsung-mi's reaction to the radical way Shen-hui's teaching had been adapted by some of the Szechwan Ch'an traditions.

7. Conclusion

Tsung-mi's analysis of the different contexts in which the terms "sudden" *(tun)* and "gradual" *(chien)* operate does much to make sense out of what often seems to be a hopelessly confused and confusing issue. For this reason alone it is worth our attention. Yet, ironically, it is just its ability to render the tangle of controversy intelligible that, in the final analysis, betrays Tsung-mi as a gradualist. His approach to the sudden-gradual issue is fully congruent with his approach to Buddhist doctrine—that is, he tries to reconcile conflicting interpretations by uncovering a more comprehensive framework in which they can all be harmoniously sublated. His theory of sudden enlightenment followed by gradual cultivation integrates the experience of sudden enlightenment into a comprehensive vision of a progressive path of spiritual cultivation, one that emphasizes the importance of a sudden "leap" of insight within a larger philosophy of progress.[75] By so doing, Tsung-mi, in effect, domesticates the experience of enlightenment. But this is precisely what the subitist claims can never be done, for there is a profound sense in which enlightenment can never be accounted for, because to do so is to place it, as Tsung-mi does, within a conceptual structure with its own strictures of rationality. The subitist insists that enlightenment is an experience of breaking through all such structures—and for that reason it is ultimately ineffable. To say anything at all *about* enlightenment is to impose structure upon it, no matter how deftly or obliquely done. A necessary corollary to any thoroughgoing and consistent attempt to apply the subitist stance would thus be an apophatic approach to language. In the end, the subitist relies on silence—but even this must be regarded as symbolic, for silence can only be interpreted within some context of discourse. When taken seriously, subitism is a position that by its very nature transcends articulation, for to articulate it coherently is to resort to the expedience of linguistic convention, in which both explicit and implicit conceptual structures are inextricably embedded.

Subitism, then, for all the appeal of its uncompromising stance, leads to a set of curious and intractable problems when it is applied to practice.[76] The apophatic rhetorical posture makes it impossible to say anything concrete about the actual experience of the practice of meditation. Taken by itself, it is easy to see how it might be possible for such a posture to be interpreted in a way that undermines religious and ethical practice. Tsung-mi seems to have been well aware of this possibility, since he came from a part of China where a number of extreme applications of Ch'an doctrine had gained currency by his day.

Nevertheless, it would be wrong to characterize Tsung-mi simply as a gradualist. The doctrine of suddenness is essential to his own sense of identity as a successor in Shen-hui's teaching line, and the experience of sudden enlightenment serves as his criterion for gauging the authenticity of Ch'an teachings on practice. Tsung-mi's own position is too complex and subtle to be categorized as simply that of a subitist or a gradualist—just as his use of the essence-function paradigm makes it impossible to characterize his thought as conforming to either a dualistic or a nondualistic model.

Tsung-mi's position on the sudden-gradual issue seems in many respects to be unique. For example, in his explanation of the nature and function of religious language, Tsung-mi claims that the sudden teaching is precisely that which is able to reveal the essence with a single word. He defines the ultimate teaching, which he identifies with the Ho-tse line, as that which reveals the nature immediately; because it reveals the nature without resorting to expedients, it is also sudden. And it does so by using the single word "awareness" *(chih)*. Tsung-mi interprets the famous phrase, "the single word 'awareness' is the gate of all mysteries," which he attributes to Shen-hui, to mean that Shen-hui used the single word directly to reveal the truth. The sudden teaching is therefore the teaching that enables one to experience sudden enlightenment.[77] He thus defines suddenness in terms of its ability to use language positively to reveal the truth.

In a very broad sense, we can see the sudden-gradual polarity as part of a larger dialectic in Buddhism. On the one hand, there is a need to create structures to give meaning and direction to practice. As a soteriological system deeply concerned with the practical task of motivating and guiding its followers, Buddhism requires a coherent vision of the nature and structure of the path. Such conceptual maps orient the practitioner, locating him in relation to his ultimate goal and thereby clarifying his task. Since such maps may also ground their pictures of the course of practice within a broader understanding of the ontological structure of reality—as Tsung-mi's threefold theory of insight, cultivation, and realization does within his understanding of the fundamental nature of the mind as the ultimate source of all appearances—they may also serve to motivate and sustain practice by giving the practitioner confidence in his ability to realize the goal, because the path he is following is part of the very nature of things. On the other hand, it is easy to lose sight of the fact that conceptual maps are only expedient devices that must be cast aside after they have served their purpose. If the practitioner becomes attached to any map as being a true picture of reality, it becomes an obstacle thwarting the very realization of that to which it is intended to lead. Buddhism thus has the equally important need continually to deconstruct those very structures it is called upon to create. From the "hard" edge of the subitist position, all means (upāya) must be rejected as conceptual traps. Given these seemingly discordant attitudes (often represented in Buddhist discourse by the distinction between conventional and ultimate truth), one could say that both stances are needed for balance, that a one-sided subitism can subvert practice just as a one-sided gradualism can stifle realization, and that what is crucial is the vitality of the tension generated between them—but to say this is to take a tack not unsimilar to that of Tsung-mi and, of course, to side with the gradualists.

Appendix 1
Ch'eng-kuan's Scheme of Sudden-Gradual Combinations

Tsung-mi's analysis of the five permutations of sudden and gradual as applied to enlightenment and cultivation is derived from Ch'eng-kuan. In his *Hua-yen ching yen-i ch'ao* (*T* 36.164c8–16) and *Hua-yen ching hsing yüan p'in shu* (*ZZ* 1/7/3.252a17–b11), Ch'eng-kuan gives two slightly different, but overlapping schemes, which, when combined, result in the five permutations outlined by Tsung-mi. Most importantly, Tsung-mi adopted Ch'eng-kuan's distinction between *chieh-wu* and *cheng-wu*. Nevertheless, even though Tsung-mi takes over the five permutations enumerated by Ch'eng-kuan, his description of their content is often quite different. He also uses them for a different purpose. Whereas Ch'eng-kuan's account claims to be purely descriptive and makes no value judgments as to the relative merits of the various positions, Tsung-mi's analysis serves to demonstrate the superiority of

Shen-hui's teaching. The differences between Ch'eng-kuan's and Tsung-mi's analyses is also discussed by Chinul in his *Pŏpchip pyŏrhaeng nok chŏryo pyŏngip sagi*. For bibliographical references see note 17 below. In order to provide a basis for comparison, a translation of the relevant sections from Ch'eng-kuan's two works follows.

1. Sudden enlightenment and gradual cultivation from *Hsing yüan p'in shu* (252a17–b1):

The case of sudden enlightenment and gradual cultivation involves enlightenment of insight *(chieh-wu)*. That is to say, in the case in which one clearly intuits the nature of the mind and then engages in the training of gradual cultivation so as to make oneself come into full accord with it, enlightenment is like the shining of the sun [following Chinul; *ZZ* has "moon"], which suddenly illuminates all things, and cultivation is like the wiping of a mirror, which becomes gradually more lustrous and bright.

from *Yen-i ch'ao* (164c8–12):

Sudden enlightenment and gradual cultivation is like seeing a nine-story tower: although it is seen suddenly, it is only after one has ascended the stairs that one reaches the top.

2. Gradual cultivation and sudden enlightenment from *Hsing yüan p'in shu* (252b1–4):

The case of gradual cultivation and sudden enlightenment means that only after having first assimilated objects so that there is only mind and then observing the intrinsic purity of the mind are mind and its objects both tranquil. There is then not even the slightest stirring of thought and the succession of past and future [thought] is sundered: [the mind] is as limpid as a calm ocean and as vast as empty space. Since this case involves enlightenment of realization *(cheng-wu)*, cultivation is like polishing a mirror and enlightenment is like the mirror's luminous reflectivity.

3. Sudden cultivation and gradual enlightenment from *Yen-i ch'ao* (164c12–3):

Sudden cultivation and gradual enlightenment is like burnishing a [bronze] mirror: although one burnishes the entire surface at a time, its becoming bright and clear is gradual. Although the myriad practices are suddenly cultivated, enlightenment is only gradually perfected. This case involves enlightenment of realization *(cheng-wu)*.

4. Gradual cultivation and gradual enlightenment from *Hsing yüan p'in shu* (252b4–5):

The case of gradual cultivation and gradual enlightenment also involves enlightenment of realization *(cheng-wu).* Here cultivation and enlightenment are both like ascending a tower: as one gradually climbs higher, one's gaze gradually extends further.

from *Yen-i ch'ao* (164a16–17):

Gradual cultivation and gradual enlightenment is like cutting sections of bamboo: the sections are not the same.

5. Sudden enlightenment and sudden cultivation from *Hsing yüan p'in shu* (252b6–11):

The case of sudden enlighenment and sudden cultivation includes three meanings.

(a) In the case of being suddenly enlightened and subsequently engaging in cultivation, a broad and sudden intuition is called enlightenment and fully merging with the way without either observing or purifying [following Chinul, *ch'eng; ZZ* has *cheng*], controlling *(shou)* or assimilating *(she),* is called cultivation. This is a case of enlightenment of insight *(chieh-wu)* and it takes samādhi as its means of access. Again, it is like a mirror which is of itself luminously reflective without having to be wiped or polished.

(b) In the case of intially engaging in cultivation and subsequently being enlightened, abruptly seeing the nature of the mind as a result of having previously engaged in cultivation is called enlightenment. This is a case of enlightenment of realization *(cheng-wu)* in which cultivation is like taking medicine and enlightenment is like curing the ailment.

(c) In the case where cultivation and enlightenment are simultaneous, when no-mind is shining in forgetfulness, it is naturally tranquil and aware. This is a case of samādhi and prajñā operating concurrently. No-mind, like a luminous mirror, suddenly reflects all things. Here enlightenment encompasses [following Chinul, *t'ung; ZZ* has *tao*] both insight *(chieh)* and realization *(cheng).*

from *Yen-i ch'ao* (164c13–16):

Sudden cultivation and sudden enlightenment is like a sharp sword cutting silk: when a thousand strands are cut, they are all simultaneously severed. Or again it is like dying a thousand strands of silk: when they are all simultaneously [immersed in] the dye, they at once become colored. Thus when the myriad practices are all cultivated, they are simultaneously brightly enlightened.

Appendix 2
The Structure of the *Awakening of Faith*

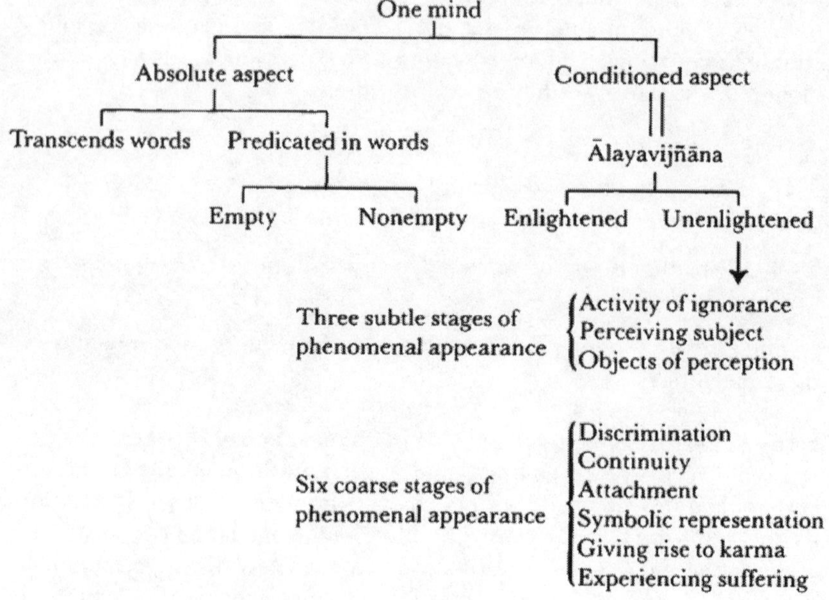

Appendix 3
A Comparison of Tsung-mi's Stages of Phenomenal Evolution and the *Awakening of Faith*

Awakening of Faith	*Tsung-mi*
One mind	
Ālayavijñāna	
Enlightened mode	1. Intrinsic enlightenment
Unenlightened mode	2. Unenlightenment
Activity of ignorance	3. Arising of thoughts
Perceiving subject	4. Arising of the perceiving subject
Perceived objects	5. Manifestation of perceived objects
Discrimination Continuity	6. Attachment to things
Attachment Symbolic representation	7. Attachment to self
	8. Defilements
Generating karma	9. Generating karma
Suffering of karmic bondage	10. Experiencing the consequences

Notes

1. This chapter is based primarily on two texts by Tsung-mi: the *Chung-hua ch'uan-hsin-ti Ch'an-men shih-tzu ch'eng-hsi t'u* (Chart of the Master-Disciple Succession of the Ch'an Gate That Has Transmitted the Mind Ground in China) and *Ch'an-yüan chu-ch'üan-chi tu-hsü* (Preface to the Collected Writings on the Source of Ch'an), referred to throughout this chapter as *Ch'an Chart* and *Ch'an Preface,* respectively. The *Ch'an Preface* appears in vol. 48 of the *Taishō shinshū daizōkyō* and the *Ch'an Chart* appears in series 2, case 15, vol. 5 of the *Dainippon zokuzōkyō.* Both texts have been edited, annotated, and translated into modern Japanese by Kamata Shigeo in vol. 9 of the Zen no goroku series under the general editorship of Iriya Yoshitaka (Tokyo: Chikuma shobō, 1971); Kamata's edition will be cited as "K" throughout. Jeffrey Broughton has included a complete translation of the *Ch'an Preface* in his "Kuei-feng Tsung-mi: The Convergence of Ch'an and the Teachings" (Ph.D. diss., Columbia University, 1975); this translation will be cited as "B" throughout. The *Ch'an Chart* is quoted extensively by Chinul in his *Pŏpchip pyŏrhaeng nok chŏryo pyŏngip sagi;* I have used the edition published by Yanagida Seizan in *Kōrai hon: Zemmon satsuyō; Zengen shosenshū tojo; Hōjū betsugyō roku setsuyō* (Kyoto: Chūbun shuppansha, 1974). The *Ch'an Chart* is also included in *P'ei Hsiu shih-i wen,* published by Ishii Shūdō in *Zengaku kenkyū,* vol. 60 (1981), 69–104.

2. See *Ch'an Chart,* 433d11–13; K, 277.

3. Ibid., 434a16–17, d1–3; K, 282.

4. Ibid., 434b11–14; K, 282.

5. Ibid., 438b5, K, 341.

6. See *Ch'an Preface,* 402b2–3; K, 81; cf. B, 142.

7. Ibid., 399c7; K, 30; cf. B, 99.

8. Ibid., 402b4; K, 81; cf. B, 143.

9. See, for example, *Ch'an Preface,* 402a10–19; K, 78. Cf. B, 139–140.

10. For an example of Tsung-mi's ecumenical approach, see *Ch'an Preface,* 400c10–22; K, 49. Cf. B, 118–119.

11. *Ch'an Preface,* 408a9–12; K, 191. Cf. B, 249.

12. See *Ch'an Preface,* 407c12–13; K, 191. Cf. B, 244.

13. See my article "The Place of the Sudden Teaching within the Hua-yen Tradition: An Investigation of the Process of Doctrinal Change," *Journal of the International Association of Buddhist Studies* 6, no. 1 (1983): 31–60.

14. See *Ch'an Preface,* 407b15–17; K, 184. Cf. B, 238.

15. See *Ch'an Preface,* 407b21–c2; K, 185. Cf. B, 240–241. This corresponds to what Tsung-mi refers to as the sudden teaching that was expounded in response to beings of superior capacity *(chu-chi tun-chiao),* which, in the *Ch'an Preface,* he distinguishes from the sudden teaching as a method of exposition *(hua-i tun-chiao),* which applies exclusively to the *Avataṃsaka-sūtra.*

16. See *Ch'an Preface,* 407b17–20; K, 184. Cf. B, 238.

17. The following summary is based on the account found in the *Ch'an Preface* (407c12–408a7; K, 191; cf. B, 244–249) but also makes use of the more detailed account found in Tsung-mi's subcommentary to both his commentary and abridged commentary to the *Scripture of Perfect Enlightenment* (*Yüan-chüeh ching ta-*

chu ch'ao, ZZ 1/14/3.280b–281a, and *Lüeh-shu ch'ao, ZZ* 1/15/2.132a–c), which will be referred to as *TSC* and *LSC* hereafter. The five major positions enumerated by Tsung-mi derive from both Ch'eng-kuan's subcommentary to the *Avataṃsaka-sūtra* (*Ta-fang-kuang fo-hua-yen ching sui-shu yen-i ch'ao, T* 36.164c) and his commentary on Prajña's translation of the chapter on the practice and vows of Samantabhadra from the *Gaṇḍavyūha* (*Hua-yen ching hsing yüan p'in shu, ZZ* 1/7/3.251d–252b). Ch'eng-kuan outlines four different major positions in each work; when both are combined, there are a total of five. Whereas Ch'eng-kuan merely outlines the different positions without evaluating them, Tsung-mi, of course, argues for the orthodoxy of sudden enlightenment followed by gradual cultivation. See Ishii Shūdō, "Tongo zenshū ni tsuite," *IBK* 29, no. 2 (1981): 586–591. For an analysis of Ch'eng-kuan's position, see Yoshizu Yoshihide, *Kegonzen no shisōshi-teki kenkyū* (Tokyo: Daitō shuppansha, 1985), 249–266. See Appendix 1 for a translation of the relevant passages from Ch'eng-kuan. The differences between Tsung-mi's explanation of sudden enlightenment and gradual practice in the *Ch'an Chart* and Ch'eng-kuan's discussion of these terms in his *Hua-yen ching hsing yüan p'in shu* are discussed extensively by Chinul in his *Pŏpchip pyŏrhaeng nok chŏryo pyŏngip sagi* (158b ff.); cf. the excellent translation by Robert Buswell in his *Korean Approach to Zen: The Collected Works of Chinul* (Honolulu: University of Hawaii Press, 1983), 278ff. Tsung-mi's enumeration of the five possible permutations of sudden and gradual as they apply to enlightenment and cultivation is adopted by Yen-shou in his *Wan-shan t'ung-kuei chi, T* 48.987b–c.

Actually, Tsung-mi seems to give a sixth position in the *Ch'an Preface:* that the terms "sudden" and "gradual" apply only to human capacities, not to the dharma (see 402a14; K, 78; cf. B, 139 and 408a5–6; K, 191; cf. B, 248). This position would seem to be that of the *Platform Sūtra* (see Philip B. Yampolsky, *The Platform Sutra of the Sixth Patriarch: The Text of the Tun-huang Manuscript* [New York and London: Columbia University Press, 1967], 137), although Tsung-mi does not so identify it. In fact, it is significant to note that, as far as I can discover, Tsung-mi never refers to the *Platform Sūtra.* Since this position is not enumerated in the corresponding sections of either the *TSC* or *LSC* and since it does not involve a permutation of the terms "sudden" and "gradual" as they apply to enlightenment and cultivation, it has been ignored for the purposes of this chapter.

18. *T* 46.1c23, as translated by Neal Donner in "*The Great Calming and Contemplation* of Chih-i. Chapter One: The Synopsis" (Ph.D. diss., University of British Columbia, 1976), 45. See the passage from Chih-i's *Fa-hua hsüan-i* (*T* 33.806b24–25) as translated in the chapter by Donner in this volume: "In the perfect and sudden meditation one takes ultimate reality as the object of contemplation even from the time that the thought of enlightenment makes its first appearance."

19. *TSC,* 280b9–10. Tsung-mi borrows the distinction between *chieh-wu* and *cheng-wu* from Ch'eng-kuan; see *Hsing yüan p'in shu,* 252a16–17.

20. Tsung-mi links this position with that of the Ox-head line of Ch'an.

21. A similar statement can be found in Shen-hui's *Yü-lu;* see Hu Shih, ed., *Shen-hui ho-shang i-chi* (Taipei: Hu Shih chi-nien kuan, 1966; repr. 1970), 121.

22. The first quotation can be found in *Ho-tse Shen-hui ta-shih yü* as quoted in *Ching-te ch'uan-teng lu*, *T* 51.439c1; I have been unable to locate the second.

Tsung-mi gives three different interpretations of this case in *TSC* (280d8–281a6) and *LSC* (132c1–16). In the first, enlightenment precedes cultivation and is therefore that of insight *(chieh)*. In the second, enlightenment succeeds cultivation and is therefore that of realization *(cheng)*. In the third, enlightenment and cultivation are simultaneous, and enlightenment encompasses both insight *(chieh)* and realization *(cheng)*. Tsung-mi's explanations basically amplify Ch'eng-kuan's treatment in his *Hsing yüan p'in shu* (see Appendix 1).

23. See my "Tsung-mi and the Single Word 'Awareness' *(chih)*," *Philosophy East and West* 35, no. 3 (1985): 249–269.

24. 407c21–22; K, 191. Cf. B, 246.

25. *Ta-sheng ch'i-hsin lun*. See *T* 32.576c11–14; cf. Yoshito Hakeda, trans., *The Awakening of Faith* (New York: Columbia University Press, 1967), 41.

26. 407b26–27; K, 185. Cf. B, 240–241.

27. 407c19; K, 191. Cf. B, 245.

28. See *Ting shih-fei lun*, *Shen-hui ho-shang i-chi*, 287 (quoted in sec. 6 below).

29. 407c19–20.

30. See *Ch'an Chart*, 438b8–9; K, 341.

31. Both the *Zokuzōkyō* and Kamata versions of the text read: *chuan-fan ch'eng-sheng chi* tun-wu *yeh*. I have emended this passage to read: *chuan-fan ch'eng-sheng chi* chien *yeh* in light of *P'ei Hsiu shih-i wen*, 95, and Chinul's *Pŏpchip pyŏrhaeng nok chŏryo pyŏngip sagi*, 158b. According to traditional mārga theory, the transformation from *pṛthagjana (fan)* to *ārya (sheng)* takes place at the stage of *darśana-mārga*. If Tsung-mi's theory of the three stages of religious cultivation can be correlated with traditional mārga theory, then he has the transformation from *pṛthagjana* to *ārya* taking place not at the stage of *darśana-mārga* (i.e., *chieh-wu*), but at the completion of *bhāvanā-mārga* (i.e., *chien-hsiu*).

32. 437d17–438a3; K, 340.

33. See Isshū Miura and Ruth Fuller Sasaki, *Zen Dust* (New York: Harcourt, Brace & World, 1966), 254.

34. *T* 10.272c4–7 and 272c25–273a2. The chapter of the *Avataṃsaka* from which this passage is quoted seems to have originally circulated as an independent scripture, the **Tathāgatatotpattisambhava-nirdeśa*, which was translated into Chinese as the *Ju-lai hsing-hsien ching* (*T* #291) by Dharmarakṣa in the late third century. According to Takasaki Jikidō's reconstruction of the development of the tathāgatagarbha doctrine, this passage served as the basis for a similar passage in the *Tathāgatagarbha-sūtra* (*Ju-lai-tsang ching;* see *T* 16.457b28–c10), the first scripture to expound the tathāgatagarbha doctrine explicitly (see *A Study of the Ratnagotravibhāga*, Serie Orientale Roma 33 [1966], 35–36).

35. K, 340. This passage is missing from the *Zokuzōkyō* text. Kamata has supplied it from the *Pŏpchip pyŏrhaeng nok chŏryo pyŏngip sagi*. It can also be found in *P'ei Hsiu shih-i wen*, 96–97. "Reducing it and further reducing it" *(sun chih yu sun)* is an allusion to *Lao Tzu* 48.

36. The following characterization is indebted to the discussion of these terms by Robert Gimello, "Chih-yen and the Foundations of Hua-yen Buddhism" (Ph.D. diss., Columbia University, 1976), 212–337.

37. The *locus classicus* for the doctrine of an innately pure luminous mind can be found in *Anguttara-nikāya* 1.10, which F. L. Woodward renders as follows (*The Book of Gradual Sayings* [London: Pali Text Society, 1970], 1:8): "This mind, monks, is luminous, but it is defiled by taints that come from without; that mind, monks, is luminous, but it is cleansed of taints that come from without."

38. *T* 31.117a8–9; see Gimello, 262–266.

39. *T* 32.576b8–9. For further discussion of this text see my "The Problem of Theodicy in the *Awakening of Faith*," *Religious Studies* 22 (1986): 63–78.

40. *T* 45.710b8–13. For a diagram of the structure of the *Awakening of Faith* see Appendix 2; for a comparison of how Tsung-mi's stages of phenomenal evolution correspond to those in the *Awakening of Faith* see Appendix 3.

41. See Tsung-mi's narrative explanation of the processes of enlightenment and delusion at the end of the *Ch'an Preface* (407b6–408a3; K, 217–218 and 222–223; cf. B, 269–278) as well as the relevant portion of the diagram itself (410–411). See also *Yüan-jen lun*, *T* 45.710b. A more primitive version of the stages of phenomenal evolution can also be found in Tsung-mi's commentary and subcommentary to the *Scripture of Perfect Enlightenment* (116c16–117c4 and 264a16–267b5) and his commentary to the *Awakening of Faith (Ta-sheng ch'i-hsin lun shu), Dai Nippon kōtei daizōkyō,* case 31, vol. 8, div. 5, pt. 2, p. 14v. See my "What Happened to the Perfect Teaching?—Another Look at Hua-yen Buddhist Hermeneutics," in Donald S. Lopez, Jr., ed., *Buddhist Hermeneutics,* Studies in East Asian Buddhism, no. 6 (Honolulu: University of Hawaii Press, 1988).

42. *T* 32.577b11–14; cf. Hakeda, 37.

43. See ibid., 577a8–10; cf. Hakeda, 44. Tsung-mi identifies this and the following stages of phenomenal evolution with the stages in the evolution of consciousness as described in the *Ch'eng wei-shih lun.* This stage corresponds to the essence *(tzu-t'i)* of the ālayavijñāna, which then divides into subjective and objective modes.

44. See ibid., 577a10–11; cf. Hakeda, 44. This stage corresponds to the subjective mode *(chien-fen, darśanabhāga)* of the ālayavijñāna as described in the *Ch'eng wei-shih lun.*

45. See ibid., 577a11–12; cf. Hakeda, 44. This stage corresponds to the objective mode *(hsiang-fen, nimittabhāga)* of the ālayavijñāna as described in the *Ch'eng wei-shih lun.* According to that text, the ālayavijñāna transforms itself internally into the body of the senses *(ken-shen, sendriyakakāya)* and externally into the receptacle world *(ch'i-shih-chien, bhājanaloka).* It defines the body of the senses as "the sense organs and the body that serves as their support" and the receptacle world—i.e., the environment—as "the place which serves as the support for all sentient beings" (see *T* 31.10a13–16).

46. See ibid., 577a13–15; cf. Hakeda, 44–45. This stage corresponds to what the *Ch'eng wei-shih lun* refers to as *dharmagrāha.*

47. See ibid., 577a16–17; cf. Hakeda, 45. This stage corresponds to what the *Ch'eng wei-shih lun* refers to as *ātmagrāha.*

48. See ibid., 577a17–18; cf. Hakeda, 45.

49. See ibid., 577a18–19; cf. Hakeda, 45.

50. See ibid., 577a19–20; cf. Hakeda, 45.

51. See E. B. Cowell, ed., *Buddhist Mahayana Texts* (New York: Dover Publications, 1969), 152–155.
52. See *T* 32.581c14 ff.; cf. Hakeda, 93–95.
53. See ibid., 582a16 ff. and 582c15 ff.; cf. Hakeda, 96–102.
54. The *Awakening of Faith* defines ultimate awakening as "awakening to the source of the mind" *(chüeh hsin-yüan)* (576b16–17; cf. Hakeda, 38). It then goes on to say: "When the bodhisattva stages have been completed and one has fulfilled the expedient [practices], one becomes unified in a single moment of thought *(i-nien hsiang-ying)*. Having become aware of the first stirrings of the mind, one's mind is without the first phenomenal appearance [of the arising of thoughts]. Because one is far removed from the subtlest thought, one sees the nature of the mind—that the mind is eternal—and that is what is called ultimate awakening" (576b23–26; cf. Hakeda, 39).
55. *TSC,* 280b17–c8 and *LSC,* 132a10–b1.
56. 435c13–18; K, 298. The verse by Shen-hsiu that Tsung-mi here quotes is that made famous by the *Platform Sūtra*'s story of the exchange of "mind-verses" that decided the issue of who the sixth patriarch was to be. It is especially curious that Tsung-mi, who identified so strongly with Shen-hui's lineage, never cites or refers to Hui-neng's matching verse. As already noted, to the best of my knowledge Tsung-mi never refers to the *Platform Sūtra.* Ch'eng-kuan quotes half of Shen-hsiu's verse, but also fails to refer to Hui-neng's, in his *Yen-i ch'ao* (see *T* 36.164c5).
57. 435d1–2; K, 298.
58. 403b26–27; K, 104.
59. *ZZ* 1/7/4.399d3 ff.
60. Ibid., 399d6–7.
61. Ibid., 400c5.
62. Ibid.
63. *TSC,* 277c14.
64. *Ch'an Chart,* 436b3–5; K, 315.
65. 435d4–6; K, 307.
66. 435d17–18; K, 307. Neither the *Zokuzōkyō* nor Kamata version of the text has "Buddha-nature" *(fo-hsing).* This has been supplied from *P'ei Hsiu shih-i wen,* 85, and *Pŏpchip pyŏrhaeng nok chŏryo pyŏngip sagi,* 152d.
67. 436a4–9; K, 308.
68. 438a18–b4; K, 341.
69. 437d5–7; K, 336.
70. 437d8; K, 336.
71. See "The *Li-tai fa-pao chi* and the Ch'an Doctrine of Sudden Awakening," in Whalen Lai and Lewis R. Lancaster, eds., *Early Ch'an in China and Tibet* (Berkeley: Berkeley Buddhist Studies Series, 1983), 13–49. I have also dealt with the importance of Tsung-mi's reaction against these radical Ch'an movements in Szechwan in my essays "Tsung-mi and the Single Word 'Awareness' *(chih)*" and "What Happened to the Perfect Teaching?" For Tsung-mi's characterization of the Pao-t'ang teachings see *ZZ* 1/14/3.278d.
72. Hu Shih, *Shen-hui ho-shang i-chi,* 287; cf. 175.
73. Ibid., 120–121.

74. See the chapter by Luis Gómez earlier in this volume.

75. To borrow Karl Potter's terminology; see *Presuppositions of India's Philosophies* (Englewood Cliffs, N.J.: Prentice-Hall, 1963).

76. For a sensitive and insightful discussion of this problem, see Carl Bielefeldt, "Ch'ang-lu Tsung-tse's *Tso-ch'an i* and the 'Secret' of Zen Meditation," in Peter N. Gregory, ed., *Traditions of Meditation in Chinese Buddhism,* Studies in East Asian Buddhism, no. 4 (Honolulu: University of Hawaii Press, 1986).

77. See Gregory, "Tsung-mi and the Single Word 'Awareness.' "

Glossary

a-mo-lo-shih 阿末羅識
ch'a-na fa-hsin 刹那發心
Ch'an 禪
chan-chuan chih-mo 展轉枝末
Chan-jan 湛然
Ch'an-yüan chu-ch'üan-chi tu-hsü 禪源諸詮集都序
chen 眞
chen-hsing 眞性
chen-ju 眞如
chen-ju i-hsin 眞如一心
cheng 證
ch'eng 澄
ch'eng-fo 成佛
Ch'eng-kuan 澄觀
Ch'eng wei-shih lun 成唯識論
cheng-wu 證悟
chi-ming-tzu 計名字
ch'i-shih-chien 器世間
chi te cheng-wu 即得證悟
ch'i-yeh 起業
chiai-chien 階漸
chiao 教
chiao-ch'an i-chih 教禪一致
chieh 解
chieh-wu 解悟
chien 漸
chien-ch'i 見起
chien-fen 見分
chien-hsiu 漸修
chien-hsiu chien-wu 漸修漸悟
chien-hsiu tun-wu 漸修頓悟
chien-hsiu yin-yüan 漸修因緣
chih (awareness) 知
chih (discrimination) 智
chih-ch'ü 執取
chih-hui tzu-jan chien-chien tseng-chang 智慧自然漸漸增長
chih-liao chien-hsing 直了見性
Chih-yen 智儼
ching-chiai 境界
ching-ch'i 境起
ching-yüan-ch'i 淨緣起
Chinul 知訥
chiu-ching chüeh 究竟覺
ch'u yin chieh-wu 初因解悟
chu-chi tun-chiao 逐機頓教
chuan-fan ch'eng-sheng chi chien yeh 轉凡成聖即漸也
chuan-fan ch'eng-sheng chi tun-wu yeh 轉凡成聖即頓悟也
chuan-i 轉依
Chung-hua ch'uan-hsin-ti ch'an-men shih-tzu ch'eng-hsi t'u 中華傳心地禪門師資承襲圖
chüeh 覺
chüeh hsin-yüan 覺心源
fa-chih 法執
Fa-hsiang 法相
fa-hsin 發心
fa-hsin yu tun chien 發心有頓漸
fa-hsing 法性
fa-k'ung 法空
Fa-tsang 法藏

fan (counteract) 翻
fan (ordinary) 凡
fan-nao 煩惱
fei-chen 非眞
fo-hsing 佛性
fu-hsin mieh-wang 伏心滅妄
Ho-tse 荷澤
hsi 習
hsiang 相
hsiang-fen 相分
hsiang-hsü 相續
hsin chen-ju 心眞如
hsin-jen ch'ing-hsing 信任情性
hsin sheng-mieh 心生滅
hsin-tzu-tsai 心自在
hsing 性
hsing-ch'i 性起
hsing man kung yüan 行滿功圓
hsiu wu-hsing 修五行
hsün-hsi 熏習
hua-i tun-chiao 化儀頓教
Hua-yen 華嚴
Hua-yen ching 華嚴經
Hua-yen ching hsing yüan p'in shu 華嚴經行願品疏
Hua-yen ching hsing yüan p'in shu ch'ao 華嚴經行願品疏鈔
Hua-yen ching yen-i ch'ao 華嚴經演義鈔
Hui-neng 慧能
Hung-chou 洪州
huo-jan hsaio-wu 豁然曉悟
i-chen-ling-hsing 一眞靈性
i-hsin 一心
i-nien hsiang-ying 一念相應
i wu hsiu hsing 依悟修行
jan ching yüan-ch'i chih hsiang 染淨緣起之相
jan-yüan-ch'i 染緣起
Ju-lai hsing-hsien ching 如來興顯經
Ju-lai-tsang ching 如來藏經
k'ai-fa 開發
ken-pen wu-ming 根本無明
ken-shen 根身
Kuan-ting 灌頂
Kuei-feng Tsung-mi 圭峯宗密
k'ung 空
li-nien 離念
liu ts'u-hsiang 六麤相
Lüeh-shu ch'ao 略疏鈔
mi chi lei-chieh 迷即累劫
mi wu yu ch'ih chi 迷悟有遲疾
ming 明
mo 末
Mo-ho chih-kuan 摩訶止觀
neng-chien 能見
ni 逆
nien-ch'i 念起
ning-jan 凝然
Pao-t'ang 保唐
p'an-chiao 判教
pen 本
pen-chüeh 本覺
pen-mo 本末
P'ei Hsiu shih-i wen 裴休拾遺門
pien ch'eng cheng-chüeh 便成正覺
Pŏpchip pyŏrhaeng nok chŏryo pyŏngip sagi 法集別行錄節要並入私記
pu-chüeh 不覺
pu-i pu-i 不一不異
pu-kung wu-ming 不共無明
pu-pien 不變
san hsi-hsiang 三細相
se-tzu-tsai 色自在
she 攝
She ta-sheng lun 攝大乘論
Shen-hsiu 神秀
Shen-hui 神會
sheng 聖
sheng-mieh teng fa pu-kuan chen-ju 生滅等法不關眞如
shih-chüeh 始覺
shou 收
shou-pao 受報
shun 順
sui-yüan 隨緣
sui-yüan ying-yung 隨緣應用

sun chih yu sun 損之又損
Ta-sheng ch'i-hsin lun 大乘起信論
tan-tao chih-ju 單刀直入
tao 道
t'i 體
t'i-yung 體用
T'ien-t'ai 天臺
tsao-yeh 造業
tu-hsing wu-ming 獨行無明
tu-t'ou wu-ming 獨頭無明
tun 頓
tun-chiao 頓教
tun-chien fo-hsing 頓見佛性
tun-hsiu chien-wu 頓修漸悟
tun-wu 頓悟
tun-wu chien fo-hsing 頓悟見佛性
tun-wu chien-hsiu 頓悟漸修
tun-wu tun-hsiu 頓悟頓修
t'ung 通
tzu-hsing pen-yung 自性本用
Wan-shan t'ung-kuei chi 萬善同歸集
wang 妄
wang-nien pen wu 妄念本無
wo-chih 我執
wo-k'ung 我空
wu chi hsü-yü 悟即須臾
wu-ming yeh 無明業
wu-nien 無念
wu-shih ken-pen 無始根本
yeh 業
yeh-hsi-ku 業繫苦
Yen-shou 延壽
yung 用
Yüan-chüeh ching 圓覺經
Yüan-chüeh ching ta-shu ch'ao 圓覺經大疏鈔
yüan-ch'i 緣起
Yüan-jen lun 原人論
yün-hsin 運心

The "Short-cut" Approach of *K'an-hua* Meditation: The Evolution of a Practical Subitism in Chinese Ch'an Buddhism

Robert E. Buswell, Jr.

In exploring the ramifications of the sudden-gradual debate in Chinese culture, we find in the evolution of the Ch'an school a prototypical example of how these concepts framed indigenous religious dialogue. The preceding chapters in this volume have shown that the imputed tension in the dichotomy between "sudden" *(tun)* and "gradual" *(chien)* styles of practice and rhetoric was used by the Ch'an school in part to forge an autonomous sectarian identity for itself. I propose in this chapter to focus on one aspect of this process of self-definition: the development of distinctive techniques of meditation unique to Ch'an. Ch'an's presumption of contemplative expertise—as the adoption of the name "Meditation" *(ch'an, dhyāna)* for the school implies—compelled it to create forms of meditation that it could claim exclusively as its own, by breaking away from the practices common to the earlier Sino-Indian Buddhist schools.[1] It accomplished this by condemning earlier Sino-Indian techniques as gradual while claiming that Ch'an taught more direct approaches to meditation. Along with its attention to Buddhist praxis, Ch'an also experimented with new types of religious language, demonstrating at the conceptual level the autonomy of Ch'an from the rest of the Buddhist tradition. Ch'an eventually abandoned the complex descriptive terminology of Sino-Indian Buddhism in favor of a terse rhetoric that it considered to be proleptic and transformative.[2] These new modes of expression were in turn applied to Ch'an teaching as well, resulting in radical pedagogical styles unknown to rival schools of Buddhism. Through this two-pronged evolution in both praxis and rhetoric, Ch'an during the Sung dynasty (960–1279) was able to justify its own paradigmatic vision of itself as, first, an independent transmission of Buddhism separate from the doctrinal teachings *(chiao-wai pieh-ch'uan / pu-li wen-tzu)* and, second, as an abrupt approach to spiritual attainment that involved nothing more than the direct vision of the enlightened nature of the human mind *(chih-chih jen-hsin / chien-hsing ch'eng-fo).*[3]

These two currents of change merged in the Hung-chou school of Ma-tsu Tao-i (709–788) and its collateral Lin-chi line, founded by the eponymous Lin-chi I-hsüan (d. 866). John McRae has explored in this volume the polemical uses of the term "sudden" in the school of Ho-tse, as promulgated by Shen-hui (684–758). The rhetorical purity McRae sees as one of the foci of Shen-hui's teachings was further elaborated by his contemporaries in the Hung-chou school. There, more illocutionary forms of discourse became not merely a rhetorical device but also a unique pedagogical technique: that of "encounter dialogue" *(chi-yüan wen-ta).*[4] The Hung-chou school attempted to use this new style of religious repartee as a means of catalyzing enlightenment in its students. The wider implications of this rhetoric and pedagogy were subsequently explored by later teachers in the Lin-chi line, who attempted to reconcile them with Ch'an praxis as well. This attempt led to the development of a "sudden" style of meditation: that of *kung-an* (public case) or *hua-t'ou* (critical phrase) investigation.[5] Exemplifying the Lin-chi approach to practice, this meditative technique was called *k'an-hua* Ch'an (Ch'an of observing the [critical] phrase) by Ta-hui Tsung-kao (1089–1163), its most prominent Sung dynasty advocate.[6] With no direct analogue in the extensive Indian meditative repertoire,[7] *k'an-hua* Ch'an is a uniquely sinitic form of meditation adapted to indigenous sensibilities regarding religious praxis.

Modern scholars, with some support from within the Ch'an tradition itself, have often asserted that the evolution of the *kung-an* technique was the product of an "internal crisis" in Sung dynasty Ch'an, brought about by the degeneration of the tradition after the demise of the charismatic Ch'an masters of the T'ang.[8] This interpretation masks, however, implicit trends in soteriology and discourse within the Ch'an school which may themselves have been sufficient to prompt the emergence of this new system of practice. Rather than treating *kung-an* and *hua-t'ou* as the products of a process of degeneration, I shall show in this chapter that they may more fruitfully be viewed as the products of an internal dynamic within Ch'an that began in the T'ang and climaxed in the Sung. *K'an-hua* Ch'an may thus be seen as the culmination of a long process of evolution in Ch'an whereby its subitist rhetoric came to be extended to pedagogy and finally to practice.

My focus here on internal developments in Ch'an is by no means meant to imply that there were not secular influences that may have contributed to this evolution. No one after all, not even the cloistered monk, is hermetically sealed off from his age. The transition to the urbanized, modern society of the Sung provided the social context within which radical changes in religion and philosophy could occur. Ch'an adepts during this period are well known to have had close connections with the Sung literocrats *(shih-ta-fu)*, who were then at the apex of their political and economic power, and the tack these masters took in presenting Ch'an to them was certainly affected by the strong concerns of that elite class for scholarly erudition, social propriety, and benevolent government.[9] The distinguished teachers of this period, like Yüan-wu K'o-ch'in (1063–1135) and his disciple Ta-hui, were especially concerned with cultivating contacts within the *shih-ta-fu* class and did much to clarify the common interests of the literocrats and Buddhist clergy.[10] The scholar-officials' elevation of classical learning and intellectual ability over family wealth and the privileges of aristocratic birth opened up the sources of secular power to the common people to a degree never before seen in China.[11] Indeed, it is intriguing to speculate to what extent this social mobility of the Sung may have prompted a comparable spiritual mobility within Buddhism, in which its elite practices focusing on insight were made accessible to all people, lay and ordained alike.

In spite of the intrinsic interest of these issues, however, I believe it will be instructive to concentrate on developments within Ch'an that led to more direct approaches to meditation. Accordingly, this chapter first surveys some of the major features common to the sinitic Buddhist tradition as a whole, as a background for the consideration of the distinctive Ch'an contributions to doctrine and praxis. It then explores the response to, and ultimately the rejection of, Indian meditative techniques that took place during the formative and transitional periods of Ch'an. In that context I examine the conceptual problems Ch'an Buddhists found in the Indian concepts of samādhi (concentration) and prajñā (wisdom) that may have contributed to their awareness that a new, truly Chinese system of contemplative practice was needed. I take the cultivation of no-thought *(wu-nien)* to be a specific example of such a Chinese form of practice. Because the intellectual context within which the method of no-thought evolved was itself superseded by new developments in Ch'an rhetoric and pedagogy, I subsequently focus on later experiments in praxis undertaken during the middle Ch'an period that eventually evolved into the *kung-an* form. Finally, to illustrate how the "terse" rhetoric of the Hung-chou–Lin-chi line was reified into the "short-cut" meditation of *k'an-hua* Ch'an, I undertake an in-depth examination of the ways in which *kung-an* were employed in Sung dynasty Lin-chi practice.

The Sinification of Buddhist Doctrine and Meditation

The Buddhism that evolved in China, and thence the rest of East Asia, was a complex amalgam of Indian and Central Asian Buddhism along with indigenous religious, philosophical, and cultural traits. The process by which Buddhism adapted, and was adapted, to China is a fascinating tale of religious acculturation with few parallels in world history. Given the immense gulf separating India and China geographically, culturally, and linguistically, it took several centuries and all the creative imagination the Chinese could muster before they made the alien Buddhist religion their own. The assimilation of Buddhism was all the more difficult because of the fragmented state of the religion that entered China. Buddhism was not a monolithic tradition imported wholesale from what the Chinese termed the "Outer Regions" (Wai-yü, viz., India and Central Asia). By the first century A.D., when the transmission began in earnest, the religion had already split into a number of competing schools of dogma and practice, each ostensibly Buddhist yet often diametrically opposed to one another in premises and approaches. As representatives and texts of these different schools trickled into China, the Chinese were hard put to reconcile their disparate teachings. This problem compelled the Chinese from the Six Dynasties period (early third–latter sixth centuries) onward to attempt to develop interpretive taxonomies *(p'an-chiao)* that could incorporate these varied doctrines into more comprehensive systems of thought. This process led to the creation of sinified schools such as the Nieh-p'an (Nirvāṇa) and, later during the Sui and T'ang periods, the T'ien-t'ai and Hua-yen. This hermeneutical reworking of Buddhism was not just a reaction to the religion's foreignness, and the Chinese schools that developed through this process were not mere recastings of originally Indian teachings. Rather, they were attempts to fashion new forms of Buddhist theology, without precise Indian antecedents, that would be more directly relevant to Chinese religious concerns and cultural presumptions.

These new sinitic theologies accepted the this-worldly orientation of Chinese culture for the most part and sought ways to allow the adherent to practice his or her religion while fulfilling expected social roles and filial duties. To accommodate the lay practice of Buddhism, many of these new schools adopted a relatively minor strain of Mahāyāna thought that never developed into a formal school in India—that of tathāgatagarbha (*ju-lai-tsang* 'embryo of Buddhahood')—as the basis of their doctrinal frameworks.[12] Tathāgatagarbha doctrine conceived of all sentient beings as being already Buddhas and thus inherently enlightened.[13] With this conception of enlightenment, the Chinese in turn envisaged spiritual beatitude not as a state of otherworldly transcendence—either apophatically as the cessation of conditioned things or kataphatically as the direct experience of the bliss of nirvāṇa—but as the recognition of the individual's multivalent interconnection to all things in the world. This state is what the Hua-yen school termed the "unimpeded interpenetration between all phenomena" *(shih-shih wu-ai).*

Since enlightenment was in this wise made coextensive with mundane life, it was not considered necessary for the adept to complete a lengthy spiritual regimen in order to achieve Buddhahood. Rather, Buddhahood could occur in the present life without requiring the adept to abandon his place in the world. This interpretation of Buddhist soteriology is the notion of "sudden enlightenment" *(tun-wu)* to which most of the Chinese schools of Mahāyāna subscribe, albeit to varying degrees.[14] Sudden enlightenment implies, of course, that there is a more direct means to awakening than the complex, intricate series of steps taught in Indian Buddhist texts. But most importantly for Chinese Buddhists, it also made the *summum bonum* of Buddhism readily accessible to ordinary people living active, engaged lives in the world, and not just to religious specialists ensconced in isolated mountain monasteries.

This accommodation is commonly seen in Chinese religious writings directed at a lay audience, the most prominent examples being Pure Land and, as we shall see later in this chapter, Ch'an texts. The openness of Chinese Buddhism to the prospect of laypeople achieving enlightenment differs strikingly from the Indian traditions. The Theravāda school current today in South and Southeast Asia, for example, generally does not regard enlightenment as a viable goal for most of the laity, and lay practice is commonly reduced to merit-making. Even ordination as a monk becomes not simply a means to personal liberation, but a way of producing and transferring merit to one's ancestors and family.[15] The openness of Chinese Buddhists to the prospects of a liberating lay vocation was not prompted solely by altruistic motives, however. As an alien religion, Buddhism suffered periodic attacks from nativistic elements within the Chinese governing bureaucracy, and the charge was frequently made that Buddhism's support of monasticism was destroying the family system that was the basis of the Chinese way of life. In asserting that enlightenment was available to people in all walks of life, Chinese Buddhism not only rebutted such charges but also helped to assure itself the continued interest and support of secular society.

But if this Chinese ideal of a sudden, immediately available approach to enlightenment was to become accessible in practice, the contemplative techniques that catalyzed awakening had also to be sinified. Buddhism has traditionally prided itself on its pragmatic outlook toward religion, in which its doctrinal positions are presumed to derive from, and be supported by, explicit meditative programs. Since it is impossible to separate the ontology of Buddhism from its soteriological schemata and meditative practices, it was inevitable that Buddhist meditation would also come within the purview of the sinification that was occurring on the doctrinal front. The earliest interest of the Chinese in Buddhism in fact derived from the spiritual technologies brought by early Buddhist missionaries. In the same way that modern Westerners often view Buddhism as a type of self-help psychology, second-century Taoists saw in Buddhism a form of internal alchemy. Taoist thaumaturges were always on the lookout for new methods of prolonging the lifespan *(ch'ang-shou),* and Buddhist meditative methods such as contemplation of the breath *(ānāpānasmṛti)* seemed to share many affinities with their own practices. Only a few decades were necessary before the Chinese learned that the real purpose of Buddhist meditation was not physical immortality but spiritual liberation. But this initial interest in Buddhist meditation gave the Buddhists a foothold in China, based on which they could begin to hone their message and thence disseminate their religion throughout East Asia.[16]

Just as early Chinese Buddhists had first to understand, and then adapt, Indian Buddhist doctrine to their own ways of thinking, so too was it with Indian contemplative techniques. This sinification of meditation began in the T'ien-t'ai school,[17] as Neal Donner has shown in his chapter in this volume. But it was the Ch'an school that undertook the most protracted experiments at adapting Indian meditative practices to China. These attempts may even have begun at the very inception of the tradition. For example, Tao-hsin (580–651), the putative fourth patriarch of Ch'an, is said to have incorporated Taoist *shou-i* (guarding the one) practices in his own descriptions of meditation.[18] In the eighth century, such experiments began to take place in earnest, coinciding with the emergence of distinct Ch'an schools with self-conscious (if not self-created) identities. These intrasectarian controversies within the Ch'an movement are represented by the archetypal debate between two rival soteriologies: the "gradual" approach of the Northern school of Shen-hsiu (606?–706) versus the "sudden" approach of the Southern school of Hui-neng (638–713). While it is now common knowledge that this controversy cannot be considered historical fact, the record of the debate nevertheless provides a valuable retrospective paradigm of Ch'an's overriding concern with excising any trace of "gradualism" from its teachings. The two eighth-century schools that traced their lineage to the Southern branch of Ch'an both advocated "sudden" enlightenment. These were the Ho-tse school of Shen-hui, who claimed to be the successor to Hui-neng, and the Hung-chou school of Ma-tsu

Tao-i, who was allegedly connected to Hui-neng through the obscure Nan-yüeh Huai-jang (677–744). Since the Hung-chou line was the only one of the earlier schools of Ch'an to survive the Hui-ch'ang persecution in 845, the majority of the mature Ch'an houses trace their origins back to Hui-neng through the Hung-chou school. Hence, classical Ch'an in all its guises claims to adhere to a "sudden" approach. Hung-chou eventually matured into the Lin-chi school, which traces its lineage from Ma-tsu Tao-i to Po-chang Huai-hai (720–814), Huang-po Hsi-yün (d. ca. 850), and finally Lin-chi I-hsüan.

The reader will note here that this periodization of Ch'an history differs somewhat from the bipartite division between early and classical Ch'an which John McRae proposes earlier in this volume. McRae has made a convincing case in his pioneering works on the Northern school for equating early Ch'an with that school, representing the formative stage of Ch'an,[19] but I suggest that we further distinguish a middle Ch'an period, ranging from the middle eighth to the middle ninth centuries, preceding the emergence of classical Ch'an. Many of the Ch'an schools that flourished during this period were reacting to the Northern school's formulations of doctrine and practice, and this transitional age is noted as a time of experimentation with new, even radical, interpretations of Buddhist praxis. Tsung-mi (780–841), the prolific chronicler of this period, mentions some seven major schools of Ch'an in his time, which flourished in different areas of China. These include the schools of Hung-chou, Ho-tse, Niu-t'ou, and the Korean Musang's (684–762) Szechwan line, which was the earliest Ch'an tradition known to the Tibetans.[20] Given the proliferation of Ch'an schools during this period, as well as the pronounced regional character of those schools, to intimate that post-Northern school Ch'an refers solely to the Hung-chou line oversimplifies the vibrancy of Ch'an during the eighth century. Of course, identifying such a transitional period is not to deny that Hung-chou was the most important of these middle Ch'an schools in the later evolution of the tradition. Nor does it reject the notion that some of the distinguishing characteristics of Hung-chou, such as encounter dialogue, came to typify mainstream Ch'an during the Sung dynasty. But it was not until such repartee was codified into the *kung-an* form that it can be termed "classical"; in Ma-tsu's time it was still one of a number of variant forms of Ch'an, all of which had a chance at predominance. Overlooking the diversity present during this transitional period obscures the many tentative steps that had to be taken before Ch'an became a mass religious movement during the Sung.

Classical Ch'an in the periodization I propose, then, would refer to the systematizations of Ch'an lineage, doctrine, practice, and institutions that were completed during the Sung, and that descended, in large part, from the Hung-chou school of middle Ch'an. Specifically, classical Ch'an refers to the Five Houses (Wu Chia) of the mature Ch'an tradition: Lin-chi, Ts'ao-tung, Yün-men, Fa-yen, and Kuei-yang. Since these schools evolved over a protracted period of time, there can be no precise terminus a quo for this period; but the late T'ang–Five Dynasties interregnum provides a convenient working date (mid-ninth to early tenth centuries). It should also be noted that the Sung dynasty is known primarily as a period of neoclassicism in Confucianism, as defined by its several retrospective systematizations of that religious tradition, Chu Hsi's (1130–1200) being the most prominent example. It thus seems appropriate to consider the systematizations of Ch'an that took place during the Sung as representing the classical period of Ch'an Buddhism as well.

The Challenge of Indian Meditative Models: Samādhi and Prajñā

From early in its history, and particularly during the middle Ch'an period, Ch'an is distinguished by experimentation with meditative praxis. The representative text of this period, the *Platform Sūtra of the Sixth Patriarch (Liu-tsu t'an ching),* provides a striking example of Ch'an reactions to Indian contemplative techniques. One of its most prominent sections seeks to reinterpret the prototypic Indian meditative concepts of samādhi (concentration) and prajñā (wisdom) in a manner more amenable to the Chinese penchant for subitism. Indian soteriological tracts typically portray samādhi and prajñā as specific constituents of a gradual regimen of spiritual maturation leading from morality *(śīla)* to concentration, and finally to wisdom.[21] Given the nonsequential approach of Ch'an, however, it is obvious that a major reconceptualization of samādhi and prajñā was in order. Ch'an accomplished this by interpreting samādhi and prajñā as being, not stages in practice, but states of mind present in all moments of thought. This redefinition allowed Ch'an adherents to claim, as in fact the *Platform Sūtra* did claim, that "the mind-ground that is without distraction is the samādhi of the self-nature. The mind-ground that is without ignorance is the prajñā of the self-nature."[22] It could then be explained that samādhi and prajñā, as states of mind, are not themselves different varieties of cultivation but are in fact both operative at all levels of practice. As Tsung-mi notes:

> From the initial activation of the *bodhicitta* until the attainment of Buddhahood, there is only calmness [i.e., samādhi] and only awareness [i.e., prajñā], unchanging and uninterrupted. It is only according to the respective position [on the bodhisattva path] that their designations and attri-

> butes are somewhat different. At the moment of [understanding] awakening [i.e., the first level of the ten faiths] they are called noumenon and wisdom. (Noumenon is calmness; wisdom is awareness.) When one first activates the *bodhicitta* and begins to cultivate [i.e., the first stage of the ten *vihāras*], they are called *śamatha-vipaśyanā.* (*Śamatha* brings external conditioning to rest and hence conforms with calmness; *vipaśyanā* illuminates nature and characteristics and hence corresponds to awareness.) When the practice continues naturally in all situations [i.e., from the seventh *bhūmi* onwards], they are called samādhi and prajñā. (Because of its effect of stopping all conditioning and fusing the mind in concentration, samādhi is calm and immutable. Because of its effect of illuminating and giving rise to wisdom, prajñā is aware and undiscriminative.) When the defilements are completely extinguished and the consummation of meritorious practices has led to the attainment of Buddhahood [viz., *buddhabhūmi*], they are called bodhi and nirvāṇa. ("Bodhi" is a Sanskrit word meaning enlightenment; it is awareness. "Nirvāṇa" is a Sanskrit word meaning calm-extinction; it is calmness.) Hence it should be known that from the time of the first activation of the *bodhicitta* until the final achievement of Buddhahood, there is only calmness and only awareness.[23]

Tsung-mi elsewhere goes so far as to claim that samādhi is actually an abbreviation for both samādhi and prajñā;[24] thus Ch'an (viz., "Meditation" or samādhi) was by implication the epitome of all Buddhist meditative culture. This collapsing of samādhi and prajñā into Ch'an suggests that the movement was seeking to define a single, overarching experience in which the entire Buddhist path *(mārga)* would be subsumed.

The nondual nature of samādhi and prajñā in Ch'an writings is explained in an influential section of the *Platform Sūtra.* There the awakening to the nature of the mind is prajñā while the cultivation of that awakening is samādhi.

> Good and learned friends. My approach to dharma has samādhi and prajñā as its foundation. It is absolutely essential that you do not deludedly claim that prajñā and samādhi are different. Samādhi and prajñā are one in their essence, not two. It is precisely samādhi that is the essence of prajñā; it is precisely prajñā that is the functioning of samādhi. Whenever there is prajñā, samādhi is present within that prajñā; whenever there is samādhi, prajñā is present within that samādhi. Good and learned friends. The meaning here is just that samādhi and prajñā are equivalent. Those people who are cultivating the path, pay heed: do not say that the arising of prajñā is preceded by samādhi or that samādhi and prajñā are each distinct. For one who entertains this [deluded] view, dharmas are characterized by duality.[25]

As attractive as this interpretation of samādhi and prajñā may have been, the quandary in which it left Ch'an was in many ways worse than the solution it purported to offer. The Ch'an emphasis on direct insight left little place for the progressive development of samādhi and prajñā. Ultimately, what need was there to retain such terms if samādhi and prajñā were collapsed into one another, or were said always to be present?

The conceptual baggage that inevitably accompanied the use of these Indian concepts was so overwhelming that Ch'an eventually discarded both of them. Samādhi and prajñā were condemned as having only provisional value for dullards who were as yet unprepared spiritually for the more sophisticated techniques of Ch'an. Approximately one generation after the redaction of the *Platform Sūtra* a Korean Sŏn (Ch'an) monk named Muyŏm (799–888), who studied in China with Ma-ku Pao-ch'e (b. 720?) in the Hung-chou lineage, made one of the more evocative denunciations of samādhi and prajñā in his *Musŏlt'o-ron* (Treatise on the Tongueless Realm):

> Furthermore, as far as the Buddha-realm [i.e., the "tongued" teachings of the doctrinal schools] is concerned, wearing the clothes of samādhi and prajñā one first enters the cave of glowing lamps; then, removing the clothes of samādhi and prajñā, one stands in the arcane land. Therefore [the scholastic teachings] still have traces. The realm of the patriarchs [of Ch'an, i.e., the "tongueless realm"] is originally free from liberation or bondage. There one does not wear even one strand of thread. Hence it is vastly different from the Buddha-realm.[26]

Note the provocative imagery Muyŏm adopts here, so unlike that used by exegetes in other sinitic Buddhist schools. "Wearing and removing clothes" refers to the various techniques taken up and put aside by the Buddhist practitioner in the course of his training. "Glowing lamps" suggests the effulgence of mind that is realized through following those techniques.[27] "Arcane land" calls to mind the ineffable state of liberation, so mysterious that it transcends all possible description. But Muyŏm leaves no doubt as to the provisional nature of samādhi and prajñā: the doctrinal teachings demand that one first put on something that must later be removed. To the Ch'an adept, committed to a sudden approach to liberation, the obvious response is: if something must eventually come off anyway, then why put it on in the first place?

Because Ch'an did not rely on any provisional characterizations of practice, Muyŏm conceived of his school as a "tongueless" approach to Buddhism. It was far superior to the "tongued" theologies—and their quintessential meditative concepts, samādhi and prajñā—precisely because it provided a way for the adherent to reach enlightenment without going through an unnecessary costume change. The Sung Fa-yen theorist Yung-ming Yen-shou (904–975) in his magnum opus, *Tsung-ching lu* (Mirror of the Source Record), describes the provisional nature of samādhi and prajñā and how the Ch'an approach transcends them both.

> Samādhi is the essence of one's own mind. Prajñā is the function of one's own mind. . . . The two approaches of samādhi and prajñā are the essentials of practice; they are the primary teachings of the Buddhas and patriarchs and are explicated in all the sūtras and śāstras. Now, according to the teachings of the patriarchs, there is one further approach that is the most concise of all. It is no-mind. . . .[28]

Toward a Distinctively Ch'an Style of Meditation: No-thought Practice

With the exception of later Ch'an syncretists like Yen-shou in China and Chinul (1158–1210) in Korea, Ch'an theorists abandoned the terms samādhi and prajñā in their descriptions of meditation practice, advocating instead the practice of no-thought *(wu-nien)* or no-mind *(wu-hsin).* As Yen-shou suggests, no-thought was considered "the most concise [approach] of all" because it involved no conceptual mediation. According to Tung-shan Liang-chieh (807–869), "No-mind conforms with the [supramundane] path."[29]

The fact that no-thought had no explicit meditative connotations within the Indian tradition may at least partially explain why Ch'an explored its potential as a more direct vehicle of soteriological development. In the *Platform Sūtra,* which once again provides the *locus classicus* for this new description of meditation, the discussion of samādhi and prajñā is followed by a treatment of no-thought. The *Platform Sūtra* defines the term quite simply: "No-thought is not to think even when involved in thought."[30] As laconic as this description may be, it intimates something vital about the term's significance. For Ch'an, thought (or "mentation") is not the issue but rather the attachment to thought—the mistaken belief that the concept of a thing is the thing itself. Conceptualization *(hsi-lun, prapañca)* is a form of projection, of imputing one's own vision of the world to the world itself, and assuming that to be the sole reality. Concepts are convenient for ordering the overwhelming chaos of sensory impression and for allowing reasoned response to those perceptions. But this very convenience prompts the person to view the world through arbitrary stereotypes—treating everything always in terms of what it means *to him,* rather than what it actually is.[31] But suppose a person were able to enjoy the benefits of using concepts while keeping his mind free from the problems they create. That is, if one could conceptualize while remaining in a state of nonconceptualization, wouldn't one then be free of the pathological effects of concepts?

Such a state is not unknown in Indian materials, which mention the peculiar mental condition of the enlightened person who remains unconscious but can still think.[32] But it is Ch'an, as exemplified in the *Platform Sūtra,* that made this goal its *raison d'être.*

> Thought after thought is nonabiding. Previous thoughts, present thoughts, and future thoughts continue along, thought after thought, without being cut off or interrupted. If one thought is cut off or interrupted, the dharma body is then separate from the physical body. During each and every moment of thought, one should not abide in any dharma. If even one thought abides, then each and every thought will abide; this is termed "bondage." But if successive thoughts do not abide in any dharma, this then is "freedom from bondage."[33]

The principal point of the section in which this passage appears is that the mind should not dwell on sensory experiences and become entranced thereby—"abide" in them. The Tun-huang reading may be construed as suggesting that thought also is not to be forcibly repressed ("cut off") through concentration techniques. This clause would then be an implicit criticism of the Northern school's presumed style of practice, which was attacked in an earlier portion of the *Platform Sūtra* as clinging to quietude rather than freeing the mind for engaged action:

> The deluded man . . . sits without moving and casts aside delusion without activating his mind. . . . This kind of practice is the same as insentience and the cause of an obstruction of the Tao. Tao must be something that circulates freely; why should it be impeded?[34]

No-thought then is nondualistic, not distinguishing between "wrong" thoughts, which should be suppressed, and "right" thoughts, which should be encouraged. It instead allows the mind to flow freely, without any of the obstructions or value judgments that would impede the Tao. Since no-thought practice can thus be allowed to develop spontaneously, it provided a critical stage in the evolution of a sudden style of cultivation in Ch'an.

No-thought is achieved when the perceptions of sense-objects no longer reverberate in the chambers of one's mind,[35] becoming in the process reified into concepts:

> To be untainted in regard to all sense-objects is called no-thought. If you constantly keep your own thoughts free from all sense-objects, then the mind will not arise concerning those sense-objects. If you don't cogitate *(ssu)* on the hundred things, thoughts *(nien)* will be exhausted and cast aside. [But if] one thought is cut off, then you will die and be reborn in another realm.[36]

The *Platform Sūtra* suggests here that tainted thoughts (thoughts that arise as a result of sensory impingement) should be allowed to exhaust themselves through a natural process of disengagement, keeping one's thoughts free from sensual attachments ("don't cogitate on the hundred things"). If instead one contrives to eradicate thought, compelling the mind to be free from mentation, one will continue to be subject to transmigration ("you will die and be reborn in another realm").

Rather than leading to aphasia, then, no-thought restores the natural clarity of mind; and, because this clarity allows the adept to see through the chimeric display of concepts, he is free to use them without attachment. This sense that effort is ultimately an obstruction to liberation is a common theme in literature propounding subitist positions, as Luis Gómez has shown in his chapter in this volume. We can thus see in the middle Ch'an emphasis on no-thought a tentative step toward a practical subitism, one that would not require the student to complete a series of steps that eventually culminate in enlightenment.

For the transitional Ho-tse school of middle Ch'an, it was the capacity of no-thought to foster unattached action that made it the principal constituent of that school's description of cultivation. In Tsung-mi's account of the Ho-tse interpretation of the "sudden" teaching—in sharp contrast to the Hung-chou view, as we shall see below—the student is encouraged toward an initial sudden understanding-awakening *(chieh-wu)* to the truth of his own innate Buddhahood. However, just knowing that he is a Buddha does not necessarily mean that he will act like one, so the student subsequently continues to develop all varieties of bodhisattva practices, maturing his comprehension, until finally complete enlightenment is achieved. But because the student remains in a state of no-thought after his initial awakening, he has neither attachment to those bodhisattva practices nor any "gradualistic" idea that they are the proximate causes of his eventual realization of complete enlightenment. It is therefore thanks to no-thought that he can both cultivate all wholesome actions and yet remain completely unattached to that cultivation, as well as eradicate all defilements without conceiving that there is anything to be eradicated. As Tsung-mi says, following Shen-hui:

> Even though we cultivate the manifold supplementary practices [of the bodhisattva], they all have no-thought as their core. If we can only maintain no-thought, liking and disliking will naturally fade away, and compassion and wisdom will naturally grow in brightness; wrong actions will naturally come to an end, and meritorious deeds will naturally be augmented. . . . It will be called the cultivation whereby nothing is cultivated. . . . A calm radiance will appear and our responsiveness will be unlimited. This is called Buddhahood.[37]

This approach of sudden awakening-gradual cultivation was to be severely criticized by later teachers in the Hung-chou and, later, the Lin-chi lineages, who followed a different interpretation of the "sudden" teachings. But it became extremely influential in the Sŏn school of mid-Koryŏ dynasty (937–1392) Buddhism in Korea, which attempted to combine *k'an-hua* Ch'an with this long-outmoded soteriological schema.[38]

No-thought retained an extremely important place in Ch'an soteriology long after it was superseded by the meditative techniques of the classical Ch'an schools, which we shall turn to at the conclusion of this essay. The importance of no-thought derives from its recognition as the "access to realization" *(cheng-ju),* catalyzing the direct confirmation of the student's innate Buddhahood.[39] Since realization-awakening *(cheng-wu)* meant the experience of the unconditioned *(wu-wei, asaṃskṛta),* it perforce was nonconceptual. A parallel with the Ch'an exegesis of samādhi and prajñā can be discerned here. Like samādhi and prajñā, no-thought was regarded as both the consummation of all other types of practice and the catalyst of the final moment of realization—it too remained valid at all levels of practice. But the simultaneous evolution of a distinctive style of Ch'an rhetoric during the middle Ch'an period was ultimately to lead to the creation of a new type of Ch'an meditation that would supersede even no-thought.

The Distinctive Rhetoric and Pedagogy of Ch'an

Because of the intimate connection between doctrine and practice in Buddhism, it was perhaps inevitable that Ch'an's response to Indian meditative models would be accompanied by new ways of referring to the doctrinal concepts of the Sino-Indian tradition. As we have already seen, one of the principal concerns of the sinitic tradition of Buddhism was the idea that secular life could be the ground of enlightenment. Ch'an sought both to draw out the practical implications of this idea and to make it its own by framing it conceptually in a way unique to Ch'an. Within the Ch'an tradition, the Hung-chou–Lin-chi lineage took the most influential strides toward, first, developing a new rhetoric with which to express sinitic Buddhist concepts, and second, creating unique styles of meditation that would correspond to that rhetoric.

It was the special place of Ch'an, as we have seen, to envision itself as separate from the rest of the Buddhist tradition, a school that was as much "Chinese" as it was "Buddhist." One way to assert that independence was to express Buddhist doctrines in a new way, using language more in keeping with the Chinese preference for concrete, laconic descriptions over the abstract, periphrastic formulations more common in Indian philosophy.[40]

> A monk asked Yün-men Wen-yen (d. 949), "What is the Buddha?" Yün-men replied, "A dried shit-stick."[41]

This mode of philosophical discourse, regarded as indigenous to China, may be said to have been licensed by such examples as the renowned description of the Tao in the *Chuang-tzu.*

> Master Tung-kuo asked Chuang Tzu, "This thing called the Way—where does it exist?" Chuang Tzu said, "There's no place it doesn't exist." "Come," said Master Tung-kuo, "you must be more specific!" "It's in the ant." "As low a thing as that?" "It's in the panic grass." "But that's lower still!" "It's in the tiles and shards." "How can it be so low?" "It's in the piss and shit!" Master Tung-kuo made no reply.[42]

A simple correlation of the distinctive terms developed within Ch'an to refer to Sino-Indian concepts illustrates the radical change in vocabulary and rhetoric that took place during the middle Ch'an period. Chinul, a Korean Sŏn master with strong sympathies for the *k'an-hua* approach of Ta-hui, lists a number of terms from both the doctrinal and Ch'an traditions that he construes as being synonymous with "true mind" *(chen-hsin).* The doctrinal terms, deriving ultimately from Indian Buddhist texts, are all abstract and conceptual: tathāgatagarbha (embryo of Buddhahood), dharmadhātu (realm of reality), buddhadhātu (Buddha-nature), nirvāṇa, tathatā (suchness). Comparable Ch'an terms, Chinul says, would be "moon of the mind," "inextinguishable lamp," "bottomless bowl," "sword that splits a wind-blown hair," and "the old master."[43] The contrast is striking, readily illustrating the Ch'an penchant for substantive metaphor.

This characterization of Ch'an discourse stands in contrast to a suggestion Luis Gómez makes in passing in his chapter above: that Ch'an's unique rhetorical styles were not really doctrinal statements but rather special illocutionary uses of language. Chinul's analysis, however, suggests that the metaphors appearing in Ch'an texts refer to the same kinds of doctrinal ideas expressed more periphrastically in the scholastic literature. The only difference is that Ch'an sought to employ locutionary styles more in keeping with the ineffable quality of the state of enlightenment. Later Ch'an syncretists like Tsung-mi, Yen-shou, and Chinul even go so far as to attempt to link expressions of Ch'an enlightenment experiences with specific stages in the complex mārga mappings of Buddhist scholastic texts. Although such correlations were vehemently criticized by many Ch'an masters, their attacks seem to be not so much a denial of the truth of those correlations as an expression of concern that such interpretations of Ch'an rhetoric would themselves become a source of intellectual fascination and clinging.

Gómez goes on to suggest that even if Ch'an words are an advanced form of religious rhetoric, one would still have to concede that they are rather parsimonious in providing explicit practical instructions. Yet Ch'an texts frequently assert that it was precisely to avoid such instructions that Ch'an adopted its peculiar form of rhetoric. The only "practical" instruction for Ch'an was the direct experience of enlightenment; any other instruction would be a hindrance—an "impediment to the Tao" as the *Platform Sūtra* would have it. Hence, Ch'an words are intended to convey the experience and content of enlightenment; and if that experience is ineffable, then the language used to describe it must strive to be equally ineffable. Indeed, any other type of description would contradict the experience itself.

Thus the unique rhetoric developed by Ch'an is distinguished above all by its "terseness" *(sheng-lüeh).*[44] That is to say, the meaning of Ch'an discourse comes not from intelligibility or clarity of expression but from its utility in prompting what Tsung-mi called "mysterious penetration" *(hsüan-t'ung)*[45]—in other words, from its transformative quality. Over against the prolixity of Indian Buddhist texts and sinitic exegetical treatises, Ch'an claimed that its language offered a direct revelation of the nonconceptual state of enlightenment, an access that was otherwise unavailable in Chinese Buddhism. Ta-hui indicates the soteriological motive of Ch'an rhetoric—its power to catalyze an awakening—when he declares that "Ch'an discourse is coextensive with Ch'an practice."[46]

There are certainly grounds for questioning, however, whether Ch'an's criticism of abstract descriptions of truth does not equally apply to Ch'an rhetoric as well. Ch'an writings themselves provide evidence that encounter dialogue could as easily become a focus of attachment and conceptual reification as any expressions of the scholastic schools; in fact, the literature abounds in criticisms of students who ignorantly ape their masters' words and actions without understanding their significance. One of Tsung-mi's major criticisms of the Hung-chou approach is that its alleged "spontaneity" was often misinterpreted by ignorant students as advocating antinomianism.[47] Furthermore, it must be admitted that *any* description, no matter how "terse," is inadequate to describe something that is fundamentally indescribable. As we shall see in our discussion of the *k'an-hua* technique, this inherent frustration over the incapacity of language was used by the mature Ch'an school as a soteriological tool.

The distinctive rhetoric of Ch'an developed in tandem with a new pedagogical style, pioneered by Ma-tsu and Lin-chi. This nonconceptual, illocutionary style of teaching—by beating, shouting, or virtually any other kind of physical gesture, in order to rouse students from complacency and catalyze their enlightenment—is well illustrated in the story of Po-chang Huai-hai's enlightenment at, quite literally, the hands of Ma-tsu.

> [One day when Ma-tsu] was walking in attendance on Po-chang, a flock of wild geese flew off overhead. Ma-tsu asked Po-chang, "What is that?" Po-chang replied, "Wild geese, master." Ma-tsu: "Where did they go?" Po-chang: "They've flown away." Ma-tsu turned his head and, seizing Po-chang's nose, violently tweeked it, so that Po-chang cried out in pain. The master asked, "How could you say that the wild geese have flown away? They have been here from the very beginning." Through these words, Po-chang awakened.[48]

Ma-tsu was also not above using a swift kick at times on his students, as the following encounter with Hung-chou Shui-liao (d.u.) suggests.

> While they were out gathering rattan, Master Shui-liao asked Ma-tsu, "What is the real meaning of Bodhidharma's coming from the West?" Ma-tsu replied, "Come closer and I'll tell you." When Shui-liao was quite close, Ma-tsu kicked him in the chest, knocking him to the ground. In a daze, Shui-liao got up, clapping his hands and laughing loudly. Ma-tsu asked, "What insight did you have that has made you laugh?" Shui-liao said, "Hundreds of thousands of teachings and immeasurable sublime meanings are on the tip of one hair; today I have completely understood their source."[49]

Subsequent masters in Ma-tsu's lineage adopted this iconoclastic teaching style with a vengeance, expanding it in virtually every conceivable direction. Whenever students questioned Ma-tsu's immediate disciple, Shih-kung Hui-tsang (d.u.)—who had been a hunter before ordaining—about the dharma, he would take up his old bow and arrow and take aim right between their eyes. A seventh-generation successor, Chin-hua Chu-ti (d.u.), always raised one finger, while Hsin-chou Ta-ti (d.u.) would strike the ground.[50] Huang-po Hsi-yün is said to have beat his student Lin-chi to bring him to enlightenment,[51] and Lin-chi himself is best known for his use of a loud shout *(ho)* as a teaching device, of which he distinguished four different types.[52] The refinement, if that is the word, of this teaching style continued unabated, and in the records of Lin-chi and his disciples we find several encounters that seem almost parodies of Ch'an teaching methods; the following example is typical:

> The Master asked a monk, "Where do you come from?" The monk shouted. The Master saluted him and motioned him to sit down. The monk hesitated. The Master hit him.
>
> Seeing another monk coming, the Master raised his whisk. The monk bowed low. The Master hit him.
>
> Seeing still another monk coming, the Master again raised his whisk. The monk paid no attention. The Master hit him too.[53]

By now the Indian antecedents of Ch'an Buddhism have faded deeply, so thoroughly synthesized with Chinese modes of thought that they are difficult to distinguish any longer. Although Chinese doctrinal schools such as Hua-yen and T'ien-t'ai retained at least something of the distinctive Sino-Indian Buddhist vocabulary, even that has largely vanished in the Hung-chou–Lin-chi line of Ch'an, to be replaced by proleptic shouts, beatings, and farce.

Cultivation in the Hung-chou and Lin-chi Schools

But what kind of formal practice was actually advocated by the Hung-chou–Lin-chi line to accompany this innovative rhetoric and pedagogy? The "discourse records" *(yü-lu)* and "transmission of the lamp" anthologies *(teng-lu),* from which most of our material on early masters in this line derives, rarely include such concrete information. Both these genres of Ch'an literature, like the *kung-an* anthologies to which we shall soon turn, were not compiled until the Sung period, several centuries after the lives of the teachers they purport to describe. The anecdotal formats of "discourse records" and "lamp anthologies" were intended not so much to preserve information about the unique teachings of specific masters as instead to convey, respectively, the particular "house style" *(chia-feng)* of each of the Five Houses of classical Ch'an or the "collective experience" of the larger Ch'an tradition.[54] The historical difficulties surrounding these materials should not, however, obscure their value in detailing Sung Ch'an's retrospective perceptions of its own evolution; indeed, the testimony of these discourse records tells us a great deal about the concerns of their Sung authors, and the specific influences they perceived from their eminent T'ang predecessors.[55] However, any conclusions these accounts suggest concerning practices current during this transitional period of Ch'an are necessarily tentative and must await further study. Given the limitations of our material, let us examine what the discourse records of Ma-tsu and Lin-chi have to say about the approaches to practice of the Hung-chou and early Lin-chi schools.

Ma-tsu's *Record* portrays a teacher whose system is totally oriented toward the experience of awakening, to the complete deprecation of cultivation.[56] True insight does not come about from maturing specific wholesome causes that lead to corresponding results. Such an approach would reduce the experience of the unconditioned *(asaṃskṛta)* to that of a conditioned *(saṃskṛta)* result, meaning that the unconditioned would be governed by the same causal processes as the conditioned realm. Such a conclusion, Ch'an claimed, reflects an inferior perspective on spiritual training, such as would be held by the mediocre *śrāvakas* of the much maligned "Hīnayāna" branch of Buddhism.

> The path does not involve cultivation. If it is claimed that it is achieved through cultivation, that cultivation results, in turn, in disaster. This is just what happens to the *śrāvakas*. . . . The *śrāvakas* don't know that the sanctified mind originally is free from stages and positions, causes and effects, steps and levels. It is a mental presumption and misconception that one cultivates causes and realizes their effects.[57]

For Ma-tsu, there is no hint of any sequence of practices that leads the student from one stage to another, progressively abandoning unwholesome actions and cultivating wholesome conduct, until those stages reach their consummation in perfect purity of mind. As he frequently reiterates, the Ch'an adept "should neither cling to the wholesome nor reject the unwholesome."[58] Hence, effort is not necessary to achieve enlightenment; rather, one should simply free the mind from artificial constraints so that it will be open to that prospect, and thus "allow the Tao to circulate freely," as the *Platform Sūtra* said.

Since there are no causes that result in awakening, the student can do nothing to effect his own enlightenment, Ma-tsu remarks, except simply to "have faith in the fact that his own mind is a Buddha."[59] Ma-tsu saw everything in life as a manifestation of the fundamentally pure nature of the mind; there is no need to think that one has to control, alter, or create anything in order to achieve enlightenment.[60] The fact that a person is sentient is proof enough of his innate enlightenment, and of the fact that his ordinary, everyday mind is itself the enlightened mind.[61] If the student will just allow his mind to be enlightened, as it in truth already is, rather than trying to shape it into that form by removing defilements and cultivating wholesome states of mind, the need for cultivation will be obviated. Then, the supramundane path will be achieved naturally, without expending any effort:

> For one who wants to directly experience this path, the normal mind *(p'ing-ch'ang hsin)* is the path. What is meant by "normal mind"? [It is the mind that is] free from construction and production, right and wrong, clinging and rejection, annihilationism and eternalism, ordinary and saint. . . . It is your everyday walking, standing, sitting, and lying down, your personal encounters and contacts with things, which are all entirely just this path.[62]

Ma-tsu's teacher, Nan-yüeh Huai-jang, reiterated this claim that there was nothing the student could develop that would allow him to achieve enlightenment when he criticized Ma-tsu for seeking Buddhahood through meditating. In a famous exchange, Huai-jang is said to have seen Ma-tsu sitting in meditation in front of his hermitage. Going over to him, Huai-jang picked up a brick and began grinding it against a stone. When Ma-tsu asked what he was doing, Huai-jang replied that he was grinding the brick into a mirror. Ma-tsu, surprised, demanded, "How can you make a brick into a mirror by polishing it?" Huai-jang in turn asked, "How can you ever achieve Buddhahood through meditation?"[63]

Since everything that occurs to the individual is an expression of the functioning *(yung)* of the essence *(t'i)* of the inherently enlightened Buddha-nature, the student need only allow that nature to express its innate state in order to be enlightened. Thus he may come to awakening without having to cultivate anything: there would be no need either to control unwholesome tendencies of mind or to develop wholesome states of mind. Hence, cultivation, such as it is for Ma-tsu, "means simply to allow the mind to act spontaneously."[64]

Ma-tsu's soteriological program—in which awakening receives exclusive emphasis and cultivation is reduced to "spontaneity" *(tzu-jan),* that is, simply allowing one's innate enlightenment to operate freely—is the second principal interpretation of the "sudden" teaching of the "Southern school" of Ch'an. As we have seen, Shen-hui's interpretation of the sudden teaching as sudden awakening-gradual cultivation presumed that further spiritual development would be necessary after the initial awakening in order for the adherent to learn how to express his enlightenment in practical terms. Ma-tsu's approach is usually characterized instead as "sudden awakening-sudden cultivation" *(tun-wu tun-hsiu),* in which awakening and cultivation are both perfected simultaneously. Awakening to the essence of the mind is claimed to occur instantaneously; and since cultivation is just the functioning of that essence, it too is instantaneously perfected, leaving nothing further either to develop or to overcome.[65] Hence, the student need not concern himself at all with cultivation but should instead give full attention to awakening.

Ma-tsu, however, provides few practical hints on what precisely the student was to do in order to have that experience of sudden awakening-*cum*-cultivation. His *Record* mentions only one catalyst that might prompt such an experience of complete enlightenment: the encounter with an enlightened master.

> If one is a person of the highest spiritual faculties, he might unexpectedly encounter the instructions [lit., "direct pointing," *chih-shih*] of a spiritual advisor and, through those words, gain understanding. Then, without having to pass through any further steps or stages, he would suddenly awaken to his original nature.[66]

Thus it would seem that encounters with enlightened teachers, such as are glorified in the many anecdotes preserved in the later *kung-an* collections, were the principal technique of "cultivation" used in the Hung-chou school; and it is the reliance on this technique that marks the transition to what would eventually become the classical forms of Ch'an.

Such encounters were intended to prod the student out of the misconception that he is not enlightened and allow him to see that everything is a manifestation of his innate Buddha-nature. But by asserting that everything is enlightenment itself and that nothing wholesome need be cultivated and nothing unwholesome removed, Ma-tsu's approach is open to the criticism that it too easily lends itself to antinomianism, a major hindrance to the student's awakening. This critique of Hung-chou soteriology was in fact made by theorists belonging to rival schools of Ch'an, as Peter Gregory has shown in his chapter on Tsung-mi in this volume. The approach of the Hung-chou school was further subject to charges of elitism as well, since Ma-tsu explicitly states that his approach is intended only for "a person of the highest spiritual faculties." Thus no attempt was made to accommodate the breadth of character types and abilities supposedly encompassed within the great compassion of Mahāyāna.[67]

Exegetes within the Ch'an tradition have also suggested that the Hung-chou stress on spontaneity had effectively shifted the focus of Ch'an away from the internal essence of mind to its external functioning. Hence, rather than "seeing the nature and achieving Buddhahood"—the paradigmatic statement of Ch'an gnoseology—the Hung-chou school instead maintained that it is through the functioning of the mind that its nature is seen. Tsung-mi, for example, portrays the Hung-chou position as claiming that "the mind cannot be pointed out; it is through such properties as its capacity for speech and so forth that we can prove its existence and become aware of the presence of the Buddha-nature."[68] The Hung-chou school, according to Tsung-mi's critique, recognizes the "adaptive functioning" *(sui-yüan ying-yung)* of the mind—the myriad ways in which the mind manifests externally—but ignores its "innate functioning" *(tzu-hsing pen-yung)*—the direct manifestation of the essence itself. Tsung-mi compares this relationship to a bright mirror, where the surface of the mirror is the essence, the natural reflectivity of the mirror its innate functioning, and the images reflected by the mirror its adaptive functioning.[69] Hence Ma-tsu's approach, in being so concerned to allow the things and experiences of ordinary life to occur spontaneously, neglects to teach the student that such experiences are the end products of a process that leads back to the essence of mind itself.[70]

The teachings of Lin-chi I-hsüan, a fourth-generation successor in the Hung-chou lineage, can in some ways be interpreted as correcting this potential misconstruction of Ma-tsu's intent. Lin-chi provided for a specific type of cultivation that would complement awakening, which the student himself could develop. This was faith *(hsin),* a practice that occupies a prominent place in the extant materials concerning Lin-chi's teachings.[71]

Faith for Lin-chi was not blind acceptance of an external deity or submission to the authority of one's teacher, but rather a faculty inherent in each and every sentient being. As numerous exhortations in Lin-chi's *Record* suggest, faith was seen as the beneficial influence constantly emanating from the enlightened nature, prompting all conscious beings toward enlightenment.[72] Lin-chi's faith is therefore equivalent to the "innate functioning" of the mind-essence, which Ma-tsu's soteriology was alleged to have neglected. Lin-chi frequently admonishes his charges that if only their faith in the truth of their inherent Buddhahood were sufficient, they would *be* enlightened instantaneously, and would not have to *become* enlightened. This is because all persons are in fact already enlightened, and only mistakenly believe that they are not; hence, enlightenment involves nothing more than simply accepting that fact—believing it wholeheartedly. As Lin-chi remarks: "Attainment is attained instantly, with no time required, no practice, no realizing, no gain, no loss. . . . The resolute man knows full well that from the beginning there is nothing to do. Only because your faith is insufficient do you ceaselessly chase about; having thrown away your head, you go on and on looking for it, unable to stop yourself."[73] But with sufficient faith, the student at once realizes the inherently enlightened essence of his own mind, which Lin-chi termed the "true man of no rank" *(wu-wei chen-jen).*[74] This form of cultivation restores to Ch'an practice the school's fundamental focus on the direct experience of the essence of mind, as expressed in the injunction to "see the nature and achieve Buddhahood."

Faith for Lin-chi was thus both the means and the end of practice, the catalyst of enlightenment as well as its consummation. By developing faith, the student comes to understand the fundamental premise of Chinese Buddhism: that his natural state of mind is enlightenment itself. When all doubts about this inherent Buddhahood are resolved through the perfection of faith, faith and enlightenment are realized to be coextensive. In this wise, the Lin-chi school can be seen to sustain the Hung-chou school's soteriology of sudden awakening–sudden cultivation in which awakening and cultivation (here, faith) are perfected simultaneously.[75]

Lin-chi's interpretation of faith as the functioning of the inherent nature of the mind recalls the important place of tathāgatagarbha doctrine in sinitic Buddhist thought in general, and Ch'an practice and rhetoric in particular. In tathāgatagarbha thought, faith is the principal soteriological tool prompting realization of immanent enlightenment. According to the *Ratnagotravibhāga,* the main Indian treatise on the system: "The highest truth of the Buddhas can be understood only by faith; the blind indeed are unable to see the blazing orb of the sun."[76] Like the "true man of no rank," the concept of tathāgatagarbha also suggests that "there is nothing to be removed, and absolutely nothing to be added. The truth should be perceived as it is, and he who sees the truth will be liberated."[77] This reduction of Buddhist religiousness to the single factor of faith offered Ch'an a way to make practical its hallmark of inherent enlightenment, as well as to justify the Hung-chou approach of sudden awakening–sudden cultivation.[78]

The role of faith carried over into later Ch'an, but without quite the same degree of emphasis that it received in Lin-chi's own thought. The systematizer of *k'an-hua* Ch'an, Ta-hui Tsung-kao, for example, reiterates Lin-chi's notion that insufficient faith *(hsin pu-chi)* causes one to distrust the truth of one's own inherent enlightenment.

> If you want to study this path, you must have stable faith, so that your mind is unaffected whether it encounters favorable or adverse sensory objects. Then and only then will you go in the right direction. . . . If you're half clear and half unclear, half believing and half unbelieving, then whenever you come in contact with sensory objects and meet with events, your mind will give rise to doubt and confusion. This is the mind that is attached to the sense-spheres. Unable to be absolutely free of doubts concerning this path, or to eradicate the root of defilement and leave all difficulties far behind—all these problems derive from lack of stable faith and from being vexed by one's own *skandha-māra.*[79]

But whereas Lin-chi expected that his students would have to try continually to strengthen their faith, Ta-hui seems to have had a rather more realistic view of the human condition. People may in truth be enlightened, but they have had an infinite number of lifetimes in the past to convince themselves that they are not. Hence, rather than developing an approach to practice that requires the student to perfect his inherent facility for faith, Ta-hui instead bases his approach to Ch'an firmly on the *doubts* normally experienced on the path. As Ta-hui says, "The roads of Māra themselves are the route of enlightenment by which the person escapes from birth and death."[80]

K'an-hua Ch'an and a "Short-cut" to Enlightenment

To this point we have seen that Ch'an shared many features in common with other schools of sinitic Buddhism. Ch'an accepted a similar ontology of mind, had adopted the subitist soteriology common to most of the Chinese schools of Buddhism, and had tried to adapt traditional Buddhist meditative terminology. Ch'an's independent identity during the middle Ch'an period derived to a large extent from its unique rhetorical and pedagogical styles, and it was the development of these styles that justified its claim of being an independent transmission of Buddhism. By the inception of the Sung dynasty in 960, however, Ch'an had become a full-blown "tradition" in its own right, as concerned with the integrity of its teachings, practices, and institutions as any of its rivals. This long-coveted legitimacy gave Ch'an considerable influence among the political and intellectual elites and allowed Ch'an practitioners to make seminal contributions in areas of secular culture such as literature and the arts. But a sinification process that had begun in order to open Buddhism to Chinese in all strata of society had now resulted paradoxically in an increasing insularity of Ch'an from the masses.[81]

It was in this context that Ch'an masters of the classical period began to look within the history of their own school for teaching methods that would be suited to Ch'an's view of its own exalted pedigree. Stories about the earlier patriarchs and teachers—which were termed "old cases" *(ku-tse)* or, more commonly, "public cases" *(kung-an)*[82]—provided an especially fecund, and uniquely Ch'an, source of pedagogical material. As itinerant Ch'an monks wandered from teacher to teacher, they inquired about stories handed down concerning earlier patriarchs and masters. Sometimes too they would query those teachers about the enigmatic remarks made by other masters they had met in the course of their travels, and ask them for their own responses. These sayings, exchanges, and variant explanations were collected and shared among the brethren, and eventually came to be used by Ch'an masters for instructing their students and testing the depth of their understanding. Teachers even began to assign such exchanges as themes to be contemplated during meditation.

Two of the earliest Ch'an masters to use *kung-an*[83] in instructing their students were Yün-men Wen-yen (d. 949), the founder of the Yün-men school, and Fen-yang Shan-chao (947–1024), who revived what was at that time a moribund Lin-chi school. Fen-yang himself compiled three separate collections of *kung-an* in his *Record:* one hundred "old cases" *(ku-tse)* with explanatory verses by Fen-yang; one hundred original *kung-an* by Fen-yang himself, to which he appended his own answers; and one hundred old cases with Fen-yang's alternate answers.[84]

It is of course the Lin-chi school that is most closely associated with the use of *kung-an,* and the majority of *kung-an* anthologies belong to that school. The largest of these anthologies is the *Pi-yen lu* (Blue Cliff Record), compiled in final form by Yüan-wu K'o-ch'in, a tenth-generation Lin-chi successor who belonged to the collateral Yang-ch'i lineage of that school.[85] The *Pi-yen lu* itself is an expansion and elaboration of an earlier work by Hsüeh-tou Ch'ung-hsien (980–1052) entitled *Po-tse sung-ku* (One Hundred Cases and Verses to the Old [Cases]),[86] a collection of one hundred anecdotes concerning earlier Ch'an masters to which Hsüeh-tou appended explanatory verses and annotation. Some sixty years later, Yüan-wu added his own introductory "pointers" *(ch'ui-shih)* to each case along with further explanations of, and commentaries to, both the case and Hsüeh-tou's verses, to form his larger anthology. A typical case in the *Pi-yen lu* begins with a "pointer" by Yüan-wu to direct the student toward the important issue raised in the *kung-an;* this is followed by the *kung-an* itself, with Yüan-wu's interlinear annotation, Yüan-wu's exposition of the *kung-an,* explanatory verses by Hsüeh-tou with Yüan-wu's interlinear notes, and a concluding commentary to the verses, also by Yüan-wu. A more complex genre of literature can hardly be imagined, rivaling any of the exegetical commentaries of the doctrinal schools. These collections of stories, most of which were compiled during the Sung dynasty, constitute one of the largest bodies of writings of any of the Chinese schools of Buddhism. Any pretense Ch'an may have still retained about being a teaching that "did not rely on words and letters" was hardly supportable given the rapid proliferation of such anthologies within different teaching lineages.

The compilation of *kung-an* collections, with their distinctive language and style, illustrates the tendency in Sung dynasty Ch'an toward refined literary activity, which was termed "lettered Ch'an" (*wen-tzu* Ch'an).[87] These literary endeavors helped to bring Ch'an into the mainstream of Chinese cultural life and also led to a fertile interchange between Ch'an and secular belles lettres. But this tendency toward greater and greater erudition was also anathema to later teachers in the Lin-chi school: if Ch'an "did not rely on words and letters," what was the need for these massive anthologies of Ch'an words? Yüan-wu's own successor, Ta-hui Tsung-kao, vehemently lashed out at Sung *wen-tzu* Ch'an, as epitomized in his teacher's *Pi-yen lu,* for fostering, he claimed, the mistaken idea that Ch'an was merely clever repartee and elegant verse. In perhaps the ultimate expression of contempt for this literary type of Ch'an, Ta-hui, according to legend, tried to keep the *Pi-yen lu* out of circulation by having the xylographs from which it was printed burned.[88]

Unfortunately the notoriety of Ta-hui's provocative action with regard to his teacher's writings has tended to obscure the revolutionary step made by Yüan-wu in the use of *kung-an*. Yüan-wu was apparently the first to teach that *kung-an* were not simply the dead records of exchanges with ancient Ch'an masters, and thus suitably the focus of literary endeavors. Rather, they should be used as if they were directly pointing *(chih-chih;* alt. *chih-shih)* to the mind of each and every individual—that is, as a statement of immediate, contemporary relevance *(hsien-ch'eng,* J. *genjō)*[89] guiding one toward enlightenment. As Yüan-wu warns in his *Hsin-yao* (Essentials of Mind): "Do not look for the living road in the words and phrases, bury yourself in the *kung-an* of the ancients, or make a stratagem for living in the ghost cave or beneath the dark mountain. It is important only to access awakening and have profound realization."[90] Despite the number of *kung-an* that had been compiled in anthologies like his own *Pi-yen lu,* Yüan-wu insisted that any one case represented all other cases, since each was the presentation of a Ch'an master's enlightened mind. Hence, a single *kung-an* contained all the past and present teachings of Buddhism and Ch'an and was sufficient in itself to bring the student to awakening. As Yüan-wu states: "If one generates understanding and accesses awakening through a single phrase [i.e., the *hua-t'ou*], a single encounter *(chi),* or a single object, then immeasurable, innumerable functions and *kung-an* are simultaneously penetrated."[91]

This change in the concept of the *kung-an* was crystallized with Yüan-wu. And with Ta-hui fully elaborating the viewpoint of his teacher, *kung-an* emerged not as literary foils but as contemplative tools for realizing one's own innate enlightenment. Hence, through the influence of Yüan-wu and Ta-hui the proliferation of *kung-an* collections eventually slowed as the need to consider a multitude of ancient cases in the course of one's training was obviated in the radical reduction of Ch'an meditation to looking into *(k'an)* but a single *kung-an.*[92]

Chung-feng Ming-pen (1263–1323), a Yüan dynasty Ch'an monk in the Mi-an branch of Yüan-wu's line, describes the use of the *kung-an* as a catalyst for enlightenment in one of the most renowned passages of Ch'an literature:

> The *kung-an* is something that can be used only by men with enlightened minds who wish to prove their understanding. They are certainly not intended to be used merely to increase one's lore and provide topics for idle discussion. The so-called venerable masters of Ch'an are the chief officials of the public law courts of the monastic community, as it were, and their collections of sayings are the case records of points that have been vigorously advocated. Occasionally men of former times, in the intervals when they were not teaching, in spare moments when their doors were closed, would take up these cases and arrange them, give their judgment on them, compose verses of praise on them and write their own answers to them. Surely they did not do this just to show off their erudition and contradict the worthy men of old. Rather . . . they stooped to using expedient means in order to open the wisdom eye of men of later

generations, hoping thereby to make it possible for them to attain the understanding of the great dharma for themselves in the same way.[93]

In *kung-an* investigation, according to Ta-hui, rather than reflect over the entire *kung-an* exchange, which could lead the mind to distraction, one should instead zero in on the principal topic, or most essential element, of that exchange, which he termed its "critical phrase" *(hua-t'ou)*. Ta-hui called this new approach to meditation *k'an-hua* Ch'an—the Ch'an of observing the critical phrase—and alleged that it was a "short-cut" *(ching-chieh)*[94] leading to instantaneous enlightenment.

The distinction between *kung-an* investigation as a pedagogical tool and *k'an-hua* practice as a meditative technique can be illustrated by examining the *kung-an* Ta-hui most often taught: the *wu* of Chao-chou Ts'ung-shen (778–897).

Once a monk asked Chao-chou, "Does a dog have Buddha-nature or not?" Chao-chou replied, "No!" *(wu)*.[95]

The entire exchange between Chao-chou and his pupil would constitute the *kung-an,* while its "critical phrase," or "principal topic" *(hua-t'ou),* would be just the word "no."[96] Because Chao-chou's answer contradicts the most fundamental tenet of sinitic Buddhist doctrine, which insisted that the Buddha-nature is innate in all sentient beings, investigating the reply "no" provides a jolt to the student's ordinary way of thinking. Single-minded attention to that one word "no" then creates an introspective focus that eventually leads the meditator back to the mind's enlightened source—a process that Ch'an terms "tracing back the radiance emanating from the mind" *(hui-kuang fan-chao)*.[97] Once the student has recovered his mind's source by this counterillumination, he will know the intent *(i)* with which Chao-chou made his response—and, by extension, the enlightened mind that framed that intent—and will consummate in himself the very same state of enlightenment.[98] Looking into the *hua-t'ou* thus leads to the nondual, enlightened source of the mind from which all discriminative thought arises.[99] The adept can then act as Chao-chou and will understand all the *kung-an* intuitively. Hence, in this new method, *hua-t'ou* practice seeks to emulate the enlightened mind of previous masters, not to explain (by literary means) the meaning of their remarks. It is as if the student were instructed to pattern his mind after that of the enlightened master who appears in the *kung-an,* until they think as one.

It may seem curious that Lin-chi Ch'an, after developing a style of teaching that was less reliant on conceptual explanation, should ultimately embrace a contemplative technique that explicitly employs words, especially when compared with standard Indian meditative approaches that made no recourse to language, such as following the breath or visualizing the parts of the body. It is therefore worth reiterating that Ch'an considered these *hua-t'ou,* or meditative locutions, to be "live words" *(huo-chü),* because they led to awakening, and the conceptual teachings of the doctrinal schools "dead words" *(ssu-chü),* because they led only to intellectual understanding. Yüan-wu warns: "Examine the live word; don't examine the dead word. One who adheres utterly to the live word will not forget for an eternity of kalpas. One who adheres utterly to the dead word will never be able to save himself. If you want to take the patriarchs and Buddhas as your masters, you must clearly choose the live word."[100] Ch'an words, such as those that appear in a *hua-t'ou,* were thus conceived of as a form of spiritual homeopathy, using a minimal, but potent, dosage of the "poison of words" to cure the malady of conceptualization. Hsü-yün (1840–1949), a renowned Ch'an master of the Chinese Republican era, explains:

> The message of the Ch'an sect prior to the T'ang and Sung dynasties was contained in one phrase of half a line, "understand the mind, see one's nature," which brought realization of the path. The transmission from master to disciple involved nothing more than "stamping" *(yin)* [the master's] mind on the mind [of his disciple]. There was no other technique. Ordinarily, the disciple would ask instruction and the master would reply. [The master] just used the appropriate technique to release [the disciple] from his bonds, as for an illness one prescribes medicine.
>
> After the Sung period, the capacity of people degenerated, and while they were taught, they wouldn't do anything. For example, if told to "renounce everything," or "do not have thoughts of good or evil," they would not renounce anything, and thought not of the good, but only of the evil. At that time, the patriarchs and teachers, from unavoidable necessity, *selected a method that used poison to counteract poison* [emphasis added]. They taught students to investigate the *kung-an* and to observe the *hua-t'ou.*[101]

A *kung-an* or *hua-t'ou* was therefore conceived of as nothing more than an expedient; there was absolutely nothing arcane or mystical about it. Its purpose was simply "to open up the eyes of patched-robed monks of this world."[102] Anything in fact could serve the same purpose as the *hua-t'ou* in catalyzing the experience of awakening: a story of an ancient master's enlightenment, the scriptures of Buddhism, even the ordinary activities of day-to-day life *(jih-yung ying-yüan).*[103] As an expedient, the *hua-t'ou* had no ultimate meaning, and there was no specific, predetermined answer to the *kung-an* such as the Japanese Rinzai tradition is commonly portrayed as expecting.

The reader might wonder at this point whether calling the *hua-t'ou* an expedient contradicts the Lin-chi claim that *k'an-hua* Ch'an is a sudden approach to enlightenment. This is not the case. One common simile for sudden cultivation, which Ta-hui uses in his own writings, is that of an archer shooting arrows at a target: even though it may take thousands of attempts before his aim is accurate and he is able to hit the bull's-eye consistently, it is the same act of shooting that is repeated time and again. The repeated observation of the *hua-t'ou* (shooting the arrows) will catalyze awakening (hitting the target consistently), but that result does not occur after progressive development through a series of stages. It is worth noting that much of traditional Chinese apprenticeship took place in the same way, learning to do the whole job properly over a long period of time rather than mastering a series of smaller steps. Ta-hui himself is extremely careful to avoid any implication that *k'an-hua* Ch'an involves any sort of graduated progress. Ta-hui does mention different experiences that are engendered by observing the *hua-t'ou,* such as perplexity, bursting, power, and interfusion. But while such experiences "may be called 'constantly illuminating in silence,' or 'a person who experiences the Great Death,' or 'an event that occurs before your parents are born,' or 'an event that occurs before the void-kalpa,' "[104] Ta-hui warns that these are merely different perspectives from which *hua-t'ou* investigation *may* be described depending on the aspiration and talent of the individual, not stages that are *invariably* undergone on the way toward enlightenment.

Further, while the conceptual form of a *hua-t'ou* may involve linguistic convention, it is still a "live word" because it is designed to lead to an experience of ultimate validity. Hence it is not the expedient that renders a soteriology either sudden or gradual, but the attachment thereto. As Ta-hui says, "While one can access the path through the gate of expedients, it is a sickness to conserve expedients and not discard them."[105] If anything, Ta-hui views *hua-t'ou* as a "sudden" expedient, intended to catalyze an equally "sudden" awakening.[106]

The purpose of the *hua-t'ou,* then, is to enable the student to transcend the dualistic processes of thought in a single moment of insight, without requiring that he "progress gradually through a series of steps or stages."[107] For this reason Ta-hui refers to *k'an-hua* Ch'an as a "short-cut" approach to meditation:

> If you want to understand the principle of the short-cut, you must in one fell swoop break through this one thought—then and only then will you comprehend birth and death. Then and only then will it be called accessing awakening. . . . You need only lay down, all at once, the mind full of deluded thoughts and inverted thinking, the mind of logical discrimination, the mind that loves life and hates death, the mind of knowledge and views, interpretation and comprehension, and the mind that rejoices in stillness and turns from disturbance.[108]

Any kind of intellectualization of the *hua-t'ou,* any attempt to understand it in terms of ordinary conceptual thought, was repeatedly denied by Ta-hui.[109] The significance of this warning becomes especially clear when Ta-hui's intimate associations with the powerful Sung intelligentsia are taken into account.[110] Ta-hui admonished these members of this elite class that the intellectual abilities they had cultivated throughout their careers could themselves become the most implacable of obstacles to enlightenment.

> Nowadays the literocrats, despite a hundred attempts or a thousand tries, are never able to experience direct penetration of this matter. This is solely due to the fact that their natures are too clever and their opinions too multifarious. When they meet a master of our school, as soon as he opens his mouth and flaps his tongue they immediately presume that they understand. Therefore it would actually be much better for them to be stupid, without so much evil understanding and evil awareness. . . . The clever are actually obstructed by their cleverness, and can't gain a sudden breakthrough.[111]

Ta-hui repeatedly cautions his learned students not even to try to resolve the *hua-t'ou;* instead they should just give up the conceit that they have the intellectual tools that would allow them to understand it. This admonition Ta-hui reiterates in his advice on how to proceed with the contemplation of several different *hua-t'ou.* With reference to Yün-men's "dry shit-stick," Ta-hui warns, "When you examine this, don't use your usual intelligence and perspicacity." Discussing Chao-chou's "cypress tree in the courtyard," Ta-hui remarks, "Suddenly with regard to this cypress tree, the mind and mind-consciousness will come to an end and the breath will stop. This is where the [*hua-*] *tou* is penetrated." Ta-hui has even listed some eight defects in the examination of Chao-chou's "no," several of which involve the use of the rational mind to determine the meaning of the *hua-t'ou.*[112] Thus there is nothing that the student can ultimately understand about the *hua-t'ou* as long as he employs his habitual processes of thought; in perhaps the ultimate paradox, it is only when he finally abandons all attempts to understand the *hua-t'ou* that its real significance becomes clear.

In these descriptions of the central place that nonconceptualization occupies in *k'an-hua* Ch'an, we have further intimations of the subitist character of this approach to meditation. *K'an-hua* Ch'an is termed a "short-cut" because it does not require a gradual unfolding of truth, but can be understood in a single instant of insight. Echoing Ma-tsu's conception of a cultivation that is simultaneously perfected in one overwhelming experience of awakening, Ta-hui too says: "Understanding one is understanding all; awakening to one is awakening to all; realizing one is realizing all. It's like slicing through a spool of thread: with one stroke all its strands are simultaneously cut. Realizing limitless teachings is just the same: there is no sequence whatsoever *(wu tz'u-ti).*"[113]

There is nothing that need be developed; all the student must do is simply renounce both the hope that there is something that can be achieved through the practice as well as the conceit that he will achieve that result.

This state beyond hope, where "there is no place to put one's hands and feet," Ta-hui remarks, "is really a good place." It is a "good place" because it is there that conceptualization is brought to an end: "Without debate and ratiocination they are at a loss, with no place to put their hands and feet."[114] Only then can the student make the all-important transition from the conditioned to the unconditioned, which is likened to a death-defying "leap off a hundred-foot pole."[115] One need only recall the role of no-thought as the access to final realization-awakening to see how thoroughly that earlier account of meditation has been subsumed by the *hua-t'ou* technique.

The leap off the hundred-foot pole from the conditioned to the unconditioned is perhaps the quintessential expression of what Ch'an means by a sudden style of cultivation and meditation. As we saw previously with Ma-tsu, sudden cultivation demands that there be no hint of any sequence of practices that would lead the student from one stage to another, progressively abandoning defilements and cultivating wholesome actions, until he achieves perfect purity of mind. The jump off the hundred-foot pole suggests the radical nonattachment, even to one's own body and mind, that Buddhism has always expected as a prerequisite to enlightenment. Ch'an does not deny that it might take time for one to build up the courage necessary to take that ultimate plunge. But its lack of sequence at least freed it from charges of being gradualistic.[116]

Ta-hui's interpretation of "sudden cultivation" is perhaps even more radical than was Ma-tsu's earlier description based on spontaneity. Both claim that total relinquishment, which is final enlightenment, cannot be achieved by undertaking any kind of practice. But whereas Ma-tsu stresses the need "to be free of defilement" and "spontaneous," Ta-hui refuses even to posit the necessity of maintaining an undefiled state, which the ordinary person might find daunting. For Ta-hui, nothing at all need be perfected to achieve enlightenment: not purity, not samādhi or prajñā, not even the bare faith of Lin-chi. Ta-hui insists instead that the practice must begin and end amid the typical afflictions of ordinary life—especially ignorance, delusion, insecurity, and stress. *K'an-hua* Ch'an in fact encourages the student to foster all the confusion and perplexity he can muster, for it was expected that the ordinary person, when first faced with the *hua-t'ou,* would indeed be puzzled as to its significance. This puzzlement is what Lin-chi Ch'an terms the "sensation of doubt" *(i-ch'ing),* and building that sensation is the main purpose of investigating the *hua-t'ou.* This peculiar Ch'an emphasis on doubt had a rather long history by Ta-hui's time. One of the earliest usages of the term appears in the enlightenment poem of Lo-han Kuei-ch'en (867–928), the teacher of Fa-yen Wen-i (885–958), who refers to enlightenment as shattering the "ball of doubt" *(i-t'uan).*[117] Ta-hui's grand-teacher, Wu-tsu Fa-yen (1024?–1104), also taught his students to keep the great ball of doubt.[118] But it was Ta-hui who drew out the full implications of this idea, making it the core of his approach to formal meditation practice.

Doubt is the perplexity the student feels from his inability to resolve the riddle of the *kung-an.* Doubt acts as the force that pressures the mind to break out of the complacency engendered by its habitual ways of thinking. Doubt places the person at a disconcerting loss, for he soon finds that his ordinary ratiocinative processes are inadequate to the task of penetrating the *hua-t'ou.* Because the person ordinarily assumes that he is "in control" (a notion attacked in Buddhism's virulent critiques of theologies positing an eternal self, or *ātman*), the insecurity created by the *hua-t'ou* becomes frustrating and unnerving, a feeling likened to "a mosquito atop an iron ox."[119] But it is precisely this sensation of doubt that *hua-t'ou* are intended to produce, and after it is present, their purpose is fulfilled.

When the doubt becomes unqualified, it and the *hua-t'ou* become indistinguishable; as the Korean Sŏn monk T'aego Pou (1301–1382) says, "The doubt and the *hwadu* [*hua-t'ou*] fuse into one."[120] From this point continued investigation of the doubt-*cum-hua-t'ou* will eventually trap the mind in an unmoving state of perfect concentration.[121] That is to say, when the sense of frustration over one's inability to resolve the *hua-t'ou* through ordinary logic has brought an end to random thought, intense one-pointedness of mind is engendered, which eventually produces the experience of no-thought. Ta-hui compared this state of being existentially, implacably "stuck" to a rat stuck in the narrowing taper of a cow's-horn trap, burrowing ever deeper to get at some oil placed inside its tip, until finally the rat is caught.[122]

The power of doubt in cutting off conceptualization is stressed repeatedly by Ta-hui: doubt is that state of perplexity "where intellect cannot operate and thought cannot reach; it is the road through which discrimination is eradicated and theorizing ended. . . . [Doubt makes the mind] puzzled, frustrated, and tasteless [i.e., lacking in any intellectual interest]—just as if you were gnawing on an iron bar."[123] Kao-feng Yüan-miao (1238–1295), a Yüan dynasty master in the Mi-an branch of the Lin-chi school, and teacher of Chung-feng Ming-pen, clarifies how doubt leads to a state of no-thought:

> As the sensation of doubt is perfected little by little, there then is no mind that initiates actions. And once there is no mind that initiates actions, the

> objects of thought are then forgotten. This ensures that the myriads of conditions naturally expire, but without bringing them to an end. The six windows [of the senses] are naturally calmed, but without calming them. Without countering the dust [of sensory objects] one suddenly accesses the no-mind samādhi.[124]

Ta-hui interprets the story of Bodhidharma's instruction to his disciple Hui-k'o (487–593) as a paradigm of the way Ch'an statements are intended to frustrate the mundane mind of the student so thoroughly that they serve as a catalyst for supramundane awakening. Bodhidharma first instructed Hui-k'o, "Bring all conditioning to rest outside, and keep the mind without panting inside." "But," Ta-hui explains, "Hui-k'o quoted texts and thereby sought certification. For this reason, Bodhidharma rejected each and every one of his statements; finally, when there was no place left [for Hui-k'o] to use his mind, he was able to step back and consider [those words]. . . . Suddenly, all conditioning was ended, and he then saw the moon and forgot the finger."[125]

As the story illustrates, the sensation of doubt must become all-consuming. In such a state, all the perplexities of everyday life are rolled into one existential "great doubt" *(ta-i)*, produced through examining the *hua-t'ou*. As Ta-hui says, "Whether a thousand doubts or a myriad doubts, they are all just one doubt. If you break through your doubt concerning the *hua-t'ou*, then a thousand or myriad doubts are all abruptly destroyed."[126]

Ta-hui viewed the unique rhetoric of Ch'an in the same way. In the only *kung-an* ascribed to him personally, he illustrates the distinctive use of Ch'an language:

> If you call this a bamboo comb, you are stuck to it. If you don't call this a bamboo comb, you have turned your back to it. Don't speak, but don't stay silent. Do not cogitate and do not guess. Do not shake your sleeves [in disapproval] and walk out. Anything you do is wrong. . . . Once I was likened to an official who confiscated all of someone's wealth and property and then demanded still more. I find this analogy particularly sublime. Truly, I demand that you hand over everything. When you have nowhere to escape, you will have to beg to take the road of death. Throwing yourself into the river or jumping into fire, you will die when your time comes. Only after you are dead will you gradually come back to life.[127]

Because mental stress and existential quandary were exactly the states that Ta-hui sought to foster through *k'an-hua* Ch'an, it is no surprise that he embraced ordinary life as the ideal venue for Buddhist meditation practice. Alluding to the simile drawn by Vimalakīrti, the quintessential Mahāyāna lay adept, he says, "The high plains do not produce lotus flowers: it is the mud of the lowlying marshlands that produces these flowers."[128] But Ta-hui's vision of the ordinary, afflicted condition of humankind as the way to enlightenment is a radical departure even for Mahāyāna Buddhism. Ta-hui saw the world as the ideal training ground for religious practice because it provided a plethora of situations in which frustration, doubting, and insecurity would appear—all weapons in the arsenal of *hua-t'ou* meditation. Moreover, the obstacles facing the householder were so ubiquitous and seductive (sex, wealth, fame, and so on, ad infinitum) that a person who was able to withstand them developed a tremendous "dynamism" or "power" *(li)* that was far superior to that of the sequestered monk, who faced few obstacles in his daily practice and so needed to expend only a modicum of effort to overcome them.

For Ta-hui, dynamism plays a pivotal role in consummating the process of *hua-t'ou* investigation because it is the energy that shakes the student loose from everything he had identified with previously. And again, it is by living in the world, yet remaining detached, that one develops dynamism: "As soon as you become aware of gradually conserving power in the midst of the dusty afflictions of daily life, this then will be where you gain power. This is how you achieve Buddhahood and become a patriarch."[129] If, on the other hand, the student permits himself to become entangled in worldly affairs, he loses his dynamism by allowing his energy to become dissipated in mundane distractions and wandering thoughts.[130]

Given the prominent place of faith in earlier Ch'an thought, as exemplified by Lin-chi, it is rather striking the extent to which Ta-hui has deemphasized faith in favor of doubt.[131] While there are passages in Ta-hui's writings where he does acknowledge the role of faith as a support of practice, he seems on the whole to have had a rather poor opinion of the prospects of the ordinary person attempting to rely on faith. More typically, Ta-hui maintains that practice has its inception in doubt, is enhanced through dynamism and the application of effort *(ching-chin, viryā),* and develops into faith only as those preceding factors mature. In his "directive" *(shih)* to the nun Miao-yüan, for example, Ta-hui says: "If you want to transcend birth and death and cross the sea of suffering, you must raise straight the banner of effort. Directly beneath it, faith will become sufficient. Only where this faith has become sufficient will the event take place of transcending birth and death and crossing the sea of suffering."[132]

To succeed in *hua-t'ou* practice, a strong sense of urgency about one's practice, rather than faith, is what is first required. In a refrain found frequently in his writings, Ta-hui says: "You should constantly paste the two words 'birth' and 'death' on your forehead. Whether drinking tea or eating rice, when sitting or lying down, when directing the servants, when coordinating your household affairs, when happy and when angry, when walking and when standing, when entertaining guests—

[throughout all these events those two words] must not be removed."[133] Ta-hui even goes so far as to dismiss the need for faith, since diligent practice will corroborate the teachings of Buddhism whether one begins by believing them or not.[134] Ta-hui's emphasis on the place of effort eventually became the "great zeal" *(ta-fen-chih)* discussed by Kao-feng Yüan-miao in his *Ch'an-yao* (Essentials of Ch'an), a synopsis of Ch'an practice that enjoyed wide currency in the post-classical Ch'an schools of the Yüan and Ming dynasties. In that text great faith, great zeal, and great doubt are treated together as the "three essentials" *(san-yao)* of *k'an-hua* Ch'an.[135]

Through the application of effort, then, the doubt engendered by the *hua-t'ou* becomes so intense that all distracting thoughts come to an end. When this condition is reached a final "burst"[136] is all that is needed to catalyze the experience of enlightenment. In other words, when the "one great doubt" produced with reference to a single *hua-t'ou* becomes the locus around which all other doubts accumulate, intense pressure is generated on the meditator's intellectual processes and on his own sense of self-identity and self-worth. The coalescence of all the meditator's thoughts and actions into that doubt—which resonates with the connotation of "absorption" (samādhi) in Sino-Indian Buddhism—produces the power (here, almost the courage) necessary to abandon himself seemingly to ultimate disaster: his own personal destruction.[137] When the student's consummate dynamism carries him beyond the point where he can cope with the pressure created by the doubt, the doubt explodes *(p'o),* annihilating the student's identification with body and mind. While ordinary language may be unable to describe this achievement, it is an experience that is readily available to all; Ta-hui compares it to "a man drinking water: he himself knows whether it is cold or warm."[138]

The explosion of the doubt destroys the bifurcating tendencies of thought as well. Whereas previously all of one's experiences were seen to revolve around one's self, and interpreted as either self or other, through *k'an-hua* practice the mind opens into a new, all-inclusive perspective from which the limiting "point of view" that is the ego *(ātmavāda)*[139] is eliminated. Awareness now has no fixed locus. The distinctions ordinarily perceived between self and other disappear, and consciousness expands infinitely, encompassing the entire universe both spatially and temporally: "Throughout boundless world systems, oneself and others are not separated by as much as the tip of a hair; the ten time periods of past and present, from beginning to end, are not separate from the present thought-moment."[140]

This expansive vision restores the perfect clarity of the mind, and all actions become expressions of the enlightened mind:

> A patriarch [Bodhidharma] said, "If mind and consciousness are quiescent and extinct, without a single thought stirring, this is called right enlightenment." Once enlightenment is right, then throughout the twenty-four hours of your daily activities, when seeing forms, hearing sounds, smelling scents, tasting flavors, feeling sensations, or knowing mental objects, whether walking, standing, sitting, or lying down, whether speaking or silent, active or still, there's nothing that is not clear. . . . Once you've attained purity, when active you manifest the function of clarity, and when inactive you return to the essence of clarity.[141]

In seeing the macrocosm of the universe reflected in the microcosm of the individual, the Ch'an conception of enlightenment is framed in terms evocative of the *summum bonum* of Hua-yen philosophy, the "multivalent interfusion of all phenomena." Moreover, as the goal of a practical subitism, the *k'an-hua* technique epitomizes the Chinese conception of the immanence of enlightenment within the mundane world.

K'an-hua Ch'an may thus be viewed as one of several products of the sinification of Buddhism, whereby the highest reaches of Buddhist spirituality were made accessible to Chinese adherents of both lay and monastic persuasions. Its evolution was prompted by critiques of Sino-Indian meditative concepts and hastened by the rhetorical and pedagogical experimentation that occurred during the middle Ch'an period. The *k'an-hua* technique, as standardized during the classical Ch'an period, exemplifies the Hung-chou conception of a "spontaneous" practice which is perfected not through a graduated regimen of cultivation but through instantaneous insight; and Sung accounts of *hua-t'ou* investigation purport to be a definitive enunciation of the soteriology of sudden awakening–sudden cultivation, in which all traces of "gradualism" have been rigorously excised. *Hua-t'ou* meditation thus emerges as a practical application of the subitist teachings that had been the hallmark of the Ch'an school since early in its history.

K'an-hua Ch'an became virtually synonymous with Lin-chi praxis from Ta-hui's time onward, and the approach was transmitted to Korea within a generation and, some decades later, to Japan. Understanding the theoretical foundations of this technique is therefore vital not only for drawing out the wider implications of the meaning of sudden enlightenment in Chinese Ch'an, but also for comprehending the subsequent evolution of Ch'an throughout East Asia. In the final analysis, *k'an-hua* Ch'an did not evolve because of the degeneration of the pristine message of some elusive Ch'an "golden age," but instead was the consummation of forces set in motion centuries before, propelled by the sudden-gradual debate.

Notes

The research for this paper was supported by a grant from the Committee on Research of the Academic Senate, University of California, Los Angeles. Its assistance is gratefully acknowledged. I would like to express my thanks to Peter Gregory and John McRae for their valuable comments on an early draft of this chapter. Any errors of fact or interpretation that may remain are, of course, my own responsibility.

1. There were strong intersectarian pressures on Ch'an that contributed to this process. This is well exemplified in the virulent Ch'an reactions to attempts by some doctrinal schools of Chinese Buddhism to subsume Ch'an within their classification of a "sudden" teaching *(tun-chiao)* theoretically inferior to the "perfect" teaching *(yüan-chiao).* For a discussion of Ch'an's response, see my essay "Ch'an Hermeneutics: A Korean View," in *Buddhist Hermeneutics,* ed. Donald S. Lopez, Jr., Studies in East Asian Buddhism, no. 6 (Honolulu: University of Hawaii Press, 1988).

2. Frederick J. Streng discusses these two types of religious language in "Language and Mystical Awareness," in *Mysticism and Philosophical Analysis,* ed. Steven T. Katz (New York: Oxford University Press, 1978), 150–157.

3. This conception of Ch'an's identity was formed during the Sung dynasty and attributed retrospectively to the putative founder of Ch'an, Bodhidharma. For the textual history of this passage, see Daisetz T. Suzuki, *Essays in Zen Buddhism,* First Series (1927; reprint, London: Rider, 1970), 176; and Isshū Miura and Ruth Fuller Sasaki, *Zen Dust: The History of the Koan and Koan Study in Rinzai (Lin-chi) Zen* (New York: Harcourt, Brace, Jovanovich, 1966), 228–230. For Yüan-wu K'o-ch'in's explanation of the significance of this verse, see *Fo-kuo K'o-ch'in ch'an-shih hsin-yao* (hereafter *Yüan-wu hsin-yao*) 4, *HTC* 120.389a6ff., 390d10ff.

4. A rendering of the term suggested by John McRae; see his translation of Yanagida Seizan, "The 'Recorded Sayings' Texts of Chinese Ch'an Buddhism," in *Early Ch'an in China and Tibet,* ed. Whalen Lai and Lewis Lancaster, Berkeley Buddhist Studies Series, no. 5 (Berkeley, 1983), 192–194, 204 n. 25; see also McRae, *The Northern School and the Formation of Early Ch'an Buddhism,* Studies in East Asian Buddhism, no. 3 (Honolulu: University of Hawaii Press, 1986), 298 n. 190.

5. One of the best studies on the development of *kung-an* and *hua-t'ou* practice is Furuta Shōkin, "Kōan no rekishi-teki hatten keitai ni okeru shinrisei no mondai," in *Bukkyō no kompon shinri,* ed. Miyamoto Shōson (Tokyo: Sanseidō, 1956), 807–840. Furuta correctly distinguishes between the use of *kung-an* during the T'ang as a teaching targeted at specific individuals in specific situations (what I characterize as a rhetorical or pedagogical use) and the use of *kung-an* in a rationalized system of practice during the Sung; see especially pp. 813–818. Sekiguchi Shindai failed to make this distinction in his discussion of the development of *kung-an* in his *Daruma no kenkyū* (Tokyo: Iwanami shoten, 1967), 335–343, and drew the strong criticism of Yanagida Seizan, *Yaburu mono* (Tokyo:

Shunjūsha, 1970), 236; see the mention at McRae, *Northern School,* 302 n. 239. Kagamishima Genryū proposes that *hua-t'ou* practice developed out of the dual foci of Sung dynasty Ch'an: first, viewing Ch'an as a separate transmission outside the teachings, but, second, also bringing Ch'an together with the doctrinal teachings of Buddhism. See Kagamishima's *Dōgen Zenji no in'yō kyōten goroku no kenkyū* (Tokyo: Mokujisha, 1965), 98–99 (noted in Miriam Levering, "Ch'an Enlightenment for Laymen: Ta-hui and the New Religious Culture of the Sung" [Ph.D. diss., Harvard University, 1978], 303 n. 1). As an example of the plentiful, if often suspect, polemical literature in Japanese on the background of kōan practice, see Kurebayashi Kōdō, "Kanna Zen to Mokushō Zen," *Zen* 1 (1941): 1–40; Kurebayashi manages to trace the origin of the *kung-an* system to somewhere between Bodhidharma and Hui-neng's time (p. 12)! The process leading up to *kung-an* has been outlined in Ishii Shūdō, "Daie Sōkō to sono deshitachi (go)," *IBK* 22 (1973): 291–295. Sung *kung-an* study is interpreted in more psychological terms in Heinrich Dumoulin, *Geschichte des Zen-Buddhismus Band I: Indien und China* (Munich: Francke Verlag Bern, 1985), 223–244. See also Akizuki Ryūmin, *Kōan: jissenteki Zen nyūmon* (Tokyo: San'ichi shobō, 1965); Hayashiya Tomojirō, "Kōan no mikata to tokikata," and Itō Kokan, "Zen no kōan," both in *Zen no kōan to mondō, Zen no kōza,* vol. 3, ed. Inoue Tetsujirō, Ui Hakuju, and Suzuki Daisetsu (Tokyo: Shunjitsuyōdō, 1952); the latter book was unavailable to me and I could not consult it in preparing this chapter.

The best study in English of *kung-an* practice, especially in Japanese Zen, is Isshū Miura and Ruth Fuller Sasaki, *The Zen Koan: Its History and Use in Rinzai Zen* (New York: Harcourt, Brace & World, 1965), 3–16, reprinted in the same authors' *Zen Dust,* 3–16. They have culled much of the relevant Japanese secondary material in preparing their work.

6. Surveys of Ta-hui's life and thought appear in Abe Chōichi, *Chūgoku Zenshūshi no kenkyū* (Tokyo: Seishin shobō, 1963), 467–484; Kajiya Sōnin, "Daie," in *Zen no rekishi: Chūgoku,* Kōzan Zen, vol. 3, ed. Nishitani Keiji (Tokyo: Chikuma shobō, 1974), 259–274; and Chün-fang Yü, "Ta-hui Tsung-kao and *Kung-an* Ch'an," *Journal of Chinese Philosophy* 6 (1979): 211–235. Dated, but with useful citations, is Nukariya Kaiten, *Zengaku shisōshi,* vol. 2 (1925; reprint, Tokyo: Meicho kankōkai, 1969), 361–384. Miriam Levering's excellent dissertation on Ta-hui, "Ch'an Enlightenment for Laymen: Ta-hui and the New Religious Culture of the Sung" (Harvard, 1978), is especially good in detailing the important influences of the contemporary secular environment on Ta-hui.

Ta-hui's collected sermons and writings appear in *Ta-hui P'u-chüeh ch'an-shih yü-lu, T* 47.811a–943a. Ta-hui's *Letters* have been translated into Japanese by Araki Kengo, *Daiesho,* Zen no goroku, vol. 17 (Tokyo: Chikuma shobō, 1969), who has drawn on traditional Japanese commentaries to the text for his interpretation. Araki gives an outline of Ta-hui's life and thought in his appendix (pp. 245–268).

Because Ta-hui's *Letters* is the first of a collection of four major Ch'an texts *(Sa chip)* studied in Buddhist lecture halls in Korea, there is an extensive Korean secondary literature on the text, starting in the mid-Koryŏ dynasty. The standard, punctuated Korean edition, which includes an accompanying Korean reading, was prepared by An Chinho, *Hyŏnt'o chuhae: Sŏjang* (Seoul: Pŏmnyunsa, 1974). Useful annotation to that edition appears in Yi Chigwan, *Sajip sagi* (1968; reprint, Taegu: Haein ch'ongnim sŭngga hagwŏn, 1974), 1-132. An annotated, vernacular translation has been made by Han Chŏngsŏp and Chŏng Chich'ŏl, *Sa chip yŏkhae* (Seoul: Pŏmnyunsa, 1976), 21-244. Ta-hui is extensively cited in the works of Chinul, with interesting commentary; these discussions appear especially in two of Chinul's texts: *K'anhwa kyŏrŭi-ron* (Resolving Doubts about Observing the *Hwadu*) and *Pŏpchip pyŏrhaeng-rok chŏryo pyŏngip sagi* (Excerpts from the Dharma Collection and Special Practice Record with Personal Notes), both translated in *The Korean Approach to Zen: The Collected Works of Chinul,* trans. Robert E. Buswell Jr. (Honolulu: University of Hawaii Press, 1983), 239-261, and 263-374, respectively.

Portions of Ta-hui's writings excerpted in *chüan* thirty-one and thirty-two of the *Chih-yüeh lu* (*HTC* 143.335b-371d) have been translated in a creative and powerful rendering by Christopher Cleary, *Swampland Flowers: The Letters and Lectures of Zen Master Ta Hui* (New York: Grove Press, 1977). Cleary has a clear, if sometimes intuitive, understanding of the implications of Ta-hui's text, and conveys accurately its spirit and style, if not its letter. He unfortunately has chosen to use an outdated edition of Ta-hui's works and freely edits and paraphrases the material to suit his own literary purposes. While this makes for a fluent, well-presented text that may be read with profit by nonspecialists, it is all but useless for scholarly purposes. Where possible, I have tried to indicate corresponding passages in Cleary's translation so that they may be consulted by those who cannot read the original Chinese.

7. I continue to be intrigued by the possible resonances with *kung-an* and *hua-t'ou* in both Indian and Chinese religion and philosophy. There are several concepts in Sanskrit philosophy of language that may be worth comparing with *hua-t'ou* to illustrate the linguistic quality of certain mystical experiences. These include *sphoṭa* (the preconceptual, nonverbal level of thought), *rasa* (the "impression" intuited by the audience of a Sanskrit drama), and *śabda-brahman* (the absolute element present in all speech). Some aspects of *k'an-hua* practice may have evolved from Tantric influences in early Ch'an; cf. Bernard Faure, "The Concept of One-Practice Samādhi in Early Ch'an," in *Traditions of Meditation in Chinese Buddhism,* ed. Peter N. Gregory, Studies in East Asian Buddhism, no. 4 (Honolulu: University of Hawaii Press, 1986), 115-116.

8. The "internal crisis" is mentioned by Chün-fang Yü, "Ta-hui," 218, who notes that by the Sung "the golden age of Ch'an now passed away." Daisetz Suzuki also claims that it was thanks to the development of the *kung-an* system of practice that Ch'an was able to survive the death of the eminent masters of the T'ang; see *Essays in Zen Buddhism,* Series Two (London: Rider and Co., 1970), 90ff.; noted in Yü, "Ta-hui," 219. Similar claims within the tradition will be discussed in the concluding section of this essay. Frankly, from my own study, I believe that if Ch'an had any such "golden age," it was the Sung. Of course, the Chinese traditionally have looked back to some idyllic earlier time as the source of all that was good in their world. For perspective on this issue, it is worth noting that even during the time of Lin-chi I-hsüan (d. 866), perhaps the

quintessential T'ang Ch'an master, there was a tendency to see the ancient masters as far superior to contemporary people; see *Lin-chi lu*, *T* 47.499b19–21; Ruth Fuller Sasaki, trans., *The Recorded Sayings of Ch'an Master Lin-chi Hui-chao of Chen Prefecture* (Kyoto: Institute for Zen Studies, 1975), 19.

9. For a general description of the associations between Sung Ch'an and the *shih-ta-fu*, see Yanagida Seizan, "Chūgoku Zenshūshi," in *Zen no rekishi—Chūgoku*, Kōza Zen, vol. 3, 92–93. For a survey of *shih-ta-fu* culture, see Patricia B. Ebrey, *Family and Property in Sung China: Yüan Ts'ai's Precepts for Social Life* (Princeton: Princeton University Press, 1984), 3–14; and for the impact of the *shih-ta-fu* on indigenous philosophy, ibid., 156–171.

10. See Yanagida, "Chūgoku Zenshūshi," 98–100; Araki Kengo, *Bukkyō to Jukyō* (Kyoto: Heirakuji shoten, 1962), 194–228. This role of Ta-hui has been argued compellingly in Miriam Levering, "Ch'an Enlightenment for Laymen," passim.

11. See the comments of James T. C. Liu and Peter J. Golas, eds., *Change in Sung China: Innovation or Renovation?* (Lexington, Mass: D. C. Heath, 1969), 83.

12. For an erudite and incisive characterization of what Yūki Reimon termed the new Buddhism of the Sui and T'ang, see Robert M. Gimello, "Chih-yen (602–668) and the Foundations of Hua-yen Buddhism" (Ph.D. diss., Columbia University, 1976), 93–118. The way the Chinese used the tathāgatagarbha concept to justify a subitist soteriology was of course not the only interpretation possible. Tathāgatagarbha is a multivalent term, and was thus easily amenable to gradualistic interpretations as well (see Luis Gómez's treatment of the "purifying gold" metaphor in this volume). These differences illustrate the difficulty, as Gómez cautions, of assigning doctrines exclusively to either the sudden or the gradual camps.

13. As the Chinese apocryphon *Ta-sheng ch'i-hsin lun* (*T* 32.575c21–22) states, "Enlightenment is the mind of the sentient being; this [ordinary] mind includes in itself all states of being of the phenomenal world and the transcendental world"; Yoshito Hakeda, trans., *The Awakening of Faith* (New York: Columbia University Press, 1967), 28.

14. This is not to imply that the concept of sudden enlightenment is unknown in Indian texts, though it is clearly the Chinese who have sought to draw out the full implications of the notion. Perhaps the earliest Indian reference to the term appears in *Mahāvastu: . . . abhisaṃboddhavyaṃ sarvan tam* ekacittakṣaṇasamāyuktayā prajñayā *anuttaraṃ samyaksaṃbodhim abhisaṃbuddho* (All that was to be fully realized. . . . Complete, perfect enlightenment was realized *by means of wisdom that was centered in one single thought-moment*); E. Senart, ed., *Mahāvastu*, vol. 1 (Paris: Impr. Nationale, 1882), 229; cf. J. J. Jones, trans., *The Mahāvastu*, Sacred Books of the Buddhists, no. 16, vol. 1 (London: Luzac, 1949), 185. This of course need not imply an Indian provenance for the Chinese idea of sudden enlightenment as Brian Galloway has suggested in his article "Sudden Enlightenment in Indian Buddhism," *Wiener Zeitschrift für die Kunde Südasiens und Archiv für indische Philosophie* 25 (1981): 205–211; see Luis Gómez's discussion in his chapter above. A parallel subitist position is also criticized in the Vaibhāṣika *Abhidharmamahāvibhāṣā* (*chüan* 90, *T* 27.465b–c):

> Some have this grasping: When the *vajropamasamādhi* appears, it suddenly eradicates all the defilements of the three realms of existence that may be cut off by insight and cultivation. All the stages before those can only subdue them, and cannot yet cut off all the outflows. Like the śramaṇas [who advocate] such sudden eradication, these [people] advocate *sudden enlightenment (tun-chüeh)* and attainment of the *aśaikṣaphala.* This is like waking from a dream: one suddenly abandons one's torpor and lassitude.

To counter this wrong view, the *Mahāvibhāṣā* advocates eighty-nine stages in eradicating the *anuśayas.*

15. For the role of merit-making and merit transference in contemporary Theravāda Buddhism, see Stanley J. Tambiah, *Buddhism and the Spirit Cults in North-East Thailand* (Cambridge: Cambridge University Press, 1970), 141–151; Richard R. Gombrich, *Precept and Practice: Traditional Buddhism in the Rural Highlands of Ceylon* (Oxford: Clarendon Press, 1971), esp. 226–240; and cf. idem., "Temporary Ordination in Sri Lanka," *Journal of the International Association of Buddhist Studies* 7 (1984): 41–65.

16. See the discussion in Henri Maspero, *Taoism and Chinese Religion,* trans. Frank A. Kierman, Jr. (Amherst: University of Massachusetts Press, 1981), 257–262, 400–412.

17. For a recent survey of T'ien-t'ai meditation, see Daniel B. Stevenson, "The Four Kinds of Samādhi in Early T'ien-t'ai Buddhism," in Gregory, *Traditions of Meditation,* 45–97.

18. For Tao-hsin and *shou-i* practice see Faure, "One-Practice Samādhi," 112–114; and David W. Chappell, "The Teachings of the Fourth Ch'an Patriarch Tao-hsin (580–651)," in Lai and Lancaster, *Early Ch'an in China and Tibet,* 96–100, 114; McRae, *Northern School,* 138–144. McRae has questioned the authenticity of the ascription of *shou-i* to Tao-hsin in his *Northern School,* 119–120.

19. The Northern school's putative predecessor, the East Mountain school (Tung-shan fa-men), could also be included in the early Ch'an period. The objection to this extension would be that virtually everything that is known about that school derives from Northern school literature. However, related Ch'an-oriented materials that predate Northern school doxologies corroborate their accounts of the East Mountain teachings. This evidence suggests that the East Mountain line did have distinctive doctrinal perspectives which played a role in the development of early Ch'an. This is a point I elaborate in my account of the apocryphal *Vajrasāmadhi-sūtra;* see Buswell, "The Korean Origin of the *Vajrasamādhi-sūtra:* A Case Study in Determining the Dating, Provenance, and Authorship of a Buddhist Apocryphal Scripture" (Ph.D. diss., University of California, Berkeley, 1985), 184–209.

20. These seven schools are mentioned in Tsung-mi's *Yüan-chüeh ching ta-shu ch'ao, ZZ* 2/14/3/277c–280a; translated in Yün-hua Jan, "Tsung-mi: His Analysis of Ch'an Buddhism," *T'oung Pao* 58 (1972): 42–50; see also Buswell, *Korean Approach,* 39, and the chapter by Peter Gregory in this volume. Tsung-mi's *Chung-hua ch'uan-hsin-ti Ch'an-men shih-tzu ch'eng-hsi t'u* (*HTC* 110.435c–436c) provides a detailed description of the four principal middle Ch'an schools; I

have translated these portions from the Korean recension of that text (entitled *Pŏpchip pyŏrhaeng-rok*) in *Korean Approach,* 265–277, and discussed their significance in the introduction to that volume, 39–49. I will not be able to treat all these experiments here; the two I do discuss, however, are representative of those movements within Ch'an toward more explicitly sinitic formulations, and exerted the greatest long-term influence on Ch'an.

21. For a general characterization of this process, see Robert M. Gimello, "Mysticism and Meditation," in Steven Katz, *Mysticism and Philosophical Analysis,* 187–188.

22. *Liu-tsu t'an ching, T* 48.342b26–17; cf. *T* 48.358c12–13. Cf. also Philip Yampolsky, trans., *Platform Sutra of the Sixth Patriarch* (New York: Columbia University Press, 1967), 164.

23. *Ch'eng-hsi t'u, HTC* 437c2–6, translated in Buswell, *Korean Approach,* 111, and cf. 276. For Yŏndam Yuil's (1720–1799) Korean commentary to this passage, see 346 n. 61.

24. *Ch'an-yüan chi tu-hsü* 1, *T* 48.399a18. Tsung-mi's commentator Chinul even tries to show that Ch'an is equivalent to *śīla,* samādhi, and prajñā; see Buswell, *Korean Approach,* 104–105.

25. *Liu-tsu t'an ching, T* 48.338b6–12. Cf. Yampolsky, *Platform Sutra,* 135, who cites parallel passages in other middle Ch'an literature at n. 54.

26. *Sŏnmun pojang-rok* 1, *HTC* 113.990a18–b16; see also the parallel version in *Tsu-t'ang chi* 17, 108a–b, in *Pulgyo sahak nonch'ong,* Hyosŏng Cho Myŏnggi paksa hwagap kinyŏm (Seoul, 1965), appendix.

27. It also calls to mind the similar imagery of the *Platform Sūtra* (*T* 48.338b26–27): "Good friends, how then are samādhi and prajñā alike? They are like the lamp and the light it gives forth." Yampolsky, *Platform Sutra,* 137, with minor changes.

28. *Tsung-ching lu* 45, *T* 48.679c14–18, 680b27–28. Note here once again the alignment of samādhi and prajñā with the doctrinal formulations of Buddhism.

29. Following the Korean interpretations of this passage; see Buswell, *Korean Approach,* 286. For the original quotation, see *Tung-shan yü-lu, T* 47.525a24; William F. Powell, trans., *The Record of Tung-shan,* Classics in East Asian Buddhism, no. 1 (Honolulu: University of Hawaii Press, 1986), 58. See also the discussion in Yi Chongik, "Chosasŏn e issŏsŏ ŭi musim sasang," *Pulgyo hakpo* 10 (1973): 241–243; and idem., *Kankoku bukkyō no kenkyū: Kōrai Fujō kokushi o chūshin to shite* (Tokyo: Kokusho kankōkai, 1980), 364–379.

30. *Liu-tsu t'an ching, T* 48.338c5; Yampolsky, *Platform Sutra,* 138. McRae suggests that antecedents for no-thought appear in Northern school writings; see "The Northern School of Chinese Ch'an Buddhism" (Ph.D. diss., Yale University, 1984), 393.

31. See Bhikkhu Ñāṇananda, *Concept and Reality in Early Buddhist Thought* (Kandy, Sri Lanka: Buddhist Publication Society, 1971), esp. 2–22.

32. "Dependent on all that [four elements, etc.] he thinks not, and yet he does think" *(tampi nissāya na jhāyati, jhāyati ca pana); Aṅguttara-nikāya* v.324–325; quoted in Ñāṇananda, *Concept and Reality,* 53. See also idem., *Magic of the Mind: An Exposition of the Kālakārāma Sutta* (Kandy: Buddhist Publication Society, 1974), 68–80; and *Concept and Reality,* 57–62.

33. Translated from the Tun-huang recension of *Liu-tsu t'an ching, T* 48.338c5–9; Yampolsky, *Platform Sutra,* 138. The vulgate of the same passage provides some slightly different nuances:

> During each thought, one does not cogitate on the objects [that appear] in front [of oneself]. If previous thoughts, present thoughts, and future thoughts continue along thought after thought without being cut off, this is termed "bondage." But if thought after thought does not abide in any dharma, then this would be "freedom from bondage." (*Liu-tsu t'an ching, T* 48.353a15–17)

This is one of a number of problematic passages in the no-thought section of the *Platform Sūtra,* which will only be resolved through further research on the text and its variant recensions. My interpretation of the Tun-huang version of this passage is tentative, since "the separation of the dharma body from the form body" need not carry the negative connotations I have implied; it may simply suggest that the attachment to ("abiding in") thought, and identifying oneself with mentation, would be the same as identifying the eternal dharma body with the transient form body. Conversely, when one brings an end to the attachment to thoughts, one would no longer identify with mentation and would in turn not mistakenly equate the dharma body with the form body. This may in fact be the reading the editors of the vulgate were attempting to bring out in their redaction of this section. The vulgate seems almost to imply that thoughts should be cut off, so that they will not continue on perpetually and lead to bondage.

34. *T* 48.338b19–22; translation is from Yampolsky, *Platform Sutra,* 136, with revisions.

35. Here I draw on the interpretations of Ñāṇananda, *Concept and Reality,* 57–62.

36. I follow the Kōshōji edition of the text in Nakagawa Taka, trans., *Rokuso dangyō,* Zen no goroku, vol. 4 (Tokyo: Chikuma shobō, 1976), 62; the vulgate for this passage (*T* 48.353a19–22) is virtually identical, differing by only a single logograph. There are problems in the text of the Tun-huang version that Yampolsky translates at *Platform Sutra,* 138.

37. *Ch'eng-hsi t'u, HTC* 110.436c5–9; translation is from Buswell, *Korean Approach,* 266, with revisions.

38. See Buswell, "Chinul's Systematization of Chinese Meditative Techniques in Korean Sŏn Buddhism," in Gregory, *Traditions of Meditation,* 203–207.

39. See ibid., 227–228.

40. Chad Hanson (*Language and Logic in Ancient China* [Ann Arbor: University of Michigan Press, 1983], 37) also notes that "Classical Chinese philosophical theories had no role for abstractions." See the characterization in Hajime Nakamura, *Ways of Thinking of Eastern Peoples: India-China-Tibet-Japan,* ed. Philip P. Wiener (1964; reprint, Honolulu: University Press of Hawaii, 1978), 178–180. While Nakamura's book has been slighted for its many oversimplifications, it is useful heuristically for outlining the general contours of Chinese and Indian Buddhist thought. See also Robert Gimello's characterization of Indian locu-

tionary styles in "Mysticism in Its Contexts," in *Mysticism and Religious Traditions,* ed. Steven T. Katz (Oxford: Oxford University Press, 1983), 74.

I do not mean to suggest here that such paradoxical formulae are unknown in Indian religious literature. For an especially provocative resonance in non-Buddhist literature, see *Taittirīya Āraṇyaka* 1.11.5: "The blind one found the jewel,/ The one without fingers picked it up./ The one with no neck put it on./ And the one with no voice gave it praise" (quoted in Heinrich Zimmer, *Philosophies of India,* ed. Joseph Campbell [Princeton: Princeton University Press, 1969], 409). Still it is generally true that the preponderance of mature Indian philosophical writing is more analytical and speculative.

41. *Wu-men kuan,* case 21, *T* 48.295c5.

42. Burton Watson, trans., *The Complete Works of Chuang Tzu* (New York: Columbia University Press, 1968), 240–241, with slight changes.

43. Buswell, *Korean Approach,* 163–164. Note also the correlations drawn by Chinul's descendant T'aego Pou (1301–1382): "This one thing . . . may expediently be called 'mind,' or 'path,' or 'king of the myriad things,' or 'Buddha.' " *T'aego Pou kuksa pŏbŏ chip,* trans. Yi Yŏngmu (Seoul: Han'guk pulgyo T'aegochong chongmuwŏn, 1974), 98.

44. For further discussion of this characterization of Ch'an discourse as "terse," see Buswell, "Chinul's Systematization," 223–226.

45. "The teachings of the Buddha [i.e., the doctrinal schools] are intended to support tens of thousands of generations [of future practitioners]; hence their principles have been demonstrated in detail. The admonitions of the [Ch'an] patriarchs involve an immediate crossing over to liberation; they aim at producing mysterious penetration." *Ch'an-yüan chu-chüan chi tu-hsü* 1, *T* 48.400a3; translated, with Chinul's explication, in Buswell, *Korean Approach,* 321–322.

46. Araki, *Daiesho,* 234; Cleary, 98.

47. Cf. *Ch'eng-hsi t'u, HTC* 110.435d4–436a12; translated in Buswell, *Korean Approach,* 273, and see Yŏndam Yuil's commentary at 345–346 n. 55. Peter Gregory's chapter above also discusses Tsung-mi's critique of the Hung-chou school.

48. *Hung-chou Po-chang ch'an-shih yü-lu, HTC* 119.409b; translation from Chang Chung-yuan, *Original Teachings of Ch'an, Selected from the Transmission of the Lamp* (New York: Pantheon Books, 1969), 132, with revisions.

49. Translated from Ta-hui's recension of the story (Araki, *Daiesho,* 37; Cleary, 106); see Buswell, *Korean Approach,* 178, 247. Cf. also *Ching-te ch'uan-teng lu* 8, *T* 51.262c.

50. For these three, see Buswell, *Korean Approach,* 167, and 188 n. 43 for specific references to the literature. See Sasaki, *Lin-chi,* 30, for Lin-chi's own account of these various styles.

51. Sasaki, *Lin-chi,* 50–52. Te-shan Hsüan-chien (780–865), in the lineage of Ch'ing-yüan Hsing-ssu (d. 740), was most closely identified with beatings, earning him the sobriquet "Master of Thirty Blows." See *Ching-te ch'uan-teng lu* 15, *T* 51.317c; D. T. Suzuki, *Essays in Zen Buddhism,* First Series, 276.

52. See *Lin-chi lu, T* 47.504a26–28; Sasaki, *Lin-chi,* 47; Miura and Sasaki, *Zen Dust,* 157 n. 12. For Lin-chi's *ho,* see Abe Chōichi, *Chūgoku zenshūshi,* 279.

53. *T* 47.503a29–b2; translation from Sasaki, *Lin-chi,* 41.

54. Following William Powell's characterizations of these genres; see his introduction to *The Record of Tung-shan,* 4–7. See also Yanagida Seizan, "The 'Recorded Sayings' Texts," 185–205.

55. See Powell's caveat concerning the teachings of Tung-shan's "discourse record" in *The Record of Tung-shan,* 8.

56. For Ma-tsu's thought, see Abe Chōichi, *Chūgoku zenshūshi,* 24–39; a good survey of Ma-tsu's life and thought appears in Honda Chōkō, "Baso," in *Zen no rekishi,* Kōza Zen, vol. 3, 157–170. See also Tsung-mi's analysis of the Hung-chou school in *Ch'eng-hsi t'u, HTC* 110.435d4–436a12.

57. *Chiang-hsi Ma-tsu Tao-i ch'an-shih yü-lu, HTC* 119.406a13–14, 406b7–8.

58. "Do not choose what is good, nor reject what is evil, but rather be free from purity and defilement"; *Ma-tsu yü-lu, HTC* 119.406a5. See also *Ching-te ch'uan-teng lu* 6, *T* 51.246a10–11; translated in Chang, *Original Teachings,* 149. Cf. also Ma-tsu's statement that the student "need not cling to wholesomeness or reject the unwholesome" (Chang, ibid.).

59. *Ma-tsu yü-lu, HTC* 119.405a18. Note also the parallel statement of Yüan-wu in his *Hsin-yao* 3, *HTC* 120.376a2–4.

60. See *Ch'eng-hsi t'u, HTC* 110.435d4–436a12; translated, with Chinul's comments, in Buswell, *Korean Approach,* 266–267. See also Peter Gregory's chapter in this volume.

61. For the equation drawn in Ch'an between "sentience" and "enlightenment," see Buswell, "Chinul's Systematization," 214–216. Note also Ta-hui's statement: "Everything that has a mind attains Buddhahood" (Araki, *Daiesho,* 73).

62. *Ma-tsu yü-lu, HTC* 119.406a7–8. For an interesting explication of the meanings of "normal" and "abnormal" mind, see Chinul's "Straight Talk on the True Mind," in Buswell, *Korean Approach,* 181.

63. *Ma-tsu yü-lu, HTC* 119.405a; discussed in Chang, *Original Teachings,* 131. See also Ta-hui's explanation of this exchange in *Ta-hui yü-lu, T* 47.910b.

64. *Ch'eng-hsi t'u, HTC* 110.436a8–9; translated in Buswell, *Korean Approach,* 267. Note also Ma-tsu's statement: "If you are aware of this mind, you will dress, eat, and act spontaneously in life as it transpires, and thereby cultivate your spiritual nature" (*Ching-te ch'uan-teng lu* 6, *T* 51.246a16–17), translated in Chang, *Original Teachings,* 149.

65. Although there are some inconsistencies in Tsung-mi's treatments of the four principal schools of middle Ch'an, he evaluates Ma-tsu's Hung-chou school as a sudden awakening–sudden cultivation approach, with its closest parallel being the earlier Niu-t'ou school. Tsung-mi says, in describing the Hung-chou approach:

> Since the principles realized through awakening are all impeccable and natural, the principles by which we cultivate should accord with them. We should not give rise to a mind that intends to excise evil and cultivate good, however, nor to a mind that wants to cultivate the path. . . . Although this school is near the approach of sudden awakening, it does not quite reach it; as far as the approach of gradual cultivation is concerned, however, it is completely off the mark [i.e., it is a sudden-cultivation approach]. (*Ch'eng-*

hsi t'u, HTC 110.436a, 438b; translated in Buswell, *Korean Approach,* 267, 269)

The Niu-t'ou was treated as an inferior variety of sudden awakening-gradual cultivation: "It halfway comprehends the approach of sudden awakening; since it advocates the relinquishment of passion, it has no shortcomings in regard to the approach of gradual cultivation" (*Ch'eng-hsi t'u, HTC* 110.438b; translated in Buswell, ibid., 269). See also the discussion in Peter Gregory's chapter in this volume.

66. *Ma-tsu yü-lu, HTC* 119.406b10–11.

67. Note Tsung-mi and Chinul's critique (translated in Buswell, *Korean Approach,* 297–304) that sudden awakening-sudden cultivation is intended only for those of most advanced capacity; for the great majority of students, sudden awakening-gradual cultivation is more appropriate.

68. *Ch'eng-hsi t'u, HTC* 110.437d10–11; translated in Buswell, *Korean Approach,* 277.

69. *Ch'eng-hsi t'u, HTC* 110.437d; translated in Buswell, *Korean Approach,* 277. This treatment of Hung-chou in terms of function is also discussed by Peter Gregory in his chapter above.

70. Note also how Tsung-mi's interpretation differs from that of D. T. Suzuki. Suzuki proposes that Ma-tsu's overemphasis on function (he does not specify which type) prompted Lin-chi to stress instead the "person" (the "true man of no rank"). Lin-chi's point was to restore Ch'an's original emphasis on the essence, as in the injunction "see the nature, achieve Buddhahood." The implication in Tsung-mi is that emphasis on function would be fine provided that it was the innate functioning of the mind that was meant, since that type was based directly on the innate essence of mind. See Suzuki Daisetsu, *Rinzai no kihon shisō: Rinzai-roku ni okeru "nin" shisō no kenkyū* (Tokyo: Chūō kōronsha, 1949), summarized in Abe Masao, "True Person and Compassion: D. T. Suzuki's Appreciation of Lin-chi and Chao-chou," in Abe, *Zen and Western Thought,* ed. William R. LaFleur (Honolulu: University of Hawaii Press, 1985), 69–80.

71. Note also Ma-tsu's *Record:* "Have faith in the fact that his own mind is a Buddha"; *Ma-tsu yü-lu, HTC* 119.405a18.

For general surveys of Lin-chi's thought, see Furuta Shōkin, *Rinzairoku no shisō* (Tokyo: Shunjūsha, 1956); Ōtsu Rekidō, "Rinzai," in *Zen no rekishi,* Kōza Zen, vol. 3, 203–222; Heinrich Dumoulin, *Geschichte des Zen-Buddhismus,* 167–193. For a thoughtful interpretation of the place of faith in Ch'an thought, see Sung Bae Park, *Buddhist Faith and Sudden Enlightenment* (Albany: State University of New York Press, 1983), 55–77. I would like to thank John Chan for suggesting to me the potential significance of the *Lin-chi lu* in bridging middle and classical Ch'an soteriology.

72. "The Master addressed the assembly, saying: 'Men who today study the Way must have faith in themselves. Don't seek outside!' " *Lin-chi lu, T* 47.499a4; Sasaki, *Lin-chi,* 16. "Since you students lack faith in yourself, you run around seeking something outside." *Lin-chi lu, T* 47.497c9; Sasaki, *Lin-chi,* 7.

73. *Lin-chi lu, T* 47.498b; Sasaki, *Lin-chi,* 13. The simile derives from the tale of Yajñadatta who, believing he had lost his head, went everywhere throughout the town in search of it; cf. the apocryphal *Śūraṅgama-sūtra, Shou-leng-yen ching, T* 19.121b20–22.

74. "The Master said: 'Over this lump of red flesh [the body or the heart] is a true man of no rank who is always going in and out of the face of every one of you. Those who have not yet realized him, look, look!' " *Lin-chi lu, T* 47.496c10–11; Sasaki, *Lin-chi,* 3. For Lin-chi's conception of "true man of no rank," see Furuta Shōkin, *Rinzairoku no shisō,* 83–88; and Abe Masao, "True Person and Compassion."

75. On this twofold role of faith, see Yanagida Seizan, "Kanna Zen ni okeru shin to gi no mondai," in *Bukkyō ni okeru shin no mondai,* ed. Nihon bukkyōgakkai (Kyoto: Heirakuji shoten, 1963), 141–163. The essay has been summarized in Morris J. Augustine, "The Buddhist Notion of Faith" (Ph.D. diss., Graduate Theological Union, 1978), 158–165.

76. Jikidō Takasaki, trans., *A Study on the Ratnagotravibhāga (Uttaratantra), Being a Treatise on the Tathāgatagarbha Theory of Mahāyāna Buddhism,* Serie Orientale Roma, vol. 33 (Rome, 1966), 296, with revisions; the overriding role of faith in tathāgatagarbha doctrine is discussed in detail at pp. 380–389. For the role of faith in tathāgatagarbha thought, see David S. Ruegg, "On the Knowability and Expressibility of Absolute Reality in Buddhism," *IBK* 20 (1971): 495–489 [sic].

77. Takasaki, *Ratnagotravibhāga,* 300, with revisions.

78. Even if Lin-chi demanded that faith be continually perfected, this need not imply gradualism. Ch'an had always insisted that cultivation was sudden provided that it only involve the continued repetition of a single activity over and over again until it was perfected, not the cultivation of a series of steps that had to be perfected in sequence. As we have seen, a common simile for sudden cultivation was target practice, in which one shoots arrows over and over again at the same target until the bull's-eye is hit consistently. Tsung-mi usually uses this simile to refer to a "sudden cultivation–gradual awakening" approach (see the translation of *Ch'eng-hsi t'u* in Buswell, *Korean Approach,* 295; see also Peter Gregory's chapter in this volume), but Ta-hui uses it even when referring to *k'an-hua* practice (as at Araki, *Daiesho,* 102; Cleary, 55).

79. *Ta-hui yü-lu* 20, *T* 47.894a; Cleary, 101. *Skandha-māra* (lit., "aggregate-devils") refers to the dangers inherent in one's own constituents of personality —that is, their inevitable demise.

80. *Ta-hui yü-lu* 20, *T* 47.894a; Cleary, 102.

81. This has been argued with considerable insight by Carl Bielefeldt, "Ch'ang-lu Tsung-tse's *Tso-Ch'an I* and the 'Secret' of Zen Meditation," in Gregory, *Traditions of Meditation,* 147–148.

82. The meaning of the term *kung-an* is akin to the use of the term "case" in law, as is attested in the popular detective-story genre spawned during the Ming; see Y. W. Ma, "Themes and Characterization in the *Lung-t'u Kung-an,*" *T'oung Pao* 59 (1973): 179–202.

83. Scholars have sometimes suggested that the first Ch'an usages of the term *kung-an* appear in stories concerning Huang-po Hsi-yün (d. ca. 850) and

his disciple Ch'en Tsun-su (780?–877?); see Furuta Shōkin, "Kōan no rekishi," 811, and Miura and Sasaki, *Zen Dust,* 153–154 n. 9. Both of these references appear, however, in literature from the Sung period (*Wu-chia cheng-tsung tsan, ZZ* 2/8/5/458a2, and *Ching-te ch'uan-teng lu, T* 51.291b17, respectively), so it remains unclear when the term was first used to refer specifically to a Ch'an exchange. Different homonyms for *kung-an* are given at Kurebayashi Kōdō, "Kanna Zen," 10.

84. *Fen-yang Wu-te ch'an-shih yü-lu, T* 47.595c–629c. This is discussed in Furuta, "Kōan no rekishi," 815–816; Miura and Sasaki, *Zen Dust,* 12.

85. *Pi-yen lu, T* 48.139a–225c. The complete text has been translated by Thomas and J. C. Cleary, *Blue Cliff Record,* 3 vols. (Boulder: Shambhala, 1977).

86. Translated by Iriya Yoshitaka, Kajitani Sōnin, and Yanagida Seizan, *Setchō juko,* Zen no goroku, vol. 15 (Tokyo: Chikuma shobō, 1981).

87. This rendering of the term has been suggested by Robert Gimello, "Poetry and the Kung-an in Ch'an Practice," *Ten Directions* 7, no. 1 (Spring/Summer, 1986): 9–10.

For Ch'an influences on Sung literature, see J. D. Schmidt, "Ch'an, Illusion, and Sudden Enlightenment in the Poetry of Yang Wan-li," *T'oung Pao* 60 (1974): 230–281.

88. See *Pi-yen lu Hsi-lu hou-hsü, T* 48.224c; translated in Levering, "Ch'an Enlightenment for Laymen," 32–33 n. 2, who tentatively accepts that the story has at least some factual basis. For a popular account of this story see Daisetz T. Suzuki, *An Introduction to Zen Buddhism* (Kyoto: Eastern Buddhist Society, 1949), 128–129; Ogisu Jundō, "Daie zenji no *Hekiganshū* shoki ni tsuite," *IBK* 11 (1963): 115–118 (cited in Levering, ibid.).

89. The first use of the term *hsien-ch'eng* 'immediately present' (J. *genjō*) with reference to *kung-an* is usually attributed to Ch'en Tsun-su, who is reputed to have said, "As an immediately present *kung-an,* I spare you from thirty blows" (*Ching-te ch'uan-teng lu* 12, *T* 51.291b17; translated in Miura and Sasaki, *Zen Dust,* 154 n. 9). As the *Ch'uan-teng lu* was not compiled until after Yüan-wu's time, however, I believe *hsien-ch'eng* to be actually a Sung locution.

90. *Yüan-wu hsin-yao* 2, *HTC* 120.367b14–15; see also *Ta-hui yü-lu* 19, *T* 47.892a19–28. *Yüan-wu hsin-yao* is a neglected text describing Yüan-wu's own interpretation of Ch'an practice, to which Ta-hui's approach clearly owes a great deal. While Ta-hui deservedly receives the lion's-share of attention in the development of *k'an-hua* practice, Yüan-wu's contribution should not be underestimated. The significance of this new interpretation of *kung-an* is discussed in Furuta, "Kōan no rekishi," 824.

91. *Yüan-wu hsin-yao* 3, *HTC* 120.379d9–10; cited in Furuta, "Kōan no rekishi," 822. For Yüan-wu's contribution to the development of *kung-an* as a meditative device, see Furuta, 819–825.

It would be worth exploring the resonances between Yüan-wu's view that a single *kung-an* subsumes all teachings and the Hua-yen doctrine that all the Buddha's words are incorporated in a single "complete sound" (*yüan-yin*). There are also provocative parallels with the conception of *dhāraṇīs* in Buddhist Tantric literature.

92. See the discussion in Furuta, "Kōan no rekishi," 831. The reader will note the contrast between Sung *kung-an* practice and the Japanese kōan system of Hakuin, in which kōan investigation becomes the virtual Ch'an equivalent of Ābhidharmika *dharmavicaya* (investigation of phenomena).

93. From *Shan-fang ye-hua* (Evening Talks in a Mountain Room), in *T'ien-mu Chung-feng ho-shang kuang-lu* 11, *Manji zokozōkyō* (Kyoto, 1884) 31/7/606a18–c10; translation from Miura and Sasaki, *Zen Dust,* 4–6, with revisions. This passage is cited in virtually all major studies of the development of the *kung-an* system; perhaps the best discussion of the implications of the passage, however, appears in Furuta, "Kōan no rekishi," 808–809.

For a comprehensive study of Chung-feng and his times, see Chün-fang Yü, "Chung-feng Ming-pen and Ch'an Buddhism in the Yüan," in *Yüan Thought: Chinese Thought and Religion Under the Mongols,* ed. Hok-lam Chan and Wm. Theodore de Bary (New York: Columbia University Press, 1982), 419–477, and esp. 430–444 for his Ch'an teachings. See also Fujishima Tateki, "Genchō bukkyō no ichiyōsō: Chūhō Myōhon o meguru kojitachi," *Ōtani gakuhō* 57, no. 3 (December 1976): 147–163.

94. Alt. *chih-chieh,* lit. "direct slicing"; I adopt this more liberal rendering to bring out better the connotations of the terms. The terms are used in Yüan-wu's *Hsin-yao, HTC* 120.372b4, 377b8, 385c7; and by Ta-hui in *Ta-hui yü-lu* 26, *T* 47.921c2 et passim.

95. This *hua-t'ou* receives extensive discussion throughout Ta-hui's writings; one of the better treatments appears at *Ta-hui yü-lu* 26, *T* 47.921c. Chao-chou's *wu* was certainly the principal *hua-t'ou* taught by Ta-hui, adumbrating its eventual selection by Wu-men Hui-k'ai (1183–1260) as the first of the forty-eight *kung-an* collected in his famous *Wu-men kuan* (*T* 48.292c). The strong emphasis on the *wu hua-t'ou* in Lin-chi Ch'an seems to have begun with Ta-hui's grand-teacher, Wu-tsu Fa-yen (1024?–1104); see Furuta, "Kōan no rekishi," 830, and Yanagida, "Chūgoku Zenshūshi," 101–104.

96. I have discussed this distinction in *Korean Approach,* 67–68.

97. A common refrain of teachers in the Yang-ch'i lineage: see *Yüan-wu hsin-yao* 4, *HTC* 120.394d3; *Ta-hui yü-lu* 19, *T* 47.893a11, and 26, *T* 47.922c et passim. I have discussed the significance of *fan-chao* in Ch'an thought in "Chinul's Systematization," 213–216. Note also the following statement by Ta-hui: "Just turn your light around and reflect back: where does the one who entertains such thoughts come from? What shape does he have when acting?" (Araki, *Daiesho,* 102; translation from Cleary, 54). Such counterillumination must be allowed to occur naturally, as in the *Platform Sūtra*'s "letting the Tao circulate freely": "You must diligently reflect back on this, but without struggling with it as you reflect back—if you struggle, you waste power. Didn't the Third Patriarch say so? — 'When you try to stop motion to return to stillness, the stopping causes further commotion' " (Araki, *Daiesho,* 102; translation from Cleary, 55).

98. See Kuroda Akira, "Zen no shinri," *Zen* 1 (1941): 41, who discusses this idea that the goal of observing the *wu hua-t'ou* is to understand the enlightened intent of Chao-chou. Note also T'aego Pou's remark: "How did *the idea to say 'no'* arise in Chao-chou?" (*T'aego Pou chip,* 109 et passim).

99. For the common etymology of the term *hua-t'ou* as referring to the "head

of speech," and thence thought, see Hsü-yün, *Hsü-yün ho-shang fa-hui,* comp. Ch'en Hsüeh-lü (1953; reprint, Hong Kong: n.p., 1961), 155, 166. See also the discussion in Chün-fang Yü, "Ta-hui," 220–221, following the Taiwanese scholar Nan Huai-chin.

100. *Yüan-wu hsin-yao* 1, *HTC* 120.350c5–6. For further discussion of this distinction, see my essay "Ch'an Hermeneutics." Note also the similar refrain in Ta-hui: "Students of meditation must investigate the live word; do not investigate the dead word. If you stay fixed on the live word, you will not forget it for an eternity of kalpas; but if you stay fixed on the dead word you will not be able to save yourself" (*Ta-hui yü-lu* 14, *T* 47.870b).

101. Hsü-yün, *Hsü-yün ho-shang fa-hui,* 155; translated also in Charles Luk, *Ch'an and Zen Teachings,* First Series (Berkeley: Shambhala, 1970), 22–23. Hsü-yün's fascinating autobiography has been translated by Charles Luk in *Empty Cloud: The Autobiography of the Chinese Zen Master Hsü Yün* (Rochester, N.Y.: Empty Cloud Press, 1974). We see in this passage that there is support from within the Ch'an tradition for viewing *k'an-hua* Ch'an as a product of Ch'an's degeneration.

102. *T'aego Pou chip,* 125.

103. Cf. *Ta-hui yü-lu* 19, *T* 47.891a22ff. et passim; see also Cleary, 13.

104. *Ta-hui yü-lu* 19, *T* 47.892a21–23.

105. Araki, *Daiesho,* 27.

106. Later advocates were not so reticent, however, to talk about stages of development in *k'an-hua* Ch'an. In Korea, for example, Chinul describes two distinct levels of *hua-t'ou* investigation: investigation of the meaning of the *hua-t'ou,* and investigation of just the word itself; I have discussed these levels in "Chinul's Systematization," 220–223. Such a bifurcation was necessary because Chinul was seeking to graft *k'an-hua* practice onto a sudden awakening-gradual cultivation soteriological schema. Like Ta-hui, however, Chinul still insisted that all *hua-t'ou* are essentially the same—catalysts of doubt and thence awakening—and any one *hua-t'ou* is as good as any other for this task.

In Japan, Hakuin divided Ta-hui's account of *k'an-hua* practice into three explicit stages: doubt, great death, and great rebirth. To this, he appended a still more structured sequence of kōan study, in which the student was to work through a series of some 1700 kōans, in five distinct repertoires, before enlightenment was consummated. Hakuin's approach is a systematic reading of Ta-hui that is not always traceable in Ta-hui's own presentation. See the treatment of Hakuin's system in Thomas P. Kasulis, *Zen Action/Zen Person* (Honolulu: University of Hawaii Press, 1981), 104–124. Kasulis' presentation of Hakuin's approach to kōan study is valuable for explaining the psychological dimension of Ch'an training. But it is also a structured interpretation of Hakuin—and, by extension, Ta-hui—that Ta-hui at least would certainly have rejected.

Some of these later "gradualist" interpretations of Ta-hui may derive from inconsistencies in Ta-hui's own accounts of soteriology. At times Ta-hui's words do seem to suggest gradualist schemata, which could have been used with justification to create a structured system of *hua-t'ou* investigation. Kajitani Sōnin ("Ta-hui," 268ff.), for example, discusses accounts of sudden awakening-gradual cultivation in Ta-hui, and Ta-hui himself uses analogies that involve sudden cultivation-gradual awakening (Araki, *Daiesho,* 102; Cleary, 55). But the preponderance of evidence shows clearly that Ta-hui's fundamental intent was to create a sudden style of cultivation oriented exclusively toward instantaneous insight.

107. *Yüan-wu hsin-yao* 4, *HTC* 120.384c4.

108. *Ta-hui yü-lu* 26, *T* 47.921c2–6.

109. "Training on this path is not bothered by a lack of intelligence; it is bothered by excessive intelligence. It is not bothered by a lack of understanding; it is instead bothered by excessive understanding" (*Ta-hui yü-lu* 29, *T* 47.935a23–24).

110. For the background of this tendency in Sung dynasty Ch'an, see Yanagida Seizan, "Chūgoku Zenshūshi," 92–93. For Ta-hui's connections with the intelligentsia, see the discussion in Araki, *Daiesho,* 252–255. The ways in which those contacts affected Ta-hui's presentation of Ch'an are discussed in Levering, "Ch'an Enlightenment for Laymen," 246–260.

111. *Ta-hui yü-lu* 26, *T* 47.922c5–12. See also Ta-hui's criticism in Araki, *Daiesho,* 110; translated in Levering, "Ch'an Enlightenment for Laymen," 257.

112. The respective sources for these quotations: "dry shit stick," Araki, *Daiesho,* 195, and cf. 130–131, translated in Levering, 303–304; "cypress tree," *Ta-hui yü-lu* 23, *T* 47.910a16–17; "no," *Ta-hui yü-lu* 26, *T* 47.921c, and cf. Cleary, 50.

The Korean Sŏn master Chinul discusses all eight of these defects and suggests that Ta-hui actually listed ten; see Buswell, *Korean Approach,* 338, and cf. 245–246. The defects are (1) Do not understand *wu* to mean yes or no. (2) Do not consider it in relation to doctrinal theory. (3) Do not ponder over it logically. (4) When the master raises his eyebrows or twinkles his eyes, do not think he is giving instructions about the meaning of the *hua-t'ou.* (5) Do not make stratagems for solving the *hua-t'ou* through the use of speech. (6) Do not busy yourself inside the tent of unconcern. (7) Do not consider it at the place where you raise the *hua-t'ou* to your attention. (8) Do not look for evidence in the wording. (9) Do not take *wu* to mean true nonexistence. (10) Do not grasp at a deluded state, simply waiting for enlightenment to come.

113. *Ta-hui yü-lu* 27, *T* 47.925c19–21. See also the parallel statements of Yüan-wu at *Yüan-wu hsin-yao* 3, *HTC* 120.372d13, 377b12–13. Yüan-wu also notes that Ch'an "does not posit stages and steps" *(pu-li chieh-chi); Yüan-wu hsin-yao* 3, 372d8. The metaphor of slicing through a spool of thread ultimately derives from Shen-hui; see *Shen-hui ho-shang i-chi,* ed. Hu Shih (Taipei: Hu Shih chi-nien kuan, 1971), 121. This metaphor is also discussed in the chapters by John McRae and Peter Gregory above.

114. Araki, *Daiesho,* 106; Cleary, 57.

115. *Ta-hui yü-lu* 22, *T* 47.903c6, and *Yüan-wu hsin-yao* 2, *HTC* 120.368a9. Note also Ta-hui's common refrain (903c3–4): "This one word [no] is the knife that slices through the road of birth and death"; and see the discussion of this analogy in Kuroda, "Zen no shinri," 41.

The metaphor of the "hundred-foot pole" was first used by Ch'ang-sha Ching-ts'en (d. 868); see *Ching-te ch'uan-teng lu* 10, *T* 51.274b8.

116. See Karl H. Potter's useful distinction between "leap" vs. "path" sote-

riologies in his *Presuppositions of India's Philosophies* (Englewood Cliffs, N.J.: Prentice-Hall, 1963), 36–46 and 236–256. This death-defying jump off a hundred-foot pole is perhaps the most evocative illustration of the meaning of a "leap" soteriology known to Buddhism.

As I suggest here, Ch'an's denial of sequence need not imply that a subitist approach is temporally faster than the much-maligned gradual paths. While the experience of enlightenment might in theory require only a single moment, the subitist may need a long time (dare I say "in practice"?) before he has that instantaneous experience—perhaps even longer than would the gradualist. One might thus reasonably ask—as Tsung-mi courageously does, in the face of what he must have known would have been vitriolic Ch'an indignation—whether a subitist position does not mask a long process of gradual development previously (i.e., in past lives), which prepares the way for that eventual sudden experience. The viability of the subitist position would demand that, regardless of whether any preparatory practices were undertaken previously, those practices have nothing whatsoever to do with the experience of enlightenment. Only in so claiming would the subitist avoid the inevitable implication that unconditioned nirvāṇa is somehow "caused" by the progressive perfection of earlier stages—an implication that plagues all gradualistic formulations of the path. See the discussion in Tsung-mi's *Ch'an-yüan tu-hsü* 3, *T* 48.408a3–5, translated in Buswell, *Korean Approach,* 297; for a sensitive treatment of this issue and its implications by Chinul, Tsung-mi's apologist, see *Korean Approach,* 297–304.

117. *Ching-te ch'uan-teng lu* 11, *T* 51.288c19–25; translated in Miura and Sasaki, *Zen Dust,* 247 n. 25.

118. Ogisu, "Shoki," 115; cited in Levering, "Ch'an Enlightenment for Laymen," 283 n. 1.

119. *T'aego Pou chip,* 166.

120. Ibid., 130. T'aego Pou received transmission in the indigenous Kajisan school of Korean Sŏn prior to receiving sanction from the Chinese Lin-chi master Shih-wu Ching-kung (1272–1352). He was thus the successor to both national traditions of Ch'an.

121. *T'aego Pou chip,* 130. Cf. also Ta-hui's statement, "Keep investigating until your mind has nowhere to go" (Araki, *Daiesho,* 121; Cleary, 61).

122. Araki, *Daiesho,* 127. T'aego uses several other colorful similes about the intensity of *k'an-hua* practice: it is like a cat stalking a mouse, a hen sitting on her eggs, a starveling thinking of food, or an infant longing for his mother. See *T'aego Pou chip,* 91.

123. *Ta-hui yü-lu* 19, *T* 47.891a23–25, sentences inverted. Cf. also *T'aego Pou chip,* 161: "The mass of doubt destroys the hundreds of random [thoughts]."

124. *Kao-feng Yüan-miao ch'an-shih ch'an-yao, HTC* 122.352d12–14. Kao-feng's *Ch'an-yao* is the third of the four major Ch'an texts studied in Korean Buddhist lecture halls, and, like Ta-hui's *Letters,* it also enjoys an extensive commentarial literature. The Korean edition of the text is edited with Korean punctuation by An Chinho, *Hyŏnt'o chuhae: Sŏn'yo* (1938; reprint, Seoul: Pŏmnyunsa, 1956). For Yüan-wu's explanation of *wu-hsin* and *wu-nien,* see *Yüan-wu hsin-yao* 3, *HTC* 120.374b7–8.

125. *Ta-hui yü-lu* 27, *T* 47.925b17, 29-c4; translated in Buswell, *Korean Approach,* 336.

126. Araki, *Daiesho,* 127. Other relevant passages from Ta-hui's corpus are translated in Levering, "Ch'an Enlightenment for Laymen," 302. Note also Yüan-miao's parallel comments in *Kao-feng ch'an-yao, HTC* 122.356b17-18:

> Of those past and present spiritual advisors in the west and in this land [of China] who were disseminating this ray of light [of the teachings], there are none that did anything more than simply resolve the one doubt. Whether it is a thousand doubts or a myriad doubts, they are all just this one doubt. One who resolves this doubt will doubt nothing more. And once he has no further doubts, [he will be identical] to Śākyamuni and Maitreya, Vimalakīrti and Old Man P'ang [P'ang Yün (740-808)].

127. *Ta-hui yü-lu* 16, *T* 47.879c11-13, 19-23; cf. the translation by Chün-fang Yü, "Ta-hui," 227. Ta-hui refers to this as a *hua-t'ou* at Araki, *Daiesho,* 27.

128. Araki, *Daiesho,* 24; Cleary, 39, quoting *Vimalakīrtinirdeśasūtra, Wei-mo-chieh so-shuo ching* 2, *T* 14.549b6; cf. Robert A. F. Thurman, trans., *The Holy Teaching of Vimalakīrti* (University Park: Pennsylvania State University Press, 1976), 66. This same passage is also quoted in *Kao-feng ch'an-yao, HTC* 122.356c11-12. The *locus classicus* for this lotus metaphor is *Dhammapada* (Pupphavagga), vv. 58, 59.

In his acceptance of the possibility of a viable lay practice, I do not believe that Ta-hui intended to impugn cenobitic training. Rather, he was countering a persistent bias in Buddhism toward celibate monastic life. On the one hand, Ta-hui wanted laypeople to know that there is nothing intrinsically superior about monasticism; family life in fact has certain advantages that can actually aid one's practice. On the other hand, Ta-hui was challenging the complacency of monks who thought that merely keeping their vocation would be conducive to enlightenment.

129. Araki, *Daiesho,* 103; Cleary, 56. The same phrase appears in *T'aego Pou chip,* 91, and "conserving power" is mentioned at *Yüan-wu hsin-yao* 3, *HTC* 120.374a17.

130. As Ta-hui notes, "Do not fatigue the dynamism of the mind" (Araki, *Daiesho,* 79).

131. I believe Chün-fang Yü overstates the place of faith in Ta-hui's thought when she notes that faith is necessary "before a person can successfully take up koan meditation" ("Ta-hui," 226). My own reading of Ta-hui suggests that just the opposite is the case: Ta-hui stresses the role of doubt in his account of Ch'an practice, with faith occupying very much a secondary place.

132. *Ta-hui yü-lu* 23, *T* 47.909b3-5.

133. *Ta-hui yü-lu* 22, *T* 47.903c10-13. Note also: "In one's daily activities, one should paste the words 'life' and 'death' on one's forehead and feel as if one owes someone a million strings of cash and the debtor is right outside the door asking for payment" (*Ta-hui yü-lu* 23, *T* 47.910c16-17; translation from Yü, "Ta-hui," 226). *T'aego Pou chip,* 111, also offers the clarification that fear of death is an important impetus to Ch'an practice. The "confrontation with mor-

tality" in Chung-feng Ming-pen's presentation of Ch'an is discussed at Chün-fang Yü, "Chung-feng Ming-pen," 435–437.

134. "If you just don't engage in any kind of evil you then will understand these words, whether you believe in them or not" (*Ta-hui yü-lu* 19, *T* 47.890b19–20; Araki, *Daiesho,* 5, and cf. 142).

135. *Kao-feng ch'an-yao, HTC* 122.357c17–d4; the passage is translated in Miura and Sasaki, *Zen Dust,* 246–247 n. 24. See also the Korean monk Sŏsan Hyujŏng's (1520–1604) discussion in *Sŏn'ga kugam* (Speculum on the Ch'an School), trans. Pŏpchŏng, Chŏngŭm mun'go, no. 131 (Seoul, 1976), 44.

136. The terms used by Ta-hui vary; they include *p'en-ti i-fa* (Araki, *Daiesho,* 105; Cleary, 57) and *pao-ti i-p'o* (*Ta-hui yü-lu* 26, *T* 47.921c3).

137. See *T'aego Pou chip,* 91: "Beneath this great doubt, one must let go of both body and mind." Hakuin later reified this experience as a specific stage in practice; see Kasulis, *Zen Action/Zen Person,* 112–116. Dōgen (1235–1237) relates this "casting off of body and mind" to the final leap off the hundred-foot pole; see *A Primer of Sōtō Zen: A Translation of Dōgen's* Shōbōgenzō, trans. Reihō Masunaga (Honolulu: University of Hawaii Press, 1971), 93–94.

138. Araki, *Daiesho,* 105; Cleary, 57. This common metaphor is also used at *T'aego Pou chip,* 57.

139. Here I draw on the intriguing interpretation of Ñāṇananda, *Concept and Reality,* passim.

140. *Ta-hui yü-lu* 9, *T* 47.848a, quoting Li T'ung-hsüan (635–730), *Hsin Hua-yen ching lun* 1, *T* 36.721a; translated in Buswell, *Korean Approach,* 213. Cf. also *Yüan-wu hsin-yao* 2, *HTC* 120.367c13–14: "Worldly dharmas and Buddhadharmas fuse into one mass. Each and every thing and person has a way to freedom."

The Korean Sŏn master Chinul used such descriptions of the Ch'an awakening experience to posit a fundamental harmony between the approaches of Ch'an and Hua-yen, as epitomized in their similar accounts of this concept of interfusion. Such similarities justified, he felt, his attempts to combine those two main streams of Koryŏ Buddhist thought in a comprehensive system of Buddhist doctrine and praxis. See Buswell, *Korean Approach,* esp. 246–253; and "Chinul's Systematization," passim.

141. Araki, *Daiesho,* 80; Cleary, 41–42.

Glossary

ch'an 禪
Ch'ang-sha Ching-ts'en 長沙景岑
ch'ang-shou 長壽
ch'an-shuo 禪說
Ch'an-yao 禪要
Ch'an-yüan chu-chüan chi tu-hsü 禪源諸詮集都序
Chao-chou Ts'ung-shen 趙州從諗
cheng-ju 證入
cheng-wu 證悟
chen-hsin 眞心
Ch'en Tsun-su 陳尊宿
chi 機
chia 家

chia-feng 家風
Chiang-hsi Ma-tsu Tao-i ch'an-shih yü-lu 江西馬祖道一禪師語錄
chiao-wai pieh-ch'uan/pu-li wen-tzu 教外別傳不立文字
chieh-wu 解悟
chien 漸
chih-chieh 直截
chih-chih 直指
chih-chih jen-hsin/chien-hsing ch'eng-fo 直指人心見性成佛
chih-shih 直示
Chih-yüeh lu 指月錄
ching-chieh 徑截
ching-chin 精進
Ching-te ch'uan-teng lu 景德傳燈錄
Ch'ing-yüan Hsing-ssu 青原行思
Chin-hua Chu-ti 金華俱胝
Chinul 知訥
chi-yüan wen-ta 機緣問答
Chu Hsi 朱熹
ch'ui-shih 垂示
Chung-feng Ming-pen 中峰明本
Chung-hua ch'uan-hsin-ti Ch'an-men shih-tzu ch'eng-hsi t'u 中華傳心地禪門師資承襲圖
Dōgen 道元
fan-chao 返照
Fa-yen 法眼
Fa-yen Wen-i 法眼文益
Fen-yang Shan-chao 汾陽善昭
Fen-yang Wu-te ch'an-shih yü-lu 汾陽無德禪師語錄
Fo-kuo K'o-ch'in ch'an-shih hsin-yao 佛果克勤禪師心要
genjō 現成
Hakuin Ekaku 白隱慧鶴
ho 喝
Ho-tse Shen-hui 荷澤神會
hsien-ch'eng 現成
hsi-lun 戲論
hsin 信
Hsin-chou Ta-ti 忻州打地
Hsin Hua-yen ching lun 新華嚴經論
hsin pu-chi 信不及
Hsin-yao 心要
hsüan-t'ung 玄通
Hsüeh-tou Ch'ung-hsien 雪竇重顯
Hsü-yün 虛雲
Huang-po Hsi-yün 黃蘗希運
hua-t'ou 話頭
Hua-yen 華嚴
hui-kuang fan-chao 廻光返照
Hui-neng 慧能
Hung-chou 洪州
Hung-chou Po-chang ch'an-shih yü-lu 洪州百丈禪師語錄
Hung-chou Shui-liao 洪州水潦
huo-chü 活句
hwadu 話頭
i 意
i-ch'ing 疑情
i-t'uan 疑團
ju-lai-tsang 如來藏
Kajisan 迦智山
k'an 看
k'an-hua Ch'an 看話禪
K'anhwa kyŏrŭi-ron 看話決疑論
Kao-feng Yüan-miao 高峰原妙
Kao-feng Yüan-miao ch'an-shih ch'an-yao 高峰原妙禪師禪要
kōan 公案
Koryŏ 高麗
Kuei-yang 潙仰
kung-an 公案
ku-tse 古則
li 力
Lin-chi 臨濟
Lin-chi I-hsüan 臨濟義玄
Lin-chi lu 臨濟錄
Li T'ung-hsüan 李通玄
Liu-tsu t'an ching 六祖壇經
Lo-han Kuei-ch'en 羅漢桂琛
Ma-ku Pao-ch'e 麻谷寶徹
Ma-tsu Tao-i 馬祖道一
Mi-an 密菴

Miao-yüan 妙圓
Musang 無相
Musŏlt'o-ron 無舌土論
Muyŏm 無染
Nan-yüeh Huai-jang 南嶽懷讓
Nieh-p'an 涅槃
nien 念
Niu-t'ou 牛頭
p'an-chiao 判教
P'ang Yün 龐蘊
pao-ti i-p'o 嚗地一破
p'en-ti i-fa 噴地一發
p'ing-ch'ang hsin 平常心
Pi-yen lu 碧巖錄
p'o 破
Po-chang Huai-hai 百丈懷海
Pŏpchip pyŏrhaeng-rok 法集別行錄
Pŏpchip pyŏrhaeng-rok chŏryo pyŏngip sagi 法集別行錄節要並入私記
Po-tse sung-ku 百則頌古
pu-li chieh-chi 不立階級
Sa chip 四集
san-yao 三要
Shan-fang ye-hua 山房夜話
sheng-lüeh 省略
Shen-hsiu 神秀
Shen-hui 神會
shih 示
Shih-kung Hui-tsang 石鞏慧藏
shih-shih wu-ai 事事無礙
shih-ta-fu 士大夫
Shih-wu Ching-kung 石屋清珙
shou-i 守一
Shou-leng-yen ching 首楞嚴經
Sŏn'ga kugam 禪家龜鑑
Sŏnmun pojang-rok 禪門寶藏錄
Sŏsan Hyujŏng 西山休靜
ssu 思
ssu-chü 死句
sui-yüan ying-yung 隨緣應用
Sŏn 禪
T'aego Pou 太古普愚
T'aego Pou kuksa pŏbŏ chip 太古普愚國師法語集
ta-fen-chih 大憤志
Ta-hui Tsung-kao 大慧宗杲
Ta-hui P'u-chüeh ch'an-shih yü-lu 大慧普覺禪師語錄
ta-i 大疑
Tao-hsin 道信
Ta-sheng ch'i-hsin lun 大乘起信論
teng-lu 燈錄
Te-shan Hsüan-chien 德山宣鑑
t'i 體
T'ien-mu Chung-feng ho-shang kuang lu 天目中峰和尚廣錄
T'ien-t'ai 天台
Ts'ao-tung 曹洞
Tsung-ching lu 宗鏡錄
Tsung-mi 宗密
Tsu-t'ang chi 祖堂集
tun 頓
tun-chiao 頓教
tun-chüeh 頓覺
Tung-shan fa-men 東山法門
Tung-shan Liang-chieh 洞山良价
tun-wu 頓悟
tun-wu chien-hsiu 頓悟漸修
tun-wu tun-hsiu 頓悟頓修
tzu-hsing pen-yung 自性本用
tzu-jan 自然
Wai-yü 外域
Wei-mo-chieh so-shuo ching 維摩詰所說經
wen-tzu Ch'an 文字禪
wu 無
Wu Chia 五家
Wu-chia cheng-tsung tsan 五家正宗贊
wu-hsin 無心
Wu-men Hui-k'ai 無門慧開
Wu-men kuan 無門關
wu-nien 無念
Wu-tsu Fa-yen 五祖法演
wu-tz'u-ti 無次第
wu-wei 無位

wu-wei chen-jen 無位眞人
Yang-ch'i 楊岐
yin 印
Yŏndam Yuil 蓮潭有一
yüan-chiao 圓教
Yüan-chüeh ching ta-shu ch'ao 圓覺經大疏鈔
Yüan-wu hsin-yao 圜悟心要
Yüan-wu K'o-ch'in 圜悟克勤
yüan-yin 圓音
yü-lu 語錄
yung 用
Yün-men 雲門
Yün-men Wen-yen 雲門文偃

III
Analogies in the Cultural Sphere

The Sudden and the Gradual in Chinese Poetry Criticism: An Examination of the Ch'an-Poetry Analogy

RICHARD JOHN LYNN

The following passage appears in the *Tai-ching t'ang shih-hua* (Discussions of Poetry from the Hall of Him Who Always Has the Classics by His Side) by Wang Shih-chen (1634–1711):

> Hung Sheng, [whose courtesy name is] Fang-ssu [1646?–1704], once asked Shih Yü-shan [Shih Jun-chang, 1619–1683] about the method of composing poetry *(shih-fa)*. He replied by first relating what I had once said about the main principles of poetry *(shih ta-chih)*: "Your teacher says that poetry is like an exquisite and towering Pagoda that appears at the snap of the fingers or like the twelve towers of the five cities of the immortals that ephemerally exist at the edge of heaven. I do not agree. To use a metaphor, poetry is like someone building a house out of tiles, glazed bricks, wood, and stone—he must put them all together, one by one, on solid ground." Hung then replied: "This constitutes the difference between the meaning of sudden and gradual enlightenment of the Ch'an sect" *(ch'an-tsung tun chien erh-i)*.[1]

By the seventeenth century it had become commonplace to discuss poetry in terms of Ch'an, to say that poetry in some way or ways "is like" *(ju)* Ch'an; the corollary, Ch'an "is like" poetry, also occurs, though not so commonly. As widespread as this habit was, from the Sung era (960–1279) on through the end of the Ch'ing in the early twentieth century, it still always had detractors and opponents. The interplay between advocates and opponents of this Ch'an-Poetry analogy makes fascinating reading, for many basic assumptions concerning both Ch'an and poetry thus come to light, assumptions whose implications touch, in turn, various fundamental aspects of Chinese literary and intellectual culture in general. Readings in the sources where this analogy occurs have indicated that the "sudden-gradual" polarity in Chinese poetics is something that cannot be understood adequately apart from an appreciation of the range of meanings inherent in this analogy, for it is there in this context that statements very often appear concerning the sudden and the gradual. This is especially true during the initial stages of the analogy's popularity as a critical concept during the earlier Sung—there, with few exceptions, they only appear in this context. Gradually, however, as Neo-Confucianism begins directly to affect the way people talk about poetry, from the second half of the twelfth century on, there also occur statements about the sudden and the gradual achievement of poetic "success" or "genius" which seem more attached to Neo-Confucian concerns; with these, the context appears to be: "the attainment of perfection in poetry is like the achievement of sagehood."[2] With the incorporation of the Buddhist concept of *wu* (enlightenment) within the philosophical writings of many Neo-Confucians, especially Lu Chiu-yüan (1139–1193) and later Ch'en Hsien-chang (1428–1500) and Wang Yang-ming (1472–1529), some writers with a critical interest in poetry who do not like the Ch'an-Poetry analogy actually take over this "secularized" concept of *wu* and say things such as: "it is all right to talk of poetry in terms of *wu* but not in terms of Ch'an" and "there has always been *wu* in great poetry, but this has nothing to do with Ch'an." However, the Ch'an-Poetry analogy continued to be the most usual context for the concept of enlightenment—sudden or gradual—as it occurred in critical writings throughout the rest of the traditional era, whatever the extent of "secular" opposition might have been. Actually, opposition cannot be understood in terms of Neo-Confucian opposition to Buddhism in general, though at times that surely plays an important part. There were intrinsic aesthetic and literary-historical forces operating within the tradition of poetry itself which sometimes argued against the Ch'an-Poetry analogy and which attempted to emancipate *wu* from its Buddhist context. The most serious challenge to the analogy, in my opinion, lay here and not in in any extrinsic philosophical force. As such, "enlightenment" in poetry from Sung times on can have any one of three basic orientations: the Buddhist (Ch'anist), the Neo-Confucian, and the literary-aesthetic. These all overlap or interpenetrate to varying extents, though it is usually possible to see which one prevails. We should also be aware, however, that lying behind *all* of them are the Taoist concepts of the spontaneous and the natural, especially as they appear in the *Chuang-tzu.*[3] Nevertheless, it is my view that by Southern Sung times, Taoist ideas as they appear in critical writings on poetry—and perhaps as well in painting and calligraphy criticism—had largely ceased to operate independently of the mainstream intellectual currents of the day, principally Ch'an and Neo-Confucianism. Philosophical Taoism, of course, was a major force in shaping these other two traditions, and Taoist ideas were certainly very much alive in Sung and post-Sung times, but there no longer seems to have been a purely Taoist context operating—ideas from philosophical Taoism become borrowed ideas in literary aesthetics, borrowed via Ch'an and Neo-Confucianism. Furthermore, these ideas should be distinguished from references in critical writings to Taoist alchemy and the search for immortality *(hsien),* for occasionally critics have compared the attainment of genius in poetry with the achievement of the Taoist adept —Huang T'ing-chien (1045–1105) and Ch'en Shih-tao (1053–1101) are probably the most famous critics who discussed poetry in these terms—something, as we shall see, that involved a different attitude toward poetry than the *natural* spontaneity inspired by the *Chuang-tzu,* though it did share things in common, in a strategic or operational sense, with views of poetry that took a gradualist approach—in the contexts of both the Ch'an-Poetry and the Confucian Sagehood-Poetry analogies.

Obviously, these are complex issues, and it would be best if in this essay I attended primarily to surveying the sources in such a way that we begin to know, simply, such things as who said what, when did he say it, and what other critics were subsequently influenced in either a positive or negative way.[4] In its original form this essay presented and discussed poet-critics through the end of the nineteenth century, but limitations of space will only allow us to consider figures through the end of the Southern Sung era in the survey which follows, including the poet-critic who in many ways is the Sung era culmination of this entire trend—Yen Yü (ca. 1195–ca. 1245). It is also beyond the scope of the present essay to determine *why* critics took the approach they did, for this would involve detailed analysis of each critic's family, social, educational, bureaucratic-professional (if applicable), and geographical affiliations—that web of overlapping relationship that resulted in one particular orientation rather than another. Of course, it would also involve an in-depth appreciation of the complete range of each critic's writings in poetry and prose—often very extensive—in order to determine what personal and individual elements were operating in his criticism. Such analysis and appreciation could only adequately happen in monograph-length studies on the individuals involved; it cannot be done here.[5] Therefore, focusing upon the Sung era, the following survey, while rather extensive, should be regarded as a preliminary exercise that attempts, at best, to bring the most important features to light, as mountain tops might be seen above a thick layer of mist which keeps the great mass of the range still obscured.

Although the custom of discussing poetry in terms of Ch'an begins in earnest only during the Sung period, it can also be found occasionally during the T'ang (618–906), that great era of Ch'an and poetry when people seem to have been more concerned with practicing Ch'an and poetry than talking about how to do it! The following Sung era seems, on the other hand, to have stood rather in awe of both the Ch'an and the poetry of the T'ang; a great deal of ink, in any case, was spent in trying to determine "how the T'ang people did it"—just how did those great Ch'an masters reach and teach enlightenment, how did those great T'ang poets write the poetry they did? Statements linking Ch'an and poetry on a theoretical level constitute one of the most common features of Sung poetry criticism—this is a fairly rare thing in T'ang letters themselves, in spite of the fact that many prominent T'ang poets were interested in Ch'an and associated with Ch'an monks. One such figure was Liu Yü-hsi (772–842), and we do find among his writings something that anticipates the later craze for the Ch'an-Poetry analogy:

> The term *śramaṇa (sha-men)* in Sanskrit is equivalent to the expression *ch'ü yü* (eliminate desires) in Chinese. Only when one is able to quit the desires will his mind become *hsü* (empty, *śūnya*), and when it is empty, the myriad forms of phenomenal reality will enter it *(wan-hsiang ju)*. When they enter it, there is sure to be something that will break out *(hsieh)*, and it is this which consequently will take form in verbal expression *(nai hsing hu tz'u)*. If verbal expression would be marvelous *(miao)* and profound *(shen)*, one must be sure to make it fit with the rules of tonal prosody *(sheng-lü)*. Thus, from the time of near antiquity on, disciples of Śākyamuni who have become famous throughout the world because of their poetry have followed one on the heels of the other. Through samādhi (*ting*, a composed mind) one achieves a *viṣaya* (*ching*, a mental realm) which consequently reaches a purity through a soaring freedom *(hsiao-jan i ch'ing)* and which, in accordance with prajñā (*hui*, wisdom), charges words with meaning *(yu hui erh ch'ien tz'u)*. Therefore such a one attains beauty through the essence of art *(ts'ui-jan i li)*. Believe in the flowers that bloom in the forest of Ch'an and shun the pearl and jade that might be fished up out of the river![6]

Liu obviously admires the poetry of Ch'an monks and masters, and he ascribes its marvelousness, profundity, and beauty to the enlightened state of mind achieved by the poets involved, a state in which the interdependent functions of perception and verbal articulation attain a perfect and natural spontaneity.

The Northern Sung Era

Su Shih (1037–1101), the great painter, poet, calligrapher, writer of prose, and statesman of the Northern Sung era, wrote a great deal about the nature of creativity and the way to artistic success in all the literary and art forms he himself practiced.[7] In poetry he believed that the poem and the creative force that brings it into being should leap forth from the poet in an unpremeditated and uncontrollable fashion—the poet, in effect, should, indeed must, tap into the well-spring of Nature itself, and the primordial creative force to which he gives himself over should take hold of him, and the poetry which results should be a "natural event." Although Su often spoke of literature and art in terms derived from philosophical Taoism,[8] he also spoke of them in terms of Ch'an, as his *Sung Ts'an-liao shih* (A Send-Off Poem for Master Ts'an-liao) reveals:

> Your Eminence has studied the bitterness and illusory nature of things—
> Hundreds of reflections whose ashes have long become cold.
> A sword hilt will only produce a feeble wheeze,[9]
> So why ever try to contend with one's contemporaries
> To see whose writing will be the most magnificent!
> A new poem should be like the most white of snows,
> Its articulation at once so pure it's startling—
> T'ui-chih [Han Yü, 768–824] criticized cursive calligraphy thus:
> Since the myriad affairs of life are impossible to avoid
> And sorrow and grief are sure to upset one's equilibrium,
> All of this will come to be lodged in the rush of one's galloping brush!
> I'm rather astonished at the way the Buddhists
> Regard the self as if it were a dried up hilltop well—
> Submissively, they give voice to their blandness and placidity *(tan-po)*
> But who provides for the expression of heroism and valor *(hao-meng)*?[10]
> After careful consideration, I don't think this is true—
> Genuine skill is not just a matter of illusions and shadows.
> If you want to make the language of your poetry marvelous *(miao)*,
> Don't ever reject emptiness *(k'ung)* and quietude *(ching)*.
> Being quiet, you can bring all possible movements to completion;
> Being empty, you can internalize a myriad realms.
> Experiencing the human world, you walk among your fellow men;
> Contemplating the self, you lie upon some cloudy mountain.
> Mixtures of salty and sour satisfy every preference,
> But among them there is an ultimate flavor with an everlasting aftertaste.[11]
> Since poetry and the dharma can do no harm to one another,
> I must again ask your opinion about what I have said here![12]

Like Liu Yü-hsi, Su advocates the cultivation of the Ch'an form of consciousness, characterized by emptiness and quietude, as a prerequisite to success in poetry. He rejects Han Yü's assertion that great art can only be produced by one who is profoundly and emotionally involved with the vicissitudes of life and ends by declaring that the way of poetry and the Buddhist dharma are complementary approaches to the problem of human existence and self-realization. Su also argues for individuality and spontaneity in poetry and warns against both imitation of the works of others and letting extrinsic motives (fame, recognition) influence the course of one's art. Although he does not seem to have ever explicitly formulated a "sudden" approach to poetic success or "enlightenment," the many references to freedom and spontaneity in his writings indicate that he surely would have been in the "sudden" camp if he had to choose sides.

By contrast, Su's contemporary Huang T'ing-chien was a thoroughgoing "gradualist." Although like Su he advocated spontaneity, he believed that spontaneity could only achieve valid results if it operated "within the rules," and "rules" for Huang meant the precepts one could derive from a tradition of "correct" models in the tradition of poetry—the great masters of the past, especially Tu Fu (712–770).[13] Time and again Huang encouraged his associates and disciples to read and assimilate the great works of the tradition, gradually adding the fruits of earlier efforts by the masters to his own potential until the time for his own ripeness occurred; he did not use the Ch'an-Poetry analogy to express this view but a Taoist Alchemy-Poetry analogy:

> Language of one's own invention is the most difficult thing to achieve of all. In Old Tu's [Tu Fu's] composition of poetry and T'ui-chih's [Han Yü's] composition of prose, there is not one single word that does not have a precedent somewhere. It is just that later people read books less and so, unwittingly, say that Han and Tu themselves invented this expression or that. Successful writers in antiquity were really able to mold and forge the myriad things of existence, and, although they were in the habit of appropriating well-worn phrases of people ancient to them in their own literary compositions, this was the way alchemists use but one grain of magical cinnabar to touch iron and turn it into gold.[14]

Huang's disciple Ch'en Shih-tao employed both the Taoist Alchemy/Immortality-Poetry analogy and the Ch'an-Poetry analogy in his writings. In one of his poems, *Tz'u yün ta Ch'in Shao-chang* (Poem Sent in Reply to One from Ch'in Shao-chang [Ch'in Kou, 1049–1101] Following the Same Rhyme Scheme), this couplet occurs: "Studying poetry is like studying how to become an immortal *(hsien)*, / For when the time is ripe your bones will change all by themselves!"[15] *Huan ku* (change the bones) was originally a Taoist term for what is supposed to happen after one has taken the true elixir of immortality (or "manufactured" it within one's own body)—one's bones become transformed into "immortal's bones" *(hsien-ku)*. Whether concocted externally or manufactured internally, the process is supposed to be a long and arduous one, but when it finally happens, it happens all at once and perfectly. *Huan ku* was also used by Huang T'ing-chien as a term to designate one particular mode of creative variation in poetic composition:

> Shan-ku [Huang T'ing-chien] said: "There are no limits to the number of ideas that might be expressed in poetry, but human talent does have a

> limit, so to use this limited talent to pursue a limitless number of ideas is something not even Yüan-ming [T'ao Ch'ien, 365–427] or Shao-ling [Tu Fu] could do. Nevertheless, when one does not alter the idea of a poem and but creates new language for it, this is called the *huan ku fa* (changing the bones method), and when one takes the idea of a poem as a general model and gives it a new shape, this is called the *to t'ai fa* (appropriating the embryo method)."[16]

In either case, Huang implies that the poet's ability to transform elements of the tradition is a magical one, of the same order as the practices of the Taoist adept. *To t'ai* (appropriating or snatching away the embryo [of another]) alludes to the Taoist belief that through breath control and certain dietary and sexual practices one can form the Mysterious Embryo within oneself; it is this embryo that, thus nourished, grows into a new and pure body; it is this that is released from the impure corpse when the adept is transformed into an immortal—when he "seemingly" dies.[17] Huang's analogy here is especially intriguing: one poet can "appropriate" the idea of a poem by another poet, an idea that the other had been "nourishing," and use it—in a kind of shortcut method—to reach the same goal of "perfection" as the original poet!

However, this way of talking about poetry in terms of Taoist practices never seems to have really caught on, probably because it was eclipsed by the general upsurge of interest in Ch'an during this time, something that made the Ch'an-Poetry analogy far more popular. Writing more than 150 years later and from the vantage point of an already long tradition of Ch'an-imbued poetics, Lin Hsi-i had this to say about both analogies in an essay dated 1266, *Huang Shao-ku chi pa* (Colophon to the Collected Works of Huang T'ing-chien):

> Hou-shan [Ch'en Shih-tao] once said: "Studying poetry is like studying how to become an immortal, / For when the time is ripe your bones will change all by themselves!" However, I say that studying poetry is like studying Ch'an, where little enlightenment can mean nothing but little success *(hsiao-wu pi hsiao te)*. Becoming an immortal can only result from an accumulation of earnest efforts *(chi-kung)*, whereas in Ch'an there is the teaching of sudden enlightenment *(tun-chiao)*, something that can be expressed metaphorically as "upon rolling up the screen you see the way" *(chüan lien chien tao)* or "upon extinguishing all doctrines you understand your own mind" *(mieh chiao ming hsin)*—something that can be called "with one surpassing leap enter directly into it" *(i-ch'ao chih-ju che)*. To be sure there was an eighty-year-old wandering monk as Ch'an-chou[18] and a white-haired incarnation as the fifth patriarch,[19] yet the young Sudhana (Shan-ts'ai t'ung-tzu) and the young Lin-chi, with one look around the dwelling and with one twist of the tiger's whiskers, straightaway stood equally with all the patriarchs.[20] How could these ever be topics for mere specious discussion![21]

Lin regards the Taoist practice of immortality as a gradualist method, likens it to the "little" enlightenment of the Hīnayāna *(hsiao-sheng),* Northern, and gradualist Ts'ao-tung tradition (as a follower of the "orthodox" Lin-chi sect would have looked at it), and rejects both as analogies for success in poetry in favor of the sudden enlightenment of the Lin-chi tradition. During the intervening 150-odd years a great number of poet-critics had discussed poetry in terms of Ch'an, however, including Ch'en Shih-tao himself, as for example in a letter he once wrote to the same Ch'in Kou:

> You, regretfully, wish to receive my teaching [concerning poetry]—why do you seek teaching from an inferior source! Long ago Śākyamuni plucked a flower and showed it to his disciples, and Kāśyapa smiled at him. Śākyamuni then said: "I entrust my teaching to this disciple."[22] This giving and the receiving of Śākyamuni's teaching was conducted in this way —although it is something great, it can be expressed by something small. If you work hard at poetry, perhaps I can congratulate you with a smile![23]

Ch'en had begun his letter with an account of how he had struggled with success in poetry until he met Huang T'ing-chien, one whose "learning is very broad," who "obtained his poetic method from Tu Shao-ling [Tu Fu]," and who "could imitate Shao-ling but does not do it." Ch'en then goes on to say:

> Thus, while his poetry remains close to Tu's, his own advances in poetry never come to an end. I once declared that Yü-chang's [Huang's] poetry is just like the way he himself is—one might be closed to both yet cannot become intimate, and one might try to keep one's distance yet cannot become estranged. . . . It is because of him that I, a person bearing a heavy load on the road of poetry, managed to have it eased.

Ch'en seems to be giving Ch'in two pieces of advice: (1) one cannot have poetry explained or taught to him by someone who has achieved success in it, and (2) although one can assimilate from the study of some master's poetry his "method" of greatness, one cannot simply apply that method wholesale and unaltered to one's own work. As in Ch'an, the teaching of poetic enlightenment is something beyond the words of any teacher or the scriptures of any dogma, and one can only profit from an association with a master by adopting a posture of individuality and freedom on some middle ground between intimacy and estrangement. However, the general drift of Ch'en's advice seems undeniably *gradualist,* with such emphasis on learning and on an extensive master-disciple relationship, as Huang had with Tu Fu and Ch'en himself had with Huang, Huang's through immersing himself in Tu's works, and Ch'en's through following Huang's example as well as his immersion in Huang's own works.

Huang T'ing-chen's influence was extremely widespread during his own day and for the rest of the Sung era.[24] Learning from "the ancients"—especially, but not only, Tu Fu—was an axiom of his which quickly seems to have begun to develop into a notion much like the idea of an orthodox patriarchy in Ch'an, or, for that matter, of an orthodox succession of teachers in the Confucian tradition (something which began to be a principal concern of the Sung Neo-Confucian movement). Fan Wen, whose dates are unknown but, since his father, the prominent statesman and historian Fan Tsu-yü (1041–1098), was a contemporary of Huang T'ing-chien and Ch'en Shih-tao, was probably active during the late eleventh and early twelfth centuries, wrote a work of poetry criticism entitled *Ch'ien-hsi shih-yen* (A Connoisseur's Guide to Poetry from the Hidden Stream) which is very much in Huang's and Ch'en's tradition. Although the work has not survived into modern times, Kuo Shao-yü has been able to reconstruct a great deal of it in his *Sung shih-hua chi i* (Sung Discussions of Poetry, A Reconstruction of Lost Works); one of these parts deals with the question of how to "learn from the ancients," relating it to the Ch'an concept of the true dharma eye *(cheng fa-yen):*

> Shan-ku [Huang T'ing-chien] said that if the student of poetry does not discern where the ancients concentrated their intent *(yung i ch'u)* but only gets at their superficial aspects *(ch'i p'i-mao),* he will as a consequence be so much the more removed from them. For example, "A breeze blows the willow catkins, filling the wineshop with fragance"—even if someone were again able to compose this line [as it were for the first time], it would still not make him a T'ai-pai [Li Po, 701–762]! As for "A barmaid of Wu presses out wine and urges us guests to try some"—anyone else would still find the words "presses out wine" difficult to reach. "My young Chin-ling friends come to see me off, / Each of us, whether leaving or not, drains his cup"—this is even more unusual. "Won't you gentlemen try to ask the easterly flowing water / Which will be longer—it or the feelings of us parted friends!"—with this we really come to the place where T'ai-pai's marvelousness *(miao)* lies, and we ought to immerse ourselves in it. As one can see, the student must first make judgment (the power to discriminate, *shih*) his master *(chu);* this is just like what the Ch'anists call the true dharma eye. One must but embody this power of vision *(yen-mu),* for only then will he be able to enter the way *(ju tao).*[25]

Fan does not give explicit advice as to *how* one should go about trying to acquire this perfect power of judgment, but from the rest of what remains of the *Ch'ien-hsi shih-yen* it is obvious that intensive and extensive study of "correct" masters of the tradition is what lies at the bottom of his idea of poetic success. As such, this too is a gradualist approach—enlightenment, for him the state in which one can exercise the correct dharma eye, is reached through systematic and thoughtful study and practice, and this, of course, is quite in keeping with what we have seen of the poetic theories of Huang T'ing-chien and Ch'en Shih-tao.

Another way of looking at the relationship between the individual poet and the tradition, for that in a very important sense is what all these statements we have been examining are concerned with, is to look at it in terms of individuality and freedom of expression, on the one hand, and adherence to the rules and the conventions of the tradition on the other. In the particular tradition that began with Huang T'ing-chien, freedom and individuality are by no means denied, but they are to be obtained and exercised within the *rules*, or rather, they are what result after a perfect learning process has taken place—one assimilates the rules and then transcends them. Lü Pen-chung (1084–1145) was another follower of Huang T'ing-chen, and his critical works on poetry are an important source for our knowledge of the general trend of poetry during the Northern Sung era. One work in particular is germane for our concerns here, his *T'ung meng shih-hsün* (Instruction in Poetry for Our Untutored Youth)—another lost work which Kuo Shao-yü has managed to reconstruct.[26] In it Lü makes a number of statements about freedom-individuality-spontaneity and rules-tradition-studied-and-crafted excellence in poetry. One passage is particularly intriguing, for in it Lü declares that the poet's poet, Tu Fu, achieved perfection sometimes spontaneously and sometimes through conscious craft:

> Old Tu at times exhibits in his poetry spontaneity that achieves the ultimate of perfection without preliminary draft and, at other times, a meticulous craftsmanship in the use of language that also reaches the ultimate of perfection. Poetry such as "So dedicated to painting he's unaware old age is coming, / Status and wealth to him are just so many floating clouds"[27] is an example of the former, and "Golden gongs and great bells arrayed in the East Palace Wing / Where an armillary, its vessel stopped with ice, hangs in the crisp autumn air"[28] is an example of the latter.[29]

As with Huang T'ing-chien and Ch'en Shih-tao, Tu Fu is the great teacher for Lü, in particular because he went "by the rules" and these rules—which mark the way to true poetic perfection—are recoverable by intense study of his poetry. His spontaneity is something that Lü believes also can be learned, since it too always "operates within the rules," and even the marvelous achievements of a Su Shih, whose way of poetry seemingly defies all rational analysis, can, through the same kind of intense study, provide the student with "a place to get started":

> In Old Tu's ballads *(ko-hsing)* one can readily discern the main threads, the ins and the outs and the beginnings and the ends, but in Tung-p'o's seven-

syllabic ancient-style verse *(ch'ang-chü)* the waves are enormous and the transformations unfathomable; here it is as if he were performing in stage entertainment *(tso tsa-chü),* making startling entrances with sudden jokes and then leaving immediately with more unexpected bits of raillery. Su's *San-ma tsan* (Eulogy on a Painting of Three Horses) says: "Shaking their manes, they give out long neighs, and all other horses are struck mute."[30] What this means is that they had something marvelous that could not be taught. However, if the student can manage to swim in this kind of language, naturally, he will have a place to get started *(tzu-jan yu ju-ch'u).*[31]

Intense study over a long period of time will provide the key to unlock any door—even the doors which, at first, do not even seem to exist. This suggests that Lü believed that there are always rules in great poetry, sometimes irreducible to rational statement to be sure but always there for the student who would spend enough effort and time to uncover them. In another passage Lü states quite explicitly that "enlightenment" can be learned:

In writing, one must have a sense of enlightened apprehension *(wu-ju ch'u),* something that comes only from working hard at it *(kung-fu)* and that is not something one can get by mere chance. For example, Old Su [Su Shih] in prose and Lu-chih [Huang T'ing-chien] in poetry both thoroughly realize this principle *(chin tz'u-li).*[32]

Over all, however, Lü advocates a fusion of the seemingly irreconcilable opposites of freedom and regulation—freedom within the rules, rules that enhance rather than restrict freedom:

Reading the *Chuang-tzu* makes one's ideas expand and thoughts grow large so that one dares to take initiatives, whereas reading the *Tso-chuan* makes one very mindful of rules and regulations so that one will not dare do things just to suit one's ease and convenience. One must not neglect either of these two works, and, in modern times, readings of the poetry of Tung-p'o and Lu-chih will, respectively, have exactly the same effects.[33]

The poetry of Huang T'ing-chien, like that of Tu Fu, is a repository of rules whose application will prevent the student of poetry from falling prey to the arbitrary willfulness of ego; Lü seems to place the *prose* of Su Shih in this category of model writings as well (see the previous passage), but Su's poetry belongs with the *Chuang-tzu*—it is an inspiration rather than a guide.

In addition to remarks made in the *T'ung meng shih-hsün,* Lü Pen-chung made an important contribution to Sung dynasty poetics by his use of the term *huo-fa* (live method)—something which later critics associate in particular with the highly individualistic and, seemingly, thoroughly spontaneous poetry of the Southern Sung poet Yang Wan-li (1127–1206). It seems to first appear in criticism in Lü's *Hsia Chün-fu chi hsü* (Preface to the Literary Works of Hsia Chün-fu [Hsia Ni, fl. ca. 1120]), which is partially preserved in Liu K'o-chuang's (1187–1269) *Chiang-hsi shih-p'ai hsiao-hsü* (Short Introductions to Poets of the Kiangsi School):

> In studying poetry, one must know what the live method is. What I mean by "live method" is this: although a poet is fully equipped with the rules, he still can transcend them, or, in other words, one's transformations in poetry may be unfathomable, yet they never are in violation of the rules. This is the way of poetry. It both has a fixed method yet lacks one, has no fixed method yet has one. Only if someone understands this can you discuss the live method with him.[34]

Lü may have derived his idea for the "live method" in poetry from the expression *huo-chü* (live utterances) that is used in Ch'an to designate ways of speaking that transcend the boundaries of rational discourse and the false distinctions drawn among phenomena—and that supposedly get at the fundamental identity of all things. The opposite, of course, is *ssu-chü* (dead utterances). This is discussed, for instance, in a statement made by the Yüan-ming Ch'an master, Yüan-mi of Te-shan temple, Ch'ang-te in Hunan (Yüan-ming's dates are unknown—probably a late T'ang figure): "You should only deal in *(ts'an)* living utterances; do not deal in dead utterances. When a live utterance goes forth, it keeps winning at the gambling mat [of understanding] forever without stopping."[35]

A contemporary of Lü's, his friend Tseng Chi (1084–1166), in his *Tu Lü Chü-jen chiu-shih yu huai ch'i-jen tso shih chi chih* (After Reading an Old Poem by Lü Chü-jen [Lü Pen-chung] I Felt a Longing for Him, so Wrote This Poem to Send to Him) praises Lü's poetry in terms drawn from both Ch'an and Taoist alchemy/immortality:

> Studying poetry is like penetrating to the truth *(ts'an)* of Ch'an—
> One certainly must be careful not to deal in dead utterances *(ssu-chü).*
> To be full of vigor and freedom *(tsung-heng)* so that one can do anything at all—
> This is to be found where there is a sense of ecstasy *(huan-hsi ch'u).*
> It is also like studying how to become an immortal—
> One has to labor arduously for so long it seems he will never reach it,
> When, suddenly and all at once, one's hair and bones are transformed,
> Just because in chanting the magic formula *(k'ou-chüeh)* he got it exactly right.
> You, Chü-jen, talk about the live method,
> Your main purpose being a wish to bring people to enlightenment *(wu).*
> Those in antiquity who composed poetry using vernacular sayings—
> Each and every one of them followed this same road.
> Of course, not only do you talk in this way,

You also actually create poetry with beauties of its own.
Its roundness *(yüan)* is perfect and smooth as a metal crossbow pellet,
Which goes after its target as fast as an escaping rabbit,
It is a wind blowing clouds in a spring sky,
Which, in an instant, take many different shapes,
It tinkles exquisitely as the music of *ch'in* and *chu* [two zither-like instruments]
Played between courses of an eight-treasure feast *(pa-chen chü)*—
Who could possibly so lack the mouth or ear
That he would not rise in admiration and delight!
Whenever a poem of yours falls into my hands,
I'm so greedy to read it I can't bear to put it down.
I've always suspected that your insides
Contain only the wind and dew that you've eaten and drunk.[36]
It's been an entire year now that we haven't had a chance to get together,
And my mind's been so filled with tedious worldly affairs!
When will I hear the sound of your footsteps approaching?
For then I shall surely keep saying—"come in" over and over again!
This humble fellow ought, in order to be near you,
Move his household and live somewhere within the seven districts of Min [Southern Chekiang and all of Fukien]![37]

The Southern Sung Era

Despite Tseng's references in this poem to Taoist alchemy/immortality, the Southern Sung era in poetry criticism rapidly became dominated by the Ch'an-Poetry analogy. In particular, a group of poets roughly spanning three generations represent this trend: Han Chü (ca. 1086–1135), Wu K'o, Kung Hsiang, and Li Ch'u-ch'üan (all of whom flourished about the year 1126), Yang Wan-li (1127–1206), and Chao Fan (1143–1229). With these figures, the analogy starts to take more precise form; with Han for instance, the idea of comparable "orthodoxies" emerges:

> The way of poetry is like the Buddhist dharma—one must distinguish in it a greater vehicle (Mahāyāna) and a lesser vehicle (Hīnayāna), the *māras* (*hsieh-mo* 'evil demons and spirits'), and the heterodox *(wai-tao)*. Only those who understand this can talk about these things.[38]

Han also describes the nature of poetic enlightenment in a poem he presented to Chao Po-yü, a relative of the Sung royal family:

Long ago, you knocked on my gate like a woodpecker rap-tapping on a tree—
There you were in a blue ceremonial gown, wearing a high, square cap!
You announced that you were a first-degree scholar seeking permission to become my disciple,

I was astonished that you, with your family connections, could have such tastes as this,
But, if it were a matter of what you harbored in your bosom, I was sure there were no vulgar thoughts there!
In Ching-chou you already knew the works of Kao and Huang[39]
And could chant the lines of these two masters so that it sounded like the jingling and tinkling of pure jade.
That a young student could have learned poetry so well was really awesome—
And I so worn out with merely talking about it and never getting anything of it across!
You ought to study poetry in the same way as when beginning to study Ch'an—
For the time being before enlightenment comes, work at all possible kinds of practices,
But once enlightenment happens you'll have the true dharma eye,
And trusting your hand to do as it pleases, everything you pluck out will be perfect poetry![40]

As in Ch'an, the student of poetry works hard at all possible "practices," when, suddenly, all this potential that has been building up explodes in "enlightenment"—which here seems to mean perfect intuitive control over the poetic medium. Long preparation precedes enlightenment—a view much in keeping with what we have already seen expounded by Huang T'ing-chien and Ch'en Shih-tao in mixed Taoist-Ch'an analogy—and thus it appears to be a gradualist approach to a sudden, once and for all event.

Wu K'o's poetry criticism is to be found in both his *Ts'ang-hai shih-hua* (Discussion of Poetry by the Recluse Who Hides by the Sea) and in various of his own poems on poetry. Only one passage in the *shih-hua* mentions Ch'an, but a set of three poems presents an extensive statement of the Ch'an-Poetry analogy; here first is the passage:

> All in all, writing poetry is like practicing Ch'an in that one must have a gate to enlightenment *(wu-men).* When I was young, I studied the poetry of Jung T'ien-ho [active during the Yüan-yu era (1086–1093)][41] and on one occasion failed to understand what one particular couplet meant: "I'm grateful to the chattering sparrows / Who at times come and shatter my loneliness." One day, I was sitting in a pavilion situated amidst bamboos when suddenly I saw a flock of chirping sparrows swoop down—then I experienced sudden enlightenment *(tun-wu)* of what the above couplet meant! From that time on, whenever I have read poetry, I have never failed to grasp its meaning.[42]

This seems to be more like the sudden enlightenment of the Lin-chi school—not training or study but the accidental or arbitrary device will shock or startle one into enlightenment; no building up of potential is involved, no inevitable explosion of accumulated learning. Wu does not deny that a long time and much effort may be involved before such enlightenment happens, but with him there does not seem to be the sense of necessary, inevitable linkage between time/effort and enlightenment that we find with, say, Lü Pen-chung. This emerges, I believe, from the set of three poems:

> Studying poetry is just like *(hun-ssu)* studying how to realize the truth of Ch'an—
> It means a bamboo bed and a rush meditation mat for more years than you'd dare count.
> But when you yourself finally grasp it once and for all,
> Without thinking, you'll pluck [poetry] out and it will be transcendent *(ch'ao-jan)*.
> Studying poetry is just like studying how to realize the truth of Ch'an—
> Merely keep placing one head on top of another and such poetry will never make it.
> Jump out of that mold that Shao-ling [Tu Fu] cast—
> A great man's aspirations, after all, ought to soar to the skies!
>
> Studying poetry is just like studying how to realize the truth of Ch'an—
> Since antiquity there have only been a few absolutely perfect couplets.
> A line such as "the pond's banks with their spring shrubbery,"
> Startling heaven and shaking earth, has been on everyone's lips right up until now![43]

"Pluck" translates *nien*—it is likely that an allusion to the account of the first transmission of the true dharma eye from Śākyamuni to Kāśyapa is intended here.[44] That is, just as Śākyamuni was able to convey the truth perfectly to Kāśyapa by plucking a flower, so the poet who "plucks" out perfect poetry can convey his intentions in such a way that he transcends all verbal obstacles and limitations. "Place one head on top of another" *(t'ou-shang an t'ou)* is an expression used by Ch'an masters, as for instance in a statement made by Master Yüan-an (834–898): "Now, say, I have cited a particular matter *(i-shih)* and ask you about it. If you say that this is so, then you are placing one head on top of another, but if you say it is not so, then you are cutting off a head and seeking life *(chan t'ou ch'iu huo)*."[45] That is, if a disciple simply accepts his master's pronouncements, he is placing another's head on top of his own, thus compounding his own illusions, but if he rejects his master's pronouncements, he is on the way to independence and enlightenment, for in so doing he "cuts off" his own head full of illusions and becomes spiritually "alive." As far as poetry is concerned, Wu is saying here that one should follow no master, not even Tu Fu, but must make it on one's own—enlightenment means total independence and freedom.

Kung Hsiang seems to be even more radical in his rejection of views associated with Huang T'ing-chien and Ch'en Shih-tao, going so far as to say that it is a waste of time to try to "touch iron and turn it into gold"—a direct slap at one of the favorite slogans of the Kiangsi school. Kung's position is made quite clear in the following set of three poems:

> Studying poetry is just like studying how to realize the truth of Ch'an—
> Only when you reach enlightenment do you realize it has taken as many years as this!
> Touching iron and turning it into gold will then seem such a great waste of time,
> Since high mountains and running streams, as always, can manage on their own!
>
> Studying poetry is just like studying how to realize the truth of Ch'an—
> Before, words might be put into their proper places but meaning didn't come across,
> But now, since intuitions transcend the bounds laid down by prosody,
> There's no longer any need to melt stones and mend the sky!
>
> Studying poetry is just like studying how to realize the truth of Ch'an—
> Just how many times have you ransacked your guts to find a way to match a couplet!
> You want to know what makes Shao-ling's [Tu Fu's] poetry transcendent marvel?
> To begin with, there are no words which can explain it to anyone else![46]

Here, enlightenment in poetry seems to mean the total discovery (or, perhaps, recovery) of the natural and the spontaneous which lie within each individual—and which cannot be taught in words to anyone else. In the first poem, Kung rejects the Taoist Alchemy/Immortality-Poetry analogy as, apparently, something teaching artificiality, an unnatural "trick." Instead, he likens poetry directly to nature—to the way mountains soar and rivers run. The allusion in the second poem is to the story of how the goddess Nü-kua melted stones to repair a broken part of the sky; here it is used to mean that after enlightenment the poet will no longer have to exert superhuman strength to patch up his poems—since they will achieve perfection "naturally."

Li Ch'u-ch'üan was another poet of the times who compared poetry to Ch'an, but he took a rather different tack, in part, by warning the student of poetry that if one practices poetry as an isolated monk practices Ch'an it will not only be a long and lonely path but also will probably result in a total lack of fame and a failure to contribute anything significant to the tradition of poetry. Here is Li's *Hsi-tseng Hsün-lao* (Playfully Presented to Hsün-lao)—Hsün-lao was probably one of Li's brothers or cousins, since his own *tzu* or personal name was Hsün-po:

Studying poetry is like studying Buddhism *(hsüeh fo)*—
Outside the scriptures there's a separate transmission.
At home you must attain enlightenment on your own,
For only then will your mental ground *(hsin-ti)* become unfettered and free
(k'uo-jan),
Then, after becoming enlightened, you have to keep on with quiet sitting
And face the wall for thirty years more!
But remember, that petal of incense used in bygone days
Could never have been for some old and lonely fellow who practices Ch'an![47]

The allusion at the end of the poem is to a couplet by Ch'en Shih-tao, from his *Kuan-yüeh Wen-chung kung chia Liu-i t'ang t'u-shu* (Viewing the Library of the One Among Six Hall at the Residence of His Honor Wen-chung). This was the library of the late Ou-yang Hsiu (1007–1072), that great statesman and writer of the generation prior to Ch'en's own. His couplet reads: "With that one petal of incense used once long ago / He was honored by Tseng Nan-feng [Tseng Kung, 1019–1083]."[48] Thus, Li warns Hsün-lao that a reclusive Ch'an-like practice of poetry will never gain him disciples such as Ou-yang's disciple Tseng Kung (a great writer in his own right).

Before dealing with Yang Wan-li, one of the major literary figures of the Southern Sung era, I wish to take a brief look at two relatively minor poets—Chao Fan, a younger contemporary of Yang's, and Shih Mi-ning, whose dates are unknown but who probably lived roughly at the same time as Yang as well. Shih actually wrote a poem entitled *Shih-Ch'an* (Poetry and Ch'an) which seems to be very much in the Lü Pen-chung tradition, since in it he talks about the "live method" and encourages the student of poetry to seek the enlightenment necessary for it in studying the great monuments of the tradition—in this case, the *Book of Odes (Shih-ching)*:

The live method of the poet is like the secret truth of Ch'an *(ch'an-chi)*—
Who gets to know just what one should work at to reach enlightenment!
But if you seek the secret mechanism *(kuan-lieh-tzu)* to unlock it,
It's not hard to trace it in the *Airs of the States* (*Kuo-feng*), the *Elegentiae* (*Ya*),
and the *Hymns (Sung)*![49]

By contrast, Chao Fan emphasizes independence from the tradition and glorifies the spontaneity of the moment:

Studying poetry is just like studying how to realize the truth of Ch'an—
Discriminate between your first years at it and your last.
No matter how skilled, how can a woodworker carve in rotten wood?
And, once mightily ablaze, how could you ever want to become dead ashes
again!

Studying poetry is just like studying how to realize the truth of Ch'an—
Want to keep intact things passed from master to you or which you heard from others?
How could autumn chrysanthemums and spring orchids ever wish to trade places?
But the pure wind and the bright moon actually share the same sky!

Studying poetry is just like studying how to realize the truth of Ch'an—
Those who tie themselves up in fetters would rather talk about lines and couplets,
But how vivid and fresh is our country with its nine great divisions and four seas—
After thousands and even tens of thousands of years, who was ever responsible for handing it down without a break![50]

All the formal skill in the world will avail nothing if one's wood (i.e., his individual substance) is not sound. (This is a direct disparagement of the Kiangsi school, which placed so much emphasis on formal training.) Moreover, one's wood ought to be kept blazing continuously—one should be living and writing poetry in a state of ecstasy. The second poem disparages the whole learning/emulation process—why should anyone try to be like someone else? As the chrysanthemums and orchids are both completely different yet completely beautiful, so should poets achieve their own individual beauties; and poetry, like the sky itself, is large enough to accommodate more than one kind of beauty, as such. The third poem takes this all a step further and disparages the whole idea of poetic tradition and formal prosodic rules—just as the land itself (the sum of nature of the known world) perpetuates itself without any help from human society, so poetry will last forever without any codified tradition and succession of "orthodox" masters.

Yang Wan-li is a significant figure both in the history of Chinese poetry and in the tradition of Chinese literary criticism.[51] He started off his career as an ardent follower of the Kiangsi school, admired the poetry of Huang T'ing-chien and Ch'en Shih-tao, and thought that poetry was a matter of skill whose secrets could be reached through systematic study and the assimilation of models. Later in life, however, Yang experienced "enlightenment" *(wu)*—to use his own term for it—and arrived at a state of poetic accomplishment or maturity where he no longer needed rules, tradition, models, or any of the other means he had been practicing earlier. It is at this point that his poetic theory seems to converge with that of Su Shih and such later figures as Wu K'o, Kung Hsiang, and Chao Fan—all of whom might be said to form a tradition of poetry of the "spontaneous and the natural." Although Yang's later theoretical pronouncements on poetry emphasize the free and spontaneous character of "enlightened" poetry, he never rejects, as a process still necessary for others to follow, the route which brought him to it—in effect, *sudden* enlightenment is only possible after a long period of *gradual* preparation rooted in rules, tradition, and models. His *Ch'eng-chai shih-hua* (Discussions of Poetry from the Studio Devoted to Sincerity), which reflects his later, mature *practical* interest in poetry criticism, is filled with remarks with which a Huang T'ing-chien or a Ch'en Shih-tao would have been in complete agreement, and we need not deal with it here. It is in his other later prose writings and in his later poetry that he presents his theoretical views, very often in terms drawn from Ch'an, which we shall examine.

Yang's mature theoretical views have much in common with those expressed in the next generation by Yen Yü (ca. 1195–ca. 1245), whose *Ts'ang-lang shih-hua* (Ts'ang-lang's Discussions of Poetry) exerted such a tremendous influence on the rest of the tradition of Chinese poetry. However, whereas Yen, as we shall see, is extremely careful about the proper route to enlightenment, the gradualist preparation stage—the masters of the High T'ang era (i.e., Li Po, Tu Fu, and others who were active during the K'ai-yüan and T'ien-pao era, 712–755) for him constitute the unique group of "best" models for the student, who should stay away from later T'ang poets and those of the Kiangsi school—Yang is more concerned with the end of the preparation process than the means to get there and is thus more catholic in his tastes and preferences as far as the earlier tradition is concerned. In fact, he remains very fond of the Kiangsi school poets and greatly appreciated Late T'ang poets as well—preferring them, it seems, to all others. Both Yen and Yang used the Ch'an-Poetry analogy, but they employed it quite differently when it came to final judgments of taste—this will become readily apparent after we have examined their theoretical writings. Yang also differs, in another respect, from Su Shih. Although he came to share Su's commitment to freedom of expression, he seems to have arrived at this through a long and arduous process—in contrast to Su's native genius. One has the feeling, in both Yang's critical writings and in his own verse, that he is by far the more self-conscious—his freedom was won only after long struggle, something he never forgot. Let us hear his account of what happened:

> In poetry I first emulated that of the members of the Kiangsi school and then emulated the five-syllabic regulated verse of Hou-shan [Ch'en Shih-tao]; after that I turned to the seven-syllabic quatrains of Pan-shan lao-jen [Wang An-shih, 1021–1086], and latest of all I emulated the quatrains of the T'ang poets. The more effort I had been putting into it, however, the fewer poems I seemed to write. . . . In the summer of that year [1177] I took up an official post at Ching-hsi [Kiangsu] and straightaway got

involved in looking over lawsuits and in managing local revenues—nothing but red ink [i.e., "red tape"] for me! From time to time I had ideas for poetry and really wanted to write but never found time to do so. On New Year's Day of the *wu-hsü* year [1178], it being a holiday, and, having been granted leave from official duties, I had little public business to attend to and so began to write poetry. Suddenly, it was as if I had undergone enlightenment *(wu),* and at this I abandoned the T'ang poets and no longer even dared to emulate any of the Kiangsi poets, Wang, or Ch'en. Afterwards I was delighted at what had happened. As an experiment, I had my son write while I orally composed several poems—they flowed out clear and fresh without any more of that awful machinelike creaking that I suffered from before. From then on, every afternoon when the clerks had gone home and the courtyard was empty, I took up a fan and either strolled in the garden at the rear of the compound, climbed the ancient city wall, went picking boxthorn and chrysanthemum leaves or clambered up places for flowers and bamboo. Thus, the myriad phenomena of nature came and presented me with material for poetry—as much as I tried to wave them away they would not leave me alone, and before I could deal with those in front, the ones behind were already pressing forward! As if I were water which had just thawed from ice, I was no longer mindful of the difficulties in writing poetry—for there would soon come a day when my poet's illness [i.e., the craving to write] would leave my body![52]

Yang expressed basically the same idea in a poem as well, one entitled *Ta Hsü Tzu-ts'ai t'an chüeh-chü* (A Poem in Reply to Hsü Tzu-ts'ai):

As a young student, I first practiced what Pan-shan [Wang An-shih] could teach
But finally had to jump back into the Late T'ang era.
From there I wasn't far from the *Airs of the States,*
And unlocking the secret mechanism *(kuan-lieh)* of poetry seemed but the most common of things![53]

This is much like Shih Mi-ning's poem "Poetry and Ch'an," where the *Book of Odes* is also proposed as the key or "secret mechanism" which unlocks poetic enlightenment.[54] In another poem, *Sung Feng-ning chu-pu Lo Hung-ts'ai chih-man ju ching* (A Send-Off Poem for Lo Hung-ts'ai, Secretary in Fen-ning [Kiangsi] Who Has Completed the Tenure of His Post and Is Going to the Capital to Fill a New Position), Yang equates practicing poetry in the Kiangsi school with practicing the Ch'an of the "Southern school" founded by the sixth patriarch Hui-neng (638–713) in the Ts'ao-ch'i region of Kwangtung—the so-called "orthodox" school which stressed sudden enlightenment:

You should know that a poet who practices in the Kiangsi school
Is just like a monk who practices Ch'an in the Ts'ao-ch'i tradition.
If you didn't go to the Nan-hua and Hsiu River regions,[55]

How would you ever have had the means to transmit the dharma—or even to hand down the mantel![56]

This poem may date from earlier in Yang's career when he was still an adherent of the Kiangsi school himself; another poem which surely dates from his mature "post-enlightenment" period, *Pa Hsü Kung-chung, Shao-kan chin-shih* (Colophon to Regulated Verse by Hsü Kung-chung, Shao-kan), takes a very different view of tradition:

I feel ashamed for those who keep the authority of schools and patriarchs alive,
For each poet ought to have his own individual style *(ko tzu i feng-liu)*.
Don't come to a halt at Huang's or Ch'en's fence,
But distinguish yourself at the vanguard of T'ao's and Hsieh's army![57]

That is, the student of poetry should not allow himself to be fenced in by affiliation with any school, in particular the school associated with Huang T'ing-chien and Ch'en Shih-tao—the Kiangsi school—but should strive to become a great independent master who *leads* that tradition of individualist poets which includes such poets as T'ao Ch'ien and Hsieh Ling-yün.

Turning to two late poems entitled *Ho Li T'ien-lin* (Rhyme Following Li T'ien-lin), we see Yang again dealing with the tradition-individual polarity:

The way to learn poetry is to come to understand it completely and then transcend what you know,
To trust your own hand and stand aloof and alone.
Since a monk's robe and begging bowl have never changed nor ever will,
The most massive hill or mountain can always become as light as a feather.[58]
In your lines, ponds shall ever be graced with shrubs—[59]
Nuances which extend beyond words always rich in the most sensitive of perceptions.[60]
Just what is this delicious poetry like?
Frost-frothy crabs served up with a bit of wine dregs!

It's impossible for heaven to keep secret the dharma of poetry—
All you must do is work harder at it!
Though, while still practicing it, it will remain the mystery of the cedar,
Once enlightenment happens, why should you ever need a peach blossom again!
I'd like to share the jade-white thing [wine] with you,
But we seem to be north and south on opposite shores.
Won't you come and chat with me about this?
We'll sit off by ourselves on some sandbank which belongs to the white gulls![61]

Now, for a final statement of Yang's view of the spontaneous and the natural, here is the third poem in a set entitled *Wan-han t'i hsien-hua ping hu-shan* (Chill of Evening, a Scene of Narcissus Together with Lake and Mountains), dated 1190:

How could one ever do without furnace and hammer to refine his lines,
But lines so written won't necessarily realize all the resources of the
phenomenal mind *(yüan-ch'ü)*,
Whereas this old fellow doesn't go looking for lines of poetry,
The lines themselves come looking for him.[62]

Yen Yü's *Ts'ang-lang shih-hua* is probably the most important work of literary criticism produced in the last thousand years of the traditional period; it is the theoretical cornerstone of the whole archaist *(fu ku)* movement in the poetry of Ming and Ch'ing times, so much so that it is no exaggeration to say that most theoretical writings of the archaist critics are footnotes or commentaries to what Yen Yü said.[63] Much of this, however, is outside the scope of our interests here, though a great deal of post-Sung critical writings that deal with the Ch'an-Poetry analogy, archaist-oriented or not, refers in some way or other to the *Ts'ang-lang shih-hua*. It is essential, therefore, that we examine those parts of Yen's work which deal with the analogy—they will be presented here in the order of their appearance in the collated and critical edition prepared by Kuo Shao-yü, the *Ts'ang-lang shih-hua chiao-shih*.[64]

The most Ch'an-imbued—and theoretical—part of the *Ts'ang-lang shih-hua* is the first section, entitled "Shih-pien" (An Analysis of Poetry). It begins with Yen's injunction to the student of poetry that judgment *(shih)* should be his master—an idea he may have got from Fan Wen[65]—and that he must be able to discriminate between the "orthodox" masters he should study and emulate from the Han (206 B.C.–A.D. 220), the Wei (220–265), the Chin (265–420), and the High T'ang eras and shun those inferior, heterodox masters from the time after the High T'ang and thus prevent "the devil of inferior poetry" *(hsia-lieh shih-mo)* from "entering his bosom"—a way of looking at the tradition that may have stemmed from Han Chü.[66] Then, Yen prescribes a course of study which covers the entire tradition from the very beginning of the tradition up through the High T'ang:

First, one must thoroughly recite the *Ch'u-tz'u* [Elegies of Ch'u, third century B.C. and later], singing them morning and night so as to make them his basis. When he then goes on to recite the *Nineteen Ancient Poems* [Han Dynasty], the four sections of music bureau ballads,[67] the five-syllabic verse of Li Ling [d. 74 B.C.], Su Wu [ca. 143–60 B.C.], and the other poets of the Han and the Wei, he must do them all from beginning to end. After that, he will take up the collected poems of Li [Li Po] and Tu [Tu Fu] and read them until, lying on top of one another, they become his pillows, just as it happens when the people of today study the *Classics*. Next, he will take up all the famous masters of the High T'ang, and after he has allowed all of this to ferment in his bosom for a long time, he will become enlightened spontaneously *(tzu-jan wu-ju)*. Although he might not attain to the ultimate end of study, still he will not have gone off the correct road. This is nothing less than to work from the "top of the head" *(ting-ning)*,[68] and I say that it is the "one road that leads upwards,"[69] that it "cuts directly to the basic nature of things,"[70] that it is the "gateway to sudden enlightenment," and that it is the "single sword-thrust to the heart."[71]

In the tradition of the Ch'anists there are the greater and the lesser vehicles, the Southern and the Northern schools, and the heterodox and the orthodox ways *(tao yu hsieh cheng)* [again like in Han Chü's statement]. There, the student must follow the very highest vehicle, embody the true dharma eye, and experience enlightenment of the first order *(wu ti-i i)*.[72] However, if it is lesser vehicle Ch'an, the fruit of the śrāvaka (hearer) or the pratyekabuddha (individual seeker), it will never be orthodox. Discussing poetry is like discussing Ch'an. The poetry of the Han, Wei, Chin, and the High T'ang represents enlightenment of the first order. Poetry from the Ta-li era [766–779] on [i.e., of the Middle T'ang, 766–835] corresponds to the lesser vehicle and has fallen into enlightenment of the second order. The poetry of the Late T'ang [836–906] belongs to the śrāvaka or pratyekabuddha. One who studies the poetry of the Han, Wei, Chin, and the High T'ang is a follower of the Lin-chi school; one who studies the poetry of after the Ta-li era is a follower of the Ts'ao-tung school.[73] In general, the way of Ch'an is concerned with marvelous enlightenment *(miao-wu)*, and the way of poetry is also concerned with marvelous enlightenment. Thus, Meng Hsiang-yang [Meng Hao-jan, 689–740] was far inferior to Han T'ui-chih [Han Yü] in knowledge but in poetry alone he was the superior, and this was all due to his sense of marvelous enlightenment. Only when one is enlightened can one be a real expert and show his real stuff. However, there are different depths and different scopes of enlightenment. There is thoroughly penetrating enlightenment *(t'ou-ch'e)*, and there is enlightenment that only achieves partial understanding *(i-chih pan-chieh)*. The Han and the Wei are indeed supreme, for they did not have to depend upon enlightenment at all! Poets beginning with Hsieh Ling-yün and including the masters of the High T'ang possessed thoroughly penetrating enlightenment; although there were others who might have achieved enlightenment, it was never that of the first order.[74]

Yen then advises the student to look at both the "superior" and "orthodox" and the "inferior" and "heterodox" parts of the tradition —that is, all those poets who do not belong to the Han, Wei, Chin, and High T'ang—finishing up with the followers of Su Shih and Huang T'ing-chien (decidedly "inferior" and "heterodox"), and declares to him that if he succeeds in "penetrating" all of this thoroughly:

What is really right and wrong with any of this will be unable to remain hidden from you. However, if you still do not see what this is all about, then you must be someone for whom true knowledge is obscured by wild fox heterodoxy *(yeh-hu wai-tao),* and you will never reach enlightenment![75]

Poetry is concerned with a different kind of talent that has nothing to do with book learning and involves a different kind of interest *(ch'ü)* that has nothing to do with the principles of things *(li).* However, if one does not read books widely and thoroughly investigate the principles of things, one will never be able to reach the ultimate meaning of poetry *(chi ch'i chih).* That which has been called "don't travel on the road of principles and don't fall into the fish trap of words"[76] is the superior way. Poetry is the expression of original nature *(ch'ing-hsing),*[77] and the poets of the High T'ang were solely concerned with inspired feeling *(hsing-ch'ü).* They were like antelopes who hung by their horns, leaving no tracks by which they might be found,[78] and their poetry is utterly marvelous because it is transparent as crystal, something that defies rational analysis;[79] it is like an echo in the air or the play of color in phenomenal appearance,[80] like the moon seen reflected in water or an image in a mirror,[81] and the words come to an end but the meaning is limitless.[82]

Yen then goes on to condemn the poetry of his own era, the Sung, for failing to meet these standards, granting only marginal approval for various poets of the early Sung who emulated the T'ang masters—Wang Yü-ch'eng (954–1001), Yang I (974–1020), Liu Yün (fl. ca. 1016), Sheng Tu (d. 1041), Ou-yang Hsiu, and Mei Yao-ch'en (1002–1060). He especially condemns Su Shih and Huang T'ing-chien for "bringing forth their own ideas in order to make up poetry"—something he believed to have caused the T'ang style to undergo a "change" *(pien),* that is, it became "deviant" and "heterodox." Following this, Yen notes that certain poets of his own day have taken up the habit of emulating Late T'ang poets, but this too elicits his censure:

It is not generally realized that they [these emulators of Late T'ang poetry] are merely the offspring of the śrāvaka and the pratyekabuddha, so how could they ever dare hope that they had come to possess the true dharma eye of the great vehicle of the masters of the High T'ang! Alas! It has been a long time since the transmission of the true dharma eye was interrupted![83]

Yen ends "An Analysis of Poetry" with this statement:

Therefore, without particular thought to my own limitations, I have attempted to determine the main tenets of poetry, borrowed Ch'an as an analogy, and, tracing the main source of poetry from the Han and the Wei on down, I say with complete confidence that we must take the poetry of the High T'ang as our dharma *(fa).* [Yen's original commentary:] The fact that here later on we set aside the poetry of the Han and the Wei and designate that of the High T'ang alone is because [in the High T'ang] poets reached perfection both in the ancient-style form and in the regulated-verse form. Even if I have to offend all good gentlemen in the world by doing so, I will not recant![84]

In general, Yen's analogy seems to function in three different ways: (1) in organizational terms, (2) in operational terms, and (3) in substantive terms. When the analogy expresses itself in *organizational* terms, it expresses the idea that the truth of Ch'an and the truth of poetry are organized in similar ways. Each has a method or way *(fa)* which the student must assimilate and internalize, and the transmission of this *fa* and its preservation are accomplished through a succession of masters or patriarchs in both organizations or systems. The "masters," of course, are those who have achieved enlightenment: in Ch'an there are Ch'an masters, and in poetry there are masters of poetry. The substances of the respective *fa* in Ch'an and in poetry may or may not have anything in common; what matters is that their organizations are similar. Within each, truth is one and immutable, and each organization has a tradition that both defines its truth and protects it against the snares and delusions of heterodoxy. When the analogy expresses itself in *operational* terms, it expresses the idea that the truth of Ch'an and the truth of poetry are learned or acquired in similar ways. This is concerned with *how* truth is transmitted but not with truth *per se.* The way the student of poetry learns poetry is just like the way the student of Ch'an learns Ch'an; their respective organizations offer similar programs or operations for the student to follow. The operation of acquiring enlightenment in poetry, where enlightenment is understood as *spontaneous* control over the *correct* poetic medium, is the same kind of operation of acquiring enlightenment in Ch'an, where enlightenment is understood as the achievement of pure consciousness, self-transcendence, mystical experience, and so forth. The ends of these two operations may or may not have anything in common, but that does not matter here; what does matter is that the operations are similar, since the student in both is advised to go through the same stages: conscious learning to assimilation and internalization to transcendency and sudden enlightenment. When the analogy expresses itself in *substantive* terms, it expresses the idea that the truth of Ch'an, Ch'an enlightenment, and the truth of poetry, poetic enlightenment, are in some way or ways similar. It is this dimension of the analogy which has attracted the most attention in traditional and modern times.[85] Elsewhere I have suggested that poetic enlightenment in the later "orthodox" archaist tradition of poetry which was based on the *Ts'ang-lang shih-hua* meant essentially two things:

> In formal terms enlightenment *(wu)* meant the achievement of perfect intuitive control over the poetic medium, but in psychological or spiritual terms it meant the attainment of a state of being where subjective self, medium of communication, and objective reality became one.[86]

As such, intuitive control and intuitive cognition seem to be opposite sides of the same coin, the "coin" being the poem *in toto,* the fusion of a spontaneous and effortless poetic *act* with a poetic medium that can perfectly articulate immediate "pure experience." It is in these respects that poetry (as Yen and those who shared his views saw it) and Ch'an exhibit substantive or ontological similarity. Effortlessness or spontaneous naturalness and the transcendence of all discriminations, perceptual and conceptual, between the absolute and phenomena, between nirvāṇa and empirical existence, are the two principal (and inseparable) dimensions of Ch'an enlightenment.[87] Intuitive control in poetry is, thus, analogous to effortlessness in Ch'an, and intuitive cognition *as it is articulated* in poetic language is analogous to the transcendence of discriminations in Ch'an enlightenment, though in poetry the objects of cognititon do not necessarily extend to the absolute or nirvāṇa. It might be argued that the "transcendental" landscape poetry of a poet such as Wang Wei (701–761) attempts to do just this, but Yen does not limit his view of poetic enlightenment to this kind of poetry alone and includes in it all poetry that he regards as having incorporated the true *fa* of poetry, poetry often far removed from that of Wang Wei—that of Li Po and Tu Fu, for instance, which he regarded as the very best poetry ever produced.

Yen characterized the highest attainment as something that "enters spirit" *(ju shen):*

> There is one ultimate attainment *(chi-chih)* in poetry: to enter spirit. When poetry enters spirit, it is perfect and complete, and nothing more can be added to it. Only Li and Tu managed to do this, and if others ever do, they will be very few indeed![88]

The term *ju shen* occurs often in art and literary criticism in traditional China—both before and after Yen Yü as well as in his own time. It has two different, though interrelated and complementary, meanings: (1) entering the "divinely-inspired" realm of perfect, intuitive artistry, the highest possible attainment in painting, calligraphy, poetry, or prose, where effortlessness and "natural" control over the medium involved allow the artist to transcend mortal limitations of articulation and technique and thus reach a state of communion with the very workings of nature itself (i.e., intuitive control) and (2) entering into the "spirit" of things, intuitively apprehending their essences, penetrating the appearances of the material world to reach the *tao* that lies immanent in all things (i.e., intuitive cognition)—but this *tao* cannot simply be equated with the Buddhist concept of nirvāṇa, for while some theorists seem to have done just that, others, including Yen Yü, did not.[89] The fact that Yen here immediately goes on to say that only Li Po and Tu Fu had achieved this in poetry is especially significant, for if he had not it would be easy to identify *ju shen* exclusively with the "transcendental" landscape poetry of the Wang Wei tradition that is so concerned with articulating flashes of self-transcendent insight into the *tao* of the natural world—something rich in Taoist-imbued Ch'an implications. This, in fact, is Wang Shih-chen's (whose statement about sudden and gradual enlightenment opened this essay) interpretation of what Yen meant by *ju shen,* taking it as something interchangeable with *ju Ch'an* (enters Ch'an).[90] Ch'ien Chung-shu has taken Wang to task for replacing Li Po and Tu Fu with Wang Wei and Wei Ying-wu (ca. 735–ca. 835) as the ultimate representatives of excellence in poetry and for his complete misunderstanding of what Yen meant by *ju shen.* Ch'ien says that *ju shen* is the highest attainment in *all* modes of poetry, not just in modes associated with serene and placid landscape poetry.[91] Ch'ien seems to be correct, for the *Ts'ang-lang shih-hua* is concerned with all modes of poetry, and, while Yen admires the poetry of poets such as Wang Wei and Wei Ying-wu, he never grants to it a preeminent status—certainly not above that of Li Po and Tu Fu. In fact, flashes of insight into the *tao* of the human world are for Yen, if anything, *more* important than success in pure landscape poetry.[92]

In spite of Yen's equating the best of poetry (that of High T'ang) with the Lin-chi school, he seems to be a thoroughgoing gradualist at heart, at least in the sense that he advocates a long and arduous gradual preparation for the sudden breakthrough. His spontaneity is a spontaneity within the rules, his individualism is an individualism conditioned by the extensive emulation of models, and his freedom is a freedom within clearly defined boundaries. He believed that the greatness of a Li Po or a Tu Fu could potentially be recaptured through a programmatic and formulaic approach—not a rational approach to be sure, but surely one whose organization and operation could be discussed in rational and systematic terms. The substance defies rational analysis, but Yen got around this by proposing a program of exposure and conditioning by models that he was sure would lead the student to success through what in modern terms might be called unconscious internalization. Something like this may also have been in the minds of those who compiled the collections of sayings by and anecdotes about the T'ang Ch'an masters in Sung times; the whole phenomenon of the "literary Ch'an" of the Sung was surely an attempt to present students of Ch'an with material for such unconscious exposure and subsequent conditioning, since, like poetry, Ch'an's meaning also defies rational exposition.[93]

Yen seems to believe, therefore, that the attainment of "perfect" poetry is impossible to reach except through a program of study and assimilation such as he provides in *Ts'ang-lang shih-hua*—no longer is it possible *not* to "depend upon enlightenment." Any attempt to do so would, in his words, end up in "wild fox heterodoxy," and he warned students of poetry away from those who tried to do so (and perhaps succeeded, though he would not have admitted it)—as, for example, Su Shih. The whole later archaist movement in poetry takes the same tack, and, interestingly enough, Su Shih becomes the great heretic for such archaist critics—the great genius who ignored the rules.[94] Pao Hui (1182–1268) a contemporary of Yen's who may have had some influence on him,[95] though stressing the necessity of gradualist study, *did not* rule out the possibility of independent and natural genius:

> I have never been proficient at poetry, so how could I have any critical knowledge of it! However, from what I have heard I think that poets in general take *wang-yang* (oceanic expansiveness) and *tan-po* (perfect tranquility) as marks of the [two] highest achievements in poetry. This can take two forms: that in which *tsao-hua* (transformation) has not yet occurred and that in which it has already occurred.[96] Both attain perfect naturalness *(tzu-jan)* in such a way that one cannot tell how it takes place. That which I call "without the occurrence of transformation" happens when there is an occasion of nebulous and unreflective experience *(ch'ung-mo yu chi)* and the silent workings of the mind leave no trace *(ming-hui wu-chi)*. Just like echoes in the air or the play of color in phenomenal appearance, one wishes there were something there to grasp, but it just cannot be done.[97] Though completely dead and lifeless, it suddenly turns into a dragon full of life and vigor, and, though absolutely still and silent, it suddenly rings out in peals of thunder. That which I call "with the occurrence of transformation" happens when true scenes appear before one, and thoughts thus brought to life manifest themselves whole and complete as if produced by heaven itself, the poem a natural thing in no need of mending, free of seams and with no marks of carving and engraving, possessing such purity and truth that it transcends mere likeness and such a totality of what it is that it surpasses simple resemblance. Therefore when you read such poetry, though it might seem the most substantial *(shih)* thing in the world, it is actually the most flowery *(hua)*, and, though it might seem the most meager thing *(k'u)*, it is really the richest *(yü)* thing possible. Although, for example, P'eng-tse's [T'ao Ch'ien's] branch of poetry, which springs from the very secret springs of nature,[98] approximates this state, how could it ever manage to be always in perfect accord with it! However, only those with heavenly endowed talent *(t'ien-ts'ai)* and innate knowledge *(sheng-chih)* of it and who never indulge in pretense can be up to such poetry as this, and the rest must try to enter it through study—and study invariably means practice! I fear that this is never an easy thing to accomplish and is why people of earlier generations coined the saying: "Studying poetry is just like studying how to realize the truth of Ch'an."

> Although there certainly is such a thing as sudden enlightenment in realizing the truth of Ch'an, there still must first be gradual cultivation and a beginning to such realization. Sudden enlightenment is like when a child is first born. One day its limbs and body are completely formed, then, gradually after a long period of nourishment, it becomes an adult, and only years after that is its *ch'i-chih* (ambition/moral will) finally established. Although this is a manner of speaking borrowed from a heterodox teaching, it still contains a principle that can be applied to poetry.[99]

Enlightenment, if one is not already born with it as a natural genius, can only come, for Pao, at the end of a long and difficult process of effort and maturation. It is interesting to note here that the Ch'an-Poetry analogy has become so widespread by the thirteenth century, in South China at least, that even a Confucian scholar and philosopher such as Pao Hui avails himself of it—though not without a qualifying apology!

There are two more figures worth considering in the Sung era. One, Ko T'ien-min, was a friend of Yang Wan-li who wrote a poem in praise of Yang's poetry which employed the Ch'an-Poetry analogy in a positive fashion, and the other, Liu K'o-chuang (1187–1269) is perhaps the first writer of note to condemn the practice of comparing poetry to Ch'an—for reasons that in one form or another will be repeated by some critics in later ages—as a minority "opposition." First, here is Ko's poem, entitled *Chi Yang Ch'eng-chai* (Sent to Yang Ch'eng-chai):

> Penetrating to the truth of Ch'an and studying poetry for you don't involve two separate dharmas,
> So you know how to make any dead snake wriggle and writhe with life!
> Spirit upright, mind emptied and ready to hold all things, your vision is naturally exhalted,
> And your hair-splitting sword, without moving, is capable of sparing or taking any life.
> Your well-spring of talent *(sheng-chi)* is so great you needn't eschew well-worn phrases—
> In modern times there's only Yang Ch'eng-chai who's up to this!
> Your talent is so lofty that it can be entrusted to public opinion forever;
> Your poetry is so romantic *(feng-yüeh)* people will use it to convey delight and grievances in all four seasons.
> I know that you, sir, have embodied an eye in the crown of your head,
> And thus achieve thorough penetration into Ch'an as well as compose poetry perfectly.
> The Ch'an of Ch'ao-chou[100] is always on the edge of your lips,
> And the poetry of Yüan-ming [T'ao Ch'ien] inscribes marvels in your breast.
> When serving in office you're so devoted to your sovereign as to put him above Yao and Shun;[101]

When retired, you water your garden in Lu-ling [Kiangsi].
The sixty-four hexagrams you reduce to only two strokes,
And the three hundred fifty *Odes* you condense to just one word.
Though I am somewhat acquainted with you, Ch'eng-chai,
I didn't realize how very fond you were of government service.
I did, however, know you could go all out and endure hunger for seventy years,
Your backbone like iron, your heart as firm as a rock.
You've never bent your knee to anyone, nor knit your brow in dismay,
And you don't hold literary works in hand while composing poetry.
For a reincarnation of Yü-ch'uan [Lu T'ung, d. 835] you're not strange at all,
But for a Lo-t'ien [Po Chü-i, 772–846] on earth for a second time you manage to be most unusual!
We're a thousand *li* apart, oh, but we share the same moon—
Wouldn't it be so much better if we could poke at cold ashes across from each other.
Why must you, sir, want to have my friendship?
I'm merely someone who lacks the hair that you have on the top of your head![102]

Ko T'ien-min, as the last line implies, was a monk when this poem was written; later in life he reentered secular life. While a monk, his name was I-hsien (Sharp Cutting Edge of the Truth). Ko's whole poem seems built on the premise that Yang's interests in Ch'an and in poetry reinforce each other and that the integration of these two disciplines are responsible for his success as an official and as a strong, self-realized individual. Ko also attributes genuine enlightenment to Yang, for such is the implication of his declaring that he has an eye in the crown of his head (the "wisdom eye") and that his "hair-splitting sword" (*ch'ui mao chien,* a sword so sharp that a hair blown against it will be cut—a metaphor for prajñā [perfect wisdom] that can "take or spare any life") can defeat any enemy (illusion) at will. Later in the poem Ko compares Yang's poetry to that of Lu T'ung, a Middle T'ang poet famous for his bizarre imagery, and of Po Chü-i, whose prosy and casual style anticipated much of the major trend of Sung dynasty poetry. (Po was also an extremely prolific poet who could write easily and quickly.) In effect, Ko here praises Yang for combining the best features of both earlier poets—he could bring off startling, extremely imaginative poetry in quantity and at ease.

The almost unbroken confidence with which Sung era critics of poetry used the Ch'an-Poetry analogy, Ko's poem to Yan Wan-li being a typical example, seems to have finally been challenged toward the end of the Southern Sung era by no less a literary figure than Liu K'o-chuang, whose *Hou-ts'un ta-ch'üan-chi* (The Great Collection of Literary

Works by [the Retired Scholar of] Hou-ts'un) contains forty-eight fascicles of poems, the largest individual collection of poetry that survives from the Sung! Liu is also known for his historical and critical survey of the Kiangsi school of poetry, the *Chiang-hsi shih-p'ai hsiao-hsü* (Short Introductions to Poets of the Kiangsi School).[103] Liu's views on the Ch'an-Poetry analogy are stated explicitly in an essay entitled *T'i Ho hsiu-ts'ai Shih-Ch'an fang-chang* (On First-Degree Scholar Ho's Abbot's Hall of Poetry-Ch'an). Scholar Ho apparently named his studio the *Shih-Ch'an fang-chang* and fancied himself, a secular poet, the equivalent of an abbot in a Ch'an monastery:

> Poets regard Shao-ling [Tu Fu] as their first patriarch, someone who once said: "If my words can't startle people, I won't stop working at it until I die."[104] Ch'anists regard Bodhidharma as their first patriarch, someone who said: "My tradition is not founded upon words and letters."[105] In the same way that poetry cannot be Ch'an, so Ch'an cannot be poetry. However, Mr. Ho would combine the two into one thing, something I cannot understand, for the marvelous faculty of mind *(miao-i)* [in Ch'an] which would stretch words beyond the ultimate *(chih yen)* certainly cannot be rendered into written language *(yen-yü wen-tzu)*. Nevertheless, he sets aside the actual and concrete *(chen-shih)* and chases after what is ephemeral and elusive *(hsü-huan)*, despising what is near and familiar *(ch'ieh-chin)* and longing after what is wide-open and remote *(k'uo-yüan)*, tarrying there so long that he forgets to return. I am afraid that Mr. Ho's Ch'an is advancing nicely, but his poetry is retreating! Mr. Ho should really heed what I say![106]

Liu offers essentially two objections to the Ch'an-Poetry analogy: (1) The truth of Ch'an cannot be expressed in words, but poetry's very being depends upon words—Bodhidharma thus eschewed them, and Tu Fu worked hard at them for his whole life. (2) Ch'an is concerned with the ephemeral, the elusive, and what is wide-open and remote from ordinary human existence, whereas poetry is concerned with the actual, the concrete, and what is near and familiar to ordinary human existence. These same objections are often raised among critics opposed to the Ch'an-Poetry analogy in later ages—something which advocates of the analogy, of course, defend against. However, as interesting as all this is, we have to leave these later poet-critics for another time.

Notes

1. Wang Shih-chen, *Tai-ching t'ang shih-hua*, ed. Chang Tsung-nan (1872 reprint of the 1760 ed.), 3.8a.
2. See Richard John Lynn, "Orthodoxy and Enlightenment: Wang Shih-chen's Theory of Poetry and Its Antecedents," in Wm. T. de Bary, ed., *The*

Unfolding of Neo-Confucianism (New York: Columbia University Press, 1975), 217–269, esp. 218–236.

3. See James J. Y. Liu, *Chinese Theories of Literature* (Chicago: University of Chicago Press, 1975), 31–34.

4. I am greatly indebted to two modern scholars of Chinese literary criticism for the guides they have provided to the sources involved: Ch'ien Chung-shu in his *T'an i lu* (Hong Kong: Lung-men Shu-tien, 1965 reprint of the 1948 ed.), esp. 115–120, 234–247, 308–312, 368–370, 374; and Kuo Shao-yü in his *Chung-kuo wen-hsüeh p'i-p'ing shih* (Taipei: Wen-shih-che ch'u-pan-she, 1979 reprint of the 1934–1947 ed.), 402 and *passim*. A more compact introduction to the sources of the Ch'an-Poetry analogy is found in Kuo's notes and commentaries to Yen Yü's (ca. 1195–ca. 1245) *Ts'ang-lang shih-hua,* his *Ts'ang-lang shih-hua chiao-shih* (Peking: Jen-min wen-hsüeh ch'u-pan-she, 1961), esp. 15–23. Tu Sung-po, *Ch'an-hsüeh yü T'ang Sung shih-hsüeh* (Taipei: Li-ming wen-hua shih-yeh kung-ssu, 1978) has also been useful, especially chaps. 5 and 6—though it should be pointed out that a very great deal of the material presented here appears earlier in exactly the same form in the above works by Ch'ien Chung-shu and Kuo Shao-yü.

5. My forthcoming translation and study of Yen Yü and the *Ts'ang-lang shih-hua* attempts to do this in part—as well as survey all the principal figures involved through the end of the Ch'ing era.

6. *Ch'iu-jih kuo Hung-chü fa-shih ssu-yüan pien sung-kuei Chiang-ling yin* (Preface to the Poem "Paying a Visit on an Autumn's Day to the Temple of the Dharma Master Hung-chü, I Then Send Him Off Back to Chiang-ling [Hupeh]"), *Ch'üan T'ang shih* (Peking: Chung-hua shu-chü, 1960 reprint of the 1707 ed.), 357.4015–4016.

7. See Susan Bush, *The Chinese Literati on Painting: Su Shih (1037–1101) to Tung Ch'i-ch'ang (1555–1636)* (Cambridge: Harvard University Press, 1971), 26–43.

8. Perhaps the most striking of Su's statements concerning the spontaneous and natural features of writing is his Taoist-inspired essay "On Writing": "My writing is like a spring with a ten thousand gallon flow gushing forth without choosing the place—then to run out on level ground a veritable torrent able to cover a thousand miles in a single day with no trouble at all! When it twists and turns around mountain rocks, it acquires shapes from what it encounters—and there is no way to predict what these will be. However, what can be known is that it will always move when it should move and stop when it should stop—this is all there is to it. As for the rest, even I do not know how to explain it!" See *Ching-chin Tung-p'o wen-chi shih-lüeh* (Peking: Wen-hsüeh ku-chi k'an-hsing-she, 1957), 57.946.

9. "Blow on a flute and you get a nice shrill note; but blow on the ring of your sword hilt and all you get is a feeble wheeze"—from the *Chuang-tzu*; cf. Burton Watson, trans., *The Complete Works of Chuang Tzu* (New York: Columbia University Press, 1968), 285.

10. These seven lines paraphrase a passage in Han Yü's *Sung Kao-hsien shang-jen hsü* (Preface to "Seeing Off His Eminence Kao-hsien"); cf. *Ch'in-ting ch'üan T'ang-wen* (Taipei: Hua-lien ch'u-pan-she, 1965 reprint of the 1814 ed.), 555.19b–20b.

11. This alludes to a passage in the writings of the poet-critic Ssu-k'ung T'u (837–908): "Prose is difficult, but poetry is even more difficult. . . . I think if we make distinctions according to flavors, we can then discuss poetry. South of Chiang-ling [beyond the pale of proper Chinese culture] whatever can be eaten, such as sour things, are certainly sour, but they are only sour and nothing more, and salty things are certainly salty, but they are only salty and nothing more. These are things which proper Chinese stop eating as soon as their hunger is slaked—since they know that these things lack the richness and excellence that lie beyond simple saltiness and sourness." See *Ssu-k'ung Piao-sheng wen-chi* (*SPTK* ed.), 2.9a, and Lynn, "Orthodoxy and Enlightenment," 240–242 and 263 n. 91.

12. *Su Tung-p'o chi* (*Kuo-hsüeh chi-pen ts'ung-shu* ed.), 10.87. For a different translation of the last ten lines, see J. D. Schmidt, *Yang Wan-li* (Boston: Twayne Publishers, 1976), 39.

13. Huang literally worshiped Tu Fu; see his *Ta-ya t'ang chi* (Record of the Hall of Great Literary Culture), *Yü-chang Huang hsien-sheng wen-chi* (*SPTK* ed.), 17.22b–23a.

14. From Huang's *Ta Hung Chü-fu shu* (A Letter Written in Reply to Hung Chü-fu), *Yü-chang Huang hsien-sheng wen-chi*, 19.22b–23b; cf. Schmidt, *Yang Wan-li,* 44.

15. Ch'en Shih-tao, *Hou-shan chi* (*SPPY* ed.), 2.2b.

16. From remarks made by Huang T'ing-chien and recorded in the *Leng-chai yeh-yü* (Night Chats from the Cold Studio) by the monk Hui-hung (1071–1128), quoted in Wei Ch'ing-chih, *Shih-jen yü-hsieh* (Jade Chips [Pearls of Wisdom] from the Poets), preface dated 1244 (Peking: Chung-hua shu-chü, 1959), 190–191; cf. Liu, *The Art of Chinese Poetry,* 78.

17. See Holmes Welch, *Taoism: The Parting of the Way* (Boston: Beacon Press, 1966), 109.

18. I.e., the Ch'an master Ts'ung-shen (778–897), the abbot of Kuan-yin monastery in Ch'ao-chou, Hupeh, who hitherto had been a wandering monk until his eightieth year.

19. I.e., Hung-jen (602–675).

20. Sudhana was one of the *ssu sheng-shen* (four with victorious bodies) who were born free from physical taint and who attained spontaneously to Buddhahood; when he was born, as sign of his innate and natural powers, all kinds of treasures burgeoned forth in the birth room after he took one look around it; he was also the pilgrim of the *Avataṁsaka-sūtra (Hua-yen ching)*. Lin-chi I-hsüan (d. 867) was the founder of the so-called Southern Lin-chi school—I-hsüan had resided at the Lin-chi temple in Chen-chou, Hopeh. "One twist of the tiger's whiskers" *(i chiang hu-hsü)* alludes to his encounter as a young novice with Huang-po after Huang-po had sent him to Ta-hui, where he had his great enlightenment. I-hsüan returned to Huang-po and told him what had happened—that is, that he had discovered that there "was not much to Huang-po's Buddha dharma." Huang-po then said he was going to beat I-hsüan, but I-hsüan hit him first instead, and at this Huang-po declared: "This madman has actually come here to twist the tiger's whiskers!" See *Lin-chi lu, T* 47.504c–505a.

21. Lin Hsi-i, *Chu-hsi chüan-chai hsü-chi* (*Ssu-k'u ch'üan-shu chen pen,* 2d series, ed.), 13.3a–4b.

22. This concerns the first transmission of the true dharma eye *(cheng fa-yen),* one account of which is given in the *Wu-teng hui-yüan,* compiled by the monk P'u-chi (Taipei: Kuang-wen shu-chü, 1977 reprint of the original 1253 ed.), 1.8b–9a: "Śākyamuni was at Spirit Mountain where, before his assembled disciples, he plucked *(nien)* a flower and showed it to everyone, who all remained silent. Only the noble one Kāśyapa broke into a smile. Śākyamuni then said: 'I possess the treasury of the true dharma eye, that marvelous mind *(miao-hsin)* which experiences nirvāṇa, that mysterious *(wei-miao)* gate to the dharma *(fa-men)* that teaches that reality *(shih-hsiang)* is formless *(wu-hsiang).* This is something that cannot be stated in words and that belongs to a separate tradition that has nothing to do with texts and formal instruction *(chiao-wai pieh-ch'uan)*; I now entrust it to the great Kāśyapa.' "

23. *Hou-shan chi,* 9.5a–5b.

24. His followers came to be called the Kiangsi school (Huang's native province was Kiangsi), which continued for generations afterwards; cf. Lü Penchung (1084–1145), *Chiang-hsi shih-she tsung-p'ai t'u* (The Sect Lineage of the Kiangsi Poetry Society), as it is described and compared with other lists of Kiangsi school affiliation in Cheng Chen-to, *Ch'a-t'u-pen Chung-kuo wen-hsüeh shih* (Hong Kong: Commercial Press, 1965), 3:511–512.

25. Fan Wen, *Ch'ien-hsi shih-yen,* in Kuo Shao-yü, *Sung shih-hua chi i, Yen-ching Journal of Chinese Studies,* monograph series no. 14 (1937), 1:392–393. The quotations in this passage are all, in order, to Li Po's famous poem *Chin-ling chiu-ssu liu-pieh* (A Keepsake Poem Left in a Wineshop in Chin-ling), *Ch'üan T'ang-shih,* 174.1784.

26. Kuo Shao-yü, *Sung shih-hua chi i,* 2:235–252.

27. From Tu Fu's *Tan-ch'ing yin* (On Painting), *Ch'üan T'ang-shih,* 220.2322.

28. From Tu's *Chi P'ei Shih-chou shih* (A Poem Sent to P'ei Shih-chou), *Ch'üan T'ang shih,* 221.2335.

29. Kuo Shao-yü, *Sung shih-hua chi i,* 2:236.

30. Su Shih, *Su Tung-p'o chi, hou-chi,* 9.17.

31. Kuo Shao-yü, *Sung shih-hua chi i,* 2:240.

32. Ibid., 244.

33. Ibid., 242.

34. Liu K'o-chuang, *Chiang-hsi shih-p'ai hsiao-hsü* (*Hsü li-tai shih-hua* [I-wen yin-shu kuan] ed.), 4b; cf. Schmidt, *Yang Wan-li,* 56.

35. *Wu-teng hui-yüan,* 15.18a.

36. Wind and dew are supposedly the "food" of cicadas which can shed their exoskeletons, the way Taoist adepts can supposedly shed their physical bodies; thus the cicada is a symbol for the Taoist immortal.

37. Tseng's poem is preserved in Ch'en Ch'i (late Southern Sung) ed., *Ch'ien-hsien hsiao-chi shih-i* (A Supplement Which Amends Omissions to "Little Collections of Poetry of Former Worthies"), 4.2b–3a; this work forms part of Ch'en's *Nan-Sung ch'ü-hsien hsiao-chi* (Little Collections of Poetry by All the Worthies of the Southern Sung) (1801 ed.).

38. Quoted in Wei Ch'ing-chih, *Shih-jen yü-hsieh,* 122.

39. I take this to refer to Kao Ho (fl. ca. 1100), a personal poetry disciple of Huang T'ing-chien, and to Huang himself.

40. Han Chü, *Ling-yang chi* (*Ssu-k'u ch'üan-shu chen-pen,* 3d series, ed.), 1.13a–13b; for a different translation of the last four lines see Schmidt, *Yang Wan-li,* 39.

41. See Wu K'o, *Ts'ang-hai shih-hua* (*Hsü li-tai shih-hua* ed.), 8b (last item).

42. Ibid., 8b.

43. Wu's three poems are quoted in Wei Ch'ing-chih, *Shih-jen yü-hsieh,* 8. The quotation in the third poem is actually a paraphrase of the first line in the famous couplet which occurs in Hsieh Ling-yün's (385–433) *Teng ch'ih-shang lou* (Climbing the Tower by the Pond): "The pond's banks grow their spring shrubbery, / And the garden willows change their singing birds." See *Ch'üan Sung-shih (Ch'üan Han San-kuo Chin Nan-pei-ch'ao shih),* 3.8a; the first of these three poems is translated somewhat differently from Schmidt, *Yang Wan-Li,* 40.

44. See above, note 22.

45. Tao-yüan, *Ching-te ch'uan teng lu* (Chronicle of the Transmission of the Lamp, Compiled During the Ching-te Era [1004–1007]), *T* 51.332a.

46. Kung's three poems are also quoted in the *Shih-jen yü-hsieh,* 8.

47. Li Ch'u-ch'üan, *Sung-an chi* (Collection of Poetry from High Mountain Retreat) (*Ssu-k'u ch'üan-shu chen-pen,* 3d series, ed.), 2.7b.

48. Ch'en Shih-tao, *Hou-shan chi,* 1.2b–3a.

49. Shih Mi-ning, *Yu-lin i-kao* (Second Draft Collection [of Poetry] by Yu-lin [One Who Befriends the Forest]) (*Ssu-k'u ch'üan-shu chen-pen,* 4th series, ed.), 25b.

50. Chao's three poems are also quoted in *Shih-jen yü-hsieh,* 8.

51. An extensive treatment of Yang and his literary career appears in Schmidt, *Yang Wan-li.*

52. Yang Wan-li, *Ch'eng-chai chi* (A Collection of Writings from the Studio of Sincerity) (*SPTK* ed.), 80.7b–8b; most of this passage has been translated somewhat differently in Schmidt, *Yang Wan-li,* 40–41 and 42.

53. Yang Wan-li, *Ch'eng-chai chi,* 35.5b; cf. Schmidt, *Yang Wan-li,* 45.

54. See above, note 49.

55. Secretary Lo actually had served in offices in these southern regions, the Hsiu River valley in Kiangsi being the place of his last appointment. Nan-hua Mountain is in the Ts'ao-ch'i area of Kwangtung and is the site of the Nan-hua temple, the base from which the sixth patriarch spread his teaching.

56. Yang Wan-li, *Ch'eng-chai chi,* 38.15a; this is only the first third of the entire poem—the rest does not have anything to do with the Ch'an-Poetry analogy.

57. Yang Wan-li, *Ch'eng-chai chi,* 26.18a; cf. Schmidt, *Yang Wan-li,* 44.

58. Learning poetry is analogous to learning Ch'an. Every poet and every monk starts out with the same "equipment"—the monk with his robe and begging bowl and the poet with language and the rules of prosody, and no one has any advantage over or disadvantage to any monk or poet who has ever lived, or ever will live. Enlightenment in both cases is open to all, and one should never be intimidated by those who might have already achieved it—the "hills and mountains" of the respective traditions—for once enlightenment happens, such

hills and mountains will seem light as a feather. Cf. Chou Ju-ch'ang, ed., *Yang Wan-li hsüan-chi* (Shanghai: Chung-hua shu-chü, 1962), 43 nn. 3 and 4.

59. An allusion again to Hsieh Ling-yün's poem "Climbing the Tower by the Pond"; see above, note 43.

60. This translates *tzu-wai mu chü hao* which literally means "outside the words eyes always artemisia-like." *Hao-mu* (artemisia-eyed) is an expression usually taken to mean "to be concerned with the world's ills." The *locus classicus* is the *Chuang-tzu:* "The benevolent men of the present age are artemisia-eyed and are concerned about the world's ills." There has been much debate about what the term *hao-mu* actually means (cf. Chou Ju-ch'ang, *Yang Wan-li hsüan-chi,* 43 n. 6; Schmidt, *Yang Wan-li,* 154 n. 11; and Burton Watson, trans., *The Complete Works of Chuang Tzu,* 100), but it is usually glossed as *luan* 'disordered, confused'—men are so upset about the world's ills that their sight has been affected. This is Chou Ju-ch'ang's interpretation, in spite of the fact that he cites the *Erh-ya i* to the effect that *hao* should be taken literally—the eyes have the qualities of the artemisia whose leaves are fragile, glossy, and moist, so that dust easily adheres to them. This is what I think Yang had in mind—sensitive eyes that miss nothing—with no political or moral overtones involved. See also *Chuang-tzu* (*Nan-hua chen-ching* ed.), 4.5a–5b.

61. Yang Wan-li, *Ch'eng-chai chi,* 4.1b–2a; cf. Schmidt, *Yang Wan-li,* 41–42.

62. Yang Wan-li, *Ch'eng-chai chi,* 29.6b; cf. Schmidt, *Yang Wan-li,* 42.

63. See Richard John Lynn, "Orthodoxy and Enlightenment," 217–218, 232–236, 238–243, 251–254; "Tradition and the Individual: Ming and Ch'ing Views of Yüan Poetry," in Ronald C. Miao, ed., *Chinese Poetry and Poetics* (San Francisco: Chinese Materials Center, 1978), 1:327–335; "Alternate Routes to Self-Realization in Ming Theories of Poetry," in Susan Bush and Christian Murck, eds., *Theories of the Arts in China* (Princeton: Princeton University Press, 1983), 317–340; and "The Talent-Learning Polarity in Chinese Poetics: Yen Yü and the Later Tradition," *Chinese Literature: Essays, Articles, Reviews* 5 (1983): 157-184, which also deals with Yen Yü's influence upon the later tradition of poetry and poetry criticism.

64. See above, note 4.

65. See above, note 25.

66. See above, note 38.

67. It is uncertain to which ballads Yen refers by the expression *yüeh-fu ssu-p'ien* (four sections of Music Bureau ballads)—something that has puzzled all the commentators, since there is no known collection by that title. However, it is my guess that it may refer to the four groups of Han and Wei ballads that occur in the *Wen-hsüan* (Anthology of Literature), ed. Hsiao T'ung (501–531) and annotated by Li Shan (d. 689) (*SPPY* ed.), in fasc. 27: (1) *Yüeh-fu san-shou,* (2) *Yüeh-fu erh-shou,* (3) *Yüeh-fu erh-shou,* and (4) *Yüeh-fu ssu-shou.* The *yüeh-fu* that appears in the next fascicle are all post-Wei pieces.

68. *Ting-ning* (top or crown of the head) is an allusion to a statement Ch'an Master Chieh-ch'en (1080–1148) made to his disciples: "You pass through the monk's hall and enter the temple, but do you also know how to pick your way in danger and difficulty over the pass through the Iron-Encircling Mountains [on the edge of the world, filled with demons]? Even if all of a sudden you spring off from the top of Śākyamuni's head or kowtow with a forehead worthy of the holy

monk [Mañjuśrī], you can't help but be in for a disastrous time!" See *Wu-teng hui-yüan,* 18.40a. That is, the way to enlightenment is so fraught with dangers that even with the advantages of a Śākyamuni or the wisdom of a Mañjuśrī the seeker will have a terrible time of it. In Yen's passage, to work "from the top [of Śākyamuni's] head" means that the student of poetry, if he follows the program of study outlined by Yen, will start off his own search for poetic "enlightenment" with the greatest of advantages. However, Kuo Shao-yü has also noted the similarity between the expression *ting-ning* and the expression *ting-men yen* (eye in the crown of the head)—which refers to the so-called third eye of wisdom that the enlightened have, sometimes referred to simply as *i-chieh yen* (the single eye)—in distinction to the pair of eyes used for ordinary sight. Kuo cites (*Ts'ang-lang shih-hua chiao-shih,* 2 n. 7) a statement made by Ch'an Master Te-chih (1080–1135): "If anyone can discern what this means, we shall grant that he has an eye placed in the crown of his head!" The context is worth citing in full: "[The Ch'an master addressed his disciples:] Last night yellow-faced Gautama took an entire chiliocosm and swallowed it it one gulp—just like when someone drinks down hot soup, not a trace was left. When its time came, it vanished. The great bodhisattvas, the śrāvakas, the arhats, and all sentient beings were completely unaware that it happened; only Mañjuśrī and Samantabhadra caught it in the wink of an eye, and, although they did get to see it, it was a vague and amorphous event, just as if something had bobbed up and down in the middle of the vast ocean—now you see it, now you don't. Well, gentlemen, tell me what this is all about! If anyone can discern what this means, we shall grant that he has an eye placed in the crown of his head! It indicates the way to nirvāṇa. Where does the smoke from a monk's funeral pyre go? It all becomes *śārira* (relics, remains), its stūpa, Ssu-k'ung Mountain, and its scattered resting places, Tieh-shih (Cairn) Plain." That is, the previous night a monk died and a "world" vanished. Cf. *Wu-teng hui-yüan,* 14.43a. If this is the context Yen had in mind, then his implication is that his program can provide the student of poetry with a "wisdom eye"—ability to discern the most profound truths about his art.

69. This is an expression attributed to Ch'an Master Pao-chi (720–814): "As for the one road that leads upwards, the thousands of enlightened worthies [who travel it] do not leave behind directions to it, so students who wear themselves out trying to have the right appearance [i.e., imitating what an enlightened worthy is supposed to look like] are not any better than monkeys trying to catch their own shadows." See *Ching-te ch'uan teng lu, T* 51.253b. Yen, however, claims that his program *can* provide the student with the correct directions to the road that leads to poetic enlightenment!

70. This is an expression that occurs in the *Cheng tao ko* (Song of Witness to the Way) by Ch'an Master Chen-chüeh (665–713): "Cutting directly to the basic nature of things is what marks a Buddha / Whereas even the mere plucking off of leaves to find a branch is beyond my power." Cf. *Ching-te ch'uan teng lu, T* 51.460a. "The basic nature of things" translates *ken-yüan,* which literally means "the roots [of plants/trees] and the source/spring [of water]"; however, in keeping with the tree-truth analogy of the entire couplet, *ken-yüan* might best be translated as "tap root."

71. *Ts'ang-lang shih-hua chiao-shih,* 1. The last allusion is to a statement made

by Ch'an Master Ling-yu (771–853): "If one can achieve a single sword-thrust straight [to the heart], whether saint or sinner, all passions will cease, and he will completely manifest the true and eternal Buddha-truth." See *Wu-teng hui-yüan,* 9.4b. That is, one should overcome illusion (of duality, etc.) by striking directly at it, just as one should try to kill an enemy with a single blow, avoiding as it were any roundabout plotting (calculation, reason, etc.). Yen's program for the student of poetry constitutes the "sword" with which he can cut directly to the truth.

72. *Wu ti-i i* can be more literally translated as "comprehend the first (supreme) *artha* (meaning)." *Ti-i i* is actually a short form of the expression *ti-i i ti* (*satya* [truth] in its ultimate meaning): *paramārtha-satya,* veritable truth of reality, the possession of the enlightened, as opposed to *saṃvṛti-satya* (*su-ti* or *shih-ti*), ordinary ideas of things, the meaning of statements as if phenomena were real. Kuo Shao-yü draws attention to the occurrence of the term *ti-i i ti* in Ch'an Master Hsi-yün's (Huang-po, d. 850) *Ch'uan hsin fa-yao* (Essentials of the Dharma That Can Only Be Passed from Mind to Mind) (*Ts'ang-lang shih-hua chiao-shih,* 12 n. 7): "Don't you know that mind *(hsin)* is the dharma *(fa)* and that dharma is the mind! One cannot use the mind to seek something further from the mind—even after millions of kalpas there will never be a day when this can be done. It would be better to achieve *wu-hsin* (no-mind), which is the dharma in its fundamental truth *(pen-fa)*. . . . Since students of the way are deluded about what the original mind *(pen-hsin)* is and do not recognize that it is the Buddha, they consequently seek for it outside themselves, working at what they think are meritorious works and efficacious practices, thus relying on gradual progress to realize attainment. They might in this way diligently seek for countless kalpas but will never accomplish the way. It would be better to achieve *wu-hsin.* Know for certain that the all-dharmas possesses nothing which has real existence, has nothing which one can obtain, nothing in which one can abide, nothing on which one can rely, no ability to transform, and nothing to be transformed. If one does not engage in such erroneous thinking, one will realize bodhi (enlightenment), and when one thus realizes the way it will be but to realize that one's originial mind is Buddha. . . . This is why the Buddha said: 'There is nothing I obtained from *anuttarāsamyaksaṃbodhi* (complete, perfect enlightenment).' However, afraid that people would not believe him, he consequently led people to the truth by means of what the five kinds of vision [i.e., human, deva (gods), Hīnayāna wisdom, bodhisattva truth, and Buddha vision] could see and what the five kinds of those who testify to the truth [the Buddha, the bodhisattvas, the śrāvakas, men, and things] could say. This is *tattva* (reality) and not mere baseless talk; it is *satya* (truth) in its ultimate meaning *(ti-i i ti)*." See *Ching-te ch'uan teng lu, T* 51.271b. Enlightenment of the first order should be distinguished from that of "the second order" *(ti-erh i),* something which Yen immediately below compares to poetry written after the Ta-li era (from the Middle T'ang on). The expression *ti-erh i* is a short form of *ti-erh i men* (gateway which consists of truth of the second order). For example, the *ch'ui-shih* (instructions given) to the fifth *kung-an* (case) commented on in the *Fo-kuo Yüan-wu ch'an-shih pi-yen lu* (Record of Lectures Made at the Blue Cliff by Ch'an Master Fo-kuo Yüan-wu [1063–1135]) (first published in 1128) uses it in the fol-

lowing passage: "Whoever supports and propounds our teaching . . . for him, noumena *(li)* and phenomena *(shih)* are not two, and the conditional and temporal *(ch'üan)* and the fundamental and real *(shih)* both unfold at the same time. However, he puts aside this first and primary move *(i-chu)* and sets up instead the gateway which consists of truth of the second order, for, if he were to cut straight through all complications at once, students who try to follow him, they being at the preliminary stage of their potentiality, would find it most difficult to find anything to hang on to *(ts'ou-po).*" See *T* 48.144c.

73. There is no actual division of Ch'an into a greater (Mahāyāna) and a lesser vehicle (Hīnayāna), and both major schools, the "Southern" Lin-chi and the "Northern" Ts'ao-tung, are founded firmly upon systems of meditation found in the great Mahāyāna sūtras. By Yen's time, the Lin-chi school had become dominant, regarded itself as "orthodox," and regarded the Ts'ao-tung school as "heterodox" and a teaching of the mere Hīnayāna. Kuo Shao-yü suggests (*Ts'ang-lang shih-hua chiao-shih,* 11 n. 2) that Yen here probably had in mind the (Mahāyāna-fostered) popular distinction between Hīnayāna and Mahāyāna sūtras—that the were the teachings of the Buddha for those of lesser intelligence and thus shallow and easy to understand, and that the latter were for the more intelligent and thus profound and difficult. "Lesser vehicle Ch'an" was a pejorative term used by adherents of the Lin-chi school to attack the Ts'ao-tung school. In this same passage Yen implies that the śrāvaka and the pratyekabuddha are orders of Ch'an lower or more inferior than the lesser vehicle, whereas *they are* the lesser vehicle. To make his analogy work, Yen has to stretch things here and there; while this does mischief to Ch'an, it does not necessarily invalidate his view of T'ang poetry.

74. *Ts'ang-lang shih-hua chiao-shih,* 10.

75. *Ts'ang-lang shih-hua chiao-shih,* 11.

76. This alludes to the *Chuang-tzu*: "The fish trap exists because of the fish; once you've gotten the fish, you can forget the trap. The rabbit snare exists because of the rabbit; once you've gotten the rabbit, you can forget the snare. Words exist because of the meaning; once you've gotten the meaning, you can forget the words. Where can I find a man who has forgotten words so I can have a word with him?" Translation by Watson, *The Complete Works of Chuang Tzu,* 302.

77. *Ch'ing-hsing* may suggest other implications drawn from the then contemporary world of Neo-Confucianism. For instance, the term might also be understood as signifying two dimensions of human personality and consciousness: individual and personal sensibilities *(ch'ing)* and general and basic human nature *(hsing),* a distinction made with something like the following definitions formulated by Shao Yung (1011–1077) in mind: "To view things from the viewpoint of things is *hsing;* to view things from the viewpoint of the viewer is *ch'ing. Hsing* is clear and open; *ch'ing* is dark and closed (or 'secret,' 'surreptitious')." See *Kuan wu wai-p'ien, Huang-chi ching shih hsü-yen* (*SPPY* ed.), B.8B.16a; translation by Siu-kit Wong, "Ch'ing in Chinese Literary Criticism" (Ph.D. diss., Oxford University, 1969), 124. Yen Yü's theory of poetry seems in general to eschew the direct expression of highly individualized personal emotion; it stresses instead the apersonal nature of poetry and its function of articulating

transcendent and universal states of mind as well as heightened and magnanimous emotional states. It is unlikely, therefore, that we can take *ch'ing-hsing* here to mean simply "emotions." The *locus classicus* for *ch'ing-hsing* in Chinese poetry is the *Ta-hsü* (Great Preface) to the *Book of Odes:* "The record-keepers of the states sang forth their *ch'ing-hsing* in order to criticize their superiors." See *Mao-shih* (*SPTK* ed.), 1. Here *Ch'ing-hsing* seems to mean "moral indignation," a far more restricted and didactic sense than its occurrence here in the *Ts'ang-lang shih-hua;* nevertheless *both* occurrences signify something other than self-centered personal emotion.

78. Certain Ch'an masters of the T'ang often alluded to the antelope which supposedly could jump up and escape its enemies by hanging from tree branches. For instance, Master Tao-ying (d. 902) once addressed his disciples thus: "You are like good hunting dogs who only know how to find animals which leave tracks and which now have come across an antelope which hangs by its horns; not only are there no tracks, you don't even recognize its scent!" See *Ching-te ch'uan teng lu, T* 51.335b. Here the master warns his students not to get caught up in the literal meaning of what he is saying, for sense and reason are useless—there are no "tracks" for them to follow. Yen suggests that the same is true for great poetry, the real meaning of which lies beyond the reach of reason and the limitations of literal language.

79. "Something which defies rational analysis" translates *pu-k'o ts'ou-po.* The exact meaning of *ts'ou-po* is unclear, and there has been considerable disagreement over its translation; see Liu, *Chinese Theories of Literature,* 151 n. 111. In some instances it seems to mean "join together," "assemble," or "piece together," as, for example, in a statement made by Ch'an Master Shan-chao (ca. 950–ca. 1027): "When nirvāṇa-illumination *(chao)* and its function *(yung)* come at the same time, how can one ever set one off from the other *(tang-ti),* and when nirvāṇa-illumination and function do not come at the same time, how can one ever join them together *(ts'ou-po)?*" See *Ching-te ch'uan teng lu, T* 51.305a. *Ts'ou-po* literally means "gather and moor" or perhaps "moor in calm waters." This is how it is understood at least by certain traditional Japanese commentators on Ch'an texts who seem to think that such an action is analogous to reflective, rational thought—the mind gathers together thoughts and fixes them in place, something, of course, condemned in Ch'an. Cf. Paul Demiéville's review of Günther Debon, *Ts'ang-lang's Gespräche über die Dichtung* in *T'oung Pao* 49 (1961–1962): 471. As such, *pu-k'o ts'ou-po* could mean "does not allow one to keep his moorings (i.e., rational bearings) in it." Some instances are quite ambiguous, as, for example, in a statement by Chu Hsi (1130–1200): "I also do not have any friends with whom I can discuss things, and, from time to time, when I do have one or two, then the dull witted have difficulty in *ts'ou-po* (piecing together/keeping their moorings or bearing in what I say) and the clever do not have any patience for it." See Chu's *Ta Fu Han-ch'ing* (A Letter in Reply to Fu Han-ch'ing), *Chu-tzu wen-chi* (Literary Collection of Master Chu) (*Ts'ung-shu ch'i-ch'eng* ed.), 1.40. We have also seen *ts'ou-po* used in a statement by Ch'an Master Fo-kuo Yüan-wu where it was translated as "hang on to" (see above, note 72). "[Something which] defies rational analysis" as a translation attempts to effect a compromise among these possibilities.

80. *Ju k'ung-chung chih yin, hsiang-chung chih se*—Yen has borrowed this from a critique made of the poetry of Wang An-shih by Chang Shun-min (ca. 1034–ca. 1100): "The poetry of Wang Chieh-fu is like an echo in the air or the play of colors in phenomenal appearance; however much you might want to pin down its meaning, you just cannot do it!" See Chao Yü-shih, *Pin-t'ui lu* (*Ts'ung-shu ch'i-ch'eng* ed.), 2.21, where Chang's critique is quoted.

81. A monk asked Ch'an Master Yüan-hsiang: " 'One should respond to something as it manifests itself in the phenomenal world just as if it were a reflection of the moon in water, but just what do we do with this moon?' The Master simply raised his fly whisk." See *Wu-teng hui-yüan,* 8.40b. Another possible source for this passage is the *Wen-shu-shih-li wen p'u-t'i ching* (Mañjuśrī Asks about Bodhi Sūtra), *T* 14.482: "Now, this manifestation of bodhi is like an image in a mirror, like a flame at its hottest point, like a shadow, like an echo, or like the moon seen reflected in water. It must be like these things when one manifests the bodhi-mind." Schmidt draws attention to the *Ta-chih-tu lun* (*T* 25.101c): "[The enlightened] understand all dharmas to be like a sleight of the hand, a mirage, the moon in the water *(jala-candra),* the void, an echo, a *gandharva* city, a dream, a shadow, the reflection in a mirror, a transformation." Schmidt then goes on to translate the commentary to this passage in the *Ta-chih-tu lun:* "As for its being like the moon in the water, the moon is really in the sky, but its reflection appears in the water. The moon, like the mark of the real dharma, is as if in the 'sky' of the reality of the true dharma nature. In the 'water' of the mind of all gods and men there appear the marks of the ego and all that belong to the ego, and for this reason it is said to be like the moon in the water. Moreover, if a small child sees the moon in the water, he is glad and wishes to grab it, but when an adult sees this, he laughs." See *T* 25.102b and Schmidt, *Yang Wan-li,* 78–79.

82. *Ts'ang-lang shih-hua chiao-shih,* 23–24.

83. Ibid., 24

84. Ibid., 24–25.

85. Kuo Shao-yü believes that it can be best understood in terms of *miao-wu* (marvelous enlightenment) in which there are two dimensions: *ti-i i chih wu* (enlightenment of the first order), which is concerned with the perfect apprehension of how to write, to intuitively control, formally correct poetry (with that of the High T'ang as model), and *t'ou-ch'e chih wu* (thoroughly penetrating enlightenment), which is concerned with the intuitive apprehension of reality. Wai-lim Yip deals with the substantive dimension of the analogy in "Yen Yü and the Poetic Theories in the Sung Dynasty," *Tamkang Review* 1, no. 2 (1970): 183–200, where he concludes that poetry resembles Ch'an in the respect that (1) it should be the product of "free activity" or "spontaneous expression" (p. 192), "a poem is best when no human effort is present" (p. 193), and (2) a poem should "grasp and give forth with immediacy the *mind picture as it is* without going through the logical, discursive and informative aspects of the words" (p. 196), it should also be "a mind-picture complete before and after the expression" (p. 197).

86. Lynn, "Orthodoxy and Enlightenment," 219.

87. A perceptive critique of D. T. Suzuki's characterization of Ch'an (Zen)

enlightenment, comparing it to William James' understanding of the mystic state and to C. G. Jung's psychology of the unconscious, appears in Heinrich Dumoulin, *A History of Zen Buddhism* (Boston: Beacon Press, 1963), 276–281.

88. *Ts'ang-lang shih-hua chiao-shih,* 6.

89. Discussions of the occurrences of the term *ju-shen,* including its *locus classicus* in the *Classic of Changes* can be found in the following: Liu, *Chinese Theories of Poetry,* 37–38 and 44; Lynn, "Orthodoxy and Enlightenment," 250–254. Both Ch'ien Chung-shu (*T'an i lu,* 49) and Kuo Shao-yü (*Ts'ang-lang shih-hua chiao-shih,* 8–10) reject the notion that *ju shen* in poetry is exclusively concerned with either Buddhist nirvāṇa or the transcendent Tao of nature of classical Taoism.

90. See Lynn, "Orthodoxy and Enlightenment," 250–253.

91. Ch'ien Chung-shu, *T'an i lu,* 48–49.

92. Kuo Shao-yü quotes with approval a statement in T'ao Ming-chün's *Shih-shuo tsa-chi* (Random Notes on Critiques of Poetry) which attempts to explain the difference between Yen Yü's two essential characteristics *(ta-kai)* of poetry: "It [poetry] must either flow freely and not be restricted *(yu-yu pu-p'o)* or it must be thoroughly imbued with deeply moving expression *(ch'en-cho t'ung-k'uai)*" (*Ts'ang-lang shih-hua chiao-shih,* 6). T'ao's statement reads: "From ancient times on there have indeed been many poets, and all possible *t'i* (forms) of poetry have occurred! But the two large delimitations Mr. Yen has formulated are actually sufficient to cover them all without a single omission. . . . 'Flowing freely without restriction'—this characterizes the form associated with T'ao [T'ao Ch'ien] and Wei [Wei Ying-wu]; it is relaxed and casual and free and easy, a manner of complete serenity and composure. . . . As for being 'thoroughly imbued with deeply moving expression' . . . Like grain spilling out from an overfilled granary, words without forethought are uttered on impulse. . . . When one writes in this form, he must make it gallop along in enthusiasm . . . and must make the reader's mind be moved by it and his emotions stirred by it, so that he cannot prevent himself from clapping his hands in rhythm and singing it at the top of his voice. The poetry of Tu Shao-ling [Tu Fu] is profound and forceful, a perfect marvel the likes of which no one else has ever managed to achieve since time began, and if you ask how he managed to do this, the answer can only be found in the words *ch'en-cho t'ung-k'uai*" (*Ts'ang-lang shih-hua chiao-shih,* 8 n. 5). Since Tu Fu's poetry is thoroughly oriented toward the human world with all its pain and ecstasy, the implication here is that T'ao Ming-chün thinks that Yen Yü, by placing Tu's poetry at the top of all possible poetic achievement (as he does throughout the *Ts'ang-lang shih-hua*), accords his greatest respect for poetry concerned with the human world, the human *tao.*

93. For a brief account of the background of the rise of "literary Ch'an" during the Sung, see Kenneth Ch'en, *Buddhism in China* (Princeton: Princeton University Press, 1973), 403–404.

94. See Lynn, "Tradition and the Individual," 346, for example, where Wang Fu-chih (1619–1692) is noted as having declared that Su Shih's poetry is "wild fox Ch'an"—i.e., "heterodox."

95. Cf. Yip, "Yen Yü and the Poetic Theories in the Sung Dynasty," 194–196. Pao was a member of a family dedicated to the study of Neo-Confucian-

ism. His father, Pao Yang, and two uncles, Pao Yüeh and Pao Sun, were first disciples of Lu Chiu-yüan (1139–1193), then, after Lu died, they became followers of Chu Hsi. As a youth Pao studied with all his relatives and is supposed to have achieved a profound understanding of the *Ta-hsüeh* (Great Learning). Later in life he wrote a commentary to the *Chou-li* (Rites of Chou), which is now lost, but many items in his collected works, the *Pi-chou kao-lüeh* (Draft Works of Sweepings from a Worn Out Broom) are of interest to the historian of Neo-Confucianism. An account of the Neo-Confucian activities of the Pao family can be found in fasc. 77 of the *Sung Yüan hsüeh-an;* see also Kuo Shao-yü, *Chung-kuo wen-hsüeh p'i-p'ing shih,* 469–470.

96. Lo Ken-tse suggests that this assertion of Pao's should be interpreted in terms of a passage in the *Chung-yung* (Doctrine of the Mean): "While there are no stirrings *(wei-fa)* of pleasure, anger, sorrow, or joy, the mind may be said to be in a state of EQUILIBRIUM *(chung).* When those feelings have been stirred *(fa),* and they act in their due degree, there ensues what may be called the state of HARMONY *(ho).*" See James Legge, trans., *The Doctrine of the Mean (The Chinese Classics),* 384. Lo notes that both Lu Chiu-yüan and Chu Hsi greatly venerated the *Chung-yung* and that this veneration was passed on to Pao Hui through his father and uncles. See Lo Ken-tse, *Chung-kuo wen-hsüeh p'i-p'ing shih,* vol. 3 (Shanghai: Ku-tien, wen-hsüeh ch'u-pan-she, 1961), 216. In the light of this, it appears that *tsao-hua chih wei-fa che* would mean "when emotions have not been stirred and transformed and the stuff of poetry reflects this" and that *tsao-hua chih i-fa che* would mean "when emotions have already been stirred and transformed into the stuff of poetry." The former exists in poetry that reflects a tranquil and dispassionate state of mind/heart, and the latter exists in poetry that expresses emotions which have been stirred by things but which are still in harmony with them—the one free of emotional overtones, the other infused with balanced emotions "proper" in their response.

97. This is almost word for word the same as Yen's statement concerning the quality of High T'ang poetry and Chang Shun-min's critique of the poetry of Wang An-shih; see above, note 80.

98. The text is *lai tzu t'ien-chi* (sprang from heavenly millet). *T'ien-chi* (heavenly millet) is supposed to be the root ancestor of all grain crops; the idea here is that T'ao Ch'ien's poetry (and that of his tradition) shares in the primordial nature of "original" poetry.

99. Pao Hui, *Pi-chou kao-lüeh* (*Ssu-k'u ch'üan-shu chen-pen,* 3d series, ed.), 2.1a–2b. The analogy here between gradual cultivation following a sudden experience of enlightenment and the long period of nourishment following birth as a child becomes an adult originally comes from Shen-hui. See his *T'ing shih-pei-lun,* in Hu Shih, ed., *Shen-hui ho-shang i-chi* (Taipei: Hu-shih chi-nien kuan, 1968), 287.

100. See above, note 18.

101. This line is modeled after a line in the first of Tu Fu's *Feng-tseng Wei tso-ch'ieng chang erh-shih-erh yün* (Twenty-Two Rhymes Respectfully Presented to the Executive Assistant of the Left in the Department of State, My Senior Mr. Wei [Wei Chi]): "You're so devoted to your sovereign as to put him above Yao and Shun." See *Ch'üan T'ang-shih,* 216.2251–2252.

102. Ko T'ien-min, *Wu-hai hsiao-chi* (*Nan-Sung ch'ün-hsien hsiao-chi* ed.), 1b.

103. See above, note 34.

104. From Tu Fu's *Chiang-shang chih shui ju hai-shih liao tuan-shu* (The Waters of the Yangtse Stretch Out with the Force of the Sea—A Trifling Effort to Portray It in a Short Composition); see *Ch'üan T'ang-shih,* 226.2443.

105. Tradition attributes the following verse to Bodhidharma: "A separate tradition outside the scriptures / Not founded upon words and letters. / By pointing directly to one's own mind, / Thus seeing into his true nature, / One attains Buddhahood." Though different parts of this verse appear in early Ch'an texts, as a whole it first occurs in the *Tsu-t'ing shih-yüan* (Collection of Matters from the Courtyard of the Patriarchs), 1st edition of 1108, compiled by Mu-an Shan-hsiang. Cf. Isshū Miura and Ruth Fuller Sasaki, *Zen Dust: The History of the Koan and Koan Study in Rinzai (Lin-chi) Zen* (New York: Harcourt, Brace, and World, 1966), 229–230.

106. Liu K'o-chuang, *Hou-ts'un ta-ch'üan-chi* (*SPTK* ed.), 99.1b.

Glossary

Ch'a-t'u-pen Chung-kuo wen-hsüeh shih 插圖本中國文學史
Ch'an 禪
ch'an-chi 禪機
chan t'ou ch'iu huo 斬頭求活
Ch'an-hsüeh yü T'ang-Sung shih-hsüeh 禪學與唐宋詩學
ch'an-tsung tun chien erh-i 禪宗頓漸二義
ch'ang-chü 長句
Chang Shun-min 張舜民
Chao Fan 趙蕃
Chao Po-yü 趙伯魚
Chao Yü-shih 趙與時
ch'ao-jan 超然
chen-shih 眞實
Ch'en Ch'i 陳起
Ch'en-cho t'ung-k'uai 沉着痛快
Ch'en Hsien-chang 陳獻章
Ch'en Shih-tao 陳師道
Ch'eng-chai shih-hua 誠齋詩話
Cheng Chen-to 鄭振鐸
cheng fa-yen 正法眼
chi ch'i chih 極其至
chi-chih 極致
chi-kung 積功
ch'i-chih 氣志
ch'i p'i-mao 其皮毛
Chiang-hsi shih-p'ai hsiao-hsü 江西詩派小序
ch'ieh-chin 切近
chih yen 至言
Ch'ien Chung-shu 錢鍾書
Ch'ien-hsi shih-yen 潛溪詩眼
chin tz'u-li 盡此理
Ch'in Kou 秦觀
Ch'in-ting ch'üan T'ang-wen 金定全唐文
ching 境
ching (quietude) 靜
Ching-chin Tung-p'o wen-chi shih-lüeh 經近東坡文集事略
Ching-te ch'uan-teng lu 景德傳燈錄
ch'ing-hsing 情性
Chou Ju-ch'ang 周汝昌
chu 主
Chu Hsi 朱熹
Chu-hsi chüan-chai hsü-chi 竹溪鬳齋續集
Chu-tzu wen-chi 朱子文集
ch'ü 趣
Ch'u-tz'u 楚辭
ch'ü yü 去欲
chüan lien chien tao 捲簾見道

Ch'üan Han San-kuo Chin Nan-pei-ch'ao shih 全漢三國晉南北朝詩
Ch'üan T'ang shih 全唐詩
Chuang-tzu 莊子
ch'ui mao chien 吹毛劍
Chung-kuo wen-hsüeh p'i-p'ing shih 中國文學批評史
ch'ung-mo yu chi 沖漠郁際
fa 法
Fan Tsu-yü 范祖禹
Fan Wen 范溫
feng-yüeh 風月
Fo-kuo yüan-wu ch'an-shih pi-yen lu 佛果圓悟禪師碧巖錄
fu-ku 復古
Han Chü 韓駒
Han Yü 韓愈
hao-meng 豪孟
hao-mu 蒿目
Hou-shan chi 後山集
Hou-ts'un ta-ch'üan-chi 後村大全集
hsia-lieh shih-mo 下劣詩魔
Hsia Ni 夏倪
hsiao-jan i ch'ing 翛然以清
hsiao-sheng 小乘
hsiao-wu pi hsiao te 小悟必小得
hsieh 泄
Hsieh Ling-yün 謝靈運
hsieh-mo 邪魔
hsien 仙
hsien-ku 仙骨
hsin-ti 心地
hsing-ch'ü 興趣
hsü 虛
hsü-huan 虛幻
Hsü li-tai shih-hua 續歷代詩話
hsüeh fo 學佛
hua 華
huan-hsi ch'u 歡喜處
huan ku 換骨
Huang-chi ching-shih hsü-yen 皇極經世續言
Huang T'ing-chien 黃庭堅
hui 慧
Hui Hung 惠洪
Hui-neng 慧能
hun-ssu 渾似
Hung Sheng 洪昇
huo-chü 活句
huo-fa 活法
i-ch'ao chih-ju che 一超直入者
i-chih pan-chieh 一知半解
I-hsien 義銛
i-shih 一事
ju 如
ju Ch'an 入禪
ju shen 入神
ju tao 入道
Jung T'ien-ho 榮天和
Kao Ho 高荷
ken-yüan 根源
ko-hsing 歌行
Ko T'ien-min 葛天民
ko tzu i feng-liu 各自一風流
k'ou-chüeh 口訣
k'u 枯
kuan-lieh 關捩
kuan-lieh-tzu 關捩子
kuo-feng 國風
Kuo Shao-yü 郭紹虞
k'uo-jan 廓然
k'uo-yüan 闊遠
k'ung 空
kung-fu 工夫
Kung Hsiang 龔相
Leng-chai yeh-yü 冷齋夜語
li 理
Li Ch'u-ch'üan 李處權
Li Ling 李陵
Li Po 李白
Lin-chi lu 臨濟錄
Lin Hsi-i 林希逸
Ling-yang chi 陵陽集
Liu K'o-chuang 劉克莊
Liu Yü-hsi 劉禹錫
Liu Yün 劉筠

Lo Ken-tse 羅根澤
Lu Chiu-yüan 陸九淵
Lu T'ung 盧仝
Lü Pen-chung 呂本中
Mei Yao-ch'en 梅堯臣
Meng Hao-jan 孟浩然
miao (marvelous) 妙
miao-i 妙意
miao-wu 妙悟
mieh chiao ming hsin 滅教明心
ming-hui wu-chi 冥會無迹
nai hsing hu tz'u 乃形乎辭
Nan-Sung ch'ün-hsien hsiao-chi 南宋羣賢小集
nien 拈
Ou-yang Hsiu 歐陽修
pa-chen chü 八珍具
Pao Hui 包恢
Pi-chou kao-lüeh 敝帚稿略
pien 變
Pin-t'ui lu 賓退錄
Po Chü-i 白居易
sha-men 沙門
Shao Yung 邵雍
shen 深
sheng-chi 生機
sheng-chih 生知
sheng-lü 聲律
Sheng Tu 盛度
shih (judgment/discrimination) 識
shih (poetry) 詩
shih (substantial) 實
shih (phenomenon) 事
Shih-Ch'an 詩禪
Shih-ching 詩經
shih-fa 詩法
Shih-jen yü-hsieh 詩人玉屑
Shih Jun-chang 施閏章
Shih Mi-ning 史彌寧
Shih-Pien 詩辨
Shih-shuo tsa-chi 詩說雜記
shih ta-chih 詩大指
ssu-chü 死句
Ssu-k'ung piao-sheng wen-chi 司空表聖文集
Ssu-k'ung T'u 司空圖
ssu sheng-shen 四勝身
Su Shih 蘇軾
Su Tung-p'o chi 蘇東坡集
Su Wu 蘇武
Sung 頌
Sung-an chi 崧菴集
Sung shih-hua chi i 宋詩話輯佚
Sung Ts'an-liao shih 送參寥師
Sung Yüan hsüeh-an 宋元學案
Tai-ching t'ang shih-hua 帶經堂詩話
T'an-i lu 談藝錄
tan-po 淡[澹]泊
T'ao Ming-chün 陶明濬
tao yu hsieh cheng 道有邪正
T'ao Ch'ien 陶潛
t'ien-ts'ai 天才
ting 定
ting-ning 頂顊
to t'ai fa 奪胎法
t'ou-ch'e 透徹
t'ou-shang an t'ou 頭上安頭
ts'an 參
Ts'ang-hai shih-hua 藏海詩話
Ts'ang-lang shih-hua 滄浪詩話
tsao-hua 造化
Ts'ao-tung 曹洞
Tseng Chi 曾幾
Tseng Kung 曾鞏
Tso-chuan 左傳
tso tsa-chü 作雜劇
ts'ou-po 湊泊
ts'ui-jan i li 粹然以麗
tsung-heng 縱橫
Ts'ung-shen 從諗
Tu Fu 杜甫
Tu Sung-po 杜松柏
tun-chiao 頓教
tun-wu 頓悟
T'ung meng shih-hsün 童蒙詩訓
tzu-jan wu-ju 自然悟入

tzu-jan yu ju-ch'u 自然有入處
wai-tao 外道
wan-hsiang ju 萬象入
Wang An-shih 王安石
Wang Fu-chih 王夫之
Wang Shih-chen 王士禎
Wang Shou-jen 王守仁
Wang Wei 王維
wang-yang 汪洋
Wang Yang-ming 王陽明
Wang Yü-ch'eng 王禹稱
Wei Ch'ing-chih 魏慶之
Wei Ying-wu 韋應物
Wen-hsüan 文選
wu 悟
wu-ju ch'u 悟入處
Wu K'o 吳可
wu-men 悟門
Wu-teng hui-yüan 五燈會元
wu ti-i-i 悟第一義
Ya 雅
Yang I 楊億
Yang Wan-li 楊萬里
yeh-hu wai-tao 野狐外道
yen-mu 眼目
Yen Yü 嚴羽
yen-yü wen-tzu 言語文字
yu hui erh ch'ien tz'u 由慧而遣辭
Yu-lin i-kao 友林之稿
yung i ch'u 用意處
yü 腴
yüan 圓
Yü-ch'ang Huang hsien-sheng wen-chi 豫章黃先生文集
Yüan-an 元安
yüan-ch'ü 緣渠
Yüan-mi 緣密
Yüeh-fu ssu-p'ien 樂府四篇

Tung Ch'i-ch'ang's "Southern and Northern Schools" in the History and Theory of Painting: A Reconsideration

JAMES CAHILL

The theory of the Southern and Northern schools *(nan-pei tsung lun)* by Tung Ch'i-ch'ang (1555–1636) is, along with Hsieh Ho's fifth-century "Six Laws of Painting," one of the crucial and influential formulations in Chinese painting theory. It was probably composed in 1595, and was published in the early seventeenth century.[1] Most Chinese theorists of painting after that time echo it, or argue with it, or are somehow affected by it. Recent scholars have tended to criticize it as ahistorical and biased in the version of early painting that it presents, while recognizing its importance in the history of theorizing. A recent, groundbreaking study has treated it, along with Tung Ch'i-ch'ang's ideas on painting more generally, in the context of late Ming literary theory and Neo-Confucianism.[2] This paper will consider it once more, in relation to the theme of the volume, the sudden-gradual polarity in Chinese Buddhism, especially Ch'an. I have previously characterized the relationship as analogical rather than substantive, and still believe it is essentially that—Tung was not, that is, implying a Ch'an aesthetic basis for his "Southern school," as has sometimes been supposed,[3] nor is he suggesting any Buddhist content for landscape painting. But we can still ask why this particular analogy was chosen—why Tung could offer the formula "Painting of Type A is to painting of Type B as Sudden Enlightenment (Southern) Ch'an is to Gradual Enlightenment (Northern) Ch'an" and have it hailed as though it were a great historical truth. In exploring some aspects and implications of Tung's Southern and Northern schools theory, we will begin outside and move inside —begin, that is, by seeing it as a strategem within a continuing controversy over opposing trends in painting, and end by considering its real significance with respect to the practice of painting by Tung himself and others. Like a work of art, which can play a dynamic role in a historical pattern while enjoying an absolute existence as an object, a theory or idea can function and carry meaning on various levels, some contingent and time-bound (the idea in historical interaction with others), and some intrinsic (the idea as embodiment of some measure of truth).

The Southern and Northern Schools Theory

Tung Ch'i-ch'ang's fullest statement of the theory is to be found in the *Hua chih* or "Purport of Painting," a collection of his writings on painting compiled around 1650.[4] It reads:

> In Ch'an Buddhism there are two schools (or lineages), the Southern and the Northern, which first separated in the T'ang period. The Southern and Northern schools of painting also separated in the T'ang. But it is not that the artists [in these two schools] were of [geographically] southern or northern origin. The Northern school is that of the colored landscapes of Li Ssu-hsün and his son Chao-tao; it was transmitted to Chao Kan, Chao Po-chü and his brother Po-su in the Sung period, and on to Ma Yüan and Hsia Kuei and their group. The Southern school is that of Wang Wei, who first used graded washes [in ink monochrome painting] and thus completely transformed the outline-and-color technique. This was continued by Chang Tsao, Ching Hao and Kuan T'ung, Tung Yüan and Chü-jan, Kuo Chung-shu, Mi Fu and his son Yu-jen, down to the Four Great Masters of the Yüan.
>
> It is like [Ch'an Buddhism, in which], after the sixth patriarch, the Ma-chü, Yün-men, and Lin-chi lineages flourished, while the Northern school slipped into unimportance. The essential thing, as Wang Wei says, is that the "misty peaks and boulders issue from the workings of heaven, and the patterns of the brushwork partake of natural creation." Also, Su Tung-p'o, in an encomium on wall paintings by Wu Tao-tzu and Wang Wei, wrote that "in the case of Wei, I can find no fault." These are true words.

The Southern and Northern Schools Theory as Rhetoric and Strategem

Tung Ch'i-ch'ang's theory was the last and most successful in a series of Ming dynasty schematic histories of painting, constructions usually of a tendentious character, in which old masters were arranged in groups or lineages, and the superiority of one kind of painting over another was argued or implied, often in large binary formulations that opposed one period or tradition or stylistic lineage of painting to another. I have outlined these theories elsewhere, and they need not occupy us here at length.[5] The basis for division in these binary formulations was sometimes period, Sung painting versus Yüan painting; sometimes socioeconomic, painting by professional masters versus that done by literati artists or scholar-amateurs; sometimes stylistic, with looser, more spontaneous styles contrasted to the careful and detailed. These criteria of division, moreover, tended to interlock into grand unhistorical patterns in which Sung dynasty professionals working in detailed, decorative, academic styles were opposed to Yüan dynasty amateurs working in free, spontaneous styles. Stated that way, of course, the issue would appear one-sided; but the Sung academicians also had their proponents, and throughout most of the Ming the argument remained open. Tung Ch'i-ch'ang's Southern and Northern schools theory was meant as an ultimate salvo from the side of Yüan, amateurism, and spontaneity (his preferred Southern school being, of course, equatable in this loose system of correspondences with those), and it did in fact carry the day, although opposition to it had begun to build again by the middle of the seventeenth century.[6]

We can best understand its success by seeing how it avoided the weaknesses of its predecessors. Without attempting to characterize individually the old masters who appear in the groupings and lineages constructed by Ming writers, which would divert us too far from our theme, we can note that they do not fall neatly into place in any of these systems; the arrangements were necessarily more or less artificial, if not arbitrary, and so open to criticism. No single objective criterion could produce a lineage that would stand up to scrutiny. (The question of why such a lineage need be produced at all will be considered later; it is enough to say, for now, that it served artists as precedent for their practice, collectors as justification for their preferences, and theorists as validation for their contentions.) The artists whom any particular critic chose to include in his preferred lineage, that is, could not be shown to be all active in a single dynasty, or all from some particular region, or all amateurs or professionals, or even all clearly relatable in style.

One formulation that probably preceded Tung Ch'i-ch'ang's by a year, and parallels it strikingly, was written in 1594 by Tung's older contemporary Chan Ching-feng (1520–1602). Chan takes the amateur-professional distinction as the basis for his dichotomy, but presents it in new terms: the *i-chia* or "liberated masters" versus the *tso-chia*, "makers" or "fabricators." He writes:

> In landscape painting there are two lineages. One is [made up of] the liberated masters, the other of the fabricators. These can also be called the professionals and the amateurs. The liberated masters began with Wang Wei . . . and later included Ching Hao, Kuan T'ung, Tung Yüan, and Chü-jan. . . . Mi Fu and Mi Yu-jen belonged to this "blood line," but after them it was cut off for nearly two hundred years, after which the Four Great Masters of the Yüan—Huang Kung-wang, Wang Meng, Ni Tsan, and Wu Chen—distantly took up this current and continued it. In our dynasty Shen Chou and Wen Cheng-ming followed this tradition in their paintings.
>
> The fabricators began with Li Ssu-hsün and Li Chao-tao, and continued with Li Ch'eng and Hsü Tao-ning. After them, Chao Po-chü and

> Chao Po-su . . . all belonged properly in this lineage. In the Southern Sung, Ma Yüan, Hsia Kuei, Liu Sung-nien, and Li T'ang belonged to this "blood line." In our dynasty Tai Chin and Chou Ch'en continued it.
>
> Of those who combined the excellences of the liberated masters and the fabricators, Fan K'uan, Kuo Hsi, and Li Kung-lin were the founding fathers; Wang Shen . . . , Chao Kan . . . , and in the Southern Sung, Ma Ho-chih were all of this lineage.[7]

Compared to earlier formulations, this one was a move in the right direction: since *i-chia* and *tso-chia* are not objectively definable categories, no one could quarrel with the writer's choice of the artists he assigned to each of them, and the additional group of those who "combined the excellences" of the two disposes of those masters who did not fit into either lineage. But the equation of the *i-chia–tso-chia* distinction with the amateur-professional one reintroduces the old problem: too few of the major landscapists before the Yüan could reasonably be classified as amateur painters. Ching Hao and Kuan T'ung, Tung Yüan and Chü-jan were in fact no more so than Li Ch'eng or Hsü Tao-ning. The terms *i-chia* and *tso-chia,* by deflecting the emphasis of the dichotomy slightly away from status toward style or creative approach, partly answered this problem, but not completely. What were needed were even more vague and accommodating categories, and these are what Tung Ch'i-ch'ang found in his choice of the Ch'an Buddhist analogy for his Southern and Northern schools theory.

The virtual equivalence of his Southern school with the scholar-amateur current in painting cannot have escaped any reader familiar with earlier constructions of painting history—the Four Great Masters of Yüan are placed at its core, and the artists who precede them are the ones commonly cited as their stylistic predecessors. The general correspondence of the list to Chan Ching-feng's list of "liberated masters" (or amateurs), moreover, makes Tung Ch'i-ch'ang's intent clear. But he stops short of defining the artists in this lineage openly as amateurs, and so avoids the unjustifiable classification of such masters as Ching Hao and Kuan T'ung, Tung Yüan and Chü-jan, as nonprofessionals. Likening them somehow to practitioners of "sudden enlightenment" Ch'an, by contrast, was uncontestable. The Southern and Northern schools theory has sometimes been dismissed by present-day writers as ahistorical: in fact, its transcending of mere history was its triumph.

The Southern and Northern Schools Theory: The Buddhist Analogy

Analogies with Buddhism, and especially Ch'an Buddhism, were often used by theorists and critics of painting in their discussions. To ask why these were chosen would raise a question even larger than the one dealt with in this paper: what do painting and Buddhism, or (even more broadly) art and religion, have in common that allows recognizable affinities or formal resemblances between beliefs and tendencies and movements in them? The simplest answer would be: although both can be discussed in rational terms, truly significant choices in both must be made on nonrational grounds; and on these choices may hang one's spiritual fulfillment, one's very "salvation." The last term, in reference to art, is only partly metaphorical; the highest creative achievements apparently break on the consciousness of their artists as a kind of enlightenment, and failure, or partial failure, is perceived as falling short of a spiritual goal. When Tung Ch'i-ch'ang, in an inscription written in 1630, laments that after fifty-two years of painting he is still unable to achieve an even level of quality in his works, he likens himself to the Buddha Śākyamuni who, after preaching the dharma for forty-nine years, regretted that he had not yet "turned the wheel of the dharma," or put his teachings into practice to accomplish the salvation of mankind.[8] Levels of achievement in painting can similarly be perceived as stages of spiritual attainment. "The painter who imitates ancient masters," Tung writes, "already belongs to the upper vehicle *(shang-sheng)*. Advancing one more step, he adopts nature as his teacher."[9]

The analogy of Ch'an, with its iconoclastic attitude toward scriptures and logical arguments, could be used by artists and critics in defense of an inspired freedom from ordinary rules and conventions in the pursuit of artistic originality; it could also be used in warning against the excesses that might result when painters adopted that attitude too enthusiastically. By Tung Ch'i-ch'ang's time, the "amateur ideal" was being invoked in defense of a great deal of sloppy painting, and several seventeenth-century writers express alarm over this erosion of old standards. Li Jih-hua (1565–1635), after praising the artists of antiquity for planning and executing their compositions in a painstaking manner, has this to say of the late Northern Sung pioneers of the scholar-amateur movement:

> When we come to the Su Tung-p'o and Mi Fu circle, however, artists suddenly begin to rely on their talents to flourish [the brush] in a bravura manner, taking brush and ink as playthings. These artists did their pictures when tipsy, or while engaged in conversation, following their inclinations. Nothing they did was less than marvelous; still, this was like the working of heaven, or the performance of an illusion—not, in the end, true painting. One can liken them to Buddhist priests who become saints outside the monastic discipline *(san-seng)*—they eat meat and get drunk on wine, spitting out dirt which all turns to gold. When other people try to

imitate them, however, they end up as nothing more than monks who have broken their vows.[10]

Artists who used aberrant styles and flaunted their unorthodoxy were frequently likened to "wild fox Ch'an" practitioners. The painter Kung Hsien, in an inscription written in 1669, associates the "heterodox" masters of his time (among whom he probably counted himself) with Buddhist monks and Taoist priests, and the orthodox masters, presumably, with Confucian scholar-officials (which indeed, in many cases, they were). He writes: "The way I would argue . . . the 'heterodox' group may not belittle the 'orthodox' one. If all our contemporaries belonged to the 'heterodox' group, there would be only Buddhist monks and Taoist priests in our country, and there would be no official [*i-kuan* 'full dress'] works of art."[11]

The Ch'an Buddhist analogy and related terminology were thus used by different writers for different purposes; parallels between religious and artistic doctrine and practice were not so neat as to preclude a variety of associational patterns.

It may seem odd—and has been perceived as paradoxical[12]—that "sudden enlightenment" Ch'an should be paralleled, in Tung Ch'i-ch'ang's formulation, to a tradition-based manner of painting that evolved, by Tung's design, into an orthodoxy. But in making this association, Tung was only accepting (no doubt from his Ch'an teacher Tz'u-pai Chen-k'o [1543–1603] among others) the conviction that Southern school Ch'an was itself a "correct lineage," and so offered a useful model for his own attempt to establish one for painting. The sectarianism of Ch'an, that is, provided a pattern for factional arguments in painting, as it had already done in poetry.[13]

The Yüan period writer Jao Tzu-jan, in the preface (dated 1340) to his *Shan-shui chia-fa,* anticipates Tung Ch'i-ch'ang in recognizing the appropriateness of the Ch'an analogy. The preface begins:

> Yen Tsang-lang [Yü] says that to study poetry is like studying Ch'an; you have to enter by the right gate [i.e., choose the right master, or lineage]. If you enter by the wrong gate, you are sure to take the outer road of the wild foxes, and fail to reach enlightenment by the upper vehicle. I likewise say: studying painting is like studying poetry; you have to follow some particular school. Then you won't aim at a false goal, and can proceed upward.[14]

The Southern and Northern Schools Theory as Basis for an Orthodoxy

As Wai-kam Ho has pointed out,[15] the idea of an orthodox or legitimate lineage *(cheng-t'ung)* in landscape painting, which is central to the arguments of many Ming-Ch'ing writers on painting, especially after Tung Ch'i-ch'ang,[16] is patterned on doctrinal lineages in both Ch'an Buddhism and Neo-Confucianism. In painting as in Ch'an, arguing for the correctness of one's *practice* on the basis of the correctness of one's *lineage* was, in a sense, the only argument open; in neither case could rational reasons for one's choice be effectively advanced. Tung Ch'i-ch'ang makes this kind of contention in a passage that parallels his statements of the Southern and Northern schools theory but shifts the grounds of argument to legitimacy of succession:

> The painting of the literati began with Wang Wei. Later, Tung Yüan, Chü-jan, Li Ch'eng, and Fan K'uan were his "proper issue" [lit., "children by legal wife," *ti-tzu*]. Li Kung-lin, Wang Shen, Mi Fu, and his son Yu-jen all stemmed from Tung and Chü. From there [the succession] goes straight on to the Four Masters of Yüan: Huang Kung-wang, Wang Meng, Ni Tsan, and Wu Chen. They all belonged to the correct (orthodox) line of transmission. In our dynasty Wen Cheng-ming and Shen Chou have also distantly succeeded to the robe and begging-bowl [i.e., the symbols of succession in Buddhist sects]. As for Ma Yüan, Hsia Kuei, Li T'ang, and Liu Sung-nien, they belong to the lineage of Li Ssu-hsün; they are nothing that we officials ought to study.[17]

Here the overt Buddhist reference is limited to the "robe and begging-bowl" metaphor; but the whole alignment of old masters like patriarchs is reminiscent of Ch'an formulations of the transmission of the doctrine. By the late Ming, of course, sectarian disputes in Ch'an lay far in the past, and the prominent masters tended instead to harmonize their differences. The closest parallel to the contentious situation in painting theory is in discussions of literature, where the question of orthodoxy was similarly still at issue among the proponents of opposing schools and trends.[18]

A lineage of enlightened masters was essential to Ch'an because the ultimate doctrine could not be transmitted through the written word so as to spread laterally to all who could read and comprehend. It could be passed only through a master-to-pupil relationship—hence the emphasis on *mien-shou,* "receiving [the doctrine] face to face." The same could not be literally true in the transmission of painting styles and practices, since the master-pupil mode of learning was more typical of professional traditions than of Tung's "Southern school" of scholar-amateurs. Tung himself acknowledged no teacher, and no significant predecessor after Wen Cheng-ming, who died when Tung was four years old; his real masters were in the fourteenth century and earlier. But the study and true understanding of the old masters' paintings could lead to a *shen-hui* or "spiritual meeting" across the centuries, and accomplish the same end as face-to-face meeting. Shen Chou, writing a poem on a copy by

Wu Chen of a bamboo painting by Su Tung-p'o, put it this way: "Men of today and those of the past cannot see each other. But, through surviving works [of former painters], it is as if they had never died."[19]

The Southern and Northern Schools Theory: Levels of Enlightenment

Establishing a single "school" or artistic direction as the only right one raises the question of how to deal with alternative directions: are they, then, to be regarded as all wrong? Ch'an doctrine, and its extension into literary theory in the writing of Yen Yü, provided the answer. There are different levels of enlightenment, to be reached through different routes or vehicles; by choosing and practicing the correct vehicle one can reach the highest form of enlightenment, while the choice of a lesser vehicle limits one's attainment to enlightenment of the second order.[20]

Although Tung Ch'i-ch'ang puts the T'ang period master Li Ssu-hsün at the head of his Northern school, which is, in his system, the "lesser vehicle," he admired Li's paintings and even advised that they could be taken as models on occasion: "If you are painting rocky seascapes, you must use the senior general Li Ssu-hsün's method . . ." and "Paintings such as the 'Shu River' and 'Waiting for the Ferry in Autumn' by Li Ssu-hsün are both 'teachers and friends of spiritual communion in my studio.' Whenever I go, I take these along with me."[21] The manner of painting associated with Li Ssu-hsün and his son Li Chao-tao, a precise and detailed drawing in fine line with the addition of heavy mineral pigments, could not, however, be taken as a basis for one's whole practice of painting. In another passage Tung warns against it, and makes the Buddhist analogy explicit, naming the Southern school masters Tung Yüan, Chü-jan, and Mi Fu as the correct "upper vehicle" models: "The school of Li Chao-tao was carried on by Chao Po-chü and Po-su; it is detailed and skillful in the extreme, and has the 'gentleman's spirit.' However, when later people imitate it, they get its skillfulness but miss its refinements." Tung traces the school through the Yüan period to the early sixteenth-century professional master Ch'iu Ying, whose paintings are "like screens ornamented with hairpins and bangles, an almost painful kind of artifice," and continues: "He died at fifty. So we know that this school of painting is definitely not to be practiced. These artists are like [Northern school] Ch'an practitioners who eventually become bodhisattvas through long, cumulative effort. They are not like the three masters Tung Yüan, Chü-jan, and Mi Fu, who could with a single leap attain salvation [lit., "enter the Tathāgatā state," *ju-lai*]."[22]

The idea of painters attaining "salvation" by a sudden leap is striking and attractive, but begs several questions. What, in painting, corresponded to "salvation"? Tung Ch'i-ch'ang would have been as hard-put to describe it as theorists before him had been. The difficulty of defining and communicating the content of literati or "Southern school" painting parallels the ineffableness of Ch'an enlightenment, providing another dimension to Tung's analogy, and another reason why he chose to make his point by analogy at all, instead of attempting to spell it out on its own terms. In trying to state or describe an equivalent for spiritual enlightenment in painting, theorists tended to fall back on such terms as *ch'i-yün* (spirit-resonance), which, although it may well have carried some relatively clear meaning for its originator Hsieh Ho and his early readers, had become by the later centuries an ill-defined criterion of quality invoked when the writer wanted to avoid being more specific. In any case, whatever the equivalent in painting, it was no one-time attainment, no "moment of truth," unless we count that moment when the artist first feels he has mastered his art. So Tung Ch'i-ch'ang's analogy raises also the question: sudden what? Gradual what?

One answer might be: sudden versus gradual in the *attainment* of mastery in painting, or in the learning process. In theory, this process was shortened for the scholar-amateur by his background, and by his lack of concern with displaying fine technique. The Southern Ch'an belief that Buddhahood is inherent from the beginning in the practitioner, so that he need only experience it immediately to reach enlightenment, must have had, for Tung, some counterpart in painting, although he never spells out what it was. Some quality or set of qualities, that is, must have been already present in the cultivated amateur artist, in Tung's view, which allowed him to cut through the long process of technical training and reach the highest attainments in painting directly. These qualities were, of course, exactly the fruits of Confucian self-cultivation and literary refinement to which the literati laid claim; hence the virtual equation of the Southern school with *wen-jen hua*. Endowed with these, the literatus-artist need acquire only a modicum of facility with the brush—some of which, thanks to his long practice of calligraphy for both practical and aesthetic purposes, he already possessed—to accomplish a Ch'an-like leap to the loftiest levels in painting. So, at least, in theory: in practice, Tung Ch'i-ch'ang's writing and paintings testify eloquently to his lifelong struggle with forms and images and the structures he made of them, a process that hardly accords with sudden enlightenment.

The gradual approach to painting (again in theory) was a matter of measured progress within the art of painting itself, a process that did not draw on the same outside resources as the amateur's moves toward mastery, and that contained distinctions and discontinuities like those characteristic of Northern school Ch'an. The artist, like someone mastering a craft or a technique, advanced by stages toward a predictable end, proficiency of a definable kind.

Tung Ch'i-ch'ang and like-minded writers and painters were not blind to the achievements of the professional masters, but they regarded these achievements as reflecting a kind of second-class enlightenment, and as suitable for others but not for themselves. Tung, at the end of his passage on literati painting quoted above, disposes of the Southern Sung academy styles (Ma-Hsia, Li T'ang, and Liu Sung-nien) in that way: they "belong to the lineage of Li Ssu-hsün" and are "nothing that we officials ought to study." Tung Ch'i-ch'ang's expressions of admiration for the works of some of his contemporaries whose styles are outside the Southern school limits—Lan Ying, Ting Yün-p'eng, Ts'ui Tzu-chung, and others—are presumably to be understood in such terms: it is all right for *them* to do such painting, but would not be all right for *us*.

The Southern and Northern Schools Theory, Ch'an, and the Practice of Painting

It might be expected that the last section of this paper would deal with actual Ch'an content in painting theory, ways in which Ch'an modes of apprehending the world might have affected theoretical formulations of how the painter perceives and represents it. But the argument stated at the outset that Tung Ch'i-ch'ang's use of Ch'an in the Southern and Northern schools theory is basically analogical, like Yen Yü's for literature, works against any supposition of Ch'an content in it or its theoretical ramifications; and I believe, with Wai-kam Ho and others, that Neo-Confucian ideas, especially those of Wang Yang-ming and his late Ming followers, make up a much more pertinent intellectual setting for Tung's beliefs.

The idea of Ch'an content in Tung's representations of landscape is similarly one that I will raise here only to dismiss. It might be claimed, through another overreading of the Southern and Northern schools theory (and especially in view of Tung's study of Ch'an in his early years), that Tung's pictures embody some mode of apprehending the phenomenal world that derives from "sudden enlightenment" Ch'an. But the wrongness of that idea, I believe, will be realized immediately when we look at Tung's paintings themselves, and compare them with landscape paintings for which a claim of that kind *can* validly be made, the so-called Ch'an paintings of the late Sung period, by or ascribed to Buddhist monk-artists such as Mu-ch'i and Yü-chien. For these we can argue, not that they are direct expressions of a Ch'an-enlightened state of mind—their artists may not, in fact, have been Ch'an practitioners at all, enlightened or otherwise[23]—but rather that the paintings present, through analyzable artistic means, a vision of nature and of natural phenomena that is consistent with the Ch'an mode of experience. By radically reducing the materials of the picture and rendering them in broad brushstrokes, more suggestive than descriptive, that allowed no fine detail, as well as by controlling ink tonality so as typically to concentrate dark accents in one area of the composition, the artist reproduces in forms the experience of apprehending reality in a single, sudden act of perception, instead of reading and absorbing it part by part. The loose ink-monochrome style of the paintings suggests a world not made up of clearly delineated, discrete entities, but perceived as a field or continuum within which the parts are fused into organic unity. And so forth—this is not the occasion for a discourse on how one can reach a workable definition of Ch'an painting. Our point is that none of this is true of Tung Ch'i-ch'ang's paintings, which, seen in themselves, are nearly as inimical to Ch'an ideals of direct, unmediated experience as those of Ch'iu Ying. Both the elaborateness of his compositions and his constant engagement with old styles work against any Ch'an-like immediacy. The latter obstacle might seem to be removed, on a theoretical level, by Tung's argument for creative transformation of the old masters' styles instead of close imitation of them; but in practice, introducing this additional level of stylistic reference to the painting drops a further screen between it and the world it ostensibly represents, rendering more difficult any Ch'an (or Neo-Confucian) sense of identity of perceiver and perceived.

We can, however, draw another kind of analogical relationship between the sudden-gradual polarity in regard to enlightenment and the amateur-professional distinction in painting, one that applies more directly than any so far discussed to the actual practice of painting, and that elucidates further Tung Ch'i-ch'ang's choice of this analogy. The practitioner of sudden enlightenment Ch'an aims at breaking through barriers of ignorance or errors in perception to a direct realization of the Buddhahood already inherent in him; his goal is inner, personal. Gradual enlightenment Ch'an involves (at least as characterized by its opponents) progress through spiritual stages toward an outer, preset goal, the bodhisattva state. How these two paths might be paralleled in the amateur and professional modes of reaching proficiency in painting has already been suggested in the preceding section. Is there a parallel as well in the actual practice of painting by artists of the two types?

Here again Chan Ching-feng's *i-chia–tso-chia* distinction can mediate between the sudden-gradual and the amateur-professional ones, providing a formulation to which both can be seen as somehow congruent. *Tso* (to make or fabricate) implies a preexisting image or model of what is to be made; one makes a chair (or, as the Taoists would say, an axe-handle) with the finished object in mind. And we can say, without venturing onto the treacherous ground of trying to describe the creative process as it actually takes place in the minds of artists, that landscape paintings in the detailed, heavily colored "blue and green" manner associated with Li Ssu-hün and Chao Po-chü, or the technically polished works of Southern Sung academicians such as Li T'ang and Ma Yüan, seem to have come into being in a similar way. These paintings exhibit a kind of perfect finish and compositional balance which suggest that the artist had an image much like the finished picture in his mind (and, no doubt, in his preparatory sketches) before he began, and executed it with such faultless technique that no signs of indecision, or changes of plan during the course of painting, are visible in the finished work. Typical paintings by the amateur or *i-chia* masters "liberated" from such constraints, by contrast, seem to have taken form in a more improvisatory way, growing unpredictably beneath the artist's hand as he responded to impulses of the moment, to transient moods, to the flow of thought and sensation in his own mind.[24] Paintings produced in this way are less likely to impart that impression of inevitability or "rightness" that the best works of the *tso-chia* convey, although they, too, can hit it sometimes. But the incorporation of signs of process, even (in the case of Tung Ch'i-ch'ang and others) of struggle, into the fabric of the picture can be exciting and moving. It can, moreover, permit varieties of expressiveness that are usually denied to the *tso-chia* by their method.

A comment by Kung Hsien is pertinent here: "There are two schools of painting today, the *tso-chia* (fabricators) and the *shih-ta-fu* (scholar-officials). Paintings by the *tso-chia* are stable *(an)* but not strange (or unexpected, *ch'i*); paintings by the *shih-ta-fu* are strange but not stable."[25] The strange or unexpected *(ch'i)* was also the quality preferred in the Kung-an school of literary criticism, and is regarded there as the basis of true originality. Tung Ch'i-ch'ang saw the amateur-professional distinction in painting as one "between 'painting by intuition' (*shuo-i* 'to follow the idea wherever it goes') and 'painting by design' (*tso-i* 'to make up and build up an idea from without')."[26]

Pursuing further the implications of this polarity takes us into parallels and sources and resonances more pertinent to Confucian thought than to Ch'an. The theoretical basis for this "painting by intuition" was the idea of the internalizing and subjectivizing of experience, which erased inner-outer distinctions.[27] If the nature of the finished painting was not (as in the Northern school pattern) predetermined by careful compositional planning and by the necessity to conform with traditional canons of style, but was instead determined during the actual process of painting by the operation of the artist's thoughts and aesthetic impulses, the painting could serve as a record of such internal experience, whether through its imagery or through the expressiveness of form and brushwork.[28] Such a process was entirely in keeping with the Confucian ideal by which the active potential of the cultivated man was manifested in spontaneous, sometimes unmotivated actions, not regulated by preexisting rules but guided by the inner order of his mind. It allowed creativity on the highest level by opening the creative process to the whole mind of the artist, instead of narrowing it to what had been learned at length and could now be reproduced.[29] The painter's involvement with the styles of his favorite old masters could be channeled into the creative mix—not through faithful replication, such as a learning student or a forger might do, but in a manner reflecting mature absorption and personal transformation. So could other aspects of the artist's inner life—his belief in *feng-shui* or geomancy, or his sense of design and personal handwriting developed in the practice of calligraphy, or his experience of mountain scenery or attachment to the characteristic terrain of his homeland, or even his political and social attitudes, through symbolic representations and associational references. Any one of these or any combination of them, following no "rules of relevance" as the mind follows none, could affect the painting and contribute to its meaning and expression. But none determined the content of the painting directly, in the sense that a straightforward portrayal of a theme or imitation of an old style took its meaning from that theme or style. The complexity of content in *wen-jen hua* at its best derives both from the multiplicity of kinds and sources of meaning and from an obliqueness of expression that results from the imposition of thought and reflection upon them. In academy and professional painting, the meaning of the work was typically set by the wishes of the imperial or other patron, or by the function the painting was to serve, or by some other constraint. "Liberated" from such constraints, the *i-chia* artist could respond to a wide range of impulses, guided only by the standards that his study of old painting instilled in him, and by the same Confucian cultivation that guided, ideally, all his actions.

It is significant, finally, that all this body of ideas, and the Southern and Northern schools theory itself, are directed to landscape painting and not to painting of other subjects. Mi Fu in the eleventh century had already recognized that while acceptable pictures of animals and people could be produced in a relatively simple way by copying their appearances, "landscape [painting] is a creation of the mind, and is intrinsically a superior art."[30] Landscape offered an incomparably richer field than figure or bird-and-flower or bamboo painting on which to work out the concerns outlined above. It was richer both intrinsically—the elaborate formal constructions and manipulations of space it encouraged, the diversity of textures and shapes that could be rendered in types of brushstrokes—and historically or culturally, in the stylistic lineages that the artist could draw on, and in the regional and other associations that had attached to them. It dealt, albeit very faintly in the more conventionalized styles, with the grandest theme of all, that of being-in-the-world. And on its loftiest levels it could reward the artist and his audience with a sense of partaking in the creative operation of nature itself. The hills and rivers and trees that owed their being to the internalization of sensory experience and the transmutation of it into artistic form should, when practice matched theory, seem less man-made, more like the products of natural creation, than more accurately descriptive or "true-to-life" images might be. Tung Ch'i-ch'ang makes that claim for his Southern school when, at the end of his basic statement of the Southern and Northern schools theory translated at the beginning of this paper, he quotes Wang Wei in defining the "essential thing" in landscape painting as that the "misty peaks and boulders issue from the workings of heaven, and the patterns of the brushwork partake of natural creation." At this point Tung leaves Ch'an behind, moving beyond analogy to a position in harmony with the *Doctrine of the Mean*'s statement that man can "participate in the transforming and nourishing operations of heaven and earth." The position is on the edge of a true mystical identification of artist and heaven as creative forces; it was left for Shih-t'ao in the next generation to go over the edge, in this as in all things.

Afterword

Since this paper was written, two more ways of looking at Tung Ch'i-ch'ang's Southern and Northern schools theory have come to my attention. One is Yü Chien-hua's stimulating suggestion, which somehow escaped my notice until recently, that Tung's choice of Wang Wei and Li Ssu-hsün as "founders" of his two schools, and his favoring of the former, reflect an ongoing struggle between scholar-official circles and the inner court circles which centered on the imperial family but were often dominated by eunuchs, and to which court painters were attached.[31] The suggestion is borne out by the composition of Tung's lineages: Li Ssu-hsün was himself a relative of the T'ang imperial family, and later court painters dominate the Northern school lineage through the Sung and down to the Che school in the Ming; in the Southern school lineage, Wang Wei as a literateur-official is followed by a succession of others, down to Tung Ch'i-ch'ang himself.

Secondly, Howard Rogers has recently pointed out that when the monk Shen-hui was endeavoring to establish Hui-neng as the true successor to Hung-jen and thus to validate Hui-neng's sudden enlightenment as the right path, it was Wang Wei whom he asked to write a biography of Hung-jen in which it was explicitly stated that Hung-jen had regarded Hui-neng as his legitimate successor.[32] Wang Wei also painted a picture of "Huang-mei [Hung-jen] Emerging from the Mountains," in which the older monk leads the younger Hui-neng out of the monastery to safety after transmitting to him the doctrine and the robe. Wang Wei's close association with the establishment of Southern Ch'an probably influenced Tung's selection of him as "first patriarch" in his Southern school of painting.

Notes

1. The problems of the date of formulation of Tung's Southern and Northern schools theory and its publication in various collections (in one case, falsely ascribed to his older friend Mo Shih-lung) are beyond our concern here. See Wai-kam Ho, "Tung Ch'i-ch'ang's New Orthodoxy and the Southern School Theory," in Christian Murck, ed., *Artists and Traditions: Uses of the Past in Chinese Culture* (Princeton: Princeton University Press, 1976), 113–129; and Shen Fu, "A Study of the Authorship of the 'Huo-shuo': A Summary," in *Proceedings of the International Symposium on Chinese Painting,* (Taipei, 1972), 85–115. The date of 1595 has been proposed recently by Hironobu Kohara, who argues persuasively that Tung's formulation of the theory was occasioned by his excited discovery in that year of a painting ascribed to Wang Wei which revealed to him Wang's method of painting in graded ink washes. See "Tō Kishō ni okeru Ō I no gainen," in Hironobu Kohara, ed., *Tō Kishō no shoga* (Tokyo, 1981), 3–24; on this point, p. 15.

2. Wai-kam Ho, *Tung Ch'i-ch'ang's New Orthodoxy.* I am very much indebted to this article for my own understanding of the theory as it is discussed in this paper.

3. E.g., by Joseph Levenson, "The Amateur Ideal in Ming and Early Ch'ing Society: Evidence from Painting," in John K. Fairbank, ed., *Chinese Thought and Institutions* (Chicago: Chicago University Press, 1957), 326. For my arguments against this overreading of the analogy, see my "Confucian Elements in the Theory of Painting," in Arthur F. Wright, ed., *The Confucian Persuasion* (Stanford: Stanford University Press, 1960), 116; and "Style as Idea in Ming-Ch'ing Painting," in Maurice Meisner and Rhoads Murphey, eds., *The Mozartian Historian: Essays on the Works of Joseph R. Levenson* (Berkeley: University of California Press, 1976), 139.

4. The *Hua-chih* is contained in Tung's literary collection *Jung-t'ai chi* (*pieh-chi,* ch. 4); this passage is on 6a–b. A shorter and probably earlier version is in a brief collection of Tung's notes on painting titled *Lun-hua so-yen,* published in 1627; see Wai-kam Ho, *Tung Ch'i-ch'ang's New Orthodoxy,* 116. Neither book is likely to have been composed in its present form by Tung himself; both appear to be collections of his recorded statements, colophons to paintings, etc.

5. In my book *The Distant Mountains: Chinese Painting of the Late Ming Dynasty* (New York: Weatherhill, 1982), 6–12.

6. For the background to Tung's theory and later responses to it, see Yü Chien-hua, *Chung-kuo shan-shui-hua ti nan-pei tsung lun* (Shanghai, 1963).

7. Chan Ching-feng, colophon to Jao Tzu-jan's *Shan-shui chia-fa.* Quoted in Ch'i Kung, "Li-chia k'ao," *I-lin ts'ung-lu,* no. 5 (1964): 196–205. The Jao Tzu-jan work, with its colophons, exists in a rare printed version preserved in Peking. Its authenticity is still in question; I use it here tentatively and hesitantly, in the expectation that further research will clarify the reliability of this potentially important text.

8. Inscription in an album of landscapes dated 1630 in the Princeton Art Museum. The inscription is translated and discussed in my *The Distant Mountains,* 117–118.

9. *Hua chih,* 10a–b.

10. Li Jih-hua, *T'ien-chih-t'ang chi,* ch. 39, 8bff.

11. Translation from Aschwin Lippe, "Kung Hsien and the Nanking School," part 2, *Oriental Art,* n.s. 4, no. 4 (1958): 3.

12. By Joseph Levenson, *The Amateur Ideal,* 320–341.

13. Wai-kam Ho, *Tung Ch'i-ch'ang's New Orthodoxy,* 116–118.

14. *Shan-shui chia-fa,* preface; after a copy of a manuscript copied from the printed edition of 1630 in the Bureau of Cultural Properties, Peking. The colophon by Chan Ching-feng dated 1594, partly translated above, is appended to this same work. The authenticity of both, as noted in note 7, is still uncertain.

15. Wai-kam Ho, *Tung Ch'i-ch'ang's New Orthodoxy,* 116.

16. See my article "The Orthodox Movement in Early Ch'ing Painting," in Christian Murck, ed., *Artists and Traditions,* 169–181, esp. 177–181 ("Appendix: The Orthodox View of Orthodoxy").

17. *Hua chih,* 4a–b.

18. See Richard John Lynn, "Orthodoxy and Enlightenment: Wang Shih-chen's Theory of Poetry and Its Antecedents," in Wm. T. de Bary, ed., *The Unfolding of Neo-Confucianism* (New York: Columbia University Press, 1975), 217–269; and "Alternate Routes to Self-Realization in Ming Theories of Poetry," in Susan Bush and Christian Murck, eds., *Theories of the Arts in China* (Princeton: Princeton University Press, 1983), 317–340.

19. Shen Chou, *Shen Shih-t'ien chi, ch'i-yen ku* section, 10B.

20. Lynn, "Orthodoxy and Enlightenment," 221, 223.

21. Shen Fu, "A Study," 92.

22. *Hua chih,* 48a–b. I should here correct my earlier statement that "the painting of the 'northern' professionals was no gradual path to *satori;* it was no *satori* at all" ("Style as Idea," 140). Tung and similarly inclined theorists frequently argue as though that were their belief, but a few passages, like the present one, do allow the possibility of "gradual enlightenment" in painting.

23. I am skirting here the whole question of the problematic character of the designation "Ch'an painting." Yü-chien was probably a T'ien-t'ai monk, Mu-ch'i perhaps a monk of the Lü sect, Liang K'ai was a master in the Imperial Academy for whom there is no evidence that he practiced Ch'an, and so forth. A usable definition of Ch'an painting can be made if we concentrate on quali-

ties in the paintings and relate these qualities to Ch'an; the outline of such an argument is given below.

24. Cf. my discussion of Huang Kung-wang's "Fu-ch'un Mountains" scroll of 1350. *Chinese Painting* (Geneva: Skira, 1960), 109–112.

25. Inscription recorded in P'ang Yüan-chi, *Hsü-chai ming-hua hsü-lu* (1924), ch. 3, 3a–b.

26. Wai-kam Ho, *Tung Ch'i-ch'ang's New Orthodoxy,* 124–125.

27. See Wei-ming Tu, " 'Inner Experience': The Basis of Creativity in Neo-Confucian Thinking," in Christian Murck, ed., *Artists and Traditions,* 9–15.

28. I follow here, in an attempt to understand and explicate the Chinese theorists' ways of thought, a theory of expression in which the qualities of the paintings derive more directly from the artist's inner experience than in fact I believe they do. My own belief about expression in art would put more emphasis on the artist's ability to utilize forms and images which carry by convention certain meanings and feelings that he wants to convey in his work, without supposing simply that these need be identical with the feelings and thoughts that make up his inner life.

29. I state the matter here in extremes, of course, as a theoretical construct; I am not denying, nor would Tung Ch'i-ch'ang deny, creativity to the "Northern school" masters. Tung would add that it was likely to be creativity of the second order; whether or not we would agree is a question of critical judgment irrelevant to our present concerns.

30. Mi Fu, *Hua shih,* quoted by Shen and Marilyn Fu, *Studies in Connoisseurship: Chinese Paintings from the Arthur M. Sackler Collection* (Princeton: Princeton University Press, 1974), 57.

31. See Yü's *Chung-kuo shan-shui-hua ti nan-pei tsung lun,* 96–102.

32. See Howard Rogers, "The Reluctant Messiah: 'Śākyamuni Emerging from the Mountains,' " in *Sophia International Review* 5 (1983): 21–22.

Glossary

an 安
Chan Ching-feng 詹景鳳
Ch'an 禪
Chang Tsao 張璪
Chao Po-chü 趙伯駒
Chao Po-su 趙伯驌
Chao Kan 趙幹
cheng-t'ung 正統
ch'i 奇
ch'i-yün 氣韻
Ching Hao 荆浩
Ch'iu Ying 仇英
Chou Ch'en 周臣
Chü-jan 巨然
Fan K'uan 范寬
feng-shui 風水
Hsia Kuei 夏珪
Hsieh Ho 謝赫
Hsü Tao-ning 許道寧
Hua chih 畫旨
Huang Kung-wang 黃公望
Hung-jen 弘仁
i-chia 逸家
i-kuan 衣冠
Jao Tzu-jan 饒自然
ju-lai 如來
Jung-t'ai chi 容臺集
Kuan T'ung 關同

Kung Hsien 龔賢
Kuo Chung-shu 郭忠恕
Kuo Hsi 郭熙
Lan Ying 藍瑛
Li Chao-tao 李照道
Li Ch'eng 李成
Li Jih-hua 李日華
Li Kung-lin 李公麟
Li Ssu-hsün 李思訓
Li T'ang 李唐
Lin-chi 臨濟
Liu Sung-nien 劉松年
Lun-hua so-yen 論畫瑣言
Ma-chü 馬駒
Ma Ho-chih 馬和之
Ma-Hsia 馬夏
Ma Yüan 馬遠
Mi Fu 米芾
Mi Yu-jen 米友仁
mien-shou 面授
Mo Shih-lung 莫是龍
Mu-ch'i 牧谿
nan-pei tsung lun 南北宗論
Ni Tsan 倪瓚
san-seng 散僧
Shan-shui chia-fa 山水家法
shang-sheng 上乘
Shen Chou 沈周
shen-hui 神會
shih-ta-fu 士大夫
Shih-t'ao 石濤
shuo-i 率意
Su Tung-p'o 蘇東坡
Tai Chin 戴進
Ting Yün-p'eng 丁雲鵬
tso 作
tso-chia 作家
tso-i 作意
Ts'ui Tzu-chung 崔子忠
Tung Ch'i-ch'ang 董其昌
Tung Yüan 董源
Tz'u-pai Chen-k'o 柴柏眞可
Wang Meng 王蒙
Wang Shen 王詵
Wang Wei 王維
Wang Yang-ming 王陽明
Wen Cheng-ming 文徵明
wen-jen hua 文人畫
Wu Chen 吳鎮
Wu Tao-tzu 吳道子
Yen Tsang-lang 嚴滄浪
Yen Yü 嚴羽
Yü-chien 玉澗
Yün-men 雲門

Afterword
Thinking of "Enlightenment" Religiously

Tu Wei-ming

D. T. Suzuki, in his reply to Hu Shih's critical reflection on Ch'an (Zen) Buddhism in China, stated that in the Ch'an movement "the Chinese mind completely asserted itself, in a sense, in opposition to the Indian mind. Zen could not rise and flourish in any other land or among any other people."[1] Although the famous Hu-Suzuki exchange clearly shows that they shared few points of convergence in their approach to Ch'an, either as a historical movement or as a spiritual form of life, they both agreed that it is uniquely Chinese.

Scholarship on Ch'an in the last thirty years has significantly advanced our understanding of the complexity of Ch'an as a cultural phenomenon. Virtually all widely accepted conventional explanations of the origin, transformation, and development of Ch'an have been challenged. Very few Buddhologists now take the Bodhidharma legend seriously; an increasing number of scholars find the story of Hui-neng problematical; and new research indicates that Shen-hui's alleged revolution to establish the "Southern lineage" may have been short-lived, if at all influential as a localized sectarian effort. Indeed, the basic Ch'an texts—their transmission, roles, and functions in pedagogy and spiritual significance—have also generated much discussion. Most of Ch'an scholarship is controversial, but the primacy of "enlightenment" as the ultimate concern of Ch'an spiritual training remains unquestioned. Yet, despite obvious advances in textual, historical, and cultural analysis, very little has been (and perhaps can ever be) said about "enlightenment" in the scholarly community.

If the Ch'an masters, their immediate students, and the laity were actively involved in the quest for the enlightening experience as their raison d'être, the monastic order, the rigorous mental as well as physical discipline, the "encounter dialogues," the shouting and beating must all be conceived of as expedient means for achieving that end. Since scholars, as professional academicians, are more equipped to deal with the observable "facts" rather than the ineffable experience, the question of "enlightenment" (which entails a personal knowledge of what it purports to be) is often relegated to the background. This is not to say that students of Ch'an do not "experience" what they study, for many of them experience it through practice. But a concerted effort to analyze "enlightenment" as a scholarly enterprise is rare. Having benefited from the enormous erudition on this subject that the preceding chapters have demonstrated, I would like to offer a personal note as a token of my appreciation.

If Suzuki and Hu were right in characterizing Ch'an as uniquely Chinese, and if our understanding of Ch'an as the quest for enlightenment is on the mark, there must be a peculiarly sinitic mode of approaching the enlightening experience. In a way, all the essays written for this volume are variations on the theme of defining enlightenment in Chinese culture. I would like to participate in this intellectual venture by providing some preliminary reflections on the assumptive reason underlying the uniquely sinitic approach to enlightenment. This may serve as a step toward the development of a communal critical self-consciousness among students of Chinese thought and religion who take "enlightenment" seriously as a task of human self-understanding as well as a subject of academic pursuit.

The seemingly naive faith of Ch'an (Zen) practitioners in East Asia that one can achieve enlightenment in one's own lifetime through one's own effort is perhaps unique in human salvific history. Particularly intriguing, in a comparative religious perspective, is that this premium on self-reliance is predicated on the paradox that the total annihilation of the self is synonymous with the complete affirmation of the self through ultimate self-transformation. No reference is made to a transcendent reality that provides a real fiat for this incredible human capacity. Rather, the enlightening process occurs in the structure of the self in this world in common activities such as eating, walking, and resting. The highest achievement of personal knowledge is not separable from what we normally do in our practical daily living.

This Ch'an approach to enlightenment obviously has deep roots in indigenous Chinese cosmological thinking. Take, for example, the veneration of the person as a co-creator of the universe. If humans are the most sentient of all the beings in the world, the human body is intrinsically spiritual. Since there are no standards of human perfection outside the human community except the natural transformation of the cosmic order of which the human body is a microcosm, the spiritual resources inherent in human nature are sufficient for self-transformation. We might ask, why is there any need for self-transformation if human nature is already endowed with sufficient spirituality? The answer could be that the person, who is not only the body but also mind-heart, soul, and spirit, is a process of becoming rather than a static structure. To the extent that the person is becoming, and thus an activity, a path for self-transformation is necessarily involved. A person cannot but transform. Any static notion of the self, as in the case of an unchanging selfhood, fails to accommodate the dynamic process of growth as a defining characteristic of the person.

In classical Confucian thought, the primary purpose of learning is for the sake of the self as a center of relationships.[2] However, it is misleading to interpret the Confucian way of learning to be human as a form of social ethics, for the purpose of education in the Confucian tradition is self-cultivation. Social harmony and humane rulership are natural consequences of self-cultivation. Priorities are clearly established: only by strengthening the root (self-cultivation) will the branches (regulation of the family and governance of the state) flourish. If we reverse the order by first imposing peace upon society with the anticipation that people will learn to live harmoniously among themselves, we not only violate the natural process of moral education but rely on an external political ideology rather than the trust of a fiduciary community. This is ineffective, for social harmony can only be attained through personal self-cultivation.[3]

The common belief that Confucian self-cultivation is elitist in the sense that only the privileged few have access to the symbolic resources of the society—such as literary training—is also misleading. The primary concern of Confucian education is learning to be human. Education is more broadly conceived than merely learning to read and write. People who have no opportunity to learn to read or write, as well as those who do, can and should pursue their education as human beings. *Hsüeh* (learning), in its etymological sense, is *chüeh* (enlightening).[4] To learn is to be enlightened; to teach is to enlighten.

This classical Confucian sense of learning as enlightenment is compatible with the Taoist idea that in the pursuit of Tao we must learn to lose ourselves.[5] The aspects of the self that both Confucians and Taoists would like to see us lose include self-centeredness, selfishness, opinionatedness, stubbornness, obsessiveness, possessiveness, material desires, and attachment to mental or physical objects. To lose these acquired dispositions in ourselves is not to practice self-denial, as in the spiritual discipline of inner-worldly asceticism, but to open ourselves to the experience of a deeper and more expansive selfhood. The two senses of the self, one private and limited and the other public and open, are shared by Confucians and Taoists even though their approaches to learning are significantly different.

Obviously, while learning as enlightenment does not imply a process of rigorous monastic discipline for the sole purpose of achieving the enlightening experience as an ultimate religious concern, its underlying assumption about human nature is profoundly relevant to our understanding the kind of enlightenment experience witnessed in the Ch'an tradition. For example, the deceptively simple claim that human nature is perfectible through self-effort provides us with both a conceptual basis and motivating energy for undertaking self-cultivation as an act of the will. Without a faith in human perfectibility, there is no intelligible basis for initiating the process of self-realization as a personal responsibility. Without a faith in self-effort, there is no inner strength that can be independently mobilized for the purpose. The pivotal difference between this Confucian, Taoist, and Ch'an faith in self-effort on the one hand, and the reliance on an outside source in devotional religions on the other, lies in the perception of human nature. Confucians, Taoists, and Ch'an Buddhists all believe that, although we are not what we ought to be, what we are is both the necessary and sufficient condition for us to become what we ought to be. We can, through enlightening self-transformation, become what we ought to be.

To say that we are not what we ought to be is to recognize and acknowledge the gap between what we are existentially and ontologically. To say that what we are ontologically is the necessary condition for us to become what we ought to be existentially is to realize that human nature as it presents itself to us must be the point of departure for our ultimate self-transformation. To say that what we are ontologically is the sufficient condition for us to become what we ought to be existentially is to affirm our faith in the transformability and perfectibility of human nature.

Enlightenment, in this sense, is self-illumination. It is the light and warmth of human nature for self-disclosure, self-expression, and self-realization. Indeed, human nature is dynamic; an activity as well as a being. It is not an entity latent in the consciousness of the human mind waiting to be discovered. Rather, it discloses itself, sometimes loudly, often subtly, when we consciously respond to the world around us. It is not forever hidden, as the thing-in-itself which can only be known by appealing to its multifarious appearances, for we are constantly in touch with it in our ordinary daily life. Although, due to external influence and self-deception, we may distort and not clearly see the face and hear the voice of our nature as it is, if we sincerely examine and cultivate ourselves by applying the right effort at the right moment, our true nature will automatically reveal itself. We have no need to search for outside support to realize what we originally have. Our human nature is self-disclosing, self-expressing, and self-realizing.

However, even though what we ought to be is what our human nature originally is, we existentially are neither. This human predicament presents a challenge: although we are born humans, we must continuously learn to be human; although our human nature has intrinsic resources for our ultimate self-realization, we must learn the way to tap them for our own "salvation." The counterpart of the theodicy question in Chinese thought is that, if human nature is truly good in the sense that it can be perfected by its own effort, how is human evil explained? The answer is not found in theories about the vindication of divine justice in allowing evil to exist. Since an omnipotent God, as the Creator, is not postulated, the relationship of man (in the gender-neutral sense) to heaven is never posited in terms of a creature's innocence to its awe-inspiring Maker. Man cannot blame heaven for his own failings. As a co-creator, he is instrumental in bringing about the state of affairs that defines his existential condition. Evil is not an active force independent of the human community; evil cannot exist outside humanity. The mutuality between Heaven and man is such that, if we fail to fully realize ourselves, we fail not only humanly to disclose, express, and realize that which our nature impels us to do but also cosmologically to assume our responsibility of a co-creator.

Evil, in this sense, does not have ontological status. It is but an existential description of what has gone wrong. Evil occurs when we fail to fully realize ourselves. Since we can never fully realize ourselves in an existential situation, evil is always present as an integral part of human existence. Although our nature, in its ontological state, knows no evil and is purely good, the concrete process by which it is realized entails limitations. Evil symbolizes the distortion and inertia involved in the self-realization of our nature. As a result, the course it takes (the human way) is a tortuous one. It is also precarious. This, however, does not negate the fact that human nature is the necessary and sufficient condition for us to learn to be fully realized as human beings.

Human nature, as conferred by the mandate of heaven, is actually a concrete manifestation of the tacit "covenant" between man and heaven. The heaven that is inherent in our nature is, strictly speaking, not "divinity circumscribed" because, as the microcosm of the cosmos, it is heaven in its authentic self-manifestation. Since the creativity of heaven is natural to the extent that nothing can be added on to or subtracted from it, the real difference in the world is made by man. The Confucian dictum that "man can enlarge the Tao; the Tao cannot enlarge man"[6] simply reiterates the point that Tao, as the unfolding of the heavenly way, can benefit from human participation.

It is important to note here that the assertion "man can enlarge the Tao" is meant to be an injunction about human duty, lest it should be misread as an expression of grandiose anthropocentrism. The human ability to form a unity with heaven and earth is predicated on a cosmic vision: the continuity of being.[7] According to this vision, all modalities of being form an organismic whole in which the vital forces interchange in a continuous flux; human beings are integral parts of nature. What we do as humans is natural in the sense that no other intelligence can set the standards for us to emulate. While this may sound anthropocentric, the underlying impulse is the recognition that human beings must not alienate themselves from the cosmic wholeness as if they were in a privileged position to rule over the universe. If we choose to do so, we can allow the collective selfish will to dominate. Yet, once our instrumental rationality takes control, the mechanism of domination inevitably turns nature into a wholly externalized other. Exploitation of nature becomes unavoidable. The belief in knowledge as power rather than as wisdom (which has contributed to transforming human beings into the most dangerous destroyers in the universe) is not compatible with the cosmic vision of continuity of being.

Each person, in the holistic cosmic vision, forms an affinity with the total environment as a filial son or daughter of heaven and earth. The particular enlightenment that is available to the person is self-discovery. Self-discovery takes the form of re-presenting that which one originally has as one's birthright. The idea is not a fundamental rejection of all one has been but an affirmation of that which underlies the core of one's true existence.

Enlightenment as self-disclosure, self-expression, and self-realization does not rely on a supernatural or superhuman agent or the confrontation of something or someone radically different from ourselves. Nor does it come through a sensuous experience of rich color, sound, and smell as if one encountered a fundamentally different world of the senses. Rather, it is recovering the lost self and returning home. The paradigmatic mystic experience, in this connection, is the unity experience—like a drop of water falling into the pond—rather than the union experience—like the consummation of a love affair.

The process that leads to enlightenment is always gradual, whereas the experience itself, no matter how well one is prepared, is always sudden. Enlightenment occurring as an unintended consequence is inconceivable. If we do not seek it consciously and conscientiously, we can never be enlightened. Implicit in all stories of sudden enlightenment is the prolonged spiritual preparation preceding the event. Since there is no transcendent creator outside the human community to bestow enlightenment as an intrinsically undeserved grace, no one has ever received enlightenment as a gift. On the other hand, since the enlightenment experience can never be fully anticipated, and it is a surprise even if one has the premonition that it may occur momentarily, the sense of suddenness is inevitable. This seems to suggest that the sudden-gradual distinction is not particularly significant in the actual process leading to the enlightenment experience.

However, the subitists' faith is so deeply rooted in the indigenous traditions of Chinese thought and religion that an explication of its underlying logic is in order. Lest we should misconstrue sudden enlightenment as an easy way out of the rigorous spiritual discipline required of all serious students of Ch'an, let us assume that the sudden-gradual debate is not about the necessity of practice but, given the centrality of diligent spiritual discipline, about what the authentic method of achieving enlightenment ought to be. The subitists insist that scripture, tradition, ritual, and teaching are in the last analysis supplementary. One never experiences enlightenment (the full awakening of the true self) by means of reading sūtras, adhering to the tradition of a particular school, observing established rituals, or following the instructions of a master. The illumination of the mind, like drinking water to quench thirst, must be experienced immediately and directly. No mediation, no matter how valuable and how lofty, is allowed. The demand for personal participation is absolute. Whether you are in or out of the realm of possibility, whether or not you have experienced the taste, whether or not you know what you are doing are clear-cut cases with no borderline instances to be determined. A situation in which a judgment call is required is difficult to imagine. After all, the only arbitration possible is the subjective decision to be in, to have it, and to know. Indeed, truth is subjectivity.

The open-mindedness with which the subitists decide to pursue a certain course of action or to abandon a well-traversed path gives the impression that there is a great deal of arbitrariness in their approaches to the enlightenment experience. How can anyone be sure of the way to proceed? The academic community, dedicated to the programmatic pursuit of knowledge, is not at all suited to appreciate the seemingly situational and inspirational pedagogy derived from them.

The matter is complicated by the implicit demand that we must try to take an inside participant's point of view if we are to make sense of enlightenment as a religious experience. Surely we do not find it convincing to say that the only respectable scholarly mode of analysis is from the perspective of the disinterested observer. But to learn to be religiously musical is one thing, to actually experience enlightenment is another—something, to say the least, extraordinarily difficult. The gradualists, in outlining the procedure by which enlightenment study is to be pursued, provide us with a way of applying our sophisticated conceptual apparatus of classification and analysis. The subitists, without giving us any handle by which we can exert our research effort, compel us to dismiss them as unintelligible.

Yet, if Suzuki and Hu were right, the uniquely sinitic approach to enlightenment should be better represented by the subitists than the gradualists. Even if historically we can never be sure what Hui-neng's teaching was all about, his alleged claim that sudden enlightenment is the authentic way still merits our attention.

It may be helpful to note that the Mencian line of Confucian teaching, the Taoist thought of Chuang Tzu, and the Ch'an of the subitist school all share one basic conviction: the spiritual resources at our disposal are necessary and sufficient for us to become enlightened. The ultimate ground of our self-realization and the actual process by which we become fully realized are inseparable. Our nature, an anthropocosmic reality, is not only our ground of being but also the creative and transformative activity that makes us dynamic, living, and growing persons. Despite our existential alienation from our true nature, we have never totally departed from it and should dedicate ourselves to fully return to it. We do not become what we are incrementally; we become, therefore we are. In the becoming process, suddenly and simultaneously, we see our true nature face to face.

This is what Mencius recommended as the authentic way of learning to be human. We first establish that which is great in our nature.[8] We do not depart from where we are here and now in order to appropriate what we do not have. Rather, the way is near at hand and inseparable from the ordinary experiences of our daily lives. Paradoxically, we must make the existential decision to find our way; otherwise, we will lose it to the extent that we become unaware that it is originally ours. Nevertheless, because it is originally ours, we can get it by simply exercising our will to do so. Willing is the necessary and sufficient condition for us to get it. The way is ours, suddenly and simultaneously, when we will that this be done.

However, although the Confucians assume that ontologically the way is within us, they never underestimate the intellectual and spiritual discipline required for regaining the "lost heart."[9] Chuang Tzu's "fasting of the heart,"[10] in this Confucian perspective, makes a great deal of sense. Its single-minded attention to "nourishing the heart," despite the vicissitude of emotions and discriminating consciousness, is in accord with the Mencian teaching of making our desires few.[11] To get that which is originally ours by simply willing is, in a common Ch'an expression, "the Great Matter."[12] Existentially nothing is more urgent, difficult, and tormenting than this Great Matter. The strength of the subitists lies in their ontological insight into the original nature (the thusness) of this Great Matter and their existential awareness that, without commitment of body and soul, an external procedure, no matter how ingeniously designed, will not work.

The deep-rooted sinitic faith in the perfectibility of human nature through self-effort underlies the teachings of Mencian Confucianism, Chuang Tzu's Taoism, and the subitist Ch'an. This faith, informed by the ontological insight that human nature is not only a ground of being but also a transformative and creative activity, enables the Confucians to perceive human beings as earthbound yet striving to transcend themselves to join with heaven, the Taoists to perceive human beings as embodiments of the Tao taking part in the cosmic transformation as connoisseurs of undifferentiated wholeness, and the Ch'an Buddhists to perceive human beings as capable of true enlightenment in a living encounter with ordinary daily existence.

Notes

1. "Zen: A Reply to Hu Shih," *Philosophy East and West* 3 (1953): 40.

2. *Analects* 12:25. For an explication of this important idea in Confucian education, see Wm. Theodore de Bary, *The Liberal Tradition in China* (New York: Columbia University Press, 1983), 21–24.

3. The statement in the "text" of the *Great Learning* makes this point abundantly clear:

> From the Son of Heaven down to the common people, all must regard cultivation of the personal life as the root or foundation. There is never a case when the root is in disorder and yet the branches are in order. There has never been a case when what is treated with great importance becomes a matter of slight importance or what is treated with slight importance becomes a matter of great importance.

For this translation, see Wing-tsit Chan, *A Source Book in Chinese Philosophy* (Princeton: Princeton University Press, 1969), 87.

4. Since one of the basic glosses on *hsüeh* is *chüeh* in Hsu Shen's *Shuo-wen,* a first-century dictionary, this etymological reading is presumably pre-Buddhist.

5. *Lao Tzu (Tao Te Ching),* chap. 40.

6. *Analects* 15:28.

7. For an introductory note on this cosmological concept, see Tu Wei-ming, "The Continuity of Being: Chinese Visions of Nature," in *On Nature,* ed. Leroy S. Rouner (Notre Dame, Ind.: University of Notre Dame Press, 1984), 113–129.

8. *Mencius* VIA:15.

9. *Mencius* IVB:12.

10. *Chuang Tzu,* chap. 4. See Burton Watson, trans., *Complete Works of Chuang Tzu* (New York: Columbia University Press, 1968), 57–58.

11. *Mencius* VIIB:35.

12. In *The Record of Tung-shan,* the master asked a monk, "What is the most

tormenting thing in this world?" "Hell is the most tormenting thing," answered the monk. "Not so. When that which is draped in these robe threads is unaware of the Great Matter, that I call the most tormenting thing," said the master.

For this translation, see William F. Powell, trans., *The Record of Tung-shan,* Classics in East Asian Buddhism, no. 1 (Honolulu: University of Hawaii Press, 1986), 57.

Contributors

Robert E. Buswell, Jr. is an assistant professor in the Department of East Asian Languages and Cultures at the University of California, Los Angeles. He received his doctorate in Buddhist Studies from the University of California, Berkeley in 1985. He is currently revising his dissertation into a book on East Asian Buddhist apocryphal scriptures, with special reference to the *Vajrasamādhi-sūtra.* His principal publication to date is *The Korean Approach to Zen: The Collected Works of Chinul.* He is also editor of, and contributor to, *Buddhist Apocryphal Scriptures.*

James Cahill received his Ph.D. in art history in 1958 from the University of Michigan. He was curator of Chinese art at the Freer Gallery of Art, Washington, D.C. from 1957 to 1965 before becoming a professor in the History of Art Department at the University of California, Berkeley. His many publications include *Chinese Painting;* a number of scholarly catalogs for exhibitions of Chinese and Japanese painting; *The Compelling Image: Nature and Style in 17th Century Chinese Painting,* which was based on the Charles Eliot Norton lectures given at Harvard University and won the College Art Association's Morey Prize for the best art history book in 1982; and three volumes in a projected series of five on later Chinese painting.

Paul Demiéville (1894–1979) was one of the most eminent Sinologists and Buddhologists of this century. He was a professor at the Collège de France, rédacteur-en-chef of the *Hōbōgirin,* and director of *T'oung Pao,* among his many distinguished positions. His publications include *Le Concile de Lhasa,* which still remains the classic discussion of the sudden-gradual debates in Tibet. Some of his more important contributions to Sinology and Buddhology have been collected in *Choix d'Études sinologiques* and *Choix d'Études bouddhiques.*

Neal Donner received his Ph.D. in Buddhist Studies in 1976 from the University of British Columbia for an annotated translation of the first chapter of Chih-i's *Mo-ho chih-kuan.* His translation (with Shotaro Iida) of Yensho Kanakura's *Indo tetsugaku-shi* has been published as *Hindu-Buddhist Thought in India.*

Luis O. Gómez is professor of Buddhist Studies and chairman of the Department of Asian Languages and Cultures at the University of Michigan. He received his doctorate from Yale University in 1967 for a study and translation of selected verses from the *Gaṇḍavyūha.* In addition to a wide range of articles in the field of Buddhist Studies, he is coeditor of *Problems de Filosofía* and *Barabudur.* He is currently interested in form criticism of sūtra literature and analysis of Buddhist ritual texts. He is also involved in the Higashi Honganji translation project, *Jōdo sambu-kyō.*

Peter N. Gregory is director and executive vice-president of the Kuroda Institute for the Study of Buddhism and Human Values and assistant professor in the Program in Religious Studies and Center for East Asian and Pacific Studies at the University of Illinois, Urbana. He earned his Ph.D. from Harvard University in 1981 with a dissertation on Kuei-feng Tsung-mi. In addition to a number of articles on Hua-yen and Ch'an, he is editor of *Traditions of Meditation in Chinese Buddhism* and coeditor of *Studies in Ch'an and Hua-yen.* He is currently finishing a study of the life and thought of Tsung-mi as well as an annotated translation of the *Yüan-jen lun.* He is also working on the libretto for an operatic adaption of the *Vimalakīrti-nirdeśa.*

Whalen Lai is an associate professor in the Program in Religious Studies at the University of California, Davis. He received his Ph.D. from Harvard University for a dissertation on the *Awakening of Faith.* He has published over forty articles on a wide variety of themes in Chinese Buddhism and comparative thought. He is currently doing research at Tübingen University on the encounter between Christianity and Buddhism. He is also collaborating with Hans Küng on two book projects.

Richard John Lynn is director of Corporate Asian Language Training in Palo Alto, California. He received his Ph.D. from Stanford University, has taught at the University of Auckland, the University of Massachusetts, and Indiana University, and was senior lecturer and head of the Department of Chinese at Macquarie University in Sydney. He has authored *Chinese Literature: A Draft Bibliography in Western European Languages, Kuan Yün-shih,* and *Guide to Chinese Poetry and Drama,* in addition to numerous articles, book sections, and reviews in the fields of Chinese literature, history, and thought. He is currently engaged in a book-length study and translation of Yen Yü's *Tsang-lang shih-hua.* His *The Classic of Changes: A New Translation with Traditional Commentaries* is soon to be published by Shambala.

John R. McRae is currently a post-doctoral fellow and lecturer at Harvard University. He took his doctorate at Yale University in 1983. A revised version of his dissertation has been published as *The Northern School of Ch'an and the Formation of Early Ch'an Buddhism.* In addition to a number of articles on Ch'an, he is presently completing two book-length manuscripts: the first a study of Ma-tsu and the transition from early to classical Ch'an, and the second an annotated translation of the complete works of Shen-hui.

R. A. Stein has been a professor at the Collège de France since 1966. A scholar of wide-ranging interests and extensive linguistic training, he has written on a broad array of themes on Tibetan and Chinese culture and thought, including Tibetan epic poetry and culture, Chinese popular religion, Taoism, and Tantra. His *La Civilisation tibétaine* has been published in English as *Tibetan Civilization.*

Tu Wei-ming taught at Princeton University and the University of California, Berkeley before becoming professor of Chinese history and philosophy at Harvard University. He received his doctorate in 1968 from Harvard University for a study of Wang Yang-ming, a revised version of which was subsequently published as *Neo-Confucian Thought in Action.* His book-length study of the *Chung-yung* appeared under the title *Centrality and Commonality.* Some of his numerous articles on Confucianism and comparative thought have been collected in *Humanity and Self-Cultivation: Essays in Confucian Thought* and *Confucian Thought: Selfhood as Creative Transformation.*

Index